Joseph G. Knapp

Economist for

the People

To Carol

EDWIN G. NOURSE—ECONOMIST FOR THE PEOPLE.
Copyright © 1979 by The Interstate Printers & Publishers, Inc. All rights reserved. Printed in the United States of America.

Library of Congress Catalog Card No. 79-83504

ISBN 0-8134-2080-6

through making as much use as possible of his own expressions from his writings and from interviews with him. In attempting to explain his thinking as it developed I have copiously quoted him, for he expressed himself precisely in effective prose. . . .

"I have also tried to keep this book in historical perspective. Dr. Nourse's life of 91 years reached nearly halfway back to the ratification of the Federal Constitution; when he was born in 1883, our population was but one-third of what it is today. Therefore I have attempted to portray Dr. Nourse's career in the framework of this intensely interesting period in which he lived—from the time when this country was predominantly rural to the time when it had become the leading industrial nation of the world. His relationship to his times is indicated by some of his professional attainments. He helped establish the Brookings Institution as a great research center in economics and political science and was its Vice-President in 1946 when President Truman appointed him as the first Chairman of the Council of Economic Advisers. He served as President of the American Farm Economic Association in 1924 and of the American Economic Association in 1942. From 1942 to 1945 he was Chairman of the Social Science Research Council, and following his service with the Council of Economic Advisers, he was long Vice-Chairman of the Joint Council on Economic Education.

". . . I must admit a certain bias in favor of my subject, for if I had not thought Dr. Nourse an extraordinary man I would not have devoted so much of my life to this effort. I have, however, endeavored to present the man fairly and humanly, as he persevered in trying to make this a better world. It is my hope that this book will help Edwin G. Nourse continue to live in the minds and hearts of his countrymen and cause many to turn to his writings for a fuller understanding of his views."

EDWIN G. NOURSE —
Economist for the People

EDWIN G. NOURSE —

 The Interstate
Printers & Publishers, Inc.

Danville, Illinois

FOREWORD

Why is a biography of Edwin G. Nourse pertinent in the confused state of the world today? My answer is that there are lessons to be learned from his life that can help us meet many of our economic and social problems. Dr. Nourse believed in the light of reason, and he demonstrated how much one man could accomplish if he set his mind to it. It is important that we catch and record the meaning and richness of his life before it is obliterated by myths and misinterpretations. That is why I have undertaken to write this biography in the light of my long association with him. How I came to undertake this "labor of love" and the methods of my approach are here set forth.

Soon after I came to work with Edwin G. Nourse at the Institute of Economics (now the Brookings Institution of Washington, D.C.) on September 1, 1926, it became evident to me that he was a man with rare intellectual and moral gifts. My admiration of him grew as I observed and came to recognize his competence in agricultural and general economics and in the theory and practice of cooperative business enterprise; his leadership in the field of social science; his great capacities in research administration and adult education; his pioneer contributions in public service; and overriding all, his character as a man.

It was my privilege to have an intimate relationship with Dr. Nourse as his life evolved from the time of our first meeting to its culmination 48 years later. This book had its beginnings in 1954 during a luncheon conversation at the Cosmos Club. I then asked him if he would have any objection if I undertook to set forth his life in a biography. He replied that he didn't see how he could stop me, and from then on we would have talks on occasion with this ultimate object in view. However, both of us were so busy on our own affairs that we had little opportunity for sustained interviews before 1962, when I was able to make use of a voice recorder. At that time I also began to assemble letters from those who could provide information on certain phases of his life.

By 1966 I had acquired the 12 books and many of the articles he had written. He was then assembling his papers for the Truman Memorial

Library and the Cornell University Archives, and he gave me duplicates of many of his articles and talks, which largely completed my library of his writings. Then in 1966, after my retirement from government service, I was asked to interview Dr. Nourse for the Cornell Oral History Project. It was agreed that the object would be to provide a chronological record of Dr. Nourse's life, and that a transcript of the recordings would be furnished for my use in writing my projected biography. These oral history sessions were carried on at Dr. Nourse's home with a tape recorder over a period extending from September, 1966, to January, 1971, and the transcribed record ran to some 800 typed pages. This record has proved invaluable to my purpose, for it explains how Dr. Nourse saw events as they occurred and how he viewed them in retrospect. I believe that anyone who reviews the transcript will be impressed with his power of recall, clarity of expression, and choice of words and sentences as he spontaneously discussed persons or situations with me. The full flavor of these conversations can best be obtained by listening to the tapes themselves, for one can there feel the spirit and enthusiasm of the man.

Because of other commitments I was not able to begin direct work on this biography until the fall of 1973, and I had completed only a few draft chapters when he died in April, 1974. While I was not able to read these chapters to him, I had promised to do so when we could find a mutually agreeable time. I recall his jaunty response: "Yes, to retain perfect objectivity you must have the views of the victim."

In making this study, I have been primarily interested in finding out how his mind functioned and how his work evolved in the light of his genealogy, upbringing, social and economic environment, and educational, political, and other influences. In a way, this book is a record of an intellectual pilgrimage. The emphasis is on Nourse's professional and public career, and it does not aspire to cover his rich social and family life. To me his life is a saga of intellectual achievement that throws much light on the 91 years in which he lived. His career indicates how a man influenced, and was influenced by, his environment. One of the guiding principles of his life was expressed by a statement of Edmund Burke that sat on his desk: "All that is necessary for the triumph of evil is that good men do nothing."

In this biography I have endeavored to explain Dr. Nourse's life as he saw it unfold through making as much use as possible of his own expressions from his writings and from interviews with him. In attempting to explain his thinking as it developed I have copiously quoted him, for he expressed himself precisely in effective prose. I have tried to keep notes to a minimum so as not to impede the interest of the reader, but I believe that scholars who may wish to dig deeper into any aspect of his life will be sufficiently guided for that purpose.

I have also tried to keep this book in historical perspective. Dr. Nourse's life of 91 years reached nearly halfway back to the ratification of the Federal Constitution; when he was born in 1883, our population was but one-third of what it is today. Therefore I have attempted to portray Dr. Nourse's career in the framework of this intensely interesting period in which he lived—from the time when this country was predominantly rural to the time when it had become the leading industrial nation of the world. His relationship to his times is indicated by some of his professional attainments. He helped establish the Brookings Institution as a great research center in economics and political science and was its Vice-President in 1946 when President Truman appointed him as the first Chairman of the Council of Economic Advisers. He served as President of the American Farm Economic Association in 1924 and of the American Economic Association in 1942. From 1942 to 1945 he was Chairman of the Social Science Research Council, and following his service with the Council of Economic Advisers, he was long Vice-Chairman of the Joint Council on Economic Education.

In closing this Foreword, I must admit a certain bias in favor of my subject, for if I had not thought Dr. Nourse an extraordinary man I would not have devoted so much of my life to this effort. I have, however, endeavored to present the man fairly and humanly, as he persevered in trying to make this a better world. It is my hope that this book will help Edwin G. Nourse continue to live in the minds and hearts of his countrymen and cause many to turn to his writings for a fuller understanding of his views.

Joseph G. Knapp

Bethesda, Maryland
June, 1979

AUTHOR'S ACKNOWLEDGEMENTS

This book is a monument to the memory of Edwin G. Nourse. I could not have written it without his cooperation in explaining much of his life to me. While I prepared the manuscript after his death, his spirit hovered over me as I coped with the problems of fairly presenting his career.

In working on this task I have been fortunate in having the generous encouragement and assistance of many persons who knew Dr. Nourse well. I wish to recognize especially the help of two of his longtime friends, Dr. Murray R. Benedict, Emeritus Professor of Agricultural Economics and Agricultural Economist for the Giannini Foundation, University of California, Berkeley; and Dr. Ewald T. Grether, Flood Professor of Economics Emeritus, and Emeritus Dean of the Schools of Business Administration (undergraduate and graduate), University of California, Berkeley. Both Benedict and Grether read all my chapters and gave me their beneficial comments and suggestions as the chapters were completed in draft form. A brief review of their professional careers will indicate why their help has been indispensable to me.

Benedict's friendship with Nourse developed from 1921 to 1928 when Benedict was Head of the Department of Agricultural Economics at South Dakota State College. During this period he served as Secretary of the South Dakota Farm Bureau Federation and as Secretary-Treasurer of the Cooperative Wool Growers of South Dakota. Thus they had a common background of interests. Benedict's brilliant record as a Social Science Research Council Fellow at Harvard University in 1929 gained for him the Ricardo Fellowship in 1930 and a lectureship the following year. He then began his long service as Professor of Agricultural Economics at the University of California, where he taught courses in farm finance and agricultural policy and demonstrated his research competence in many bulletins and articles. He was elected President of the American Farm Economic Association for 1941, and in 1943 he began his long-continuing connection with the National Planning Association as a member of its Agriculture Committee. In 1944 he served as chairman of a committee of consultants that recommended plans for the reorganization of the Farm Credit Administration. He also advised California and federal agencies on many problems relating to subjects such as agricultural education, statistical methodology, and natural resources use. In 1952 he served with Nourse on the committee of agricultural economists that prepared the Farm Foundation's "Search Light Report" on Farm Policy. Benedict's national reputation is based primarily on his penetrating analyses of national agricultural policy made from 1951 to 1956, while he was Research Director of the Farm Policy Study sponsored by the Twentieth Century Fund. His volume, *Farm Policies of the United States, 1790-1950,* is a classic in agricultural economics and agricultural history literature. Following his retirement, he was honored by the University of California in 1961 with the LL.D. degree, and in 1962 he was named a Fellow by the American Farm Economic Association.

Grether's friendship with Nourse began in 1944 when his review of Nourse's book, *Price Making in a Democracy,* opened up a continuing correspondence. Their friendship ripened when Grether came to Washington in 1948 to direct economic mobilization planning, domestic and foreign, for the Truman Administration, and they had offices on the same floor of the Old State Building. They shared many interests. Both recognized the importance of marketing, the value of competitive enterprise, the social responsibilities of business organizations, the significance of price policy, and the desirability of a social science approach ranging beyond economics.

It is impossible to encapsulate Grether's productive professional life in a few sentences. As an innovative economist in the field of marketing at the University of California, he established himself with his book, *Retail Price Maintenance in Great Britain* (1935). From 1939 to 1941 he was managing editor of the *Journal of Marketing* and from 1941 to 1943 he was its editor-in-chief. From 1941 to 1961 he was the organizing Dean of the Undergraduate and Graduate Schools of Business Administration at the University of California, Berkeley. Twice, in 1955 and 1975, he received the Paul D. Converse Award for Contribution to the Theory of Marketing, an honor also given Nourse in 1955. His internationally-known book, *Marketing and Public Policy,* published in 1966, the year of his formal retirement, expressed his faith in our private enterprise system. The following year, when he was awarded the Honorary LL.D. degree at the University of California, Berkeley, he was characterized as "a pioneer in the study of marketing economics who has bridged the gap between economic theory and marketing" and as a "scholar, administrator, and academic statesman par excellence." In June, 1977, the Marketing Science Institute held a symposium at Harvard University in his honor, in recognition of his "half century of teaching and research in marketing in the public interest."

I wish also to express my sincere appreciation to Grether's wife—Carrie Virginia Grether—for reading my manuscript chapter by chapter and giving me her independent and useful comments.

I wish also to thank my son, Dr. John Laurence Knapp, Director of the Economic Research Division, Tayloe Murphy Institute, University of Virginia, for considerately reading all of my manuscript and giving me his frank and useful suggestions.

Furthermore, I am deeply indebted to the following for graciously reading substantial portions of my manuscript and giving me most helpful criticisms and suggestions:

Dr. Wayne D. Rasmussen and David Brewster, Agricultural History Branch, U.S. Department of Agriculture, Chapters I-VIII.

Dr. Gould P. Coleman, University Archivist, Cornell University Libraries, Chapters I–IV.

Leon H. Keyserling, former Vice-Chairman and Chairman, Council of Economic Advisers, Chapters X–XIII.

Dr. Monroe Newman, Professor of Economics, The Pennsylvania State University, Chapters XIII–XVI.

J. Tyler Nourse, who has kindly reviewed Chapters XV and XVI and assembled photographs for my use. I have greatly appreciated his warm encouragement of this biography of his father.

Many others generously provided me with information and stimulation through conversations or correspondence. Among them I wish to mention: Dr. Martin A. Abrahamsen; J. Kenneth Anderson; Dr. Henry B. Arthur; Albert H. Atwood*; G. Derwood Baker; C. Candy Balderson; Dr. George Washington Bell; Dr. Karl Brandt*; Miss Esther Breck; Louis Brownlow*; Dr. Arthur F. Burns; Dr. Robert D. Calkins; Dr. Mollie Ray Carroll; Chris L. Christensen*; Prof. Colin Clark; Dr. Gerhard Colm*; Dr. Joseph S. Davis*; Lynn R. Edminster; Dr. Lloyd C. Elam; Dr. Russell C. Engberg; Dr. Henry E. Erdman; Dr. Joseph L. Fisher; Sen. Ralph E. Flanders; Herbert L. Forest; Dr. Moe L. Frankel; Mrs. Jeanne Franklin; Kelsey B. Gardner*; Dr. Robert Aaron Gordon*; Bertram Gross; A. H. Hausrath; Dr. R. B. Hefflebower; Dr. Walter W. Heller; Paul G. Hoffman; Dr. Jerome H. Holland; Dr. Paul Homan*; Dr. Calvin B. Hoover*; Lyman S. Hulbert*; Mrs. Eleanor C. Isbell; Dr. O. B. Jesness; Dr. Dexter Keezer; Lewis H. Kimmel; Dr. Erich O. Kraemer; Joseph A. Livingston; Karl D. Loos; Dr. Lewis L. Lorwin; Dr. Isador Lubin*; Judson P. Mason; Hellen Hill Miller; Dr. Raymond W. Miller; Dr. Harold G. Moulton*; Dr. Willard F. Mueller; Dr. William I. Myers*; Robinson Newcomb; Dr. William H. Nichols; George N. Pederson; Professor Frank Robotka*; Dr. Harold B. Rowe; Stanley H. Ruttenberg; Dr. Walter Salant; Dr. Roscoe Saville; Dr. Theodore W. Schultz; Hon. John Snyder; Dr. Joseph J.

Spengler; Mrs. Beryle E. Stanton; Dr. John Steelman; Dr. Herbert Stein; J. Kenneth Stern; Dr. George W. Stocking; Dr. Henry C. Taylor*; George Terborgh; Dr. Harry C. Trelogan; Dr. Jacob Viner; Dr. Ralph J. Watkins; Dr. Frederick C. Waugh; James E. Webb; Dr. Harry Wellman; and Prof. Edwin B. Wilson.

It is not possible to express here appreciation of the many books and articles that I have found helpful or inspirational in writing this biography. In small part my appreciation is recorded by citations. It pleases me to here record that the Bethesda Public Library, under the direction of Ellen Fenstermaker, has provided me with very efficient and friendly library service.

I also wish to thank Mrs. Anne Wood, Mrs. Peggy Gagan, and Mrs. Barbara Shivnan for their most helpful typing service.

I am most grateful also for the confidence in this book expressed by Owen Hallberg, President of the American Institute of Cooperation and by Dr. Kenneth D. Naden, President of the National Council of Farmer Cooperatives. With their help, sufficient advance orders have been assembled from cooperative associations to ensure its publication.

Furthermore, I wish to express my great appreciation to Russell L. Guin, Chairman of the Board of The Interstate Printers & Publishers, Inc., and his associates Ronald L. McDaniel, Editor, Gregory J. Ottarski and Penny J. Ellis, Editorial Assistants, and V. L. Thomas, Marketing Manager, for all they have done to bring forth this book as I would like it. No one could have a more cooperative publishing firm.

This book has been prepared without subsidy, except for $400 provided by the Farm Foundation to defray part of my typing costs. I have greatly appreciated this expression of interest.

Altogether, the preparation of this book has been a cooperative undertaking in which many have generously given of their time and resources. However, I must accept full responsibility for the plan of the book, its content, and its shortcomings.

Finally, I wish to thank my wife, Carol, for sticking with me on my ninth book. Her encouragement and good counsel have sustained me, and I take pleasure in dedicating this volume to her as an expression of my continuing affection.

---

*deceased

OTHER BOOKS BY JOSEPH G. KNAPP

The Cooperative Marketing of Livestock
[with Edwin G. Nourse]
(1931)

*The Hard Winter Wheat Pools:
An Experiment in Agricultural Marketing Integration*
(1933)

E. A. Stokdyk: Architect of Cooperation
(1953)

*Seeds That Grew:
A History of the Cooperative Grange League Federation Exchange*
(1960)

Farmers in Business
(1963)

Great American Cooperators
[with associates]
(1967)

*The Rise of American Cooperative Enterprise:
1620-1920*
(1969)

*The Advance of American Cooperative Enterprise:
1920-1945*
(1973)

TABLE OF CONTENTS

Part One. THE PATH TO PUBLIC SERVICE (1883-1946)

I.	The Mold for the Man	3
II.	College Days—Lewis Institute and Cornell University (1902-1906)	18
III.	Finding His Way (1906-1915)	28
IV.	His Feet on the Ladder (1915-1918)	47
V.	Building a Reputation (1918-1923)	62
VI.	Gaining National Distinction (1923-1928)	85
VII.	Probing the Farm Problem (1928-1940)	116
VIII.	Return to General Economics (1928-1940)	148
IX.	Rounding Out a Professional Career (1940-1946)	174

Part Two. FIRST CHAIRMAN, COUNCIL OF ECONOMIC ADVISERS (1946-1949)

X.	Laying the Foundation (1946-1947)	205
XI.	Building an Institution (1947-1948)	242
XII.	Sticking to His Guns (1948-1949)	277

Part Three. NEW FRONTIERS (1950-1974)

XIII. Economist at Large (1950-1959)   333

XIV. Economics Practitioner and Philosopher (1960-1972)   393

XV. Searching to the End (1965-1974)   440

XVI. The Man and His Work   465

Appendices

A. I Must Believe   487
   A Triptych by Edwin G. Nourse

B. The "Unfinished Symphony"   491

C. Selected Bibliography of Nourse Writings   506

Notes   511

Index   533

Part One

THE PATH TO PUBLIC SERVICE
(1883-1946)

Chapter I

THE MOLD FOR THE MAN

Edwin Griswold Nourse was born in Lockport, New York, on May 20, 1883, but his formative years were spent in the suburbs of the rapidly expanding city of Chicago. He once referred to himself as a "casebook American," in that all of his ancestors on both sides "for ten generations were purely Anglo-Saxon families."

The Family Heritage

Nourse got his name from Francis Nurse, who immigrated in 1642 to Salem Village—now Danvers—near Salem, Massachusetts, from Yarmouth, in the county of Norfolk, England. Francis was an artisan, a "tray maker," which, in today's parlance, would be a cabinet maker. As a "selectman" he was well known in the community for his ability to see both sides of a question. Soon after coming to the new country, Francis married Rebecca Towne, who also came from Norfolk, England. She was the same Rebecca Nurse who was excommunicated from the church and then hanged as a witch during the hysteria that swept the area around Salem in 1691. When Rebecca, then in her seventies, was pressed to confess being a witch, she steadfastly refused, saying: "I know nothing of this foul thing. Would you have me belie myself?" Her execution helped bring a revulsion of thinking toward the mania that was blighting the name of Massachusetts, and from then to the present day, she has been esteemed as a martyr, if not as a saint.[1]

Francis and Rebecca had several children, including the progenitor of Edwin Nourse. In succeeding generations, Nourse's male ancestors were mostly farmers living in Massachusetts and southern Vermont. His grandfather—who changed the spelling of the name "Nurse" back to the original English spelling "Nourse"—moved to a farm in New York State, near Utica, where Nourse's father, Edwin Henry Nourse, was born in 1842.

Nourse's Parents

Edwin Henry Nourse, who was called "Henry" by Edwin's mother, was not cut out to be a farmer. His grandmother, who had been a teacher, taught him to play the piano. His mother and sisters were musical, and they all would sing and have great times together while Henry's father would sit quietly aside and occasionally growl: "I don't see what you have so much to laugh about." It was a happy family environment, and Henry naturally became interested in choir music and in the community sings that were becoming common at that time.

Like other country boys of this period, Henry attended a one-room school in his neighborhood. However, he was able to attend Whitestown Seminary and attain about the equivalent of a high-school education. To acquire some formal musical training, he also spent several months at a choir training school in northern Pennsylvania. Here he was in the same class with Ira D. Sankey, who later became the musical partner of Dwight L. Moody, the great evangelist. It was a matter of lasting satisfaction to Henry that he won in a musical competition over "the great Ira D. Sankey."

Although Henry's heart was not in farming, his parents needed him on the farm, so he resigned himself to that occupation. During the Civil War, he could not leave his aged parents who depended on him to run the farm, and furthermore, by then he had a wife and an infant son to care for. Since he could not serve in the Union Army, he was forced to pay for a substitute to take his place. In later life he would recall how he paced up and down on a moonlit night, mortified that he could not help defend his country, while the Southern troops were marching on Washington.

With the death of his first wife in 1867, Henry left his son "Rafe" with his wife's people and went west to spend two years in Wisconsin on an unsuccessful basket-manufacturing venture.[2] He then returned to farm but he continued to show an active interest in music. Soon he was a member of a quartet that sang at country weddings and funerals, and he took an active interest in improving church choirs. When the opportunity arose, he became a teacher of music in the Lockport, New York, public schools. Here he met Harriet Augusta Beaman, the principal of a grade school, and they were married in 1876. Like Henry, Harriet was proud of her pioneer heritage, which she could trace back to early colonial times. As a girl she had shown her pluck and determination by opposing the will of her father, who did not believe in higher education for women. With borrowed money she attended the Oswego State Normal School, where she graduated in 1871. It was quite an attainment for her to be promoted to the position of grade school principal in a city school while she was in her early thirties. She once demonstrated her strong sense of fairness by insisting that a student called up for discipline should be given an opportunity to explain his side of the case. She was a cultured person endowed with a pleasing personality.[3] She was a fine helpmate for Henry in every way, and she was able to assist him with his reports and speeches. They had three children: Mary Augusta, born on March 11, 1880; Alice Louise, born on January 28, 1882; and Edwin Griswold, born on May 20, 1883. All were destined to become successful in their independent careers.

Henry gradually made a name for himself at Lockport as one of the pioneers in the tonic sol-fa method of teaching people to sing without forcing them to learn to read music. When Edwin was Chairman of the Council of Economic Advisers in the late 1940s, he received a letter from an old lady in Lockport who, as a girl, came under his father's influence. She said: "It opened up a whole new world to me and I have been grateful all of my life to him."

Henry's novel teaching methods attracted the attention of public school officials in the towns of Englewood and Hyde Park, Illinois, then suburbs of Chicago, and in 1883 the two towns joined together to employ him as "Superintendent of Public School Music." This is how Edwin Nourse went west as a baby in the fall of 1883.

Childhood in Englewood

Until Edwin was six, the Nourses lived under rather modest circumstances in a rented cottage in Englewood. During this period, Henry prepared a set of graded song books with a teaching manual to go with them that were published by the Chicago firm of Oliver Ditson and Company. With the added income from his books, Henry was able to build a rather pretentious two-story house on a lot that he had acquired in the same locality. This was a real step up for the family just as Edwin was entering the first grade. His sister Alice has well described the new home as she first saw it.

> The day we moved my sister and I wheeled our doll carriages . . . to our very own home with central heating and gaslighting. We looked with amazement at the wide staircase with its newel post supporting a handsome gas fixture. The two parlors were carpeted from wall to wall in soft blue. Under the bay window, in the back parlor stood a sofa done in red plush. . . . Behind the hall was my father's study, with a table under the window covered with green baize. At one end was his mimeograph on which he copied instructions to be used with his books.[4]

Edwin was a chubby-faced, healthy little boy who enjoyed his first two years of school at Englewood, but otherwise these years made no distinct impression on him. He recalls that his father then spent much time in his study preparing his musical exercises. His father was much concerned with the question of whether Englewood and Hyde Park would be annexed to Chicago. He opposed this because it would bring these communities under the control of wicked, wet Chicago. The first long word that Edwin came to know was "annexation."

When Edwin was eight years old, his father traded the new house in Englewood for a house and seven acres of land in Downers Grove, a little town of 2,500 some 32 miles west of Chicago. It was the terminus of the Burlington's commuter trains, so it was readily accessible to the city. The move did not interfere with Henry's teaching work, for he was able to transfer his duties to districts on the west side of Chicago.

Although the home in Downers Grove was primitive compared with the modern home in Englewood, it held many attractions. The lot, which was formerly a nursery, had stately pine trees and a small orchard and vineyard, and it was in a pleasing small-town environment. It was just the kind of place that Henry had long desired, for as a farm-reared boy with many generations of farming ancestors, he loved the land and had long dreamed of getting out into the country. As his wife philosophically said: "Henry always wanted a farm on the corner of State and Madison."

There was another factor that influenced Henry in making the decision. His wife had been stricken with an incurable heart disease which led to her early death. This impending disaster greatly concerned him, for he did not see how he could manage in the big Englewood house without her. He concluded that he could better care for his children under the simpler and safer conditions at the little farm in Downers Grove. Although his wife loved her attractive and comfortable home in Englewood, she was a farm-reared girl herself, and she understood Henry's longing for the land. She also respected his judgment that the move would be best for bringing up the children.

Growing Up in Downers Grove

Not long after the move to Downers Grove, Edwin's mother died. His memories of her are rather hazy, for he was only eight years old, and she had been an invalid for several months before her death. He was, however, aware of her tender affection and of her concern for his future. He realized that she loved books and that she was a creative person, and he always attributed to her his propensity toward scholarship and writing.

The move to Downers Grove opened up for Edwin a new world of adventure. A horse named "Prince" came with the property, and Edwin's father soon bought a cow to provide fresh milk for his ailing wife and growing children. He also raised a flock of chickens. Thus there were plenty of chores for a boy to do, and it was not long before Edwin took over the milking. "The Place," as the family called the little farm, gave him the pleasures and experiences of growing up in the country. His sister Alice later said: "To Edwin and me it was seven acres of magic."

While his mother was ill, his sister Mary, three years his senior, had largely looked after Edwin and their sister Alice. Mary was a self-reliant little girl, and after their mother's death she became something of a "housemother" for her younger sister and brother. She looked on them as her charges, and she accepted many responsibilities that would have fallen on their mother. At that time, Henry was so busy with his professional work and the problems of getting the home established that he could devote little time to his children. Edwin remembered how Mary used to read to him and Alice. When she came to a big word that she couldn't pronounce, she would call it "something." This amused her father, who once said: "It seems to me that every other word you read is 'something.'"

Mary introduced Edwin and Alice to the books that were favorites with children at the time, such as *Little Men*, *Little Women*, and *Black Beauty*. She also read to them articles from the *Youth's Companion*, a magazine that Henry subscribed to for its educational and moral influence. This became a great favorite with all members of the family.

Soon after the death of his wife, Henry was able to get a distant relative, "Cousin Clara," to serve as housekeeper. She was not a warm, outgoing person, and the children quickly built their own tight little circle with Mary as their champion. At the beginning, Cousin Clara tried to be nice to the children, partly because she saw herself as a possible replacement for their mother. However, when Henry showed little disposition to accept her into the family, she became irritable and took out her resentment on the children. Looking back, one of the good things that came out of Cousin Clara's two-year reign was that it drew the children together against her as the common enemy. The unusually close attachment of Edwin to his sisters was strengthened by this situation. Alice later recounted an incident of this period which shows how Edwin was developing a character of his own. One day Cousin Clara was upset because Edwin had not emptied the grape skins from a bowl. To discipline him, she commanded that he take each grape skin separately to the chicken house. Edwin did as he was told, but in a very distinctive way. He made a ceremony of it by carrying each grape skin daintily above his head in a salute as he took it out to the chicken yard, to the admiring amusement of his sisters. This, of course, infuriated Cousin Clara, but Edwin was following the letter of the law. Already his spirit of independence was manifesting itself in an original way.[5] Henry did not perceive the dislike of his children for Cousin Clara until she was away during the summer holidays, when he could look after things himself. Then the children, fearing her return, expressed their pent-up feelings. At last aware of the situation, Henry wrote to Cousin Clara that she need not return.

For the next few years, a Miss Cook presided over the house in a fair-handed and competent way. But she gradually took a liking to Henry that he couldn't fully reciprocate, so she left. Then there was a succession of housekeepers until Edwin was a sophomore in high school. At that time Henry married a Chicago public school teacher, partly because he thought she would be a good mother for his children. She sought to merit their affection, and the girls and Edwin gradually came to accept her as "Mother Nourse."

An intangible, but important, influence on Edwin as he grew up in Downers Grove was the Nourse family tradition of honesty, going back to Rebecca Nurse. As a boy he was conscious of Rebecca's place in history and proud of her, although he never knew the full facts until they were later developed through research. He liked to think that he inherited her steadfastness of character, and in later life he was to reflect on the effect her example had on him and his sisters in a delightful essay, "Witch's Brood," presented to the Literary Society of Washington on May 23, 1964. It began: "I am a son of a witch." In this essay he paid tribute to Rebecca for her "imperturbable calm in the midst of mass hysteria" and her "intellectual self-respect—or commonsense—in the face of ideological cant or judicial incompetence." Like so many things imbedded in one's childhood, the example of Rebecca Nurse helped give direction and meaning to Edwins life.

Another conditioning influence on Edwin was the pioneering record of his family. Francis and Rebecca had come to America to improve their lot, and their descendants were always on the move to better themselves. Edwin's father had expressed his strong pioneering instinct by trying his luck in Wisconsin, and then he had returned to help develop the new field of public school music. Edwin's mother had demonstrated her pioneering temperament by going out on her own in the teaching field. Thus the pioneering spirit was deeply imbedded in Edwin, and it was to have a significant effect on his career.

The dominant character in his formative years was his father. Henry Nourse was a man of spare build, nearly six feet tall. In Edwin's words, he was "one of the beavers of his time with a full beard that he chopped off when I was about 10. After that he wore a spade beard which he finally reduced to a greying mustache." Family photographs show him as neat, well groomed, and dignified in appearance. Henry was a man of principle who took moral problems seriously. A strict, almost fundamentalist Baptist, he "had no truck" with drinking, smoking, or dancing, although he became more tolerant after Mary took up dancing at the University of Chicago. He objected to strong language of any sort, although he occasionally would say "pshaw." With all his strictness, he had a saving sense of humor, and he used to tell how he was once reprimanded by his aunt for using strong language. He had been helping her lay a carpet, and it was difficult to stretch smooth and tight. When finished, she complimented him on a fine job but added: "Henry, I was very sorry that if you hit your thumb, you'd say 'Pshaw.'" Henry didn't allow any deviation in his son. Edwin was helping his father on a hot summer day, when in exasperation, he said: "Confound it." His father couldn't let this go, so he reprimanded him for using this vulgar expression. Henry couldn't tolerate dishonesty in any form. He once chastized Edwin for giving him an excuse that he thought was untrue. These incidents provide some idea of the puritanical atmosphere in which Edwin was brought up, with its strong emphasis on duty, propriety, and industry.

Although Henry Nourse was stern in his demands on his children, he was considerate of their needs and wishes. He had ambitions for himself and his children. He felt responsible for giving them guidance and educational opportunities which would enable them to amount to something. He was economical and more concerned with the pleasures of living than with making money. He liked people and was highly respected by all who knew him. He was proud of his profession of music, which brought happiness to people. One of his qualities was a stoical acceptance of life. Clearly Edwin held his father in high respect and had a considerable affection for him. They were comrades as they worked on carpentry jobs and as they did other things around The Place. Edwin once mentioned a walk that he had with his father "just for the company of it." His father guided him, but did not keep him under too tight a rein. Edwin did what he wanted to do, but he felt responsible to his father for doing what he thought was necessary.

One of Edwin's early friends who exerted a healthy influence on him while he was growing up was Matt Diener, a man hired by his father to help prune and harvest the acre of grapes that came with The Place. Henry wanted to have someone around Edwin as a surrogate father, since he would be away all day in the city with his school work. Matt was just the man he needed, for he came from Alsace-Lorraine with vineyard experience and was a deacon in the German Evangelical church. Edwin and Matt came to be much attached to each other, to the great satisfaction of Edwin's father.

Edwin's sisters, Mary and Alice, also played a very important role in conditioning his life. From his infant days they were intensely proud of him, and this attitude continued throughout their lives. Mary was the pacesetter who provided an example and guidance for her younger sister and brother. What Mary could do, she expected them to do. Alice was handicapped by illnesses during much of her childhood, losing a grade in school as a result. This brought Edwin and her together in the freshman year of high school, but because of more illness, Alice graduated one year later than he.

Edwin and Alice shared a very close affinity during the time they lived at Downers Grove. They were very fond of each other, and both shared a talent for writing. Because of Alice's periods of ill health, a tender relationship developed. Edwin's strong sense of empathy grew through association with a sensitive person such as Alice. In high school they were often rivals in the same class. Although she admired her tall, handsome brother, she was somewhat envious of his "precious gift," his ability to write. They liked to think of themselves as "twins." Edwin once said: "When H. G. Wells later wrote a story about two devoted siblings called 'Peter' and 'Joan,' we adopted the names. As long as Alice lived she opened her letters to me as 'Dearest Peter,' and I would sign my letters to her 'Peter.'"[6]

When Edwin was a boy in Downers Grove, the "sense of the Civil War was pervasive," and he was "thoroughly imbued with the Civil War spirit." Veterans of the war but a quarter century past were an "important element in the community." A volunteer company had been raised in the area, and there was a GAR (Grand Army of the Republic) post with a hall in Downers Grove. Edwin was thrilled when the pastor of the Baptist church promoted a Baptist Boys' Brigade, of which he was proud to be Second Lieutenant. Looking back on this experience, he said: "Our drill master was Sergeant Gene Farrar, who had been with an Illinois regiment that had marched with 'Sherman's Bums' to the sea. On Memorial Day, while the parade was forming, we youngsters of the Boys' Brigade were allowed to go up into the GAR Hall to mix with the veterans and see the war prints and other Civil War mementos." Nourse's deep interest in American history which developed while he was a child was no doubt amplified by these early contacts with those who had helped make history.

Church played a very important role in Edwin's early life, and his strict religious training helped build his outlook on life. His father, active in the church, led the choir, and he expected his children to attend Sunday school and church services on Sunday mornings, and meetings of the Baptist Young Peoples Union on Sunday evenings. When his father was home they had morning prayers, and on Wednesday nights—after the children had joined the church—they were expected to attend prayer meetings and testify. Edwin accepted this environment without any deep religious convictions, and he later was grateful that his religious background gave him a fund of biblical knowledge and literary allusions of use in his professional career.

When he was about 10 years old he joined the church. It happened in this way. Alice, who was highly emotional, had been fired by the cantata "Esther" put on by her father at the church and later by some revival meetings. She requested his permission to join the church, which he granted. Mary, who didn't like to have her younger sister join before she did, followed suit, and Edwin, not wishing to be left out, decided as a social necessity to take advantage of the opportunity. He never took his conversion seriously, and when asked if he had ever contemplated becoming a minister, he replied with emphasis: "Definitely not."[7]

Without question the dynamic city of Chicago had a tremendous effect on Edwin as a boy. He grew up in the outskirts when the city was going through its greatest period of expansion. Its population, only half a million in 1880, reached more than a million by 1890 and one million seven hundred thousand by 1900. It was in these years that the city's great industrial and mercantile enterprises boomed—the big livestock packers, the large terminal grain marketing firms, the Pullman Company, Marshall Field and Company, Montgomery Ward, and Sears and Roebuck. In 1892 the first steel skyscraper in the world reared its head in Chicago and in the same year the elevated railway began to knit the sprawling city together.

Along with economic progress came great social and cultural developments. A notable cultural event in 1889 was the completion of Louis Sullivan's auditorium then called "the most famous building on the American continent." In the same year, Jane Addams began her work at Hull House, the world-famous social service center. In 1891 the Chicago Symphony Orchestra under Theodore Thomas brought a wave of musical appreciation to the city, and in 1893 the Art Institute of Chicago was built along the lake front. Chicago's most impressive civic achievement was the holding of the World's Fair—The Columbian Exposition—in 1893, which astounded the world with Chicago's energy and progressiveness.

George Ade, who was a Chicago reporter at the time, summed up the World's Fair with this comment: "The world's greatest achievement of the departing century was pulled off in Chicago. The Columbian Exposition was the most stupendous, interesting and significant show ever spread out for the public. As a demonstration of civic pride, community enterprise and nation-wide cooperation—revealing the progress and culture and creative impulses of the world—it has not been matched."[8] Nourse later said: "The World's Fair was a breakthrough. Chicago broke its neck to get itself registered in the world as something more than a backwoods community."

Not everything was glorious in Chicago. In the 1890s it was the most crime- and vice-ridden city of the nation. The situation was so bad in 1893 when the World's Fair was held that W. T. Stead, an English editor and author, wrote a book which threatened the city with damnation—*If Christ Came to Chicago.* Robert Morss Lovett called this book "the most terrific arraignment of any city since the Hebrew prophets denounced Babylon."[9] To Henry, Chicago was the wicked city from which he had to protect his young. To Edwin, it was the outside world that had to be explored and examined.

Of particular interest to Henry Nourse and his family was the creation of the University of Chicago, which formally opened on the Midway in October, 1892, in the shadow of the white buildings being constructed for the World's Fair. Within a few years, with the munificent backing of John D. Rockefeller, it had become one of the great educational institutions of the world. Edwin thus was able to watch the university grow from the ground up. His father, as a good Baptist, took a possessive interest in the university's progress, for he saw it as a place where his family might get their college education at reasonable cost, without jeopardizing their morals.

When the children outgrew the *Youth's Companion,* Henry subscribed to McClure's magazine, "which brought the world into the home." The only other magazine subscribed to was the *Baptist Examiner*, which Henry read "religiously," but which had little appeal to Edwin. Henry did not subscribe to a Chicago newspaper, for he bought one at the station to read on his way to work. Edwin and his sisters "got their stimulation mostly from the *Downers Grove Reporter,*" which carried little outside news.

Books were always important to Edwin. Although there was no public library in Downers Grove, he had access to many books at home, which he later referred to as one of the few family libraries in town. Some of the volumes, mostly relating to poetry, had been collected by his mother before her marriage, while others were accumulated by his parents. Among these books were Mark Twain's *Roughing It*; Parkman's *Oregon Trail*; *Quo Vadis*; and *Uncle Tom's Cabin*. As a boy he came to know and enjoy these books. Two books that made a definite impression on him were gifts to his father in appreciation of his participation in commencement exercises. One was Ulysses S. Grant's two-volume *Autobiography*, which Grant wrote in order to pay his debts, when he was dying of cancer. The other was Fisk's *American Revolution*.

Edwin's mother had been determined that her children would have college educations, and his father sought in every way to carry out her wishes, either expressed or inferred. He also had a very strong desire to give his children all possible cultural opportunities as they were growing up. He recognized that there were many educational advantages available in Chicago that were not to be found in a small community like Downers Grove, so he made it a point to take the children to "the City" for frequent excursions to satisfy their needs. He would take the girls and Edwin separately, for their tastes and interests were quite different. Edwin was particularly excited by his visits to the World's Fair in the summer of 1893, when he was 10. When his father asked him: "Where do you want to go?" Edwin's first choice was the Transportation Building and then the Manufacturer's Building, and of course, he wanted to go to the Midway, where all the shows were. Edwin recalled that he saw Buffalo Bill and Annie Oakley and real live Indians in the flesh, but not Little Egypt, the exotic dancer who was the most popular attraction at the fair. His father did not think this kind of entertainment suitable for a boy of 10. "Pure refined entertainment we got, and particularly music, but he drew the line on the theatre and opera, for my mother had frowned on such frivolous activity."

As a boy Edwin was little affected by the national political controversies of the time. His father was a member of the ineffective Prohibition Party and was little concerned with the issues that divided the Democrats and Republicans. Because of his father's affiliation with the Prohibition Party, Edwin marched in the 1896 Chicago parade for the Prohibition presidential candidates and wore the party's campaign badges and buttons, but this was more of a lark than a commitment. In the same year, out of curiosity, he attended a large gathering in Englewood addressed by William Jennings Bryan, so that in later life he could say that he heard the great Commoner during this campaign.

Although his father was only passively interested in national politics, he was definitely concerned with local politics. Shortly after the family moved to Downers Grove, he successfully ran for the local school board to ensure better educational standards for his children, and he was several times reelected. He was particularly concerned with keeping the "wets" from gaining control, and he enlisted Edwin's help in obtaining information that would be helpful. This experience gave Edwin an awareness of the importance and nature of political action.

Although Edwin was too young to be conscious of the Haymarket Square anarchist riots which shocked the nation in 1887, the event left an aftermath of bitterness and dissention which came to a head in 1893 when Governor Peter Altgeld pardoned three of the Haymarket "anarchists" on the grounds that the evidence did not prove their guilt. While Edwin did not fully understand the issues involved (for he was but 10), the controversy which was aroused by Governor Altgeld's action gave him, as he later said, "an outlook on the question of anarchism, civil rights, and the powers of the governor to pardon."

The economic depression of 1893 taught Edwin the importance of business conditions. His father's salary was cut from $1,800 to $1,600, and this strained the family finances and aroused much concern as to the future. The following year he became aware of the labor problem when Eugene Debs, the President of the American Railway Union, called a strike of the Pullman Company workers which threatened to paralyze the railroad industry. The refusal of the Pullman Company to consider the strikers' demands led to rioting and burning of cars in the Hawthorne freight yards midway between Downers Grove and the city. Edwin was to remember how his father sent him out to buy the morning papers so he could keep in touch with developments. To stop the spread of rioting and keep open the mails, President Grover Cleveland took the extreme measure of calling out federal troops and camping them on the lake front. To Governor Altgeld this was an infringement of state power, and a bitter controversy arose that attracted national attention. This historic confrontation gave realism to Edwin's later interest in the labor movement. The experience at least taught him that there was more than one side to a labor dispute.

Edwin was a normal boy in most respects, and his childhood was a generally happy period. He loved The Place, and it gave him plenty of outlet for exercise and fun. As a boy he was taught to work, and he accepted this as a matter of course. Any task that he did around The Place was for the common good, and he had little money to spend. His father provided for his essential needs, but this didn't cover luxuries. His greatest extravagance was to buy two bicycles for the children—a boy's bike for Edwin and a girl's bike for his two sisters. If Edwin was given any money, he was expected to explain how it was spent. Not until he left home for college did he make or have any money for himself.

Edwin got along well in school, but he wasn't a grind. Only one course made a lasting impression on him, and this was grammar in the seventh grade, taught by Miss Dollinger from the high school staff. Nourse later remarked: "Unlike most kids, who think it loathesome, I was fascinated with the classes in grammar. She must have been a good teacher." By the time Edwin graduated from grade school, he was beginning to shoot up, and within a year or so he attained his full height of six feet one inch "in his stocking feet" and six feet two "with his shoes on."

High School Education

Edwin was fortunate in having good mental stimulation and social encouragement during his four years in high school. He came along at a very propitious time, as he later explained:

> When we went to Downers Grove, father was quite concerned about the quality of education, and whether it would be sufficient to prepare us for college. He soon got himself on the school board and there was a gradual upgrading process. Even when Mary was getting near college age, she was forced to go away to an academy for a year and a half to fit herself for the University of Chicago. By the time Alice and I came along, three years later, the high school was in position to meet college entrance requirements.

When Edwin began his freshman year at 14, the principal of the high school, who was also superintendent for the Downers Grove school system, was Mr. Rassweiller, a long-time friend of his father. He took an interest in Edwin and did what he could to further his nascent interest in chemistry by buying supplies so that he could dabble in experiments described in a book that was in the five-foot shelf of books that was the eighth-grade library. With Mr. Rassweiller's death early in the school year, Mr. O. M. Searles, a young man working for his doctor's degree in psychology at the University of Chicago, was brought in as principal and superintendent. This was a fortunate appointment for Edwin, for Searles was to have a definite influence on his future career. He was a dynamic, alert person who soon injected a new spirit into the high school. Although he taught little himself, he recruited competent young teachers and did much to raise the quality of education while promoting a healthy social environment among the students.

Searles took a great interest in what the high school students were doing, thinking, and planning, and he urged those warranted by ability to go on for university training. Edwin soon got to know him well, for he was a good friend of his father and was frequently a guest at the Nourse home. His father looked to Searles for guidance on the educational problems of his children, and Searles gave Edwin unstinted encouragement to go on for university training. Edwin's sister Alice has concisely provided her impressions of the impact made by Searles on Edwin and herself.

> Into Edwin's and my life now stepped Mr. Searles, the new superintendent, a humble man—short, stocky, with unruly black hair, wonderful blue eyes, awkward movements. His name still invokes in me, and in Edwin, exciting new vistas of the mind. Standing somewhat awkwardly before the high school students—his clothes never seemed to fit—Mr. Searles would talk about books, about writing. Under his guidance Edwin and I read avidly—Dickens, Scott, Thackeray—I was even stirred by Burke's speech on *Conciliation,* difficult though it was, which Mr. Searles had us study. He introduced us to poets other than Whittier and Longfellow—Shelley, Keats and, of course, Tennyson, so admired in that day. For the first time I heard about style in writing. He made us express ourselves, sometimes praising, sometimes criticising our efforts, but always believing in us.[10]

Edwin was particularly fortunate in having Miss Edith Neal, a recent graduate from the University of Chicago, as his English teacher during his freshman year. She used to keep his essays to buoy her up when she became discouraged in trying to teach English to her less responsive students. She brought out the best in him, and he began to develop pride in his writing ability. In later life he was to refer to his work with her "as a step forward in my intellectual development."

Edwin's interest in studying German, encouraged by his friendship with Matt Diener, got a boost during his sophomore year under Mable Messner, a Northwestern University graduate who came from a German-speaking family. To familiarize himself with the language, he attended Matt's German-speaking church and played German hymns on his horn.

Latin was a subject that gave him difficulty, and he had to repeat one book of Caesar. However, he went through the four-year course—the grammar year, Caesar, Cicero, and Virgil—and later in college he was to take further work in the subject "to keep up the classical tradition." He discovered early that Latin was essential to good English writing. Edwin also enjoyed his work in history, civics, mathematics, and other customary high school subjects. He then had no interest in the field of economics. However, he remembers that when in high school he overheard a man tell his father that he had a library made up entirely of books on economics. This aroused his curiosity, and the word stayed in his memory. Altogether, for the times, he got a well-rounded high school education.

High school also opened up Edwin's social life. The young teachers brought in by Searles believed that social activities were essential to a complete education, and evening school parties were introduced. Edwin recalled how, one time in his sophomore year, the students dressed up the schoolrooms to entertain the visiting football team. "We had a real evening party with some sort of non-alcoholic punch and sandwiches and cookies and music. It was really an eye-opener to us. That's the first thing of that sort I'd ever attended." He went on to say: "Encouraged by this new spirit, about 10 or a dozen of us who were particularly congenial formed a little club just to have a party at the home of one of the members on Saturday night once a month. When they formed a dancing class, I was not permitted to join it because of Father's fundamentalism."

He looked back on this phase of his high school life with much satisfaction: "I think it was just about as wholesome and idyllic a life as a youngster in high school could have—very different from the teen-age life of this affluent age in our big-city schools."

Edwin took a great interest in athletics while in high school. He played center on the football team, which had no coaching other than that given by "a local yokel" who "told us a little about the game." Edwin was at that time quite an organizer, and he was active in introducing basketball and promoting track meets. He liked to play on all the teams, but he wasn't in his words, "a born athlete. I never won anything." He was never able to develop a real competitive spirit in athletics.

During his high school days, his inseparable chum was Harry Slusser, who later became a Chicago attorney. In the winter they promoted skating and tobogganing parties, which were very popular in those days. Edwin had several girl friends, but as he explained: "We had just the sweetest boy-girl friendships. You didn't go steady in those days." He admitted, however, that he became "a little attracted" to a girl who afterwards married Harry, and that he became for a time "much attached" to a dashing young girl who came to town, and "mildly interested in another girl in a brotherly sense."

Taking everything into account, high school was a very stimulating time in Edwin's life. He was then a handsome young man, popular with his teachers and classmates. He liked his courses and got the most out of them. He was finding himself as a person and beginning to demonstrate qualities of intellectual and social leadership. He was preparing for he knew not what—but he was content that whatever he learned would come in handy.

Graduation day was a big event in his life. He gave the class oration, and that night the graduating class met at the Nourse home for a party. It wasn't a large group, for there were only a dozen in the class.

At this time, Edwin's future looked bright. What would he make of it?

Chapter II

COLLEGE DAYS—LEWIS INSTITUTE AND CORNELL UNIVERSITY (1902-1906)

When Edwin Nourse graduated from high school, he didn't want to go on to college. He wanted to work on the little Downers Grove farm, but his father would not listen to "any such talk." As Edwin later explained: "There was no question. His discipline was strong enough so that I just dropped the idea. He had found out about Lewis Institute, where I would be able to live at home and commute there and pay a very low tuition. So my first year at college was at Lewis Institute—now the Illinois Institute of Technology."

Lewis Institute—First Year

Thus in the fall Nourse began going to Lewis Institute. This involved a two-mile walk to the college from the suburban station. Lewis Institute was a coeducational school founded in 1896 on the western fringe of Chicago by Allen C. Lewis, a Chicago traction magnate. It offered vocational and general liberal arts courses and gave an associate in arts degree after two years of training. It was something like a junior college of today, and it was a good arrangement for Nourse. Although he commuted from home, he got into the wider cultural life associated with Chicago. Looking back Nourse said: "I didn't have a real goal at that time. I wasn't preparing for a career. I didn't have any professional orientation and I picked up courses in high school fashion. I was just going to college."

However, Nourse found the city students congenial, and he soon joined the Parnassions, the men's literary society. He also became a member of the Dafdalians, a local fraternity founded by Professor Lewis on the Daedalus tradition of high respect for skills in the arts and sciences. Nourse later said: "I had a very good time at Lewis Institute and was very much in the spirit of the school. I think it was a very good choice."

At Lewis Institute, Nourse took courses in English, Latin, German, history, trigonometry, and wood shop. He had "puttered around at carpentry" with his father but he wanted "to get the thing on a little more professional basis." An old Scotsman ran the woodshop, and he was pleased that Nourse was more patient and careful in his work than most students. So he assigned him the task of making a little fumed oak chair. Nourse later conceded that he did "a pretty nice job on it" and "was gloating over the thought of having it around the house" when he found that it was being made for George Carmen, the Director of the Lewis Institute, who was taking it to his summer home in Wisconsin.

At Lewis Institute, Nourse came under the beneficial influence of Dr. Edwin Herbert Lewis, the Head of the English Department, who recognized his literary talent. Lewis had a system of marking papers with an *H.* for Honors and an *H.H.* for High Honors, and Nourse was able "to catch an *H.H.* from him every now and then." Lewis had resigned as assistant professor at the University of Chicago to take the Lewis Institute position. While at Chicago he had written the university's famous alma mater, which contained the classic words:

> The City White hath fled the earth,
> But where the azure waters lie
> A nobler city hath its birth,
> The City Gray that ne're shall die.[1]

Nourse has given us this portrait of Lewis and his relationship to him:

> Professor Lewis felt that Lewis Institute had a good deal of engineering and tradesmen's son atmosphere and he wanted to give it a little more cultural, spiritual outlook. He was the son of a minister I believe. And he was quite a dramatic figure, bald headed, with a Van Dyke beard and a noticeable resemblance to William Shakespeare, a resemblance of which he was amusingly proud. He favored himself a little bit as a tenor singer. He had all these endearing qualities and he spotted me as being more responsive to that sort of thing than many of my classmates, and after only a quarter or so there, he asked me if I would like to assist in one of his English classes for my tuition which I did. So that was the beginning of my teaching experience."[2]

Nourse never lost his appreciation for the lift that Professor Lewis gave to his life. In his 1953 commencement address for the Illinois Institute of Technology, the successor to the Lewis Institute, Nourse paid tribute to Lewis's contribution to the cultural side of the Institute's progress, and in 1966 he established a fund for an Edwin Herbert Lewis English prize to commemorate Lewis and to emphasize the fact that the Illinois Institute of Technology was not merely an engineering school, but a well-balanced university.

Nourse's year at Lewis Institute was very rewarding in every respect. It greatly increased his social proclivities, for he learned to dance and participate in a more general environment. This year also fired his ambition to go on for further education to a recognized college, and he settled on Cornell University. Nourse has explained his thinking at this time:

> I wanted to go to an eastern school and preferably in a real college town. My first choice was Yale but I found from the catalogue that they required Greek as well as Latin. So I picked out Cornell for two main reasons. (1) the glamour of the crew, and (2) the fact that it was an eastern school in a small college town. Poor boy that I was, my ambitions were limitless and I went there with the idea and did enroll for a six year course in civil engineering which involved getting a B.A. before a C.E. I had read in a Chicago Sunday paper of the exciting work of the Civil Engineers and that appealed to my sense of getting around in new country and also to my mechanical turn of mind.[3]

He did not find Professor Lewis enthusiastic about his "engineering slant." Lewis was "apprehensive that at Cornell I might get that way and lose what he thought was a discernible bent toward English. Later in life he was pleased that I had made something of the literary side of economic exposition."

Nourse knew that he would largely need to pay his own way at Cornell, for he could count on no help from his father, who was overwhelmed by his own financial problems. His only help was a loan of $100 (later made into a gift) from a friend of the family, Mrs. Griswold, from whom he got his middle name. With this loan, along with what he could earn during the summer in carpentry work and what he hoped to earn while going to college, he felt that he could get by.

To understand his home situation, it should be realized that just as he was completing his work at Lewis, the Chicago school board discontinued his father's job as an economy measure. This was a serious blow, for his father had meager savings, and since he was over 60, there was little other work to be found. He and his wife could count only on small monthly teacher's pensions of $20 each as a means of support, and Alice was now ready for college and needed financial help. The loss of his position deeply affected his father, for he had been proud of his work, and it was the source of much of his happiness. However, he met the disaster with fortitude and dignity, and during the fall he was able to find a few part-time teaching jobs in nearby suburban towns.[4] That summer Nourse and his father added a new front porch to the house, which made the home more comfortable and attractive.

Cornell—First Term

Nourse was captivated by Cornell from the beginning. It was everything he hoped it would be. The spirit of Cornell, with its social life and victorious athletic teams, was all that any student could desire.[5]

Andrew D. White, the founding president, still lived on the campus and brought eminence to it, and Jacob Gould Schurman, who was then president, was held in high respect by the whole academic community. He was nationally ranked with Elliot of Harvard, Jordan of Stanford, and Harper of the University of Chicago among the outstanding college presidents of the day. It was the general belief at Cornell that students should enjoy their studies, be enthusiastic in the learning process, and not be compelled to take only required courses. White encouraged students to be self-supporting, and there was no stigma attached to working one's way. He and Ezra Cornell had been determined to make Cornell "a people's school" rather than "a gentlemen's school."

When Nourse set off for Cornell, his father was greatly concerned that he not get started on the wrong track. He was very much afraid that Edwin might slip away from the church when he got to a "Godless State University," so he arranged to have his "letter of membership" transferred to the Ithaca Baptist Church. He enclosed it with a personal letter to the pastor, and he instructed Edwin to call on him when he got to Ithaca. His father informed the pastor that Edwin would have to earn his own way, and he requested his help in finding a job for him. Fortunately the pastor was able to find work for him to earn his board waiting tables at Cascadilla Hall, which Nourse later termed "a job I loathed from my boots up."

Nourse soon found a place to stay in a third-floor attic bedroom on Eddy Street, which he got rent-free for taking care of the furnace and shoveling snow from the walks. He found that he could cook for himself in his room, so he freed himself from the unpleasant Cascadilla job. He picked up a little money from various odd jobs.

Although he matriculated for the engineering program, his first courses were primarily in liberal arts—English, French, mathematics, and history. The only course directly related to engineering this first year was one in mechanical drawing under Johnny Parsons, who was famous on the campus for his promotion of ice hockey. Rather than take military training, Nourse joined the band to be under the famous leader Pat Conway. Nourse went out for football, but he didn't impress coach Pop Warner, so he gave this up. Nourse never had any great interest in competitive athletics, and this early college experience demonstrated to him that he could better spend his energies on other things.

Altogether, Nourse enjoyed his first term at Cornell. He loved the university's beautiful setting in the hills on Lake Cayuga, and he liked the small-town atmosphere of Ithaca. He found pleasant his contacts with fellow students from all parts of the nation, and he liked Cornell's joyous college spirit.

The Typhoid Setback

Nourse was just completing his first term in January, 1903, when he was caught by the notorious typhoid epidemic that ravaged Cornell from the middle of January to the end of March. As a fellow student later said: "For weeks the campus was fanned hourly by the wings of death." During the epidemic, 131 students came down with the dread disease, and 13 died. In addition, about 160 stricken students fled Cornell for their homes and, of these, 16 died. Nourse was among those who left for home. Aware that he was coming down with typhoid, he finished his work for the semester in a half-sick condition and then found his way home. He got there just in time, for the following day he was put to bed with a high fever.[6]

For the next six weeks he was in a delirious condition and it was touch-and-go as to whether he would survive. In March, while Edwin was still in bed, his father died from an illness no doubt aggravated by his fear that his son would not recover. During this period of great strain, Edwin was cared for by his stepmother and Miss Whitcomb, a trained nurse who had been Alice's nurse. When Alice called on her for help, she dropped everything and came at once. It was due to their devoted care that Edwin pulled through. He later said: "To these two women, I have an immeasurable debt."

For several weeks after the illness Nourse convalesced at home. His weight had fallen from 175 to 125 pounds, and he was not able to resume normal activities until late in the fall.

At this time when the economic costs of his illness made it seem impossible for him to ever return to Cornell, he was heartened by an act of generosity and sympathy from Andrew Carnegie, who had himself been a victim of typhoid. Carnegie realized that the Cornell students stricken by typhoid had been penalized by a catastrophe beyond their control, and so, through a fund provided to the university, he arranged for restitution to be made to them of the costs and losses they had suffered. In this way the doctors' bills and other expenses of Nourse's illness were largely met by a reimbursement of about $800.[7]

Even with this assistance Nourse was not strong enough to return to Cornell the following academic year, so he decided to take further work at the Lewis Institute. With this additional work he was able to meet the requirements for the two-year certificate which was granted him by Lewis Institute in June, 1904. During the following summer and fall he endeavored to make a little money doing carpentry work and painting before returning to Cornell. One of his jobs was to help build a parsonage.

Resumption of Work at Cornell, 1905-1906

When Nourse came back to Cornell in January, 1905, it was a relatively small university in terms of what it is today. It then had about 3,000 students, mostly undergraduates, and mostly men, although the number of women students was on the increase. Professors had time to have talk sessions with their students, and it was not uncommon for students to visit professors in their homes. The professors knew their students —their aspirations and abilities. Research was something that professors did largely on their own time and initiative. It had not yet become a separate branch of university activity. In describing the informal conditions that then prevailed, Nourse has said: "I remember how Professor Sill told us in class that anyone who wanted to, could come to the office and we would have a little party. He had pipes and tobacco there, and we sat and smoked and talked in his office."

This was an invigorating period in Nourse's life, and he made the most of it. He was now past 21, and he no longer felt responsible to his father for moral guidance. He even began to take up pipe smoking, although on the whole, he was a pretty tame individual by today's standards. His religious conversion as a boy had been only skin-deep, and he no longer was under any parental pressure to attend or support a church. He had long been cynical of the dogmas of the Baptists, and one day he dropped in at the Unitarian church, which he found much more to his taste. However, most of his churchgoing was at the Sage Chapel on the Cornell campus, where distinguished ministers from different faiths preached the sermons.

While Nourse was at Cornell, it was primarily a "man's school" and there wasn't anything like the sort of mixing found today in a typical state university. His social contacts with girls came through church or college affairs, and he didn't form any serious attachments. The romantic side of his life was not to blossom until he got to Utah.

Cornell was then known as one of the most progressive universities in the nation, and its tradition of "Freedom and Responsibility" was well established.[8] Students were allowed a great amount of latitude so that they could take whatever courses might interest them, and the spirit of independence was also deeply rooted in the faculty. Professors were given a free hand to develop their courses as they wished, and they looked upon themselves as the guardians of the university.

Under Cornell's elective system, "a student might take any courses that he pleased, in whatever order, provided only that he pass a certain number of hours. . . . The freedom of the Arts student was nearly absolute. Many found their way, by their own efforts and errors, to the kind of education they sought; and many of those who profited by this freedom were ever afterwards grateful for it."[9] Nourse was among this group, for it suited his temperament.

Nourse now was not so pinched financially as he had been when he first arrived as a student. Not only had he made and saved a little money, but he had $500 as his share of the payment made on his father's life insurance policy. His greater affluence made possible a more normal standard of living, which permitted him to devote more time to his studies. During this period at Cornell he lived in a rooming house and received his board free by managing a boarding house club.

Rather than going home during summer vacation in 1905, Nourse decided to save the travel costs and get better acquainted with his native state. He roamed from town to town, paying his expenses and making a little money by carpentry or similar work. One of his jobs was to help build a boat, and another was to help rebuild a barn destroyed by fire. It was a summer of adventure that whetted his appetite for more study and experience.

Nourse's professional training now began to expand rapidly. He was much more mature, and he had a better understanding of what he wanted to get out of college. He gave up his intention of getting a degree in civil engineering and centered his attention on history and other social sciences, which strongly appealed to him. However, he took a number of elective courses in which he had some special interest. For example, he studied surveying in his junior year, and in his senior year he took two courses related to agriculture—field engineering and economic entomology. He later explained his interest in these courses by saying: "I had or had from my father acquired this farm instinct."

Nourse learned a valuable lesson in the entomology course that he was never to forget. As he later recalled it: "I remember very distinctly how the professor in talking about spraying for orchard pests said there were a few sprayers powered with internal combustion engines but that they were unsatisfactory, and he didn't think they would ever displace hand pumps." In the future, Nourse never underestimated industrial progress.

It should be pointed out that there was no separate agricultural campus when Nourse was at Cornell. This came shortly afterwards, with the great period of expansion in the College of Agriculture under Dean Liberty Hyde Bailey, whom Nourse used to see around the campus. In 1906-1907, the regular enrollment of agricultural students was only 145. By 1910-1911, it had increased to 597. There was then little instruction available in agricultural economics. Otherwise, in view of his general agricultural interests, he could have well elected to take farm management, which rapidly developed after 1907 under Professor George F. Warren.[10]

Nourse was singularly fortunate in his selection of history teachers.[11] He studied American History with Professor Charles Hull and Modern European History with Professor Ralph Catteral. He also found of absorbing interest a Greek Politics course given by Professor Harry Sill. This course introduced him to Walter Bagehot's *Physics and Politics*, which had as its theme "the necessity of society forming a crust of custom that would give a discipline, and then being able to break the crust so that we could go forward in social evolution." Nourse liked the idea, and in his later years he said: "It's been in the background of my thinking ever since." At this time in his college career, Nourse was finding of much interest Darwin's *Origin of Species*, and the books by Herbert Spencer. His interest in sociology was beginning to emerge. Nourse didn't take a course in philosophy, but he had the "Great Titchener's" course in psychology. However, he was not impressed with Professor Edward B. Titchener's "mechanistic theories."[12]

Nourse was also highly fortunate in his selection of economics professors. He didn't take Professor Frank Fetter's course in general economics, which was reputed to be dull, but he did take his course in sociology—Philanthropy and Corrections—which he found fascinating. In this course he came to know Fetter well through field trips made to the Auburn Penitentiary and to a state insane asylum. He also had very stimulating courses with Professor Walter F. Willcox, who had served as Director of the Census for 1900. This started a friendship that continued until Willcox's death in 1964. (Nourse attended Willcox's 100th birthday party at the Cosmos Club in Washington, D.C., in 1961.) Nourse also became well acquainted with E. A. Goldenweiser, Willcox's assistant who later became Chief Economist for the Federal Reserve System. In later life, Goldenweiser proudly claimed Nourse as one of his students. Nourse also had several courses with Professor Jeremiah Whipple Jenks, an authority on anti-trust problems, who drew on his vast experience as an economic and political advisor to various European and South American governments. Nourse found Jenks "an attractive, folksy sort of lecturer."

Of particular significance to his later career were two courses on labor problems in his senior year with Professor Robert Franklin Hoxie. Nourse liked his fresh, psychological approach to studies of labor organization. His thinking, Nourse later said, "represented a real breakthrough in that field. He was getting away from the mechanistic sort of analysis of the past to a study of labor organizations in their institutional setting." Nourse was later to apply this same approach to the study of agricultural and cooperative institutions.[13]

Nourse had no further work in English after his return to Cornell except for a course in public speaking, which was "primarily devoted to giving orations." However, the essay-type examinations in the social science courses gave him practice in composition, and his prose often attracted the favorable attention of his professors.

Nourse also took full advantage of the many good outside lectures that were available. One that made a definite impression on him was "on the institutionalizing of the big corporation" by James B. Hill, the great corporation lawyer, who, in Nourse's words, was "the man who put together the New Jersey Corporations with a 'purpose clause' so broad that they could do anything." Another lecture of great interest to him was one on industrial medicine.

At Cornell, Nourse began to develop something of a social philosophy. Part of it he attributed to his father's moralistic approach to public questions, and part he saw as his own response to "the emerging spirit of liberalism represented by the 'muckrakers' that was beginning to see the possibilities of a better society—if not a great society." He was becoming aware of the great issues shaping up in our national life, and he was forming his ideas on how they might be met. Theodore Roosevelt was then president, but Nourse didn't "climb on his bandwagon." As he later explained: "There was nothing in my family background that gave me a reformist line of interest in the major parties. It was a spontaneous reaction, a bit of aloofness, rather than a judgment."

In his senior year, two of his friends were avowed socialists, and their arguments caused him to "ponder very seriously whether this was the wave of the future." After giving the question much consideration, he did not find socialism "congenial as a form of economic organization." As he put it: "This was not my pitch."

Finally, in the spring of 1906, he came to graduation. He then had no definite plans on what he would do next, although he was beginning to look forward to graduate work. His main immediate concern was to make a little money to help his sister Alice with her college education. As he walked down the sidewalk on his way to the graduation exercises, he ran into Professor Catteral, who fell in step with him. "What are you going to do now, Mr. Nourse, teach?" Nourse replied: "My father was a teacher; my mother was a teacher; all of my aunts have been teachers. If there is anything I am not going to be, it's a teacher." Three months later, Nourse was on his way to Ogden, Utah, to start his teaching career.

Probably if he had not responded so cockily, Professor Catteral might have told him that he and Professor Sill were impressed by his work and were hoping to work out plans to offer him a fellowship so that he could take graduate work in history. Without this encouragement, as will be explained in the next chapter, Nourse returned home and found that the best way to make a little money was by teaching. Thus when the fellowship offer came later in the summer, he was committed to a teaching job. If he had received the fellowship and gone on for graduate work in history, he "probably would have become a historian." Although his experience in the next few years was to draw him to economics and sociology, he never lost his love for history.

Nourse always looked back on his years at Cornell with great satisfaction. It was there that his mind was opened up to the intellectual joys of work in the social sciences and the opportunities that this field held for a man with his interests, abilities, and temperament. His courses at Cornell gave him a "fine momentum" to go on for graduate work as soon as he could arrange to do so. To pick up a little more experience, he routed himself home via Washington, D.C., to see the national capital.

Without question, Cornell had a great influence on Nourse's life. I once asked him: "What do you feel was the contribution Cornell made to you?" He responded: "It satisfied my hopes and dreams of my college life very fully—friendships, broader acquaintanceships, good fellowship, expanding interests, intellectual stimulation, sense of direction . . . I *really* got a college course out of it."

Chapter III

FINDING HIS WAY
(1906-1915)

Nourse was not quite sure of the way he wished to direct his career following his work at Cornell. He knew that he needed to broaden his experience and get further training, but he was inclined to let his life unfold and to feel his way, taking advantage of opportunities for advancement as they might arise.

Utah Interlude, 1906-1908

As noted in Chapter II, Nourse's main concern was to make some money after he graduated from Cornell. Attractive jobs were scarce, and he talked his problem over with O. M. Searles, his high school friend and teacher, who was now working for a teachers' employment agency. Searles told him of an opening for a teacher in history and civics at the Ogden, Utah, high school that would pay $90 a month—not a bad salary at that time. The opportunity appealed to Nourse, for this would enable him to get acquainted with the Great West, and so he "grabbed" it.

The train trip to Utah made a deep impression on him. He later said:

> I remember perfectly well coming off the Nebraska plains into Colorado and the foothills of the Rockies one fall afternoon near sunset, and my first view of the big mountains. It thrilled me to find Ogden nestled right in the foothills of the Wasatch Mountains which are some of the most beautiful in that western highland.

Nourse found Ogden a congenial place to live, for it was an up-and-coming railroad and industrial center of about 10,000. It was very much a western town, and when he cashed his first paycheck, the cashier, with a six-shooter he could easily reach, paid him in gold pieces. Nourse was fascinated by the population "with its particular Mormon ingredient," and he was pleased with the high quality of the high school. His colleagues struck him as first-rate and cosmopolitan, and later he was to observe that he didn't see how such a good faculty was assembled at the salaries paid.

Almost immediately Nourse moved into the Bachelor's Club, which was a good place to live, for the principal of the high school and the teacher of chemistry and physics (who coached the football team) also lived there. It was not very long before the three—all of whom were well over six feet tall—were good friends. Moreover, there were a number of rising young businessmen in the club, and this provided contacts with a somewhat different group. One was a lawyer who became assistant attorney, and Nourse did a little work for him in bill collecting. The Bachelor's Club greatly broadened Nourse's moral standards. As he later said: "While it wasn't a wild crowd, it was a group of western young men, and I began then a very moderate sort of drinking which was quite foreign to my earlier experience."

The high school itself was a more complete school than he had attended at Downers Grove, and most of the students were non-Mormon, for the Mormons attended their own parochial schools and academies. However, there was little feeling of apartness in the community, and Nourse soon had many friends among the Mormons. They had quite a lively social life of their own essentially separate from that of the gentile community, and there was a definite consciousness of the separation between the two groups. However, Nourse found no sense of strain or friction or segregation, "and the mingling of business and professional life and to quite an extent, social life, was quite pervasive."

Nourse was soon enjoying a pleasant life, for several of the teachers had friends among the local people.[1] There were often card parties and other affairs in the evenings. Through these meetings Nourse became acquainted with Ray Tyler, an Ogden girl and a recent Wellesley graduate, who was then teaching in Salt Lake City. He met Ray when she came to visit an old girl friend, and this was the beginning of their romance.

Nourse soon became greatly interested in Mormon history and in the accomplishments of the Mormons in irrigation "which made the desert bloom." He was also impressed by the Mormon community enterprises, which were not technically organized as cooperatives, but which had many cooperative characteristics. He later was to say "they were contributors to our lore and practice of cooperation in this country, and I drew upon this experience as I began to get identified with cooperative farming activities in the Midwest." To him, "Brigham Young was a real entrepreneur and industrial promoter who could have been the head of General Motors."

Nourse was well qualified by his work at Cornell for teaching the history and civics courses, and he found this experience very enjoyable, for it stabilized what he had already learned. When summer vacation arrived, Nourse decided instead of traveling home to accumulate some earnings so that he could later take graduate work in economics at the University of Chicago. He had chosen Chicago for it was then outstanding in the social science field, and he was disposed to follow Professor Hoxie, who had accepted a position in the economics department there. During the summer Nourse had two jobs. The first was as a timekeeper with a construction gang that was installing automatic electric block signals on the Southern Pacific Railroad west of Ogden. The crew that he joined was working on the salt flats of the Nevada desert, and there was little for him to do at night, so he read in his bunk Arthur T. Hadley's text on economics and some of the books by Herbert Spencer, which then had great appeal to him. When this job gave out, he got another as local representative for the International Correspondence School at Ely, Nevada, then a revived mining town. He was employed to collect on the payments of quite a number of young men who were taking simple engineering courses. While he was on this job, he had his first trip on a stagecoach and got some idea of life in a mining camp, with its casual labor, or hobo, class. His interest in economics in its historical and geographic setting was beginning to develop. Looking back in later life, he said: "That is the kind of economics I find congenial. I never have been an economic technician, econometrician, natural science type of economist. Out of this western experience and my natural interests I began to have my orientation shaped."

After two years of teaching, Nourse resigned to take up graduate studies in the fall at the University of Chicago. To make a little more money and get more experience, he stayed on to work as a clerk and cashier for the hotel and dining car service of the Harriman (Union Pacific) lines first at Pocatello, Idaho, and then at Rawlings, Wyoming. This gave him an opportunity to see a rising agricultural center in Idaho and to get some idea of cowboy-and-Indian life in Wyoming.

Nourse has always looked back with satisfaction on these two formative years in the West. It gave him a sense of maturity, brought him in contact with the wide-open West, stabilized his thinking and ambitions, and gave him funds to go on for further academic training. Of even greater importance, it provided him with a sweetheart—Ray Tyler—who was to become his life's partner. Nourse said of this period of his life: "It opened up a whole new world to me."

University of Chicago—First Year, 1908-1909

One of Nourse's professors at Cornell University had once said in class that an education should be like a slice of bacon with a strip of lean then a strip of fat. This idea of interlarding formal education with practical experience appealed to Nourse, and now, with some experience under his belt, he was ready for another strip of lean at the University of Chicago. He was now 25.

On his trip east, Nourse stopped off at Lawrence, Kansas, where his sister Alice had taken a position as YWCA secretary at the University of Kansas. She reported that her attractive brother made a good impression on the girls under her supervision.

When he arrived at the University of Chicago, Nourse was disappointed to find that Professor Hoxie was taking a year *in absentia* to work with labor organizations. Since Nourse had relied on having Hoxie's counsel and courses, this was a serious blow. Nourse also found that the fellowship that he had counted on to solve his financial problems was not available. When he was able to see Hoxie, he found out what had happened. Hoxie remonstrated: "You damned fool. You were supposed to make an application for a fellowship in economics, but when I went to see that it was approved and carried through, it hadn't been received. I did find that there was an application from you for a fellowship in sociology." Nourse had not known the ropes. He thought that he should make application for a fellowship in sociology, since he wanted to get a broad view of social structure and social problems before he specialized in economics.

Hoxie got busy and found him a working fellowship in economics, which covered his tuition for a few hours' work a day in the library. His Utah experience helped him obtain the fellowship, for he was required to submit an essay on an economics subject. Nourse took for his topic the effect of the national money panic of 1907 on the rather isolated banking centers of Utah. The reviewers commented that the essay showed promise, although it was rather general.

At the university, Nourse lived in Snell Hall, one of the men's dormitories in the quadrangle. This brought him to the center of university life, for Arnold B. Hall, the head of the dormitory, had been assistant to Harry Pratt Judson in the Political Science Department, and Judson was now president of the university. Hall was later to become President of the University of Oregon and a member of the staff of the Brookings Institution when Nourse was its vice-president.

Nourse found Chicago a very interesting laboratory for a young social scientist. It had become a great industrial and cultural center. It gave him the opportunity to participate in its social life and satisfy his interests in music and the drama. During this year he got acquainted with the work of Jane Addams at Hull House. While he was at the university, his stepmother and half brother were living on The Place at Downers Grove, so frequently he would spend weekends with them and keep in touch with his old home friends.

The Head of the Department of Economics at the University of Chicago was then J. Lawrence Laughlin, one of the best-known economists in the country. However, he was away most of the year in the downtown Loop district, as he was head of the Chicago Sound Money Crusade, which was then laying the foundations for the Federal Reserve System. Because of this situation, Nourse was not able to have much contact with him during his first graduate year. The main courses that he had in economics were one in statistics with a particular emphasis on demography under James A. Field, a delightful and cultured scholar who never let his pupils forget that although figures cannot lie, liars can figure; and another in economic history under Chester Whitney Wright, a painstaking student of this subject. This course gave him a fine grounding on the economic development of the United States, which came at a good time, following his western experience.

Although Nourse's economic pickings were not impressive during his first year of graduate work, he was fortunate in having courses with some of the nation's outstanding sociologists and social thinkers. Among them were Albion W. Small, who was then highly respected by sociologists throughout the world, and W. I. Thomas, who was rapidly gaining fame as a social thinker. He also had a stimulating course in social psychology with George Edgar Vincent, who soon was to become President of the University of Minnesota.

In this course, Nourse prepared a rather long term paper on "Rural Conservatism," which gives a good idea of the direction of his thinking at that time. In this paper he examined the causes underlying the attitudes of farmers. He held that the farmer was inclined toward conservatism for three main reasons—the isolation of his life, his distinctive family relationships, and the influence of migration. He summarized these views in the following paragraph.

> Here, then, we have in brief our dialectic of rural stagnation: (1) Sep-

aration from the varied stimuli of closely compacted population, scant competition, and few patterns for imitation; (2) longer and closer family attachments, economic dependence on the father, and leadership and direction in the hands of the old; (3) selective migration of the vigorous, aggressive, and original parts of the population, leaving the more torpid and stationary members to shape the standards of the group.

However, Nourse did not think that the conservatism of the rural population was a real barrier to progress. He saw no need for antagonism between city and country. In fact, he believed that

economically the country is the partner of the city. In a mutually beneficial division of labor, it naturally takes up the extractive industries, furnishes the raw material for the city. The latter works this up into the finished product, which supplies the consumption of city and country alike. Socially, the same general relations hold. The country furnishes raw material—strong vigorous young life.

Although the paper was somewhat labored, it showed academic thoroughness and ingenuity of expression. It effectively used supporting literature and gave indication of Nourse's growing ability to express himself in a fresh and cogent way. Its emphasis on the copartnership relationship of industry and agriculture was a theme that Nourse was to build on as his career unfolded. It is significant that Professor Vincent thought so well of this paper that he suggested that Nourse read it to the class. Professor Small suggested that it be shortened for the *American Journal of Sociology,* of which he was then editor, but Nourse never settled down to the job of revising it.

On the whole, Nourse's first graduate year at the University of Chicago was rewarding. It got him into the swing of university life again and provided him with the courses that he desired, under very able men. In effect, he completed a sociological minor to be followed by an economic major. This had been his original ambition, and circumstances made the plan feasible.

His good record during the year was attested by an offer of an instructorship at the University of Pennsylvania for the following year, based upon the recommendations of his professors at Chicago. He had gained a foothold.

Wharton School Instructor, 1909-1910

Edward Sherwood Mead, Professor of Finance at the Wharton School of Finance of the University of Pennsylvania in Philadelphia, had received his doctor's degree in economics at the University of Chicago. When he needed a young man to serve as his assistant, he naturally turned to his alma mater. Although Nourse had not taken courses in money and banking or corporation finance, Professor Laughlin tapped him for the job, which paid $1,200 for nine months. This was a definite step up from the $90 a month received at Ogden. Moreover, he would be able to do a substantial amount of graduate work.

To prepare for the new job, which was largely to conduct quiz sections for Mead's courses in money and corporation finance, Nourse studied during the summer the books that would be used. When he arrived at the Wharton School, he found Mead to be a very pragmatic character who was not exacting in his demands. (Mead also did quite a lot of consulting work for business firms, and this gave a practical tinge to his work.) Nourse also was required to assist Thomas Conway, Mead's close associate who was teaching real estate economics and who was also active in real estate promotion. The work that he did in assisting Mead and Conway thus broadened his training in important areas of economic development.

One of the courses taken by Nourse was with Simon Patten who, in Nourse's words, "was quite a figure at the time." Nourse remembers Patten as "a fresh voice and a unique individual. He was 'the son of the middle border,' a shovel-footed, tall, gawky sort of individual whose method of lecturing was quite of a reminiscent sort. He was a heretic, repudiating all of the Malthusian doctrine out of his Midwest experience of the great productivity of our western country. He said this idea of pressure upon the food supply by the population was utter nonsense." His incurable optimism on the future of the American economy and his independence in thinking were highly stimulating to a young man like Nourse, who was endeavoring to find his way as an embryo economist. Nourse recalls that one evening in one of Mead's classes a student asked: "How do you explain Patten's views, which are not quite in line with what you have said in your lecture?" and Mead's "characteristic" response was: "The answer is simple. It simply is that Patten's mind moves like the mind of no other man born of woman."

Of particular interest to Nourse was a seminar that he had with Professor J. Russell Smith in economic geography. Nourse found Smith "a very human sort of Quaker," and he felt free to talk with him about his own awakening interest in the economics of agriculture. Smith encouraged Nourse by taking him on trips to eastern Pennsylvania and western New Jersey, where Smith's brother was managing a chain of truck farms. This gave Nourse a good understanding of the economic problems of a settled and prosperous agricultural region.

Although Nourse got along quite well at the Wharton School, he saw it only as a stepping stone in his career. He did not find it the kind of place where he could settle down and make a career. He also planned to get married as soon as possible, and making a home in Philadelphia didn't appeal to him. At Christmastime he wrote to his fiancée, Ray Tyler, that he didn't feel that this was a congenial atmosphere for his future. He said: "The University of Pennsylvania was here a couple of centuries before I got here and it'll make its mark on me rather than give me any chance to make a mark on it. I'd rather go out to some smaller place where I can do something of my own." At that time, the Wharton School was the leading business training college in the United States. It had developed an elaborate proliferation of business courses of great practical value, but to Nourse they seemed "extremely technical and commercial rather than economic in any analytical or philosophical sense." In the letter to his fiancée, he said that the Wharton School had given him a vision of how he could shape his career toward agricultural economics. He went on to say: "This sort of approach to business or any branch of industry has perhaps been overdeveloped here on city occupations, but certainly underdeveloped as to the great industry of agriculture and I would like to use the insights from the training I have got here to see what could be done toward developing something in the way of a comparable agricultural economics."

While Mead contemptuously referred to the agricultural West as "the short grass country," Professor Smith encouraged Nourse in his ambition to apply economics to agriculture and helped him find what he wanted in the way of an opportunity to "get out into the short grass country." He also encouraged the idea of marriage. Mead said to Nourse at the time: "I know you want to get married and you are thinking of discontinuing your appointment here. This new job will give you good experience, and if you want to come back to us, you will be welcome." As to his marriage plans, he said: "I know it seems a long time to postpone that another year, but you'll find that you'll be married a hell of a long time afterwards and you may as well wait." Nourse said of this comment: "This gives you a sample of the personality of Edward Sherwood Mead, who incidentally was the father of Margaret Mead, who has made such a distinguished career as an anthropologist. I saw her as a chick."

Nourse didn't take Mead's advice seriously, so he and Ray Tyler were married in Oakland, California, on August 17, 1910. After a honeymoon in Colorado Springs and a few days at Downers Grove, he and his bride proceeded to the University of South Dakota, where he had accepted a position as Head of the Department of Economics and Sociology. When he got there, he was somewhat surprised by an announcement in the local newspaper of his arrival. It said that Professor Nourse "is an indefatigable worker." Nourse didn't know how they found this out, but he said it helped him get off to a good start.

University of South Dakota Professor, 1910-1912

In 1910 the University of South Dakota at Vermillion was a small institution. There was an administration and classroom building and a science building. A new law school building had just been completed; Nourse held his classes there. Vermillion was a simple country trading community only a dozen or so miles from Sioux City, Iowa. It then had a population of less than 3,000, and the student body of the university was well under 1,000. Although small, the university had great plans.

Nourse was head of the Department of Economics and Sociology, but the staff of the department consisted only of one young instructor who largely taught business subjects. Nourse taught both the economics and the sociology courses. Although his department was small, he was for the first time in his life a big toad in a small puddle. As a full-fledged faculty member, he could attend faculty meetings as a "professor," and this gave him insights on how a university was administered.

The faculty was small but congenial. It was presided over by President Gault, a social man of scholarly outlook. The "active spirit" was Dean Perisho, who traveled around the state "assiduously promoting" the university. Thomas J. Sterling, the Dean of the Law School, was "an admirable and able person" whom Nourse was to know later in Washington, D.C. The School of Music was under Dean Grabil, who was also a rampant single taxer. Professor Cotton, an excellent violinist, was the piano teacher and was "worth more than he was paid." There wasn't much of a social science faculty. The most important member was Professor Christophemeier, who changed his name to Christol, and "who could blame him." Nourse worked with him in training the debating team. There was also a very capable man in the Chemistry Department.

Nourse's salary of $1,800 was in line with the salaries being paid at that time, so with low rent and low grocery bills, the Nourses were able to live well and save something. When they first arrived in Vermillion, they boarded with a retired farmer whose wife recounted to Mrs. Nourse tales of the terrible hardships of the pioneering days not long past. The Nourses soon were able to rent a small-frame house which had been built of green cottonwood. It had shrunk a great deal, and when the cold weather came, it was hard to keep the house warm.

His teaching schedule gave him little time for outside activity. One major exception was a talk that he gave in the fall of 1910 at the instigation of Dean Perisho to the Dry Farming Congress at Pierre, South Dakota. Nourse had been reading a series of articles on cooperation in agriculture running in the *Saturday Evening Post*, and he had been struck by the success of cooperative dairy marketing in Denmark, where all of the cooperative creameries were using effectively the same brand for marketing butter as a standardized, high-quality product. On the basis of the information in these articles, Nourse formulated a talk for the Dry Farming Congress on the suitability of cooperative organization for handling farm business, and he endeavored to make his talk concrete by telling his audience: "You should look forward to the day when you are selling South Dakota products under your own brand." He later admitted that it was a very sterile speech, "a long ways from the threshold of those wheat farmers," but it is important that it started Nourse thinking on the subject of cooperation in a serious way.[2]

That Nourse was beginning to think deeply on economic matters in 1911 is evidenced by a carefully prepared address that he gave to the student assembly of the university in December of that year. He took as his topic, "The Ethical Value of the Economic Process." His interest in this subject grew naturally out of his experience, plus his reading and reflection. He had become greatly interested in the ethical problems of our society through the challenges of the "muckrakers" and through the courses he had in sociology and economics at Cornell and Chicago. This interest was augmented by his practical business experiences in Utah and other western states and his observations and contacts at the Wharton School, with its strong pro-business environment which excited further interest in the subject.

This address was not an amateur effort, and it is surprising that Nourse didn't submit it as an article for publication in a general magazine. It reflected much study and analysis and it was presented in lucid, effective prose. He opened his address by saying: "It may seem rather a hardy undertaking for one to appear to plead the ethical value of economics." He then said: "Probably never more than today have we been aroused to the unethical conduct that is current under guise of 'business practices.' . . . But, I believe that there are some truths which we are prone to overlook which may be brought out by considering the phenomena of our economic activities, and that is what I wished to suggest by wording my topic 'the economic process,' as I have." He went on to explain that "the economic process includes the production, consumption, exchange, and distribution of material goods and valuable services. It takes more than a casual glance to perceive that here is the very cradle of our ethical values." Later in the address he said: "Function determines structure, and ethics is a social institution developed through the needs of many . . . whose predominant activities come within the economic process."

Nourse did not question the criticisms made against many business practices, for he considered them healthy. He said: "We should welcome all indictments against the present order as essential to the most rapid righting of its wrongs. But at the same time it is well to remember that the loudest tumult in the forum does not mark the period of lowest moral ebb so much as the awakened public conscience and the dawn of better conditions." He paid his respects to the adage "honesty is the best policy" by saying that while it was "not the highest motive toward right conduct," it still has "ethical value in that it drills in the practice of right action and thus prepares men for voluntary exercise of such virtues." Nourse maintained: "I am not here as a special pleader. I am not trying to distort plain facts through an impossibly optimistic interpretation. We want the blessed sunshine of truth let in, instead of engilding what is ugly with a film of sentimental moonshine. But I believe that the general viewpoint I have urged is true as well as optimistic."

He concluded his address with these words:

> Ethics deals with the relation of man to his fellows, and the range of ethical values have therefore their being within the compass of the total social process. Since the economic process is a large, if not indeed the dominant, segment of the social process, its value for ethics is proportionately great. We concede that the work is badly done today even as we have had bad philosophers and false priests. By so much does the economic process fall short of the full measure of its own prosperity and its possible service to mankind.

Nourse was never to lose his faith in the economic process evolving under American conditions. He realized then, as later, that it was far from perfection, but he saw it as a response to the needs and character of our people—always subject to modification and improvement.

Although his work was going well, Nourse decided in the spring of 1912 not to return the following year. When he informed Dean Perisho of his decision, the dean gave him "a promotional spiel on the great future of the university," but it left Nourse cold. "Dean," he said, "those things will all probably happen in God's good time, but the clods will rattle down on my coffin before that happens here and I can't wait." From this conversation it might be assumed that Nourse intended to continue work for his doctor's degree so as to fit himself for a larger opportunity, for he was moving toward a promising career in economics. He was now 29, and a fine professional future seemed assured.

Then something happened to his academic ambitions that is logically difficult to explain. It is best told in Nourse's own words. "I then had a violent outcropping of the agricultural interest and practical spirit that almost deterred me from going on to college from high school." Perhaps it was a call from his farming ancestry, but whatever it was, Nourse decided to take over the operation of the little 7-acre farm of his father's in Downers Grove. He arranged to buy out his sisters' interests, acquired a little more land in the area, and began a new career as a commercial poultry farmer.

Before going on, it is important to report that Nourse's experience at the University of South Dakota did prove valuable in the long run. It gave him fine teaching and limited administrative experience, it gave him contact with the agriculture and industry of a western prairie state, and it started his mind working on the possibilities of cooperation in agriculture.

Back to the Land, 1912-1914

Nourse came back to Downers Grove in June, 1912, fired with enthusiasm. His stepmother and half brother had been living on The Place for several years, but it was not an operating farm. The vineyard had gradually gone out of cultivation, and most of the land was back in grass. There were a few fruit trees and bushes, but there was no produce for market.

When he took over, he had definite ideas of what he wanted to do. He decided that his main operation would be producing eggs for market. He also planned to develop The Place as a small truck farm, so he planted about an acre in tomatoes, beans, and other truck crops. He also felt the need for more land, so he acquired two small acreages of about 10 acres each for producing corn and wheat for the poultry operation. Since he was going to specialize in raising chickens to produce eggs, he needed to supplement his flock, buy an incubator and brooder, and make adjustments in the farm buildings. To do all of these things, he had to have capital, and to obtain this, he arranged a loan with the local bank.

In the summer of 1912, Nourse was happy with his farming prospects and contented with his existence. He remembered later how one day he looked over his fields and in sheer joy said to himself: "This is the life." Mrs. Nourse gave her full support to the venture, and in view of the fact that it was to be mainly a poultry farm, she gave it a name, "C-a-d-a-c-u-t," to express phonetically the peculiar sound made by chickens.

During the fall and winter months, the Nourses got The Place shaped up for full-scale operations the following year. Then in the spring, disaster struck. As Nourse has told the story:

> Just as I was getting my spring hatching operations underway in the basement of my house and I was delivering a dry cow to a butcher-buyer on the other side of town with a wagon I borrowed from a neighbor, and just as we got back into town, a bolt dropped out from the thills and got down on the horse's heel and he started running away down the hill into town. I got thrown out and landed in an angle of the concrete curb with all my weight behind an ankle which was shattered into at least seven pieces. I was taken from there directly to the train into the Presbyterian Hospital in West Chicago and was out of commission. We had a heavy rain that night and Mrs. Nourse went down to the basement the next morning only to see a flood of water, with scores of dead baby chicks floating on the surface. You can see why this ended my farming experience.[3]

The seriousness of the injury did not show up until the following year, but it did make impossible the resumption of active farming operations. Nourse was laid up in a succession of casts for the entire summer, but he was able to get around on crutches and "learned to navigate with the cast pretty effectively." In the late summer it was obvious to him that he had "to create some visible means of support." Teaching seemed the best possibility, so he got in touch with his old friend O. M. Searles, who found a job for him as teacher in economics and sociology at Ripon College in Ripon, Wisconsin—the town where the Republican Party was founded. It was a very pleasant small college town, mostly composed of people from New York State who had moved west. While at Ripon, Nourse produced his first article to be published. It grew out of his own experience and interest in a problem that was gaining national attention—the so-called back-to-the-farm movement. The article drew heavily on his training in sociology and economics. Although the article was accepted for publication in the summer of 1914 by the *North American Review*, one of the prominent national magazines of that time, it was not published until early in 1915 after revision to take into account the effect of the world war which broke out in August, 1914. The Nourses were elated to have the article accepted while their future was so uncertain.

It had become obvious while he was at Ripon that another operation on his ankle was imperative. If Nourse had been able to get modern day orthopedic surgery when he was first taken to the hospital, things might have turned out differently. Unfortunately, the distinguished pioneer plastic surgeon, Dean Lewis, was away giving a lecture on plastic surgery at a medical convention, so Nourse had been turned over to a less skilled man who was not able to effect a complete recovery. As it was, the bone material, when nature was trying to remedy the break, filled in the joint and formed what is called an interarticular callus. This led to a very painful condition that grew progressively worse.

His experience at Ripon brought him up with a jerk. He was now nearing 30, and his leg injury made it impossible for him to continue in farming. By the spring of 1914, he said to himself: "Well, fella, you are certainly in the bush leagues now. You'd better make a fresh start and you'll have to do it by getting back into the mainstream." So he decided to write to Professor Laughlin, with whom he had been in casual touch since his first year at the University of Chicago. Laughlin advised him to go on and earn the doctor's degree. Nourse saw the wisdom of this counsel, but he was in great need of financial assistance, and he made this clear to Laughlin. He enquired: "What kind of fellowship could I get?" Laughlin was definitely interested in Nourse's career possibilities, so he wrote back that he could "do something a little bit better than a fellowship." He said: "You will be appointed for next year not to a fellowship, but to an assistantship under my direction." It would pay $500 and cover tuition charges.

With arrangements made for the next year, Nourse went back to the Presbyterian Hospital where Dean Lewis put him on the table for a lengthy operation, which proved strikingly successful in view of the experimental stage that plastic surgery was then in. In looking back on this experience, Nourse philosophically remarked: "There are always two possibilities. I had the bad luck of the break, the good luck of eventually getting into the hands of one of the pioneers in plastic surgery—who instead of letting the thing go on to amputation, which was the sure outcome, gave me a double bone transplant so that at times people have been unaware for some time that I once had a crippling injury."

Who can say what would have happened to Nourse's career if he had not had this serious accident. At any rate, it shocked him back into a professional career. Looking back on this farming experience, Nourse said: "It was a perfectly fantastic undertaking with the almost nonexistent capital that I had."

So in the fall of 1914, two weeks after the normal opening of the university, Nourse rented a room on Ellis Avenue and presented himself, on crutches, for the wind-up of his doctor's degree.

University of Chicago—Final Year, 1914-1915[4]

Thus, Nourse resumed his graduate work at the University of Chicago.
As the graduate work he had done at Chicago and at the Wharton School largely fulfilled the course requirements for the doctor's degree,

his main problem was to complete the foreign language requirements and write a satisfactory thesis prior to coming up for the written and oral examinations. However, to round out his academic credits, he found it desirable to take a few more courses during the fall and winter quarters. The course that he remembered most vividly was on the history of economic thought given by Walton Hale Hamilton, who impressed him as a "youngish-looking, gimlet-eyed man with a rather nonchalant and non-academic manner." He found this a very stimulating and delightful course. Each member of the class was required to write a paper on one of the "ancient worthies," and Nourse chose Thomas Aquinas. He also took one more sociology course with Albion W. Small, whom he greatly admired, and another on economic history with Chester Whitney Wright. The problem of passing the language requirements was not great, for he had a good grounding in German, and with a little special preparation he was able to pass French. Then, as now, the reading requirements were nominal.

As assistant to Professor Laughlin, his main responsibility was to attend his money and banking classes and seminars and to mark the term or intermediate papers that were turned in. This was not a heavy duty, and it enabled him to get a good understanding of Laughlin's thinking on economic matters. During this year at Chicago, Nourse shared an office with John B. Canning, a fellow graduate student, in the East Tower of the Harper Library, which was then the home of the Department of Social Sciences. Canning was an accounting major who later developed a pathmaking book on the economics of accountancy. They became fast friends and shared many mutual interests.

After getting his general program underway, Nourse consulted Professor Laughlin on plans for his thesis. "Diplomatically" he suggested a subject in the field of money and banking that he thought would appeal to Laughlin. However, Laughlin, after listening quietly, asked: "Have you any other topics in mind?" Nourse replied: "Yes, but I suppose it's a wild shot. Now in Father's time and in my time, I've had experience on the producer's problem of using the South Water Street market for perishable products. Like all my neighbors and fellow shippers, I found it a very unsatisfactory price-making apparatus. I would like to make a study of this market as a market mechanism, as a factor in price determination." After musing a little, Laughlin said: "Well, that sounds very interesting and it has a personal original character which appeals to me." He continued: "Now, I will be of *no* assistance to you whatever in the content of this thesis and I doubt if there is anyone in our group here who can help you very extensively. However, I and others can be of critical assistance to you on the workmanship of your thesis. If you want to go ahead on this subject and think you can do it, why, I'll approve it." This remark taught Nourse that Laughlin was not "a dried up old theorist as was sometimes alleged."

The problem of obtaining the data for his thesis was not easy, but as Nourse later remarked: "I always had to do things the hard way." He went on to say: "So on crutches, I started to go down to the South Water Street market—a seven mile streetcar trip—and to probe around on the slippery sidewalks, among the boxes and bales and with the not always literate and often unfriendly personnel of the market to get the understanding of what the market structure was and what influence it had on the market process that was being empirically worked out there. I subscribed to the *Producer*, the trade journal, and I clipped and I talked and I pondered and I wrote."[5]

It was an enormous job, and in May, when the study was almost completed, Walton Hamilton, who had been following Nourse's progress in writing the thesis, said to him: "Nourse, why don't you submit this to the Hart, Schaffner and Marx prize contest? You may not get anything out of it, but I have been the reader for Professor Adams at Michigan University who is on the awards committee and this is at least better than much of the stuff submitted."

So with this encouragement, Nourse did his utmost to complete the manuscript for submission before the deadline. On the evening of the last possible day, he submitted the manuscript to Professor Laughlin, who was also a member of the awards committee. Although he didn't get the first or second award—which both paid cash—he was granted a special honorary mention, which carried the right of publication, which would defray the cost of publishing his thesis. How this book was prepared for publication and eventually published will be described in the next chapter.

Three other important developments in Nourse's career occurred while he was completing his doctoral work. In February, 1915, the article that he had written largely at Ripon College was published by the *North American Review* under the title, "The War and the Back to the Land Movement." Nourse had submitted the article under the title, "The Folly of Back to the Land," but the emerging World War I situation made desirable a shift in the article's emphasis to take into account the war's probable impact.

The publication of the article gave Nourse several benefits. It brought his writing to national attention and to the attention of his professors, and this heightened his prestige at the University of Chicago. It also raised his morale, for it was his first published work for which he was paid, and the $50 he received helped make ends meet.

The article itself merits attention, for it represented a comprehensive and cogent analysis of an important problem that was calling for attention. In the article, Nourse held that "the financial lure of the land" had been exaggerated in that various studies failed to bear out the claims of those who rhapsodized on the financial opportunities in agriculture. He maintained that at this stage of industrial development, a back-to-the-land movement "was *not* a generalized remedy for a problem that was emerging." He concluded his article with this sentence: "If America is to realize the largest measure of her economic powers, it must be by concerted effort to upbuild our trade and industry and by an increase of economic organization and industrial efficiency in agriculture, not by a debouch upon the land."

The second important development came about in this way. In the December issue of the *American Economic Review* appeared an article by Irving Fisher, the nationally-known Yale economist, entitled "Fourteen Objections to the Compensated Dollar" in which, in Nourse's words, he "disposed of all of his critics to his satisfaction." Nourse felt that one important objection had been overlooked, so he wrote an article which he called "A Fifteenth Objection to the Compensated Dollar" and submitted it to Davis R. Dewey, the editor of the *American Economic Review*. His point was that if the community knew that the dollar was to be compensated by a change in its gold content, it would accept that factor in its calculations and discount the change so that inflation would take place just the same. In February, the article was returned with a letter from Dewey which said: "[Your manuscript] was submitted to two of my associates, who do not consider your argument sound." However, Dewey sweetened his letter by saying: "It was not on this ground that we feel it unwise to accept your article at the present time, but due to pressure of other articles and the feeling that we should not give further room to the subject until Professor Fisher has published his book. . . ."

When he showed the letter to Professor Laughlin (who himself had not been overimpressed with Nourse's argument), Laughlin "blew his top," saying: "What right does the editor of the *American Economic Review* have to exclude publications on the basis that a particular group regards the argument as unsound? This is a scientific, well-written article and he should have added it to the controversy." Although Nourse didn't get his views in print, his spunk and initiative made a good impression on Laughlin and the economics faculty.

It was about this same time that the *Journal of the Canadian Bankers' Association* asked Laughlin, as the distinguished leader of the Sound Money Crusade in the United States, to prepare an article for publication. Laughlin responded, according to Nourse, in his "true Laughlin best manner," saying: "This article I do not have time to prepare, but I have turned it over to my assistant, Mr. Nourse, and he will send you an article." In Nourse's words: "He didn't ask them whether they would accept a substitute or not. He *told* them." So Nourse prepared the article, which was published early in 1915 under the title, "The Agricultural and Industrial Balance in the United States." For his effort he received $50, which came in handy.

In this article, Nourse considered a problem that was growing in significance with the boom conditions arising from the war in Europe. What should be the attitude of industry toward agriculture? It was his view that the conditions of the time required "occupational balance" between agriculture and industry. He maintained that "the nation . . . must make its industries complementary, in order to employ national resources and human power to best advantage, to save wastes of needless transportation, and keep above the stage of diminishing returns." The last sentence of his article reflected his growing opinion that the basic importance of agriculture should not be ignored by statesmen, bankers, and educators if the nation as a whole was to prosper. He said: "Agriculture is always the economic foundation and without a firm foundation the national structure is insecure, but it is not less true that the justification of a good foundation is to be found in the structure which it upholds."

During the academic year, Nourse made two lasting and significant friendships in the faculty, although he had courses with neither of them. The first was Dean Leon C. Marshall, who was just getting the School of Business under way. He was an innovative, social-minded type of person, and he and Nourse hit it off well. The other friendship was with Harold G. Moulton, a protégé of Laughlin and soon-to-be editor of *The Journal of Political Economy*, who was beginning to build his national reputation in the field of financial organization. His infectious enthusiasm and competence favorably affected Nourse and would lead to a lasting intellectual partnership.

This is a good place to take a look at Nourse as he was beginning to hit his professional stride. Mollie Ray Carroll, a contemporary graduate student, recalls him as "perhaps the most outstanding of the able graduate students in economics. So scholarly was he and so competent in clear exposition that the rumor among his fellow graduate students was to the effect that he had already received his doctorate in English." To her, he was a most personable and gracious young man who knew where he was going.[6]

As he came to the end of the school year, Nourse let himself go on the written examinations that were required before the oral examination for the doctor's degree and made a favorable impression for his knowledge, independence, and originality. His oral examination by a group of top people from the economics and sociology faculties was more of an ordeal, and when he waited "on a stiff little chair in the hall for the verdict of his examiners," he said to himself: "This is the end. I have not made a showing sufficiently impressive to justify being given the doctor's degree."

But he was self-deprecatory. When he was invited back into the examiner's room, Dr. Laughlin informed him that the examiners had considered his record and the results of his written and oral examinations and had come to agreement that he should be awarded a doctor's degree, magna cum laude. Shortly afterwards, when a fellow student asked him the result, Nourse replied: "I squeaked through."

It was a beautiful June day when the degree was awarded him in the court of Hutchinson Commons. To Nourse it represented the culmination of his long struggle to attain a professional foothold. He was now 32 and on his way.

Chapter IV

HIS FEET ON THE LADDER
(1915-1918)

As Nourse neared completion of his graduate work at the University of Chicago, he began to consider his next move. Professor Laughlin proposed that he stay on as an instructor in the Department of Political Economy, while Dean Leon C. Marshall offered him an instructorship in the School of Business. He also had nibbles from the University of Pittsburgh and Iowa University—both in the field of money and banking. In discussing his future with Laughlin, Nourse said:

> I was born in New York, reared in Illinois, went to college at Cornell, did some teaching at the University of Pennsylvania, and the University of South Dakota and in Wisconsin, and I've had some contact with life in Utah, Nevada, Wyoming, and California but I don't know the South. I feel that a man going into economics and political science should know all sections of the country, not as a tourist, but as one who lives and works in the environment. So I've not closed my mind on these other offers but I am still hoping that I can find an opening in the South.[1]

As Nourse later explained, he definitely didn't propose to stay on at the University of Chicago "because I felt that the youngster who grows up in a department and continues there remains a youngster, and I wanted to achieve maturity where I could be a big toad in a small puddle, rather than a small toad in a big puddle."

Shortly after this conversation, Nourse got a telephone call from Laughlin. "Mr. Nourse," he said, "President John C. Futrall of the University of Arkansas is here with me at the Quadrangle Club and he has a strange opening at his university. Would you like to acquaint yourself with it?" Nourse said: "I'll be right over." The position available was that of Professor of Economics and Sociology and Head of the Department of Economics and Sociology in the College of Arts and Sciences, University of Arkansas.

It happened that Hillman Brough, then the head of this department, was taking a leave of absence for the next year to run for the nomination for Governor of the State of Arkansas. If he got the nomination, which was tantamount to election, and was elected, and if Nourse "liked them and if they liked him," the position would be continued. The proposition appealed to Nourse, and he accepted with a salary of $2,200, "payable in script of a state which was still in default on the payment of its Civil War bonds." However, he stipulated that he must have an opportunity to become acquainted with the state and investigate some of its economic problems. Although the university did not have specific funds for research, President Futrall said: "We will make the best arrangements we can to carry out that purpose."

With his work completed at Chicago and a job lined up for the fall, Nourse spent the summer with his wife in California, where he broadened his knowledge on far-western economic and social problems. He was now 32 and ready to move up on the professional ladder.

Getting Started

The Nourses were pleased with their new environment in Fayetteville. It was a pleasant, attractive town located in a beautiful natural setting, and the people were warm and friendly. The university was somewhat larger than the University of South Dakota, and the faculty and community were highly congenial.

Although his title as professor and head of a department was somewhat impressive, Nourse was the only professor in the department, and his staff consisted of but one assistant—Julian S. Waterman, who taught the more technical business courses. Nourse didn't even have a private office. He had to make do with a desk in a classroom and a cupboard for storing his books and records.

During his first year at the University of Arkansas, Nourse taught the economics courses already scheduled by Professor Brough, and since he had already given these courses at the Wharton School, the University of South Dakota, or Ripon College, they didn't represent a heavy teaching burden. Most of the classes were small, with only 15 or 20 students. At this time his interest in agricultural economics was "blossoming," so he did everything possible to broaden his agricultural foundations by getting acquainted with members of the agricultural faculty and by attending their seminars and sessions. In view of his continuing interest in the operations of the Chicago produce market, he also acquainted himself with the marketing methods of the apple and strawberry growers near Fayetteville. This gave him an opportunity to see something of the shipping of very perishable produce. Nourse found that "they had a 10-day strawberry season, following the Texas season and preceding the Missouri and northern shipping seasons. They had there the migrant workers, as pickers, who followed the crops from Texas on up through and into other crops in the northern Mississippi Valley. That gave me an interesting sidelight on labor economics." He also visited a little Italian colony, Tonittown, in the northwest corner of the state. "This was a pure Italian wine-growing community. It was a communal effort of this immigrant group." Nourse was not able during his first year to examine closely the cotton economy of the state, "of which I knew absolutely nothing." This greatly intrigued him, but he had to wait until other things could be done.

Economic Adviser

When Nourse arrived in Fayetteville, he found his predecessor, Hillman Brough, actively running for the governorship. Brough promptly called on Nourse for assistance. He said to Nourse: "The first thing that I want to do after my election is to introduce a sound tax measure and get it through the legislature. I want you to work with me on that." So Nourse helped him write a tax bill, which was ready when Brough was elected governor in November. Work on this problem led Nourse to write an article on the effort being made to get the finances of state on a sound basis, and this was published in the June, 1917, Bulletin of the National Tax Association under the title, "Progress in Arkansas." This article is of special interest in the light of Nourse's later work as Chairman of the Council of Economic Advisers. In it he held that Arkansas was "waking up" under the progressive and businesslike administration of Governor Brough, which promised to end "the sway of peanut politics." After describing what had already been accomplished in solving the state's financial problems, he claimed that Arkansas "has made a serviceable beginning." He concluded by saying: "Probably the most pressing need at the moment is for intelligent public discussion preparatory to the meeting of the constitutional convention and of the next legislature."

Brough also was politically interested in the problem of tenancy, for he wanted to find out whether the time merchant system associated with the plantation economy of the state was exploiting sharecroppers and other small farmers. Brough's concern with this problem led Nourse to undertake a study of tenancy in Arkansas, which continued intermittently throughout his three years with the university. How he worked on this study and with what final results will be described later in this chapter.

When Nourse completed his work at the University of Chicago, it was understood that his doctoral thesis would be published by the Houghton Mifflin Company who issued the Hart, Schaffner and Marx prize essays; Melvin T. Copeland of the Harvard Graduate School of Business was assigned to assist Nourse in preparing his thesis for publication. From time to time during his first year at Arkansas, Nourse worked on the revision of his manuscript and corresponded with Copeland on problems that arose. This led Copeland to invite Nourse to Harvard for a few days of consultation in the spring of 1916.[2] However, Nourse deferred active work on this book until he could complete work on another book that he felt was more urgently needed.

Agricultural Economics

Agricultural Economics was a book of readings for this relatively new field. He had got the idea of preparing this volume from the book of readings on economics published by the Chicago University Press for his professors at the University of Chicago—Leon C. Marshall, Chester Wright, and James A. Field. He liked the plan of their book, and he saw the need for a comparable one on agricultural economics. The preparation of this book became Nourse's absorbing interest during his first year at Arkansas, although he did not let it interfere with his academic duties as professor and department head.

It was an enormous high-pressure undertaking, for the book was largely completed during the academic year plus the summer months spent at the University of Chicago, where library facilities were more adequate. It is hard to believe that this book was completed so that it could be published by the University of Chicago Press late in 1916, for the book ran to 896 pages and consisted of 290 "readings" grouped into 17 chapters, and much of the book called for introductory and interpretative comments by Nourse. Nourse later had this to say about its preparation: "I began to shape up my interest, and it's amazing with the limited library facilities at my command that I did get as presentable a group of readings and did as much of the structural part of the book as I did in that short period of time. I was a fiend for work."

While Nourse was working on this book, he wrote an article, "What is Agricultural Economics," for the April, 1916, issue of *The Journal of*

Political Economy. This article, which he adapted as an introduction for his book under the title, "The Aims and Scope of Agricultural Economics," represented a challenge to the rapidly developing field of agricultural economics. At that time, there were only two textbooks on the subject, and neither of them presented the field in a broad economic framework. It was Nourse's contention that "agricultural economics is not a science distinct from other economic science, nor, on the other hand, is it merely an art devoid of scientific implications and responsibilities." It was his view that "the best hope we can venture for agricultural economics is that it will take and maintain its proper place of dependence and assistance, and that *general economics may be both its point of departure and the goal of its return.*" (Emphasis added.) Moreover, Nourse was concerned that agricultural economics should develop as a broad field of study for the important questions relating to agriculture. For example, he said: "Agricultural economics should teach us to think through the utopia of cooperation." He finished the article by expressing the belief that the importance of agriculture in our whole industrial system justified "at least one solid course in agricultural economics in the curriculum of every great university even though it has no professional school of agriculture."

Nourse called his book *Agricultural Economics,* but its subtitle provided a more accurate description of its nature and content: *A Selection of Materials in Which Economic Principles Are Applied to the Practice of Agriculture.* In a conversation in 1973, Nourse explained to the author that the subtitle "did very definitely express what I thought I was doing. I was trying to get away from the purely descriptive material that was then available on the economics of agriculture. I didn't get suggestions. This was a one-man job with a limited library, so I bulled it through according to my own ideas with what material I could get hold of. I didn't then teach a class where I could try out the book on students."

The chapter titles show the extensive coverage of the book: I. The Emergence of the Problem of Agricultural Economics; II. Consumption; III. Land and Other Natural Agents in Agricultural Production; IV. Human Effort as a Factor in Agricultural Production; V. Capital Goods as a Factor in Agricultural Production; VI. Organization and Management of the Agricultural Enterprise; VII. Records and Accounts as Measures of Efficient Management; VIII. Principles of Value and Price as Related to Farm Products; IX. Market Methods and Problems; X. Transportation and Storage Facilities as Factors in the Marketing of Farm Products; XI. The Rent and Value of Farm Land; XII. Land Tenure and Land Policy;

XIII. Interest on Farm Loans; XIV. Rural Credits; XV. Agricultural Wages; XVI. Some Problems of Agricultural Labor; and XVII. Profits in Agriculture.

The introductory statements for each chapter and the selected readings displayed Nourse's catholic point of view and his extensive knowledge of the literature relating to the economic problems of agriculture. Moreover, the book carried many perceptive comments on vital matters where he felt it necessary to round out the materials available on the subject. In some cases he wrote the "reading." One such instance was his statement on "The Possibilities of Cooperation," which examined the general character of the cooperative as a form of business organization, and then concluded: "It seems possible that it is the most potent single force at work upon our agricultural system today." Another illustration was a helpful explanation of the newly passed Federal Farm Loan Act.

One of the most interesting parts of the book was its preface, which explained that the book was designed to combine many of the desirable features of a source book with a text. In fact, Nourse termed the book "a composite text." He also said: "The purpose of the book will be achieved if it is found to be a reservoir for diverse needs." He offered the book "as food for thought and a stimulant to the thought-process, not as a scripture to be learned by rote."

To make the book more usable as a textbook, Nourse developed an accompanying manual for teachers, which was published in 1917.

Agricultural Economics was a landmark achievement which soon gained for Nourse national recognition as a comer in this new field. Professor George L. Putnam of the University of Kansas, in reviewing the book for the *Journal of Political Economy* (March, 1917), said: "Teachers of agricultural economics will welcome this collection of materials. [While it] can hardly be regarded as a first class textbook . . . it represents by far the best attempt that has yet been made to satisfy this need."

Although the book did much to conceptualize the field of agricultural economics, there was no big market for the book such as there was for the practical type of farm management book by George Warren. At this time, the subject of agricultural economics was just beginning to gain acceptance as a college course. The American Farm Economics Association had not yet been established, and there was no general consensus on what the field consisted of.[3]

The Chicago Produce Market

With the publication of *Agricultural Economics* and the manual for teachers, Nourse could devote his full attention to the revision of his doctoral thesis for publication. This was largely a matter of updating material and bringing the subject matter into better literary focus. Professor Copeland gave Nourse a free hand, for it was evident that he needed little help. As indicated by the preface, he completed the book on May 31, 1917. The book was issued in 1918 under the apt title, *The Chicago Produce Market*.

Nourse recognized in his introduction the growing appreciation of the importance of economic analysis for agricultural problems. He then said:

> Not least among the services rendered by this economic analysis of our agricultural industry has been the directing of more careful study to those parts of the process which have to do with the marketing of the product. Whereas the agricultural scientist was prone to measure results in terms of weight or bulk at the farm, the agricultural economist is concerned with cash results in the market. The technical process ends with harvest, but the economic process of agricultural production cannot be regarded as complete until the goods are put into the hands of the consumer. To achieve efficiency merely in growing a crop is not enough. Economies so laboriously brought about in the early part of the process may be entirely swallowed up by wasteful methods of marketing. Our eyes have at length been opened to see that the *mechanism of the market* needs to be as carefully designed and as skillfully operated as any other part of our producing machinery. [Emphasis added.]

Later in the introduction Nourse said: "The slow and careful process of scientific study of the market problem is now demanded. This must rest upon an adequate analysis of the task to be performed, full and accurate knowledge of present systems and their complicated working, and an appreciation of how and why they have come into their present situation." Nourse then went on to say that this study of the Chicago Produce Market was undertaken "as a modest venture . . . in the field of marketing investigation. . . . It aims by the careful examination of a selected problem of limited scope to derive some understanding of the principles involved and of the part played by a particular *market mechanism* in determining the prices of certain agricultural products." (Emphasis added.)

The body of the book was presented in 10 chapters. Four dealt with the wholesale aspects of the market. These described its location and equipment, personnel, organization, and transportation and storage facilities. Another dealt with the retail structure and operations of the market. After this description of the somewhat complicated Chicago Produce Market, two chapters were devoted to "The Effect of the Market System on Prices." This analysis was the heart of the book. Nourse opened these chapters by saying: ". . . Our vital interest centers, not in the structure of the machine nor in the way its wheels revolve, but in the quality of the work which it turns out. The significant problem is: How well does this *market mechanism* perform its appointed task? And the test of its efficiency is to be found in the prices which it brings to pass." (Emphasis added.) Then followed a chapter on "The Chicago Municipal Markets Commission" and another on "Other Projects for Improving the Market System." In his concluding chapter, Nourse maintained that a "mere do-nothing policy is by no means admitted. The city must make conditions favorable to the proper functioning of our market system." He emphasized this point by saying: "It is of the utmost importance that the tremendous stake which the public has in that development be recognized."

This was a seminal study. It was the first serious attempt to explain the nature of a marketing mechanism in the light of its institutional setting. This was a pathmaking book in the field of marketing. E. T. Grether, in his essay on "Edwin Griswold Nourse" in the series of profiles on "Pioneers in Marketing" (*The Journal of Marketing*, April, 1958), described *The Chicago Produce Market* as "an institutional exploration into the workings of one aspect of the mysterious mechanism and forces operating between farmers and city consumers in one important market." Nourse had no pattern to work by, and it represented an original empirical approach to the study of an important marketing institution. Some years later, Secretary of Agriculture Henry A. Wallace termed the book a model for marketing studies.

The following sentences from the introduction convey something of the objectivity of Nourse's approach in making this study. "The slow and careful process of scientific study of the market problem is now demanded. This must rest upon an adequate analysis of the task to be performed, full and accurate knowledge of present systems and their complicated workings, and an appreciation of how and why they have come into their present situation. Only by such a preparation shall we qualify ourselves to estimate deficiencies and plan improvements."

Nourse's study of the South Water Street market and his marketing explorations in Arkansas made him skeptical of some of the "truths" of economic theory. He found that "perfect markets" as assumed in the theory of normal price did not generally exist for agricultural commodities where production was already fixed. This idea obsessed him, and so in the spring of 1918, he fashioned an article on how markets for agricultural products actually worked. Nourse called his article "Normal Price as a Market Concept," and he was elated to have it accepted by the prestigious *Quarterly Journal of Economics*, published by Harvard

University. In this article (which was published in September, 1919, after Nourse joined the staff of Iowa State College) he pointed out that "writers have habitually given us a production-adjustment concept of price normality and have generally had their minds filled with industrialized processes of production, in which the flow of goods is continuous, or, at least, has its stoppings and startings, its expansion and curtailment, largely under control toward the end purpose of making supply such as to command a remunerative price." He went on to say:

> This is all very well so far as it goes. But the concern has been too exclusively with the normality of supply conditions, and little or nothing has been said about the normality of the demand which comes to effective expression in the market, or concerning the adequacy of the market mechanism to bring about normal adjustments of actual supply and actual demand conditions. The stark cost-of-production concept of normal price is insufficient to the economist's need in attacking the problem of market systems and methods as a favor in price determination. And this inadequacy is particularly evident in the case of those extractive products which are not produced by highly industrialized processes and for which, there, the conditions of supply are highly adventitious.

It was Nourse's view that normal price would be one that kept the flow of production at the optimum relation to successive demands of the total market. He believed that all suppliers of a product should have a market mechanism which would give all equal exposure to all the possibilities of the market, and that, on the other side, every consumer or industrial user of a product should be served by a market mechanism which gave him equal knowledge of and access to all the economically reasonable sources of supply.

Nourse's article was accepted in the economics profession as a sound theoretical statement, and it earned him recognition as one of the developers of market theory and of practical marketing methods and devices. It provided him with a foundation for much of his later work with cooperative marketing associations, and it served as a forerunner for the emphasis that was later to be given by students of marketing to the concept of market structure. As one of the best-known theorists in the field of marketing later said: "To [Nourse] the market was not a passive or neutral factor in the price-making process but, by its structure and practices, went far to determine which demands were brought in touch with which sources of supply. Markets and marketeers therefore were dynamic forces in activating and guiding consumer or user demands and in discovering, stimulating, and aiding suppliers."[4]

Academic Career

While Nourse was preparing these books and articles, his teaching program was going well, and at the end of his first year his academic standing was well established. By then he was a member of the "Honors" and "Intercollegiate Debating" standing committees of the University Senate, and he was free to determine the courses offered by his department. According to the university catalogue for 1916-1917, he personally gave the following courses: Elementary Economics, Economic History of the United States, Current Economic Problems, Theory and Practice of Banking, Public Finance, and Agricultural Economics. The last course reflected his growing interest in this field, and it was described in the catalogue as follows:

> The principles of economics as applied to the concrete problems of rural life; the relation of agriculture to other industries of our country; economic organization of the business of agriculture, transportation and the marketing of farm products; rural credits and cooperative enterprises; the problem of distribution as touching rents and values of farm land, farm labor and wages, rates of interest and profits in agriculture. Designed for all persons identified with rural communities, teachers, merchants, bankers, as well as those who expect to engage directly in farming.

Nourse's new courses for the academic year 1917-1918 reflected his developing intellectual interests. In Natural Resources and Their Administration, he offered a subject which was gaining national importance. He described this course as "a study of the economic qualities of land and its appurtenances, and the technical conditions of their utilization; private ownership and other forms of control; rent and the value of land; conservation and land policy." Another new course, Forms of Business Organization, indicated Nourse's developing interest in the cooperative form of business enterprise. He described this course as "a critical discussion of the individual, the partnership, the corporate and the *cooperative* methods of organizing the factors of production into business enterprises; the economic reasons for the growth of trusts; the *cooperative movement here and abroad*; scientific management as a factor in operating efficiency; the size of the most productive unit." (Emphasis added.) He also offered two other new courses: Money and the Price System; and Capital and Its Institutions.

Up to this point we have focused attention primarily on Nourse's professional progress at the University of Arkansas. However, he did not neglect his teaching responsibilities, for he held them of primary importance. In fact, he greatly enjoyed this phase of his work, and there is abundant evidence that he was highly respected and liked by his students.

One of them, Joe C. Barrett, who later gained national eminence for his work in international law, was an undergraduate under Nourse during all the time he was at the University of Arkansas. He has recorded his appreciation of Nourse's contribution to his career in the following sentences:

> At the beginning of University studies most, if not all, students are quite malleable. Adult character and mental and emotional attitudes are formed and developed during college years. It is during that time that young men, like rockets, are mounted on launching pads, and the trajectory aim is formulated. Nourse was extraordinarily good at this, even though our age differential was not too great when I became his pupil. I still bear the imprint of his mold....[5]

Barrett has recalled how he nearly became involved in a student rebellion being fomented against the university administration, particularly the president. Concerned about what to do, he visited Nourse at his home, where Nourse gave him wise counsel that kept him from making a "senseless move." On another occasion, Nourse "generated a small loan" that enabled Barrett to achieve a desirable end.[6]

Another of his students, Brooks Hays, who gained national prominence as a congressman and government official, remembers that "few professors made as strong an impression on the state during the brief time he was at the University."[7]

Charles S. Stewart, who succeeded Nourse as head of the department at the University of Arkansas, later pointed out that "several who continued their courses with me bore witness to the inspiration Nourse brought to them. I soon came to know something of the greatness of Edwin as a teacher of undergraduates."[8]

Finding the Facts

As noted in Chapter III, Nourse had obtained a promise from President Futrall that the university would do everything possible to help him do research on the agricultural problems of the state, although the university had no funds for field research. Futrall kept his promise by what Nourse later described as a "bootlegging" operation. To assist Nourse in his research explorations throughout the state, the university provided travel funds and expenses in two ways: (1) by having him visit high schools as University Visitor to recruit future students, and (2) by giving him assignments to work with the Extension Service on educational programs being conducted in the rural areas of the state. It was through such arrangements that Nourse was able to make a rather ambitious analysis of the tenancy problem in Arkansas.

Most of the work on this study was done during the summers of 1917 and 1918. As Nourse explained in the foreword to the study, when published after he left Arkansas: "The material presented in the following pages was secured through field work done during August 1917 and August 1918, supplemented by two brief trips at other times and by investigations carried on from Fayetteville during the University year and the early part of the summer of 1918."

Most of the data for this study was obtained while Nourse was a member of Extension Service teams that traveled throughout the state on educational programs. In the summer of 1917, it was Nourse's job to explain how the new Federal Farm Loan Act could be used by farmers to improve their economic condition. In the summers of 1917 and 1918, the university was giving much attention to the "Food Will Win the War" campaign, so Nourse also was called upon to give talks on ways to increase food production. One by-product of this experience was an article by Nourse on "The Cheapest Source of Increased Food Production" in the *Scientific Monthly* for February, 1918. In this article, Nourse maintained that low-cost food production could be obtained most economically by the improvement of farm technology.

Nourse greatly enjoyed his participation in this extension activity, which brought him in intimate touch with agricultural conditions over much of the state. Nourse recalls how in one county where there was no railroad, the Extension Service team traveled on horseback. "I remember one trip in which we had eight people and a cavalcade of seven horses and/or mules that we'd recruited, so that we would ride ahead and one man would tie his steed to a tree and the man would go on on foot while a man who was on foot would pick up the mount and go ahead."

Nourse was stimulated by the comradeship of the other members of the Extension Service team. One of them was Ruby Tenneson, a "very presentable and delightful girl," who dealt with problems of the rural home. She came from a real hillbilly background, and it gave her much pleasure to help Nourse learn about living conditions in the somewhat primitive areas of the state. One evening while the group was chatting in the hotel, Nourse remarked that he didn't know anything about the customs of these mountain people, and that he was enjoying the opportunity to learn more of their distinctive life. Miss Tenneson spoke up and said: "Well, Dr. Nourse, I'm just a little hillbilly girl. I grew up in a cabin with a punch floor and I'd be very happy to tell you anything that I can and answer the questions that you have about our life."

Sometimes when the members of the group were out beyond the reach of any hotel, they were entertained overnight by country families. Nourse remembered how one mountaineer told of his coming to the area, saying: "Why, when I came here, them hills was just working with deer and bear." Nourse found that conditions were still quite primitive. "Some of them had lived in these hills for several generations and never built a privy. The woods were ample to their wants."

"The Revolution in Farming"

During his last year at the University of Arkansas, Nourse drafted a manuscript that he called "Making the Farm Safe for Democracy." This was published in the *Yale Review* for October, 1918, as "The Revolution in Farming." Its literary quality and pertinence were attested by issuance in this recognized "highbrow" journal. This article shows the direction of Nourse's thinking at this time. The last sentence of his first paragraph stated its theme: "Faced with a rural exodus, depleted fertility, diminished exports, a rocketing cost of living, and the imperative necessities of war, we are now being brought to realize that American agriculture must be thoroughly reorganized upon the basis of modern industrial efficiency." He then said: "The vastness of that task is enough to stagger."

Nourse saw developing a new agriculture—"scientific," "capitalistic," and "commercial"—that was rendering "the simple technical and business methods of the past obsolete." To meet its needs, he saw two types of agricultural organization evolving. The first was the incorporated, or corporation, farm, designed "to repeat upon the farm the success it had earlier achieved in the factory." While recognizing its claims for business efficiency, Nourse questioned its superiority for the industry of agriculture on both economic and social grounds. Moreover, he did not look upon the corporation farm as the only means of escape from inefficiency in agriculture. He saw another method of agricultural reorganization embraced in the term agricultural cooperation "being worked out with much success." He maintained that "under this new regime, the individual farmer, whether owner or tenant, continues as master of his own business with his personal interest and fortune bound up in its success or failure. This form of organization performs the specialized services required by farmers at minimum cost."

Nourse also saw the individual family farm benefited by many educational, research, financial, and other services that could be provided by the government through its research and extension facilities. He believed that these "socialized services" could well complement the work of farmers' cooperative organizations.

In agricultural cooperation Nourse saw "something as big as 'big business,' as 'stupendous as socialism.'" "Yet," he said, "it is neither. Rather, it is the antidote for both, and this because of the fact that it combines the proven merits of both." Nourse completed his essay with this prophetic sentence: "It may be that out of what we have regarded as the most individualistic of all callings there shall come the pattern for an effective socializing of our economic life." This article marked a new stage in Nourse's development. From then on, he was to be one of the most articulate advocates and champions of the cooperative form of agricultural enterprise.

Nourse was quite content with life in Arkansas, and he made no direct move to get another position. He was much attached to the southern people, and he and Mrs. Nourse enjoyed the pleasant living conditions in Fayetteville. Yet, he was an ambitious man, and he realized that he was preparing himself for larger responsibilities. His work had begun to attract attention from other universities, and when an offer came to develop the field of agricultural economics at Iowa State College, one of the leading land grant colleges, he could not resist it. So his work at the University of Arkansas terminated in the summer of 1918.

The Tenancy Report

Before settling into his new position, Nourse prepared a report on his study of land tenure in Arkansas, for he never liked to leave any work unfinished. This report, which carried the title "A Preliminary Survey of Land Tenure in Arkansas," was the first economic bulletin published by the University of Arkansas. It carried a foreword by Nourse, written from Iowa State College on October 14, 1918. In this, Nourse explained how the study had been made and expressed the hope that even in its incompleted form, "the bulletin may serve to give persons outside the state a juster appreciation of land tenure conditions in Arkansas, and ... be of some service in directing the thought of her own citizens along lines of intelligent and hopeful effort and bring about the best possible adjustment of economic relations dealing with the land."

This bulletin of 76 printed pages was a remarkable professional performance, in view of the difficult conditions under which much of the material for it had to be gathered on casual trips. It divided the state into geographical types of farming areas and examined the agricultural conditions and organizations within those regions. In the concluding section of the bulletin, Nourse raised the question: "Is Tenancy a Menace in Arkansas?" He concluded that the question of tenancy was clouded by an unfortunate misunderstanding of definitions and statistics. He held that under certain conditions, tenancy might be to the economic advantage of both the tenant and the community, and that ownership was not necessarily an economically desirable condition. It was his view that "much work must be done over a period of years before we shall be able to say just what is the most effective size of farm enterprises in the various sections of the state and with various types of farming." However, he thought it "evident that many owners are scrubbing along on undersized farms, when a little industry and foresight would enable them to rent or buy enough additional acres to get a farm of effective size."

He concluded the report with this incisive paragraph:

> Here are problems a-plenty—problems of old plantation days, problems of new pioneer development, a wide variety due to a diversity of soil, climate and social conditions. The state owes it to herself and to the nation in these tremendously important days of reconstruction, to inaugurate and follow out a constructive policy with reference to its land, whether forest area, power sites, mineral resources or farm lands. This bulletin is merely a first attempt to survey the field and state some of the issues as they relate to farm land. They should be met as promptly as possible by a constructive policy which will mean in some cases legislative action; but practical measures will be safe and helpful only in proportion as they are based upon searching study of the specific problems which confront us.

This report foreshadowed Nourse's long interest in the conservation and wise use of natural resources, which he was to emphasize after World War II while Chairman of the Council of Economic Advisers.

Nourse got just what he wanted from his three years at the University of Arkansas. This period rounded out his experience by giving him knowledge of the people, institutions, and customs of the South. It enabled him to develop his special interest in agricultural economics and establish himself as a pioneer in this emerging field. It gave him an opportunity to demonstrate his capacity in the academic field and improve his administrative abilities. Moreover, it provided him with stimulating and favorable conditions for intellectual growth and for completing two important books and writing several articles of recognized importance. In short, this period at the University of Arkansas gave Nourse his bearings and opened the way for his expanding career. Iowa State College was to provide just the challenge he then needed.

Chapter V

BUILDING A REPUTATION
(1918-1923)

In the spring of 1918, Nourse received a letter from John H. Brindley, the Head of the Department of Economics at Iowa State College, inviting him to come to Ames to examine how work in agricultural economics might be expanded. At this time, the acute economic problems of Iowa agriculture growing out of the war called for an outstanding scholar in agricultural economics to develop properly this field at Iowa State College.

Nourse was receptive to this call, and on his visit to Ames he met Dean C. F. Curtis, who promptly made him a definite offer under which he would be in charge of agricultural economics teaching and an agricultural economics section in the experiment station. This arrangement "fitted in quite perfectly" with Nourse's aspirations, and the salary of $3,000 on an 11-month basis was also attractive. So, in the fall of 1918, he took up his new job at Ames.

Establishing Himself, 1918-1920

At this time, work in rural economics and sociology was under Professor Brindley in the Department of Economic Science in the Division of Industrial Science. Although Nourse was to be nominally under Brindley, he was also to be responsible to the College of Agriculture. In fact, his salary was "distributed between the experiment station, the college and Extension Service." This dual administrative arrangement was not a happy one, especially for Brindley, for responsibility gravitated naturally to Nourse, who later admitted that he "was inclined to go ahead independently with as much rope as I could get from Director Bliss of Extension and Dean Curtis of the College of Agriculture, so as to shape up an integrated organized unit of agricultural economics. I had enough support all around and enough youthful brashness so that Brindley was not able to do much more than plaintively ask me once in a while if I knew who was head of the department."

Although Nourse was interested in teaching, he was equally interested in research and extension work. He believed that teaching, research, and extension work in agricultural economics should be co-ordinated administratively to the extent possible. In keeping with this philosophy, Nourse favored joint appointments among the college, the experiment station, and the Extension Service on the grounds that it was appropriate, especially in a marketing subject, to have "a man split three ways" so that his teaching could be "enriched by more intensive work on experiment station projects and by experience in carrying them into areas of application through the Extension Service." At first, Dean Curtis was much opposed to this idea, for it was "his doctrine that a man was *either* a teacher, or a research worker, or an extension specialist," but under Nourse's persuasion he "grudgingly acceded" to the idea that staff members could perform teaching, research, and extension duties.

When Nourse took over the agricultural economics work at Ames, he inherited a small amount of farm management and land tenure work being carried on by two men, along with a one-man post in rural sociology. Within a couple of years, Nourse was able to consolidate these programs and enlarge them with new staff appointments into what in effect became a department of agricultural economics, farm management, and rural sociology in the College of Agriculture, although he continued to be nominally responsible to Brindley. Looking back some 50 years later, Nourse proudly asserted: "I can modestly say that it was then the first well-rounded course of social science that had won a place in an agricultural college and experiment station set up."

In developing his teaching program, Nourse did not need to devote specialized attention to instruction in farm management and land tenure, for these subjects were already covered by staff members. This left him free to devote his energies to the development of courses in agricultural economics, marketing, and cooperation, his fields of special interest. During his first year he gave a course in agricultural economics in which he used his own *Agricultural Economics* as the textbook. For agricultural marketing he used as a text L. D. H. Weld's *Agricultural Marketing*. For agricultural cooperation he drew on G. Harold Powell's book, *Cooperation in Agriculture,* and other source materials.

One of the advantages that attracted Nourse to Iowa State College was the opportunity to engage in research and extension work on important farm problems. Upon arrival, he found that the situation was made to order, for Iowa was seething with activity among farmers in their efforts to bring about a more satisfactory adjustment to a rapidly changing market economy. Nourse quickly sensed and identified the major problem areas in his new economic environment. Marketing was a matter of major concern for all of the state's major commodities—grain, livestock, and dairy products—and he was soon actively developing research and extension work in these areas.

Frank Robotka, who came to work with Nourse in 1920, gives us this interpretation of the way Nourse looked at things at that time:

> Nourse was essentially a pragmatist. He held that the meaning of economic concepts, for example as they related to marketing, was to be sought in the market place and their validity was to be tested by their practical consequences. His major emphasis was on problem solving, rather than on mere academic or theoretical speculations about them. He believed strongly in the efficacy of getting to the root of problems by studying them in the areas where they had their roots. This approach, he believed, revealed the nature and impact not only of economic forces but of environmental and institutional factors which theoretical analysis could not reveal, yet an understanding of which was essential for problem solving. He was impelled by a keen sense of urgency with respect to whatever problem that engrossed his attention at a given time.[1]

Conditions were ripe for Nourse when he took up his work in Iowa, for the state's farming community was in ferment. The Iowa Farm Bureau Federation had just been formed, and it was beginning to grow vigorously. Nourse lost no time in getting acquainted with the leaders in the federation who were closely allied with the college's Extension Service. He early established friendships with James Howard, the president, and John Coverdale, the secretary, who became respectively the President and Secretary of the American Farm Bureau Federation when it was established late in 1919 to bring business organization and methods to the nation's agriculture. He also entered into a congenial relationship with Henry C. Wallace, the editor of the influential *Wallace's Farmer*, who was to become secretary of agriculture under President Harding. Nourse became a friend also of his son, Henry A. Wallace, who was to take over the editorship of *Wallace's Farmer* and later become a secretary of agriculture under President Roosevelt.

At this time, cooperative marketing in Iowa was rapidly gaining strength. There was a thriving interest in cooperative elevators, livestock shipping associations, and other kinds of cooperative activity. Nourse was greatly interested in these organizations and was soon in close touch with their leaders. Before discussing the research and extension programs that he devised to help strengthen such organizations, it is important to see the broad framework of Nourse's thinking at this time.

"The Place of Agriculture in Modern Economic Society"

Of particular concern to Nourse was the importance of clarifying the issues confronting agriculture with the close of the war. He had been intrigued by the relationship of agriculture to industry since 1915, when he considered this problem for the *Canadian Journal of Banking*. Now, in the light of changes brought on by the war, he was ready to examine the questions involved in a more painstaking way. This led him during his first year at Ames to develop two articles on "The Place of Agriculture in Modern Industrial Society," which were published in *The Journal of Political Economy* in April and July, 1919. He evidenced his purpose by the following introductory statement: "It becomes a highly practical endeavor, and no mere academic pastime, to draw up the most searching formulation we can of the place of agriculture in a modern industrial society such as we are fashioning in America."

Nourse presented his views in a broad historical framework, which made clear how the long-held "agrarian bias" had given way to a "mercantile bias," which was still evident.

> Just as the prevailing sentiment of their times was reflected in the writings of the earliest political economists, so the persistence of a like mercantilist viewpoint is strikingly revealed in the fact that modern textbooks on economics have been so exclusively treatises on manufactures, trade, transportation, and public finance, and the business of farming has received such slight attention, that at length certain economists felt the need of setting forth separate expositions of rural economics as a means of bringing agriculture within the purview of economic science.

Nourse saw a new day dawning in which the importance of both agriculture and industry would be recognized. He said: "America is challenged today as never before with the need of effecting a skillful adjustment of all the parts of her economic life in that harmonious proportion which alone can give an equal measure of well being to all her parts, and health and vigor to the whole body politic." To him it was "an obvious truth that our civilization is one and inseparable."

After a careful examination of the agricultural-industrial policies of France, England, and Germany, Nourse found that "at the opening of the twentieth century American agriculture stood in just the same subservient position to American industrialism that the colonies had occupied toward England a century and a quarter before." Although this "imbalance" had been somewhat corrected by improved agricultural conditions and new technical developments, "the future was still not clear." Nourse held that "agriculture must secure countervailing aid and support or find itself in an artificially unfavorable position and steadily losing ground in the unequal struggle." He also maintained that agriculture needs "education, capital, and organization, and to get them we must have a wise public policy, not penny-a-line misinformation."

In an explanatory note at the end of his concluding article, Nourse said: "The present paper does not aspire to present any solution of the present agricultural-industrial problem of the United States, but it does seek to set this problem in its proper perspective." He also said: "Those who attempt to bring the light of sound social science to bear upon the rural problem must be thoroughly conversant with the technique of modern farming, which has changed and is today changing with considerable rapidity. . . ."

"Harmonizing the Interests of Farm Producer and Town Consumer"

Nourse could not leave this general subject without giving it further attention. In October of the following year, he dealt with it more comprehensively in another article for the *Journal of Political Economy* which he aptly titled "Harmonizing the Interests of Farm Producer and Town Consumer."

Concerned with the trend of developments following the "subsidence of the war boom," he examined the probability of a clash "between the townsman and his country cousin." In this article he pointed out that "perhaps the most salient feature of change since [pre-war days] is the rise of strong organizations of farmers which have quietly but swiftly sprung up with the avowed purpose of preventing the resubmergence of their members in the low economic and social estate [of past periods]." He continued: "They force upon our attention the burning question whether agricultural producers can so organize their industry as to secure for themselves a high standard of life and at the same time not establish the cost of living, of food and clothing and farm produced raw materials upon so high a level of cost as to exert a retarding or even blighting effect upon that important part of our civilization which emanates from town."

Nourse believed that the farmer's chief source of discontent was "to be found in the position of economic, social, and political inferiority accorded the farmer in civilization's scheme of things." He pointed out that "the American farmer feels that his voice is no longer heard in the affairs of our country as it was in the earlier days of the republic." He didn't see as possible an alignment of farmers with organized labor, for "the main objectives of organized labor and those of the farmer are, in fact, diametrically opposed." But he thought "the present moment is opportune to mobilize the farmers of America for the maintenance of a high average standard of income and living. The whole idea of economic adjustment based upon competitive equilibrium stands upon a pragmatic footing. The rural class must to a large extent work out its own salvation."

To Nourse, the current high prices and rural income did not warrant complacency. He foresaw that the conditions confronting the coming generation would defeat the farmers' aspirations "unless effective organization on his part plus an intelligent and generous attitude on the part of the non-agricultural public shall be promptly brought about." He also said: "Unless the farmer himself sees to it that we equate our urban and industrial life toward a relatively small but intelligent, well trained and amply equipped class of farm producers, it will inevitably gravitate toward a large class of ignorant, inefficient, and ill-equipped yokels."

Two possibilities of integrating agriculture into the economic system of the country were apparent to Nourse. One was "by integrating agriculture downward or backward from the consumer." The other, "which offered a way of escape," was by working "upward or forward from the farm producer seeking to merge adjacent economic processes into . . . organizations under his own control." An illustration of what could be done was afforded by the methods of the California Fruit Growers Exchange.

Nourse thought it "high time that the industrialization movement which had progressed so far in other lines of economic endeavor should be brought to a corresponding stage of development in agriculture." He did not anticipate that the integration movement of farmers would get out of control, for he was impressed with the constructive attitude of farm leaders with whom he worked. In this article he was asking for reasonableness from all parts of our economic society. But primarily, he believed that the problems of rural welfare had to be the concern of the farmer himself, through his own political and economic organizations.

The Challenge of Corporate Farming

In his article, "Harmonizing the Interests of Farm Producer and Town Consumer," Nourse had examined the possibility of integrating farming "downward or backward" from the consumer by means of corporation farms which had sprung up during World War I. He concluded that a more promising development would be for farm producers to merge "upward or forward" so as to bring "adjacent economic processes under his own control" by means of cooperative organization.

Nourse developed this idea more fully in an article for *The Youth's Companion* (April 15, 1920), under the title, "Corporate and Cooperative Farming." In this article he said: "Through the practice of cooperation the farmer has found and put to practical use a principle of economic organization as effective in its sphere as that of the proudest trust." With a considerable foresight he concluded his article by saying:

> It is a merry race that corporate and cooperative farming are scheduled to run in this twentieth century. The corporation will doubtless dash ahead along certain favorable stretches of the road with a swiftness and an agility that come of centralized power and will seem permanently in the lead. But those will be mere sprints, spectacular rushes to attain the profits of successful "promotion." In due time it will probably appear that cooperative methods will irresistibly drag the heavy body of general farming to a permanent place of leadership.

This article was one of several that Nourse wrote about this time for *The Youth's Companion* and other general publications. He believed that it was important to reach general readers as well as professional workers in the field of agriculture.

"Will Farm Prices Fall?"

In the two years following World War I, industry and agriculture enjoyed abnormal prosperity. While boom conditions prevailed, it was not popular to predict that the level of prices might fall. As Nourse observed the contemporary situation, it became apparent to him that supply and demand conditions could not long sustain the high prices for farm land. When he voiced this view in mid-1919 in a *Wallace's Farmer* article entitled "Raising the Rent on Iowa Farmers," Dean Curtis "took a somewhat jaundiced view" and remarked: "Well, Mr. Nourse, I've been here much longer than you have and in my experience, the price of Iowa land has always advanced and I'm sure it always will." On the other hand, the article attracted favorable editorial mention by Henry C. Wallace.

Soon afterwards, Nourse's University of Chicago friend, Harold G. Moulton, published an article, "Will Prices Fall?" in *The Journal of Political Economy*. As Nourse later said: "This article triggered me to write a follow-up article on 'Will Farm Prices Fall?'" As Moulton gave only brief attention to agricultural prices, Nourse felt that it was essential "to scrutinize carefully this agricultural phase of the price outlook" in view of the significant influence of farm prices upon "the effective demand of one-half of our people," as well as upon labor and raw materials costs for industry. He presented his analysis and findings in the March, 1920, issue of *The Journal of Political Economy* before the drastic decline in farm prices set in later that year.

In this article he raised the question of whether farmers through their organizations could maintain the current high level of prices. Although aware of the growing strength of organized agriculture and sympathetic to the needs of farmers, he perceived certain conditions that might bring about a significant fall in farm prices. For one thing, he saw a contraction of abnormal European demand as the war-torn countries got back into normal agricultural production. Moreover, it appeared to him that the strong home demand for agricultural products resulting from the unusual prosperity of industry was showing signs of weakening. With less apparent demand for agricultural products, he also saw a threatening supply situation brought about by the war-induced advancement of production techniques and by greater supplies in prospect from agricultural raw materials-producing countries. It seemed to Nourse that "the immutable facts of economics impose an insuperable barrier to the maintenance of present prices (or their further advance) if effective demand be seriously impaired, while supplies increase, remain stationary, or fail to be proportionately reduced."

As to the demand for American products in the world market, he held that "the outlook is most certainly not bright." Moreover, he saw the outlook for home demand "impaired by the waning of extraordinary wartime demand" and by the "probability of a less rapidly expanding urban population in the next epoch of American history," along with "the keen competition that our manufacturers must meet in disposing of their goods in the markets of the world." He considered even more important the increase in production brought about by the fuller application of the modern techniques of scientific agriculture. He thought this would bring about in the years ahead "a relatively low price level for farm products comparable to that of the latter part of the nineteenth century." He did not believe that farmers, no matter how well organized, could protect themselves from this general situation. He said: "Organized farmers cannot force the issue in a weak market any more than organized labor can win a wage strike on the eve of an industrial depression."

Under these circumstances, what was the farmer to do? Nourse held that "the most promising line of endeavor would seem to be in the direction of protecting the farmer's net return by seeing to it that costs move down in conformity with inevitable declines in selling prices." He believed that the farmer's organizations could help bring this about "by fostering all efforts which look toward productive efficiency on the farm and in the market handling of agricultural products." He concluded his analysis by saying: "A level of education and a high standard of organization together with excellent natural resources must make up in efficient production the balance compared with the lower standard of living of other peoples or the fresher fertility of other lands. Of such a program we may say: ' 'Tis not so wide as a tariff door nor so deep as a well of subsidy; but 'tis enough, 'twill serve.' "

Nourse's article attracted widespread attention among farmers and farm leaders, although as a bearer of the reverse of good tidings, it disturbed those who preferred nostrums to logical analysis.[2] Many of his friends in the college and in the Iowa Farm Bureau were highly critical of him for voicing such negative views, until events vindicated the logic of his position.

Study of West Coast Cooperatives

While Nourse was working on these articles and getting his teaching, research, and extension program under way, the American Farm Bureau Federation was formed in November, 1919, and one of its immediate interests was the creation of strong cooperative marketing associations. Its first major effort of this type was to develop a cooperative plan for grain marketing, and in response to its call, a mammoth national grain marketing conference was held in Chicago on July 23 and 24, 1920. This resulted in the establishment of a Committee of 17 to work out a national grain marketing plan.[3]

There were then two dominant schools of thought on the kind of national cooperative grain marketing plan that was needed. One advocated building on the experience of the existing cooperative elevator movement, while the other favored the more dramatic proposal of state and national centralized pooling organizations espoused by Aaron Sapiro, the dynamic California cooperative lawyer. At the Chicago conference Sapiro made a deep impression with his arguments for "Cooperation—American style," under which cooperatives would become strong business organizations capable of controlling prices.

Before the Committee of 17 got down to the work of developing a national plan for grain marketing, a group of midwestern state farm bureaus financed a study group to examine in some depth the experience of California and other West Coast cooperatives to obtain ideas that might be useful in improving grain marketing methods in the Midwest. Although cooperative marketing of grain was of most immediate importance, the study group was also directed to obtain information that would be helpful in marketing livestock and other commodities.

The secretary of the Iowa Farm Bureau Federation, E. H. Cunningham, was at this time greatly interested in encouraging the best forms of cooperative organization for Iowa conditions, and from his associations with Nourse he had a high respect for his ability. He therefore named him to represent the Iowa Farm Bureau on the group and authorized him to gather additional information that might be useful for solving Iowa problems.[4]

During September and October, the group visited most of the major cooperatives operating in California, Oregon, and Washington, where all requested information was made readily available. This trip was of great value to Nourse in helping him clarify his views, for the team visited such prominent cooperatives as the California Fruit Growers Exchange and the various "commodity type" cooperatives then in their heyday. He got well acquainted with the leaders of the western cooperatives, men like G. Harold Powell and Aaron Sapiro, the respective leaders in the divergent California philosophies of cooperative marketing. According to Nourse, "one of the highlights of the trip was a rather lavish dinner in San Francisco put on by Aaron Sapiro who endeavored to indoctrinate us with his philosophy."

In the course of the investigation, Nourse's searching and analytical mind soon made him, in effect, the leader of the group. Upon his return home, he reported his findings to the Iowa Farm Bureau Federation, and his report, with slight modifications, became the report of the full delegation to the meeting of the Committee of 17 held in Chicago on November 4, 5, and 6, 1920. At this meeting he presented the report and defended its provisions as the spokesman for the study group. His mastery of the subject—as evidenced by the transcript of the discussion following the presentation of the report—established him in national farm bureau circles as an authority on cooperative principles and procedures.[5]

The study group report was presented in four parts: (1) relation of growers and marketing agency, (2) legal structure of marketing agency, (3) commercial practices, and (4) economic and social outlook and purpose of the cooperative organizations.

Under the first heading, the group was "deeply impressed with the fact that successful western cooperatives have passed beyond the stage of local shipping-point cooperation to that centralized organization which is necessary if significant results are to be obtained in the market distribution of the crop." The group was impressed with the truly cooperative character of the western marketing associations, which were "not commercial companies trading with the general public for the profit of their members as are many of our farmers' elevators." Rather, they were mutual associations for service to their members on a cost basis. It was the judgment of the group that this exclusive membership relation of the Pacific Coast cooperatives represented the true type of cooperative organization that should be followed by midwestern organizations. Although the western cooperatives were set up either as centralized or federated associations, the group felt that the federated plan was best suited to the needs of grain growers.

Under the second heading, the group considered whether the use of marketing contracts which "tie the group to the marketing association for a period of years" should be recommended for midwestern growers. It was the general view that this would not be necessary if a greater sense of loyalty could be engendered.

Under the third heading, the group looked with favor on the commercial practices employed by the western cooperatives and saw as a model the work of the California Fruit Growers Exchange. It was found that the western associations had "secured efficient business management by employing the best trained and most successful men of practical achievement wherever they could be found." The group was also impressed with the "universal practice of pooling returns" used by the western associations, which it termed "a practice which is of the essence of the cooperative method." However, the group was not convinced "that the grain and livestock farmers [of the Midwest] were at the present time ready to renounce their individual control over the marketing process to this extent." It was believed that if such "a feature were to be incorporated into any plans advocated by the Committee of 17, a thorough program of education would have to be undertaken before it could be put into operation."

Under the fourth heading, which the study group considered the most important, it was found that the western cooperatives were operating in an "economically sound and socially right" way. However, the group was of the opinion that "any attempt to create and use a monopoly power for securing a specially favorable economic position for its members is as pernicious in a farmers' organization as in the case of the so-called trusts."

The report concluded with this sentence: "We are convinced that such [western] associations are a powerful agency in securing for their members more favorable prices than they could otherwise obtain, and that our farmers need equally good selling service in the difficult times by which we are confronted."

Building the Cooperative Program

The opportunity to study cooperative development in its most advanced stage in California, Washington, and Oregon came at an important time in Nourse's career. He was able to see for himself how these western cooperatives were organized and how they functioned, and the experience gave him many ideas that could be applied to the improvement of cooperatives in Iowa and the nation. Before going on the trip, he was well versed on the methods of the California Fruit Growers Exchange, and what he found confirmed his high regard for the achievements of this pioneer cooperative organization.

The trip also gave Nourse ideas on how the legal structure of Iowa cooperatives could be strengthened with a new state law that would provide for cooperative associations set up on a membership, rather than on a stock, basis. The Iowa "Rochdale" cooperative law of 1915 did not provide for membership-type cooperatives as favored by the 1914 Clayton Amendment to the Sherman Antitrust Act. Nourse found the Iowa Farm Bureau Federation highly agreeable to having a new state cooperative law such as he deemed desirable, and with the technical assistance of Jim Mitchell, the attorney for the federation, a law was drafted in accordance with Nourse's views. As Nourse later remarked: "I served as coach." With the support of the Farm Bureau and other farmer groups, this law was passed with little difficulty on April 5, 1921.

The Iowa Non-stock Cooperative Law of 1921 authorized the formation of associations able to operate fully as business organizations—in the same way that corporation laws provided for the establishment of business organizations. It partially reflected the things that impressed Nourse in his study of West Coast cooperatives, supplemented by an examination of other state cooperative laws. Although it was patterned somewhat on the non-stock cooperative law recommended by the United States Department of Agriculture, it included a number of novel features. In many respects the new law represented a departure from the state's general corporation law. Under it, the "capitalistic" idea, with its stock and profit features and proxy voting, were entirely eliminated. In effect, the new law was designed "to establish a self-service organization for the members on a purely cooperative plan." It provided for jointly administered sales departments, or other departments, for the farming enterprises of members to which they might delegate certain specialized tasks which they could not perform efficiently as individuals. It provided for non-transferable memberships and financing through certificates of indebtedness rather than by stock, and this permitted use of the revolving fund method of building capital. Moreover, the new law made specific provision for federated cooperative associations. In fact, it was one of the first, if not the first, state law to employ the term "federated."

While associations formed under the new law were to market only products of members, it was found desirable in 1924 to amend the law to permit cooperatives, other than for marketing livestock, to market the products of non-members to an amount equal in value to products of members. This change met the needs of existing cooperative elevators and creameries which had many non-members, and it was in conformity with the Capper-Volstead Act of 1922.

Following his trip to the West Coast, Nourse expanded work with cooperative associations. In the summer of 1920 he had induced Frank Robotka, an experienced worker with cooperatives at the University of Minnesota, to come to Iowa State College to work as a research and extension specialist in the field of agricultural cooperation. Farmers' elevators were then in need of tightening their legal structures and strengthening their methods of operation, and the livestock shipping associations were moving toward a state federation. It was an ideal time to help these organizations to get on a stronger basis. In Robotka he had a disciple who was to build a national reputation during his lifetime work with farmer cooperatives.[6]

The expansion of work with cooperatives, however, did not come without a struggle. It was deeply questioned by private concerns, who brought strong pressure on the college to stop it. As Nourse later recalled:

> We had a distinct battle at that time because the commercial marketing interests were quite alarmed at this rise of the cooperative movement. I remember that the President of Iowa State College instructed me to lay off on our promotion of cooperatives in the state until this matter could be resolved. . . .
>
> . . . And I remember well a meeting in his office, where the heads of the Farmers Grain Dealers Association and of the dairy and livestock cooperatives and the representatives of the packing houses and of the elevator interests and terminal markets were present and I made my claim to this educational interpretation of our cooperative work. Of course, the President understood what I was trying to do, but I made a very forceful explanation of the responsibility of the college to exercise its educational function by making available to farmers of the state whatever devices there were for increasing their marketing efficiency as well as their productive efficiency. We put it on a very high ground of principle and we made it stick.
>
> There was some question as to whether the State Board of Education would permit us to go on. Would the Dean of Agriculture back me up? Would the President back the Dean up, and would the Board of Education back the President up? But we won that battle and from here on, we

went forward with a campaign of education as free as possible of any promotional factor. We were not trying to get the farmers to organize cooperatives. But if the farmers saw possibilities of efficiency in dealing with their pressing economic problems by the use of cooperatives, then we from the college—Experiment Station, Extension Service—would give them the most skillful service that their institution could provide.[7]

The Livestock Shipping Association Study

The livestock shipping movement was just beginning to gather steam in 1918, when Nourse arrived in Iowa. Although the first Iowa association of this type was formed in 1904, there were in 1916 only 57 active associations in the state. Thirty-eight more were formed in 1917, and 47 more in 1918. The number of new associations jumped to 130 in 1919, and to 311 in 1920. By that time, about one-fourth of the livestock shipping business in the state was being done by cooperative associations.

This development greatly impressed Nourse and led him in early 1920 to begin a study for the purpose of learning "(1) the history and growth of the movement, (2) its present magnitude, (3) the future of the organizations and the business methods pursued by them, (4) the achievements in terms of financial saving, more efficient handling, or better market distribution, (5) the difficulties which beset the movement, and (6) the outlook for its future development." He thought that it might be well to "pool common experience" so that "future efforts may be directed more uniformly along lines of proven safety and success."

The study was continued over a period of 10 months, with visits in person by Nourse and his assistants to over 300 of the associations. The results of the study were published in July, 1921, under the title *Cooperative Livestock Shipping in Iowa in 1920*.[8] The study found that the associations were making substantial savings for members, and that the prospects for further development were excellent if the existing local associations could be welded into a "working organization which would have the state as its economic unit." When this bulletin was being prepared, a state-wide livestock shipping association was being established, and Nourse thought it might perform services for livestock producers of Iowa analagous to those performed for citrus growers by the California Fruit Growers Exchange.

The livestock shipping association study was made at a favorable time, for a national livestock marketing plan was then being developed by a Committee of 15 appointed by the President of the American Farm Bureau Federation on January 3. Without doubt, the plan of the National Livestock Producers Association, which was set up by this committee in November, 1921, definitely reflected Nourse's views. His interest in better livestock marketing, which began with this Iowa study, was to continue unabated during the decade and eventually lead to a full-scale examination of cooperative livestock marketing in the United States.[9]

The Farmers' Elevator Study

Nourse had become aware of the farmers' elevator movement soon after he arrived in Iowa. Such organizations were well established by 1918 but the movement was still active, for 30 were formed in 1918, 46 in 1919, and 51 in 1920. Having a natural interest in how institutions originated, he began to examine how the existing farmers' elevators had evolved.

With the emphasis given to the grain marketing problem by the Committee of 17, he saw the need for an analytical study to provide complete and authoritative information on the farmers' elevator movement in Iowa. This led him with members of his staff to visit practically every farmers' elevator in the state. How he worked on this project has been recalled by Frank Robotka: "On one field trip on which I accompanied Nourse in gathering data for this study, we completed our survey of the cooperative in one town several hours before the next train was scheduled to arrive. Rather than wait for the train, we walked 6-7 miles to the next town and completed our survey there before the train arrived. Autos were not as generally available then as now."[10]

This survey not only provided information on the formation and development of the existing associations of this type, but it also provided understanding of their methods of organization and operation and present problems. The bulletin that resulted in March, 1923, *Fifty Years of Farmers' Elevators in Iowa*,[11] was unusual in that it was primarily an institutional study of the farmers' elevator movement in Iowa. As Nourse explained in the bulletin:

> Here we have attempted to get a perspective of the efforts of two generations of Iowa farmers to build up a system for the country marketing of their own grain. . . . This history has been studied with care and the results presented . . . in the belief that the study of the successes and failures of the past would, on the one hand, show us the pitfalls into which farmer elevator companies may be led, and on the other hand, show the real value of the farmers' elevator company and stimulate the grain producers of the state to undertake a thoro overhauling of their grain elevator business.

"The Outlook for Cooperative Marketing"

Nourse's close study of the rapidly expanding cooperative marketing movement came to a focus in a paper entitled "The Outlook for Cooperative Marketing," which he presented at the annual meeting of the American Farm Economics Association in late December, 1921.[12] He opened his paper by saying:

> Cooperation is a form of business organization which has emerged in the slow evolution of business institutions to meet the needs of the complex life of today. It is destined, I believe, to play a part as large and as brilliant as that of the old line-corporation and the "trust" so-called.

While confident of the long-run future of cooperative marketing if conducted for the "more efficient standardization, assembly and market distribution of farm products," he was apprehensive of the current philosophy of "centralized market control," with its emphasis on price fixing that was being effectively spread by Aaron Sapiro.[13] Nourse feared that "these architects would build a massive dome, heavy with stonework, ornate with carving, and glittering afar with gold leaf, but set upon a quite inadequate substructure." He said: "Possibly the pertinent question is whether we do not need just now to build plain but commodious working quarters rather than to let our interest and effort turn so much to dome and pinnacle."

It was Nourse's view that "in its ultimate development cooperative organizations should . . . afford the means whereby the achievements of big business are made available to the farming industry." But, he warned: "We must not be so dazzled by the swift and sweeping victories of certain great captains of industry as to expect exactly to duplicate their exploits either in magnitude or speed." He continued: "The 'man on horseback' has no place in the rural scheme of things." He deemed it necessary for cooperative leaders to "take up the burden of slower education and discipline of great democratic masses such as will in time weld them into orderly, self-controlled bodies moving forward slowly but with irresistible force and with unbreakable tenacity."

To attain the end that he considered desirable, Nourse saw the need of a great expansion of cooperative education and development of expert business management for both local and overhead organizations. He saw the aim to be providing "effective competition" with private agencies serving farmers, and he did not believe that the elimination of all private agencies would be desirable. In fact, he was of the view that "the cooperative itself needs private competition to keep it from resting on its oars and lapse back into the easy ways of inefficiency." Moreover, he deemed it essential that there be "the alternative channel of private trade to keep even cooperation from becoming monopolistic and exploitative."

Nourse concluded that the great progress in recent years in building strong, democratically designed cooperatives provided a basis for optimism, as long as sound principles of organization and operation were followed. His talk was a direct attack on the then popular Sapiro philosophy of obtaining market control through big business cooperatives. It was a "stop, look and listen" speech addressed to a select audience of agricultural leaders. It marked Nourse as the outstanding champion of cooperative organizations built on "ground-up," as opposed to "top-down," methods.

"The Economic Philosophy of Cooperation"

Nourse's interest in the cooperative form of business enterprise expanded with his study of its potentialities for agricultural betterment. As he gained mastery of this field, he saw the need of a statement that would explain the aims and significance of cooperatives and gain public respect and support for them, while giving them guidance in their evolution.

In "The Economic Philosophy of Cooperation," published in the *American Economic Review* for December, 1922, Nourse achieved all of these ends. This article became the New Testament on agricultural cooperation, and is still considered a classic on this subject.

Nourse opened his article by saying: "Taken by and large cooperatives are long on practice and short on theory." He thought that more constructive results could be obtained if there were "a better common understanding of the several distinctive features of the cooperative form of organization," not only by farmers but by legislative and other public bodies. Nourse pointed out that three "fundamentals" largely constituted the "theoretical basis" of cooperative success. These were:

1. Increased efficiency or reduced costs of service; no credit, no solicitation, and gratuitous or nominally paid service by members.
2. Popular distribution of savings or profits; minimum interest paid to invested capital, any surplus to go as patronage and wage dividends.
3. Democratic control, each member voting as an individual.

He then provided a searching analysis of these "fundamentals," primarily from the standpoint of their application to agriculture, with the resulting conclusion that "agricultural cooperation offers to the inherently decentralized industry of agriculture a workable and expansible scheme of organization. . . ." He held that "there is in this cooperative philosophy something that must be reckoned with as a factor in the future evolution of our economic life." He concluded his article with this suggestion: "We should look upon agricultural cooperation . . . as a movement to be carefully fostered and directed into channels of practical success as well as social helpfulness. Like other evolutionary processes its future course depends largely on the quality of its leadership. To analyze the issues intelligently and helpfully would be a service which the economist might well feel himself called upon to undertake."

This article came out at a very propitious time. The Capper-Volstead Act had recently established the right of farmers to organize cooperative associations without being subject to persecution under the anti-trust laws, and there was a groundswell of interest in the cooperative form of business enterprise. If any one statement set the course for constructive cooperative development in the years to come, this was it.[14]

In later life, Nourse held that this article was "a very natural outgrowth of my continuing empirical study of economic problems." He went on to say:

> I'd been working quite intensively for some four years with this cooperative mechanism and I thought it was time to incorporate that experience into the general economic literature. I thought it was incumbent on me as a trained economist to see if I could develop a reasonable body of theory to explain this as an institution which had won a place and should hold a place among the marketing institutions and to a considerable extent among the financial institutions and to some extent the production institutions of our economy....[15]

In this article, Nourse disassociated himself from the "cooperative commonwealth" idea, which was then a theoretical concept popular in England under which all business would be on cooperative lines. Nourse looked upon this as a "doctrine, a creed" which needed to be debunked. It was Nourse's contention that cooperative organizations should be looked upon as a properly differentiated type of economic institution within a private enterprise economy, with government playing a complementary role. This was not the idea of a cooperative commonwealth.

Building a Department of Agricultural Economics, 1918-1923

While Nourse was extending the frontiers of agricultural economics through his writings and speeches, he did not neglect his academic and administrative responsibilities. He took great pleasure in his teaching, and his courses inspired many who were to become prominent in their later careers. Over the years, many who were his students have generously told me of their indebtedness to him for perception, encouragement, and guidance. He was always helping his students to make the most of their lives. He recognized the capabilities and ambitions of young people and encouraged many to go on for graduate training, either at Ames or at other universities. Although aware of the value of specialization, he persuaded many of them to round out their training by taking courses in other departments. His high professional standards and impressive personality also affected many who were not his direct students. One of those so impressed was A. H. Hausrath, who was to build a national reputation as an economic research analyst. As a part-time janitor while he was a student of vocational agriculture, Hausrath saw Nourse almost daily from the fall of 1920 to the fall of 1922. He has written me as follows:

> I was in his office most every day for his office was on my beat. As this work was performed in the late afternoon after classes were over Dr. Nourse was usually at work in his office. Our personal relationship was cordial and friendly, but with a bit of reserve on both sides. Out of mutual respect for each other's preoccupation, neither of us felt inclined to interrupt the other's activity, except for a cordial greeting and a short, appropriate comment or an occasional short conversation. I saw him as a warm friendly person, greatly interested in other people, modest and unpretentious himself, ready to join in scholarly discussion quietly and with patience, and with an ever present good nature. In fact, I can look back even now over some 45 years and picture him as tall and modestly dressed—usually in a gray suit and bow tie—and with a friendly twinkle in his eyes. Through these casual contacts I developed a rather definite image and impression of the man; and through some mystique I can't explain he in turn exerted a constructive influence on me. Certainly it was in part by example.[16]

Nourse's major ambition at Ames was to build a well-rounded department of agricultural economics. He was alert to the necessity of finding the best possible men for his staff to supplement his own efforts, and he drew colleagues from Ohio State University, the University of Illinois, Michigan State University, and the University of Minnesota. He was not always successful in obtaining those he wanted. Soon after he took up his work at Ames, he endeavored to recruit O. B. Jesness, then a cooperative specialist with the United States Department of Agriculture. Upon Nourse's invitation, Jesness visited Ames for inspection by the Dean and Directors of the Experiment Station and of Extension, winding up in the president's office for final clearance. All seemed favorable, but the appointment did not come through. After several weeks, Nourse had to inform Jesness that the president considered him too radical. According to Jesness: "My work in the USDA was with cooperatives and at that particular time some colleges were on the griddle for giving encouragement to farm cooperatives. The President was sensitive to this pressure."[17]

This episode reflects the problems that Nourse had in building his staff and the sensitivity of college administrators at that time to the charge that agricultural cooperation was a radical doctrine. Not long after this, Nourse gained recognition for agricultural cooperation in the college as being part of the competitive free enterprise system.

Conditions within the college were not conducive to the development of a new line of work when Nourse arrived at Ames. The old-line production-minded departments looked askance at the new field of agricultural economics, believing they could give their students any economic training they might require. It took some time for Nourse to overcome this opposition. One of his concerns was that other departments refused to permit their students to take courses in agricultural economics as electives, for he believed that to be well rounded, all agricultural students needed courses on the business side of agriculture. In this he was something of a pioneer in what has become the conception of agribusiness so popular in agricultural colleges today. To gain acceptance for this idea, not only at Ames but at other agricultural colleges, he wrote an article for the *Prairie Farmer* in 1921 entitled "Does a Pig Have More Sense than a Sophomore?"—the inference being that pigs flourish by being able to make choices in what they eat.

The problem of getting budget support was always a battle, because of the established standing of the older production departments, whose members were jealous of this rising department. In time, however, Nourse developed rapport with most of the men in the production departments and took over much of the economic training they had been giving. Frank Robotka later explained his problem in this regard:

> Nourse's aggressiveness in promoting the growth of the agricultural economics department aroused no little jealousy and opposition on the part of some of the older and well established "technological" departments. Although Nourse did not discuss his administrative problems with his subordinates, it was apparent that there were potent "opposition forces" and that Nourse spent much time and energy in his efforts to cope with them. On one occasion he let drop a few words to the effect that we staff members had little realization of the battle he had to wage in order to maintain financial support for his department and staff.[18]

Nourse had a very broad conception of what a department of agricultural economics should be. This was well set forth by Robotka:

> His interest embraced the whole gamut of specialized areas within the general field of agricultural economics from economic production on individual farms to general agricultural policy, from the pricing process in local farm markets to the pricing process in central and national markets, and in the markets for the factors of production.[19]

During Nourse's tenure, his staff steadily grew as the area of interest widened to include work in farm finance, farm prices, and farm business problems and practice. When he left the college in 1923, his staff had grown to 22, embracing workers in the college, experiment station, and extension. As Robotka said:

It is not always that one finds the interest that Nourse exhibited in all three phases of the work of a land grant college—undergraduate and graduate teaching, research and extension. Most of those on the teaching staff were also part-time research workers on the experiment station staff, and a few of the extensioners also did some teaching or research work.[20]

I. W. Arthur also said in evaluating Nourse's stewardship of economics work while at Iowa State: "Mr. Nourse had the ability to guide and stimulate his young staff to productivity in research, teaching and extension and in matters of public policy."[21]

Although his focus centered on his own work at Ames, Nourse took a great interest in helping his fellow agricultural economists in other colleges. One who benefited from his advice and counsel was Dr. Murray R. Benedict, who recalls his first contact with Nourse as follows:

My associations with Edwin Nourse extend back over a period of more than 50 years. We first became acquainted in the early 1920's. I had just been appointed as the first Chairman of a new department of agricultural economics at Brookings, South Dakota. Well aware of my very limited qualifications for such a position, I felt that it would be helpful to me to have an informal talk with Nourse who was then Chairman of the department of Agricultural Economics at Ames. Accordingly I wrote to see if that would be agreeable. This produced an immediate invitation to come down and spend a day with him, which I did. His cordial greeting and friendly attitude at once put me at ease. Though older than I, more experienced, and much better equipped professionally, there was no condescension or aloofness in his discussion of mutual problems and interests. In fact, the groundwork of a lifelong friendship was laid in that one personal interview. I felt immediately the honesty and straightforwardness of his opinions and comments and found that on many issues our thinking was surprisingly congenial.[22]

The Problem of Governmental Regulation

Nourse's last Iowa State College contribution was a paper presented at the annual meeting of the American Economic Association in December, 1922, on "The Proper Sphere of Governmental Regulation in Connection with the Marketing of Farm Products."[23] This dealt with a problem of much interest in view of the various regulatory activities that were being assumed by the federal government in the years following World War I, although the slogan of the current Republican Administration was "Less Government in Business."

Nourse examined phases of regulation under three headings: (1) "the established zone of government control," (2) "the promising field of present day experimentation," and (3) "the dubious area beyond."

In the first category he placed regulation applying to the mechanism of exchange-money and credit institutions, and standards of weights and measures. In the second category he examined the role of government in determining desirable trade practices; methods of trading, settlement, and delivery; standards of fairness, safety, and facility; and limitation upon time and place of trading and upon trading personnel. Here he found the principle of government supervision largely acceptable, except with regard to the question: "Shall government attempt to standardize trade practice?" On this question he saw an opportunity for government leadership, since "a public agency and it alone is capable of assuming a supervisory function over all the forces of self-regulation which have for some time been emerging" and which have "the fundamental weakness of being motivated by self-interest."

In his third category, "the dubious area beyond," Nourse included "prescription of commissions, service charges, or traders' margins, so as to secure uniformity and reasonableness or prevent extortion, discrimination, and evasion." He also included within this category "the fixing of prices for private trade whether otherwise regulated or unregulated." In this general area he was less confident that government intervention would be helpful, for as he pointed out, "the feeling of the economist runs constitutionally against such intrusions into the determination of market values, which seems to be fundamentally a natural rather than a mechanical process." He went on to say:

> We shrink from taking any measures calculated to reduce the flexibility of a system whose health depends upon its ability to adjust itself rapidly and fully to every changing stress or strain thrown upon it by the swift succession of outside events. For myself I would about as soon lash down the steering wheel of my car and ride on the back seat as to regulate or "fix" the prices of farm products. . . . In the long run it is doubtful if regulation directed primarily to the end of seeing that nobody makes any money will commend itself to economists any more than it does to business men.

In summarizing his paper under the heading, "The prerequisites to effective regulation," Nourse pointed out that the issue was "not one between regulated or non-regulated marketing." Rather, it was "between competent, scientific, trustworthy regulation and amateur, doctrinaire, political 'lame-duck' regulation." He believed that governmental regulation had "evolved as one of the inescapable elements in our highly complicated market organization." He did not consider it "possible to decide by *a priori* reasoning just where the frontier of public participation can most wisely be drawn. Much more work of observation, experiment, and appraisal is yet to be done. But with regulatory work placed in the hands of a trained personnel, some of them drawn from the finer elements of the trade but with a liberal sprinkling of those who have had professional training in economics, it seems safe to expect that moves will be tentative till a sufficient basis of fact can be secured on which to base a trustworthy judgment. There is big work here for the economist both in government service and outside."

Nourse's thinking at this time reflected the results of his empirical marketing studies in the light of the evolving power of government. He judiciously distinguished between useful government services and unwarranted government control of the marketing process. This paper shows how he was cautiously feeling his way on a problem that would assume great importance in his unfolding career.

The Move to Washington, D.C.

By 1922, Nourse was ready for a wider arena. At Iowa State College he had built an outstanding department of agricultural economics and gained national prominence as a thinker in the expanding field of agricultural economics. Although happy in his life at Ames, he was not adverse to a larger opportunity, should it come his way.

Just at this time, the Institute of Economics was being established in Washington, D.C., under the direction of his good friend, Dr. Harold G. Moulton. When he saw Moulton at a conference in Chicago in May, Moulton explained what the Institute was planning to do. This appealed to Nourse, who said: "You will be needing a good agricultural economist. I accept." Thus he became the first employee of the new organization and the head of its agricultural division, although he was not able to take up his work actively in Washington until early in 1923.

Before we look at his career in Washington, let us see how he evaluated his time at Iowa State College. Looking back in the final years of his life, he said: "It was a valuable part of my professional training and experience. I was here getting what I'd had in mind up to that time. It gave me more administrative experience and more active contact with farmers' organizations. I would say that it was a rounding out and maturing experience which was invaluable preparation for coming to Washington to participate in the development of the Institute of Economics."[24]

The Nourses had thoroughly enjoyed their five years at Ames. They were popular with the faculty and students and with the people of the town, and in November, 1922, an added happiness came with the birth of their son—John Tyler Nourse.

Nourse at this time was nearing 40 and in the prime of life. He had the confidence that came with proven ability to meet difficult problems, and he was full of great expectations.

Chapter VI

GAINING NATIONAL DISTINCTION
(1923-1928)

The new job in Washington, D.C., was made to order for Nourse. It gave him an opportunity to employ his creative talents on the economic problems of agriculture, then of primary national importance.

Before going on, one should realize that the Institute of Economics in 1922 represented a new and distinctive approach to the study of the nation's economic problems. Therefore, it is important that we know how the Institute came to be established as a product of the fertile mind of Robert S. Brookings, who, during World War I, served as Chairman of the Price Fixing Committee on the War Industries Board. This experience made him aware of the need for an organization to continuously study national economic problems to help guide public policy

Brookings was a remarkable person.[1] After making a fortune in business, he had retired at the age of 46 to devote his money, interest, and ability to the advancement of higher education. As President of Washington University in St. Louis, he had participated actively in the establishment of the Institute for Government Research in 1916 in Washington, D.C., to help improve the functioning of government. Although this organization, of which he was a trustee, languished during the war, Brookings recognized its importance and infused it with new spirit in 1919 through a campaign which raised adequate funds to ensure its effective operation for a period of years. As Dr. William F. Willoughby, the Institute's longtime director, later said: "If it had not been for Mr. Brookings the Institute for Government Research would have been an unmarked grave on the road to better government." As it turned out, it became the agency which largely brought into being the executive budget system and Bureau of the Budget through an act of Congress in June, 1921.

Brookings did not rest content with the successful rehabilitation of the Institute for Government Research. From his experience on the Price Fixing Committee, he concluded that economic problems were of even more vital importance than problems of government administration. He saw the need of a research institute to make impartial studies of basic economic questions. To fund such an organization, he turned to his old friend Henry Pritchett, who was then head of the Carnegie Corporation. Pritchett liked the idea and recommended it to his board, which after careful consideration, created the Institute of Economics with a sustaining fund of $1,650,000 payable over a period of 10 years. The governing body of the new institute, comprised of men of eminence in education and public affairs, held its first meeting in March, 1922, with Brookings as chairman. In announcing the establishment of the Institute of Economics, the following statement was issued by the Carnegie Corporation:

> The Institute of Economics has been founded . . . for the purpose of assembling and interpreting the economic data which form the bases of national and international policies. . . . Most of the great issues which the people in our democracy are called upon to decide are essentially economic questions. . . . It is the purpose of the Institute to aid the public in making decisions in the light of knowledge. To this end, the data assembled and the conclusions reached will be presented in as untechnical a form as possible, through books, pamphlets, and special articles.
>
> Among the subjects to which the Institute will devote attention are: international commercial policies; questions of domestic and international finance; the relations of government to business; problems of agriculture, taxation, and transportation; and the various issues relating to industry and labor. The Institute has been located in Washington in order that it may have access to the vast amount of information on economic problems that is to be found in government archives, reports of commissions, and the collections of other institutions.

The announcement also carried the following commitment not to interfere in the functioning of the Institute:

> The Carnegie Corporation of New York, in committing to the Trustees the administration of the endowment, over which the Corporation will have no control whatsoever, has in mind a single purpose—namely, that the Institution so inaugurated shall be conducted with the sole object of ascertaining the facts and of interpreting these facts for the people of the United States in the most simple and understandable form. The Institute shall be administered by its Trustees without regard to the special interests of any group in the body politic, either political, social, or economic.

It was understood that the Institute would dig into the immediate, perplexing, economic questions confronting the nation. In the first meeting of the trustees, Brookings emphasized the importance of dealing with practical problems rather than with more general ones, saying: "I have never been able to accomplish anything without having some sort of definite problem in view."

The trustees recognized that of major importance would be the selection of the executive director for the new institute, and among those considered, the name of Dr. Harold G. Moulton, Professor of Economics at the University of Chicago, stood out because of the vigor of his economic studies and his recognized administrative ability. After correspondence, Moulton visited Brookings in Washington early in May to consider what Brookings described as "the greatest opportunity for service existing in this or any other country today." Moulton then knew little of Brookings, but the adventurous character of the enterprise appealed to his pioneering spirit. One thing he knew positively: that if the Institute of Economics was to have any chance of success, "the approach of every problem must be wholly objective and the directors and staff must have a free hand."

Encouraged by this visit, Moulton went back to Chicago to think over the proposition. He then returned to Washington to satisfy himself on what he considered the vital question: "Would he be able to develop a program of scientific work, unhampered by the strong personality of Brookings and the Board of Trustees?" He had to make sure in his own mind that Brookings would give him the free hand that he considered of indispensable importance. According to Brookings' biographer, Moulton cross-examined Brookings for some seven hours before he made up his mind that "Brookings would play the game, that the scientific basis was secure."[2] The issue was soon settled by official action when the Board of Trustees declared that "the primary function of the trustees is not to express their views on the scientific investigations conducted by the Institute but only to make it possible for such scientific work to be done under the most favorable circumstances."

It was upon his return to Chicago after he had come to this understanding with Brookings that Moulton described the plans for the new institute to his friend Nourse, who jumped at the chance to develop the agricultural phases of the Institute's work.

Moulton was the ideal man to get the new organization under way. Then 38 years old, with plenty of years of active service before him, he was a dynamic, driving person who was a recognized scholar in the field of economics and business administration with a bent for practical inductive research. He was a forceful speaker and writer who could work with business and non-academic groups and who had the gift of enthusiasm, which drew colleagues toward him. No one was better fitted by temperament, interest, experience, and training for the inauguration of this great experiment in practical economic research. In Nourse he had a close friend who brought to him complementary qualities of a high order.

Finding His Place

In June, 1922, Nourse joined Moulton in Chicago to go on to New York City for a meeting of the Executive Committee of the new Institute of Economics. At this meeting, held in the office of the Carnegie Corporation on June 19, the appointment of Harold G. Moulton as staff director was affirmed, and Nourse's position as head of the agricultural division was ratified with the understanding that he would not be able to devote his full time to the Institute until he had completed his obligations with Iowa State College. At this meeting, Nourse was asked if he had any suggestions to make regarding the activities of the agricultural division. He replied that his interests largely centered on the marketing problems of agriculture, and that he thought there was an opportunity to render an important service in this direction.

From New York City, Nourse and Moulton proceeded to Washington, D.C., where the Institute of Economics was being established. Staff had to be assembled and a program launched. A building at 26 Jackson Place on Lafayette Square was already under construction to house the Institute of Economics and its sister organization, the Institute for Government Research. On this exploratory trip, Nourse began to envisage a program of work in agricultural economics for the new institute. His concern was to establish working contacts and get the lay of the land, so he used the two weeks available to make connections with the Department of Agriculture and other agencies in Washington.

When Nourse returned to Washington for two months in the winter of 1923 to get his program started, the Institute of Economics had begun to take form. A staff of some 20 was now employed, and work was going forward in two main areas: (1) international post-war problems, and (2) tariff studies closely related to agricultural products. The minutes of the trustees' meeting on January 13, 1923, stated that the work of the agricultural division was in abeyance because of the inability of Nourse to leave Iowa State College. However, the prospective work of the agricultural division was outlined as follows: "It is the purpose of this division to center attention upon the larger relations of agriculture and industry, and upon the farmers' organization movement. The problem of agricultural credit will be given early attention."

Nourse's first objective was to develop plans for a study of great national concern—the possibility of recovering or reopening the European market for agricultural commodities. He had given much thought to this question since 1920, when he expressed skepticism on the short-term improvement of foreign demand in his article, "Will Agricultural Prices

Fall?" He believed that this subject had to be disposed of before more constructive work could be undertaken. As he later remarked: "The cliché at that time was that agriculture will recover as soon as the European market comes back." This study fitted in well with the work that Moulton was projecting on European post-war readjustment, which was then a matter of much national concern. Moulton at this time was completing his book, *Germany's Capacity to Pay*, which was the first of a series to be published on reparations and war debts.

While in Washington, Nourse got his project well organized so that he could work on it as time would permit at Ames. One of his initial problems was to tactfully establish a harmonious working understanding with Brookings, who was greatly interested in the possibilities of industrialized agriculture. Brookings saw in corporation farming the solution for the farm problem—a view that Nourse considered sterile.

With his obligations met at Iowa State College, Nourse moved his wife and 10-month-old son to an apartment in Washington on September 1, 1923. He did not buy a home until early in 1926, when he obtained a commodious house on Jocelyn Street in the Chevy Chase section of Washington, D.C., which was to serve as his home for the remainder of his life. His new position brought a significant increase in income. During his five years at Ames, his salary had increased from $3,000 to $3,800. Now on the new job, it jumped to $8,500, a high professional salary at that time.

When Nourse came to work full time in Washington, he had already done a considerable amount of work on the European market study. He brought with him from Ames Elmer J. Working to work on general economic studies, and Claude Benner to make a study of the newly created Intermediate Credit System. He also employed Forest Larmer to make a study of livestock financing, a subject of much interest to Nourse.

Nourse made a good impression on his associates in the new institute. He knew where he was going. Mrs. Elizabeth Wilson, long-time personal secretary of Dr. Moulton, recalls him at this time as a dignified and earnest man who never raised his voice whatever the provocation, which was quite unlike the behavior of her extrovert "boss," Dr. Moulton.

When Moulton reported to the Board of Trustees on October 19, 1923, he stated that the agricultural division of the Institute was now actually organized. He indicated that this division was expected to serve two main purposes: "First, it will cooperate with other divisions in working out the agricultural side of those national problems other divisions are studying; second, it will undertake independent studies of its own on problems peculiar to agriculture such as marketing, cooperative organization, rural credits, and the readjustment of agricultural production." He called attention to the fact that "the condition of the American farmer is perhaps the most important question before the American public today," and then said: "One of the salient angles of the problem is the export market and the relation of the American farmer to the European situation." He pointed out that the agricultural division was endeavoring "to set forth elements of the problem in terms of the realities of American agricultural production," and said: "This study should serve to clear up a great deal of loose talk by showing the impracticability of certain proposed remedies and by focusing attention on the real problems of agricultural readjustment which lie before us." Moulton also said that the agricultural division was beginning investigation of other problems of agricultural adjustment, such as a study of intermediate credit for agriculture and of cooperative marketing organization. He anticipated that within the year, work could be undertaken dealing with the economic and legal aspects of the larger types of cooperative organization. He called attention to the fact that "the nature of their objectives, the propriety of their methods and issues of public policy involved have never been given adequate consideration."

This report by Moulton, no doubt largely prepared by Nourse, shows how Nourse was quickly beginning to establish his program in the fall of 1923. His energies were then largely absorbed in the European market study which he completed in April, 1924. Its nature and significance will be discussed later in this chapter.

In Washington, Nourse soon found himself working closely with the Department of Agriculture, especially with Dr. Henry C. Taylor and members of his staff in the newly created Bureau of Agricultural Economics. At this time, Taylor was developing the Outlook Conferences, which brought together annually representatives from the agricultural colleges and the department to examine economic factors relating to anticipated agricultural production. Nourse saw this as a very constructive activity and gave it his full support and cooperation.

"Some Fundamentals of Cooperative Marketing"

Although Nourse was busily engaged in his European market study, he could not resist an invitation to address the National Association of State Marketing Officials on "Some Fundamentals of Cooperative Marketing" at its annual meeting in November, 1923. The conflict between the "top down" and "bottom up" schools of cooperative development was at its peak, and Nourse was the acknowledged champion of "bottom up" procedures as contrasted with the "top down" methods advocated by Aaron Sapiro. Nourse distinguished the two points of view as follows:

> One doctrine places the emphasis upon the selling function. It insists upon control of from 50 to 75% or more of the product, this control to be placed in the hands of a captain of the industry who shall get benefits for a passive membership through charging all that the traffic will bear. The individual member and such local sub-divisions as may be built up for administrative purposes are viewed as merely incidental to the main purpose of getting this bulk of product into the hands of the general sales manager to be so administered in the central markets as to secure the maximum price.
>
> The other doctrine [to which Nourse subscribed] rests upon a belief that the center of gravity of the cooperative movement is to be found in the shipping function, and that the chief gains for the producer are to be made by economically assembling and efficiently distributing the product, equalizing it among different market points with as much skill as possible. It lays great stress also upon the actual participation of the grower, both for the purpose of keeping down overhead expense and of bringing back the educational value of contact with the market so as to touch the original producer and influence him in adjusting his operations to the actual needs of the market and thus to stabilize the industry.[3]

In his presentation, Nourse categorically set forth eight fundamentals of successful cooperative marketing and made clear what he meant by each.

1. Successful cooperation in the United States must be cooperation American style; that is it must take account of the peculiar genius of our people. . . .
2. The local cooperative association . . . is wholeheartedly democratic. . . . There should be no question about retaining the local self-directing group as the prime unit upon which the cooperative organization must be built if its structure is to be sound and enduring. . . .
3. Any requisite size and strength are to be obtained by the organization of self-governing locals into federations. . . .
4. Cooperative organization wisely handled can accomplish great and permanent gains in the way of net price for the grower; but it does this not by power to coerce the market so much as by skill in meeting the market. . . .
5. The cooperative organization should keep as free as possible from speculative activities. . . .
6. Cooperation is the opposite of competition. . . . [Here, Nourse was arguing against the use of unfair business tactics employed by private agencies.]
7. The cooperative organization must be free from promotional methods and from promotional expense. . . .
8. Successful cooperation demands practical and scientific study of the peculiar requirements of each particular trade organization and of each region in which the improvement is to be tried. . . .

In contending that the advantages of large-scale cooperative organization and operation could best be obtained through the federation of local cooperatives, Nourse somewhat played down the significant contributions made possible by the centralized form of organization. As the protagonist of the "bottom up" school of cooperative development, he was not inclined to give Sapiro all the credit he deserved for some of the progressive business ideas he had injected into cooperative organization. As we shall see later in this chapter, he was to modify his views with further study and experience and become less didactic in his criticisms of Sapiro and centralized cooperative marketing organizations.

In concluding his talk, Nourse pointed out that there were three groups in the cooperative movement. "First, those who are in a rut . . . satisfied with the progress they have made. . . . Second, are those in the clouds, thinking that cooperation will make everybody prosperous all the time. . . . Third, is the group of progressive reality, studious to learn the merits of each new device proposed for the bettering of our market machinery; courageous to launch upon new experiments; but sanely insisting that careful study be given to each proposed step as they proceed." Of course, Nourse identified himself with group three, and in the years to come, he was to demonstrate his faith in this general approach.

Election as President— American Farm Economic Association

Nourse's standing as an agricultural economist was greatly enhanced by his new position with the Institute of Economics, and it is not surprising that upon the nomination of Dr. Henry C. Taylor, he was elected President of the American Farm Economic Association at its annual meeting in December, 1923. The impression that Nourse made at this meeting was later recalled by Dr. Fred Waugh: "I remember that meeting very well, and especially Dr. Nourse's part in it. He spoke at a luncheon meeting, and carried on a lively discussion with such pioneers as Richard Ely, William J. Spellman, Henry C. Taylor, and George Warren. Quite evidently these men and all the other participants in the meeting looked up to Dr. Nourse as one of the strongest agricultural economists in the country."[4] Another at this meeting was Dr. Roscoe Saville, who was impressed by Nourse's dignified demeanor, his profound and practical knowledge in the field of agricultural economics, and his evident leadership capacity.[5] During the ensuing year while Nourse was president of the association, he did what he could to broaden the outlook of the organization, and this was reflected in the outstanding program he developed for the annual meeting in December, 1924.

American Agriculture and the European Market

Nourse completed his book on *American Agriculture and the European Market* in April, 1924. In the introduction he set forth his purposes as follows: "Broadly stated, the book seeks to reveal: (1) the effects of European development upon American agriculture prior to 1900; (2) the changed conditions beginning near the end of the century; (3) the effects of the World War upon our agriculture; (4) the world-wide conditions making for the present depression in American farming; and (5) the prospects for agricultural exports to Europe in the years immediately ahead." He marshalled his arguments in two parts.[6] In Part I he explained "how the present situation developed." Here he examined the agricultural problem in historical perspective from colonial days to the present. Then in Part II, he focused attention on "the problem in 1924 and thereafter." On the basis of this analysis and statistical facts, he concluded that "Europe, shorn of her credits here and our debtor on a tremendous scale, cannot be expected to be a good market at present and prospectively higher levels of costs. Hence, agricultural exports may be expected to drop still further in 1924 and thereafter. *For American agriculture to plan her future building on the foundation of an expected revival and growth of the European market would, therefore, mean building on quicksand.*" (Emphasis added.)

The book had an immediate impact. Dr. John D. Black, then Head of the Department of Agricultural Economics at the University of Minnesota, wrote Nourse on July 24, 1924: "I like it. It is a clean cut presentation of the problem, and well written and easy to read. What is more to the point, I believe that your conclusions are sound throughout." Dr. E. W. Ball, Director of Scientific Work for the United States Department of Agriculture, considered the book "a clear and comprehensive analysis of the American agricultural situation." Writing Nourse on November 10, 1924, he said: "It is the first analysis that has gone back to fundamentals. . . . I predict that this book will have a wholesome effect on the trend of thought on our agricultural problem."

Nourse was well pleased with the reception of the book. In a Brookings Institution memorandum written early in 1925, he noted that the book had been favorably reviewed in various European journals and immediately translated into German and Russian. While the American reception was less enthusiastic in that "some felt that the future of agricultural exports was painted in colors somewhat too dark," he thought this was to be expected, "because the book said frankly just what the interested parties did not want to hear." For himself, he was "amply satisfied" in that until the book appeared, "no one had had the vision and temerity to attack the amiable myth of the European trade revival." He observed that "from that time forward, opinion had perceptibly changed, and corroborative statements from the Department of Agriculture and the Department of Commerce began to appear." Without question, this book greatly enhanced Nourse's position as a national leader in the field of agricultural economics.

Now that this study was completed, Nourse could turn to a subject that intrigued his attention and one that he felt offered an opportunity for constructive work. From his experience in Iowa and elsewhere he had come to believe that there was need for a fundamental examination of agricultural cooperative marketing development, in the light of the federal and state laws that affected cooperative organization and operation. He threw himself into this study of the cooperative marketing institutions with all of his energies and was soon immersed in information gathered from the state and federal agencies and various cooperative sources.

In the summer of 1924, a delegation of important agricultural leaders, headed by Dr. Henry C. Taylor, attended the meetings of the International Institute of Agriculture at Rome. Nourse welcomed an opportunity to serve on this delegation, now that he had completed his European market study and was already at work on his study of American agricultural cooperatives. The trip by boat afforded him an opportunity to become closely acquainted with such significant agricultural and cooperative leaders as Charles W. Holman, Secretary of the National Milk Producers Federation; Oscar Bradfute, President of the American Farm Bureau Federation; Walter Robinson, President of the American Wheat Growers Association; and B. W. Kilgore, President of the American Cotton Growers Exchange. Following the meetings, which were of great interest in themselves, tours were arranged for the delegates which enabled Nourse to study first hand agricultural methods and organizations in Italy, Germany, Denmark, and other European countries. He particularly valued the opportunity to examine the organization and operating methods of the Danish cooperatives, which were then being held up as models for American cooperatives. Altogether, this experience gave Nourse a sense of reality as to the nature of European agriculture and broadened his perspective on the problems of American agriculture. It also gave him a deeper appreciation of the cultural values of European civilization.

The Brookings Graduate School of Economics and Government

While Nourse was getting his work established, a new organization closely related to the Institute of Economics was coming into being—The Robert S. Brookings Graduate School of Economics and Government. In 1923, Brookings had provided funds so that graduate students in economics and government at Washington University in St. Louis could do part of their work for doctoral degrees in these two areas in association with the staffs of the Institute of Economics and the Institute of Government Research. To facilitate this program, Brookings purchased an old private home at 1724 I Street, only a few blocks from the two institutes, as a residence for the students and pledged annual support of $1,000 for each of 20 fellowships. Before the first class was enrolled in the fall of 1924, it was apparent that this program could best be operated on an independent basis, so it was incorporated in November, 1924, as the Robert S. Brookings Graduate School of Economics and Government.

As the Brookings school was conveniently located near the two institutes, a close liaison relationship was soon established between the three bodies. Many of the graduate students developed thesis subjects of direct interest to the institutes, and staff members of the institutes helped give the school general direction, instruction, and guidance. Moulton served as vice-president and chief administrative officer of the school.

The unique character of the new school has been well described by Charles B. Saunders, Jr. in the following paragraph from his brief history of the Brookings Institution:

> Frankly experimental in nature, reflecting Brookings' personal views of the inadequacies of most graduate education, the school soon attracted wide attention for its innovations and its pioneering emphasis on training for the public service. Its doctoral program placed primary emphasis on the opportunities afforded for ready access to the course materials on public policy research and personal contact and discussion with Washington officials. Studies focused on the larger economic and political questions of contemporary culture rather than on the academic disciplines. There were no formal courses, credits, majors, or minors; students were expected to participate in a series of short seminars, undertake extensive readings, and work on practical problems of government policy with the staff of the Institutes.[7]

From its beginning, Nourse took an active interest in the work of the school, for it brought to him many of the satisfactions of university life. He liked the opportunity to meet with the students in seminars and discussions, and he counseled several on their research projects. Moreover, he felt close to the school, for the Dean of the Faculty was Walton Hale Hamilton, who had been his instructor in the history of economic thought at the University of Chicago.

A Call for Intellectual Action

In his presidential address in December, 1924, Nourse brought a new vigor to the American Farm Economics Association. Speaking on the topic "Some Economic Factors in an American Agricultural Policy," he considered it "timely and profitable for the American public to ask itself very bluntly and very honestly the question: What do we propose to do with agriculture?" He believed that agricultural economists had much to offer in helping the public deal with this question, and he maintained that "we are not powerless as to the course which our economic life should follow." He held that "our prime task as economists is to become really proficient as 'trouble shooters' for the economic machinery with which the farmer works. To do this successfully, we must first become thoroughly conversant with both the structure and the functioning of that economic mechanism." Moreover, he insisted that agricultural economists must have a "broad national viewpoint," in that "agriculture is only one part of the indivisible economic life of the nation."[8]

With this appeal to the better instincts of his fellow agricultural economists, he examined the evolution of agricultural policies and the current state of national thinking on agricultural problems. He came to the conclusion: "The time has come in the maturing of our national life when it seems desirable to establish and maintain a permanent agriculture in a position of effective coordination to other interests in our national life." He saw this as a "great task which unfolds before . . . our profession. If we are to be scientists and not apologists, professional servants of the whole society, not commercial retainers of a special interest, we must bring not merely insight and sympathy to bear upon the task, but also keen analysis, cool judgement, broad vision, and the utmost degree of intellectual honesty."

Nourse concluded his address with a statement which neatly disposed of the popular faith in current nostrums. "The longer the run of attention and effort is toward export dumping corporations, larger and easier credit extensions, and organized price control, instead of toward the individual and group enforcement of a truly American rural standard of living, the longer the valuable qualitative elements of an agricultural policy will elude the farmers' grasp." This address did much to raise the sights of the agricultural economics profession. It was a call both for idealism and intellectual competence, which deeply impressed his fellow agricultural economists.

Upon completion of his year as association president, Nourse agreed to take over the editorship of the association's quarterly, the *Journal of Farm Economics*. In accepting this responsibility he had ambitions for the development of a better journal. It was then mostly devoted to agricultural production and farm management subjects, and association dues were but $3.00 a year. So Nourse proceeded to expand the publication into a more significant organ. At the end of the year, he could report back to the annual meeting: "We are now getting on the map as a professional association and I think the four issues of the *Journal of Farm Economics* this year are the prototype of a professional journal. In bringing it up to this level, I have enlarged your debt and I think that you should now—both in view of the dignity of the association and its financial exigencies—raise dues to $5.00 so that we can make it a better journal." So the dues were raised, and Nourse continued to edit the journal for the ensuing year. When he gave up the editorship in December, 1926, the journal was recognized in agricultural circles as a very influential publication.

Birth of the American Institute of Cooperation

As soon as work was done on the European Market book, Nourse began his comprehensive study of the evolution of cooperative institutions in the United States. He wisely refrained from making it a study of cooperative marketing enterprises, which were then of dominant importance. As he got immersed in this study, he came to have a greater appreciation and understanding of all kinds of cooperative undertakings, and he became more tolerant of some of the ideas espoused by Aaron Sapiro and other leaders of the commodity cooperative marketing movement.

At almost this same time—early in 1924—it became apparent to some of the leaders in the dairy cooperative movement that the conflict of philosophy among cooperatives was doing more harm than good. The movement was being polarized rather than clarified, and the public was getting a confused idea of what cooperative organizations really stood for. Led by Richard Pattee, Secretary of the New England Milk Producers Association, and Charles Holman, Secretary of the National Milk Producers Federation, sentiment began to form for some kind of clearinghouse for cooperative ideas in the hope that a consensus might be arrived at. This sentiment finally came to a head in plans for an organization to be known as the American Institute of Cooperation.[9] It then had gained the powerful support of Dr. Henry C. Taylor, Chief of the Bureau of Agricultural Economics of the United States Department of Agriculture.

Pattee, Holman, and Taylor were quick to recognize that Nourse could be of immense importance in furthering the proposed organization, and they sought his active cooperation. He responded enthusiastically, for he believed that the type of organization they had in mind could serve as an educational forum for promoting sound cooperative principles and practices. One of the immediate needs was to obtain supporting funds to ensure the success of the project. With Holman and Taylor, Nourse visited Beardsley Ruml of the Laura Spellman Fund in New York City and helped persuade him to provide a substantial grant to cover basic expenses until the Institute could function on a self-supporting basis.

A key problem in getting the American Institute of Cooperation under way was finding a man to serve as program chairman who could enlist widespread support from cooperative officials and agricultural leaders. No one had qualifications equal to those of Nourse, for he was well known among cooperative leaders, and he had the respect of those interested in cooperatives who were associated with the agricultural colleges and other public agencies. Nourse willingly accepted this heavy responsibility, and in the spring of 1925 he was giving a great deal of time and energy to building a program and selecting speakers for the sessions to be held at the University of Pennsylvania during the summer. This was a very ambitious undertaking, and Nourse had almost complete responsibility for making it a success. He threw himself into the effort and almost suffered a physical breakdown. As Nourse later said: "I pretty nearly killed myself on the AIC for several years. But it was not my chick; I did not hatch the idea. It came to me and I tried to build a good brooder for it. . . ."[10]

The Institute brought together a wide spectrum of cooperative directors, leaders, and students interested in cooperative enterprise for a four-week period in the summer of 1925 at the University of Pennsylvania, where Nourse was, in his words, "a sort of housemother to the whole enterprise." The first institute meetings were a marked success. They did what they aspired to do—provide a clearinghouse for cooperative thought and practice—and in the process, it brought a sense of harmony within cooperative ranks. One of the important seminars was conducted by Nourse. This was designed to develop a workable definition of cooperative enterprise. While no formal definition was agreed upon, the discussion made it evident that a narrow one would not do.

The success of the first summer institute assured its continuation in later years, and for several years Nourse continued to serve as Chairman of the Program Committee. At the first institute, he had been dubbed Dean of the American Institute of Cooperation, and he graciously accepted this compliment by facetiously saying: "A dean is a mouse studying to become a rat."

In working on this project, Nourse did not lose sight of its relationship to the book he was preparing on cooperative development. In fact, this work heightened his perception of the problems and possibilities of cooperative business organizations and provided him with source materials and direct contact with current cooperative developments.

A Unifying Statement

The annual meeting of the National Association of State Marketing Officials in November, 1925, featured an address by Nourse on the "Recent Trend of Cooperation Among Cooperatives."[11] He saw the cooperative movement going through a "settling down period" with a "strong get-together" tendency among cooperatives, and he discerned "real and substantial progress" in agricultural cooperation. He then said:

> You are all aware that there was not a get-together spirit manifest in the cooperative movement a few years ago. Certain vigorous new forces had come into the cooperative movement. Some of the people who espoused the new influence, the new leadership in cooperatives expected too much. A considerable element of fight was injected. You know that as well as I do. I think there were in that period some sufferings that could be described as "growing pains." There was a great deal that was narrow-minded, that was wrong on both sides.

Nourse did not see any good in rehashing the old issues. But he did think the situation showed the need of getting together those with different shades of thought "from the most extreme progressive or radical," to work out a common ground for agreement and "incorporate some of the more progressive ideas in some way so that progress can be made with safety." He believed that the American Institute of Cooperation had provided just the forum that was needed. He observed: "It came at a very opportune time."

This address marked a significant change in Nourse's thinking since his meeting with this same body in November, 1923. He displayed a much greater tolerance for the centralized type of cooperative organization by admitting that "probably some of us failed to realize the situation as it confronted the people who had a particular problem with strong centralized types of organization." He also admitted that sound cooperative development could come from the bottom up or from the top down. He said: "I have seen buildings put up both ways. In some places the foundation is built first and the superstructure afterwards. But in some skyscrapers you see stone put on the seventh story first."

Nourse's conciliatory statement met with a good response, for the controversy between the two philosophies was fast losing its meaning. While he made clear that he was not a "die-hard" cooperative fundamentalist unwilling to grow with the times, he yielded none of his strong belief that cooperatives must be economically sound in their basic objectives and procedures. It is significant that Walton Peteet, then Secretary of the National Council of Farmer Cooperative Marketing Associations—an organization set up to promote the advancement of "commodity marketing" as espoused by Aaron Sapiro—said in an address following that of Nourse: "I can add nothing to the very clear analysis of the general trend in cooperation that Dr. Nourse has made."

In the spring and early summer of 1926, much of Nourse's attention was absorbed by his work as Chairman of the Program Committee of the American Institute of Cooperation. The success of the first institute encouraged him and his associates to plan for an even more ambitious program for the sessions to be held at the University of Minnesota from June 21 to July 17. It was decided to center attention on current problems of cooperatives in specific fields: grain, livestock, etc. Nourse took special interest in the development of a comprehensive program on cooperative livestock marketing in view of the book he had in mind on cooperative livestock marketing as a follow-up study of his forthcoming book on the legal foundations of agricultural cooperation. The Minnesota institute was also designed to emphasize training and education. The program provided for three-day short courses for managers and directors of livestock shipping associations, cooperative creameries, and farmers' elevators, and for 12 academic short courses on aspects of agricultural cooperation to be offered jointly with the University of Minnesota. The professors in these courses included such well-known agricultural economists as Dr. John D. Black, Dr. O. B. Jesness, Dr. H. Bruce Price, and Dr. Theodore Macklin. Nourse was to give the course on "The Economic and Legal Foundations of Cooperation."

Nourse was greatly pleased with the results obtained at the Minnesota institute. All went as planned, and some 500 key leaders in the cooperative field attended. One who attended this institute was Professor Orion

Ulrey, then a graduate student in agricultural economics. He well remembers the spirit of enthusiasm that pervaded this institute. Along with several other students, he lived and had meals at the Alpha Zeta House with Nourse, O. B. Jesness, Mordacai Ezekiel, and Richard Pattee. Ulrey recalls that "the discussions about cooperatives and the rural economy at meals and during the evenings, left a deep impression on the students who were searching for ideas on improved systems." In fact, Ulrey attributes his life-long interest in cooperatives to this early association with Nourse. Ulrey took his course and was impressed by him as being very "fair in his analysis of the fundamentals and possibilities of cooperative business to serve American farmers."[12]

Nourse's main participation in the institute, other than in teaching, was to serve as chairman and discussion leader of the four days of the program devoted to cooperative livestock marketing. He introduced this part of the program with a talk on "History and Structure of Cooperative Livestock Marketing," in which he said: "It is my purpose to examine the several parts of cooperative livestock marketing as it has actually developed and to raise a few questions as to how we could most helpfully contribute to its future shaping." The papers and discussions provided much useful information for the book he was then projecting on "The Cooperative Marketing of Livestock."

My Early Work with Nourse

While working for my doctor's degree at Stanford University in the spring of 1926, I submitted an article to Dr. Nourse, who was editor of the *Journal of Farm Economics*. In a few weeks I received two letters from him in the same envelope. In one, on the letterhead of the *Journal*, he accepted my article for early publication. In the other, on the letterhead of the Institute of Economics, he enquired whether I would be interested in helping him write a book on the cooperative marketing of livestock. Although my work at Stanford was not completed, I jumped at this chance, and as a result I reported to him in Washington, D.C., on September 1, 1926.

I recall how cordially Nourse received me, and from that time forward I was to enjoy a sense of empathy with him. As he was absorbed in some important task, he enquired if I could find something to do until he was free to work on our project. This suited me, for I had to find a place to live; and I wanted to get acquainted with the Library of Congress and other facilities of Washington. So, for the first month, I was very much on my own.

Then Nourse called me into his office and said: "It's about time we started work on our book." I concurred. Then he said: "I believe it is to be on the cooperative marketing of livestock." I again concurred. "Moreover," he then said, "I believe it is understood that I am going to work on it and you are going to work on it." I could but agree. With all of this settled, he continued: "Let's get that down." So he stepped to the door and said to Laura Lane, his secretary: "Come in and bring your book." After she was seated, he said: "Put at the top of the sheet in caps 'The Cooperative Marketing of Livestock.' Under that write: 'By Edwin G. Nourse and Joseph G. Knapp.'" After she had written this down, he said to her: "Please type two copies of this and give one to Mr. Knapp." After she had handed me my typed copy, he said: "I feel awfully tired. We have named the book and agreed on its authorship. That's enough for one day." So our book was launched, and soon afterwards we began to develop plans for the book and to assemble information for it.

I have given this personal account because it shows something of the personality and character of Nourse at this time.

The Institute of Economics as of 1926

The Institute of Economics was a very friendly place to work when I arrived. I was immediately given a desk in a room adjoining Nourse's office with Frank Tanenbaum, who was writing a book on the Mexican agrarian revolution. No one could have been a better companion than Frank, and he soon helped me get acquainted with the other members of the staff and his friends in the Brookings Graduate School. The only other person working on the agricultural staff under Nourse at this time was Russell Engberg, who was making a study to determine the relationship of industrial prosperity and depression to farm product prices and farmers' operating costs. His findings were to be published in a book the following year under the title, *Industrial Prosperity and the Farmer*.[13]

The Institute was then in every sense a community of scholars who were all busy on books of importance, and it was a great inspiration for me to have this close association with economists of national standing. Several of us would go out for lunch together, and this helped me get well acquainted with them. We also had staff seminars from time to time in the basement library, on matters of mutual interest, and this helped build an institutional spirit. The Brookings Graduate School was flourishing with some 30 scholars in residence a few blocks away on I Street, and this interlocking relationship of the school with the Institute gave access to stimulating lectures by men such as Graham Wallace and Carl

Becker. In his memorial tribute to Dr. Moulton in 1965, Nourse well caught the spirit and flavor of the Institute of Economics at that time. He said: "It was an exciting mental atmosphere that Moulton created in our offices and conference rooms in those early years. But there was also an easy camaraderie that ran from top to bottom of the organization. . . ."

While Nourse was getting his own program established, he was taking a great interest in the general program of the Institute. For example, he gave his best thought to books issued by other divisions of the Institute. One who remembers how Nourse helped him at this time is Dr. Lynn R. Edminster, who joined the staff of the Institute of Economics in September, 1922, to work on tariff studies relating to agriculture. His book, *The Cattle Industry and the Tariff*, was published in 1926. Nourse was greatly interested in this book, and he reviewed it critically before publication. As Edminster has remarked: "This, I can assure you he did." Not only did he offer many helpful minor suggestions, but he provided a footnote that questioned one of Edminster's assumptions. This didn't upset Edminster. "I came out of this experience," he recalls, "with a profound respect for Dr. Nourse's professional skills but also for his admirable personal qualities. His was the attitude, not of the hostile and harsh critic but of one whose only concern was to raise the questions that needed to be raised in order that the truth might be properly served. This, to my way of thinking, is the mark of a gentleman and a scholar."[14]

In the fall of 1926, Nourse had many irons in the fire. He was giving much attention to the final stages of his forthcoming book on agricultural cooperation. He was continuing his active interest in the American Institute of Cooperation, and was already making program plans for the next year's institute. He was working actively on the Agricultural Economics Committee of the Social Science Research Council, and he was giving thought to a major talk that he was scheduled to give at the next annual meeting of the American Farm Economic Association, which he saw as an opportunity to bring a fresh point of view to the agricultural economics profession.

Altogether, he was a busy man, but happy in his work and home life. His professional work was now well established, and he was enjoying the social and cultural advantages of Washington. He had taken up clay modeling for recreation, and this gave him an opportunity to express his creative and artistic abilities. He now had his own home, and this gave him an outlet for his skill in carpentry and gardening.

Life at the Institute of Economics was going well. With a small congenial staff, he enjoyed rapport with Moulton and his colleagues in the two institutes and in his associations with the Brookings Graduate School.

The Institute of Economics was building a national reputation for its excellent economic studies, and he was proud to be one of its leaders.

When I joined him, his secretary was Laura Lane, a delightful girl with an impish sense of humor that gave a pleasant ambience to his office. As he shared her services with me, I soon came to appreciate her competence and cooperative spirit. This is a good place to record that Nourse was always appreciative of help given by his secretaries. He once said to me: "There is no question but that a good secretary is a joy unto the Lord and a help to her boss." Laura Lane served him for nearly 10 years, starting in 1923. He later referred to her as "a bright girl, without college training. On the legal status book she did a lot of work looking up cases and handling material of that sort which made me press for advancement of her salary. She was an assistant as well as a secretary. She was a very good stenographer and a good typist, and she could get out very nice work very fast." His infectious enthusiasm for whatever he was writing found in her a kindred spirit.

"The Outlook for Agriculture"

The main event of the annual meeting of the American Farm Economic Association in December, 1926, was Nourse's paper on "The Outlook for Agriculture." He "curtly" announced his thesis at the start in the following terms: *"The outlook for American agriculture is far from bright, the industry being faced by portentous technological changes while its organization and institutions are such as to make extremely difficult, indeed in large part impossible, a prompt and suitable adjustment to these circumstances.* Stated as a paradox, the outlook for agricultural production is so good that the outlook for agricultural prosperity is distinctly bad." (Emphasis added.) He challenged the complacency of those who held that agricultural trends were favorable to an early resumption of farm prosperity on the grounds that "we are only just now coming into the stage of effective and widespread application of scientific methods to the production of agricultural products as a whole."

After supporting his thesis with evidence, he said: "Agriculture is in an epoch of chronic surplus rather than one of chronic deficit. . . . This situation I interpret as involving a tendency toward the decline of agricultural prices faster than costs can be reduced. . . . Doubtless the most proficient [farmers] can survive and even prosper in a mild way in such a transition period, but the main question is how the industry as a whole is circumstanced to meeting the situation, the difficulty, if you please the crisis outlined above." On this he was pessimistic. He felt that the economic organization of agriculture left farmers "exposed, practically defenseless, against the full force of this economic strain."

However, he found some constructive forces at work. These he listed as "(1) individual success in the direction of more than average efficiency, (2) readjustment of the nation's agricultural industry through the cumulation of many personally successful moves toward better farm management in the proportioning of enterprises, (3) continued shifting of workers out of farming, (4) the possible infiltration of corporate business into agriculture, and (5) the cooperative movement." While he thought that all five of these forces were to be reckoned with, he considered "none of them, nor all together—adequate to really save the agricultural situation during the next decade or so."

However, it is significant that he gave special recognition to the constructive possibilities of cooperation in his closing paragraph.

> Popular faith has of late centered most conspicuously upon the cooperative movement. In the main, however, this represents a yearning for vicarious salvation rather than any tough and seasoned knowledge of the powers and purposes of the cooperative form of economic organization. Speaking out of some years of close contact with agricultural cooperation and careful study of both its theory and practice, I am convinced that it is destined to be a plant of slow, though sturdy growth. It is a democratic and hence rather fumbling attempt on the part of agriculture to achieve for itself certain of the outstanding benefits of large-scale organization as demanded by the evolution of modern business conditions but so adapted as to meet the peculiar needs of the farming industry. This means both the introduction of a higher degree of economy and efficiency into the actual processes of production and marketing and also the effecting of units of organization large enough to permit of the averaging of returns and the scaling of operations to the needs of a market broadly studied and skillfully exploited. *I am convinced that cooperation offers in the long run one of the most important and, quite probably, the most important single opportunity for improving the economic organization of our agricultural industry as a whole....* [Emphasis added.]

Nourse's paper opened up a spirited discussion. Dr. George F. Warren of Cornell University maintained that Nourse had "considerably overemphasized the ease with which production can be increased . . . [in that] agriculture is a biological industry . . . and can never be converted into a mechanical industry." He held that the agricultural depression would have to run its course before confidence was restored, and he foresaw that "when the agricultural depression is over it is probable that we will have twenty years in which much of the program of the American Farm Economic Association will be devoted to some phase of the problems of the high cost of food." Others were in more agreement with Nourse. For example, Dr. Oscar C. Stine of the Bureau of Agricultural Economics completely supported his thesis and suggested that perhaps relief might come from the organization of a "go-to-the-city-movement." Like Nourse, he felt that cooperative marketing was not then strong enough to meet the problem.

Nourse could not resist preparing a rejoinder with the discussion of his paper in the January, 1927, issue of the *Journal of Farm Economics*. In this he pointed out that much of the discussion was "extraneous" to the issues which he had raised. He was concerned that only Stine had given much consideration to his second major proposition, "the inadequacy of existing or apparently developing agricultural institutions to effect a satisfactory adjustment to actual conditions." He then said: "Possibly the languid interest in this issue ... illuminates the problem of why the active leaders of farm organizations have proved such blind and futile captains of their host in this period of distress." He concluded by wondering "whether the issues raised in this discussion are not of such broad and fundamental significance to agricultural economists as a group that the several points of view might profitably be elaborated by their respective spokesmen in later issues of this Journal."

Nourse never shrank from controversy. In fact, before giving his paper, he had termed it "provocative rather than conclusive." To him a professional association without strong differences of opinion was apt to be of little value. He believed that a main purpose should be to stimulate thought and research so as to come to common understandings.

Nourse's views on the nature of the agricultural problems fell on fertile ground, and in the next few years the articles in the *Journal of Farm Economics* reflected much deeper thought by agricultural economists. When the American Farm Economic Association held its next annual meeting in December, 1927, Dr. George Warren presented the leading paper, "Which Does Agriculture NEED—Readjustment or Legislation?" It was his basic view that the solution to the farm problem would come in a reasonable period of time by working out economic forces. However, by this time there was developing a feeling among agricultural economists that the problem could not wait, and that a federal farm board of some kind should be given power to help bring about more favorable economic conditions. The leader in expressing this view was Dr. Joseph S. Davis, Director of the Food Research Institute of Stanford University. As a discussant of Warren's paper, he said: "I believe that both readjustment and legislation are needed, but that the two problems must be considered in relation one to the other and in due perspective. I believe that desirable readjustments could be promoted, others rendered unnecessary, and painful consequences of the depression mitigated by a Federal Farm Board with the cooperation of a Federal agricultural council."

Nourse sat on the sidelines during this discussion. The process of giving more serious consideration to the farm problem by agricultural economists was underway. However, he felt that one question required fresh study: whether the outlook for agricultural exports was more favorable than it had been four years before, when *American Agriculture and the European Market* was published. He reexamined this question in an article, "The Trend of Agricultural Exports," for the June, 1928, issue of the *Journal of Political Economy* and found that "the [export] outlook in the spring of 1928 does not seem to be such as to give the farmer much more cheer than was vouchsafed to him in the spring of 1924."

The Legal Status of Agricultural Cooperation

With the disposal of the European market question in 1924, Nourse had been able to turn to what he considered a more constructive undertaking—a study of cooperative development in the United States. This subject was of pressing national importance, for there was then a widespread belief that the agricultural depression could be largely cured through the development of strong cooperative marketing organizations.

Nourse's work in Iowa had impressed upon him the importance of having good legal foundations for cooperative development, and he had come to the belief that the cooperative form of business organization could best be studied in the light of its changing legal structure and foundations. He started out in an inductive way to examine cooperative experience as it evolved in "a legal mold," and the book finally took form as *The Legal Status of Agricultural Cooperation.*

The project required an enormous amount of research into the federal and state laws, regulations, and judicial decisions relating to cooperatives. As the book grew, Nourse sent draft chapters to many legal authorities for their suggestions and comments. In doing so, he did not ignore Aaron Sapiro. After reviewing three of the key chapters, Sapiro wrote Nourse on March 8, 1926: "I am returning the three chapters with some notations. That's a splendid piece of work." J. C. Mitchell, who had helped Nourse draft the Iowa Cooperative Law of 1921, thought that he was being too fair to Sapiro. He observed that "the earlier chapters impress me as rather too much of an exposition of the Sapiro schemes." When the book came out in early 1927, Nourse sent Mitchell a copy with the comment: "I trust that in its final form you will read the book with a reasonable degree of composure."

When the book was published, the Institute of Economics press release (no doubt prepared by Nourse) described it as follows:

> The present volume has attempted to show the evolving nature of cooperation as a modern economic institution. The outstanding conclusions of the book are: That the prolonged depression in American agriculture has had the effect of bringing cooperation to the fore as the permanent form of organization for farming as an industry; that agricultural cooperatives have achieved a reasonably stable and workable status through a long process of legal and economic evolution; and finally, that certain difficult problems have still to be faced by the cooperative movement.

The character of the volume was reflected in its four general conclusions:

(1) It is well that cooperation, even of the forceful modern pattern, has been accepted as a going institution of present day business.
(2) It is both inept and unnecessary for cooperative institutions to be developed as class legislation applicable only to agriculture.
(3) Even large and powerful cooperative organization does not constitute a public menace, owing to the presence of natural and institutional checks upon the abuse of power.
(4) No formula for the regulation of cooperative activities can be laid down in definite and final terms.

Nourse saw the book as only a step on the way. He finished it with these two sentences: "The present volume has attempted nothing beyond showing the evolving nature of cooperation as a modern economic institution. How this institution is actually being applied in particular branches of our agricultural industry—cotton, grain, tobacco, livestock, milk, or other—constitutes another, a larger, and an indefinitely continuing field of study."

Nourse was pleased with the immediate response to the book. Dr. W. I. Myers of Cornell University said in writing Nourse: "The earlier books on cooperation were of the descriptive type. While interesting and perhaps useful, they did not give anything like a critical analysis of the legal basis or economic structure of cooperative organizations. I hope that your book will prove to be a forerunner of a new series of texts on cooperation in which the various important phases of this subject will be analyzed more carefully than has been done before." L. S. Hulbert, legal authority of the Department of Agriculture, wrote Nourse: "Your book is unique and does not duplicate or resemble any previous publication on cooperation." Charles J. Brand, first chief of the United States Bureau of Markets, expressed himself in a review as follows: "This book is a real contribution to the literature of cooperative institutions. . . . It should be on the shelves of agricultural students, teachers, economists, county agents, members of the legal profession, bankers and business men, and executives of cooperative business enterprises."

Appreciative reviews came from all quarters—farm, business, economic, and legal journals. The *Economist* of England said: "It is not generally recognized by advocates of agricultural cooperation [in England] that there is more to be learned about its development by looking across the Atlantic than by looking across the North Sea." Of particular significance to Nourse were the reactions in the law reviews. Matthew Tobriner, in the *Harvard Law Review*, said: "This study presents a picture, clearcut and ably drawn of the legal status of the cooperative marketing association and of the process by which courts and legislatures have defined its powers. . . ." James Angel McLaughlin, in the *Cornell Law Quarterly*, said: "There ought to be more books like this. There will not be an embarrassing number because the production of such a study takes special training, patience, and brains." John Hanna, in the *University of Pennsylvania Law Review*, declared: "If subsequent volumes planned by Nourse maintain the standard set in the present book the Institute of Economics will have handsomely justified its existence."

Probably no reaction pleased Nourse more than that of Samuel Guard, editor of the *Breeder's Gazette*, who wrote him as follows (October 28, 1927): "I am tremendously interested in your book. It certainly strikes me as being a momentous contribution to the marketing of farm products." After expressing his deep dismay that many of his friends had lost faith in cooperative marketing, he asked: "You have not lost faith in the efficacy of cooperative marketing to solve many of our farm problems, have you?" Nourse promptly responded with a "Most positive, NO" and then set forth his views in some detail.

> I feel that a great many people took up the cooperative movement as a "get rich quick scheme" for agriculture. They were willing to *speculate* a little on something for which high pressure salesmen made extravagant claims but were too lazy or too gullible to investigate the real values and possibilities of the proposition. Now that some of these ventures have blown up either because of faulty organization or management, they easily lose faith in the whole cooperative idea. They do not have the staying qualities or the business foresight to *invest* in cooperation as a permanent producer of real but conservative dividends for the farmer.
>
> As I look at it, the cooperative form of organization offers not everywhere, but in many parts of our agricultural industry, the outstanding possibility for the future by affording long time elements of sound business organization imperatively needed if the industry is to give a creditable account of itself among other branches of modern business.
>
> To my mind, the evidence is ample that the cooperative form of organization has established itself. . . . The real issue is whether we can develop an understanding membership ready to go into cooperative enterprises and

sweat through the period of gaining experience and becoming permanently established and learning how to function under this difficult but desirable form of organization and also of selecting, weeding out, and training leaders, officials and technical staffs, who can keep these enterprises in a wholesome and progressive condition. . . . The educational effort of the next 10 or 25 years will determine the measure of success which cooperation can achieve in the United States.

Guard was greatly pleased with Nourse's reply. He wrote back (November 7, 1927): "It made me holler right out loud to find someone willing to stick by the old ideals of cooperative marketing and to believe that another 25 or 50 years will bring us a merchandising system that will really place the farmer on a new basis of economics."

The Corporation Farm Question

While Moulton was pleased with Nourse's program of work, Brookings was somewhat skeptical of its importance. He continued to think that Nourse should direct his attention to the reorganization of agriculture along big business lines. Brookings expressed his views in a letter to Moulton on January 22, 1927, as follows: "You are the only member of our organization who has appreciated the importance of selecting current acute problems for investigation and publication. Confidentially, Nourse in this respect has been a disappointment to me. Why take some phase of the agriculture problem, like its history over a period of years, or marketing, requiring a year or more for the publication of a book, which, while unquestionably a valuable contribution to the subject, cannot in my judgment compare with the most important economic problem which confronts the nation, i.e., why has efficiency as measured by production per capita developed within the past few years such a great disparity between the industries and agriculture. . . ." He went on to suggest that Nourse might "put men enough in the field to secure the facts upon which a book could be written within the time necessary to secure maximum results and render maximum service." The object would be to "ascertain what the opportunity for improved efficiency there may be in my cooperative or corporation scheme."

Nourse was not uninterested in the subject, for he had written an article on corporation farming for the *Youth's Companion* in 1922, but he felt that Brookings' "notion of salvation of agriculture by factory methods" did not take sufficiently into account a great many aspects of farming, both technical and economic. In a memo to Moulton commenting on the proposal (February 8, 1927), he said: " Personally I should enjoy working on the problem, and see only two objections: (1) my line of attack, methods of work, and conclusions (in all probability) would fall far short of satisfying Mr. Brookings; (2) I do not see how I could myself undertake it this spring without neglecting my book which is soon to go to press...."

Moulton thereupon wrote Brookings that Nourse was greatly interested in the possibilities of "industrialized farming," but that the Council (which included Nourse), after careful consideration, concluded that his proposal would necessitate a considerable departure from the program approved by the trustees, and that it should not be undertaken without the approval of the executive committee, on which Brookings was chairman. Moulton indicated that if the project was undertaken, "Nourse would himself wish to do the field work required." Although no formal project of this type was developed, Nourse did follow through by personally visiting some of the best-known corporation farms of that period and his findings were reflected in his writings during the next few years.[15]

Although Nourse realized that Brookings had some reservations on how he was developing the agricultural program, this never became a source of embarrassment to him. Late in his life, Nourse paid Brookings the following tribute: "Although he was wrapped up body and soul in the future of the two institutes and the school—the whole enterprise—he withheld his hand. He might express his view but he never intervened in management. This was a wonderful help."[16]

"The Farmer's Mysterious Malady"

In the spring of 1927, Nourse continued to cope with the farm problem. Much as he favored cooperative organization for agriculture, he did not believe that such organizations could meet the present problems of maladjustment. He placed more trust in gradual changes, such as the migration of farmers from the land and the better organization and operation of those left on farms. He saw the problem in historical perspective and its solution in the working out of long-time trends. He developed his ideas in a paper, "The Farmer's Mysterious Malady," which unfortunately never found a publisher. In it, Nourse cogently diagnosed the so-called malady, and came to the conclusion that it was not mysterious if one looked at the facts objectively. It was only mysterious because of the many nostrums being offered. The following sentences are worth quoting:

> We cannot afford to look at the matter too narrowly.... The mysterious malady of agriculture involves the whole question of the socio-economic organization of a basic industry. The economic institutions of agriculture seem peculiarly ill-suited to meet the challenge of the potent forces of scientific technique and modern economic organization.... Such answers

as have been proposed are halting, timorous, and backward-looking—not courageous, inventive, and daring. . . . Farmers need a leadership which will discard old sentimental and habitual patterns of thought and make a realistic attack on the challenging modern problem. . . . Too long have they sweated to trundle their artillery . . . in pursuit of imaginary enemies, the "deflationists," or to capture the mythical castle "Equality."

In view of the book we had underway, Nourse took much interest in shaping up a full week's program on cooperative livestock marketing for the Third Institute of Cooperation at Northwestern University, June 20-July 16, 1927. For this occasion he asked me to prepare a paper on "Direct Buying at Packers' Private Yards," a subject of much concern to livestock cooperative leaders. This called for a substantial amount of research, on which Nourse gave me a free hand, although he was always available for consultation.

I recall my impressions of him as he chaired the livestock sessions that summer. He was commanding in appearance, well dressed but not overdressed, and he always had on a natty bow tie. He presented his views clearly in a confident manner that kept his audience with him, and his enthusiasm was infectious. He never talked down to his audience or used off-color jokes, although his playful sense of humor was evident. I was struck by how he gave every subject under consideration undivided attention and how effectively he spotted strong or weak spots in positions taken.

Improving the Training of Agricultural Economists

We have observed how the profession of agricultural economics expanded rapidly in the 1920s and how it became less farm management-oriented, with more emphasis being given to marketing, cooperation, and broad economic studies. As Thomas P. Cooper pointed out in his presidential address to the American Farm Economics Association in December, 1924: "The view of the field of farm economics during the past few years has progressed to a point where consideration is given not only to the farm as a business enterprise but to the great enterprise of agriculture as a whole." The Purnell Act of 1925 dealt with this situation by providing funds for experiment station research in marketing, cooperation, and rural sociology. In this same year, the newly established Social Science Research Council recognized the importance of better-trained agricultural research workers by setting up an advisory committee on social and economic research in agriculture, with Nourse as one of the seven members of this committee. After a survey of research being done in the fields of agriculture economics and rural sociology, this committee recommended

Nourse's father, Edwin Henry Nourse, 1883.

Nourse's mother, Harriet Augusta Beaman Nourse, 1887.

Nourse's paternal grandfather, Elisha Nurse.

Nourse's paternal grandmother, Lucy Newland Nurse.

Nourse with his sisters, Alice and Mary, 1887.

Alice, Edwin, and Mary, 1893.

In high school, age 17.

Nourse in the Baptist Boys' Brigade at age 12.

In college, age 20.

Mary Augusta Nourse, 1899.

Edwin Henry Nourse, 1900.

Alice Louise Nourse, 1900.

Alice Louise Nourse, 1906.

Ray Marie Tyler, Nourse's future wife, 1906.

Nourse's home in Washington, D.C., 1926. He lived here until his death in 1974.

Mary Augusta Nourse in solarium of Nourse's home, 1926.

Nourse and son Tyler, about 1925.

Mrs. Nourse and Tyler, about 1927.

Nourse in his Brookings Institution office, 1945.

that the Social Science Research Council provide funds for fellowships to enable promising workers to complete or advance their training so as to improve the quality of social science research in agriculture. The Council approved this proposal and set up a special committee under the chairmanship of Nourse, the chief proponent of the idea. The fellowships were to be available to persons who already had at least one year of graduate work, and the stipends were to vary from $500 to $2,500, unless very exceptional circumstances justified a larger amount. Nourse described the program to be offered in the *Journal of Farm Economics* for January, 1927, and it was put into operation later in the year. During the next few years he was to devote much time and effort to its success. When he retired as chairman of this committee in 1931 because of the pressure of other work, the Social Science Research Council, in its annual report, said: "The success of the program of fellowships in agricultural economics and rural sociology has depended in no small measure on the work of the chairman of this committee, Dr. Edwin G. Nourse."

One who was to be greatly benefited by a Social Science Research Council fellowship was Dr. Murray R. Benedict, who later was to become an eminent agricultural economist. When Benedict applied for a fellowship so that he could study at the University of Wisconsin, Nourse requested that he state frankly the reasons for his choice. Benedict replied that his real preference was to go to Harvard, where he could study under John D. Black and F. W. Taussig, but this seemed impossible because of the high costs for travel and tuition that would be involved. Nourse wrote back that if a year at Harvard was what he desired, the committee would see that the stipend would be increased to make this feasible. Many years later, Benedict was to say: "I have never ceased to be grateful for this gracious and constructive nudge in a direction which undoubtedly had a profound effect on my later professional development. It is typically Nourse—selfless, generous, and understanding."[17]

"The Evolving Idea of Cooperation in the United States"

For several years, Nourse had been studying the way in which the theory of cooperation was evolving out of experience. He summarized his thinking in an address to the American Institute of Cooperation in the summer of 1928 under the title, "The Evolving Idea of Cooperation in the United States."

After stressing that American cooperation placed its emphasis upon business efficiency rather than social reform, he noted that one of the pressing cooperative problems of the day was to help in the stabilization of agricultural production. This led him to the observation that "no amount of benevolent despotism or pure efficiency of a remote management will take the place of continuous, studious participation by members in the formulation and carrying out of plans and policies." He saw "a whole new range of problems, which might be designated as the political science of cooperative organization . . . gradually working out in the hard school of experience. . . ." He thought that "the really significant issue in this phase of our cooperative evolution centers around the practical question of how far pure democracy is compatible with business success," and he attached "great significance" to the shift from "the dragnet or inclusive type of organization," which was aggressively promoted in the early 1920s, to the "more exclusive or selective type of organization," which provides for a more democratic type of active participation. He was impressed with the way in which American practice seemed to be distinctly veering toward the doctrine that a cooperative association "should be open to every member of the industry upon the showing of certain qualifications," and he believed that "one of the greatest steps in the progress of cooperative thinking in the last few years had been the swing away from the idea of 'standard marketing', a 'uniform marketing contract', and the 'model set-up' to the much more flexible idea of organization which will vary according to the character of the commodity or other factors."

While feeling that considerable progress had been made by cooperatives in modifying the arbitrary philosophy injected into the cooperative movement by Aaron Sapiro, he was concerned by what appeared to be a "revival of the 'commodity marketing' theory in the so-called 'clearinghouse movement' which would provide for combining cooperatives and non-cooperative organizations to administer the marketing of a given crop." Nourse could not agree that the objectives of cooperative and non-cooperative organizations were compatible. He held that "the producer's paramount interest is in the adjustment of production to demand and this is no interest at all of the shipper, except in a very indirect and incidental way." He went on to say: "However valuable the clearinghouse may be as a market distribution device, it does not touch the larger problem of productive organization which is the heart of the farmer's problem."

While he admitted that "the clearinghouse may be a practical expedient for meeting a concrete market situation," he warned that "in taking it up we want to be sure that we do not sacrifice the principles of cooperation." Nourse conceded that he was a "fundamentalist" in insisting that "cooperation is a distinctive form of economic organization based on personal participating membership," for "only through organizations so conceived and so operated can you secure comprehensive and constructive action on problems of group interest." It was his view that "if you are going to accomplish anything reasonably adequate toward the stabilization of a market you must have a membership which definitely identifies its connection with the group interest in that territory." He concluded his talk by saying: "I think that the cooperatives have too often taken the easy way to get a temporary commercial success instead of taking the stricter view of cooperation as a means of the lasting organization of the industry."

The impartial views of Nourse as an objective but friendly student of the cooperative form of enterprise were highly respected in cooperative circles for their perception and fairness, and they greatly helped at this juncture of development in keeping the cooperative movement from going off at a tangent. Nourse's conviction, based upon logical reasoning, that cooperative marketing was a form of business enterprise that should not be diluted to achieve temporary ends, gave him a moral standing among cooperators—and among close observers of the cooperative movement— that was held by no other cooperative leader of the day.

The Opening of a New Career

The creation of the Brookings Institution on July 1, 1928, by merger of the Institute of Economics, the Institute for Government Research, and the Brookings School, was to have a profound effect on Nourse's later career, for it brought him back into the mainstream of economics. Under the consolidation, Moulton became President of the Brookings Institution, while Nourse took his place as Director of the Institute of Economics, which became in effect a division of the greater institution.[18]

While Nourse continued to be in charge of the agricultural economics program, he was now responsible for all economic studies. This didn't involve an immediate change in his interests, for as close consultant to Moulton, he was already in touch with all of the economic work being carried on. However, from now on he would have to think of the program as a whole and assume total direction for it.

In the next two chapters we will see how Nourse's work in general economics expanded during the Great Depression and the New Deal, while he continued to be heavily involved with the acute national problems of agriculture. In Chapter VII we will continue with the agricultural phase of his career, and then in Chapter VIII we will see how his work expanded in a complementary way in the field of general economics.

Chapter VII

PROBING THE FARM PROBLEM
(1928-1940)

As director for all economic studies of the Brookings Institution, Nourse could not detach himself entirely from the absorbing problems of agriculture, which reached a new dimension in the 1930s. We will therefore devote this chapter to a continuation of his work in the area of agricultural economics, leaving to Chapter VIII an examination of his broader institutional responsibilities and his activities in the more general field of economics.

Agriculture and Recent Economic Changes

In the fall of 1928, Nourse spent several weeks intensively examining recent developments in agriculture for the report on *Recent Economic Changes in the United States*, which was published in the spring of 1929.[1] He welcomed this opportunity to examine in depth the state of agriculture in the nation, and particularly the experience of the best-known corporation farms.

Nourse's examination of the changes that had occurred in agriculture since 1922 gives us a good idea of his thinking on the agricultural problem just before the nation's agricultural policy was to be greatly modified by the passage of the Agricultural Marketing Act of 1929, and the conditions that were quickly to arise as the country was confronted by the worst economic depression in history. It should be noted that as 1929 opened, the farm situation was better than it had been for some time because of adjustments made within agriculture and the general prosperity of the nation.

In his analysis, Nourse carried forward the views expressed in his December, 1926, address to the American Farm Economic Association on the "Outlook for Agriculture." After dealing with the "disappointing demand" for agricultural products, he turned to a crop-by-crop consideration of "exuberant production" brought about by advancing scientific farming methods, and particularly the use of power farming which he considered "hardly less than revolutionary." While he found that American farmers had been waging "a courageous and resourceful battle" to readjust their industry, he could not find much cause for believing that satisfactory adjustment would soon be effectively attained. In examining costs of distribution, he credited cooperative marketing with being of productive value, but he found cooperative effort "signally unsuccessful" in adjusting supplies to market needs for the great staple crops. After considering attempts by farmers to develop organizations coextensive with the bounds of given agricultural industries, he concluded that a more determined effort might be expected "to secure authorization for marketing arrangements which would remedy the impotence of voluntary cooperation by requiring all those engaged in a given line of production to participate in a common scheme of market distribution." This statement is of interest in view of the fact that proposals for some kind of federal farm board to achieve such an end were then under political consideration.

In his statement, Nourse stressed the "comparative immobility of agriculture." While he did not foresee that the individual family farm would soon be supplanted by large corporation factory-type farms, he considered it obvious that corporate organization of farms would become of greater importance. The steady drain of workers from farms to cities struck him as a necessary economic adjustment, but he did not believe this meant that "the quality of our farmer class generally is being lowered or that they are becoming peasants." In summarizing his views, Nourse pointed out that "the process of readjustment is too fundamental and far-reaching to be accomplished in any short period of time." He thought that the problem to be addressed was "the question of what sort of permanent organization of agriculture the nation demands and should expect in the modern economic age."

This was how Nourse saw the condition of agriculture a few months before the stock market crash which ushered in the Great Depression. Few then anticipated how all parts of the economy would be drastically affected in the very near future, although Wesley Clair Mitchell, in his closing review of the general economic situation, sounded this ominous note: "Even in the face of affairs, all is not well. Perhaps no serious setback will occur for years to come. But we are leaving 1921 well behind us, and there are signs that the caution inspired by that disastrous year is wearing thin."[2]

Nourse's chapter on "Agriculture" displayed his ability to dispassionately analyze an economic and technical problem. Although he was in sympathy with the plight of farmers, he did not let his personal feelings interfere with his logical processes. To him, economic analysis required examination of all aspects of a problem, both favorable and unfavorable. Like a physician, he believed that sound diagnosis was essential to cure. Where he could help find constructive remedies, he was concerned in doing so.

The Coming of the Federal Farm Board

The election of Herbert Hoover in 1928 set the stage for a comprehensive government program designed to give agriculture equality with industry, and after months of debate, Congress passed the Agricultural Marketing Act, which became effective with the president's signature on July 19, 1929. This act had several novel features. It encouraged "the organization of producers into effective associations or corporations under their own control." It set up a Federal Farm Board of nine members "to encourage the organization, improvement in methods, and development of effective cooperative associations." It created a revolving fund of $500 million to be administered by the board to provide for setting up stabilization corporations to control any surpluses that might arise.[3]

The Agricultural Marketing Act met with Nourse's general approval, for he believed that some government program of this kind was called for. He was disposed to give the Federal Farm Board a fair trial. Looking back on the beginning of this experiment, he said:

> The whole thing was a very good illustration of the way we do things in this country, and I think it's a pretty good way in the last analysis. Trouble results in protest; protest results in the demand for very radical reform measures. . . . Then in time solid judgment and experience take over. In that agricultural depression period farmers were making extreme demands for revolutionary changes. Those demands were debated. Bills were passed, vetoed, etc., and there was a residue of decision that the federal government should take some steps, even though not drastic steps in this area. So in the first year of Hoover's administration, a relatively conservative and yet somewhat revolutionary step was taken in passing the Agricultural Marketing Act. It had two features that were definitely of a reform character or a change in our institutions and practices. One was the setting up of a top analytical and policy making body—The Federal Farm Board—as a board of strategy for national agriculture, and as they decided that more active intervention was necessary by government, it would have federal funds to implement it. Second: it represented a consensus that the automatic price-making functions of our market resulted in the collapse of prices at times of surplus supply and deficient demand, and that the government could play an active role by impounding surpluses and feeding them back

> into the market at a later time when production had curbed itself or been curbed by government advice and when demand had recovered or had been stimulated by private or public effort. Now, the logic of that was impeccable (1) of having federal funds to carry price depressing surpluses over to more advantageous times of marketing, and (2) of having a national intellectually based board of strategy to supervise this thing. On that basis, I don't recall that I ever was antagonistic to that development. In fact, it represented an exemplification of my philosophy of "Normal Prices as a Market Concept" which I expounded in my 1919 *Quarterly Journal of Economics* article.[4]

This new development made it desirable that we defer completion of the book on cooperative livestock marketing until the Federal Farm Board's influence on cooperative marketing could be evaluated. While Nourse was agreeable that I now start on a companion study of cooperative grain marketing, I felt that I needed broader experience at this stage of my career. Two opportunities arose: one at North Carolina State College, which would provide research, teaching, and extension experience; the other in business research for a western university. I was aware that Nourse favored the North Carolina job, which would give me valuable knowledge of the South and extend my work in agricultural economics, but he scrupulously avoided advising me on which position I should take. When I told him that I had taken the North Carolina post, he simply said: "This will build on the start you have made."

With its mandate from the Agricultural Marketing Act, the Federal Farm Board immediately proceeded to establish effective cooperative marketing associations by integrating many of the existing cooperatives into national federations, and within a year such national organizations were created for grain, livestock, cotton, and other commodities. While the board was thus endeavoring to strengthen the structure of cooperative marketing, it was confronted by the abnormal drop in farm prices that accompanied the onset of the Great Depression. This forced it to almost immediately enter into costly stabilization operations that impaired its ability to function in its intended manner. Under these circumstances, Nourse reserved judgment on the procedures of the Federal Farm Board while it was struggling with this emergency situation. During this period, he examined more carefully the growing significance of mechanization in agriculture.

The Impact of Mechanized Agriculture

Nourse's views on agricultural mechanization in *Recent Economic Changes* were of so much interest to Dr. Harry Millis, the President of the American Economic Association, that he invited Nourse to elaborate his thinking for the coming annual meeting of the association (December, 1929). Speaking on the subject, "Some Economic and Social Accompaniments of Mechanization of Agriculture," Nourse said: "A new psychology with reference to the whole process of farming is demanded by the introduction of power methods." He also said: "I cannot escape the conviction that the mechanization of agriculture will have profound repercussions upon the use, the values, and the institutions of land as one of the great factors of agricultural production." Of particular interest were his views on how mechanization would influence farm business management:

> It has been freely asserted that the new agricultural situation demands a new economic organization following the corporate pattern so generally adopted in other callings. The rosy pictures of quick salvation painted by the superficial students of the situation are no more convincing than the stubborn assertion by some of the ultra-conservatives that no basic change of organization is either possible or called for. . . . The managerial problem of agriculture is probably the most acute one which has arisen as a result of the mechanization movement. The great economic significance of the coming of power farming is that it permits the reduction of production costs in a way roughly comparable to what has been going on in the industrial field. I say "permits" advisedly since these possibilities can be taken advantage of only by the development of a suitable business organization within the industry.

Nourse believed that this developing situation would result in larger family-type farms able to make use of mechanical power and equipment. He thought there was much "to indicate that with the decentralized character of agricultural processes and the development of comparatively small power units adapted to farming, farms from four to possibly ten times the size of the family operating units to which we have been accustomed would make the best fit with the requirements of the new technique." He thought that even the lower figure "would permit a selective process which would result in culling out the three-quarters of our farmers who show themselves to be the poorest farm managers." He thought this process would raise "the level of entrepreneurship" in agriculture "to a significant degree." Nourse did not consider a reduction in the number of farmers undesirable. Rather, he held that it would result in more efficient independently organized farm enterprises, which could make a stronger base for "comprehensive group action."

Nourse's analysis recognized that a new element had been introduced into the agricultural industry with the passage of the Agricultural Marketing Act. He saw in the newly established Federal Farm Board an attempt to achieve economic "rationalization" through "the agency of agricultural cooperatives," but he was not convinced that the cooperative form was a workable device for the achievement of this objective. He did not "believe that a really adequate program of agricultural rationalization" could be "worked out and put into effect" through the voluntary efforts of "six and one-half million 'independent' farmers even though they be given the leadership of nine supermen in a Farm Board." To achieve any real degree of rationalization for the great staple crops, he thought there would need to be "a fair degree of concentration of executive responsibility," and that this could come only through a better "focussing of the managerial function" as farms grew fewer, larger, and stronger as economic units.

These views of Nourse indicate how his mind played on economic problems. He believed that any program of lasting significance must take into consideration the logic of economic facts. Incidentally, it is here of interest that his opinion that the number of farmers could be effectively reduced became almost a fetish of agricultural economists some 20 years later.

The New Forces in Agriculture

In March, 1930, Nourse followed up his 1929 statement on economic changes in agriculture with an address to the American Academy of Political and Social Science on "The Apparent Trend of Recent Economic Changes in Agriculture." He pointed out that three forces had "jolted" America's agriculture out of its previous course and set it upon a fresh line of economic development: (1) foreign demand and competition, (2) science and engineering, and (3) group action and rationalization.

In view of the establishment of the Federal Farm Board in the preceding year, his views on the third force are of particular interest. He saw the Farm Board's program as a continuation of the trend "from an individual to a group basis organization." He pointed out that the commodity marketing movement of the 1920s had been based on "a seller's market psychology—in the belief that, given comprehensive organization, the group could exact a satisfactory price and need not worry about the adjustment of the production department, whereas the scheme was tried out in a buyers' market." Turning to a consideration of the objectives of the Agricultural Marketing Act, he said that its central purpose "is to work out a plan of orderly production for the agricultural industry and of orderly marketing of the commodities thus produced." Stating that "any thoughtful student of the history of American agriculture can hardly fail to be staggered by the magnitude of the task which confronts the Farm Board," he held that "it must be viewed as a very interesting experiment in applying general concepts of coordinated planning and centralized control."

While Nourse hoped that the Farm Board could help bring about a better adjustment of production to market demand, he saw this as a long-run problem. Although convinced that "the pressure of recent economic changes promises to force agriculture to catch up with the modern industrial procession," and that this would call for a gradual change in the structure of agriculture to fewer but stronger economic units in farming, he was not ready to accept mandatory control of agricultural production through government action.

A few months later, in July, 1930, Nourse came to grips with the Farm Board's problem of production control in an address to the American Institute of Cooperation on "What Can the Farm Board Do Toward Production Control?" Here he examined what cooperatives had been able to do by themselves in controlling agricultural production, and what they might do with direct assistance from the Farm Board. He saw three kinds of situations: (1) where conditions were favorable to control by a cooperative, as with milk and certain specialty crops, (2) where little could be done, as with the great staple crops, and (3) where more might be done with the help of the Farm Board for livestock, tobacco, and certain other commodities. On the third situation he thought that the "Farm Board might become a better agency than any which we have previously had for gauging market requirements and for relaying this information promptly and widely to a majority of the producers." On this he said: "It remains to be seen how deep an understanding of the fundamentals of the economic organization of agriculture and the potentialities of cooperative associations the Farm Board will display over a period of years, and of how persuasive and aggressive will be the call of its leadership toward voluntary adjustment of difficulties."[5]

The Cooperative Marketing of Livestock

It will be recalled that completion of our cooperative livestock marketing study was held up, awaiting developments under the Agricultural Marketing Act. Nourse continued to work on this book in the light of Federal Farm Board operations, and upon his invitation, I spent several weeks with him during the summer of 1930 helping to bring the study up to date. I recall how careful he was to see that I had every opportunity to contribute my input and how he later sent me the galley proofs for corrections and suggestions. He followed through on our understanding that I was to be coauthor of the book.

In his preface to *The Cooperative Marketing of Livestock* published in May, 1931, Nourse, as Director of the Institute of Economics, said:

It is, of course, difficult to select any particular time for going to press with the discussion of a movement so dynamic as is cooperative marketing today. However, the broad outlines of Farm Board influence have now been revealed, the actual structure of a national system has been set up, and the issues which will confront the movement in the future are fairly well defined. The present moment therefore seems an opportune time for presenting the results of our study.

The plan of the book was presented in an introduction largely written by Nourse. In this he presented his thinking on the importance of historical research in economics as follows:

It is our belief that both the present and the future have continuity with a living past, and that the present set-up of a comprehensive livestock marketing organization under the Federal Farm Board or any other agency can be adequately appraised or even fully understood only as seen in the perspective of past events which have led up to and conditioned current developments.

He also made clear his approach to problems as an institutional economist:

The natural scientist has found that he must examine the lower forms of life as a preliminary to the study of the more complex. It is equally necessary that any really adequate study of the complicated economic institutions of today be grounded thoroughly in the evolutionary process of which they are merely the latest stage. Cooperation is much too complex an economic and social institution to flourish on mere enthusiasm. It must be grounded on patient and fearless study of its past as well as its present manifestations and disinterested discussion of the issues on their merits.

A large part of the book was devoted to the way in which cooperative livestock marketing had evolved in local and then central markets. It was presented in three parts: Cooperative Shipping, Cooperative Selling, and Current Developments. This organization of the book provided a platform for examining the program of the Federal Farm Board as it related to local, regional, and national procedures in cooperative livestock marketing, and for evaluating the current influence of the Farm Board on cooperative livestock marketing in the light of economic standards and cooperative principles. It was our contention that the efforts of the Farm Board were laudable, but it was feared that "political expediency has overcome cooperative doctrine," that "the Farm Board is intolerant of other brands of cooperative endeavor in livestock marketing," that "there is lack of a properly constituted underlying organization of producers," and that "development of a livestock marketing organization has proceeded along promotional rather than on cooperative lines."

The book was well received as a fair analysis of the Farm Board's efforts in livestock cooperative marketing, and of its approach in other commodity fields.

When the American Institute of Cooperation held its annual meeting at Kansas State College in the summer of 1931, the program featured an analysis of the Farm Board's work with cooperatives in various commodity fields. For this occasion Nourse presented "An Evaluation of the Livestock Marketing Work of the Federal Farm Board," which elaborated on some of the general positions advanced in our book. In this talk he said: "The efforts of the Federal Farm Board in the field of livestock marketing are very much of a piece with their efforts in other fields, notably grain and cotton. They reflect an exaggerated fear of the evil effects of competition between marketing agencies and an exaggerated hope of what can be accomplished through suppression of competitive selling by the several units of the system." He continued: "It is true in the case of livestock, as in other marketing fields, that there have been wastes and inefficiencies due to the small-scale, fragmentary, and unsystematized organization of the cooperatives," and he thought it "important that these be remedied by developing a harmonious system of merchandizing units of such size as is necessary for economical operation." However, he could not "escape the feeling that the Federal Farm Board does not stop here but expects to make its major gains beyond this point through the sheer strength of collective bargaining by an agency large enough to establish itself in a definitely monopolistic position. This is a recrudescence of the 'commodity marketing' philosophy preached a decade ago by Aaron Sapiro." He then made his position clear by saying: "It seems to me that the present position of the Farm Board is that the fault was not with the Sapiro price philosophy but with the inadequate strength of the organizations which attempted to carry it out, that the Agricultural Marketing Act supplies this deficiency of strength and that we shall now proceed to accomplish what was so alluringly promised in 1920."

Nourse was also of the opinion that the Farm Board, in setting up national cooperative marketing associations, was not understandingly and effectively taking advantage of the cooperative principle of business association. While following the letter of the cooperative statutes, it was bringing in more "passive patrons" than "participating members"—who give cooperation its "distinctive character as contrasted with ordinary commercial business." In brief, he feared that the Federal Farm Board was attempting to create big business-type cooperatives by compromising cooperative principles. He concluded by saying:

> Cooperation, even under the most favorable conditions, moves slowly because it is necessary to keep a large number of average individuals in step with the whole procession. We shall have to accept such rate of progress as the unfolding years show us can be made by the persons who themselves make up the movement. At the present time I fear we are

witnessing an effort to make speed by short cuts of the industrial big business type and by compromising cooperative principles. The next few years will create a demand upon all of us for a careful analytical and educational campaign.

Nourse's views were to be borne out by experience in the years ahead.

The Problem of Production Control

As the Federal Farm Board struggled to improve farm prices by price stabilization measures, Nourse raised the question: "Can Agriculture Affect Prices by Controlling Production?" in a paper presented on November 13, 1931, to the Academy of Political Science. He saw three ways in which the Farm Board, with associated agencies, might achieve some progress in this "happy consummation": (1) control through "a comprehensive system of educational and hortatory organizations," (2) control through "cooperative associations of producers widely and strongly organized," and (3) control by "government action, direct or indirect."

He did not anticipate great immediate benefits coming from the first approach. Although he saw more potential advantages from strong cooperative associations in the control of specialty crops, he thought that "control through voluntary cooperatives is hopeless for the great staple crops." He then considered how government might be brought in to help with the problem through effecting compulsory pooling, rationing of credit, or restriction of land use, or by licensing of agricultural production. He indicated that his mind was not closed to the idea that

> our institutions might, in the present state of our knowledge, be caused to develop in this direction with a considerable degree of success. Conceivably the social cost might be less under such a control system as we might be able to perfect over a period of years. On the other hand, I cannot refrain from calling attention to the fact that the attempt to centralize economic planning, thus causing the actions of a large number of people to be determined by a small group, has dangers as well as potentialities of good. When the head planners were right, great benefits would be derived, but the ills that would flow from wrong decisions would be not less extensive or widespread.

He closed his presentation with this philosophical paragraph:

> It is but natural that, in such an extraordinary period of emergency readjustments as have been thrust upon us in the past decade, many minds should dally with the possibilities of omniscient and omnipotent economic direction which would cure or mitigate these ills with great rapidity. I would hazard as my guess, however, that we shall in the end settle down to a continued reliance upon freedom of enterprise in agriculture, coupled with stronger emphasis and increased effort along educational lines in order that these individual decisions may be made as wisely

as possible. I fancy also that in the regulative sphere we shall, in terms of cooperative organization, credit extension, and land institutions make numerous modifications which will have some influence toward preventing the widest kind of aberrations of individual economic effort from the economic center of gravity. Under ordinary economic conditions such an institutional system will produce probably the most satisfactory results, and it is too much to expect that any set of institutions could guard against the difficulties of the crises which come occasionally in human affairs.

Nourse also presented his ideas on "Agriculture in Relation to Economic Prosperity" in a nation-wide radio address over the National Broadcasting Company network on November 28, 1931.[6] In this talk, he maintained that the prosperity of agriculture depended upon the prosperity of business rather than vice-versa. He said: "Until general business creates a situation of full employment, profitable operation, and free exchange of goods, the farmer's market will be cramped and unsatisfactory." This sentence is of interest, in view of its recognition of the importance of "full employment" 15 years before the Employment Act of 1946 was passed.

Further Thoughts on the Surplus Problem

In January, 1932, Nourse gave an important address at the annual meeting of the National Cooperative Council on "Agricultural Surpluses as a Concern of Cooperatives." At this time, the Federal Farm Board was holding large quantities of wheat and cotton impounded to maintain farm prices.

In opening his subject, Nourse referred to two extreme positions which cooperative thought had taken in recent years. "On the one side is the simple belief in the marvelous powers of cooperative marketing to exact a satisfactory price from consumers regardless of conditions of supply. . . . At the other pole is the despairing conviction held by many producers of farm commodities that no voluntary organization of producers is capable of accomplishing any significant improvement in the prices of their products." He saw in between these extreme positions "a third position or range of positions that represents a still-surviving faith in cooperative organization as an institution capable of exercising a more or less effective control of conditions of supply and, through the mitigation of market gluts due to relative surplus of buying demands, exercising a beneficial effect upon prices over a shorter or longer time period."

Nourse did not think the surplus problem was going to fade away, for he saw "overproduction," or "agricultural surplus," as "the outstanding feature of the commercial world in which the cooperatives must function during the next decade or so." He thought that cooperatives would have "to shape action wisely to the actual conditions" confronting them. To his mind, this called for a better understanding of the term "surplus," and he believed it imperative to distinguish local or temporary surpluses from annual surpluses. He considered the first amenable to the use of "efficient distributive marketing," while for annual surpluses he advocated that cooperatives avoid speculative risks in holding supplies for future sale. Maintaining that cooperative associations, in marketing the great staple crops, would be financially better off if they never engaged in "interseasonal holding efforts," he strongly recommended that the "Council and its constituent associations consider the wisdom of examining and reaffirming this anti-speculation principle as applicable to the annual marketing programs. If cooperatives adopt such a non-speculative policy, they will sell their product within the normal crop-moving season either to consumers or processors or to agencies which specialize in the business of speculative holding." Nourse supported his position by calling attention to the fact that while the Agricultural Marketing Act of 1929 provided for a special agency with large public funds to act as a "shock absorber between the farmer and a profoundly disturbed market," its experience was demonstrating that it "may not be possible even for government to carry this burden in periods of extreme economic disturbance."

Nourse did not anticipate a comfortable period ahead for cooperative marketing associations, for he saw them in the midst of a long campaign with "no relief expedition in sight." He believed that "the chronic surplus situation in agriculture will make cooperative marketing associations' lives a bed of thorns and not of roses in the years just ahead."

Laying Sapiroism to Rest

Nourse carried his criticism of the Federal Farm Board's big-business philosophy to a climax in a verbal clash with Carl Williams, the cotton representative on the Federal Farm Board, during the July, 1932, meetings of the Institute of Cooperation at the University of New Hampshire. In his talk on "Cooperative Structure and Farm Board Policy," Nourse attacked the board for what he called its "neo-Sapiroism." Williams, an able debater, met this charge head-on by saying he could not help but believe that Nourse's attitude expressed a "perennial recrudescence of opposition to Sapiroism." In a spirited rejoinder, Nourse said: "If I have a perennial recrudescence of antagonism to Sapiroism, it is certainly not to Mr. Sapiro.[7] When I find that philosophy being expressed, advocated, and promoted in the field of marketing, I have a constitutional reaction against it. I would not call it antagonism. I hope it is based upon a reasonably good intellectual process."

Williams responded in a gracious manner, saying:

> I think that fundamentally there is less difference between us than our remarks would indicate. We are each seeking the truth. . . . Perhaps the main grounds of difference is that Dr. Nourse has had the unexampled opportunity to sit on the outside and observe the conduct of another man or another group who by virtue of law have been forced to act and not to sit on the outside and think about it. Perhaps our viewpoints as a board would be different if we occupied the position which Dr. Nourse so wonderfully occupies. There is a difference between study from an abstract viewpoint of a problem and having to handle and solve the problem in practice in the field.

It is of practical interest that Nourse's views on the weakness of the Sapiro marketing philosophy have been borne out by the course of history, for no cooperative to this day has been able to control the production and marketing of a major crop without the intervention of government. This debate cleared the air. Soon afterwards, the Federal Farm Board acknowledged that it could not function effectively in controlling marketing without being granted powers for the control of production. A widespread acceptance of this position set the stage for stronger agricultural legislation. The Agricultural Adjustment Act of the following year was the result. While Nourse watched the development of this piece of New Deal agricultural legislation with much interest, he never took any direct credit for the form it took. In fact, on many occasions he attributed the Agricultural Adjustment Act to the foundation work of John D. Black, Mordecai Ezekiel, and M. L. Wilson, among others.

The Agricultural Credit Problem

Although the marketing problems of agriculture absorbed much of Nourse's attention during the depression, he followed closely the serious credit problems of agriculture and the attempts of the Federal Intermediate Credit Banks to alleviate them. In a national radio discussion in 1932, he called the farmer's credit problem of equal importance to his marketing problem. In this situation he saw the desirability of bringing up to date Benner's book on the Intermediate Credit System, and Frieda Baird, a former Brookings Graduate School student, was employed for this work. As a result of this foresight, the Brookings Institution was able to publish in May, 1933, a volume under the title, *Ten Years of Federal Intermediate Credits*, by Frieda Baird and Claude L. Benner. This book came out just as the Farm Credit Administration was being set up to consolidate all federal agricultural credit activities as part of the New Deal agricultural program, and it proved very valuable as a base book for its developing operations.[8]

The Initiation of the AAA Study

In the spring of 1933, while the New Deal agricultural legislation was being passed by Congress, Nourse expounded his views on "concurrent history" at a meeting of the Problems and Policy Committee of the Social Science Research Council. He maintained that this method of research provided "the best factual foundation for hypothesizing, generalizing, and formulating principles in the social science field," and he illustrated his position by describing how our book on the cooperative marketing of livestock had been prepared to take into account the concurrent developments of the Federal Farm Board.

Nourse's presentation was of so much interest to Edmund E. Day, then Director of the Laura Spellman Rockefeller Foundation, that he came to see Nourse and Moulton at the Brookings Institution. He stated that he was very favorably impressed by the conception of "concurrent history" as "a novel and promising method of social science research," and he wondered whether consideration was being given by the Brookings Institution to the continuation and expansion of its studies so as to provide a first-hand concurrent history of the Agricultural Adjustment Administration as it was developing. As the Brookings Institution was seriously limited in funds at that time, Nourse immediately responded: "Yes, if we had the money, this would be a logical development." Day answered: "I think our foundation would be prepared to underwrite a study of this size." Nourse then made one stipulation: "We could not make this study on a scientific basis unless we knew that we would have access to the process as it develops in the Department of Agriculture. I will pursue this matter with the Secretary of Agriculture." This was agreeable with Day, and Nourse found Secretary Wallace highly receptive to the proposal. In fact, he said: "We have been doing too much wishful thinking so we welcome it."[9]

Nourse considered the proposed study of such broad scope and importance that it should be conducted "under the broadest intellectual auspices we could get." He therefore asked Joseph S. Davis, Director of the Food Research Institute at Stanford University, and John D. Black, Professor of Agricultural Economics at Harvard University, to join him as codirectors. Nourse felt that the three would make a good combination in that Davis was gifted in statistical analysis, while Black was a specialist in production economics, and Nourse himself was primarily trained as a marketing economist. Both Davis and Black were held in the highest respect in the agricultural economics profession, and both had served as economic advisers to the Federal Farm Board. Black, moreover, was credited with putting the word "adjustment" into the name of the Agricultural Adjustment Administration. Nourse considered Davis more cautious and penetrating, and Black more bold and hopeful than himself and all three were known as men with strongly independent views. Nourse thought that as codirectors, the three "would act as checks and balances on each other."[10]

In announcing the inauguration of "A Concurrent Study of the Operation of the Agricultural Adjustment Act" in June, 1933, the Brookings Institution explained the nature of the undertaking as follows:

> The Agricultural Adjustment Act of 1933 launches the government upon a vast experiment in the social control or direction of a major industry. Ordinarily when such economic ventures have been undertaken, no means have been at hand for conducting a scientific study of the experiment when it was in progress. Reliance has been placed upon casual, unorganized observation and upon opinions expressed by various persons whose observation was fragmentary or who consulted a very incomplete and often distorted record of what actually had been undertaken and of the results which had actually come from the undertaking. In the present instance the Institute of Economics of the Brookings Institution felt that it would be wise if a different course could be followed. We proposed a project for the concurrent study of this experiment on a basis as nearly scientific as it could be made. The essence of this proposal was that we should undertake at once a careful and comprehensive observation of the course of the experiment and provide a record of continuous readings of the various phenomena connected with it.
>
> Before undertaking this project we ascertained from the Secretary of Agriculture that such a plan would be viewed with favor by him and his associates and that they would do whatever they could to facilitate the making of such a study.

To carry on the study, provision was made for a working force divided into two parts. The first consisted of a staff of 11 specialists, together with the necessary clerical, statistical, and stenographic assistants working in Washington. The 25 or so "resident observers" of the second group were located at various strategic points throughout the territory—mostly in agricultural colleges and experiment stations—in which the adjustment efforts were being undertaken. It was the task of the Washington staff to study the development of plans and activities of the Agricultural Adjustment Administration and to guide the collection of field observations by the resident observers.

Before describing how this project was carried on and with what results, let us examine the effect of the New Deal on agricultural cooperatives and Nourse's views on the problems that arose.

The Impact of the New Deal on Cooperative Marketing

The New Deal brought an important new question to American agricultural cooperatives: Would production control provided for under the Agricultural Adjustment Act weaken the position of cooperatives by taking from them one of their assumed principal functions? This question was of much concern at the tenth annual meeting of the American Institute of Cooperation held at North Carolina State College in Raleigh, in July, 1933, just as the New Deal's agricultural program was beginning to take shape.

Nourse gave one of the keynote talks: "The Cooperative Marketing Movement Under the New Deal." Pointing out that "the cooperative marketing movement is a dynamic and growing thing," he asked the question: "What new things have been brought into the life of the cooperative movement by the new agricultural legislation?" He also asked these questions: "Will the move toward larger and more effective cooperative organization in agriculture go forward more rapidly under the new legislation and administrative effort, or will it tend to fall farther into the background? Will the Agricultural Adjustment Act tend to supplement and stimulate or to supersede the movement toward cooperative organization as a dominant force in agriculture?"

In general, he took a hopeful position. He thought the creation of the new Farm Credit Administration held much promise for the better financing of cooperative associations, while "the cooperative movement may be stimulated rather than superseded by the government's participation in active adjustment efforts." He thought the decisions of cooperative leaders in the agricultural field would have "enormous importance both with reference to the success of the present agricultural adjustment undertaking and to the long time welfare of farmers."[11]

A year later, after the new agricultural legislation was in effect, the principal question before the American Institute of Cooperation at the University of Wisconsin in July, 1934, was: "What will be the effect upon cooperative institutions of the so-called 'New Deal' type of legislation administered with 'New Dealer' interpretations?"[12] Two divergent points of view were evident. One was represented by Glen Frank, President of the University of Wisconsin, who said:

> The farmers of the United States must choose between a sweeping regimen-

tation of agriculture from Washington and a sweeping reorganization of the total agricultural forces of the nation in cooperative units, nationally coordinated, that can think with expert leadership, speak with power, and act with authority. They cannot have both. The permanent adoption of regimentation means the prompt death of the cooperation movement. The imposed government of regimentation and the self-government of cooperation cannot exist together. One is the method of dictatorship, the other the method of democracy.[13]

The other viewpoint was expressed by Secretary of Agriculture Henry A. Wallace, who said: "The adjustment act is your baby as much as ours. If there are ways in which our plans can be shaped so as to increase your incentive, we want to know about them."[14]

In view of these conflicting viewpoints, there was much interest in Nourse's address on "The Farm, the Cooperative, and the Government." It was his view that the cooperatives were being strengthened rather than weakened by New Deal agricultural measures, especially by improved credit services and by government efforts to control production. He held that experience had demonstrated that cooperatives by themselves could not stabilize the agricultural industry and that any real degree of "economic planning and direction" would have to be on "comprehensive, not to say coercive patterns" such as those of the Agricultural Adjustment Administration. He believed that it was "in order for the cooperatives to renounce" production control as a goal of their endeavor. But he went on to say:

Does this mean that I am a defeatist or have elected myself to sing the swan song of the cooperative movement? By no means. It does mean, however, that I am suggesting to the leaders of the cooperative movement that they re-examine the question of just what are the important and attainable goals of cooperative endeavor, that they concentrate their energies upon the attainment of these objectives, and that they readjust or even reorganize their associations in such a way as to avoid duplication with the government activity and to make efforts of the cooperatives and those of the government complement each other as smoothly and effectively as possible in the service of the farmer.[15]

Nourse saw several functions that cooperatives could best perform in the marketing process, and he urged them to concentrate their efforts in this direction. He finished his address with these words: "The farmer must be reeducated to the true field of service which cooperative associations are designed to perform and as to how these services are complemented by the functions of government and not superseded by them."

By July, 1935, when the American Institute of Cooperation met at Cornell University, cooperatives had adjusted quite well to the New Deal agricultural programs. The emphasis of the meetings was on ways in which cooperatives could independently strengthen their position. Nourse used this occasion to speak on the subject, "What Cooperatives Should Know About America's Capacity to Produce and Consume." He had come to the conclusion from his work on the recently completed Brookings Institution studies, *America's Capacity to Produce* and *America's Capacity to Consume* (see Chapter VIII), that cooperative organizations were on the right track in their efforts to have goods and services produced and distributed on a cost basis. He concluded his talk by saying:

> I sometimes feel that agricultural cooperatives have of late been growing weary of well-doing and have shown an inclination to depart from truly cooperative ideals and lapse back into methods, policies, and attitudes which, as practiced by industrial and financial interests, have been retarding our national economic progress. It would be a sad ending to the story of cooperative endeavor in the United States if, through the adoption of monopolistic policies, production control, and closed shop types of group organization, it should become a brake upon our capacity to produce and thus upon our capacity to consume rather than a means of enlarging markets and enabling the whole population to produce for themselves a larger measure of material-being.

"Is the AAA Doomed?"

With the collapse of the National Recovery Administration following the Schechter decision in the Supreme Court, there was widespread interest in whether the Agricultural Adjustment Administration could survive. Nourse examined this question, "Is the AAA Doomed?" in the *Farm Journal* of August, 1935. In dealing with this question, Nourse did not concern himself with the merits of the agricultural adjustment program itself. He said: "It may be right or wrong, foolish or wise." What concerned him was the question of whether the program was likely to be continued. He saw three possible exits for the Agricultural Adjustment Administration: "murder, suicide, or death from natural causes." With regard to the second, he said: "Is this champion who took the field to win higher prices for the farmer now so weak of constitution or so crippled by external wounds or internal ailments that he is about to take to his bed and give up the ghost? Or is he tired of life and seeking to find an easy way out?"

Nourse considered this fate as being clearly outside the range of nearby possibilities. He pointed out that "Henry Wallace and M. L. Wilson, Chester Davis and Howard Tolley, and all the rest of the administrative staff of the AAA make up a living and healthy body, vital and courageous to the last degree, as full of hope and confidence in the soundness and potential efficacy of this scheme of agricultural adjustment as they ever were, and with their strength increased and toughened by the hard knocks and experience that they have had in the past two years." Moreover, Nourse could find little evidence that farmers or Congress or even consumers were ready to give up the experiment.

He therefore anticipated that the Adjustment Act would be amended and strengthened to meet possible constitutional objections, and he saw little possibility that the "Adjustment Act as a whole will fall." It seemed to him that the trend of the Supreme Court's decisions since the inauguration of the New Deal had shown the highest type of judicial tolerance. "The Court has sought to give to the Constitution a sufficient flexibility so that legislation in economic affairs may meet the changing needs of growing economic life, while at the same time protecting the vital fundamental principles on which our government is founded."

Soon after this talk was made, the Supreme Court found the AAA act unconstitutional insofar as the processing tax was concerned—but this did not preclude the revamping of the act to achieve its aims through different procedures. Basically, Nourse was right that the vitality of the program ensured its continuance under the conditions of the time.[16]

The Evolution of Agricultural Planning

The emphasis on economic planning by the New Deal made agricultural planning a subject of great national importance. For some time, Nourse had been crystalizing his ideas on this subject, so he welcomed an opportunity to express them at a meeting of the American Academy of Political Science in November, 1935. It was his general view that agricultural planning was not something entirely new in the United States. He traced its origins back to the Homestead Act of 1862 and the establishment of the land grant colleges for educational guidance. He recognized that the acute problems of agriculture in the 1920s had intensified the government's interest in helping farmers, and he thought that a constructive planning development was the inauguration of the "Outlook Reports" by the U.S. Department of Agriculture to help farmers better make farm plans. He also thought it significant that during this period, cooperative organizations introduced a certain "planfulness" by centralizing marketing operations. He held that the establishment of the Federal Farm Board under the Agricultural Marketing Act of 1929 represented a great step forward in planning, in that it "sought to coordinate distributive operations under nation-wide cooperative marketing organizations. Through its ancillary devices of credit extension and carry-over manipulation by stabilization corporations, it went considerably farther toward implementing planning than had any of the previous undertakings of government." In turn, the experience of the Farm Board opened the way for the Agricultural Adjustment Act of 1933, which "launched the government on a program of implemented planning for agriculture [with] specific production programs for most of the major agricultural products." Nourse thought the present development of planning was a result of the emergency conditions which had confronted agriculture since World War I, and he doubted whether there would be as much need for planning with the return of more normal conditions.

The Agricultural Adjustment Concept

Nourse extended his ideas on planning at the annual meeting of the American Farm Economic Association in December, 1935. Speaking on the subject, "The Fundamental Significance of the Agricultural Adjustment Concept," he said: "It was the Agricultural Adjustment Act of May 12, 1933, which first accepted as public policy the use of government authority to aid and aggressively persuade farmers to adjust their scale of production at a point designed to peg a price level legislatively determined as being a suitable objective."

After placing the Adjustment Act in "historic perspective," Nourse examined some changes "which these adjustment institutions introduce into our handling of the agricultural part of our economic machine." He said:

> Income adjustment is merely the means through which there is brought about an effective redirection of the productive process. The economic significance of this step is that it carries us from the regime of rationalized individual farm organization and management, as we have known them, to one of economic planning for the agricultural industry. The old school of advisory farm organization was negative and comparative in its character. . . . Agricultural adjustment on the other hand launched a frontal attack on the price basis. Instead of being defensive and comparative, it is offensive and categorical. It sets up a specific price objective and undertakes to attain it by production control.

Here Nourse made a very interesting point: that agricultural prosperity depends upon industrial prosperity. Believing that "agricultural adjustment in the economic planning sense cannot, no matter how powerful its control of the process of production, assure such a categorical objective as pre-war income parity in the absence of commensurate control of industry under some high command which fully accepts the validity of the income objective set up for agriculture," he concluded that "accomplishment of the stated objectives of economic planning for agriculture could be assured only in the setting up of a general planned economy." He then said:

> Those responsible for carrying out the AAA experiment have not been committed to any such sweeping general economic adjustment philosophy. The actual course of the experiment has been determined by an administrative group most of whom were practical men with their feet on the ground, by a professionally trained staff well versed in the technical requirements and limitations of the agricultural industry. . . . They have tended increasingly to direct their activities toward goals more practically attainable and more economically tenable. Greater and greater emphasis has been placed upon adjustment of the process of agricultural production toward the attainment of standards of "good farming." . . . If this evolution of thought and action be continued, it would bring us back to a position superficially similar to the scheme of economic organization which obtained under the older regime of educational guidance.

Nourse was aware that any agency empowered to control production in a democratic society would be subject to political pressures. He called attention to the fact that the experience of the United States and of all democratic countries indicated that consideration of what the government would do was "essentially academic," in that "actual decisions of a government agency endowed with power to allot large pecuniary grants will be heavily tinged by political influence." Nourse concluded his talk by saying:

> The fundamental significance of the adjustment concept embodied in the Agricultural Adjustment Act is that it shifts the theater of decision from the small individual enterprise, where it resided under systems of *laissez faire* and "assisted *laissez faire*" over to a central planning agency. . . . This scheme of agricultural direction or adjustment definitely repudiates the idea that 6,500,000 farm enterprisers can within their intellectual and institutional limitations act as "economic men" whose 6,500,000 separate decisions will add up to an economically sound answer to the nation's problem of agricultural production. It asserts that the only sound answer to a problem of national policy must be made through a national agency which, however, seeks to keep as much of intimately detailed knowledge and flexibilty in field tactics as is compatible with a unified high command. Whether such an economic balance between centrifugal and centripetal forces can be maintained by a system which of necessity must operate in a political milieu, can be determined only in the light of longer operative experience. Both the short experience under the Agricultural Adjustment Act and the general evidence of analogous situations engender some misgivings.

It is quite clear from these expressions that Nourse was skeptical on how far planning could be carried by the Agricultural Adjustment Administration.

Marketing Agreements Under the AAA

During the years from 1933 to 1936, work on the concurrent study of the Agricultural Adjustment Administration consumed a great amount of

Nourse's time and energy. In 1934, four publications in pamphlet form were issued to furnish an objective account of the AAA program during its initial year of operation. In May, 1935, results of the study began to appear in six books designed to evaluate the AAA program as it related to wheat, tobacco, dairy products, livestock, and cotton, and to marketing agreements. Three were the works of the codirectors: Davis on *Wheat and the AAA*, Black on *The Dairy Industry and the AAA*, and Nourse on *Marketing Agreements under the AAA*. The six books provided the framework for a summary volume, *Three Years of the Agricultural Adjustment Administration*, published in February, 1937, under the coauthorship of Nourse, Davis, and Black.

Here we will examine briefly the marketing agreements book which, in the words of Nourse, differed from the other AAA studies in that "the bounds of the discussion are not drawn along commodity lines but according to the method of 'adjustment' used, namely marketing agreements, licenses, and orders." Nourse was particularly interested because this phase of the agricultural adjustment program tied back "into a long history of growth in agricultural marketing institutions and cooperative endeavor." In fact, he noted that the marketing agreements, licenses, and orders were "of such distinctive character and potential importance they might almost have constituted a separate piece of legislation."

The first chapter of the book explained how the marketing agreement idea evolved from the McNary-Haugen bills and was then picked up in the Domestic Allotment bills that became part of the AAA. This chapter reflected Nourse's deep interest in the beginnings and development of an idea. The main body of the book studied operative experience under the marketing agreement program as a basis for analyzing "the possibilities of these devices as major procedures for the promotion of farm prosperity and agricultural stabilization."

The final two chapters of the book examined the basic questions involved in the "market adjustment effort of the AAA." Of particular interest was Nourse's chapter "Price Objectives and Strategy," in which he pointed out that "the parties to all such agreements and licenses are operating under the theory of monopoly price, applied to the supply within their administration." He described the situation brought about by the marketing agreement process as "controlled marketing" or as "collective price making." He held that "its general price theory is built upon the more aggressive elements of the cooperative marketing movement as that institution had developed over a considerable period of time." He pointed out that "as large federated or centralized cooperatives grew up, they tended to place their emphasis strongly on the desirability of a single coordinated control of the distribution of a given commodity so that the total supply of the whole producer group could be administered or manipulated in the market in such a way as to secure the maximum return which seemed feasible in view of the conditions of demand." The difficulties involved in "welding all individual producers into an integrated group" caused cooperatives to look for some practicable device for bringing about "compulsory cooperation," an awkward conception which implied "controlled marketing on a comprehensive basis."

The inclusion of the licensing provisions of the Agricultural Adjustment Act was "hailed as at last implementing such an undertaking on the part of producers." This section of the act was interpreted to mean that "when a substantial majority of the producers of a given commodity were agreed on a scheme of managed distribution . . . the nonadhering minority should by license be constrained to abide by and participate in this collective plan."

Nourse believed that the marketing agreement and licensing sections of the act would have a "considerable supporting value" in expanding and accelerating "the use of grading, inspection, and other similar measures for the improvement of handlers' practices." He also saw that if the marketing agreement provisions of the Adjustment Act were given permanent form, this "might result in significant innovations in market structure and functioning." He therefore thought that for certain commodities, the marketing agreements and licenses might serve as "sweeping agencies of 'market reform' or market reorganization."

In his summary chapter, "Results and Future Usefulness of Market Adjustment Devices," Nourse admitted that any attempt to appraise results so far attained under the marketing agreement and licensing provisions of the Agricultural Marketing Act was "beset with extreme difficulties." He therefore proposed to couch his views in "terms of qualitative analysis rather than statistical computation." He expressed as his purpose "to shed light on the question whether marketing agreements and licenses have introduced into our market institutions a new mechanism or agency of distinctive usefulness to farmers either temporarily or permanently."

It was Nourse's view that experience with the dairy marketing agreements had shown their potential usefulness, and that it was highly desirable that the legal authorization be continued so that efforts could be continued to improve methods of purveying fluid milk to metropolitan markets. Nourse likewise thought that experience indicated the desirability of continuation of the program for fruits, vegetables, and general crops. He made the interesting point that "the issue which is thus raised is one of political science rather than of economics, namely: Shall we permit a government agency to step in as the arbiter of economic fortunes and put the economic activities of the individual under the constraint of group organization on the grounds that the group as a whole will benefit from this governmental control of private action even though the relative or absolute position of certain individuals is prejudiced?"

Nourse saw clearly the dangers of complete control if effected by the marketing agreement procedure. It could easily result in overstimulation of prices and lead to overproduction, unless it could be wisely administered through government agencies. He made the pertinent statement: "Whether successive secretaries of agriculture would have the technical advice necessary to make wise decisions and the political fortitude to put them into effect, is a question which cannot be answered in advance, but on it the wisdom and practicability of the whole proposal must ultimately rest."

Nourse thus thought that the ultimate success of the market agreement program would necessarily depend upon the soundness of the policies followed by the Department of Agriculture. He considered the marketing agreement "a device of considerable economic promise but by no means as yet brought to a state of perfection." He believed that many years of "patient experimentation and refinement would be required to develop its full potentialities and at no time would its operations be better than the quality of the men who man it."

In this book Nourse displayed his mastery of the complex agricultural marketing process, and it immediately had a marked influence on the market agreement and licensing procedures subsequently used by the Department of Agriculture. In reviewing the book for the *Journal of Farm Economics* (1936), Dr. Henry E. Erdman of the University of California called it "a bit of concurrent history of an attempt at market reform." He found the book written "in a spirit of friendliness toward the marketing agreements" and then said "the author apparently made up his mind that they have possibilities for good and wrote accordingly. He could, of course, have magnified the inherent dangers which would arise from abuse of the plan, and, on the other hand, he could have magnified the potentialities for good on the assumption that operation would be ideal. He chose the middle course." There was much truth in Erdman's comment, for Nourse was searching for a constructive solution to an important marketing problem, and he saw this as a promising development. Nourse was himself greatly pleased with the book, for it afforded an opportunity to analyze an innovative method for meeting serious marketing problems through cooperative organizations joined by the power of the federal government. This represented a new departure in cooperative and governmental theory, and he was intrigued by its possibilities.[17]

Three Years of the Agricultural Adjustment Administration

After three years of concurrent study, the three codirectors presented their report on the Agricultural Adjustment Administration up to January 6, 1936, when its program was sharply modified by the adverse decision of the Supreme Court on the constitutionality of the processing tax.

In his director's preface, Nourse pointed out that the book should not be looked upon as a "post-mortem document since this production control experiment is only one phase in the life history of a growing national agricultural policy." He pointed out that "such value as the study may prove to have will derive in the main from its being based on an extensive 'set of readings and recordings' of the phenomena as they took place, with their meaning analyzed and findings published promptly enough so that the lessons of this experience might be made useful in the next stage of our agrarian development." He also said:

> A distinctive character of our method has been that we were seeking to proceed inductively from current recordings of a great number of observations on the phenomena of the adjustment experiment to such generalized conclusions as they might properly yield. We have sought to approach this task with receptive minds but as objectively as possible. . . . Our conclusions take the form of interpretations of the actual play of economic forces under the new institutional situations. . . . *A social agency, like a mechanical device, may be safe and useful in one man's hands or in certain circumstances and an engine of destruction as used by another or under other circumstances.* [Emphasis added.]

This general study called for fine coordinating capacity and tact on the part of Nourse. All three codirectors were authorities in their fields, men of strong wills, and individuals of independent judgment, and it was not possible for them to entirely subordinate their views into one common position. Nourse made this clear in his preface: "It was our hope that the joint authors of this volume would be able to agree on the major points of interpretation and appraisal. In the main, it has been found possible to arrive, after discussion, at a conclusion and a form of statement which was acceptable to all three collaborators." Where agreement was not attainable, divergent views were expressed frankly in footnote dissents. With reference to the concluding chapter, Nourse said: "[It] can hardly be regarded as a composite statement. The main part was written by me; Dr. Davis presents a short supplementary statement; and Dr. Black a somewhat more extended individual evaluation and statement of the general philosophy on which it is based."

In view of Nourse's primary authorship of the concluding chapter entitled "AAA Philosophy in the Light of Experience," its conclusions are of particular interest to us in this biography. This chapter attempted to synthesize the viewpoints of the authors on two questions: "whether the devices employed under the AAA were capable of attaining the objectives sought, and whether the attainment of these objectives would promote the welfare of agriculture and the national economic life." The reader was warned not to expect a simple yes or no answer as to whether the Agricultural Adjustment Administration was "good" or "bad," in that "social phenomena in a dynamic world seldom admit of this kind of neat characterization."

The authors saw much to commend in the "adjustment idea." It was their view that "while it is an obvious fact that economic forces are constantly tending to work out their own equilibrium, we believe that human knowledge has progressed to a point where social engineering can bring about equilibria more promptly, at less cost, and of a more desirable character." They thought it "not merely improbable but, for technological reasons, even impossible that other parts of our economic system can be brought to the thoroughgoing conditions of individual competition which would make automatic adjustment between them and agriculture capable of realization." Following this line of thinking, they said: "We concur, therefore, in the basic claim of the AAA that to put agriculture in a wholesome place in the national economy, we need to experiment with and, so far as possible, perfect new institutions for integrating group action on a wider scale—co-extensive with an entire commodity, such as corn or cotton, or even seeking to co-ordinate the nation's agriculture as a whole." Therefore, "on its merely conceptual plane," the authors accepted "the basic adjustment doctrine." They held it "desirable in the broad economic sense that agriculture be adjusted to a position of economic balance or equilibrium of return as compared with other branches of our national economic system." They accepted "the view that organized action of government is in our modern technical and institutional situation necessary to effect such adjustment on a socially satisfactory plane."

With this proviso, attention was directed to the significant question: "Have the measures which the AAA employed in fact promoted better balance and national economic progress?" On this question, the authors found that the AAA production control program had been reasonably effective during its initial years of application, but they emphasized that this was a time of "extreme maladjustment." They did not believe that "the gains from continuing the reduction contract procedure would be proportionate to their burdensomeness and the chances of error in more normal times." The authors therefore advocated "reserving these extreme readjustment measures for emergency situations." They emphasized this point by saying: "We would not advocate calling out the fire department to sprinkle the lawn." They also gave general endorsement to the use of marketing agreements and related procedures—but cautioned against their abuse. After examining the benefits brought by the AAA in farm relief and subsidies, the authors emphasized that what was required in an emergency could be hurtful if applied when conditions were more normal. The authors found that the AAA "had shown a growing inability to limit itself in its payment of benefits to the classes of cases in which we have argued that there is economic justification" (p. 471). They were concerned that in practice, the program had placed "minor emphasis on true agricultural adjustment and major emphasis on disbursing a very large amount of money to the maximum number of farmers." Thus the payments had "taken on the character of a political hand-out," and tended to "create vested interests" which would stand in the way of "sound economic development of the industry in the future" (p. 473). They felt that relief agencies should handle the problem of chronic rural poverty, and that for the AAA to attempt to deal with the problem would threaten the program's breakdown.

The authors looked with favor on the AAA's promotion of "economic democracy," which they saw as an "exemplification of practical 'self-government in industry,'" and they held that "in the main, results appear to have justified this phase of AAA philosophy." Looking to the future, the authors concluded that "some such agency [as the AAA] for coordinating action in this loosely organized industry is needed from this time forward."

In comprehensively reviewing the volume for the *Journal of Farm Economics* (1937), Dr. O. B. Jesness of the University of Minnesota said: "Here is the cap-sheaf to the series of books and preliminary reports published by the Brookings Institution as results of its studies of the agricultural adjustment program started soon after its inception in 1933.... The importance of the subject matter and the standing of its authors assure it of the wide reading which it well deserves." After carefully examining the contents of the volume, Jesness concluded:

> The authors and the Brookings Institution are to be commended for having made this study concurrently with the development of the adjustment program and for having brought together so satisfactorily the results in this

final volume. It should be read not only by agricultural economists but by citizens generally; such reading should serve to broaden the understanding of this phase of public policy and lead to the development of improved policy for the future.

It is of interest that the book—long out of print—was reprinted in 1971 as a "seminal work." In reviewing this volume for *Agricultural History* (January, 1974), Lowell K. Dyson said: "No serious historian of the period can afford to neglect this book."

Interlude in Europe

During 1936 and again in 1937, Nourse made trips to Europe. One was as a delegate to the International Institute of Agriculture at Rome, and the other was as a representative to a World Nutrition Conference in Geneva. These were pleasant interludes in Nourse's heavy schedule of work, and they gave him an opportunity to broaden his knowledge of European economic, social, and cultural conditions. On his 1936 trip, he was able to spend a few days at Cambridge University with his old friend, Dr. C. R. Fay, who took him to an evening seminar conducted by J. M. Keynes. In view of his experience, he was somewhat amused by the cocksure views that Keynes expressed on American agricultural problems, which to Nourse were not quite that simple.[18]

Public Adviser to Agricultural Cooperatives

With the completion of the AAA study, Nourse took the continuation of the Agricultural Adjustment Administration for granted, with such modifications as might be made through legislation or administration. He had never lost his interest in the long-run benefit of agricultural cooperative organizations to agriculture, and he had taken an active interest in their development under the New Deal agricultural program. In 1937, he resumed his active role as public adviser to cooperative associations on how they might best operate under present and anticipated governmental programs. Speaking at the American Institute of Cooperation meetings at Iowa State College in July, 1937, on the subject, "Post-War Trends in Farmer Cooperation—and Where They Are Leading Us," he expressed concern on the restrictive policies promulgated by the AAA to keep prices up through measures designed to effect control of supplies. He concluded that cooperatives were placing an exaggerated emphasis on collective bargaining power made effective by government.

He did not hold that all of the emphasis given to supply restriction by the commodity marketing movement, the Federal Farm Board, or the AAA was necessarily bad, for "farmers had to protect their interests." He recognized that "for the kind of economic society compatible with the present state of our technical knowledge we must have those kinds of organization which keep economic processes under such control as to give orderly production and marketing." He thought the restrictive policies of the AAA were called for as emergency measures, but he went on to say: "We do not want to become so concerned about controls that we cut down the power of the economic machine. We need to have brakes as well as an engine, but we want the brakes to operate as a safety device —not as a constant drag on the power plant."

Nourse saw the marketing agreement provisions of the AAA providing an opportunity for cooperatives to better adjust supply to demand, and, influenced by his current price studies, he thought that much could be done through differential pricing, so that prices would better serve the needs of consumers and increase the amount of total consumption. Believing that too much emphasis was being placed on supply restriction as a means of price raising, he hoped that cooperatives would not limit themselves to this "field of negative action," but would "explore the newer and more constructive devices of interpreting the market and expanding their field of activity in the service of the consumer."

In this talk, Nourse raised the question: "Has there been a tendency for our American cooperatives to forget the ideals and purposes of the founding fathers and to follow a line of least resistance toward emulation of the methods of speculative, profit-maximizing corporate capitalism which they originally aspired to supersede?" He went on to say: "To raise this question is not to suggest that the whole trend from commodity marketing to the Farm Board and from the Farm Board to the Agricultural Adjustment Administration was bad. I am no economic mugwump, no commercial pacifist. I fully agree that the agricultural business group cannot subsist on noble sentiments.... It must at times eat its spinach and wade in...."

"Agriculture," 1940

By 1940, Nourse had become deeply involved in the general problems of the economy, particularly the importance of industrial price policies as a controlling factor in the economic health of the nation. (See Chapter VIII.) Absorption in this area of work had forced him to give less attention to the problems of agriculture, which had reached something of a plateau, as far as public policy was concerned. Moreover, the war in

Europe promised to loosen restrictions on production, although the future was highly uncertain. It appeared to be a good time to determine how far we had come in agriculture and where we were going.

In this circumstance, Nourse welcomed an opportunity to evaluate the present condition of agriculture as part of a general Brookings Institution study published under the title, *Government and Economic Life: Development and Current Issues of American Public Policy* (1940). Nourse's 83-page chapter on "Agriculture" was a terse but full analysis of how public policies relating to agriculture had expanded from colonial days to the present. In this analysis, Nourse summarized and put into perspective what he had learned from his intensive study of agricultural development since he began work in this field at the University of Chicago in 1915. Nourse dealt with his subject both as economic historian and agricultural economist, and his essay was recognized as a masterpiece of presentation. At the request of Orris Wells, then Chief of the Bureau of Agricultural Economics, the chapter was reprinted as a separate monograph so that it could reach a wide audience of agricultural workers and graduate students in agricultural economics.

Nourse presented his views under six main headings: I. Pre-War Governmental Relations to Agriculture; II. Relations of Government to Agriculture During the World War; III. The Transition Years, 1920-1928; IV. The Federal Farm Board; V. Agriculture and Government Since 1933; and VI. Emerging Issues. It is not possible to illustrate here the wide spectrum of Nourse's positions on the many subjects covered by his analysis. However, the following quotations will convey the nature of his presentation and reflect his general attitude. With regard to the Agricultural Marketing Act of 1929, he said:

> This act was novel in moving government from the informational and analytical role in relation to individual enterprise in farming to one of vigorous propaganda as to specific courses of action, implemented, to a degree at least, by the power of [government] to grant financial assistance to or withhold it from national organizations through which individual producers made contact with the market. Novel too was the use of government credit in support of particular commodities [p. 904].

With regard to the Agricultural Adjustment Act of 1933, he said:

> This measure by no means turned its back on the educational approach traditional in government's relation to agriculture. But it adopted many of the proposals of more positive action which had been advanced by agriculturists and others during recent years. Notably it undertook to implement the mandate given by Congress to the Federal Farm Board to promote "orderly production" which, in the Board's latter days, had turned toward investigation of the possibilities of land use programs or other types of production control. The Adjustment Act also picked up many of the pro-

posals contained in the equalization fee and domestic allotment plans, which had been rejected in 1929 in favor of the Farm Board experiment [p. 913].

Nourse recognized that the Agricultural Adjustment Act had changed the character of government policy in agriculture "from the role of advisory guidance to one of over-all planning and implemented activity designed to determine both the direction and the magnitude of agricultural enterprise" (p. 915).

Under the heading, "Emerging Issues," Nourse stressed the fact that "agriculture is patently an area of special treatment by the state and federal government, particularly the latter." He partially accounted for this by the persistence of agricultural fundamentalism, a philosophy which assigns agriculture a "paramount importance" in national well-being. He also thought the "economic and technical character of the agricultural industry itself" exerted a continuing and powerful influence on the form of measures for its special treatment. This had taken form in educational and research aid to cooperatives and in various provisions of the Agricultural Adjustment Act.

Nourse was of the opinion that "the scheme of industry-wide organization of agriculture under the leadership of governmental 'action agencies' raised an important problem." He said: "If it means not merely the largest potentiality of efficiency for collective planning but also maximum power for collective bargaining or group pressure in agriculture, we shall have a scheme of organization which, in the absence of a philosophy of moderation, might conceivably be used to the end of exploiting other industries or departments of the national economy" (p. 942).

He was also concerned by the special interest political organizations that had grown up to take advantage of government intrusion in the agricultural industry. He questioned "whether any philosophy of general economic welfare can long prevail in the struggle against narrow group interest equipped with the weapons of political power" (p. 943).

Nourse maintained that "the agricultural problem does not exist in isolation but as part of the functioning of the national economy. There is not even a segment of the population which can be delimited as that to which agricultural policy is limited. Both the numbers to be dealt with and the methods to be followed under the 'farm security' program are intricately intertwined with those of the 'social security' program being experimented with in the industrial and commercial field." He held that it must be the concern of government to deal with all industry, "so as to develop the highest standards of living through the fullest utilization of our total labor force with our total natural resources and accumulated capital."

These expressions show the breadth of Nourse's thinking at this time on the agricultural problem and his keen sense of equity. They also throw light on his attitude toward national planning—which was then more highly developed in agriculture than in any other segment of the economy. By 1940, Nourse had fully established his position as one of the nation's leading agricultural economists. Now let us examine in Chapter VIII how he built a second career as a general economist during these years from 1928 to 1940.

Chapter VIII

RETURN TO GENERAL ECONOMICS
(1928-1940)

Nourse enjoyed his new post as Director of the Institute of Economics in the newly formed Brookings Institution. It widened his functions and brought him into more direct touch with broader policy questions. He now had to devote more time to directing, planning, and supervising general economic studies. The new position also enabled him to continue with his studies in agricultural economics, while it afforded him an opportunity to broaden his own work in the more general field of economics. This was not a new area of interest, since he had been trained as a general economist and he had always considered himself an economist with a special concern for the problems of agriculture.[1]

It should also be observed that Nourse's close association with Moulton in the development of the Institute of Economics had greatly stimulated his interest in general economic problems. As a member of the Institute's guiding staff council, he was brought into close association with all studies relating to labor problems, international trade, transportation, and monetary policies. Moreover, in the informal atmosphere of the Institute, all members of the staff, regardless of their special capacities, participated in free and easy discussion of the economic problems of the day, especially in the seminars devoted to studies in progress. Although the staff looked upon Nourse as primarily an agricultural economist, he was highly respected for his analytical abilities on all economic subjects. For example, Isadore Lubin, who worked closely with Nourse from the Institute's beginning into the 1930s, recalls that he never thought of him as exclusively an agricultural economist. His impression of Nourse during this formative period of the Institute is worth quoting:

> Dr. Nourse gave me my first real contact with a professional friend from the Middle West. I was much impressed by him for he was so fresh in the best sense of the word. He was interested in all kinds of problems, and I

didn't look upon him as an agricultural economist, because he had such a wide interest in the whole field of economics and other matters. He was extroverted, but it wasn't a good idea to try to fool him. He was a man who would take on Harold Moulton, and he didn't yield. I felt that he had an important indirect effect on how policies were made in the Institute by his manner and his ability to work well with Moulton.[2]

To Joseph J. Spengler, who worked at the Institute in 1928 and 1929, Nourse was not his idea of an agricultural economist. He wrote me as follows:

I was impressed when I saw Dr. Nourse sculpturing for he was the first economist so gifted to my knowledge. I was struck also by how nicely dressed he was, bow-tie and all, for that did not associate with cooperative marketing and agriculture in my then knowledge. He was a quiet, self-contained, judicious man who did not rattle easily and who carried conviction. I feel that he was responsible in part for the Institute's emphasis upon solid empirical work.[3]

Thus, when Nourse took over as Director of the Institute of Economics, he knew the staff intimately and the work being performed by each member. Moreover, the working procedures of the Institute were well established. After a project for study was accepted by the director and Council, an advisory committee was set up to work with the author or authors. This committee generally consisted of the director and one or more staff members who had a special interest or competence in the investigation. The arrangement was quite informal, the idea being that this would develop closer cooperation with the staff and lead to more effective work. Each author was granted a high degree of freedom and independence, as long as professional standards were maintained. This general procedure was continued when the Institute of Economics was incorporated into the Brookings Institution.

Early Days of the Brookings Institution

The establishment of the Brookings Institution in 1928 immediately solidified the work of the Institute of Economics and the Institute for Government Research, for they became operating divisions of the new Institution. The work of the Brookings Graduate School was continued as the training division, but it ceased granting degrees after those already enrolled were graduated in 1930.[4]

The Brookings Institution had started out with great expectations. Moulton envisaged it as a "comprehensive social science center promoting organized research and training in all the humanistic sciences; playing a constructive and practical role in the solution of economic, social, and political problems; serving as a center for visiting scholars; and fostering policy research in the country at large."⁵ However, this grand conception was nipped in the bud by the Great Depression, which made difficult even the continuation of the work heretofore carried on.

When the Brookings Institution began its operations, the work of the three divisions was continued in their old quarters until they could be housed in an impressive "eight-story limestone edifice" dedicated on May 15, 1931. This beautiful building, made possible by a generous gift from Mrs. Brookings and later demolished in the renovation of historic Lafayette Square, was well-designed to facilitate the Institution's work.

> Fronting on the square were ample offices for the research and administrative staffs, a well-equipped library, conference rooms, and publication office. Behind it, connected by an enclosed arcade with a formal court, were the club-like quarters of the residence building. In the first-floor lounge, . . . scholars, fellows, and guests mingled socially or gathered for lectures and informal talk. In the dining-room above, theorists daily tested their opinions against the experience of government officials. The private Round Table Room, where off-the-record discussions were held with distinguished guests, was to become a Washington meeting place as celebrated as Bernard Baruch's bench in the park outside. . . . On the upper floors were dormitory rooms for fellows and visiting scholars, a small gymnasium, and the best squash court in Washington, where Dr. Moulton regularly defended his unofficial institutional championship.⁶

With these commodious and prestigious quarters, the Brookings Institution soon became prominent in Washington as a non-governmental center for economists, political scientists, and other workers in the social sciences.

When the Brookings Institution moved into its new quarters, the country was well into the Great Depression, and the problem of maintaining its existing work was already giving great concern to Moulton and his close associates. Primary attention had to be paid to the maintenance of the ongoing program, and plans for expansion had to be deferred. A number of unfortunate circumstances made the problem of financing the work of the Institution critical at that time. In 1931, the 10-year grant of the Carnegie Institution for the Institute of Economics expired, and in the same year, a 7-year grant by the Laura Spellman Rockefeller Foundation to support research in government administration also ran out. Moreover, George Eastman's support of the training program, which had amounted to $50,000 annually since 1925, was terminated with his death in 1932.

Efforts were made to attract endowment funds without success, and the Institution was forced to practice stringent economy wherever possible and to find short-time studies that would finance themselves. One source of revenue that helped sustain the Institution during this difficult period was a number of studies for state governments made by the Institute for Government Research. Through his own professional competence in the field of transportation, Moulton also was able to attract funds for a major study of transportation policy.[7]

At this time when the future of the Institution was in jeopardy, help was to come from a newly formed foundation established "for the benefit and welfare of mankind." In 1929, Maurice Falk, who had made a fortune in industry and business, had established the Maurice and Laura Falk Foundation, with a trust fund of $10 million to be expended, principal and income, within 35 years, but up to 1932, no disbursement of funds had been made. Since Nourse played a major role in attracting substantial assistance from the Falk Foundation for the Brookings Institution, it is important to explain how these funds were obtained.

When the Falk Foundation was established, one of its immediate problems was to determine how it might use its resources most effectively. After many months of consideration, the Board of Trustees agreed in July, 1931, "to enter, tentatively, the field of economics, and to grant to some well-established institution the means of studying a basic problem." The general decision to work first on economic problems was greatly influenced by the depressed economic condition of the country, for it was hoped that economic analysis would reveal how the economic system might regain its health. To decide where to place its money, the Falk Foundation paid a fee of $3,000 to the Social Science Research Council to obtain suggestions "for a program of research important to the general economic well-being during the next decade." This survey brought the work of the Brookings Institution to the favorable attention of the trustees of the Falk Foundation for two main reasons: (1) its record of practical work on major economic problems, and (2) its administration by Dr. Harold G. Moulton, a man highly respected by the business community.

Moulton and Nourse were very hopeful that they could obtain a substantial grant from the Falk Foundation to maintain and strengthen the Brookings program. To accomplish this end, Nourse, with the collaboration of Moulton, proceeded to develop plans for a comprehensive project on the distribution of wealth and income in relation to economic progress. They then presented their proposed study to the trustees of the Falk Foundation in Pittsburgh, who agreed on January 8, 1932, to finance its conduct and completion. It was understood that the results of the study would be presented in four related volumes prepared by the Brookings staff under the general direction of Nourse, "who was largely responsible for the broad outline of the entire study." This new source of funds not only did much to temporarily solve the Institution's serious financial problem, but it paved the way for needed support on a wide variety of economic studies which eventually totalled more than $1,500,000.[8]

The Wealth and Income Study

During the next three years, Nourse was to give a considerable amount of his attention to the study he and Moulton had envisaged under the general title, "Wealth and Income in Relation to Economic Progress." The general objective was to help bring about "the greatest acceleration of the nation's economic progress," and the fundamental question to be considered was "whether the existing method of distributing the national income tends to evoke from our productive resources the greatest flow of goods and services of which they are capable." In carrying out the work on this project, the enquiry was divided into four "segments of manageable size and sufficient internal unity of subject matter and method," and each was to result in a publication. The titles for the four volumes to be prepared concurrently were to be: *America's Capacity to Produce, America's Capacity to Consume, The Formation of Capital,* and *Income and Economic Progress.* While each volume was to have a severely limited objective, it was understood that they would dovetail in relation to the larger study of which they were a part. *America's Capacity to Produce* was to consider our system of production realistically as a technological process. *America's Capacity to Consume* was to show how the national product was divided among the various groups in society. *The Formation of Capital* was to deal with the pecuniary aspects of the problem, such as the relation of consumptive expenditures to capital formation. The final volume, *Income and Economic Progress,* was to bring together the various segments of the investigation for "interpretation, diagnosis, and possible prescription." The project was a grand conception—imaginative and practical—and it was geared to the needs of the nation.

Nourse immediately undertook the preparation of *America's Capacity to Produce,* while getting work under way on *America's Capacity to Consume.* This involved assembling staff largely from within the Institute to work on specific assignments, supplemented by a few technical specialists. It was a team job that brought all of the resources of the Institute of Economics into play, and Nourse found himself something like a conductor of an orchestra. After this work was started, the advent of the New Deal made work on the project more urgent and opened up a need for economic analyses of various New Deal programs. I have already described how the opportunity arose for the Institute to make a comprehensive study of the Agricultural Adjustment Administration in May,

1933, and it was not long before a somewhat similar study of the National Recovery Administration was launched with the support of Rockefeller funds. As Nourse later remarked: "We were embarrassed by an abundance of riches." In view of his primary responsibility for the conduct of the AAA study, he had to give much of his time to planning and selecting personnel for this project. Fortunately, he could defer work on the volumes that would result from the AAA study until he completed his work on the "capacity to produce" volume. In view of the heavy stress caused by the convergence of the work on these studies, Moulton relieved Nourse of responsibility for directing the work on the "capacity to consume" volume, although Nourse contributed considerably to its completion.[9] Moulton assumed responsibility for the volume on the formation of capital, as this subject was in his special field. Thus Nourse was called on for little work on this volume other than to help fit it into the framework of the larger study.

It is of interest that John Maynard Keynes paid a visit to Moulton in the summer of 1934, when work was moving along on these various studies. Nourse and a few other staff members were present. Nourse reported that Keynes and Moulton were far apart on their thinking on fiscal policy, with the result that there was a spirited clash of views, since "Moulton was no mean debater." Nourse was not overly impressed with Keynes, who seemed to have a somewhat dismal impression of American economists.[10]

America's Capacity to Produce

The foundation study in the wealth and income series, *America's Capacity to Produce*, was published in June, 1934, under the authorship of Edwin G. Nourse and Associates. In his director's preface, Nourse explained "the division of labor" among those who were associated with the preparation of this volume and gave them full credit for their contributions. A foreword also described the larger study of which this book was a part. In this he said: "In the light of existing conditions and current experimentation in the realm of economic organization, the present moment seems opportune to examine anew the foundations of economic progress." He also said: "Looked at from [the] purely technical point of view, the national economic problem is simply one of using our labor supply upon our natural resources and productive equipment so fully and efficiently as to turn out, year in and year out, the largest possible dividend of goods and services. This not merely demands industry and skill on the part of the workers but also a correct direction of society's productive effort. We must strike a balance between current satisfaction of consumers' wants and the maintenance of an adequate stock of those underlying [capital] goods . . . that are essential in the process of creating consumers' goods."

The task of *America's Capacity to Produce* was explained fully in the book's introduction. In brief, it was designed to find out "whether our producing plant is adequate, inadequate, or excessive." The authors said: "We must get an understandable and reasonably accurate measure of what the capacity of this plant actually is and of the extent to which it is utilized" (p. 18). They were primarily concerned with the question of whether actual production utilized our full productive capacity for the period 1925-1929, and "if not, how much latent productivity might have been drawn upon for the satisfaction of our people's wants."

The authors were aware of the complex analytical and statistical problems involved in their procedures, and they attempted to make clear the limitations of their work. They pointed out that "in our analysis we have endeavored to arrive at capacity estimates that are attainable under the *practical operating conditions* which exist." While they believed that their methods provided "a much truer picture than is given by . . . studies heretofore made," they cautioned: "Confessedly we have employed methods of estimation, which to many statisticians and economists will seem daring if not hazardous. We believe, however, that the analysis by which we have proceeded . . . has been sufficiently buttressed by statistical measurements at all major points, and our final estimates have been checked against practical operating experience and criticism of technicians and business men to an extent that eliminates possibilities of serious error."

The body of the book examined the productive capacity of various segments of American industry for the period covered by the study. The final chapter brought the findings from these enquiries into focus. In brief, they found that "our productive system as a whole was operating at about 80 per cent of capacity in 1929," and that "if this 20 per cent of our resources not utilized could have been brought into production, it would have added goods and services to an amount one-fourth as great as the total which we were already getting from the operations of these years."

In summarizing their findings, the authors dealt with three questions. First, "Did the margin of unutilized plant capacity in the several branches of industry expand during the period from 1900 to 1930?" The answer given was: "No. There was no general tendency to pile up capital equipment in continually growing excess above what could be commercially employed." Second, "How much plant capacity under practical conditions of sustained operation was utilized in the peak year 1929 or in the prosperous period 1925-29?" The answer: "We arrive at a net estimate of 19 per cent as the amount of added production of which our industrial plant was technically capable under the conditions prevailing in 1929. This figure would need to be raised only about 2 per cent to measure the recoverable slack of the whole period 1925-29." Third, "How much unutilized labor was there in 1929, and was the practically available labor force adequate to man the unutilized plant capacity and bring it to full productivity?" The answer: "Every important branch of industry had a substantial labor slack in 1929."

In concluding their summary, the authors trenchantly said:

> Certainly our findings do not bear out the contention of those who, in the midst of the present depression, say that we were living in a fool's paradise in 1929—that we were "living beyond our means," and that disaster had to follow. Individuals, of course, were living beyond their private means as individuals always will in both prosperity and depression. But the nation was not. We were not trenching on our resources of capital goods or of labor power. Equipment was being maintained at a rate entirely suitable to the indefinite continuance of operation at the 1929 rate of activity. There was an unutilized margin which, in the perspective of the past, would appear to be about normal. Labor in general was not being so driven as to impair either health or morale. On the contrary, there was nearly 20 per cent of reasonably available labor which was not turned into the productive stream. Our economic society lacked almost 20 per cent of living up to its means.

The final sentence of the book tied it into the framework of the larger study. After pointing out that a substantial boom in individual incomes would result if our productive plant had been fully employed during the period of the study, the authors said:

> If, upon the very conservative grounds that we base our findings, such a betterment in material conditions lay within our grasp in the prosperous years of the late twenties, every alert mind must be driven to the question: What was there in the organization or functioning of our economic system which caused us even in those favorable years to fail to attain it, to say nothing of the margin four times as wide which we are failing today to make available to the satisfying of human wants: Such is the question we shall continue to explore in the subsequent volumes of this series.

There was great public interest in the book upon publication. The nation was then regaining its confidence after the Great Depression, and the book gave a psychological lift to this spirit. Economic conditions were slowly improving, and there was receptivity to ideas that would help the economy function more effectively. The study provided assurance that the country was fundamentally sound and that the economic machine, if properly operating, could increase the economic welfare of the nation. Until its publication, there were many who believed that the cause of our economic malaise was overproduction, and at that time, the National Recovery Administration was engaged in a great campaign to harness America's producing capacity with codes and other restrictive devices. The *New York Times*, in an editorial (July 4, 1934), held that the book dealt a heavy blow to the myth that the depression was the result of a tremendously overexpanded plant.

The reviews of the book in the professional journals acclaimed its significance, although some reserved judgment on its analytical and statistical procedures. Harlan L. McCracken, in the *American Economic Review* (December, 1934), called the book an important study of a major economic problem, and it impressed him as a "careful piece of work done by a competent staff." Arthur F. Burns, then a young economist at Rutgers University, after subjecting the book to searching scrutiny from the standpoint of its methodology in a review for the *Journal of Political Economy* (1935), concluded: "There is much to be gleaned from this volume about the course of capital investment . . . and no economist—whatever his specialty—can afford to overlook it entirely."

One of the most searching reviews was by Joseph S. Davis in the *Journal of Farm Economics* (February, 1935). He began by stating: "This is a book for discriminating readers." He then, after careful analysis, gave it credit for "breaking much ground," saying "probably all the work reported had to be done. The volume contributes essentially *toward* answering the questions suggested by the title and furnishes part of the foundation for a fuller answer. . . . The authors are presumably aware but do not expressly say, much more patient, penetrating thought and research on many elements of the subjects are needed before a really satisfactory synthesis on 'America's Capacity to Produce' will be possible."

The book also attracted much interest abroad. Colin Clark of Cambridge University, in a review for a German economic journal, called it "a brilliantly original attempt to assess the production capacity of the United States. This investigation is for the most part original, precise, and comprehensive." He also said that the authors showed "a profound knowledge not only of economics, but also of engineering problems." Many years later, in a letter to me, Clark indicated how he had been thrilled by the book when it came out. He said:

> I was of the generation which received "America's Capacity to Produce" and "America's Capacity to Consume" when they first came out with great enthusiasm; not only for the importance of their results, but also for their

remarkable boldness and success in pioneering new methods of analysis of economic data. The former of these books also played, for me and for others, an important part in discrediting many extravagant ideas in circulation at the time. . . . Nourse's book showed firmly that, while a great deal of productive capacity was admittedly wasted in the 1930's, nevertheless if it had been employed up to its full practical limits, it would not have increased the real income of the American people by anything like the factor usually claimed.[11]

Nourse was greatly pleased by the welcome given this book. It had provided needed information on a subject of great national importance, and it provided a foundation for determining how economic progress could be attained. He felt that no more could be asked for.

Income and Economic Progress

Nourse did not work directly on the second and third volumes of the wealth and income study, although editorially he supplied much of the connective thread that integrated them into the project as a whole. While the fourth and final volume of the series, *Income and Economic Progress*, was published under the authorship of Moulton, he said in his acknowledgements:

> The reader of this volume should be informed of the distinctive part which has been played by Mr. Nourse in connection with the entire series. As Director of the Institute of Economics he was largely responsible for the broad outline of the investigation as a whole, as well as being the primary author of *America's Capacity to Produce*. His contributions to the final volume have been such as to entitle him to joint authorship. He has written the introduction and the concluding chapter and contributed much to the organization and interpretation of other chapters.

A story lies behind this handsome admission. Nourse felt that Moulton had pushed for publication before full analysis could be completed and believed that the book as completed by Moulton placed too much emphasis on price reduction as a business practice and not enough on its economic and social importance. Many years later, in recalling this matter, Nourse said:

> Moulton was a great stickler for keeping up to a schedule, and when we got a grant we had to deliver on time. He said to me at one time, "The trouble with you, Nourse, is you have no time sense." He would say, "This is a book we've got to get out at a certain time and we've got to make it as good as we can." Well, that is what happened on that book. He went ahead and wrote it, and here his time sense came in. He was scheduled to go to Europe and he wanted to get the book off for publication first. He wanted me to appear as author and he as co-author. But as I saw the manuscript as it was developing I said: "No, I won't be joint author on it." I insisted that I would not be joint author as it was coming. As

Director of the Institute of Economics, I was chairman of the staff group to consider the book with Moulton. [Charles O.] Hardy and [Leverett S.] Lyon were the other members. About two days before Moulton was to sail, we had a consultation and the committee was unanimously in agreement that the book was not ready to be published, and should be deferred for further work after Moulton returned from his European trip. This was a most unpleasant incident, for we were the four horsemen of the thing. Moulton stormed out of the room saying: "I'm not going to have people tell me that I don't have a good book here," and he did bull the book through for publication in the face of that adverse report before he left. But when he got to the boat, he wrote me a letter saying: "Nourse, you have a better temperament than I have for handling these things, and I'm extremely sorry for the situation that developed." It was a very nice letter between two old friends, so I cabled him: "Situation fully understood, have good trip." That was the only fundamental difference that Moulton and I ever had. It was friendly. We were very good friends and coworkers, but we didn't see eye to eye on some things.[12]

In the light of Moulton's statement in his acknowledgement, we may conclude that the final chapter of the book, entitled "Economic Progress and the Democratic Ideal," represented Nourse's views. In this chapter he pointed out that the major questions in the total study had been:

> Can we not, within the limitations of our natural resources, our people, and our traditions, with only evolutionary modifications and readjustments to current conditions, restore and stabilize such a productivity of goods and services as will provide a general standard of living as high as that which we have known at the peaks of prosperity in the past? Can we not expect to improve on our best performances until every citizen . . . who cared to exert himself could attain a material standard of living equal at least to that of the so-called "middle-class" in the prosperous days before the collapse of 1929?

Nourse found that the cumulative findings of the general study had brought out the fact that "there is one type of distributive reform which in our judgment outranks all others in its promise of attaining the goal we seek. This is in the gradual but persistent revamping of price policy so as to pass on the benefits of technological progress and rising productivity to all the population in their role of consumers." He also said: "We cannot have the economics of mass production save in an economy of mass consumption. Each is the condition of the other."

Nourse also pointed out that no attempt was made in this volume to set forth the details of a low price program, for this would require "detailed examination of the peculiar situations in various industries," and the time was "not yet ripe for the presentation of anything more than general principles." However, the hope was expressed "that we may continue particularized and intensive studies in this field, supplementing them with the practical experience of business executives." These sentences make clear that Nourse was not content with the enunciation of the importance of low-price policy as a means of achieving economic progress, and that he intended to examine the possibilities of employing the policy in actual business situations. He was concerned with the practical application of the idea, and this was to be his greatest professional interest in the next decade.

Altogether, the wealth and income studies were a considerable success, and they brought credit to the Brookings Institution. For example, Walter Lippman called the series "the most useful economic study made in America during the depression."[13]

While Nourse felt that the interpretation of the final volume was "too managerial and not enough of the economy," he considered the four volumes together a significant piece of work. Many years later, he said: "The study dealt with the economy as an entity, not with any interest such as management, labor, agriculture, or consumer being paramount. Thus I think we can say that the studies were real pioneer work in the new economics of national aggregates. You see 'America's Capacity to Produce' meant maximization of the gross national product although the term was not in vogue then. I enter somewhat of a claim here that we were forward looking, forward reaching in our outlook and methodology."[14]

Brookings Institution in the Mid-1930s

In the mid-1930s, the Brookings Institution was going strong. It was busily engaged in economic and governmental problems of major national importance, and there was a high sense of mission in its staff. It was now enjoying adequate financial support from various foundations for a comprehensive program, and its attractive facilities near the White House made it a major social science center. The many problems that came with the approach of the New Deal emphasized the need for the type of realistic analysis of economic and political problems that the Brookings Institution was set up to cope with. Nourse at this time was steadily gaining recognition for his capable administration of the economic studies carried on by the Institute of Economics, and his director's prefaces displayed his deep interest in them. His practical good sense, combined with high standards of scholarship and effective presentation of results, was gaining for him the loyal support of the entire staff. His enthusiasm for good work was contagious, and he took a sympathetic interest in the problems of the individual staff members. Many of those who were associated with the Brookings Institution at this period recall instances of how Nourse helped them with writing or relationship problems. They commonly express this by saying that he was a gentleman and a scholar in the finest sense of these words. His sense of fairness made a great impression on his colleagues, while his calm, judicious temperament helped keep the program of the Institute of Economics on a healthy and even keel. As the historian of the Brookings Institution has said, referring to this period: "The Institute of Economics under Nourse was winning wide respect."[15]

Although Nourse was leading a very full professional life in the mid-1930s, he found time to enjoy his home and family. He and Mrs. Nourse carried on an active social life, and they seldom missed a good play at the National or Belasco theatres. It was at about this time that he was invited into the Washington Literary Society, which was to give him enjoyable company and intellectual stimulation throughout the remainder of his life. He took no vacations to speak of, for he looked upon the general meetings of the Social Science Research Council as opportunities for relaxation. One of the secretaries of the Council at that time recalls that he was the best dancer on the floor at these occasions. Moreover, the variety of his activities in itself kept him from overconcentration on any one project. His sister Alice and her husband, Earl Hobart, then had a summer lodge on the Potomac River above Great Falls in Virginia, and this gave him an opportunity to occasionally escape into the country on weekends and holidays. After they moved to California in the late 1930s, his sister Mary and he acquired this property, which served as a haven for him up into the 1950s.

Industrial Price Policy and Economic Progress

With the completion of the wealth and income studies, Nourse, with the collaboration of Horace Drury, undertook to bring the general theory of low-price policy "down to practical application" by examining how it was being used by big-business organizations. They published their results in June, 1938, under the title, *Industrial Price Policy and Economic Progress*. This book examined the growth of large business corporations as they had evolved in the United States, and how big-business managers had gradually gained a "larger measure of power and a large degree of discretion in executive policies." The book also paid particular attention to the price policies employed by several major corporations through case study analysis. The authors did not look upon their study as definitive, for they were then mainly concerned with opening up the subject for more comprehensive analysis.

In his director's preface, Nourse pointed out that this book represented an attempt "to discern the constructive implications of what is already being done by pace makers in this field [low-price policy] and to envisage the results to be expected if these constructive lines of business practice were widely followed." He continued: "This approach looks toward the inductive development of a positive theory of the price process in the real and dynamic world evolving about us." Nourse was not unaware of the great difficulties involved in gaining acceptance for the philosophy of low-price policy, but he thought the attempt important, in that it implied "a certain strategy for the attack on social problems." He also made clear that the focus of the book was not on "the immediate problem of depression and recovery" by saying: "Whatever its immediate applications its analysis of price policies is concerned with economic hygiene rather than emergency treatment of acute illness."

The book's introduction gives a more comprehensive statement on the relationship of this study to the wealth and income volumes which had come to the general conclusion that "the broadest and most direct road to the improvement of the general economic welfare is to be found through a consistent policy of expanding real incomes by lowering the prices of goods and services wherever advance in techniques and organization made such a course practicable." It was made clear that "economic statesmanship" would be involved in applying this policy in practice. As the authors said: "We are seeking to portray the conditions actually obtaining in the price world in which the business manager must make his decisions and to consider with him the circumstances under which and the extent to which he can contribute to national welfare by naming a lower rather than a higher price for his products."

Nourse and Drury were aware that many business executives would view their proposals for a low-price approach as "academic and impractical," but they were encouraged by the extent of interest shown by many business leaders in the conception. They recognized that their book dealt mainly with "administered prices," which were prices established by the decisions of executives. Thus they believed that the significance of their book would depend upon the degree to which it might influence the decision-making process of business executives. They hoped that their appeal for economic statesmanship would yield helpful results in economic progress.

The spirit of the study was reflected in the following statement from the book's introduction: "It was our desire to keep our feet firmly on the ground; to make realistic analyses of price problems as they actually confront the business man, exphazizing the technological conditions which underlie economic processes and the institutional framework in which business is conducted." They admitted being heartened in their efforts by the generous cooperation accorded them by executive officials and staff specialists of many business concerns.

The body of the book provided a description of the price-making process in modern large-scale industry, an analysis of the practical experience of large corporations in determining prices, and an attempt to clear up misconceptions as to the meaning of the term "low-price policy." The findings were brought together in a chapter entitled "Dynamic Price Making." This chapter pointed out how the industrial office had become the birthplace of prices for much of our economic life, and how the "price-making executive" had become the "guide and regulator of the economic process in a considerable part of our business world." The authors said: "He takes upon himself the responsibility for the standard of living for an even larger proportion of our people. Much as he generally hates the phrase, he becomes in fact the economic planner of our society rather than merely the adapter of his personal affairs as best he can to a largely automatic price mechanism."

Nourse and Drury then contrasted mechanistic and dynamic approaches to price determination by large industrial firms. Mechanistic price-making was described as "essentially conservationist in character, setting the protection of existing capital as its major goal," and not "concerned primarily with the satisfaction of consumers, or wage earners." The dynamic approach to prices, on the other hand—characterized by the use of low-price policy— called for "resourcefulness, imagination, and creative genius." They said: "By the more universal dissemination of these methods may we not hope not alone for recovery from present stagnation but for the maintenance of a more orderly and stabilized prosperity over the years to come?" (p. 259).

The authors maintained that the era of competitive capitalism had not been brought to a close by the growth of modern large-scale corporations. Rather, in their view, large-scale organizations had changed the character of competition. To them, "the competition among pigmies, which some are eager to try to restore, is puny by comparison. Competition is quite as keen and much more productive of results when we find industrial giants marshalling their mighty resources to perfect new techniques and new schemes of organization through whose use more and better goods may be put within the reach of the masses." These were brave and idealistic words. Were they ahead of their time? Were they based upon wishful thinking? At least they gave recognition to the fact that large, powerful corporations eventually must accept a higher degree of social responsibility in their procedures, a thought which has permeated the thinking of many business leaders.

In a section of the final chapter called "The Challenge of Free Enterprise," the authors made clear that they considered their arguments for low-price policy "intensely practical." They said: "Let no one suppose that what we are here expressing is a mere pious homily on some altruistic but impracticable scheme of business management. We are not proposing that business men play the role of Santa Claus and turn over their wealth to the public or that they work for only nominal pay." They clinched their argument with this statement:

> If the American business man demands the right of freedom of economic enterprise, society in granting it to him may properly ask that he use that freedom aggressively in the public interest. This, to our way of thinking, is the challenge which the industrial system makes to the industrial executive. If he cannot meet it, the system of free enterprise under private capitalism is doomed to a condition of invalidism, low vitality, and unproductiveness which is utterly incompatible with the natural resources, productive equipment, and man power which the nation has at its disposal.

Nourse and Drury did not expect an overnight change in the pricing policies of major business organizations. But they saw no reason why an appeal to the better instincts of business leaders should not be made. Realizing that many years might elapse before their views gained widespread acceptance in the business community, they asked why the educational process to achieve this end should not begin.

Industrial Price Policy and Economic Progress immediately attracted wide public attention. H. R. Baukage, the well-known radio commentator, in an article in the Washington, D.C., *Sunday Star* (July 17, 1938), said that it "already promises to be one of the most talked of publications the Brookings Institution has produced." He thought the timing of the book was "almost too perfect," in that it appeared "just as Senator O'Mahoney and his committee are about to look into the monopoly question." He went on to say: "Naturally those who view with alarm the trust investigation now going on as a potential witch hunt, [are] greatly cheered to find authority in the report for the assertion that big business isn't bad just because it is big." However, Baukage pointed out that the book was in no sense "a defense" of big business as such. He also thought that "a lot of left-wingers won't like what the Brookings experts have to say." While he thought the book "may provide grist for the anti-New Deal mill," he observed that "less reactionary readers will be pleased with the authors' emphasis on the need to preserve free enterprise as 'the American Way.'"

Baukage believed that the early response to the book indicated that it may have "a very practical effect."

The book was soon widely reviewed by technical experts in professional and business journals. For example, Ralph E. Freeman of the Massachusetts Institute of Technology, in *Mechanical Engineering* (March, 1939), said:

> There will be general agreement with the main thesis that price reduction is the best means of disseminating the benefits of technical progress and that these benefits can be disseminated effectively only if business men are courageous, imaginative, and forward looking. . . . The book is to be welcomed because it emphasizes the importance of price derangement as a cause of our failure to realize to the full the industrial plants that are available and the men and women who are willing and able to work.

Ralph S. Tucker, in the *American Economic Review* (December, 1938), said:

> This well-written and stimulating book is a refreshing contrast to many others recently published on the same subject in that it does not assume that the competitive system of free enterprise is dead or hopelessly ill, but is concerned with developing a positive theory of pricing which if more generally accepted might improve the efficiency of the system. . . . The authors' main conclusion will meet with general acceptance to all economists.

Donald Wallace of Harvard University, in reviewing the book for the American Statistical Association, said that the book's "forceful challenge to the accepted views of the problem of monopoly requires the serious attention of economists." Later in the review, he said:

> This book is important because it contains a sharp challenge to those views of the problems of big business which emphasize the ineffectiveness of competitive forces and the wastes of monopoly; and because it implies a denial of the present desirability of more Governmental control in industrial markets or of change in the antitrust laws. The authors evidently believe that problems of monopoly first need more attention from business executives.

Wallace also made the point that the authors had attacked the customary practice of approaching pricing problems from the sort of equilibrium theory which they thought failed to "emphasize the dynamic elements from which progress comes." He thought they had put their finger on a "serious shortcoming" of much of the literature dealing with the theory of monopolistic competition.

Sam H. Thompson, in the *Journal of Farm Economics* (1929), said: "The inductive development of a positive theory of pricing industrial goods . . . has been effectively demonstrated. . . . It is to be hoped that many industrial leaders will read it carefully and endeavor to apply its lessons of "economic statesmanship."

Although R. F. Kahn (a friend of Keynes at Kings College, Cambridge) found the book lacking in "theoretical treatment of the problem of pricing" (*The Economic Journal*, June, 1939), he admitted that it could be recommended for the numerous examples of pricing practice drawn from American experience.

Though gratified by the reviews, Nourse was concerned that many reviewers did not recognize the book's expressed limitations as to its coverage. In a memo to Drury, he observed that certain criticisms were predicated upon the belief that the book attempted to cover a great deal more than "we had any idea of covering." He said that the objective of the book was not to justify or even to appraise, in any complete way, the position of the large concern in the national economy or to advocate as a universal rule the lowering of prices. He noted also that the decision to undertake the book largely grew out of businessmen's reactions to the lower-price policy recommendations in *Income and Economic Progress* as a means of sharing technological advances with consumers so as to sustain prosperity. While some businessmen had claimed such a process of price reduction was impossible, others had claimed that it was in fact being actively carried on. So it was decided to go out and see what circumstances had either compelled price reduction or made it profitably possible, in the hope that we might "make some contribution to the more widespread, prompter, and smoother working of the process." Nourse did not look upon their study as a full analysis of the problem of price policy, but he thought it disclosed a tendency for businessmen to give more consideration to public needs.

While Nourse was pleased by the attention given to his views on low-price policy by professional economists and business leaders. he realized that the prevailing attitude was one of skepticism toward the idea that big business or labor organizations could be brought around to acceptance of low-price policy as being for the public good. He felt that the burden of proof remained. It should be noted here that the subject of monopoly was deemed of great national importance in the fall of 1938, when the Temporary National Economic Committee, under the chairmanship of Senator Joseph C. O'Mahoney, was then beginning its comprehensive survey of American business management and ownership. In view of the intense interest in this subject, the American Academy of Political Science devoted its annual meeting in November to a consideration of "Monopoly or Competition—Industry and Labor." In the addresses on this occasion, Nourse dealt with the topic, "Monopolistic Practices and the Price Structure."

In opening his statement, Nourse expressed concern that the hypothesis of the meeting seemed to be that government must intervene more aggressively in the price-making policies of big business to protect the public interest. He thought it more desirable to examine "the potentialities for both good and bad" which reside in four types of big-business operation—"price leadership, sharing the market, price stabilization, and price discrimination." Moreover, he believed it possible that "the practices of monopolistic competition, as we know them today, are moving toward a sounder, more enlightened and more constructive era." He based "this hope—and a certain tempered confidence" upon three factors: "(1) the sharpening of inter-commodity and even inter-industry competition through the technological possibilities created in a world of applied science; (2) the broadening and deepening of the economic wisdom of executives; and (3) the very growth of large-scale business which confers on such concerns an institutional character whose wide range of interests and permanence of life emphasize the underlying harmony between great corporate interest and public welfare."

Nourse did not believe that the "process of development toward mature and sound use of monopolistic powers" was completed. In fact, he said: "In view of the extreme youth of the big business movement, it is to be regarded as only in its beginnings." Moreover, he thought "the idea that price jurisdiction could and would be used primarily for the promotion of short-run acquisitive ends has been pushed into the background," not because of the disappearance of "original sin," but due to "a growth of understanding." He continued: "The bigger big businessmen, the more perspicacious or better educated business executives, are coming to perceive that, while such a course might promote the short-run interests of a business buccaneer, they definitely stand in the way of the comprehensive and continuing process of growth throughout the business system on which the deep and sustained prosperity of a system of free business enterprise must ultimately rest." He saw gradually developing "a widespread type of corporate administration . . . turning its attention to ways of utilizing price jurisdiction which will build business broadly and soundly because . . . this would contribute in the largest way to the service of society." This gave him hope for believing that the newer devices of monopolistic competition would eventually "promote the healthy functioning of a system of free enterprise, with only its necessary complement of government participation." He urged business executives and professional economists to "join in the intensive study of the numerous constituent problems of this type of price-making" rather than "throw up their hands in despair."

Nourse at this time was already making plans to take his own advice through undertaking a further study of the price-making process in big business. This was to result in several important papers and a major book, *Price Making in a Democracy*. This development will be discussed in the next chapter.

In an informal talk given to friends in the Farm Credit Administration in January, 1939, Nourse revealed how his study of industrial price policies grew out of his explorations in agricultural marketing. As he studied the agricultural marketing system, he questioned the assumption that farm prices were made under conditions of "perfect competition." He found that on the supply side, farmers were competing with one another while on the demand side, powerful interests—railroads, millers, packers, handlers, etc.—were able to dominate the market. This situation had led him to support cooperative organizations strong enough to deal on an equal basis with buying interests. In fact, he found that some of the larger cooperatives were capable of exerting a certain amount of monopolistic competition, comparable to that developed by large industrial concerns. His study of marketing agreements under the AAA made clear that the problems of agricultural price policy were not fundamentally different from those of industrial price policy, and this had led to his book on industrial price policy. He thought that there were great possibilities in price lowering to sustain economic progress, but that it was not a panacea. He said: "It seems to me that we live, and are going to live, in a society in which for various technical reasons it is necessary to have comparatively large units of organization . . . and that our central problem is learning how to practice economic statesmanship in the administration of prices." He pointed out that some people had criticized his industrial price policy ideas as being a whitewash of business. Nourse admitted that the "blindness, the selfishness, the stupidity" with which businessmen in the past had "abused the price-making system was almost beyond belief," but he was greatly encouraged by the extent to which modern businessmen "were beginning to pioneer longer-range, more economically sound ways of dealing with price policy." He went on to say:

> Some people tell me: "You are terribly impressed by what these businessmen are going to do; you make your hortatory talk, they put up a pious front, and you are deceived by it." I do not attempt to answer that, but I do think that qualitatively there has been a change toward a more constructive way of administering prices, and that if we could get everybody back of that we might have a considerable part of the monopoly problem

solved. I want to go just as far as I can towards intelligent self-regulation of industry.

Nourse thought that the best time to undertake a price reduction program was in a period of prosperity. He said: "The time to make positive contributions toward a broader, more liberal, more constructive price policy is when conditions are relatively favorable, as in a prosperity period. . . . The real test of the application of that doctrine is in a period of advancing prices. This must help sustain the momentum of recovery, while raising prices would nip it in the bud." He also applied his thinking to the problems of farm cooperatives. He said: "Now with somewhat better agricultural conditions, cooperatives should direct their attention primarily towards studying how they may get an adequate return for farmers by selling as much as possible of the product rather than in trying to build up farm returns through following restrictive policies which mean a small volume at a relatively high price."

Now let us turn to another very important aspect of Nourse's life which significantly influenced his professional development.

Work with the Social Science Research Council

While Nourse was busy administering the program of the Institute of Economics, he was giving active attention to the work of the Social Science Research Council, for as Moulton withdrew direct interest in the affairs of the Council, Nourse became more vitally involved. Until 1931, Nourse's Council relationship was largely in agricultural economics and rural sociology. Starting in 1931, he became a member of the Problems and Policy Committee, the guiding committee of the Council, and in the following year, he became its chairman, a position he retained until October, 1939, when he was named Vice-Chairman of the Council.[16]

His work with the Problems and Policy Committee called for frequent weekend meetings at the Council offices in New York City. This caused Moulton to chide him by saying: "Edwin, do you think you are working for the Brookings Institution or the Social Science Research Council?" To Nourse, this was a serious matter, and he testily replied that the time he devoted to Council business was his own, since Council meetings were held on Saturdays and Sundays, when the Brookings offices were closed. Furthermore, he pointed out that these meetings were helpful to him as Director of the Institute of Economics in making contacts and in getting ideas of value to the Institute. This view was substantiated (see Chapter VII) when his advocacy of "concurrent history" at a meeting of the Problems and Policy Committee brought forth funds from the Rockefeller Foundation that made possible a comprehensive study of the Agricultural Adjustment Administration and a like study of the National Recovery Administration.

During the years while Nourse was Chairman of the Problems and Policy Committee, the Social Science Research Council became increasingly important as the national center for social science research. One of its principal problems was to establish social science research as of cognate importance with natural science research, for at this time, natural scientists were inclined (and many still are) to look upon the social sciences as not being true sciences. Moreover, many social scientists were themselves uncertain as to how they should describe their work, some even taking the position that the Social Science Research Council might have been better named the Social Studies Research Council. In view of this situation, the Social Science Research Council in May, 1937, on the recommendation of the Problems and Policy Committee, appointed a special committee of distinguished social scientists to review Council policy under the chairmanship of Mark A. May of Yale University. The other members of this committee were Wesley C. Mitchell, Columbia University; William F. Ogburn, University of Chicago; Robert Redfield, University of Chicago; and Arthur M. Schlesinger, Harvard University. This committee immediately employed Louis Wirth to make a comprehensive study of the work of the Council from its inception in 1923 as a basis for offering recommendations on how the work of the Council might be strengthened.

Wirth's report—a comprehensive document of 162 multigraphed pages—provided a valuable record of the way the Council had developed and gained recognition. Wirth discerned five major stages in the life of the Council, all of which Nourse had known: (1) organization (1923-1926); (2) expansion (1927-1930); (3) consolidation (1931-1933); (4) retrenchment (1934-1935); and (5) reconstruction and planning (1936–). With regard to the last stage, which had just opened, Wirth said: "The current situation calls for resolute and critical re-examination of Council policy." He thought the appointment of the Committee on Review of Council Policy demonstrated that "the Council is searching for clarification of its policies and their more effective implementation."

Wirth noted that the Council had become "the recognized central national body of the social sciences in the United States," and that in recent years the Council's Problems and Policy Committee and the Council's staff had "devoted ever increasing attention to the exploration of ways of making the Council a more useful instrument in facilitating and stimulating social research." He thought the chief defect of the Council was, to a large extent, an underemphasis on its intellectual function. He did not believe that the Council was performing "the function of furnishing intellectual leadership to American social science" to the full extent of its capacity. To meet this problem, he suggested that there be set up a research planning committee that "would have the function of exploring and directing the Council's potential research planning activities." He also proposed the establishment of a committee on review and criticism that would have as its special function "the periodic review of research activities and accomplishments."

The Council Committee on Review of Council Policy accepted much of the Wirth report in its recommendations to the Council in September, 1937. It urged that "intellectual leadership in the facilitation and coordination of research in the social sciences be reasserted as the dominant and controlling purpose of the Council." This committee also said: "Too few of the research activities of the Council have arisen from a desire to test social hypotheses or to discover basic laws and too many have been inspired by immediate social needs or the interests and problems of other social agencies. . . . The Council's research activities have been largely in the field of human engineering." To meet this general problem, the committee therefore proposed that action should be taken toward placing "heavier emphasis on the Council's efforts to put social research on a sounder scientific basis." The committee was also of the view that "there is developing from the experience of the Council . . . a growing perception among social scientists that all of them are studying different aspects of a single subject: namely, the behavior of human beings in society. If that be the case, it follows that one of the Council's greatest opportunities to promote research lies in carrying further the cross-fertilization of ideas among men specializing in different aspects of social behavior."

The Committee on Review of Council Policy therefore recommended that there be created "a committee on research planning and appraisal," as there was no other agency "so well suited to carry on planning for the social sciences or for critically assessing its contributions to knowledge." In the discussion of this proposal by the Problems and Policy Committee, Edmund Day emphasized the need for more critical analysis of research being done in the social sciences. He challenged his colleagues as to whether they had any clearly defined idea of what social *science* research actually was, and whether they were making any sustained, systematic, or comprehensive effort to find out. In response to Day's views, the Problems and Policy Committee recommended that an appraisal committee be set up immediately under Day's chairmanship. Nourse served on this committee during its first year, and the following year he became its chairman.

The Appraisal Committee operated in this manner. Each of the seven disciplines represented in the Council was asked to select for its respective field an outstanding publication of recent years which had gained recognition for being a valuable and influential instance of social science research. The Appraisal Committee then selected one of these studies for intensive analysis and a competent worker in the same professional field was assigned the job of evaluating the research procedures used. His critique was then circulated to members of the Appraisal Committee and others interested. Thereupon a full day was given to a discussion of the study and the critique prepared on it. This discussion was recorded and edited, and then published with the critique and rejoinder of the person or persons who made the study.

The first book so selected for review was *The Polish Peasant in Europe and America*, by Thomas and Znaniecki. This was a sociological study, but it was pertinent to the work of anthropologists, psychologists, economists, and political scientists. The results were so productive that the following year, while Nourse was chairman of the committee, an economic study was selected for examination—*The Behavior of Prices*, by Frederick C. Mills. The appraisal of this book by Raymond T. Bye, the rejoinder by Mills, and the discussion of its research methodology and significance by those present at the conference were published as a full-scale book by the Social Science Research Council.[17] This record of the conference shows how skillfully Nourse, as chairman, saw that all viewpoints were fully recognized. His foreword to the volume is of special interest in giving his views on the problems of social science research and the value of the appraisal function as it was being carried out by the committee. In this he said:

> The Social Science Research Council, in seeking to discover and define its proper role of usefulness for the seven disciplines represented in its membership, is laying increasing emphasis on intellectual leadership toward improving the quality of social science research and in promoting better organization among scholars for carrying out such work.
>
> . . . .
>
> If the public is to be enlightened as to the basis on which experts distinguish between success and failure in the task of giving a scientifically rigorous quality rather than mere irresponsible ingenuity to the product of research activity—which today makes increasing demands upon our time and funds—the so-called experts must come to reasonable agreement, or at least moderately limited and specifically defined disagreements, as to their own ways of working and the criteria which they find it useful and neces-

sary for each to apply to the work of others, if he is to use their product in his own subsequent endeavors.

. . . .

Are the materials and methods used in this social science field (economics) so different in character from those of the natural sciences that it is not possible to arrive at any reasonable consensus among workers on any point? Is some such formulation necessary if the character, point of departure, and bearing of new hypotheses are to be clearly recognized and evidence in support of them as effectively presented as in the natural sciences?

. . . .

This conference illustrates with painful clarity the fact that the difficulty of arriving at consensus with reference to the validity and value of any original contribution to our store of knowledge is involved with the looseness of our current practice with reference to the definition of concepts and the verbal symbols that we attach to them. It was hardly possible for the several participants to make sure that they were talking about the same thing when they were discussing "institutionalism," "price systems," "behaviors," "stability," "normal," or "equilibrium." How complacent are economists or how complacent should they be permitted to be about going on the present rugged individualism in which each writer uses these terms in his own particular and often unclarified meaning?

After endorsing Edmund Day's warning of the year before that social science was in danger of becoming a self-contained cult, Nourse said:

If our practices tend to shrink the bounds of that cult to narrower and narrower limits till the lone worker becomes a cult unto himself, the danger is great indeed. Nor is this a purely imaginary danger today. If the growth of knowledge is to be as healthy and vigorous as possible, the individual mind must be allowed to range as widely and freely as it may be moved to do by its quest for truth; but if it is to make these explorations fruitful for society, the product of such untrammeled thinking must be put in a form that is intelligible to one's fellows.

The full scope of Nourse's leadership in the Social Science Research Council during the 1930s was reflected in his last report as Chairman of the Problems and Policy Committee, which was presented at the meeting of the Council's Board of Directors, September 12-14, 1939. On this occasion he discussed all problems of the Council with a firm grasp on his subject and audience. He described in detail the efforts of the Problems and Policy Committee to put into action the research recommendations of the Committee on Review of Council Policy and gave an informative résumé of the Appraisal Committee in performing "a useful but difficult task." It was quite clear from his effective presentation that he was intimately familiar with all aspects of the Council's operations and deeply concerned with its main preoccupation *the improvement of actual research*.[18]

With his retirement as Chairman of the Problems and Policy Committee, Nourse's interest in the work of the Council did not flag. He immediately became Vice-Chairman of the Council, and in a year its Chairman, a position he was to hold until 1945.

Nourse at 57

By 1940, 57-year-old Nourse had built an enviable record in guiding the agricultural industry in a long period of economic and technological change, and more than any other, he had given leadership to the evolving cooperative movement. He was now broadening his interests to the economy as a whole, and he was fast gaining recognition as a provocative and constructive thinker on the economic problems of industry. He was admired for the administrative guidance that he was giving the Institute of Economics on economic problems of national importance, and he was highly respected for the breadth of his scholarship displayed in his association with the Social Science Research Council. He was in fine physical and mental condition, and the economic and social problems of the future excited him.

Chapter IX

ROUNDING OUT A PROFESSIONAL CAREER
(1940-1946)

As Nourse was 57 in 1940, he could look forward to retirement at age 65 in 1948. He was at the peak of his professional form, and he was intent on rounding out his career in the area relating to the improvement of the American free enterprise system. He was primarily interested in carrying forward his explorations in low-price policy as a means of promoting economic progress, and he desired to bring to bear the methods of social science in his economic studies. He was not looking forward to retirement, but that problem could be handled when he got to it. His concern was to make the best use of the time available in the years that lay immediately before him.

An insight into Nourse's thinking in 1940 is given by an unpublished paper he prepared on "The Economist and His Job." He was then trying to formulate what the role or function of the economist should be in our society, and to do this, he divided economists into three categories: business economists, political or general economists, and social economists. In the first group he included economists who served the interests of a particular business or special types of economic organization, such as labor unions. He thought of business economists non-invidiously as "economic attorneys," in the sense that their objectives were limited to the pecuniary advancement of some form of special interest. He did not think that such economists should be classed as economists "in the same sense as those who seek to promote not private economy but political economy, that is the wealth of nations." His own area of interest was with the work of general economists, who sought "the greatest attainable flow of wealth for the social group as a whole." He looked upon such economists as "organization engineers" striving to fashion an economy beneficial to all. Nourse bracketed "social economists" with "social philosophers," in that they dealt with "the production of human welfare rather than the productivity of material wealth." While their efforts were commendable, he saw them as placing emphasis more on ethical questions than on the basic economic problems of significance to all classes of society.

Nourse saw the profession of economics in its broader sense, passing over from "the philosophic or metaphysical plane to a basis of really scientific method." He believed that economists would have "an ever increasing sphere of importance" as they attained maximum efficiency as "technicians in the field of human organization in the promotion of group wealth." This essay suggests that he was endeavoring to clarify in his own mind the somewhat ubiquitous role of the general economist, as contrasted with the more limited roles of the business or social economists. It was an exploratory effort which reflected his confidence in the procedures of social science, and it no doubt helped him define his own role as a general economist.

Brookings Institution During the War

In 1940 and 1941, the Brookings Institution helped adjust the nation to war. Charles O. Hardy's *Wartime Control of Prices*, prepared at the request of the War Department, provided invaluable information for mobilization a year before Pearl Harbor. When war came, President Roosevelt appointed Moulton to the War Resources Board, and members of the staff were increasingly drawn into work for congressional committees and war agencies. During 1942, important studies were published on industrial manpower requirements and urgent transportation problems.[1]

With funds for basic research sharply curtailed by war conditions, the Institute of Economics and the Institute for Government Research were abolished as formal divisions and consolidated into a single research staff to achieve more effective administration. In effect, this broadened Nourse's responsibilities, for as vice-president under the reorganization, he provided general supervision of the Institution's research studies and helped Moulton represent the Institution on general affairs. The reduced research program enabled Nourse to devote more of his attention to matters in which he had a direct interest, such as the work of the Social Science Research Council and the problems of the American Economic Association. During these war years, his professional output reached a peak with the publication of *Price Making in a Democracy* and many articles and papers dealing with the anticipated post-war problems of the economy.

Work with Business Leaders

Nourse's study of industrial price policies had brought him into touch with many big-business leaders who were glad to find an "academic economist" vitally concerned with the way business was actually carried on. When the National Association of Manufacturers set up an economic advisory committee in 1939, he was invited to its membership. He found this a very rewarding relationship, for it gave him an opportunity to keep in close touch with current big-business thinking, while enabling him to express his views to an influential audience who might put them to practical use. As an outgrowth of this mutually beneficial relationship, Nourse was invited to present his views on "The Nature and Future of Private Enterprise" before the Congress of American Industry in New York City on December 5, 1941—just two days before the Pearl Harbor attack. This talk was greatly appreciated by American business leaders, and it was given wide distribution as an NAM pamphlet. It also gave Nourse real satisfaction, for it enabled him to convey in capsule form much that he had learned through his studies of business organization and low-price policy. Nourse opened his address by saying:

> I shall attempt . . . to state in bald and positive terms the elements that both businessmen and economists regard as the essentials of a private enterprise system. Then I shall attempt to apply those principles logically, vigorously, dispassionately—and this I think means scientifically—to the current and emerging business situation. . . . My real focus of attention will be on how to resume private enterprise after the war and make it attain the maximum of success over a long period of the future.

He decried the widespread attitude of "bitter resignation" that free enterprise was being supplanted by government enterprise. Although Nourse conceded the validity of this line of thinking, he held that there was no going "back to normalcy." He thought that the only way private enterprise could vindicate itself was by marching forward to new economic practices and policies which "express a new sense of responsibility for general welfare." He said: "The farther I press scientific lines of economic analysis, the more am I convinced that economic efficiency demands more, not less, freedom of private enterprise." He believed that the next stage in business enterprise would be marked by a "shift from management in the aristocratic tradition of personal proprietorship to the democratic philosophy of nonpartisan administration."

Nourse admitted that "the future of private business" hung in the balance, but he thought its salvation would depend upon the ability to discharge responsibilities to its several classes of clients—consumers, workers, and capitalists. Otherwise, he was fearful that government would increasingly assume authority over business affairs. He said: "The one real chance of preserving the system is by united and daring programs of action, by exercising enterprise as well as being private."

This somber warning was expressed so earnestly and with so much hope, good will, and graciousness that it was accepted as a logical and positive contribution for business guidance. Nourse found that he could express himself frankly to a business audience, because he had something vital to say on problems of much concern to them.

Defining "Price Policy"

Nourse's explorations in pricing practices caused him to feel that the term "price policy" needed more precise definition. He therefore developed his views on this subject in a carefully prepared article, which was published in the *Quarterly Journal of Economics* (February, 1941) under the title, "The Meaning of Price Policy." It was his objective to show "why prices are what they are in a society attempting to operate a system of free enterprise mitigated by corporate consolidation, collective bargaining unions, and . . . government agencies." While recognizing that economics is "much more than a study of price structure and action," he pointed out that "the ubiquitous character of prices as a manifestation of the economic process makes price behavior an excellent frame of reference for studies of wide scope and significance."

After examining price theory as it had evolved in recent decades, he turned his attention to price-making as conducted in modern economic society. He was particularly intent on appraising the distinctive role played by the industrial executive in administering prices, and he maintained that the methods of social science might profitably be employed to get a better understanding of how prices are actually made by business institutions. He thought that "price policy studies should show the way in which the factors of rational guidance fit into the operations of business concerns."

In summarizing his examination of issues involved in the concept of price policy, he said: "Price policy studies are not put forward as a novel form of doctrine leading to some economic nostrum. I have sought rather to stress the greater richness and adequacy imparted to price theory as older lines of analysis have been complemented by studies of all price-determining factors. . . . Studies in price policy seek to discover the subjective factor in price-making within the area of price administration. . . . If this task be competently done, we shall have a much fuller and clearer account of how prices become what they are under the rationalistic ministrations of the business executive . . . the legislator, administrator, and court."

It was his view that "price policy" shifts the "focus of attention from the mechanistic and deterministic aspect of the price-making process to the volitional factor introduced by the rationalistic influence of the human participants in the process." He concluded his article with this perceptive statement:

> Technology has brought us far beyond the point where price can be relied upon to effect automatic adjustment of our economic society. Economic planning and price administration are emerging clearly as the pattern of our economic society. If such a society is to be conducted on lines of rational planning under traditionally free enterprise, businessmen must put their practical knowledge of actual operative experience . . . more fully at the disposal of professional and detached economists. . . .

He believed that this approach would greatly advance the scientific character of economics as a social study by making it "within measure an experimental science."

"Democracy as a Principle of Business"

In March, 1942, the *Yale Review* featured an article by Carl Becker, "Making Democracy Safe in the World." A second article by Nourse dealt with the same subject, under the title, "Democracy as a Principle of Business." In this he asked: "Does the democratic pattern provide a dependable and efficient way of supplying the material foundations for the good life?" Coming at a time when we were locked in a struggle for national survival with the totalitarian powers, this question demanded attention. It was Nourse's belief that the individuals concerned as laborers and employees should have a greater voice in the way business was conducted. This would change the character of labor unions and business management. As to the unions, he said: "As an economic institution, the union should exist for the worker, not the member for the union. Members should have the right of free speech (without fear) in the councils of both local and central unions and the secret ballot as a means of registering their personal views on policy, finances, and action." He was no less critical of the autocratic procedures employed by business organizations. It was his view that "the power of our economic machine comes from the working contribution, physical and mental, of all its individual participants. Efficiency demands that we draw their power forth." He held that "democracy is a major biologic principle of economic life because it bases the health of the whole organism on the appropriate nourishment, stimulation, and co-ordination of every cell in its structural and functional relationship, whether it be of bone, tissue, or organ."

Presidency of the American Economic Association

Since 1911, Nourse had taken an interest in the affairs of the American Economic Association. He was therefore greatly pleased to be elected president of the association in December, 1941, to serve for the year 1942. It was to be one of the most difficult years in the organization's history, because of the need to help government meet demands for qualified economists in the war agencies. By May, it had become evident that travel restrictions might force the cancellation of the annual meeting scheduled for late December in Cleveland, but it was not until November 17 that the meeting was cancelled by government order. Fortunately, Nourse had already found that it could be held in Washington, D.C., if postponed until early January. So, members were notified on December 7 that it would take place in Washington, D.C., from January 4 to 9, 1943. Nourse insisted that it was especially important that the economics profession register its views at this time on the nation's economic problems.

The change in time and location called for new arrangements and many last-minute changes in the program. As President of the AEA, Nourse also had the responsibility of organizing and implementing the program for the annual meeting while preparing his presidential address. As he said in writing to George Washington Bell, the long-time Secretary-Treasurer of the AEA, on November 20, 1942: "All in all this was a swell year *not* to be president of the AEA."[2]

For his presidential address, Nourse took for his subject "Collective Bargaining and the Common Interest."[3] It was his general thesis that "non-governmental organization for multilateral group bargaining presents, in the long run and over the major part of the economic field, the truest and fullest opportunity for universal self-expression combined with technical efficiency."

At this time, the nation was deeply engaged in World War II, and many in the economics profession were coming to believe that the general welfare demanded a planned economy. Nourse was not among them. He did not "accept the proposed methods of government-directed activity and government-regulated prices" as essential to a progressive economy. He saw the answer in a more constructive use of collective bargaining, which he defined as "the process by which many individuals of many talents may organize themselves for the continuous discovery of their true economic interests and the peaceful promotion of those interests." He had been impressed in his economic studies by the growing power in our economic life of large corporate concerns, national trade unions, and agricultural marketing cooperatives, and he thought it desirable "to learn how these groups could be most efficiently organized for joint voluntary action to attain a scheme of market values that would provide maximum human satisfaction for the total population." He believed that self-controlled economic organizations held many superiorities over government in business, and he held that four conditions had to be met if collective bargaining was to realize its potentialities as the mechanism best suited to advance the distinctive ends of economic life. "There must be," he said, "(1) functional equality among the parties; (2) democratic representation of individuals in local groups and of local units in overhead organizations; (3) full disclosure of facts; and (4) sincere use of professional assistance." It was self-evident to him that the price-making process in modern economic life could not depend upon the automatic reactions of individual economic men but demanded more complex and purposive action.

Nourse continued to give much attention to the work of the AEA during 1943. At the annual meeting of the American Economic Association in December, a symposium of past AEA presidents dealt with this question: "What should be the relative spheres of private business and government in our post-war economy?" On this occasion, Nourse declared: "I am an avowed minimalist in delimiting the sphere of government in economic life;[4] and an avowed maximalist as to the sphere of private business. . . . I define the role of government as that of creating a favorable milieu for the general practice of private enterprise, not actual operation except in a few limited classes of goods and services or the control of detailed direction of specific businesses." Later in his statement, he said: "The current disposition to throw major responsibility for the conduct of economic life into the lap of government suggests the search for a shortcut instead of dedicating ourselves to the hard task of working out satisfactory results within the framework of a democratic system—'by blood and sweat and tears.' "

Price Making in a Democracy

Nourse was aware that *Industrial Price Policies and Economic Progress* had opened up many questions that needed further analysis and supporting evidence. Soon after its publication, he began formulating plans for a follow-up book, and it began to assume form in 1941. To take advantage of the "active and steadily mounting interest in the modern workings of the private enterprise system," he decided to issue the book in a series of pamphlets before final publication. This would build interest in his project and afford him a feedback of suggestions and criticisms as he went along. Nourse was pleased with the results obtained. Altogether, 12 pamphlets were issued from January, 1942, to July, 1943, before the book was published in February, 1944, under the title, *Price Making in a Democracy*. This book provides the best general exposition of his views on how our private enterprise system works with special reference to the role of price policy.

The book was presented in three parts: Principles, Problems, and Prospects. Nourse aptly called the first chapter "Between Automatic and Authoritarian Price Making," to convey the idea that in our present-day economy, prices were no longer made automatically, nor were they generally made by government authority. In between automatic and authoritarian prices had developed, with the growth of large business corporations, a system of "administered prices," which had some of the "nature of both." This "in between" area was the focus of his book, and he pointed up the problem in this way:

> The economic self-interest of universally free individuals no longer acts as an Invisible Hand to guide business on the right way. This guiding hand is stayed when the free individual enterprise of the masses is superseded by the group enterprise of corporate industry, trade, and finance. Responsibility for determining the direction of the nation's economic life today and of furnishing both opportunity and incentive to the masses centers upon some 1 or 2 percent of the gainfully employed. It becomes necessary, therefore, to ask what principles of economic organization and direction the members of this small group are actually applying to this great task and what in fact are the fundamental principles which must be relied upon to guide them to the goal of success for both themselves and the economy [pp. 19-21].

In presenting his plan for analysis at the end of this chapter, Nourse raised two basic questions: (1) "Is the following of a low-price policy inherently unsound or unworkable?" (2) "Is such a course unlikely to be followed because of psychological, organizational, or legal difficulties in the way of putting it into practical operation?" (pp. 21-22).

He was aware that his views on low-price policy were considered "impractical" and "overly optimistic" by many business leaders and economists. To disarm such critics, he admitted two biases which rested, he believed, "on sound economic grounds." He stated the first as "a belief in the wisdom and economy of evolutionary growth or institutional modification and educational adaptation rather than sharply destructive revolutionary change." He thought that "we must not overestimate the thoroughness or rapidity with which improvement can be attained through adjustment and modification of existing institutions and the education and stimulation of human behavior within that institutional structure" (pp. 23-24). His second admitted bias was "a belief in the long-run superiority, in terms of high efficiency and lower social cost, of democratic private enterprise as against plutocratic or bureaucratic centralization of power." On this he said: "We are simply concerned that the reader be made fully aware that a belief in the economic superiority of democracy is a postulate of our study" (p. 25).

He concluded this first chapter by saying: "All who share a belief in the *capacity* of private enterprise to achieve national well-being should be ready to turn to the task of studying its operational requirements—to see what private capitalism must do to realize its full potentialities."

It is not possible here to examine the book in detail, but certain views expressed in the final chapter, "Company Management and Economic Stability," give some of its spirit and flavor.

> The whole economic philosophy expounded in preceding pages is based on the premise that there is an underlying solidarity of interest among all parts of an economy, and hence among all participants in its business life. Such solidarity expresses itself as a common concern for maximum production [p. 423].
>
> . . . .
>
> We believe that the attainment of what might be called "scientific" management of a system of private business would call for a systematic attempt to give all workers with hand or brain ample access to the use of natural resources and accumulated equipment at the place for which their capacities best fit them and to establish the closest approximation to an open market for the valuation of their productive contributions in these respective posts. This would lead us, in the complex technological and commercial situations of a modern industrial age, to the equivalent of freedom of individual effort (and its reward) which was embodied by Thomas Jefferson and Adam Smith in two notable documents in "the spirit of '76" [p. 434].
>
> . . . .
>
> It is evident that both the expansionists' and restrictionists' interpretations of business competition are exemplified in current business practices. But if we read the record of the last few decades, the restrictionist tendencies—under the slogan of "stabilization"—are so much in the ascendency or are so little frowned upon or combatted by responsible business leadership that they threaten again to involve us in deep and apparently incurable depression unless competition as one of the basic ingredients of the American way of economic life can be generally accepted and consistently practiced as a struggle toward superior efficiency, not merely in the qualitative sense of superior techniques but in the quantitative sense of economical and efficient utilization of the whole body of labor with efficient equipment [p. 437].
>
> . . . .

> The writer has experienced some difficulty in seeking to convey the basic importance he attaches to low-price policy as a guide to business management without seeming to offer a panacea. . . . To set low-price policy as the master key for solving . . . managerial puzzles is simply to say that the business enterprise of all our people cannot be most fully unleashed to use the knowledge that comes from advancing science . . . unless volume of production be accepted as the prime objective of economic life and price as merely the expression of trading ratios which conform to such full-scale activity [pp. 447-448].
>
> . . . .
>
> Adam Smith's recognition of self-interest as a perennial and dependable spring of human conduct is as true today as it was in his time. But the operation of self-interest on the part of officials of a highly organized economy must be on the basis of truly enlightened self-interest if the system is not to destroy itself—and hence its administrators [p. 449].

The Impact of the Book

Price Making in a Democracy attracted much attention in business and professional circles, for it dealt with a problem of great national interest: Will private enterprise be able to maintain full production and employment with the resumption of peace by means of low-price policy? While most of the reviewers were impressed with the quality of Nourse's economic analysis, they were generally skeptical on the possibilities of widespread adoption of his low-price policy proposal. However, A. B. Wolfe, in a six-page review in the *Journal of Political Economy* (March, 1945), cautioned that "if anything can make private enterprise . . . satisfactory in its public service, perhaps . . . moral conviction of high calling will do so. At any rate," he said, "Nourse's courageous faith and optimism are both stimulating and refreshing." He found the book "open-minded, courteous, and tolerant," and "beyond doubt one of the 'musts' of the present decade." George W. Stocking, in a comprehensive examination of the book for the *American Economic Review* (September, 1944), found Nourse's discussion "well knit and closely integrated," and he was impressed by the study's "high quality of economic analysis." He could not, however, accept the major conclusion "that in a society in which decisions are centralized under the control of a few price-making executives, reliance may be placed upon the unseen hand of enlightened self-interest to guide the economic processes toward the general welfare." Francis W. Coker, in reviewing the book for the *Political Science Quarterly* (June, 1945), pointed out that Nourse "is sure that business must look far ahead and at the public effects of its price making." He observed that "in his search for a way to preserve private enterprise, by harnessing it to economic democracy, his method is to consider, not how natural economic men acted in an earlier society, but how actual business men may act wisely in existing society. He realizes that private enterprise is not necessarily free enterprise and that anyone who undertakes to treat economic and political problems apart from one another is not likely to contribute much to the solution of either."

James J. O'Leary, in the *Yale Review* (Autumn, 1944), believed that "every business executive and labor leader in America should read Dr. Nourse's valuable book for the cogent arguments he puts forward on how prices should be made in a democracy. He sees the goals of the post-war American economy as being full employment of resources, maximum output of those goods and services freely chosen by consumers, and progress in the size of the real national income through technological improvements. . . . He contends, furthermore, that free enterprise not only affords the best system for attaining these objectives but also is a bulwark of American political democracy." While O'Leary held that "Dr. Nourse's ideas are eminently sound as far as they go" and that "a low-price policy would have many great advantages," he found "notably lacking . . . ideas on how the business cycle problem should be met." Moreover, he noted that "nowhere does he discuss the inevitably large role that the federal government must play in our post-war private enterprise economy." He also questioned Nourse's argument for "an enlightened industrial self-government in the interests of social welfare," saying: "We should remember . . . that industrial self-government is subject to abuses which may open the way for the destruction of democracy."

Donald C. Horton, in *Land Policy Review* (Fall, 1944), after pointing out that "a major part of the book attempts to convince business leaders that they can and should utilize the discretionary economic power inherent in control over large aggregations of productive resources to make private-enterprise systems function better both in their own and in the public long-run interests," went on to say:

> The philosophy of a low price policy is presented as a partial substitute for expanded functions of government in economic matters. Dr. Nourse presents his confession of faith in private enterprise early and often, but frankly recognizes that it must remain largely a matter of faith that cannot be subjected to scientific anlaysis. Whether others agree with him on this matter need not impair the usefulness of the central core of his economic analysis. He sets forth clearly the policies he believes private enterprise would need to follow to promote full employment. . . .

Horton also found of much interest Nourse's observations on the place of the economist in the formulation of business policy. "He would have the economist stick to his last as a social scientist and not attempt to take responsibility for final business decisions." Horton thought this implied that government economists should confine themselves to the field of objective scientific enquiry, a view that Nourse would attempt to put into practice as the first Chairman of the Council of Economic Advisers.

E. T. Grether, in analyzing the book for *Management Review* (September, 1944), said: "The distinguished author of *Price Making in a Democracy* is presenting a gospel, viz., that the American economic system of free enterprise may be saved by a conscious, deliberate low-price policy on the part of business managers." Grether thought that Nourse had supported his "dogma" well, in that "the bulk of the volume is devoted to broad, fundamental analysis and interpretation," but he went on to say: "Ultimately, he discards exposition, analysis, and scientific prediction for an all-out appeal to the intelligence and sense of responsibility of business leaders." Grether concluded his examination of the book with this challenging statement:

> *Price Making in a Democracy* cannot be read too widely, especially by business executives. Theoretically, the author's case is sound—a generalized "low-price policy" intended to maximize production and employment would be the wisest course for American enterprise. Unfortunately, however, historical perspective in relation to the inherent functioning of industrial and market competition does not allow one to be optimistic concerning Dr. Nourse's faith that business in the main may be expected to pursue the low-price course. The stronger likelihood is that free enterprise will be saved not alone by its good works but by grace . . . i.e., by government which will assume the responsibility for residual unemployment.

It is interesting to see how Nourse reacted to Grether's review. In writing him (November 11, 1944), he said: "I am struck at once by your broad characterization of the book . . . that it preaches a gospel," although this "characterization" is somewhat softened by the next sentence: "The author supports his dogma well (by) broad, fundamental analysis and interpretation." Nourse could not agree, however, that he had discarded "exposition, analysis, and scientific prediction for an all-out appeal to the intelligence and sense of responsibility of business leaders." As to "scientific prediction," Nourse said: "The predictive value of my analysis might be interpreted in two ways: (1) that I undertake to show that *if* certain conditions were met by industrial management the most successful outcome would result, or (2) that business management shows a trend toward practice which will 'produce a successful outcome.'" He admitted that he had hoped to achieve the first objective, but that on the second, he was a "complete agnostic," since the best evidence seemed to be "wholly inadequate and changing its complexion from day to day." Nourse also observed:

> I have been genuinely puzzled as to why so many economists seem to think

this sort of treatment should be given the invidious label "preaching" rather than being accepted as engineering analysis and exposition, even if it is not entitled to the more flattering phrase "scientific." . . . If an engineer makes a study of a certain building problem and his findings as to design, structural details, and construction and maintenance practice which should be followed if a building or a bridge is to stand up and accomplish the purposes desired, one would I think not accuse him of preaching to his profession or to the commercial interests concerned. Nor would his exposition of why the following of these practices would make for success be construed as a prediction that all skyscrapers or Bay bridges in the future would in fact be based upon his diagnosis. . . .

Nourse thought that two reasons largely explained this "preaching reaction": "(1) That in putting the exposition in as persuasive terms as possible to reach a business and general audience, I probably overdid it." (2) "My line of attack which holds that economics is a social science rather than . . . a system of abstract logic or of mechanistic determination . . . affronted not only the fundamentalists but even the institutionalists. . . ." Nourse believed that "the volitionary area" had to be explored with "diligence and penetration if we are to have a well-rounded theory of the economic process as it actually is."

The most searching examination of *Price Making in a Democracy* was by William H. Nicholls, in the *Journal of Farm Economics* (November, 1944). Nicholls thought that few economists would disagree except in details with the fundamental principles of low-price policy as set forth by Nourse. He thought he had put his finger upon a key weakness of current economic theory, its tendency to fall back upon "deterministic studies" of market situations with the executive conceived of as "a robot." While he thought that Nourse had rather effectively avoided the methodological biases inherent in recent theories of monopolistic competition and employment, he felt that he had skipped over too lightly some of the problems of monopoly and the attainment of full employment, which these theories were designed to solve. He held that Nourse's principal advance beyond much of current price theory was in his attempt to get business management to take what the economists call "a general-equilibrium," rather than "a particular-equilibrium," approach. It was his opinion that Nourse's major thesis was essentially "as revolutionary for our times as was Adam Smith's in 1776." He saw as the greatest weakness of the book "its complete omission of any consideration of the role of government in implementing or even making possible the generalization of low price policies." He thought he might have been more realistic, as well as constructive, had he at least considered "what positive role the government might play in saving private enterprise."

Nicholls summed up his analysis of the book by saying:

> Any shortcomings . . . are attributable in very large part, to the boldness with which Dr. Nourse has come to grips with one of the most crucial and difficult problems of our times. This book is most assuredly worth the painstaking and thoughtful consideration of every economist and business man. . . . If he succeeds in convincing more economists of the existence of a considerable area for the exercise of free will on the part of business management and if he influences even a few more strategically located business leaders to be bold conditioners rather than the less adventuresome conditioned in pushing for generalized low-price, he will be deserving of a hearty "Well done!"

The editor of the journal gave Nourse an opportunity to supply a commentary along with Nicholl's review. Nourse labelled this an "addendum" rather than a "rejoinder," in that he could take little exception to Nicholl's general views. He was particularly interested in pointing out that he had limited his book to the area of private enterprise, which was then being inadequately investigated "while a great host of economists are giving their enthusiastic attention to the public sector." He pointed out that he had specifically recognized in the book that his analysis "must remain in some details incomplete until it is carried through to the adjacent area of public policy and governmental action," and that he had said in a footnote: "I discarded a nearly completed chapter on 'Private Price Policy and the Role of Government' because it involved me in too many dicta on issues outside the scope of this book's analysis."

Nourse also saw fit to answer this question: "How optimistic am I as to the possibility of developing a socially acceptable private economic leadership within the time which will presumably be available?" He admitted that "popular demand runs strongly to quick and comprehensively operative government remedies. . . . The tides of education move slowly, whereas the winds of popular demand blow fast and hard." He had "no assurance—and not too much confidence—that time will be granted" to achieve the results he thought desirable. "But," he stoutly maintained, "I feel that it is still the obligation of the scholar to pursue without the distraction of contemporary clamors his analysis of what would constitute the most satisfactory—that is, both efficient and free—system for organizing our economic life."

Views on What Government Could Do

As explained in the previous section, Nourse had confined his book, *Price Making in a Democracy*, to an examination of what private enterprise could do to help develop a strong economy after the war and had not used a nearly completed chapter dealing with "Private Price Policy and the Role of Government." He gave his thinking on the place of government in post-war adjustment in an address to the Academy of World

Economics, Washington, D.C., on May 4, 1944, under the title, "Taxes, Prices, and Employment." Here he examined the question, "Can we handle the *public debt* as to promote, rather than to retard, full employment and the most adequate national product?" He proposed an affirmative answer, saying: "I believe that economists certainly, legislators and bureaucrats probably, and businessmen possibly today possess enough knowledge of how the economic process operates so that we can, at necessary and appropriate times, incur public debts of a constructive or facilitating character and still not have the burden of this debt or necessary service charges on it crush business or harmfully retard its general course." He continued: "I believe that a rational technique of public spending and public debt—even daring debt incurrence—puts into our kit of economic tools a device which is wholly within the tradition of vigorous economic enterprise." However, he believed that "like every power device it has potentialities of danger as well as helpfulness. Whether or not we find we have created a Frankenstein is an open question whose answer depends on the courage we display as well as on the caution we exercise."

Nourse believed that it was incumbent on him to show in his paper how the public tax program could be reconciled with voluntary pricing practices so as "to give the fullest opportunity for workers to find an outlet for their efforts in the satisfaction of their family wants." He saw taxation "as a means of maintaining employment by shifting dollars into positions of most active consumer spending," and he recognized that government could also furnish jobs directly through public works projects. He was not opposed to such action as long as funds were wisely used to provide benefits for the people, but he was not willing to accept the "Keynes dictum" that huge expenditures for public works of no direct value to the public were justifiable. He went on to say:

> I believe that we should carefully explore and diligently exploit the possibilities of a predominantly private organization of our labor force for high-level productivity rather than jumping debonairly to public direction of this process—a rocky, not a rosy, road to travel. Of course, if events prove that this industrial impasse cannot be broken or that a satisfactory level of achievement cannot be accomplished fast enough, we shall undoubtedly turn to government as an alternative agency . . . to prevent the waste of any large share of our capital and manpower resources.

Moreover, he maintained that government in the long run would have to honor its financial obligations, for he questioned whether public spending, supported by deficit finance, could provide "economic perpetual motion." He held that "the ability of the economy to carry its total national debt must be related to the ability of productive enterprise to produce income which can be detoured through the tax channel without impairing other relationships."

He saw "emerging a greater degree of agreement among economists if not among the general public, as to the relation of tax redistributions of income to the creative and manipulative efforts of private administrators of our economic process." He also thought the idea was growing that government "could help redress maladjustment in the economic process so as to have fundamentally beneficial results without involving the government in national ownership of resources or facilities or in operative functions." He also inclined to agree with the "median position" enunciated by Robert Nathan that "total spending is the key to prosperity," but that government spending should be looked to only "as a last resort."[5] His own position, he said, "would be at the side of this median band which would probably be defined as 'rightist'; where resort to such actions was taken most seldom and limited most rigorously to disbursing and not to operating activities."[6]

In another paper prepared about this same time, Nourse dealt with "The Place of Taxation in a Healthy Economic System."[7] He did not align himself with the "tax haters" who took as their slogan, "The power to tax is the power to destroy," or with the "tax lovers" who declared, "The power to tax is the power to create." He thought a more adequate view of the economic character of the taxation process might be summed up in a new slogan: "The power to tax is the power to effect adjustments in the functioning of our economy."

He believed it likely that tax collection and government spending would increase, for there "are certain types of consumption which can be provided and enjoyed only, or most efficiently, on a community, state, or national basis." He thought that these "can best be provided or provided only through the tax machinery," and that "a part of the increased national productivity which we have within our grasp is not likely to be realized after the war unless it takes the form of expanding government spending and more government jobs." Nourse then examined several areas where government spending could be beneficial, such as in public provision for recreation facilities, forms of medical care and particularly hospitalization, and programs for better nutrition. He believed that the government should place its emphasis on raising consumptive standards rather than on job-giving, and said: "If the government starts out with a sense of responsibility for jobs as such, we are almost certain to end up with grandiose public works of dubious productive value or of mere 'busy-work' of which leaf-raking is the classic example." He ended this paper by saying: "That government is best which governs most discriminatingly; not meddling in the operative arrangements of its individual citizens but creating the broad conditions of public economic health."

Helping Business Define Its Post-War Role

Nourse realized that he would need to have the support of business leaders on his low-price policy views if they were to become effective. He therefore welcomed an invitation to present a paper on "What Should Be the Post-War Price Policy of Industry?" to the Economic Advisory Committee of the National Association of Manufacturers in the summer of 1944. This occasion gave him an opportunity to follow up on the views he had expressed in *Price Making in a Democracy* and bring them into focus on the looming problem of post-war reconversion. He answered the question posed in the title of his paper by saying: "A low-price policy." He stated that this conclusion was based on four almost axiomatic propositions:

> (1) That we cannot have sustained high volume of operations except at prices as low as actual costs at full utilization of resources permit; (2) that without this high-volume production we cannot have high-level employment; (3) that if high-level employment is not achieved by business, *political* forces will demand prompt and extensive resort to public spending in whatever amount is conceived to be necessary to prevent unemployment; (4) that this public works program would entail deficit spending which, in the face of a 250 billion dollar national debt, would demoralize private venture capitalism and progessively and rapidly bring about government operation—not mere control—of business.

In the discussion which followed the elaboration of his position, he vigorously defended the practicality of low-price policy. He particularly desired to make clear that sound price policy was not a matter of altruism or of social value. "I start from the premise," he said, "that businessmen are in business to make money—as much money as they can. The whole problem I am trying to face is: What are the requirements of a private enterprise system which will enable businessmen *in the long run* to make for themselves the largest amount of profit by doing the largest business on behalf of the public?"

A few months later, Nourse participated in a number of West Coast Executive Conferences on Public Relations sponsored by the National Association of Manufacturers. They were primarily concerned with the anticipated problems of transition from war to peacetime conditions, and Nourse used as his subject, "Prices and Jobs." He spoke as a representative of the Brookings Institution without compensation, for he wished to maintain his "scientific objectivity" as an independent economist.

In opening his talks, he defined effective public relations as "doing a good job and getting credit for it." He held that only by doing a good job for the country as a whole could "individual companies prosper fully and steadily." He liked this definition, for it implied "an engineering or professional attitude toward the work of business managers rather than conceiving business as a sharp game of making big individual profits in the short run."

It was his general thesis that the coming of peace would present a great challenge to business leaders, in that business would be left in private hands "only if it demonstrated its ability to produce" a high standard of living in the post-war years. He said: "What I am concerned in showing is that there is no inherent reason why private business should not provide ample employment opportunities on wage and price bases that will support a standard of living so high that there will be a popular demand to continue that system of economic life rather than calling upon government responsibility and state control."

In these talks, Nourse examined the views of those who favored reliance on government for economic prosperity as a background for espousing his views on the desirability of low-price policy as presented in his book, *Price Making in a Democracy*. He said: "We must fit the price situation to the income situation so that a full-scale product can be currently bought, or else products will pile up and unemployment will again appear." He also said: "*Pricing for full-scale production must be an inseparable part of planning for full-scale production.*"

He concluded his talks by saying: "The gist of my whole speech can be stated very briefly: You can't beat the law of supply and demand.... Unless prices are low enough to move the whole product promptly into consumptive channels, jobs decline and the whole system of private enterprise is in trouble."

Business leaders liked Nourse's frankly expressed views, and they admired his competence and intellectual integrity. They felt that he was one "academic" economist who understood their problems and who was willing to go to bat for them as long as they were reasonable in their demands. They recognized his sincere desire to help them make the private enterprise system work without the necessity of government control or operation.

Nourse at this time was very favorably impressed with the progressive thinking on problems of post-war adjustment being displayed by the newly formed Committee for Economic Development and like organizations. It is of interest that he and Keynes differed on the importance of such groups at a small private dinner held at the home of Leo Pasvolsky sometime in 1944. The only guests were Mr. and Mrs. Herman Feis, Dr. and Mrs. Nourse, and Lord and Lady Keynes. The table was so arranged that Nourse and Keynes faced each other. As Nourse recalled the incident, Keynes was giving his view quite freely on what should be done on the whole broad problem of national economic adjustment, when Nourse managed to break into the discussion and ask: "Lord Keynes, is there nothing in England today like our Committee for Economic Development?" Keynes replied: "What's that?" After Nourse had explained how the CED had been set up by Paul Hoffman, Eugene Meyer, and other leading businessmen to help private enterprise meet problems of management and investment contemplated with the end of the war, Keynes disposed of the question by saying: "Oh yes, there are a few old Colonel Blimps that talk about that kind of thing in England." This exchange reflects the divergent economic approaches of Nourse and Keynes. While Nourse looked upon economics as an institutionalist and social scientist, Keynes saw things primarily as a classical economist. As Nourse later said: "American economists divide into two classes: the Keynes disciples and the economists who can take him or leave him." While Nourse recognized Keynes' great analytical abilities, he admitted being in the latter group.[8]

Business Leadership in the Large Corporation

While he was writing *Price Making in a Democracy*, Nourse looked forward to the completion of a companion volume by Dr. Aaron Robert Gordon. This book—*Business Leadership in the Large Corporation*—was started in 1939, but because of Gordon's war service with the Office of Price Administration, it could not be completed until January, 1945. Nourse explained how his book came to be published and its relationship to his price policy studies in a long prefatory note for this volume:

> Some five years ago I had become aware of the interest that Professor Gordon was taking in the structure of the large business corporation in relation to its economic functioning. . . . This line of research seemed to me so definitely complementary to my own studies on the content of corporate management—particularly price studies—that I undertook to bring him to Brookings so he might complete his analysis of the large corporation as it affects the role of business leadership.[9]

Nourse thought that Gordon made a real contribution in his examination of the practical behavior of businessmen. He held that "institutional" economists should not neglect "what may be called the private institutions of business," including "the company structures, practices, and policies that businessmen have themselves built up and operate within the law set out on statute books and in administrative rulings." He maintained that

> it is a merit of the author's treatment that he seeks to think through with the business man the implications of present ways of corporate life or the influence they have on the economic performance of private business managers. His treatment implies a belief that the business mechanism is constructed by business men, according to designs, whose various features must be considered with as much care and professional competence as the design of a motor or the layout of an assembly line. Only so can we have progressive engineering rather than mere Topsy growth.

Nourse noted that the book, as a "personalized, volitional, or psychological analysis of the economic process," represented a third type of economic research, complementing the "theoretical" and the "institutional." He particularly liked the concluding chapter on "The Professionalization of Business Leadership," which was highly congenial with his own views. Here Gordon said: "Efficient business leadership in the large corporation must depend on an able dynamic chief executive, supported by a competent staff adequately organized and directed."

"Business Executives as Professional Men"

While Gordon was completing his book, Nourse was starting a sequel to *Price Making in a Democracy* to be called "Business Executives as Professional Men." His primary object was to determine the extent to which business management could be professionalized and made more responsible for the direction of our economic life. He saw as his primary audience businessmen and officials of labor unions, but he hoped that the book would be of value to professors and students of business and economics, and also to general readers interested in current economic evolution. In a project statement for the book, dated April 30, 1945, he set forth his thinking on what he was trying to accomplish:

> In *Price Making in a Democracy* I attempted to outline the *content* of a sound industrial management, with maximum scope for private enterprise. R. A. Gordon, in his companion volume, *Business Leadership in the Large Corporation*, outlined the *structure* through which administrative control is exercised in our industrial society. He showed how the entrepreneur in the old textbook sense has virtually disappeared from "big business" and been replaced by a salaried managerial hierarchy. . . . But structure and content do not complete the story. The human factor or the personality of business remains to be considered. This is the task I propose for myself in the forthcoming book. Here the approach is in terms of personnel—the members of the managerial hierarchy, their background, outlook, formal training, and vocational organizations, as these determine or influence the way in which these persons will discharge their administrative functions. Thus we

round out a trilogy on modern industrialism in terms of (1) structure or organization, (2) content or economic philosophy, and (3) administrative personnel or the human agent.

I start from the premise that since corporation officials and union executives are significant directive agents, their economic philosophies and personal motives, operating through the administrative structures of business, influence the economic process in important—sometimes beneficial, sometimes disastrous—ways, though of course they operate within the broad limits set by fundamental economic forces. I therefore undertake in this book to examine a little the concepts of their own which these leaders entertain; the education, training, and research processes by which their personal characters and official conduct are shaped; and the methods of recruitment, advancement, and survival, to determine what sort of a directive corps they now make or are likely to become in the years just ahead.

As was his practice, he submitted draft chapters to qualified persons to obtain their suggestions and criticisms. Although several of these readers questioned his hypothesis that business administration could be developed as a profession, they generally agreed that the book was needed and could serve a constructive educational purpose.[10] He had completed about half of the book in draft form by July, 1946, when he was called by President Truman to head the first Council of Economic Advisers.

Leadership in Social Science

His chairmanship of the Social Science Research Council during the years 1942-1945 required much of Nourse's attention, for the war gave unprecedented recognition to the contributions that all kinds of scientists could make in the war effort. The Social Science Research Council was naturally concerned with the full utilization of social scientists in programs relating to the war and did everything within its power to help the government find the personnel that was needed. During this period the Council set up a committee on the federal government's relationship to research with public funds, and its report for 1944-1945 declared: "Probably no other single activity of the Council during the past year is of immediately equal significance." The Council was especially interested in how social science work could be made most fruitful in the post-war period through training programs.

As an outgrowth of the tremendous increase in all kinds of research activity during the war, legislation to establish a national research foundation to help promote research with federal assistance was proposed in 1945. The primary leaders of this movement were natural scientists who thought of scientific research in terms of their own fields of special interest. This caused Nourse and his associates in the Social Science Research Council to be concerned that social sciences be given full recognition under any program set up by the federal government to foster and encourage fundamental scientific research.[11]

In the hearings on science legislation (S 1292 and related bills) held on October 29, 1945, Nourse, in behalf of the Council, presented the case for recognition of the social sciences in any federal program designed to encourage scientific research. In his statement, Nourse emphasized the inherent unity of science, saying: "The basic problem of all science is to get fuller and more accurate knowledge as to the materials to be found and the forces which operate in the world, in order that they may be so controlled and utilized that mankind may have a safer and more satisfying existence." He then said:

> A mere technical or laboratory knowledge of our physical world and of biologic life does not of itself set us any considerable distance toward that goal [for] it is only as we discover effective ways of imparting that knowledge to human beings and organizing them into social institutions such as the political state, the economic agencies of business, the church, and other non-profit agencies of specialist and cultural life that we can make orderly and sustained progress toward the goals of civilized life.

Nourse maintained that formal divisions between natural, biologic, and social sciences were arbitrary and should have no place in the thinking of the national legislature when it attacks the problem of utilizing the resources of science as fully as possible "to make the nation strong." He asserted that "every problem of utilizing the resources of nature for man's safety and material satisfaction has two halves—one technological, the other economic." Many years later, in discussing this statement with me, he said that if he were to give this talk again, he would say "has three halves," so as to include the word "social."

In his testimony, Nourse pointed out how social science had been utilized effectively during the war and how it would be increasingly needed to solve the long-run problems of creating a peaceful society and peaceful world. He also stressed that the proposed legislation did not present a new departure in governmental policy and practice, for it merely proposed "to extend and more adequately subsidize the scientific work of the federal government." He supported this view by citing the long experience of the government in assisting research work in agricultural economics, rural sociology, and rural government.

While social science research was not provided for when the National Research Foundation was established in 1950, it was eventually recognized by later legislation. Nourse's thinking helped lay a foundation for this development.

Expansion of Cooperative Activities

Nourse maintained his interest in agricultural economics and cooperative enterprise during the war. He followed closely the efforts of the Farm Credit Administration to develop a cooperative credit system for agriculture, and in 1943 he arranged for Earl Butz, then a young economist at Purdue University, to evaluate the 10 years' experience of the Production Credit System. As Nourse indicated in the preface of the resulting book, *The Production Credit System for Agriculture* (1944), this system represented a "considerable departure from familiar concepts of the relation of private business and government," which called for determination "of what public policy we should adopt with reference to this new sphere of intertwined public and private activity."

During the war, the American Historical Association undertook to publish a series of pamphlets for use by the army in G. I. roundtables, and Nourse assumed responsibility for developing one on cooperative enterprise. He called on me to prepare it, and this resulted in the G. I. pamphlet *Why Co-ops*, published in 1945. I did this job quite independently of Nourse, but he liked what I did and made but few suggestions for its improvement. Growing out of our renewed relationship, Nourse invited me to undertake a study of the rapidly growing cooperative purchasing movement. To do this, I arranged for leaves of absence from the Farm Credit Administration for periods in 1945 and 1946. On this project I worked out with him a plan for the study, but he gave me a free hand as I proceeded—and as I completed draft chapters, he gave me suggestions for their improvement. I dug deeper than I had intended on historical origins, but Nourse understood what I was attempting and gave me his complete encouragement.[12]

While working closely with me on my cooperative purchasing book, Nourse invited his former Iowa State cooperative colleague, Frank Robotka, to spend some time with the Brookings Institution, making a study on the theory of agricultural cooperation. Thus in 1945 and 1946, the Brookings Institution was a hub of research activity in the field of cooperative enterprise.

During the war, the American Institute of Cooperation was forced by travel restrictions to suspend its annual sessions. When in 1944 a sentiment formed for the reinvigoration of the Institute under the leadership of Dr. Raymond W. Miller, Nourse actively aided Miller in getting the AIC reestablished on a much stronger basis so as to provide year-round research and educational services. One of the new developments was setting up a research committee, and Nourse, as a member, took an active part in its meetings which were frequently held in his Brookings Institution office.

For the AIC's volume, *American Cooperation, 1942-1945*, which was prepared to record cooperative developments during the war years, Nourse contributed a challenging article on "The Place of Cooperatives in Our National Economy." In this he said: "My recent studies in the realm of industrial structure and practice tend to strengthen my belief in the soundness of the cooperative form and to enlarge my estimate of the economic area to which it may effectively be applied." He stressed two points: (1) *"The place in the nation's business logically marked out for the agricultural cooperative is primarily that of 'pilot plant' and 'yardstick' operation. Its objective is not to supersede other forms of business but to see that they are kept truly competitive."* (2) *The true place of the cooperative is that of economic architect, not commercial Napoleon.* If its practitioners grasp the distinctive economic philosophy of this business form, they will view it as a means to improve the lot of both farmer and consumer by improving the efficiency of the economic machine, not by using group force to exact the largest possible return for a special interest."

It was his view that

> the success of the cooperative movement is to be judged more by the quality of its performance than by the size of its membership or volume of its operations. When a cooperative has to maintain its position by constant and intensive evangelicism, sentimental appeals to membership, or governmental favors and special aid, the presumption is justified that it has overgrown or outlived its true economic need and value. Cooperation is hard headed business, not an ideological crusade.
>
> Cooperation must make constructive contributions to the health of the economic system consistent with its basic philosophy of bringing equitable benefits to the worker and the consumer.

When the AIC resumed its annual sessions in August, 1946, at Purdue University, Nourse gave the keynote address, "From Dogma to Science in Cooperative Thinking." He held that cooperative leaders should take a forward scientific look at the possibilities of cooperative enterprise and not be content to follow the guiding principles that had well served cooperatives in the past.

He urged cooperative leaders to "constantly remember that economic evolution has proceeded a full century from the time at which the pioneers of Rochdale lived and wrought. In this situation, we must analyze business needs, design economic devices and appraise social purposes with as much originality and vigor as they did in their day." He maintained that this session of the AIC should signalize a definite rebirth of the cooperative movement. This new Institute should be not merely an educational or propaganda body, disseminating forms of organization and practices already worked out and conventionalized. Nor should it be content merely to serve as a commercial convention in which we can generate enthusiasm and learn of each other's operating tricks or organizational gadgets.

It should, if it is to take its place in the march of the modern scientific world, become a carefully planned and adequately financed research organization, probing more deeply into the still unfathomed mysteries of what "equitable association" of farmers means in both the political and the economic sense, not alone to their own members but to the whole society of which they are a part and from which in the long run they can expect economic reward only in proportion as they render economic service.

Nourse never lost his deep interest in cooperative enterprise, regardless of how busy he was on other matters.

Is Planning the Road to Serfdom?

With the end of the war in sight, the problem of planning the post-war adjustment assumed increasing importance. Many believed that strong government measures would be required to meet the transition to peacetime conditions, while others feared that such government intervention would impair, if not destroy, the private enterprise system. While this debate was growing in intensity, Frederich A. Hayek, a highly respected classical economist, intellectually assaulted the conception of government planning in a widely read book, *The Road to Serfdom*.[13] It was Hayek's conviction, supported by his experience in Austria under Hitler, that economic planning through government led directly to fascism or Nazism.

Nourse found this book so challenging and significant that he prepared a full review of it for the *Journal of Farm Economics* (May, 1945). In his review he said:

> The reviewer, as a notorious defender of private enterprise and one who himself has viewed with alarm some of the more ambitious "action programs" and easy reliance on fiscal policy as the means to economic security, might be expected to put himself in full support of Professor Hayek's argument. On the contrary, the book seems to me to be seriously lacking in realistic recognition of many grades of social control that in fact conserve individual freedom. I find difficulty also in accepting as valid his standard of economic purity from which a society must not at all depart if it is to keep from being drawn into the whirlpool of socialism-made-synonymous-with-totalitarianism. Hayek's norm is extreme economic individualism in the *milieu* of a free market operating automatically under the sway of some wholly objective and impersonal law of competition.
>
> It might seem unbelievable in the present day, when both technological and organizational evolution have advanced to the stage that they have,

that we should find a full throw-back to atomistic competition presented as both practicable and preeminently desirable. Yet here we find that proposition in cold and unblinking print.[14]

Although he could not agree with the book's major thesis, Nourse believed that it might "well give pause to those who have been rather actively inclined to ride 'the wave of the future' and who think that the tough problems of agriculture can be solved by the short-cut method of turning them over to the central government." He thought it would be useful "if it stimulated agricultural economists to struggle harder to demonstrate that it is possible to adjust the economic lives of farmers and of their organizations soundly—and without loss of independence—into the functioning of an advanced industrial society."

Nourse considered the questions raised by Hayek so vital that he returned to the book in a more general review article for *The Public Administration Review* (Spring, 1946), which he called "Serfdom, Utopia, and Democratic Opportunity." Here he evaluated Hayek's book, along with Herman Finer's *Road to Reaction* and Barbara Wooton's *Freedom Under Planning*. He gave this article much thought, for it served as a vehicle for expounding precisely his own balanced views on the general subject of planning.

He found all three of the books "hortatory" and "essentially idealogical in character," and he thought they clearly pointed out "the need for research into the myriad of problems the authors raise." However, he believed that none of the books provided a frame of reference for such a program of research because of one important shortcoming, namely: "Not one of these authors differentiates kinds of planning or distinguishes planfulness by government from scope of governmental action or contrasts these with implementation or execution of plans. One misses such a useful distinction as that which Lewis L. Lorwin makes between 'institutional planning' and 'operating planning.' "[15] Without giving Nourse's views on the strengths and shortcomings of the three books, it is of interest to see how he expressed his own views on how far the government might go in the planning field:

> My own studies lead me to believe that, under current practices of corporate risk-taking, some activating role on the part of government in the area of planning is necessary if we are to maintain reasonably full utilization of the nation's productive resources. This, however, does not mean "nationalization" of industry or of important branches of industry— or permanent retention in government hands of anything like the whole area of enterprise which it might find it necessary to enter for purposes of operative demonstration or initial underwriting.

It is obvious from this statement that Nourse was becoming more tolerant toward government intervention, should this be necessary to facilitate the functioning of private enterprise.

Inception of the Employment Act of 1946

Nourse was so busy on his various commitments that he took only a general interest in the legislative development of the Employment Act of 1946. However, in the initial stage of this legislation, he was called upon for testimony by Senator James E. Murray, Chairman of the War Contracts Subcommittee of the Senate Committee on Military Affairs.[16] A concern of this subcommittee was the development of "legislation to help achieve full employment after the war."

In his testimony on May 3, 1944, Nourse was asked to present his views "on the basic economic issues involved in achieving full employment in the transition and post-war period." In response, he maintained that the basic question to be answered was: "What are the fundamental operative principles according to which a system of private capitalism can be continued in successful operation in a democratic country?" He drew on his book, *Price Making in a Democracy*, to support his position that there was nothing inherently wrong with the private enterprise system if properly conceived, and he held that it was important that the war economy be liquidated as rapidly as possible so that peace activity could be resumed.

Senator Murray requested Nourse's views on whether a top planning board was needed to help in post-war adjustment. In reply, Nourse said: "Yes, I think that such a board should primarily be a broad policy board which should not attempt itself to conduct the process in any detail or to plan the details of execution." *Murray*: "But it should lay down the policies?" *Nourse*: "Absolutely." *Murray*: "Quite clearly and distinctly, and that Congress should control that?" *Nourse*: "Yes." *Murray*: "And should it lay down the policies to direct the reconversion activities?" *Nourse*: "I think the early and clear enunciation of those policies would be one of the most constructive forces we can have." *Murray*: "Thank you for your very able statement, Dr. Nourse."

Nourse was inclined to think that this testimony had a decisive influence on his appointment as Chairman of the Council of Economics Advisers. This opinion was based on a letter from Senator Murray (July 31, 1946) congratulating him on his appointment, in which he said: "I recollect your splendid testimony on post-war problems before my Military Affairs Subcommittee back in the spring of 1944. . . . In fact, before the Banking and Currency Committee met to consider your nomination, I showed your testimony to the Chairman of the Committee and pointed out that you had helped develop the philosophy which was finally embodied in the Employment Act of 1946."[17]

In the fall of 1944, there was great popular interest in "full employment" legislation to protect against the danger of massive unemployment following the war, and both President Roosevelt and Thomas E. Dewey endorsed the idea in their presidential campaigns. The idea took tangible form on January 22, 1945, when Senator Murray introduced the Full Employment Bill (S 380). This measure reflected the views of John Maynard Keynes and Alvin Hansen on how unemployment could be largely controlled, if not eliminated, by massive government spending.[18]

Nourse questioned the logic expressed in the Full Employment Bill, for he was skeptical of the ability of government to automatically guarantee full employment. When *Harper's Magazine* in February published an article with the title, "Shall We Guarantee Full Employment?" by Stanley Lebergott, one of the proponents of the bill, Nourse felt compelled to prepare an article in reply which he entitled, "Can We Guarantee Full Employment?" This was not accepted by *Harper's*, so he dropped the matter. It is significant that in this unpublished article he termed the proposed legislation "statistically fantastic and economically naive," and said: "If business is to be kept healthy and active . . . we must not rely upon government manipulation of a 'national production and employment budget.'"[19]

With the drastic modification of the Full Employment Bill later in the year to make it acceptable to the business community, he was more hopeful of its possible usefulness, but his interest was more passive than active. We will defer to Chapter X discussion of the provisions of the Employment Act of 1946, which became law in February, 1946, and the role assigned the Council of Economic Advisers in carrying out its intent.

The Call to the Council of Economic Advisers

In July, 1946, Nourse was busily engaged in his various responsibilities at the Brookings Institution, when he was tapped by President Truman to be Chairman of the new Council of Economic Advisers under the Employment Act of 1946. It was a position he could not turn down, for he believed that his training, experience, and interests uniquely qualified him for this post. Moreover, as a long-time member of the economics fraternity, he felt obligated to undertake this assignment, which recognized the growing significance of economic science in our national life.[20] As he explained many years later, he was ready for this great responsibility.

The completion of "Business Executives as Professional Men" would be the end of my Brookings career, and it was problematical what I would do after that. The appointment to the Council gave me an opportunity to go on the inside of government, which I had studied and worked with from the outside, and was a new development for which I was ready at the time. I had grown with the process of the times to the stage where I was still objectively critical, and yet open-mindedly responsive, to these new proposals, dealing in new ways with new situations. So I think this change was quite opportune.[21]

In Chapter X we will see how Nourse terminated his work with the Brookings Institution and transferred immediately all of his energies and abilities to his new position. It was to open up a new life for him.

Part Two

FIRST CHAIRMAN, COUNCIL OF ECONOMIC ADVISERS (1946-1949)

Chapter X

LAYING THE FOUNDATION
(1946-1947)[1]

In July, 1946, Nourse was busily engaged in writing the book which he tentatively called "Business Executives as Professional Men." It was designed to round out his studies in price-making and business organization. He was then 63 and he looked forward to retirement from the Brookings Institution at 65. He was giving little thought to what he would do next.

Then, as he expressed it, "lightning struck." Late Wednesday evening, July 24, he received a telephone call from his friend Charles Ross, press secretary for President Truman, enquiring whether he would consider serving as Chairman of the Council of Economic Advisers being set up under the provisions of the Employment Act of 1946. The President had not been able to find a suitable man for this important post, and he was anxious to get the Council under way so that it could provide information for the first economic report of the president called for in January, 1947.

Nourse realized that the new position would completely change his life, and he doubted whether he should allow himself to become involved. However, he could not refuse to examine the matter, so he agreed to see the president at the White House the following morning. The possibilities of the position as outlined by the president intrigued him, but he asked for time to consider the problems involved, and this was agreeable with President Truman.

In the next few days, Nourse carefully examined the Employment Act and especially the provisions relating to the duties assigned the Council of Economic Advisers. He also got assurances from agricultural and business leaders that they would welcome his acceptance of the job. From what he could learn, he assumed that he would be able to work harmoniously with the other two members of the Council who had already been selected—Leon H. Keyserling and John D. Clark. He realized that the

Council was set up as a triumvirate with no special authority being vested in the chairman, but as he had always been able to work with others, he gave this problem little concern. Anyway, this was a matter beyond his control.

While he realized that the Employment Act contained great possibilities for public service, he recognized that it could be badly interpreted and gravely misused. He wondered whether he was fitted by temperament and background for the rough and tumble of public life. On the other hand, he felt that this was a "professional opportunity that should not go by default." He finally made up his mind on Sunday at his summer place on the Virginia side of the Potomac River. As he later recalled:

> I remember very definitely going out that Sunday afternoon and paddling around in the river and then lying on one of the outcroppings of rock, looking up at the blue sky and considering whether I would take on the difficulties of this job and allow my professional career to be diverted in this manner. I finally concluded that this was a challenge to the profession, and with my conviction about the role of the economist in public service, I couldn't dodge it, although my preference would clearly have been to say 'No'.[2]

So he decided to set forth his understanding of the position and the conditions under which he would accept it in a letter which he sent to the president the next morning. He admitted later that this letter was somewhat "bumptious," but he felt that he must honestly set forth his views. If the president saw the job as he did—fine. If not, he would not be interested in it. As Nourse later said: "These were my convictions and there was a good deal of 'take it or leave it' in my attitude. I was, by no means, eager to drop the line of economic investigation that had run back through my years of Brookings connection and I was not elated."

In his letter to the president (July 29, 1946), he said:

> Last week you did me the honor of inviting me to accept your appointment as Chairman of the Council of Economic Advisers created under the Employment Act of 1946. To accept this appointment would completely disrupt the program of professional work which I had laid out for myself for the coming years. However, the importance of the task you propose for me and the possibilities which it offers of rendering public service are so great that I feel I cannot do otherwise than accept.
>
> As you remarked when I talked with you last week, the Act marks a distinct new step in the history of this country. It will be of the utmost importance that the first Council serving under it shall understand its task so wisely and organize its activities so skillfully that all members of the government and of the public alike shall be impressed with the fact that this is a well-conceived agency of democratic government and a great aid to the promotion of sustained prosperity and economic stability.

LAYING THE FOUNDATION

After stating his conception of what could properly be expected of the Council, he wrapped up his ideas in the following paragraph:

> All this adds up to saying that the Council of Economic Advisers is conceived as a scientific agency of the Federal Government. *Its prime function is to bring the best available methods of social science to the service of the Chief Executive and of the Congress in formulating national policy from year to year and from month to month. There is no occasion for the Council to become involved in any way in the advocacy of particular measures or in the rival beliefs and struggles of the different economic and political interest groups.* It should give a clearer and more comprehensive picture than we have ever had as to the economic state of the nation, as to the factors which are tending to retard prosperity, and as to the probable effect of the various remedial measures which may be under consideration by the Executive or the Congress. [Emphasis added.]

He then concluded:

> If this statement correctly interprets the Act and reflects your hopes and purposes for the Council, I feel that the position you offer me is one of unparalleled opportunity as well as responsibility. To it, if my nomination is confirmed by the Senate, I shall give my most loyal service [EPS, pp. 106-107].

Two days later, on July 31, the president announced the appointment of Nourse as Chairman of the Council and said in a note to him: "I appreciate very much your letter of the 29th. . . . I am looking forward to real results from this set-up." On the morning of August 9, Nourse and his two fellow Council members took the oath of office in front of the president's desk. After the ceremony, the president gave the Council its "sailing orders." "Now you gentleman, just keep this national income up to 200 billion dollars, and we'll be all right" (EPS, p. 109).

Nourse had little time to terminate his work with the Brookings Institution. His main concern was disposition of his half-finished book on business executives as professional men. He briefly considered publication of the part he had completed, but he decided that this might cause embarrassment in his new position. So he set the manuscript aside and never returned to it. I once remarked to him that he must have found it difficult to give up work on a book on which he had spent so much time and he replied: "The train went by."

The Nature of the Employment Act of 1946

If we are to understand Nourse's life during the next 3½ years we must know how the Employment Act of 1946, which set up the Council of Economic Advisers, came to be passed and what it undertook to accomplish. As noted in Chapter IX, there was a widespread belief during

World War II that steps should be taken to avoid a serious post-war depression with heavy unemployment. To meet this problem, Senator James E. Murray of Montana (with Senators Robert Wagner of New York, Elmer Thomas of Utah, and Joseph C. O'Mahoney of Wyoming) had introduced in the Senate on January 22, 1945, the Full Employment Bill (S 380) which was to be cited as the "Full Employment Act of 1945." This carefully designed bill reflected the great interest in economic planning that had emerged during the New Deal and World War II years, and especially the compensatory spending views of John Maynard Keynes (as popularized by Alvin Hansen) which had become gospel to many American economists and liberal leaders. It proposed a rather mechanical procedure of federal spending to maintain full employment.

To understand the implications and significance of the Employment Act of 1946 we must first examine in some detail the Full Employment Bill from which it evolved. As few readers have access to the original Full Employment Bill, it is essential to quote extensive passages from the bill itself. The Full Employment Bill was markedly different from the Employment Act of 1946, which is sometimes erroneously referred to as "the full employment act."[3]

The stated purpose of the Full Employment Bill was "to establish a national policy and program for *assuring continuing full employment* in a free competitive economy, through the concerted efforts of industry, agriculture, labor, State and Local governments, and the Federal Government." (Emphasis added.)

The intent of the bill was presented in Section 2, which declared that:

    (a) It is the policy of the United States to foster free competitive enterprise and the investment of private capital in trade and commerce and in the development of resources of the United States;

    (b) *All Americans able to work and seeking work have the right to useful, remunerative, regular, and full-time employment, and it is the policy of the United States to assure the existence at all times of sufficient employment opportunities to enable all Americans who have finished their schooling and who do not have full-time housekeeping responsibilities freely to exercise this right.* [Emphasis added.]

    (c) [This section provided that to promote the general welfare of the nation in specified ways,] it is essential that continuing full employment be maintained in the United States;

    (d) In order to assist industry, agriculture, labor and State and Local governments in achieving continuing full employment, it is the responsibility of the Federal Government to pursue such consistent and openly arrived at economic policies and programs as will stimulate and encourage the highest feasible levels of employment opportunities through private and other non-Federal investment and expenditure;

    (e) *To the extent that continuing full employment cannot otherwise be achieved, it is the further responsibility of the Federal Government to provide such volume of Federal investment and expenditure as may be needed to assure continuing full employment;* [Emphasis added.]

(f) Such investment and expenditure by the Federal Government shall be designed to contribute to the national wealth and well-being, and to stimulate increased employment opportunities by private enterprise.

The heart of the measure was Section 3, which provided for "The National Production and Employment Budget."

> [Section 3 (a) declared:] The President shall transmit to Congress at the beginning of each regular session the National Production and Employment Budget (hereinafter referred to as the "National Budget"), which shall set forth in summary and detail, for the ensuing fiscal year or such longer period as the President may deem appropriate: (1) the estimated size of the labor force . . . (2) the estimated aggregate volume of investment and expenditure . . . as will be necessary to provide employment opportunities for such labor force. [Such dollar volume was to be] hereinafter referred to as the "full employment volume of production"; (3) the estimated aggregate volume of prospective investment and expenditures. . . .
>
> (b) [This paragraph provided that when] prospective investment and expenditure for any fiscal year or other period as set forth in the National Budget . . . is less than the estimated aggregate volume of investment and expenditure required to assure a full employment volume of production . . . it would be regarded as a prospective deficiency in the National Budget. [The president was required to set forth in the National Budget] *a general program for encouraging . . . increased non-Federal investment and expenditure . . . as will prevent such deficiency to the greatest possible extent.* [He was also to include such recommendations for legislation] . . . as he may deem necessary or desirable. . . . [Emphasis added.]
>
> (c) *To the extent, if any, that such increased non-Federal investment and expenditure as may be expected to result from actions taken under the program set forth in accordance with subsection (b) of this section are deemed insufficient to provide a full employment volume of production, the President shall transmit a general program for such Federal investment and expenditure as will be sufficient to bring the aggregate volume of investment and expenditure by private business, consumers, State and local government, and the Federal government, up to the level required to assure a full employment volume of production.* . . . [Emphasis added.]

Section 4 (a) provided for the preparation of the National Budget "in the Executive Office of the President under the general direction and supervision of the President, and in consultation with the members of his Cabinet and other heads of departments and establishments."

Section 4 (c) gave the president authority to "establish such advisory boards or committees composed of representatives of industry, agriculture, labor, State and local governments, and others, as he may deem advisable for the purpose of advising and consulting on methods of achieving the objectives of this Act."

Section 5 provided for the establishment of a Joint Committee on the National Budget "to be composed of the chairmen and ranking minority members of the Senate Committees on Appropriations, Banking and Currency, Education and Labor, and Finance, and seven additional Members of the Senate to be appointed by the President of the Senate; and the chairmen and ranking minority members of the House Committees on Appropriations, Banking and Currency, Labor, and Ways and Means, and seven additional Members of the House of Representatives. The party representation of the Joint Committee shall reflect the relative membership of the majority and minority parties in the Senate and the House of Representatives." This committee was to select a chairman and a vice-chairman from among its members.

It was to be the function of the Joint Committee "to make a study of the National Budget transmitted to Congress by the President . . . [and] to report to the Senate and the House of Representatives, not later than March 1 of each year, its findings and recommendations with respect to the National Budget, together with a joint resolution setting forth for the ensuing fiscal year a general policy with respect to such National Budget to serve as a guide to the several committees of Congress dealing with legislation relating to each National Budget."

In looking back on the proposed full employment bill, it seems incredibly naive from the standpoint of practical politics and economic realities. It assumed that a national budget for full employment could be devised and put into effect with reasonable promptness and that Congress would lay down like a lamb in working with the president. From the time of its introduction it was obvious that the full employment bill would meet with stern resistance from business groups and economic and political realists. The country was not then ready for such a drastic innovation in government economic organization. Later students of the full employment bill have generally agreed that it was fortunate that the proposed act was made more flexible to meet the needs of the country, for if enacted it would have been a disastrous failure, and a good idea might have been largely lost. As Robert Lekachman has said: "Whether this mechanism could ever have worked is an open question. Political responsibility was shared between a President responsible for the forecasts and program and a Congress charged with making its own analyses and legislative proposals. Nor did any possible sanction ensure congressional adherence to the time table written into the measure."[4]

It is not surprising that the introduction of the Full Employment Bill marked the beginning of an intense political struggle which was to continue until in metamorphosed form it was enacted by Congress on February 20, 1946, as the Employment Act. The absorbing story of how the Full Employment Bill of 1945 evolved to become the Employment Act of 1946 has been well told by Stephen Kemp Bailey in his informative book, *Congress Makes a Law: The Story Behind the Employment Act of 1946* (New York: Columbia University Press, 1950). It was a contest of persons and principles, of different conceptions on the role of government, and of interpretations on what was feasible or impossible of attainment.

The Full Employment Bill did not come to a vote in the Senate until it had been carefully revised and extensive hearings had been held. It was not until September 28, 1945, that the bill in amended form was passed by a vote of 71 to 10. In the House of Representatives, the bill was introduced on February 15, 1945, by Congressman Wright Patman. After hearings which began in September, it was replaced by a substitute bill retitled the Employment and Production Act of 1946, which was passed by the House on December 14, 1945, by a vote of 259 to 126. The substitute measure eliminated all references to full employment and the National Production and Employment Budget. Instead it provided for the promotion of maximum employment and an Economic Report from the president, along with a Council of Economic Advisers to assist the president in preparing the Economic Report and to perform other advisory functions. The Joint Committee on the National Budget became the Joint Committee on the Economic Report. It was obvious that it would be difficult to harmonize the Senate and House bills through conference, but this proved possible. The Senate bill sponsors and conferees saw that the House version was better than nothing, and on February 14, they largely accepted the House measure, which, with the president's signature, became the Employment Act of 1946 on February 20, 1946.

While the Senate conferees accepted almost intact the provisions of the House bill for a Council of Economic Advisers, it is significant that one clause was deleted that would have weakened the intimate relations of the Council with the president. This clause read as follows: "The President is requested to make available to the Joint Committee on the Economic Report, if it desires, the various studies, reports, and recommendations of the Council which have been submitted to the President." The Senate managers on the bill, according to Bailey, "insisted that any provision which in any way served to make ambiguous the relation of the Council to the President would be unacceptable." It was believed that the omitted clause "would enable the Joint Committee to embarrass the President in case the Council's recommendations did not jibe with the Chief Executive's. It would enable the Joint Committee to split Executive planning into two factions and play one off against the other."[5] Obviously if this clause had been accepted, it would have largely emasculated the Council of Economic Advisers as a distinctive advisory body to the president.

The employment Act of 1946 was thus a composite product. While it stemmed from the Full Employment Bill, it differed greatly from this bill as it was first introduced and amended. In his book Bailey printed the Employment Act so as to show by different forms of type the portions taken from the original bill and from the revisions of the bill made by the Senate and the House (pp. 228-232). With this background, let us examine the major features of the Employment Act of 1946. Of primary importance was its declaration of policy (Section 2) which was expressed in the following tortuous sentence:

> Section 2. The Congress hereby declares that it is the continuing policy and responsibility of the Federal Government *to use all practicable means* consistent with its needs and obligations and other essential considerations of national policy, with the assistance and cooperation of industry, agriculture, labor, and State and local governments, to coordinate and utilize all its plans, functions, and resources for the purpose of creating and maintaining, in a manner calculated to foster and promote free competitive enterprise and the general welfare, conditions under which there will be afforded *useful employment opportunities, including self-employment, for those able, willing, and seeking to work, and to promote maximum employment, production, and purchasing power.* [Emphasis added.]

The act eliminated all references to the National Production and Employment Budget which was featured in the Full Employment Bill. Instead of being required to transmit to Congress at the beginning of each regular session the "National Budget," the president was required to submit the "Economic Report." Provision for this report was made in Section 3 (a) which required it to set forth:

> (1) the levels of employment, production, and purchasing power obtaining in the United States and such levels needed to carry out the policy declared in section 2; (2) current and foreseeable trends in the levels of employment, production, and purchasing power; (3) a review of the economic program of the Federal Government and a review of economic conditions affecting employment in the United States or any considerable portion thereof during the preceding year and of their effect upon employment, production, and purchasing power; and (4) a program for carrying out the policy declared in section 2, together with such recommendations for legislation as he may deem necessary or desirable.
> (2) The President may transmit from time to time to the Congress reports supplementary to the Economic Report, each of which shall include such supplementary or revised recommendations as he may deem necessary or desirable to achieve the policy declared in section 2.
> (3) The Economic Report, and all supplementary reports transmitted under subsection (2) shall when transmitted to Congress, be referred to the joint committee created by section 5.

Of particular importance to this study of Nourse's career was Section 4, which created in the Executive Office of the president the Council of

Economic Advisers. This was an entirely new type of agency in the federal government, and it was given a strategic role in administering the Employment Act. Since it set forth the conditions under which Nourse was to function as Chairman of the Council, it is here quoted with little change:

> Section 4 (a) There is hereby created in the Executive Office of the President a Council of Economic Advisers (hereinafter called the 'Council'). The Council shall be composed of three members who shall be appointed by the President, by and with the advice and consent of the Senate, and each of whom shall be a person who, as a result of his training, experience, and attainments, is exceptionally qualified to analyze and interpret economic developments, to appraise programs and activities of the Government in the light of the policy declared in Section 2 and to formulate and recommend national economic policy to promote employment, production, and purchasing power under free competitive enterprise. Each member of the Council shall receive compensation at the rate of $15,000 per annum. The President shall designate one of the members of the Council as chairman and one as vice-chairman, who shall act as chairman in the absence of the chairman.
>
> (b) The Council is authorized to employ, and fix the compensation of, such specialists and other experts as may be necessary for the carrying out of its functions under this Act, without regard to the civil-service laws and the Classification Act of 1923, as amended, and is authorized subject to the civil-service laws, to employ such other officers and employees as may be necessary for carrying out its functions under this Act, and fix their compensation in accordance with the Classification Act of 1923, as amended.
>
> (c) It shall be the duty and function of the Council—
>
>> (1) to assist and advise the President in the preparation of the Economic Report;
>> (2) to gather timely and authoritative information concerning economic developments and economic trends, both current and prospective, to analyze and interpret such information in the light of the policy declared in section 2 for the purpose of determining whether such developments and trends are interfering, or are likely to interfere, with the achievement of such policy, and to compile and submit to the President studies relating to such developments and trends;
>> (3) to appraise the various programs and activities of the Federal Government in the light of the policy declared in section 2 for the purpose of determining the extent to which such programs and activities are contributing, and the extent to which they are not contributing, to the achievement of such policy, and to make recommendations to the President with respect thereto;
>> (4) to develop and recommend to the President national economic policies to foster and promote free competitive enterprise, to avoid economic fluctuations or to diminish the effects thereof, and to maintain employment, production, and purchasing power;
>> (5) to make and furnish such studies, reports thereon, and recommendations with respect to matters of Federal economic policy and legislation as the President may request.
>
> (d) The Council shall make an annual report to the President in December of each year.

(e) In exercising its powers, functions and duties under this Act—

(1) the Council may constitute such advisory committees and may consult with such representatives of industry, agriculture, labor, consumers, State and local governments, and other groups as it deems advisable;
(2) the Council shall, to the fullest extent possible, utilize the services, facilities, and information (including statistical information) of other Government agencies as well as of private research agencies, in order that duplication of effort and expense may be avoided.

(f) To enable the Council to exercise its powers, functions, and duties under this Act, there are authorized to be appropriated (except for the salaries of the members and the salaries of officers and employees of the Council) such sums as may be necessary. For the salaries of the members and the salaries of officers and employees of the Council, there is authorized to be appropriated not exceeding $345,000 in the aggregate for each year.

Although Section 4 set forth functions, duties, and responsibilities of the Council in some detail, nothing was said of administration of the Council except for the sentence in subsection (a), "The President shall designate one of the members of the Council as chairman and one as vice-chairman, who shall act as chairman in the absence of the chairman." It was clear from this sentence that Nourse would have to gain acceptance of his leadership as chairman through intellectual capacity and moral force.

Section 5 created the Joint Committee on the Economic Report and spelled out the important role it was to perform in administering the Employment Act. It was "to be composed of seven Members of the Senate, to be appointed by the President of the Senate, and seven Members of the House of Representatives, to be appointed by the Speaker of the House of Representatives." The party representation on the joint committee was to reflect "as nearly as may be feasible" the relative membership of the majority and minority parties in the Senate and House of Representatives. The Joint Committee was to select a chairman and a vice-chairman from among its members. In effect this would give the chairmanship to the majority party.

Section 5 (b) declared:

It shall be the function of the joint committee—
(1) to make a continuing study of matters relating to the Economic Report;
(2) to study means of coordinating programs in order to further the policy of this Act; and
(3) as a guide to the several committees of the Congress dealing with legislation relating to the Economic Report, not later than May 1 [later changed to February 1 by the Legislative Reorganization Act of 1946] of each year (beginning with the year 1947) to file a

report with the Senate and the House of Representatives containing its findings and recommendations with respect to each of the main recommendations made by the President in the Economic Report, and from time to time to make such other reports and recommendations to the Senate and House of Representatives as it deems advisable.

Of special interest was Section 5 (d), which greatly broadened the powers of the Joint Committee. It declared:

The joint committee, or any duly authorized subcommittee thereof, is authorized to hold such hearings as it deems advisable, and within the limitations of its appropriations, the joint committee is empowered to appoint and fix the compensation of such experts, consultants, technicians, and clerical and stenographic assistants, to procure such printing and binding, and to make such expenditures, as it deems necessary and advisable. . . . [T]he joint committee is authorized to utilize the services, information, and facilities of the departments and establishments of the Government, and also of private research agencies.

This authority in effect provided for a technical staff to help evaluate the Economic Report of the President and such other reports as he might make to the Joint Committee and to perform other desired functions. Section 4 (e) authorized an appropriation for each fiscal year of $50,000 "or as much thereof as may be necessary," to carry out the provisions of Section 5 to be disbursed by the Secretary of the Senate on vouchers signed by the chairman or vice-chairman of the Joint Committee.

In his memoirs, President Truman recorded a statement prepared for his use on February 20, 1946, when he signed the Employment Act and made it law. Although he did not use the statement, which was provided by Secretary of the Treasury Fred Vinson, he said that it "reflects the hope and the confidence with which I regarded this legislation." It read as follows: "Occasionally, as we pore through the pages of history, we are struck by the fact that some incident, little noted at the time, profoundly affected the whole subsequent course of events. I venture the prediction that history, some day, will so record the enactment of the Employment Act of 1946."[6]

It should be realized that when the Employment Act of 1946 became law, the threat of immediate post-war depression and unemployment was evaporating. Industry was turning rapidly from war production to meet the delayed demands of consumers for automobiles and other scarce goods, and there seemed no great urgency for putting the Employment Act into immediate effect. Moreover, in the ensuing months, President Truman's attention was absorbed by many serious domestic problems arising from the insistent demand that price controls be abolished and from the pressure of labor unions for high wages. In view of this situation, the president did not take steps to implement the Employment Act by setting up the Council of Economic Advisers until July. His delay reflected a growing public opinion that the act was of less urgent importance than when it was conceived.

Keyserling and Clark

When the Employment Act was passed, it was an untried experiment and there was widespread skepticism on how it would work in practice. It was generally agreed that its success would depend largely upon the character, competence, and compatibility of the three men selected by the president to serve as members of the Council of Economic Advisers. It is thus necessary that we have a good understanding of the two men who were to be Nourse's partners in this enterprise. Their personal and professional backgrounds throw much light on their subsequent performance as Council members and help explain the internal problems that were to confront Nourse as chairman.

Leon H. Keyserling was 38 when he was appointed Vice-Chairman of the Council.[7] Born and reared in South Carolina, he was imbued by his parents with an ambition for public service. His father was prominent in agricultural, business, and state government circles, and his mother was active in educational and civic affairs. In 1924, when he was 16, Keyserling entered Columbia University, where he majored in economics under Professor Rexford G. Tugwell. He was an excellent student and won prizes for term papers in his junior and senior years and was elected to Phi Beta Kappa. Upon graduation in 1928, he entered the Harvard Law School to find out how economics could be used in the legislative process. Obtaining his law degree in 1931, he was offered a job with a leading New York law firm, but instead he decided to take graduate work in economics at Columbia University under Tugwell and serve as his assistant. He found this relationship very stimulating, for Tugwell at that time was advising Governor Roosevelt on economic problems. One of Keyserling's various jobs was to help Tugwell prepare a book on *American Economic Life and Means of Its Improvement*.

When Tugwell, as a member of Roosevelt's brain trust, followed him to Washington in March, 1933, he soon got Keyserling a job with Jerome Frank, Legal Counsel of the Agricultural Adjustment Administration. A few weeks later, Keyserling's participation in a conference on plans being made for the National Recovery Administration attracted the attention of Senator Robert F. Wagner of New York, the leader on much of the New Deal's economic legislation, and he became Wagner's secretary and legislative assistant. During the next four years he helped Wagner draft such important measures as the National Industrial Recovery Act, the Labor Relations Act, and the U.S. Housing Act of 1937. With the passing of the Housing Act he became General Counsel of the U.S. Housing Authority, and later he served as its Deputy Administrator. In 1942, he largely drafted the Executive Order which set up the National Housing Agency to consolidate housing activities. He then became General Counsel for this agency, and he was in this position when he was called to the Council of Economic Advisers in 1946.

While engaged directly in public housing matters, Keyserling continued his close personal relations with Senator Wagner and assisted him in preparing speeches and articles and in helping him draft the Democratic Party platforms for 1936, 1940, and 1944. His close connection with Wagner gave him standing with many senators and congressmen and made him well known in government offices. His various activities in Washington from 1933 to 1946 caused one commentator to say: "During this period Keyserling had his fingers in almost every pie baking in the New Deal ovens."[8]

During World War II, Keyserling became greatly concerned with the problem of post-war unemployment. In 1944, he expressed his views on what might be done to meet this problem in an essay, "The American Economic Goal—A Practical Start Toward Full Employment," which won Second Prize and an award of $10,000 in the Pabst Brewing Company's Post War Unemployment Essay Contest.[9] He considered this essay "an opportunity to integrate economics and political theory," and he maintained that "it was really the outline for the Employment Act."

This essay is worth detailed examination, for it gives us insight into Keyserling's thinking before and after he became a member of the Council of Economic Advisers. In his introduction he said: "We need an *American Economic Policy* and an *American Economic Goal*. . . . We must start with a proposal so plain, democratic and consistent with our way of doing things that it will appeal at once to the American people, be accepted by Congress, and be supported by a vigorous President." He proposed that Congress establish an American Economic Committee

> with 3 members from the Senate and 3 members from the House of Representatives, appointed by their presiding officers, 3 members appointed by the President from his Cabinet, and 6 members appointed by the President to represent American enterprise, including 2 each from industry, agriculture, and labor. The President would designate the Chairman. The Committee would have a small technical staff. . . . Each committee member would be called before the Congress for questioning and exposition. The Committee, in addition to representation at Cabinet meetings, would make quarterly reports to the President.

The Committee would have four main tasks: (1) to recommend to Congress, *at the earliest opportunity*, an *American Economic Policy* and periodically to recommend improvements in this Policy; (2) to define and popularize an *American Economic Goal*; (3) to outline broad tasks of research and information to help achieve the *American Economic Goal* . . . (4) to evaluate governmental tools . . . to help achieve the *American Economic Goal* in accord with the greater freedom and flexibility of the *American Economic Policy*.

This Committee would not recommend specific legislation—because that would confuse it with specialized agencies, bury it in pressure politics, and distract it from its big job. This Committee would be the first practical step in an evolving democratic teamwork by American enterprise, Congress, the Departments and the President toward an *American Economic Policy* and an *American Economic Goal*."

Under the heading "An American Economic Policy," Keyserling said:

The Congress should adopt by Joint Resolution, and the President should approve, an American Economic Policy taking into account the recommendations of the *American Economic Committee*. This policy would not be a regulatory "code" of obligations, but only a framework of reference for an affirmative purposeful economic program. To emphasize its flexibility, the Resolution would *recommend* to the President (i) that he comment upon the Policy in each Annual Message, and (ii) that whenever he signed or vetoed a major law affecting economic matters, he attach a short statement relating his decision to the Policy.

Keyserling offered 10 suggestions on what might be included in a "first *American Economic Policy*." Several deserve quotation:

(2) Maximum standards of living depend upon full employment of manpower, skills, plant and resources. This is the *American Economic Goal;*

(5) Achievement of full employment is predominantly a task for the system of American enterprise, including industry, agriculture, and labor, working in a democratic environment which encourages collective bargaining by all groups and discourages restrictive monopolies by any;

(6) The Government should provide *incentives* to American enterprise to expand toward full employment, [including "tax *incentives* where workable," research and factfinding assistance, fiscal incentives in the form of insurance or guarantees, public credits, etc.];

(8) Where all these *incentives* fail to achieve full employment by American enterprise, direct Government programs represent bedrock civilized responsibility;

(9) We should continue measures to prevent exploitation, establish decent standards of work and pay, set up systematic protection against old age, accident and illness, and maintain community services—reflecting what an expanding economy can permanently afford, rather than what a stricken economy turns to for temporary relief;

(10) America should participate in international economic arrangements, to enlarge world trade and to make our world healthier, more stable, more prosperous and more peaceful. . . .

Under the heading "The American Economic Goal," Keyserling said:

> The *American Economic Committee* should define an *American Economic Goal*, reflecting America's optimum productive capacity, national income and employment, and correlating these with an "optimum standard of living within the reach of all American families." The Goal would be a continuing inventory of our needs and resources—with sub-goals reflecting major categories. This Goal would involve neither regimentation nor compulsion. Democratically conceived by a representative Committee, it would express America's voluntary sense, of its power and promise. We would not proceed toward it under the forced draft of war "quotas." We would move at whatever pace the people approve. . . .
>
> The Committee would present the Goal to the public, in a brief, popular report, signed by Committee members and approved by the President. At intervals there would be progress reports, including timely features, such as the re-employment of veterans. The President would discuss these reports in radio talks. Thus the driving force toward the Goal, focussing continually upon the performance of both enterprise and Government, would be that prime weapon of democracy, the watchful eye of an informed people. . . .

This summation gives some conception of the idealistic, economic, social, and political thinking that Keyserling was to manifest as Vice-Chairman of the Council of Economic Advisers. He did not give up faith in his conception of "An American Economic Policy" and an "American Economic Goal" to be worked out by "An American Economic Committee."

As all contestants in the Pabst Essay Contest were limited to 2,000 words, Keyserling's plan had to be tersely presented. However, contestants were privileged to submit supporting statements, and Keyserling's statement was the only one published in full as Chapter 21 in *Planning for Jobs*, a book comprised largely of selected parts from the 36,000 essays submitted for the awards. In this statement Keyserling made clear that he considered Congress the "center of gravity" in the formulation of economic policy. He also defended the concept of economic planning as long as it was done democratically. He said: "Americans should not be afraid to plan out in the open. They should be afraid only of the confusion and dissent which enable evil and designing men to plan in secret."

With his essay completed, Keyserling turned to the implementation of his full employment ideas in legislation. At this time Senator James E. Murray's War Contracts Subcommittee of the Military Affairs Committee was beginning to develop a post-war full employment bill under the direction of its staff director, Bertram Gross, and Keyserling became one of his principal advisers. Keyserling had brought Gross into government in 1938 when he employed him in the information division of the U.S. Housing Authority, and they were intimate friends.

When the original Full Employment Bill (S 380) was introduced to the Senate on January 25, 1945, Keyserling immediately gave it his support in an article in the March issue of *Survey Graphic* which was entitled, "From Patchwork to Purpose." He did not look upon the bill as the last word on the subject, but he thought it a good beginning. He said: "Regardless of vicissitudes it may face before coming to a vote, this bill is central to public concern."

Soon after this bill was introduced, it was taken over by Senator Wagner's Banking and Currency Committee, with Gross continuing as staff director on the bill. During the summer Keyserling worked closely with Gross in revising the bill, which was passed by the Senate on September 28, by a vote of 71 to 10. However, the Senate bill was not acceptable to the House, which passed, on December 14, a substitute measure (HR 2202) which provided for a Council of Economic Advisers and made other substantive changes. A compromise was finally achieved in the Employment Act of 1946, which became law on February 20. Keyserling was not dissatisfied with the final result, for he felt that the original Full Employment Bill had "got out of hand" and "provided a specific formula for government spending as employment dropped, whereas the measure finally passed—the Employment Act of 1946—got away from any specific formula and gave the government broad powers to meet anticipated post war problems."[10]

In view of Keyserling's active work on full employment legislation, it is not surprising that he was chosen by President Truman to be Vice-Chairman of the Council of Economic Advisers before the other two members were selected. He was recognized as a vigorous, hard driving, imaginative, action-minded liberal who knew intimately the machinery of federal government. Moreover, he was considered a staunch Democrat who had the firm support of important Congressional leaders in the Democratic Party. Senator Wagner, in recommending him for appointment to the Council, said:

> He is well liked and highly regarded not only by those up here who share his liberal views, but likewise by those with different political viewpoints. . . . I gradually formed the opinion that Mr. Keyserling was not only a first-rate legal technician, but also a first-rate student of economics and of governmental problems. . . . I am enclosing a folder containing some of his quite recent speeches and articles all in support of the objectives of the present administration."[11]

John D. Clark's background can be more simply given. At the time of his appointment to the Council he was 62. Like Keyserling, he was trained as a lawyer. As a young man he was City Attorney for Cheyenne, Wyoming. Shortly afterwards he became Counsel for the Midwest Refining Company, and then for many years he was a vice-president for the Standard Oil Company of Indiana. In his late thirties, having acquired a fortune, he gave up his lucrative business career to take graduate work at The Johns Hopkins University, where he received his Ph.D. degree in 1927. His doctoral dissertation stressed the importance of the Sherman Antitrust law and was published as *The Federal Trust Policy*. After several years as a professor of economics at the University of Denver, he served for a brief period as a Democratic representative in the Wyoming legislature. During the New Deal he took an active interest in political affairs and was a member of various state and national Democratic committees. At the time of his appointment to the Council of Economic Advisers, he was Dean of the College of Business Administration at the University of Nebraska. His record indicated that he held firm convictions and pragmatic political views. He was known as a low interest rate man and an advocate of governmental planning. He was respected for his independent and unorthodox thinking, progressive outlook, and broad knowledge of business organization and practices. Although not considered personally ambitious, he was known to be greatly interested in doing what he could to advance the public interest. Personally he was regarded by his colleagues as a modest, friendly man of good judgment. As he had written little on purely economic subjects, he was not well known in the economics profession. It was commonly believed that his appointment to the Council of Economic Advisers was made upon the recommendation of his long-time friend, Senator Joseph C. O'Mahoney, one of the original sponsors of the full employment bill.[12]

This brief examination of the pre-Council careers of Keyserling and Clark reveals that both were trained in the law as well as in economics, and that both were closely attuned to the progressive wing of the Democratic Party. While Clark had practical business training, he was little informed on federal government administration. Keyserling had little practical business experience, for his career had been almost exclusively related to federal legislative and executive offices. As contrasted with Nourse, neither Keyserling nor Clark had attained recognition for sustained economic analysis, and neither was well known in the economics profession. Looking back on the careers and characteristics of the three Council members, Edward S. Flash, Jr. said: "Taken together, the differences in background and conviction of the three Council members foreordained a basic incompatibility among these presidential advisers."[13]

Getting Underway

When the Council was officially set up on August 9, it had the job of establishing itself and preparing the first Economic Report for the president by the end of the year. There was no time to lose. Fortunately, the Bureau of the Budget could provide temporary assistance on personnel matters and other details of administration until the Council could arrange such services for itself.

The problem of finding satisfactory quarters demanded immediate attention. Nourse had understood that the Council would be located in the Executive Office Building then known as Old State, adjacent to the White House, but no offices were available in it. A limited amount of space could be had in a small office building at 1712 G Street which housed the fiscal division of the Bureau of the Budget, but Nourse thought it unwise to begin the life of the Council under such inauspicious circumstances. Keyserling and Clark immediately took advantage of this temporary arrangement, but Nourse refused to leave his Brookings Institution office on Jackson Place until a more satisfactory arrangement could be worked out. He expressed his attitude as follows:

> I felt that it was important—in the protocol-conscious atmosphere of Washington—that we be established at the start in quarters whose character and propinquity to the President's office proclaimed the position that the Council was to occupy in the executive establishment. Congress had set up the Council as an independent agency working directly with and for the President, to perform functions of broad economic analyses, some of which had in recent years been experimentally developed in the fiscal division of the Bureau of the Budget. To move in on the fringe of that Bureau's domain would raise ambiguities in the minds of sharp-eyed reporters and the public generally and cause embarrassment both to us and to them. In my book, 1712 G Street was out [EPS, p. 113].

Soon afterwards, more attractive offices became available in the North Interior Building, but they had housed the defunct National Resources Planning Board, which still had a bad name with many people. Nourse felt that these offices would link the Council with the demise of that unfortunate agency, and he continued to hold out for space in the Executive Office Building. His patience, or stubbornness, paid off in early October, when, through the efforts of James Webb, Director of the Bureau of the Budget, sufficient space became available in the basement of Old State to house the Council members and some of the top staff. Thus, on October 14, the Council began its official career in the Executive Office Building, and fortunately, within a few months space became available for the Council and its staff on the third floor directly opposite the West Wing of the White House. It could not have asked for a better location.

While the Council was struggling to obtain adequate quarters, it was endeavoring to recruit professional staff of high quality. This job was largely assumed by Nourse in view of his extensive acquaintance with the personnel of the economics profession, and his fellow Council members gave him a free hand, for they were in full accord with his view that "we should recruit men in terms of their intellectual ability and their capacity to work with other agencies along problem lines and not be too much concerned with the individual's doctrinal position." As Nourse said: "They were cooperative to a fault as I dropped our net wherever I thought a good man could be lured into our staff" (EPS, p. 116).

Early in September, the professional staff began to take form with the appointment of Fred Waugh, a highly respected statistician and market economist, and he was soon joined by Paul Homan, Donald Wallace, and Gerhard Colm, all well-known economists with intensive government experience. Of particular importance was the appointment of Gerhard Colm, who was one of the top experts in the fiscal division of the Bureau of the Budget and who was internationally known for his work on national income accounts. Colm was willing to transfer to the Council, but he wanted to be recognized as Chief of Staff while the Council saw itself as being its own Chief of Staff. Colm was finally persuaded by his chief, James Webb, that it would be logical for him to transfer to the Council on its own terms in view of the fact that the Employment Act definitely assigned work on national income and fiscal policy to the Council.

One of Nourse's first problems was to develop working relations with the president. When the Council was sworn in, the president had said to him: "Mr. Steelman [then Director of the Office of War Mobilization and Reconversion] will be your principal point of contact." Not knowing the President's way of operating, Nourse felt—probably without justification—that the remark minimized the amount of direct attention he intended to devote to the Council. He soon found, however, that John Steelman, who was to be designated "Assistant to the President" in December, kept in touch with the work of many departments and agencies for the president, and Nourse's relations with Steelman proved congenial and useful. As an economist, Steelman had a direct interest in the work of the Council and did all he could to see that the president gave full attention to the activities of the Council. Moreover, Nourse found the president generally accessible for consideration of specific Council problems.

Another early problem was to establish smooth and helpful relations with the executive agencies of the federal government. To develop such liaison, the Council members immediately began a series of courtesy calls on the Secretaries of the Treasury, Commerce, Agriculture, and Labor, and on the agency heads concerned with important economic matters. As Nourse pointed out:

It must always be borne in mind that the device of a Council of Economic

Advisers in the Executive Office of the President was injected into a long-standing Cabinet system, with largely autonomous Department Secretaries. Furthermore, this system has been expanded by the addition of "independent" commissions whose heads likewise have considerable authority in formulating economic policy. . . . Since the Economic Report of the President was designed particularly to secure an integration of department or segmental policies into a truly national and internally consistent policy, it was important that any advisory function that the Council was able to achieve should begin with the separate branches of government and their policy-making heads [EPS, p. 169].

With cooperation at the top ensured, good working relations could be developed by the staff members of the Council with the professional staffs of the federal agencies. According to Nourse, "We [soon] had the fullest cooperation of staff workers and administrative officers in all branches of government—in supplying data, exploring techniques, conferring on policy issues, and collaboration on report material. . . . Our scheme of organization was designed to provide conduits through which the underlying work of hundreds of government statisticians and economists could be economically and flexibly drawn upon in the production of our top level synthesis for policy-making purposes" (EPS, p. 165).

Under the Employment Act, as mentioned earlier, the Council was empowered to "constitute such advisory committees and . . . consult such representatives of industry, agriculture, labor, consumers, State and local governments, and other groups as it deems advisable." Nourse and his fellow Council members were greatly interested in building rapport with such groups, and they immediately availed themselves of this authority. Within a month after the Council was sworn in, invitations for consultations were extended to representative agricultural, business, and labor organizations, and arrangements were made to obtain liaison with consumer groups and state and municipal bodies.

One of the Council's first meetings of this type was with the CIO Economic Policy Committee. Stanley H. Ruttenberg, who was present, has recalled how Phil Murray, Walter Reuther, Jim Carey, Emil Rieve, and other CIO leaders came to this meeting "rather reluctantly, with a feeling that little would come of the meeting." However, said Ruttenberg, "Dr. Nourse's gracious attitude, combined with his intense interest in wanting to understand in great detail the position of the labor leaders, made each of us that were there sit up and take notice. . . . Dr. Nourse would probe and probe and probe. He wanted us to know what he was thinking, but it was clear that he was sincerely interested in knowing what we had on our minds. . . . This facet of Dr. Nourse's personality, this helpful interest in striving to get a better understanding of people's ideas, was greatly appreciated by those who met with him."[14]

These consultations were to provide much helpful information on the problems of the various segments of the economy, and they soon became a regular feature of Council operations.

As the work of the Council took shape, it was apparent that the Council needed an able administrative officer. The person best qualified seemed to be Bertram Gross, a protégé of Keyserling, who had played a key role in the drafting of the original Full Employment Bill and the Employment Act. The significant contribution of Gross as staff director of the Senate committee which worked on the original Full Employment Bill was to be disclosed in 1950 by Bailey in his classic study of the Employment Act: "He was the spark plug of enthusiasm which fired the staff with a passionate zeal for the cause of full employment." Bailey also said: "There was hardly a phase of the Full Employment Bill fight, from the original drafting to final passage, that Gross and his assistants failed to touch profoundly" (*Congress Makes a Law*, pp. 66, 67). While Nourse recognized that the "identification of interests between Gross and Keyserling might tend to give a distinctive quirk to Council development," it was obvious that no one could be found who was better informed on the legislative background of the Employment Act and the intentions of its framers and also "on to the ropes" of procurement, appointments, and other administrative procedures in the federal government. Gross would have liked the title "Secretary to the Council"—a title which was accorded him after Keyserling took over as chairman—but Nourse felt that this appellation might give Gross too much independent authority. It was finally agreed that the post would be called "Assistant to the Chairman" rather than "Administrative Assistant to the Chairman," as the former would provide an opportunity for Gross "to help creatively in working out a suitable organization for this new and different agency" (EPS, p. 121).

Thus when the Council commenced its "formal labors" in the Executive Office Building on October 14, it had, in Nourse's words, "a three man Council of diverse backgrounds and outlooks, a senior staff of four full-time men and four part-time, and a high-powered executive officer." Moreover, it had already made known its presence in Washington. The prospects were encouraging. There had been working harmony in getting the Council under way, and all of the Council members agreed on the importance of establishing its program on a basis that would attract favorable public attention. As Nourse described the situation: "We were very polite to each other and all three of us had a devotion to the purpose of the Employment Act and a desire to make it an effective agency from the start."

During this initial period, Nourse had found his new responsibilities both interesting and challenging. Although he had long enjoyed intimate contact with government agencies, this was his first experience on working from the inside. This involved looking at problems in a new way, for the "orientation of the Employment Act and the attitude of those most concerned with its implementation was that of fiscal and monetary policy." While Nourse considered himself reasonably well informed on monetary policy, he realized that he had not kept up-to-date on fiscal policy, which had been going through a period of intensive development. He therefore endeavored to expand his knowledge in this field while getting the best current thinking on it for the Council's use. He was pleased that he could draw on the expert guidance of Gerhard Colm in this area. He later explained: "I was trying particularly to keep a balance between fiscal and monetary policy on the one side, the big macroeconomic forces, and the market—business and labor and agricultural or microeconomic forces—on the other side. It was a period of great growth in my thinking because I had exposure to people who were experts in many fields." Nourse felt competent on the economic problems of business, labor and agriculture, and he later said: "I was not holding back against government activism as such, but I was wanting to take a keen analytical, objective view of developments, as they were proposed or as they were put into effect."[15]

In reviewing this formative period with him many years afterwards, I said: "I get the impression that you went into this job cool, but that as you got into it, you became increasingly excited by its potential. Is that right?" He replied: "Well, of course, one couldn't be in a job of this sort without having it steam him up a good deal."[16]

Nourse's First Public Address as Chairman

In inaugurating the Council's operations, Nourse saw the desirability of doing everything possible to explain to important groups how the Council planned to function under the Employment Act. He was therefore pleased to receive an invitation from the National Association of Manufacturers to give an address on December 6 at its Congress of American Industry on the subject, "The Employment Act and the Economic Future." He saw this as an opportunity to create confidence of business leaders in the way the Council was proceeding.

Nourse realized that great significance would be attached to this address, since it would be interpreted as the views of the Administration. He therefore explained to President Truman what he planned to say and asked if he wanted him to accept the invitation. Truman replied: "Yes, of course. They need to know what we're thinking and doing about this."

When Nourse asked whether he would like to see the address when prepared, Truman answered: "No. I have perfect confidence in you as an economist. You explain it to them."

In his address Nourse expressed the view that it was essential that American businessmen should realize three things if they were to have a correct understanding of the nature and meaning of the Employment Act so that they could take full advantage of it for the future benefit of American industry.

His first point was that the act did not propose any simple panacea for business ills. The purpose of the act as he saw it was to achieve prosperity through promoting the efficiency of the nation's business "just as the purpose of a great corporation is to achieve company prosperity through efficiency of overall and spot-management, skillfully joined." He looked forward hopefully to the development of "friendly understanding and organization effectiveness" between private and public agencies, since the Employment Act called for the cooperation of industry, agriculture, and labor in a way calculated to foster free competitive enterprises. He summarized this point by saying that the work of the Council was directed toward the application of the soundest and broadest managerial principles and practices in dealing comprehensively and vigorously with the nation's business—rather than toward "monetary or any other specific formula of economic stabilization and national prosperity."

With this assurance given to private enterprise, Nourse turned to the government's responsibility under the act for promoting "maximum employment, production, and purchasing power." He thought there was nothing revolutionary in this declaration, which "simply reaffirms in clearer terms and gives new implementation to a responsibility which is part of our traditional American system."

For his final point, Nourse dealt with the responsibility of business itself in accomplishing the overall purposes of the Employment Act. He thought the act gave the system of private enterprise "a new lease on life" by making it "the foundation and cornerstone of our position as the leading nation in the post-war economy of the world." He held that business management was on probation to justify itself under the favorable conditions afforded by the act, and that it was imperative that competitive free enterprise meet the challenge of serving the nation's needs. He did not overlook organized labor as part of the system of free competitive enterprise, for he realized that monopolistic acts of labor unions could be as harmful as those of business firms. He saw no reason why collective bargaining in good faith could not work to the advantage of the total economy.

Many years later Nourse said of this talk: "This was just the message I wanted to get over. I had been expounding this philosophy of the responsibility of business executives as leaders in our modern society, and I thought this was a good opportunity to emphasize this again and indicate that it would be a guiding principle of the Council of Economic Advisers."[17]

The First Annual Report of the Council

There were two main jobs to do when the Council settled down to work in the Executive Office Building. The main task was to prepare the materials for the president's first Economic Report to be submitted in early January. Of secondary importance was the completion of the Council's first annual report to the president called for in December by the Employment Act. Since the annual report of the Council was to set the stage for the economic report of the president, it will be given first attention.

From the beginning, Nourse had realized that success of the Council would call for a close understanding with the president on how this novel agency of government would function. In his initial interview he had been somewhat disturbed by President Truman's view that the Council would be primarily a "fact finding agency," for Nourse saw it as performing a much broader service. One of Nourse's main concerns in getting the work of the Council under way was to broaden the president's understanding of the role that the Council could best perform. He also believed it incumbent on the Council to educate the Congress and governmental officials and the public on the meaning of the Employment Act of 1946 and on the way the Council proposed to operate. This was a task congenial to Nourse as an educator.

In his letter to President Truman accepting the position as chairman, he had set forth his conception of how the Council would function under the Employment Act, but he thought that a more enlightening statement for general consumption was needed. As he mulled over this idea, he saw the possibility of using the first annual report of the Council called for in December as a means of meeting this purpose as there would be little to report on operations for the first year. The idea met with approval of his colleagues, and at Nourse's first conference with the president on September 18, he explained how a report of an educational character could help condition the public mind for the president's January Economic Report. President Truman liked the idea, so Nourse indicated that he would

LAYING THE FOUNDATION

submit an outline for the report and keep him informed as work on it progressed.

One month later, Nourse informed the president that the Council was tentatively planning its first report under three headings: (1) the political philosophy of the Employment Act, (2) the economic philosophy of sustained employment, and (3) aspects of the outlook for production and jobs. President Truman was entirely satisfied with the outline, and Nourse indicated that as drafts were completed they would be submitted to him for his suggestions.

Nourse took great interest in preparing the first draft of the report, which was then revised to take into consideration the views of Keyserling and Clark. They were in general accord with the draft, although Clark thought that Nourse overemphasized the difference in schools of economic thought that were compromised in the Employment Act. He also thought that discussion in the report should be centered on "the aggressive program which the Council intended to follow." While this problem was being worked out, Nourse observed in his diary: "Clark seems to me to be disposed to advocate a more sweeping and aggressive policy than either Keyserling or I would be likely to follow" (EPS, p. 123).

On November 26, Nourse submitted the first part of the report, which the president found "just the sort of thing that would be desirable." The full text was submitted on December 4, and with only a few changes in phraseology it met with his approval. The report was thereupon put in final form for release at the president's press conference on December 18, at which time Nourse was asked by the president to respond to questions on the report.

Because of its importance as a statement of official policy, this report is here presented in some detail. The opening paragraph read as follows:

> The Employment Act of 1946 marks a distinct and important step in the evolution of our national life and our frame of democratic government. The Council of Economic Advisers, which this Act sets up in the Executive Office of the President, *constitutes an undertaking in the field of political science no less than in the field of economics.* Therefore, it seems appropriate that, in this first annual report, the Council should clearly set forth its conception of the agency which Congress has established within the executive branch and explain the Council's relations to the administrative departments and independent agencies, to the Congress, and to nongovernmental agencies in our economic system. The opening section of this report, accordingly, will deal with the political philosophy of the Employment Act of 1946. The second section will consider the economic philosophy of sustained employment and high-level production. Against this background we shall then discuss briefly a few outstanding aspects of the outlook for production and jobs during 1947 and in the years immediately following.

> It is the President's Economic Report to the Congress rather than this Council report which will contain specific economic conclusions and recommendations. [Emphasis added.]

Part I, on the political philosophy of the Employment Act, succinctly explained how the act came into being after a struggle between those who favored reliance on free enterprise and those who saw the necessity of direct action by the central government. As the report explained:

> The measure which finally emerged from this process of legislative coalition was a well-balanced and carefully drawn piece of legislation. Although frequently referred to as a "much watered down version" of the original proposal, it is in fact a broad enabling act of great flexibility as well as vigor. It is far from being a meaningless verbal compromise. The present act does not make any particular method mandatory. Nor does it legislate any specific remedy into use. Instead the law states quite fully and clearly the general purpose and intention of the Congress and lays down the principle that the executive and the legislature shall seek diligently for any method which, in the peculiar circumstances of any given situation, appears to them to be sound and to promise helpful results.

It was pointed out that the Employment Act laid a mandate on the President and the whole executive establishment and upon both houses of Congress "to pursue the goal of promoting maximum use of the Nation's resources, natural and human, so as to provide work opportunities as ample as are practicable for those who are anxious to apply their labor to the supplying of their wants." Moreover, the act was to operate in "a manner calculated to foster and promote free competitive enterprise."

The report also examined the governmental machinery through which the purposes of the Employment Act were to be attained. In describing the function of the Council of Economic Advisers, it was emphasized that "the Council as such does not have any administrative powers or responsibilities. It is purely a consultative and advisory agency." It was also made clear that the establishment of the Council "does not reallocate basic public responsibilities; it merely puts improved professional techniques and resources at the disposition of those who make national policy. Since the President must formulate his policies and shape his program within his own evaluation of the most varied and comprehensive political, as well as economic influences and considerations, it is not to be expected that his report to Congress will merely reflect the conclusions and recommendations of his economic Council. He will simply use as he deems wise such economic analysis, appraisal, conclusions, and recommendations as they prepare for him. . . ."

The second part of the Report on "The Economic Philosophy of Sustained Employment" asserted that "the passing of the Employment Act by Congress would have been no more than a senseless gesture if it did not express a considered belief that, by mobilizing our capacity of economic reasoning, and the brains and experience of business management, labor leaders, and others, we could moderate in the future the devastating periods of business depression." The report went on to say: "The three appointees who make up the initial membership of the Council, though no one of them had so much as met either of the others at the time of his selection, have found themselves in a gratifying state of like-mindedness on this matter. All of us believe wholeheartedly in the basic purposes of the Act. We believe its broad enabling powers provide a device through which practical action can be suited to the demands of changing circumstances. . . ."

The report then examined in some detail how the Employment Act accepted the broad concept of mutual adjustment, while rejecting the concepts of Spartan laissez faire or governmental intervention. Nourse saw this as a means of laying to rest the provisions of the Full Employment Bill of 1945 which would have required the government to take action in an automatic way under prescribed economic conditions.

With this explanation of the political and economic philosophy imbedded in the act, the report in Part III turned to a brief examination of the nation's economic condition under the heading, "Some Aspects of the Outlook for Production and Jobs." This section was designed to pave the way for the forthcoming Economic Report of the president.

The Council saw the economic situation as favorable because of the strong pent-up demands for producer and consumer goods. There seemed no immediate danger of recession if industry and labor followed sound economic practices. The report ended on this optimistic note:

> It is our belief . . . that enough time is afforded in which wise policy and action on the part of labor, of management, of agriculture, and of finance, with a very carefully considered complementary role by the Government, will not only raise the national prosperity to new high levels but will maintain those levels with a degree of stability which has not characterized the earlier exploratory and speculative decades of our industrial life. It is toward such a system of continuous study and collaborative guidance of the Nation's business on a basis of competitive private enterprise and economic democracy that the Employment Act of 1946 is directed. To its achievement the Council of Economic Advisers dedicates its best efforts.

On the whole, the report was well received by the press and public. It served the purpose envisaged by Nourse and did much to help establish confidence in the new Council at a time when there was much skepticism on how it would work. Without question, it also provided a foundation of interest for the first Economic Report of the president.

In later discussing this report with Nourse, I said: "It seems to me that it was drawn with posterity in mind. I take it that you were trying to get the flag up to give precedence to professional work and gain wide public approval and interest in the work of the Council." Nourse in reply said: "Well, that's true, and that was accepted by Keyserling and Clark."[18]

Preparing the President's First Economic Report

In settling down to work on the preparation of materials for the president's Economic Report, the Council had many questions to answer and few precedents to follow. These questions were resolved by a decision to prepare the report so that the president could submit it as his own report with such changes as he might deem desirable.

In working on the report, Nourse found himself in some disagreement with his fellow Council members on the procedure to be followed. Based on his long experience in directing economic research studies for the Brookings Institution, he was a strong believer in the value of teamwork and he favored giving top staff members full opportunity to develop and display their initiative. Looking back on the problems that arose in preparing the draft materials for the first report of this kind, he said:

> As I saw it, the prime task of the Council was to select the salient facts from the great flood of data available in other agencies, streamline this information into a comprehensive and consistent interpretation of the issues confronting the economy, and thereupon give a critique of proposed or possible means of dealing with the problems that would be encountered in the coming year. It seemed to me that the Council should take the lead in shaping up the area of discussion that seemed to its members most promising. I thought that the men whom we were assembling on our top staff were fully qualified to be, and should be, encouraged to regard themselves as the full team of economic advisers to the President, of which the Council members would serve as captain and quarterback. I felt, too, that frequent meetings of staff with Council members to exchange views fully around the table was the most satisfactory way of getting the issues considered from all angles and of guiding staff specialists in their further collection of materials and their consultation with the professional staffs of other agencies. Between staff meetings these specialists would draft portions of the proposed report for the President but do so with a maximum understanding of the whole situation and policy objective [EPS, pp. 135-136].

It soon became apparent to Nourse that this working procedure was not fully acceptable to Keyserling and Clark. He found that their "attitude and participation in the staff meetings ranged from bored indifference to open sabotage." He then explained:

> Frequently, if I sought to elicit a Council member's view after canvassing the staff, I would get this reply: "I consider this a matter of policy to be decided in Council meetings, and not discussed with the staff." As to the preparation of the finished draft for the President, it would quite evidently

have been appreciated if I had busied myself with the routine calls made upon the Chairman's time and had delegated the task of drafting a Council document from the memoranda secured from staff members in response to topical assignments. This draft could then be dealt with expeditiously in Council meetings. If differences of view were found within the Council, they would be resolved by a majority report. In spite of the administrative convenience of such a procedure, I could not reconcile myself to accepting it. I thought we should try to educate each other to the maximum degree of honest consensus and frankly inform the President as to differences on which we might divide—as do economists outside the Executive Office— and even the most competent technicians in all lines [EPS, p. 136].

It should be kept in mind that these views reflected the problems involved in preparing the first report while the Council was finding its way. As more experience was gained and as the professional staff expanded to include more specialists, it became possible to systematize procedures and more clearly define duties. However, as long as Nourse was chairman, he was never able to accept the executive type of procedure that Keyserling and Clark preferred. He saw the staff as being more like a university faculty group than as a band of technicians in an industrial company.

While this method of preparing the first report was somewhat cumbersome, it should be realized that the Council was then finding its way by trial and error and was inductively developing procedures suitable to its needs. One advantage of this informal unstructured approach was that it gave staff members a feeling that they were partners in preparing the report and encouraged them to display their initiative.

One of the problems that called for attention was working out a plan or outline for the content of the report. Here a problem of some concern was whether to include a section on the nation's economic budget—an area of specialized work under Colm. The Council finally agreed that this was a useful device and that it did not imply acceptance of the idea as a basis for government intervention, as was implied in the original Full Employment Bill. In fact, the presentation of this information helped to make clear that with existing knowledge of economic facts, an automatic response to economic forecasts would not be practicable.

As the Economic Report of the president began to shape up in draft form, Nourse kept the president informed on progress being made. On November 26, he arranged a conference for the Council members with the president to discuss the materials being developed for the report. Two conferences were then set up for December 3 and 10. In these meetings the Council presented its views on taxes, the budget, labor management problems, and similar matters. It appeared that the president was in full agreement with what was being prepared, and on December 17, Nourse submitted a draft of the Economic Report in tentative form with a covering letter which called attention to certain aspects of the report. He said in this letter that while the Council was improving this draft, it would be helpful to have the president's views. As there was no response to this letter, Nourse, on December 27, sent the president revised copies of the report with another covering letter. As time was running short since the report had to be presented by the president on January 6, Nourse then endeavored to find out what was happening to the draft submitted. He was informed by Clark Clifford, the president's special counsel, that the first reaction of the president to the December 17 draft was that it was "too long" and that he had turned it over to John Steelman, who had been named assistant to the president on December 12. Steelman, in turn, had turned it over to three of his staff assistants who had been members of his staff in the Office of Mobilization and Reconversion, which had been abolished on December 16 (EPS, pp. 140-141). It was natural that he would have turned to these associates for help on this matter, since the OMR had been making a quarterly report which, in Nourse's words, was "a sort of rudimentary prototype for our economic report to the President." Thus when the report was turned over to Steelman's staff assistants, they "took it upon themselves to rewrite the report. So the first big battle of the Council was to assert our priority in the role of executive advisers to the President in drafting the report and to restore as much of what we had in our draft as possible."[19]

Nourse told the story of what then happened in *Economics in the Public Service* (pp. 141-142):

> About December 31, Steelman returned to us a proposed Economic Report of the President which had been prepared from the Council's draft materials. It had been substantially shortened, drastically changed in order of presentation, and considerably "jazzed up" in style. After this text had been examined by the Council and top staff members, it was the unanimous feeling that many things that were essential to a consistent and workmanlike analysis had been omitted from the draft and that the rearrangement obscured the essential outline of the analysis.
>
> On the afternoon of Friday, January 3, Steelman convened a meeting of Council members with his assistants and with Secretaries Snyder, Harriman, and Schwellenback to consider a plan for the official draft of the President's Economic Report. . . . Following the meeting Steelman and his assistants and the assistants of the Secretaries worked on the Report and completed a draft that night which was then sent to the Government Printing Office. The following morning the galley proofs were submitted for the consideration of the Council. It was largely the draft prepared by Steelman's assistants, plus a few additions from our third draft of materials.

> The Council and staff worked diligently on this draft all that morning and early afternoon, preparing recommendations for revision and particularly proposing the restoration of important things which had been excluded. Later that afternoon the Council met with Steelman, and his three assistants, and worked until 7:00 p.m. preparing a final revision of the White House draft . . . to go to the printer that night for paging. The revision was in the main satisfactory to us.[20]

Nourse realized that while the Council had the major responsibility for preparing the Economic Report, it was not to be looked upon as the Council's report but as the report of the president. It was written in the Employment Act that the Council would assist and advise the president in the preparation of the Economic Report, but no final jurisdiction was given to the Council. Nourse was meticulous in referring to the Council's drafts for this report as "draft materials" for the Economic Report—a preciseness of expression not fully appreciated by his colleagues.

The experience on clearance of the first report made clear that the Council would have to defend its views in the reports to be issued in the name of the president. It also made clear that subsequent reports would need to be carefully drawn to take into full consideration department and agency positions so that they would not be subject to extensive revision in the White House.

The First Economic Report of the President

In introducing his first annual Economic Report to the Congress on January 8, 1947, President Truman said:

> As the year 1947 opens, America has never been so strong or so prosperous, nor have our prospects ever been brighter. Yet on the minds of a great many of us there is fear of another depression, the loss of our jobs, our farms, our businesses. . . . I reject, and I know the American people reject, the notion that we must have another depression. . . . I am referring to economic collapse and stagnation such as started in 1929. This need not happen again, and *must* not happen again.

In its review of economic conditions, the report found unemployment "probably close to the minimum" for a free economy, while production was reaching new peacetime levels. The principal problem was the rapid rise in prices which was reducing consumer purchasing power.

The report provided information on prices, wages, and profits in 1946. After examining favorable and unfavorable factors in the economic situation, the report recommended various short-range and long-range programs. Of particular interest were the long-range programs designed to strengthen the functions of the American economy: (1) Efficient utilization of the labor force; (2) Maximum utilization of productive resources; (3) Encouragement of free competitive enterprise; (4) Promoting welfare, health and security; (5) Cooperation in international economic relations; and (6) Combatting economic fluctuations.

While the report was not spectacular, it provided a common-sense presentation of the state of the economy, and its modest recommendations on what should be done were generally acceptable. On the whole, the report met with a good public reception. Truman was pleased and he called Nourse on the phone to say: "It's a dandy."

Retrospect on the First Five Months

In early January, Nourse was pleased with the way the Council was operating. It had become a going government concern, and it enjoyed the interest and goodwill of the public.

The first five months had given Nourse an opportunity to use his training and experience in a great new adventure in government. The more involved he became, the more convinced he was of the soundness and importance of the Employment Act. He had found his relations with his fellow Council members congenial, and he had enjoyed his contacts with the president, cabinet secretaries, and agency heads. He was proud of the Council's professional staff, which was building close relationships with counterpart government agencies. The consultative conferences with labor, industry, and agricultural groups were demonstrating their usefulness.

The first annual report of the Council had helped gain public understanding of the Employment Act and the work of the Council of Economic Advisers, and Nourse was particularly pleased with the warm reception given his first major address, which emphasized the significant role of free competitive enterprise in effectuating the purposes of the Employment Act. The first Economic Report of the president, prepared largely by the Council, had met with a high degree of public approval. With a good beginning, the future of the Council looked bright.

It was then Nourse's view that it would be a great mistake to try to make "a big and spectacular thing" of the Council. "My interpretation," he said, "was that it should stick to its knitting as a professional agency, establish friendly relations, gain acceptance throughout the other departments, and gradually build itself into the existing frame of government."[21] This approach had given good results in establishing the Council, and Nourse felt that the foundation was now laid for a more positive program.

The Inception and Influence of the Wardman Park Group

In view of its influence on Nourse's later career as Chairman of the Council, it is important that we here examine a political development that followed the Congressional elections of 1946. It should be realized that the mood of the country in the fall of 1946 was anti-administration. Inflation was rampant and labor unions seemed out of control. While President Truman had valiantly endeavored to maintain price controls and restrict strikes, he had lost the confidence of the electorate. The Republican Party saw its opportunity to regain power under the telling slogan "Had Enough?" It captured both the House and the Senate with workable majorities in the November elections. The Republicans were jubilant. In the words of Cabell Phillips, "Now they had two years in which to roll back the inequities which Roosevelt and his upstart successor had imposed on the nation and beyond lay the shining promise of recapturing the Presidency itself."[22]

It is here significant that in response to this situation a small "strategy group" formed itself within the administration to work "unobtrusively" for the reelection of President Truman in 1948, and that Keyserling was an important member of this select group. Little was known of this development—which was to exert an important internal influence on the Truman Administration during the next two years—until it was disclosed 20 years later by Cabell Phillips in his penetrating study of the Truman Presidency.[23]

As Phillips tells the story, "this extraordinary 'palace guard' operated quietly and almost invisibly during 1947 and 1948 to create a positive and distinctive identity for the Truman Presidency. Their short-range objective was to try to assure Mr. Truman's re-election in 1948 . . . but in the long run they sought, also, to shape the social and political development of the nation in accordance with their liberal philosophy."

We must know something of this inside group and how it functioned if we are to understand the internal White House state of affairs while Nourse was Chairman of the Council. According to Phillips:

> The nucleus of this group was composed of Oscar Ewing, Director of the Federal Security Agency, Clark Clifford, Special Counsel to the President, Leon Keyserling, member of the Council of Economic Advisers, G. Girard ("Jebby") Davidson, Assistant Secretary of the Interior, David A. Morse, Assistant Secretary of Labor, and Charles S. Murphy, an administrative assistant to the President. Read today, these names do not suggest a "junta" of revolutionary potency. But each man had power in his own corner of the Federal bureaucracy, and each could enlist support as it was needed among other constituencies. *Their collective influence could make itself*

felt in practically every important agency of the executive establishment. [Emphasis added.]

This group materialized late in 1946. They met each Monday evening in Ewing's apartment at the Wardman Park Hotel. They would have dinner about 6 o'clock and then discuss and argue until close to midnight. No notes were taken, no records were kept, and no leaks were permitted to the press. The agenda usually was restricted to one or two topics, issues currently or soon to come before the President for decision. *Clifford and Keyserling, because of their strategic location in the White House, could aim their influence directly on target—the President.* [Emphasis added.]

The active leader of the group was Clark Clifford, who, as special counsel to the president, was in a position of strategic importance. He knew what was going on in the Executive Office and he had the confidence of the president. His account of how the group worked, as quoted by Phillips, is thus of special interest:

The stinging defeat in 1946 . . . pointed up more clearly than anything else could that there just was no clear direction, no political cohesion to the Truman program—at least not in the minds of the politicians and the people. And it pointed to two more years of frustration and final defeat for Mr. Truman in 1948.

I think it was Jack (Oscar) Ewing who first suggested the idea that a few of us get together from time to time to try to plot a coherent political course for the administration. Our interest was to be exclusively on domestic affairs, not foreign. We wanted to try to develop not only policies that would be good for the country, but especially those that would have a high political appeal. We wanted to create a set of goals that truly met the deepest and greatest needs of the people, and we wanted to build a liberal forward-moving program around those goals that could be recognized as a *Truman* program.

The idea was that six or eight of us would try to come to an understanding among ourselves on what direction we would like the President to take on any given issue. And then quietly and unobtrusively, each in his own way, we would try to steer the President in that direction.

Naturally, we were up against tough competition. Most of the Cabinet and the congressional leaders were urging Mr. Truman to go slow, to veer a little closer to the conservative line. . . . We were pushing him the other way, urging him to boldness and to strike out for new high ground. . . . Well, it was two forces fighting for the mind of the President, that's really what it was. It was completely unpublicized, and I don't think Mr. Truman ever realized it was going on. But it was an unceasing struggle during those two years, and it got to the point where no quarter was asked and none given.

From the final sentences of Clifford's statement it might be erroneously inferred that President Truman was not aware of the meetings of this group. It would have been hard for him not to know of this activity on his behalf. In an interview with the author on April 5, 1975, Keyserling said:

"This was a very informal group. The president knew what was going on. He was kept informed."

Thus, while Keyserling was serving officially as a member of the Council of Economic Advisers, he was active unofficially in this secret strategy group which was concerned with influencing the political actions of the president. He did not consider this a conflict of interest with his Council duties, although it might have been embarrassing to him if it had become public knowledge. Keyserling's own account of his relationship to the Wardman Park group is given in his oral history interview for the Truman Library.[24] In this interview he provided more detailed information on how the group worked and how it led to his becoming "a drafted member of the White House team which assisted on speeches and messages for the president." Much stress was placed on the confidential nature of the meetings held. "It is surprising that although we met every Monday night at Ewing's apartment at the Wardman Park, had a wonderful steak dinner, and then spent three or four hours together, there was never a single whisper of those meetings in any press in the United States. . . . It never got out." In response to a question on how effective the group was in influencing Mr. Truman's views, Keyserling said: "That group was immensely influential."

One of the first questions to be considered by the group in the spring of 1947 was whether the president should veto the Taft-Hartley Act. "As the main draftsman of the Wagner Act," Keyserling said, "I naturally took the lead in arguing that President Truman should veto the Taft-Hartley Act. As this proceeded, it became apparent that the substantive arguments had to be reinforced with political arguments. . . . I saw that I would have to turn the argument in that direction to make any progress with it. . . . In view of the 1946 elections it was especially important that Truman identify himself clearly as a lineal successor to the New Deal." Keyserling thought that he deserved "eighty-five percent of the credit for convincing the group but Clifford deserved eighty-five percent of the credit for persuading the President. He was closest to him; he saw him all the time."

Following work on the Taft-Hartley Act, according to Keyserling, "the Ewing group branched into a wide range of other matters, which really culminated . . . in the stance of the President in the campaign of 1948, but more particularly in the message which he sent to the Congress enunciating a very far flung New Deal. Now, here again, I would say without derogation of others, that Clifford and I were the two large factors: I on the programmatic side; he on the persuasive side."

The meetings of the Wardman Park group naturally led to an intimate relationship with Clifford and Charles Murphy of the White House staff, with the result that Keyserling was called upon for help in preparing speeches or other messages for the president. As a result, Keyserling became increasingly active in promoting the social programs of the Truman Fair Deal. He said in the interview: "I wrote very many memoranda for the President on this, not in my role as member of the Council, but in my role as sort of an accepted ally of the internal White House group." He indicated that his relationship with Clark Clifford became very intimate. "Clifford and I were as close together as any two people in these jobs could be. We had confidence in each other; we worked together a great deal."

In particular, Clifford called on him for help in preparing the president's State of the Union messages. On this activity, Keyserling said: "This was one of the things that during Nourse's time he didn't like very much, but really it wasn't undercutting him. He wasn't prepared to do it. He wanted to be disassociated from the Administration. The Administration was entitled to look any place it wanted to in the government to get help in the preparation of messages of this kind, and so partly in consequence of the Ewing group or otherwise, I did it. Nourse knew about it. I talked to him about it and he never raised any explicit objection; he hardly could, but I suppose it was a source of uneasiness."

Without question, Keyserling's close alliance with Clark Clifford and Charles Murphy as their trusted confidant gave him great influence within the Administration. He actively helped on the "whistle-stop" talks given by Truman in his 1948 campaign. "It would take two forms. One form would be facts; the other form would be drafts of passages." It can be assumed that his close White House connections had some effect on the positions he took on Council matters. He realized that he had power within the Administration, and this naturally was reflected in his thinking and behavior. This situation did not make things easier for Nourse.

It was Nourse's belief that the Council of Economic Advisers should provide the President with economic advice free of political considerations. He had no political ties, and he felt no responsibility to either party. On the other hand, Keyserling had long played an active role in the Democratic Party, and he saw no reason why in a personal capacity he should not work closely with the party's political apparatus. Although he no doubt endeavored to keep his unofficial activities with the Wardman Park group and the president's office apart from his duties with the Council, it is difficult to see how his relationship would not affect his behavior as a member of the Council.[25]

Although Nourse was not aware (and evidently never became aware) of Keyserling's important role in the Wardman Park strategy group, he soon came to realize that Keyserling had developed an intimate relationship with Clark Clifford. As he saw it: "Keyserling pushed and Clifford was responsive. Papers which should have come to me—messages or public speeches that the President had in progress—for handling as head of the Council, very frequently went to Mr. Keyserling and were returned by him without his bringing them to the attention of the Council."[26] This situation was frustrating to Nourse for he felt that Keyserling was dealing with matters of concern to the Council on a personal basis. While Nourse idealistically believed that the Council members should confine themselves to providing the President with the best possible economic advice, Keyserling pragmatically looked upon himself as a political as well as an economic helper to the President and he saw no conflict in these two roles. To Keyserling Nourse's thinking on this matter was unrealistic and this difference in fundamental attitudes was to cause tension between the two. While the conflict in viewpoint was most apparent in their disagreement on whether Council members should serve as advocates for the positions taken by the President in hearings before Congressional committees, it increasingly was to influence their attitudes on other matters.

Chapter XI

BUILDING AN INSTITUTION
(1947-1948)

With the Economic Report for 1947 out of the way, Nourse could consider more general problems. One subject that called for immediate attention was determination of how the Council could best function in relationship to the Joint Committee on the Economic Report and other Congressional committees.

The Problem of Testifying Before Congressional Committees

Under the Employment Act of 1946, the Council of Economic Advisers was made directly responsible to the president and it was given no specific responsibilities to Congress. However, it was common for Congress to call on government agencies for testimony at committee hearings, although it could not require testimony from members of the president's staff. Keyserling and Clark saw no reason why the Council should not appear before Congressional committees, especially before the Joint Committee on the Economic Report. They favored this as a means of furthering the president's economic program while gaining recognition for the Council as a significant organization in itself. Nourse was more cautious. He foresaw no serious question arising as long as the Congress and the president were in basic accord, but he anticipated that trouble could arise if members of the Joint Committee might wish to cause embarrassment by finding disagreement between the thinking of the president and the members of his Council.[1]

As Nourse pondered over this problem, he came to the conclusion that it would be wise for the Council to establish a policy of not appearing before Congressional committees where danger of disagreement between the Council and the president could be exploited. He described his thinking at the time in his diary:

> As I became better acquainted with the total situation and acquired experience in the practical operation of the Council, I came increasingly to the feeling that the essential purposes of the Employment Act would be best served if the activities of the Council were beamed exclusively to the service of the President and the various agencies of the Executive Branch [EPS, pp. 203-204].

To be on safe ground, Nourse decided to talk over this question with the president on January 14, 1947, when he was consulting him on the Council's plans and activities for the coming year. He then suggested that "an immediate question seemed to be whether the Joint Committee of Congress would expect to have an active relationship with the Council and what our response should be if they sought to draw us into discussion of the Economic Report." Nourse pointed out that "the other members of the Council were inclined to welcome a rather active relationship," whereas he was "apprehensive that the Committee might seek to draw members of the Council into discussions of policy positions taken by the President in his Economic Report, some of which might not be precisely in line with the views of the individual members of the Council." He suggested "that we should establish a practice from the beginning which could be followed consistently and with safety in subsequent years when, conceivably, there might be considerable divergence between the Council's recommendations and the President's policy statement to the Congress" (EPS, p. 204).

Nourse reported that President Truman "immediately agreed that we should protect ourselves against such a situation while at the same time not remaining aloof from the work of the Committee. The formula which seemed to meet with his approval was that we should cooperate in 'elucidating' for the committee any points of fact or (with care) of interpretation relative to the President's Economic Report, but that issues of policy were to be left alone and that we should not be drawn into discussion of them." Thus the president straddled the issue. He didn't forbid appearances before the Joint Committee as long as policy questions were avoided. Since Senator Taft was to be the Chairman of the Joint Committee, the president thought it might be well if Nourse called at his office for an informal discussion of the problem. "He felt sure that the general principles outlined would be acceptable to Taft and the rest of the Committee." Nourse thereupon visited Senator Taft, who generally concurred with the president's view.[2] During the next two years while he was Chairman Taft did not press the Council to appear before the Joint Committee.

In his talk with Truman, Nourse called attention to a passage in a paper that he was presenting at the annual meeting of the American Economic Association on January 27. He thought that this passage was germane to the question of whether the Council should testify before Congressional hearings. It read as follows: "When we have brought this sort of material [objective economic analysis] to the President's desk, we shall have discharged our responsibilities under the Act as I conceive it." After reading the address including this passage, President Truman responded: "Perfectly sound." Nourse thus felt that he was on firm ground in holding that the Council should not testify before hearings of the Joint Committee on the President's Economic Report unless directly requested to do so by the president.

During the next six months, the staff of the Council developed good working relations with the staff of the Joint Committee, which was organized with Dr. Charles O. Hardy as Director on April 1, 1947. Hardy had long been Nourse's friend and colleague at the Brookings Institution, and Nourse had tried hard to persuade him to take one of the top posts on the staff of the Council. Hardy thought that he should sit in on the Council's deliberations, but the Council took the position that it was not possible for it to be "an augment of the Joint Committee's staff." However, in the words of Nourse: "We informed him that the doors of our workshop were always open to him and all the workers on his staff and we endeavored to develop most complete two-way cooperation at the staff level. The staff of the Joint Committee were invited and frequently attended our advisory conferences with labor, industry, and agricultural leaders" (EPS, p. 189).

After the adjournment of Congress, Senator Taft called a meeting of the members of the Joint Economic Committee to which the members of the Council of Economic Advisers were invited. Nourse thought that this meeting was "of some historical importance," in view of the subsequent developments in Council-Joint Committee relations. According to Nourse, Taft leaned back in his chair and said: "Well, now we've had the first run on the work of the Council and the Committee. I wonder what we've learned from that and what you gentlemen of the Council would like to discuss with us members of the Committee." Nourse commented: "Now, there was the sort of meeting between the Committee and the Council in which I could freely participate. I think it might have been a basis for communication between the two agencies of great value."[3]

Enlisting the Support of the Economics Profession

In view of his long experience in the field of economics, Nourse was anxious to enlist the support of the economics profession in promoting the objectives of the Council of Economic Advisers. He therefore welcomed an invitation to address the annual meeting of the American Economic Association at Atlantic City on January 27, where he could explain how the Council planned to operate under the mandate given it by the Employment Act of 1946. He took for his subject "Economics in the Public Service," which he explained by saying: "This phrasing reflects quite succinctly my own interpretation of the role of the Council of Economic Advisers to the President. I conceive this agency as the doorway through which the best thinking on systematic economics may be brought into clear and effective focus at the point of executive decision as to national economic policy and action."

This meeting provided an ideal setting for the purpose he had in mind. The presidential address by E. A. Goldenweiser, his friend since Cornell University days, was entitled "The Economist and the State," and he emphasized the importance of the Employment Act by declaring that February 20, 1946—the date when the Employment Act was approved by President Truman—"may mark the first step in the process of rationalizing the government on an overall basis and organizing American democracy to fit modern conditions." He said: "It is beyond doubt that the Act provides a foundation for coordinated economic policy." Goldenweiser pointed out that the Council of Economic Advisers needed particularly the support of the American Economic Association "whose former president has been appointed as Chairman of the Council." He also said: "The country cannot afford to have this promising start become lost in the mazes of official tape, or in conflicts for power among agencies. It must become the beacon light leading toward a new and more adequate machinery of government in democracy." He continued: "The Council is at present in the experimental stage. On how it is developed and how much importance it gains in shaping the country's economic policy will depend whether it will signalize a momentous step forward."

Goldenweiser was confident that the Council would become of great significance to economists. "This new instrument of government," he declared, "gives the profession of economists a broad opportunity of rendering greater service to the nation and places on them and on this Association a correspondingly grave responsibility." He maintained that Congress had said to the economist "put up or shut up. . . . The economist is out in the open and must come to grips with the problems of state."

In his address, which attracted an overflow audience, Nourse said:

> What I have to say is dictated entirely by the fact that something new has been added to our governmental system just as we stand on the threshold

of a new era of peace. . . . This step in the evolution of our economic institutions . . . came with the passage of the Employment Act of 1946 and the setting up of a Council of Economic Advisers as the doorway through which the best thinking of systematic economics . . . may be brought into clear and effective focus at the point of executive decision as to national economic policy and action.

He asserted: "The new device is installed at a point of great significance and conceivably of great influence for the economist and for that branch of social science which we call economics." Eschewing the concept of the Council as "the three wise men of economics," he said:

As I understand the matter, we have by the vicissitudes of politics, been entrusted with the task of organizing an agency through which, over the years, the Chief Executive of the United States may see the economic situation and problems of the nation in its entirety and through professional eyes. It is the responsibility of this agency to process for his consideration the materials which should be of most use to him in laying out his policy and following his course of action with reference to the national economy.

While observing that such material submitted by the Council would "be politically processed in the office of the Chief Executive and be reprocessed in a strongly political atmosphere by the Congress," he did not think that this situation "should come as a shock to realistic men acquainted with and devoted to our democratic form of government."

Nourse saw the Council of Economic Advisers as "a very small synthesizing body through which lines of enquiry can be initiated and conclusions and recommendations formulated" for answering certain economic questions for the Chief Executive. He besought the cooperation of the economics profession in helping the Council with this task. Foreseeing many problems, he said: "I cannot feel that economics in its present state is adequately prepared to render public service fully commensurate with this opportunity." He thought that the Employment Act, by "opening the door of opportunity to the discipline of economics at the point of central policy consideration for the economy, lays upon the profession as such a deep responsibility." He indicated that the Council would draw on all available agencies, government or private, for research data and assistance, and he called specifically for all possible cooperation from the American Economic Association. He also emphasized the highly significant role that teachers of economics could play in improving public understanding of the objectives and procedures called for by the Employment Act.

With regard to the act itself, he said: "Never, I venture to guess, has so much economic theory, explicit and implicit, been written into an act which covers only four small pages." He thought it highly important that the Employment Act was "premised very definitely on a theory of maximum freedom of private enterprise," while combined with this there was a "no less strong declaration of government responsibility for active and effective utilization of its resources, both natural and human."

He finished his talk by quoting the statement made by President Truman when he signed the Employment Act, starting it on its official career: "The Employment Act of 1946 is not the end of the road, but rather the beginning. It is a commitment by the government to the people. . . . We shall try to honor that commitment." Nourse commented by saying: "As I understand the meaning of economics, that commitment is quite within the almost universally accepted tradition of our profession. I trust that every member of this association has made or will make a personal commitment to that end."

Nourse's paper was very favorably received by his fellow economists. It made them aware that the Council of Economic Advisers was to be no ordinary agency of government, but a body which would represent, at least to the extent of Nourse's ability to make it so, a wise spokesman for the economics profession on the current and continuing economic problems of the nation.

Organization of Staff Work

As the staff expanded, it became obvious that steps should be taken to better organize its operations. According to Nourse, Keyserling took the lead in this work. "From the start, Mr. Keyserling had expressed a lively concern over matters of agency administration. Early in 1947, he urged that . . . we proceed to draw up an outline of specific duties and responsibilities of each of our staff people . . ." (EPS, p. 155 ff.). The plan of staff work, completed on June 17, embraced laying out areas of work which were delineated as follows: "(1) labor force and labor relations; (2) plant capacity, investment, and management; (3) agricultural and consumer economics; (4) flow of income, goods and services; (5) price relations and policies, monopoly and competition; (6) international economic relations; (7) development of human and material resources; (8) construction, housing and public works; (9) veterans, social security and welfare; and (10) taxation, debt, and banking."

Of particular interest to Nourse was a "scheme of committee organization within the staff, focused around four major problem areas or fields of concentration." Three of these committees dealt with primary areas of work: (1) stabilization devices; (2) wage-price problems; and (3) investment needs and capital formation. The fourth, the Periodic Reports Committee, functioned under three joint chairmen—Fred Waugh, Gerhard Colm, and Paul Homan, who drew upon all members of the staff groups. This committee was responsible for drafting all official reports which were brought to the review of the members of the Council. Thus this committee brought the work of the entire organization into focus. As Nourse has reported: "Keyserling took responsibility for keeping track of the progress of the staff drafts and of condensing and editing them . . . for final consideration by the Council. . . . In the last stage of drafting, the three joint chairmen of the Periodic Reports Committee and other staff specialists sat around the Council's table . . . endeavoring to reach concensus . . . on the most effective and appropriate form of statement. The Council members took full responsibility for the final form" (EPS, pp. 156-157).

Under the plan of organization developed, each member of the Council assumed responsibility for certain fields of work. The apportionment was as follows: "*Mr. Nourse* (besides responsibility for general administration and special contacts): Plant capacity, investment, and management; Price relations and policies; Development of human and material resources; Operations of wage-price committee. *Mr. Keyserling*: Labor force and labor relations; Nation's economic budget and its components; Construction, housing and public works; Veterans, social security, and welfare; Operations of stabilization committee; Operations of economic round-up committee. *Mr. Clark*: Agriculture and food; Monopoly and competition; International economic relations; Taxation and debt management; Money and banking; Operations of Federal grants-in-aid committee."

This general plan of organization provided a suitable arrangement for staff work and was to be little changed while Nourse was chairman. It laid out staff responsibilities and gave staff members an opportunity to display their initiative. It limited the general staff meetings, which were largely replaced by meetings of the working groups. Although this form of organization formalized arrangements, it still permitted a great deal of informality in procedures. Nourse continued to stress the desirability of giving all members of the staff a full opportunity to participate in the general thinking of the Council on important economic matters.[4]

The Council's Budget Problem

With the Economic Report for 1947 out of the way, the Council could proceed with the job of building its staff. This was a slow process, for it was necessary to determine what positions should be set up and then to find the persons best qualified to fill them. When the Council presented its budget justification to the House Appropriations subcommittee on April 24 for the fiscal year 1947-1948, its work force from chairman to messenger totalled but 28 persons, and 5 of them were part-time employees. The budget proposed provided for 48 staff employees with salaries aggregating $243,000, an amount well under the authorized ceiling provided in the Employment Act.

Presenting a budget justification to maintain the Council's operations was a new experience for Nourse. He thought that the budget request of $400,000 provided (only) for a modest and reasonable expansion of the Council's work, but the House Appropriations subcommittee, in his words, "took a noticeably cool, if not hostile, attitude." The chairman of the subcommittee, R. B. Wigglesworth, asked this question: "Do you realize that you have the highest average pay rate of any agency in the entire government?" Nourse replied: "That's not a surprise to me. It's entirely natural and defensible because we do not have the average run of high and low [paid] staff. We are a super staff, utilizing the work of other agencies that have lower rate people in their ranks." Congressman Wigglesworth gave little weight to this argument. The Republicans were now in control of Congress, and the Employment Act had been passed by a largely Democratic Congress.

Following the hearings, Wigglesworth followed up with a letter which instructed the Council to make no further commitments pending the action of the subcommittee. This imposed a severe handicap on the Council in obtaining personnel necessary to complete its staffing plan. In an attempt to lift the ban, Nourse wrote Wigglesworth on May 21, explaining the problem confronting the Council. In this letter he said:

> After long and careful search we had selected highly qualified economists for several very important staff positions, and they had made the decision to sever their present connections. We cannot, however, ask them to take such action when we are not in a position to make definite commitments to them. . . . Our success in offering sound advice to the President, the Congress, and the business community will depend very largely upon the adequacy, accuracy, and timeliness of our observations and interpretations of the changing business picture. The members of the Council act as our own supreme professional staff but we must have a reasonable number of carefully chosen assistants at an early date if we are not to continue to spread ourselves out too thinly over the large area of study which has been assigned to us.
>
> All of the appointments frozen in accordance with your instructions, as well as most of the others provided for in our 1947 appropriation, would have been completed some time ago had it not been for the extreme care with which the Council has moved in selecting and fitting together the members of our highly specialized staff. That careful procedure largely

explains the savings that we have been making out of our 1947 appropriation and the relatively large sum which we are expecting to return at the end of the fiscal year. [In fact, the amount later to be returned to the Treasury was over $90,000.]

No reply was made to Nourse's letter, but the subcommittee recommended a reduction in the Council's budget from the $400,000 requested to $350,000. The Senate subcommittee on the Independent Offices Appropriation Bill took a more friendly attitude and recommended a restoration of the $50,000 cut made by the House subcommittee. However, this was lost in conference, so the Council's budget was fixed at $350,000 for the next fiscal year.

With the ban lifted, the Council could make the delayed appointments so that within a few months the Council was at last manned to do its job. With the new appropriation, Nourse said: "We continued our policy of having a staff of minimum size but highest quality and economizing through the fullest use of materials available to us from other agencies." From the beginning, Nourse insisted that no appointments would be made for political considerations (EPS, pp. 152-155).

Expanding the Council's Advisory Function

At this time, the Council was concerned with the development of its program for 1947, particularly with reference to its advisory function for the president as outlined by the Employment Act. Nourse opened up this question in an interview with the president on February 12, by saying that the Council was focusing its work program on identifying danger spots in the economy and preparing special memoranda for him as occasion arose. The president in turn said that he would be glad to receive such memoranda and talk with the Council when it was prepared to bring such matters to his attention. Nourse considered this interview "very satisfactory." In his diary notes he said:

> The President seemed thoroughly pleased with what had been accomplished in our first reports and said: "We want to work right ahead along these same lines." He seemed to indicate also a great willingness to discuss with us at any time any matter which we wished to bring to his attention. . . . [However,] he did not suggest or apparently contemplate turning to the Council for advice on matters of taxation, budget, or other subjects on which he is to take policy and action positions right along [EPS, pp. 176-177].

Nourse followed up on March 7 by sending a note to the president in which he expressed concern over the upturn in prices and its impact on wage negotiations. The president responded with an "appreciative" reply on March 10, saying: "Keep your finger on the situation and keep me fully informed on the program." Just at this time, the "Truman doctrine" to provide financial assistance to Italy and Greece was being enunciated. Since the anticipated costs would affect the domestic economic situation, the Council enquired in a letter on March 19: "Should we, in the report we expect to make to you covering developments during the first quarter of 1947, leave these probable changes out of consideration?" Since this program was still tentative, the president deemed it desirable to defer consideration of its probable impact.

On April 7, the Council examined the price situation with the president in connection with its first quarterly report, and at his suggestion, the report was laid before the cabinet at its meeting on April 9.

At this time the Council was concerned with the problem of whether it would have a special and direct advisory role on legislation of major economic significance or whether such legislation would be referred to the Council for analysis through the Office of Legislative Reference of the Budget Bureau. In the case of the portal-to-portal pay bill, it was specifically referred to the Council through the president's office by Clark Clifford, whereas shortly afterwards, the tax reduction bill was referred to the Council by the Office of Legislative Reference. On this bill, the Council wrote the president on June 5 that it regarded this area one on which the Council should advise the president direct. In its letter the Council said:

> Our official duty to serve as your economic advisers . . . gives us a special concern with tax measures adopted by the Congress. What fraction of national income is withdrawn as Federal revenue has an important impact on the operation of the economy and the possibility of attaining the economic objectives set forth in the Employment Act. Hence we have been giving close attention to the probable effect of the tax reduction proposed . . . now before you for signature or veto. Herewith we submit the conclusions to which this study has brought us [EPS, p. 179].

As neither the Director of the Budget Bureau nor the president made any comment on the Council's procedure, it was repeated when the Taft-Hartley Bill came up for consideration. Thereafter it was arranged with Director Webb of the Budget Bureau that the Legislative Reference Bureau would refer to the Council any measures of possible interest, leaving it to the Council to decide whether under the terms of the Employment Act it should advise the president direct.

A significant opportunity for service came on June 22, when President Truman set up a three-part study on the foreign aid program and called for the Council to report on the impact of the proposed program on the national economy. The Council's comprehensive report, submitted on

October 18, was prepared by a staff committee of Paul Homan, Gerhard Colm, and Walter Salant and gave assurance of the economic soundness of the program under consideration. In expressing appreciation for the full study, President Truman said: "The Council of Economic Advisers played an invaluable role, not only by preparing its own report, but by furnishing staff assistance to the Secretary of the Interior and the Citizens' Committee under the Chairmanship of the Secretary of Commerce" (EPS, pp. 167-168).

The Council also thought that it should be free to offer suggestions to the president on matters of business policy. Following the settlement of the coal miners' strike, the Council drafted a statement for use by the president if he considered it "salutary" for him to issue it. On July 14, this was given out, with minor changes, as a Statement of the President. About this time, Nourse took the initiative in sending the president his personal views on a problem occasioned by the shortage of steel scrap, since there was disagreement within the Council on whether it should offer its views on this problem. Although no direct reply was made to Nourse's letter, he was pleased by the way the president handled the problem.

Thus by mid-1947, the Council had established a modus operandi in advising the president on economic problems that it considered pertinent to its responsibilities under the Employment Act.

Reaching Out to Political Scientists

In his address to the American Economic Association, Nourse had explored the importance to economists of the Employment Act of 1946. Since he thought the act had equal significance for political scientists, he gladly accepted an invitation to discuss its governmental aspects at the annual meeting of the American Society of Public Administration held on March 14, 1947, in Washington, D.C. He chose as his subject: "Public Administration and Economic Stabilization."[5]

In his introductory remarks, Nourse pointed out that the economic problems to be faced under the Employment Act could not be separated from those relating to its public administration, for neither could be "dealt with understandingly or effectively in isolation from the other." He saw the act as providing a basis for a "happy and fruitful marriage—between political science and economics," and then said:

> My gratification at the passage of the Employment Act of 1946 and my willingness to take part in the attempt to bring it into effective operation stem largely from my belief that this legislation represents a real and substantial step in the evolution of our politico-economic institutions. It seems to me to promise better coordination between private units of

economic enterprise, large and small, and other undertakings—from local to national, which, by reasons of the functions involved, need to be organized on a public or governmental basis.

He maintained that "Government is inescapably integrated into the economy," for "in the final analysis, economic well-being is the major end for which the state exists." To him, the Employment Act was "faithful both to the political traditions of our Republican form of government, with its division of powers, and to our economic tradition of maximum private enterprise, with complementary use of public agencies for economic ends." He saw the Annual Economic Report of the President as "essentially an extension of the state-of-the-union procedure." He did not think that the Employment Act altered "the traditional system" of operation in any way, since the Council of Economic Advisers "merely augments the facilities of advice formulation under the President."

Nourse did not see the Employment Act as providing "any logical or ideological rule or criterion for determining the line between private, publicly regulated, and governmental activity in the economic area." He thought the "one distinctive change" introduced by the act was "in defining the concept of a national economic goal, attempting to gauge the amount by which actual performance falls short of that goal, and declaring formal governmental responsibility for seeking every means of closing that deficiency." It was his view that

> the passage of this Act reflected a sober realization that, in the state of technological and organizational development to which we have now advanced, it is quite possible for our economic life, once it is thrown out of adjustment, to fail to rebound with the resilience of an immigrant population pioneering a virgin land during the early decades of the technological revolution. It reflects the somber possibility, revealed during the 30's, that even such smart people as we are, could be subject to even more severe spasms of depression or the chronic invalidism of low production, underemployment, and meager purchasing power. It recognizes that if we are to hold the momentum attained under the stimulus of war and convert it into a steadily held high pace of peacetime activity, economic administration must do much by way of conscious and intelligent contriving.

Nourse believed it wise that the act did not prescribe in any specific way what the government itself must do. He said:

> It is its great merit that it left the details to be filled in by the subsequent process of legislative and administrative action and did not bind either the Congress or the executive agencies to any individual panacea or particular type of remedy. Instead it enunciated its purpose in the policy clause of the Act: "To coordinate and utilize all its plans, functions, and resources for the purpose of creating and maintaining . . . conditions under which there will be afforded useful employment opportunities . . . and to promote maximum employment, production, and purchasing power."

He believed that "the very fact that this measure does not authorize the use of a specific remedy, but rather establishes a process for choosing and combining either preventative or remedial measures, emphasizes the responsibility which devolves upon public administration in the broadest sense, legislative and executive, federal, state, and local, to promote the objectives of economic stabilization on a high level of efficiency."

Nourse finished his talk by examining in some detail the way in which the Council of Economic Advisers was set up to function. He emphasized that the Council was possessed of no administrative authority or power to issue directives by saying: "Ours is a purely consultative and advisory role not merely as to the president individually but also, as a staff arm of the president, to a considerable number of administrative offices of the federal government." Moreover, he made clear that the Council's advisory role extended to state and local governments, and to private business organizations through its consultative arrangements. He posed the problem of the Council in these words:

> Thus we must live our life and develop our usefulness on the administrative level but in the scientific atmosphere of ends-and-means analysis and comparative evaluation, not in the rarefied atmosphere of authority. Far from being in a position to issue directives, we do not even voice our own recommendations publicly. To attain a large measure of usefulness we must win, not merely with the President, but also among the executive heads of departments, agencies, and commissions, a solid respect for the professional competence of our work—and also for its imperturbable realism. Finally, we must also win the confidence of the official heads of private economic organizations and of spokesman for "the public."

It was evident in this address that Nourse had great confidence in the power of reason. He believed that with goodwill and understanding, the Employment Act of 1946 could provide a means for the solution of the nation's number one domestic problem—the stabilization of the economy on a prosperous basis. In the next two years, his idealistic conception of the powers of the act and of the role of the Council of Economic Advisers in helping implement them was to be severely tested in the crucible of political realism.

Promoting Economic Sanity

During the first half of 1947, Nourse used every opportunity to promote what he considered sound economic policy. He believed that the country would pass definitely from a seller's market within the year, and he was hopeful that if American business could make this transition with orderly and skillful price and cost adjustments, it would bring some years of well-sustained prosperity. He could not then foresee the rapid resumption of government spending necessitated by the deteriorating foreign situation which was to postpone indefinitely a return to normal economic conditions.

Believing that a return to a buyer's market was logical, Nourse urged businessmen to get ready for the change. In addressing the annual meeting of the American Retail Federation on February 25, 1947, he pointed out that the Employment Act was dedicated to high production and consumption under a system of "free competitive enterprise," and then said: "It is up to all branches of business to put the principle fully into practice in 1947 and the years that follow. No one knows precisely where prices, and costs, and volume are going to find their equilibrium in the years ahead. But we do know that if we are to have sustained prosperity we must keep the throttle open for volume production and sales. We must not try to maintain either price or profit margins *at the expense* of volume. That is 'restraint of trade' and is the antithesis of maximum production, employment, and purchasing power." He did not think that the adjustment to a buyer's market would be easy. "We are not going to move from the artificial prosperity of mass buying on the basis of a national debt of staggering size to the sound prosperity of a peacetime private market without making an indefinite number of small local decisions and adjustments."

Nourse again emphasized sound business leadership in addressing the Controllers Institute of America on March 17. Taking as his subject "Three Schools of Business Thought," he said: "The year 1947 will go down in history as a year in which private business management took some decisive steps toward determining what the future of the private enterprise system is to be." He looked back on 1946 as a period of getting the economy reestablished on a provisional basis as war controls were removed. Now he saw the problem becoming "Will the natural forces of market competition promptly restore economically sound and therefore permanently prosperous business relations?" He thought the answer would be largely dependent upon business behavior, and he divided business administrative officers into three categories: (1) those who believe in getting while the getting is good, (2) those who are endeavoring to operate with a "firm price policy" so as to reduce the dangers of inflation and possible work stoppages, and (3) those who accept the responsibility of working toward business stabilization by reducing prices as steadily as high volume production and efficient management will permit. Nourse thought that the first group was doing everything possible to dig the grave of private business enterprise, while the second and third groups, and particularly the third group, were showing the power of well-trained and responsible management to perpetuate our system of private competitive enterprise. It may be said that he was preaching to this business audience, but the fact remains that private business concerns must accept responsibility for their own actions if a "private enterprise system" is to work. Nourse believed in calling a spade a spade and in giving credit where credit was due.

In an address to the American Marketing Association on June 12, 1947, Nourse stressed the importance of marketing in the process of economic reconversion. After stating the three objectives of the Employment Act—"maximum production, employment, and purchasing power"—he said: "I am inclined to think that the longer we live under and work with this measure, the more our interpretation will center on the first of these terms, namely, maximum production." But he held that the attainment of maximum production would place a heavy burden upon marketing institutions to see that consumer demands were kept in line with the nation's productive power. In his opinion, "market absorption of our enlarged post-war production" would call for more efficient procedures rather than a "back to normalcy" attitude. In the highly competitive buyer's market he saw coming, there would be need for "price reduction in step with every technological and organizational development," if consumer demands were to make possible the attainment of maximum production of goods and services.

Helping on Budget Policy

From its establishment, the Council enjoyed good relations with the Bureau of the Budget—its "sister agency" in the Office of the President. James E. Webb, the Director of the Bureau, recognized the value and complementary nature of the Council's work and did what he could to smooth the way for the Council's development. "As the Council took over and expanded the function of broad analysis of the functioning of the economy," it became obvious to Webb that the relationship of the Council and the Budget Bureau should be strengthened and systematized. Therefore, in May, 1947, he invited the Council and its representatives to sit in with him and his top aides to reconcile views on desirable budget policy for the 1948 fiscal year. This involved coming to agreement on such matters as the state of the economy, the business outlook, the trend of the national income, and prospective federal revenue. This meeting, said

Nourse, "gave us our first formal introduction into this important joint function of the two staff arms of the President's office" (EPS, p. 173).

The exploratory meeting in May led to further meetings in the early fall when the budget was being firmed up, and in December before the drafts of the President's Economic Report and his budget message were put in final form. Working harmony between the two agencies in developing these important state papers was also greatly facilitated by almost constant interstaff relationships. The procedure established in 1947 set the pattern for subsequent years.

"Organized Labor and Economic Stabilization"

Nourse attributed great importance to an address for the International Union Convention of the Brotherhood of Railway and Steamship Clerks in Cincinnati on May 14, 1947, for he saw this as an opportunity to make a "major statement as to how the policies and actions of organized labor fit into the objectives and means for obtaining them outlined in the Employment Act of 1946." He took as his subject "Organized Labor and Economic Stabilization."[6]

In this address, which was made at a time when organized labor was demanding large wage increases to meet higher prices, Nourse stressed the importance of the engineering approach in dealing with "the problem of economic adjustment under free enterprise and collective bargaining." He insisted that "we must acquire a basic understanding of the broad repercussion and long-run-cause-and-result relationships involved in business actions." He saw the basic problem of reconversion, not yet completed, as keeping the momentum of high level economic activity while converting it "to orderly market transactions on a sustaining basis."

Nourse emphasized three points in his analysis: (1) "that organized labor settlements must be the parent and not the child of economic stabilization;" (2) "that restriction of production must be definitely opposed and not even silently condoned by organized labor if the great objectives of the Employment Act are to be achieved;" and (3) that the long-feared post-war economic depression can be avoided only through "the intelligent and determined participation of organized labor, of corporate management, and of farmers and their associations," backed up by wise complementary lines of policy and action by the government. He saw no reason why the nation should not have a period of sustained prosperity, provided that as a people we are "smart, and tolerant, and well disciplined enough to work together in a democratically organized program" to realize this end.

Helping Launch the Joint Council on Economic Education

In the summer of 1947, Nourse became deeply interested in a projected program for better economic education in the secondary schools, and this was to be one of his major concerns for the rest of his life. At that time, G. Derwood Baker, a professor of secondary education at New York University, with a group of colleagues was vigorously promoting the idea of a workshop on economic education for secondary schools. He had enlisted the support of the Committee on Economic Development, then headed by Paul Hoffman, which had made a grant of $12,000 to finance "a pilot project to determine whether it would be possible in three weeks of intensive work to give public school personnel a reasonable comprehension of the fundamental aspects of our American economic system," and he was faced with the problem of planning the program and recruiting the staff, consultants, and participants. To get suggestions on how the workshop idea could best be developed, Baker turned to his old friend, A. D. H. Kaplan of the Brookings Institution, who arranged for an appointment for Baker to see Nourse. Baker has told of his meeting with Nourse in the following words:

> You can imagine that it was with a great deal of trepidation that I climbed the stairs of the Old State Department Building and approached the office of so distinguished an economist. How would he respond to my project and to my limited knowledge of the field? You will appreciate how he put me at ease. He was deeply interested in the broad problem of the economic education of the citizenry, and where better to begin than in the secondary schools which enroll all the children of all people. He explored my ideas. He was pleased that this was not to be a propaganda effort in support of "free enterprise," that all segments of the economy and society would be represented. We spent ninety minutes going over topics to be explored; and I came away with a list of fifteen individuals who would be useful as economic consultants, and with the assurance that Dr. Nourse himself would be pleased to participate in one of our sessions. From that moment on I felt assured that we were dealing with an idea whose time had arrived.[7]

During the fall and winter, Baker, with his associates, worked out a program for a three-week workshop which was held in August, 1948, on the campus of the Riverdale School in the Bronx. It was attended by 65 participants who represented city school systems and state departments of education from across the nation. Nourse served as one of the consultants, and he gave a talk on the role of government in fostering sound economic thought under the Employment Act. According to Baker: "His seasoned scholarship and his gentility were impressive. He was not a hit-and-run speaker. He stayed for three days, and entered into all of our discussions and became one of the group. When I invited Dr. Nourse to speak I expressed the hope that he would be able to stay over a day or two as our guest. After his address I told him that we had transportation to Penn Station for him. His response was typically open and disarming: 'Trying to get rid of me are you? Sorry, but I took you at your word. I am staying over until Sunday.'"

Out of this first workshop, plans evolved for the Joint Council on Economic Education, which was incorporated in January, 1949, with Baker as president and with Nourse as a charter member of the Board of Trustees. Upon his retirement from the Council of Economic Advisers, Nourse became Vice-Chairman of the Joint Council on Economic Education, a position he was to hold until 1965, when he became an emeritus trustee.

The Midyear Economic Report

In the spring, the Council had proposed the issuance of a midyear economic report to supplement the Annual Economic Report of the President. President Truman had approved this suggestion, and the report, largely prepared by the Council, was submitted to the Congress on July 26, with the following brief introduction by the president:

> When my first Economic Report was presented to the Congress on January 8, 1947, the nation was turning from the economic controls of wartime to a free economy. Now, 6 months later, it is appropriate that we consider carefully what success we have had in meeting the problems of that process, what difficulties lie ahead, and what action should now be taken. It is for this reason that I transmit to the Congress this Midyear Economic Report.

The economic situation had shown some improvement in the previous six months, in that "prices increased sharply in the second half of 1946, increased more slowly in the first quarter of 1947, and then leveled off in the second quarter. This leveling off reflected some catching up of supply with immediate demand, an increase of consumer resistance and the encouraging response of many businessmen to the Government's price advice, which they recognized to be in their own long-range interest." However, it was pointed out: "This improvement in the price situation should not blind us to further need for price reductions in some cases. In other cases, there is need to hold the price line in the face of recent developments which revive some fears of another upswing of inflation."

The report said: "Belief in the free enterprise system as expressed in the Employment Act stems from the conviction that the processes of dynamic economic life are so complicated and change so fast that a multitude of local decisions and flexible revisions are indispensable to economic health and vigorous growth." Attention was given to four special problems of immediate concern, but of particular importance was the threat of wage increases outrunning industrial productivity should the recent settlement between the softcoal miners and the mine operators set a general pattern. The report said: "One major question raised by the coal settlement is whether the wage increase for the miners will give impetus to wage demands in other fields unrelated to the specific problems and possibilities of those particular industries. If so, it could lead to a more or less general wage-price spiral, increasing and prolonging our transitional difficulties. . . . Price boosts now in pivotal areas of the industrial field . . . can only add to inflationary forces. Another general surge of inflation would have only one result—the sharp recession which it is to everybody's interest to prevent."

The Problem of Economic Reconversion

With the midyear economic report completed, Nourse could center his attention on pertinent problems of economic reconversion. In view of his background, no industry interested him more than agriculture, where he saw basic adjustments needed. He expressed his thinking in an address to the American Institute of Cooperation on August 25 under the title, "The Position of Agriculture under the Employment Act of 1946." It was his theme that "organized farmers, no less than union employees and corporate managers, have a responsibility to develop a positive program under which their operations will contribute most fully to the long-run prosperity of the country as a whole." He noted that "not only the President and the Council of Economic Advisers but the whole country will be watching with close attention the way in which the action of farmers and the policies of cooperative and general farm organizations fit into the effort to check inflation, prevent a harmful boom, and contribute to an integrated program of national economic life." After mentioning certain recent developments in agriculture that were giving him much concern, he said:

> I suspect that within not so many years farmers will be looking to the Employment Act and the President's Economic Report to find means of protecting themselves against the slings of outrageous fortune when the world's scarcity of farm products has been overcome and the surplus problem is back with us. I believe the Employment Act of 1946 should be a powerful aid to all our major economic groups, each according to its needs as part of an inter-related whole. The question that bothers me is this: Are these various groups . . . ready to use this measure with wisdom and balance to the attainment of these great ends?

He said in conclusion:

May I suggest that today is the time for agriculture to put its own house in order, for cooperatives to lead in demonstrating the ability of an economically-literate and socially-conscious farm population to play, with high responsibility and self-discipline, its part in a stabilized economy at home, articulated with steadily recovering or advancing economies throughout the world. . . . The challenge is there to be met if we are to demonstrate to the world and to ourselves that our system of free enterprise under representative government has the powers and virtues we claim for it.

In an article for *Printers' Ink* (October, 1947), under the title "The Problem-Market Absorption," Nourse turned to the problem of sustaining production. He observed that this subject was of intense interest to him, since he had started his professional career as a market economist in 1915 when he wrote his doctor's thesis on "Market Mechanisms as a Factor in Price Determination." In opening this article, he said:

People with insight have been pointing out for several years that the end of the war brings the role of the marketing man back into top billing. . . . This role may be described as distributing abundance. It has never been done in any large and general way or on any scale such as that which now challenges us.

Emphasizing that maximum employment called for maximum production, he then said: "There can be little doubt that flow of productive effort and output can be maintained if one—and only one—condition is met, namely if the market continues to take the product." He also pointed out that "the marketing expert cannot come in and save the situation after production management has made its decisions. Market wisdom must guide production, cost, and price policy." He summed up by saying that "the last five years have demonstrated the tremendous capacity of our market to absorb goods and its equally tremendous power, on the production side, to supply goods to satisfy that demand. The market is the critical spot at which those two great potentialities must be brought to fruitful union."

Nourse dealt with the vexing labor problem in an article for *Dun's Review* (November, 1947), under the title "The Employment Act and the Act of Employment." He saw the need for greater "integration of policy in the whole labor movement." While recognizing the economic function performed by labor unions, he called for forbearance in their use of power. He said: "It would seem imperative that both labor and management abandon the race for each to get strong enough to beat the other and that, instead of gang fighting, they adopt in good faith the method of collective adjustment of the economic process in which they are both partners." In a final observation, he wondered: "Shall we ever find a collective contract in which both parties will agree to share in the outcome of business ventures on the basis of an external audit of the joint product *after* it has been ascertained rather than making the acceptance of rigid demands for settlement in an uncertain future the condition of operation?"

On November 20, 1947, Nourse gave an important talk to the Economic Club of New York on the subject "The Progress of Economic Reconversion." He then had served more than a year as Chairman of the Council of Economic Advisers, and he now had a tempered view of the economic problems of the nation. He began his talk by distinguishing economic reconversion from physical reconversion:

> For the first year and a half after V-J Day, we amazed the world and rather surprised ourselves at the speed and smoothness of our post-war reconversion. Civilian workers and plants were switched from making war materials to providing peacetime goods and services, and millions of men and women were reabsorbed from army, navy, and air forces with unexpected ease. But this is only physical reconversion. It will not achieve sound prosperity for the nation or assure stabilized prosperity in the years ahead unless we combine and complement this physical reconversion with the more delicate and difficult process of economic reconversion.

Nourse explained that the problem of physical reconversion involved engineering and industrial techniques, while the problem of economic reconversion was more difficult in that it called for going from a largely controlled economy back to one freed of wartime controls. He thought that "it must be evident to any thoughtful person that economic reconversion after this upheaval cannot mean 'going back to normalcy.' In a dynamic world there is no normal to go back to. Instead we must work out a carefully considered new set of pecuniary and operative relationships among the active participants in economic life. These include the economic relations between the individual citizen and the community of citizens known as 'the Government.'"

He held that "two precious years had been lost in failing to get down to the basic problems involved in economic reconversion while the nation 'muddled through a lot of piecemeal adjustments' which were of an inflationary rather than of a stabilizing character." Economic reconversion, in his opinion, would call for a new approach on economic problems which he outlined in this way:

> It involves a change in the form of question asked as the basis of an economic decision. The question ceases to be: What will give my company or my union or my agricultural unit the biggest gain in some relatively short-run period? The question becomes: What course of action by my company, my union, or my agricultural unit will contribute most to the enlargement of national productivity and the putting of this productivity on a sustained basis? When a man or an organization puts the question thus there is the unspoken premise: Only by promoting the largest and best sustained national prosperity can I in the long run have the best market in

which to sell my product, whether goods or labor or technical and managerial talent.

Nourse found this economic philosophy embodied in the Employment Act of 1946, which declared a clear and unequivocal intention to "foster and promote free competitive enterprise."

While he did not think that economic reconversion could be accomplished immediately without some continuation of economic controls, he was hopeful that more enlightened thinking by industrial, labor, and agricultural groups would gradually establish free competitive enterprise on a sound and enduring basis. He could not see how proponents of free competitive enterprise could expect it to function effectively without self-control.

The "Special Session" on Inflation Control

As the rate of inflation rose in the late summer and early fall, President Truman stepped up his warnings on the danger of depression unless prices and wages could be brought under control. The Council gave him encouragement in its quarterly report of October 1 by urging examination of the "full armory of control measures" to supplement the emphasis being given to control through education and voluntary cooperation.[8]

Convinced that the situation required action, the president called a special session of Congress on October 23 to meet on November 17 to deal with the related problems of inflation and European aid. He followed up the next day, October 24, with a nationwide radio address to emphasize the gravity of the domestic situation. He maintained that if the spiral of inflation, which was then up to 16 percent annually, was not broken, depression would surely follow with world-wide consequences. He said: "We could choose the course of inaction. We could wait until depression caught up with us, until our living standards sank, and our people tramped the streets looking for jobs. Other democratic nations would lose hope and become easy victims of totalitarian aggression. That would be the course of defeatism and cowardice."

While the decision to call the special session was justified by economic developments, it was deemed to be good political strategy. It was realized that if constructive results were obtained, the Administration could take the credit, while if nothing significant was accomplished, the Republican Opposition could be blamed. This was the thinking of the Wardman Park strategy group, of which Clark Clifford and Leon Keyserling were dominant members. Their views were expressed in a "Confidential Memo for the President," dated November 19:

If the President recommends a bold program and the Congress refuses to go along with him, then we will be storing up valuable ammunition for a later time. . . . Our record on prices must be crystal clear because there is the ever present danger that if prices continue to go up, the people may be so irritable and irrational about the problem that they will vote the "ins" out and the "outs" in. . . . Because of the probability of increasingly high prices in 1948, it is possible that the issue will reach a climax in the summer of 1948. This would come at a highly propitious time for the President and the Democratic Administration.[9]

The Council's views on what might be included in the President's Message in opening the Special Session, prepared at the request of Clark Clifford, were presented in an 11-page memorandum on November 5. Emphasis was placed on the use of fiscal and monetary policy and standby controls. The Council's recommendations were generally accepted, although some important officials in the government favored more emphasis on voluntary restraint and less on restrictive controls.

The heart of the President's Message to Congress on the first day of the Special Session, November 17, was a 10-point program for controlling inflation. Its more controversial provisions authorized allocation and inventory control of scarce commodities and consumer rationing and price ceilings on products in short supply.[10]

After holding hearings on the president's proposed program, the Joint Committee on the Economic Report accepted several of the "less controversial" recommendations, but it deferred judgment on those relating to rationing and other controls (EPS, pp. 192-193). Before the session ended later in December, Congress acted favorably on only 3 of the 10 proposals, and they were, in Truman's words, "of minor importance compared to the others." As Goodwin and Herren said: "Regulation of credit, rationing, and price control had been denied. . . . Effective steps might not have been taken against inflation by the Special Session, but a firm political foundation had been laid for the campaign of 1948."[11] Thus, while the president lost no time in expressing his "deep disappointment" with "such feeble steps toward the control of inflation," he was not surprised or made unhappy by this outcome.

Should the Council Testify Before Congressional Committees?

The question of whether the Council should testify before Congressional committees had remained "quiescent" (to use Nourse's word) until the Senate Foreign Relations Committee tentatively scheduled the Council to appear on November 12 for "interrogation" on the Council's special report on the impact of the foreign aid program. While Nourse thought that such an appearance "would seem natural and on its face innocuous," he feared that it might initiate a precedent for the Council debating issues of Administration economic policy. Nourse explained his position to the secretary of the Foreign Relations Committee and the matter was dropped. However, as Nourse recorded in his personal diary:

> This incident revived an issue which had been smoldering in the Council since the preceding winter. Neither Mr. Keyserling nor Mr. Clark was prepared to accept my interpretation of the Council as a professional agency merely serving the President with factual and analytical material and making confidential recommendations to him, but remaining personally detached from the policies which he subsequently enunciated. They were eager to make themselves influential, particularly on the Hill, in helping to carry out those policies which they had recommended or even some different or more or less modified policy which the President might present in the absence of or contrary to our recommendations [EPS, p. 205].

Just at this time, Keyserling and Clark were sensitive on this question, for they wanted to support the president's anti-inflation proposals before Congressional committees called to consider them. Nourse explained their attitude in this way:

> It had become a matter of comment in the press that Mr. Keyserling through his personal friend Clark Clifford had participated actively in the writing of the message which the President presented at the opening of the special session of the Congress. He was particularly eager to appear in behalf of the price control and allocation recommendations, and Mr. Clark was more than anxious to break a lance on behalf of credit controls. They both seemed to feel that if we were not prepared to support the President's policies we should not continue on the Council (EPS, p. 206).

Nourse did not believe that Council members should undertake to advocate the recommendations of the president while serving as his professional economic advisers. Nourse's expression of concern suggests the extent of the disagreement in the Council that was occasioned by this incident.

At about this time, support for the views of Keyserling and Clark came in an article in the Autumn number of the *Public Administration Review* by Senator Ralph Flanders, a member of the Joint Committee on the Economic Report. Flanders thought that much would be gained in bringing into focus the President's Report if the members of the Council were to meet with the Joint Committee and "present and elaborate on the economic reasoning underlying the President's report"—even if this were to prove embarrassing to them. After studying the article, Nourse explained to Senator Flanders why he considered the proposed procedure undesirable. He followed up by going over the whole matter with Senator Taft, the Chairman of the Joint Committee. In concluding the interview,

Taft in effect said: "I am not now prepared to take a final position on the question as a matter of principle. However, I am aware of the difficulties that you point out and since you feel the matter is important to the proper functioning of the Council, I will not make any call upon you to appear before our Committee" (EPS, p. 206).

While the issue was shelved, it was not settled. It was to come up again in early 1948.

The Council's Second Annual Report

The second annual report of the Council submitted to the president in December, 1947, briefly described how the Council had developed its organization and work program during 1947. However, the great bulk of the report was devoted to a penetrating analysis of the meaning of "maximum production" and means of obtaining it. Nourse believed that it was important that the public understand the full implications of the term "maximum production" as one of the key objectives of the Employment Act, and he largely drafted this part of the report.

To obtain maximum production, it was maintained, would require "wise development of our natural resources and the proper provision of capital goods and capital funds." Moreover, maximum production would require not only provision for the best possible equipment for the use of workers but also "ability to absorb the enlarging flow of product in step with the rate of capacity enlargement." This in turn would depend upon "sagacity" and "promptness" in making "appropriate price and income adjustments." It was recognized that "cooperative efforts of labor and management" would be required "to reduce or remove restrictive practices" so as to maintain an economy of "maximum employment, production, and purchasing power" as called for under the Employment Act.

The report stressed that capacity to consume would largely determine capacity to produce. "If we are to achieve and stabilize maximum production . . . we must in future have much higher consumption in all the lower and middle ranks," for "the small number of well-to-do will not be able to absorb the possible output of consumers' goods." To achieve continuous high levels of economic activity, business leadership would need to act "wisely and vigorously." Should private enterprise fail to provide adequate productive use of the nation's resources, the federal government as required by the Employment Act would be forced to take action. But, it was emphasized, government economic programs should be "carefully designed to add to the resourcefulness, the productivity, and the growth of our business system as a whole."

According to the report, maximum production would "involve real price competition" and reliance on the profit motive to direct economic activity. The report closed with this thought: "Maintenance of a state of maximum production, once it has been reached, is absolutely inconsistent with the use of monopolistic control to exact for any organization or unit a more favorable distributive position than would be meted out to it by a system of completely fluid competition."

The *Washington Post*, in an editorial on Christmas Day, hailed the report as a "unique public document" and called it "a contribution to clearer thinking on a subject about which there is a great deal of misconception."

The Economic Report of January, 1948

The President's Economic Report of January 14, 1948, was a far more comprehensive document than the first report of a year before. The postwar boom had expanded and inflation had become the number one worry. In opening this report, the president said: "As we enter the New Year, the American people are keenly aware that inflation is the dominant problem in our economic affairs." In presenting his economic objectives, he said: "The first objective for 1948 must be to halt the inflationary trend. . . . Our second objective for 1948 should be to maintain maximum employment, achieve maximum production, and adjust the price-income structure so as to stop the inflationary spiral without production cutbacks or excessive unemployment. . . . Our third objective for 1948 should be to establish firmer foundations for the long-range growth and prosperity of our economy in the years ahead." Under long-range objectives, he listed development of natural resources and capital equipment, development of human resources and productivity, and development of institutions and practices for a high-production economy.

The body of the report provided information on price and income trends and the course of inflation. It was pertinent that wholesale prices had increased 44 percent from June, 1946 to November, 1947. Attention was given to "the nature of inflationary pressures" and to the question of why inflation is dangerous as a basis for examining various adjustments needed to combat inflation. These included fiscal and credit policies, but special emphasis was placed on the need for selective controls over prices and wages. The president held that Congress should authorize him to impose limited controls as he had requested in opening the special session of Congress on inflation in November.

The final paragraph read as follows:

> Since our first experience with the Employment Act is occurring under conditions that give priority to measures needed to counteract inflation, we are given time to consider carefully the measures that will aid in meeting the threat of unemployment in the future. But we must not fritter away the time thus granted us. We must not be complacent and believe that the job of employment stabilization has been resolved. A boom carries in it the seeds of its own destruction. We must be prepared to act in time if we want to make good our promise and prove to the world as well as to ourselves that an economic system of free institutions can be made to work steadily as well as efficiently.

Nourse was generally pleased with the report as an objective economic document, and it was well received by the public.

The Council's Budget Problem Increases Tension

When the Joint Committee held its hearing on the 1948 Economic Report in January, Senator Taft, in accordance with his understanding with Nourse, did not call on the Council for testimony. However, Averill Harriman, Secretary of Commerce, who was serving as President Truman's "field commander" to present his economic program before the various Congressional committees, assumed that Nourse would appear in support of the president's program. When Nourse demurred after explaining why he could not testify Harriman did not push the matter.

However, the problem indirectly arose in the Council's January budget hearings before the House subcommittee on the Independent Offices Appropriation bill. As explained by Nourse:

> Certain Republican members of this committee sought to confuse the question of what funds the Council needed for efficient operation with issues of whether they agreed with particular aspects of the President's economic policy, and whether the Council as a body or the Chairman personally supported these particular recommendations. I tried to show that the Council was not set up by the Congress as a policy-making or policy-implementing body but as a factual and interpretive staff for the President. But the committee took a dim view of this kind of service . . . (EPS, p. 207).

It will be recalled that a year earlier this committee had taken a very critical attitude on the work of the Council and had reduced its budget request for the fiscal year from $400,000 to $350,000 after restricting the Council's ability to complete its staffing arrangements. Largely as a result, the Council was forced to return $90,000 of the appropriation for its first year. The same attitude prevailed at the budget hearing in 1948, and the Council's request for $350,000 for the next fiscal year was reduced to $300,000. "This action," said Nourse, "was linked to the question of what role the Council was to perform. The question had two aspects: one, whether the Council as such was an essential or even a useful agency; the other, what would be the scope of its operations" (EPS, p. 209).

The negative attitude of the committee was expressed in its report as follows:

> This agency has been the subject of searching enquiry on the part of the committee, many of the members being dubious as to its value. It appears that particularly all of the information which the Council has used has been developed by other agencies of the Government and could have been made available in useful form directly to the President by the agency originating it. There is little indication that, to date, the efforts of the Council in endeavoring to co-ordinate and interpret data have produced important results. However, this is a relatively new organization and the committee has made provision for it for another year and expects to follow its activities closely. [Quoted by Nourse, EPS, pp. 209-210.]

The action of the committee was explained differently by the members of the Council. According to Nourse, "Mr. Keyserling and Mr. Clark attributed the House Appropriations Committee's cut of our budget request to the fact that my presentation did not make a case for an active role on the part of the Council." Nourse could not agree. "Personally," he said, "I think it is entirely explained in terms of partisan politics and a dislike of the whole concept of the Employment Act." He went on to say: "It seems a strain of logic to argue that by becoming protagonists of Administration programs we would have won the approval of, and a more liberal recommendation from, the Republican majority of the Committee on Appropriations. They had us either way. If we were responsible for administration policies that were personally obnoxious, we should have our power of mischief reduced or removed. If we followed a merely academic line, we were superfluous and should be pruned in the interest of economy" (EPS, p. 210).

The subject brought a heated interchange within the Council which Nourse recorded in his personal diary on February 23:

> In Council discussion Mr. Keyserling said that my tenacity in this matter raised the whole question of whether Council matters were to be decided by majority vote or whether one member could block action. I replied that if he and Mr. Clark wished to invoke a majority rule procedure, I would be entirely willing to accept it for the Council, but as a matter of principle I could not accept it for myself in the present instance. I had made it entirely clear to the President in my letter accepting an appointment to the Council that this was on the premise that the Council would be kept clear of the political arena. If it were now to be launched into that arena, it would need a chairman of different talents and tastes than mine, and I would gladly step aside so that such an appointment could be made. Both he and Mr. Clark said that this was not an acceptable alternative, and since I was "stubborn" in my position, they would abide by the result [EPS, p. 207].

However, Keyserling could not agree with Nourse's position. In his Oral History Interview for the Truman Library, he later said: "Now, although Nourse was Chairman, he was one among three equals, and what do you do on a multiple body on a matter of procedure. You go by majority vote. The chairman can be outvoted. So it was Nourse's obligation, in my view, once we outvoted him on it, either to go or have one of us go and say: 'I'd rather have one of the others do it.'" As dissention over this question could not be resolved within the Council, it was to remain a sore point until the deadlock was broken by the president during the electoral campaign in the late summer. Keyserling claimed that this situation became almost impossible because Nourse went around the country claiming that the other two members wanted to politically support the president. While there is no evidence to justify this imputation, it was realized by those who knew the inside situation that the Council members were badly divided on this issue. In view of Keyserling's close relationship with Clark Clifford and Charles Murphy it can be assumed that the White House was aware of the disagreement within the Council.[12]

Advising the President, 1948

In 1948, the Council, in Nourse's words, "extended itself, or was drawn into more active participation in several current situations" (EPS, pp. 222-228). On February 12, the Council, at the request of Clark Clifford, provided a brief statement for the White House on the abrupt decline in commodity prices. Later in the month, the president instructed the Council to analyze the economic impact of advances in steel prices, and its seven-page statement on the subject was released to the press on March 10. In a memorandum on March 24, the Council advised the president on the economic problems inherent in the new preparedness program brought on by the Communist coup in Czechoslovakia in February. Truman replied the following day: "I think you are working in the right direction. We must be very careful that the military does not overstep the bounds to a war footing—that is not what we want."

In its quarterly report on April 7, the Council examined several disturbing developments—the February break in agricultural prices, the rise in steel prices, and wage increases. Concern was expressed that Congress had reduced taxes by $5 billion annually while approving on the same day the European Recovery Plan that would cost about $6 billion. The Council thought that the president might wish to release this report to the press for the enlightenment of the public, and on the recommendation of the cabinet, it was issued from the White House. Early in May, Nourse gave the president the Council's views on the pressing steel-wage problem and received an appreciative reply. He also gave John Steelman, the Assistant to the President, his personal suggestions on a serious rail strike. He said: "I am aware that this is not a situation in which you or the president conceive that my duties need concern me or that the services of the Council are called for. However, I hope that as an older man I may be indulged in stating my views in a matter that challenges us both simply as social scientists and as citizens." Steelman phoned Nourse to thank him heartily for his views which the president and he considered sound. The foregoing incidents show that the Council was functioning effectively in advising the president as occasions warranted.

Economic Indicators

When the Council of Economic Advisers began operations in 1946, the fiscal division of the Bureau of the Budget was issuing a small chart book quarterly in multigraphed form, giving economic information under the title *Economic Indicators*, for the use of the president and administrative offices. Nourse and his fellow Council members believed that a report of this sort should properly be issued by the Council, and in the spring of 1948, the Council was in position to assume this responsibility. The Joint Committee on the Economic Report immediately saw the advantage of giving this report a broader circulation in printed form and arranged to issue it as a Committee print. The early issues published by the Joint Committee carried a letter of transmittal from the Joint Committee to the Congress, in which Senator Taft said:

> From the time the Joint Committee on the Economic Report was established, its members realized that one of its basic needs was a concise and meaningful picture of current economic trends and developments. Fortunately the Joint Committee finds that *Economic Indicators*, a set of basic charts and tables compiled monthly by the Council of Economic Advisers, admirably fills this need.

Taft then explained that the Joint Committee had for several months provided the Congress and the public with a limited number of copies of *Economic Indicators* and that the response had indicated such widespread interest that the "Committee has arranged to release *Economic Indicators* each month as a Committee print." The following year, the Joint Committee was authorized to continue issuance of *Economic Indicators* as a regular monthly publication available to the public on a subscription basis. Publication and distribution of *Economic Indicators* by the Joint Committee brought favorable attention to the Council of Economic Advisers and greatly enhanced its prestige in the business community.

The Impact of ERP and Defense Programs

At the annual meeting of the Chamber of Commerce of the United States on April 27, 1948, Nourse spoke on a subject of increasing interest to the business community, "The Impact of ERP and Defense Programs on the Domestic Economy." Noting how the costs of the European Recovery Program and growing defense needs provided a stimulant to the economy which allayed immediate fears of a recession, he was concerned that the growing increase in such expenditure might revive inflationary pressures "in menacing form." He agreed that these programs might require government funds to encourage adequate plant for anticipated production needs should private financing not be available, but he did not like the idea of putting "more industrial plant in government hands" if it could be avoided. While he thought that certain long-range benefits were foreseeable from these programs in that they constituted investments in future international trading opportunities and protection from actual destruction of our wealth, he said: "Five, ten, or fifteen billion dollars' worth of goods and services a year cannot be withdrawn from our economy during the next few years and still leave the real income of consumers as high as it would otherwise be during this period." While he admitted "in perfect candor" that the foreign aid and defense programs gave a lift to the economy, he was apprehensive that they would make more difficult the ultimate attainment of the hoped-for equilibrium of a "free and well-stocked market."

A Report to Political Scientists

As a political scientist, Bertram Gross, Assistant to the Chairman, was interested in explaining to the political science profession how the Council functioned under the Employment Act. His close relationship to the legislative development of the act and its early administration uniquely fitted him for preparing an article in the *Political Science Review*, April, 1948, on "The Role of the Council of Economic Advisers." Nourse agreed to collaborate on the article, which was published under the joint authorship of Nourse and Gross. Each prepared sections of the article but Nourse gave Gross credit for doing much of the work.

This article explained how the Employment Act evolved from the original Full Employment Bill. "The aim was broadened to include 'maximum employment, production, and purchasing power,' and in place of specific emphasis upon public spending as a method of achieving the objective, it was provided that the government 'coordinate and utilize all its plans, functions, and resources.'" The authors pointed out that the

Leon H. Keyserling, Nourse, John D. Clark, and President Truman, August 9, 1946, as the Council of Economic Advisers begins its official career. (Used by permission of the *New York Herald Tribune*.)

The Council of Economic Advisers and staff in front of Old State (the Executive Office Building), October, 1946. Behind Nourse and Clark is Margaret Quill, Nourse's administrative assistant, and behind her are Fred Waugh and Gerhard Colm, two of the top staff members.

President Truman with his cabinet and top advisers, 1947. © Harris & Ewing.

James E. Webb, Director of the Budget; W. Averell Harriman, Secretary of Commerce; Clinton P. Anderson, Secretary of Agriculture; Nourse; and John R. Steelman, Assistant to the President; in Steelman's office, 1947.

The Council of Economic Advisers: John D. Clark, Nourse, and Leon H. Keyserling, 1947. (Wide World Photos, Inc.)

Nourse; J. Edgar Hoover, Director of the FBI; Tom C. Clark, Attorney General; and W. Averell Harriman, Secretary of Commerce; stalking the steel industry, 1947. (From the *Washington Evening Star;* used by permission of Gib Crockett.)

Nourse with fellow economists, 1947. (Chase-Statler photo.)

W. Averell Harriman, Secretary of Commerce; Nourse; and Clinton P. Anderson, Secretary of Agriculture; April, 1947. © Harris & Ewing.

Nourse with Paul G. Hoffman, Chairman of the Committee on Economic Development, 1947. (*New York Times* photo.)

Nourse with H. Christian Sonne, Chairman of the National Planning Association Board of Trustees, December, 1947. (Chase-Statler photo.)

Nourse with Sen. Joseph C. O'Mahoney, November, 1948. (*New York Times* photo.)

Nourse with Charles F. Brannan, Secretary of Agriculture, November, 1948. (Associated Press photo.)

Nourse meets the press, January, 1949.

Meeting in the White House Cabinet Room (July, 1949) to discuss President Truman's Special Message are Charles S. Murphy, Administrative Assistant to the President; David E. Bell, Special Assistant to the White House Office; Leon H. Keyserling, Vice-Chairman of the Council of Economic Advisers; Robert C. Turner, White House staff consultant; Nourse; and John D. Clark, Council member.

Cartoon from Nourse's records.

Cartoon by Cloyd J. Sweigert. (Used by permission of Mrs. Cloyd J. Sweigert.)

Nourse's last year with the C.E.A.—1949.

From the *New York Herald Tribune*. (Used by permission of Dan Dowling.)

economic reports provided for under the Employment Act had "gone beyond any previous Presidential messages in laying before Congress and the country a full picture of what has been happening to the American economy, and in developing a comprehensive national policy geared to the maintenance of prosperity." They said: "The framers of the Act approached their task in terms of developing governmental machinery that would fully gear into the constitutional separation of powers between the legislative and executive branches. Rather than ignore this separation or attempt to bestride it through the creation of a composite or in-between body, they chose to set up a council to advise the President and a joint committee to perform a similar function for Congress."[13]

In their exposition the authors pointed out that the Council was strictly an advisory body, and not an administrative agency. They said:

> The purpose of the Employment Act in setting up the Council was to have an agency that would concentrate on advising the President and not be sidetracked or diverted by other responsibilities. . . . Under the Act the Council has no administrative powers or responsibilities. It does not issue directives to other agencies. It does not supervise the execution of Presidential policies. It does not engage in activities to build up popular support for the President's program. It has not taken on the task of explaining the President's proposals before congressional committees.

Emphasis was placed on the non-political character of the Council's work. "The present Council has been careful to operate on a strictly non-political plane. Whatever the personal views of its members on political issues, the Council does not become a vehicle for expressing them. Even appearances before the Joint Committee on the Economic Report or to other congressional committees to discuss economic issues under legislative consideration has been eschewed."

It is, however, of much interest that a footnote to this last sentence pointed out that this position [so far maintained by Nourse] was not unanimously held by all members of the Council. The view of Keyserling and Clark was expressed as follows: ". . . the intent of the Act will best be served if the Council extends cooperative professional assistance to the Joint Committee as . . . it comes to consider the fundamental materials contained in the President's Economic Reports as transmitted to the Congress." This was the first public expression of a difference among the Council members on the question of reporting to the Joint Committee.

The Joint Economic Committee Splits on Party Lines

The Joint Committee on the Economic Report did not complete its report on the President's Economic Report for 1948 until May 11. The

Council was pleased with the following statement in its introductory section: "The economic reports of the President give extremely valuable assistance to all those who are interested in solving the problems of continuous full employment. . . . We feel that the operations under the [Employment] Act have fully justified its passage and have given us a good start on the national economic policy guided by more information and study than we have ever had before. To the extent that we present any criticism of the reports, we do not intend to reflect in any way on the manner in which this work was done" (EPS, p. 195).

In making its report, the committee split on party lines. All eight Republican members signed the "Committee Findings," while the six Democratic members signed the statement of minority views. The Republican majority stated that "the inflation condition is due to an attempt to accomplish more than is possible at our present capacity for production. Our first recommendation is that Government expenditures be reduced." With regard to inflation controls, the majority report said: "Our committee is very much opposed to the establishment of over-all Government price controls, wage controls, or allocation controls in time of peace." The Democratic minority accepted the President's program without qualification. It was evident that nothing would be done in Congress on the president's anti-inflation program until after the coming presidential election.

"Economic Stabilization in a Troubled World"

On May 31, 1948, Nourse addressed the annual dinner of the Illinois Institute of Technology alumni association. He chose as his subject "Economic Stabilization in a Troubled World." This occasion gave him special pleasure, in view of his student days at Lewis Institute, which had evolved to become the Illinois Institute of Technology. He happily expressed this relationship in his first sentence by saying: "You may have a tepid interest in me personally as a son of Lewis Institute and thereby a son-in-law of Illinois Institute of Technology." He looked upon this address as an opportunity to explore with a serious-minded audience some of the economic issues that were confronting the Council of Economic Advisers.

As a foundation for his presentation, Nourse explained that "the great objective of the Employment Act was to devise suitable business and governmental structures and procedures to the end that we might have better sustained use of natural resources, manpower, and capital in the satisfaction of the material wants of the nation." However, he went on to say: "This did not mean merely smoothing out such highs and lows as have been encountered in the past and stabilizing their median level. It meant that we should mobilize our economic brains to fashion measures—preventive as far as possible, remedial when necessary—to combat the century-old disease of modern capitalism, the␣so-called business cycle."

Following a review of the abnormal inflationary conditions that had confronted the Council of Economic Advisers in its first two years, he said:

> As an analytical economist, I am profoundly interested in watching as objectively as possible the trend of economic behavior in this great land of private enterprise and democratic government. We have evolved to a state of gigantic corporations and massive labor unions. We have acquired a tremendous national debt through steps which were probably unavoidable and which certainly cannot be retraced. And we have created for ourselves "big government" which, if you will examine the figures, is predominantly military. It therefore becomes a fascinating question whether we have enough economic "savvy" and powers of discipline or forbearance by power groups to make it possible to curb orgies of headless speculation or to rally from sinking spells of paralyzing disillusionment and fear. In other words, can our free society manifest a healthy social adjustment, or will a manic-depressive psychosis become chronic as we pass from adolescence to maturity?

Taking a broad view, he saw grounds for optimism in the sense of responsibility being shown by industrial managements, labor leadership, banking organizations, and government in endeavoring to check the process of inflation. "I submit," he said, "that we have done a tremendous job of economic reconversion without any great amount of internal strife or more than minor sabotage. We have maintained a high level of national production, simultaneously raising the standard of living of the working population and investing tens of billions of dollars in the plant which will make labor efficient in the future. All this was done, moreover, while we were sending unprecedented exports abroad to relieve devastated countries and reconstruct the world economy."

While gratified by achievements in reconversion, he was concerned by the new problem "of how much our economic stabilization may be disturbed by the prospect of having to live in a troubled world—even though its disturbance is 'short of war.'" While fully cognizant that expenditures for national defense and foreign aid commitments were necessary for national survival, he cautioned that they must be carefully managed so as not to impair the economic strength of the nation. He saw the problem as being "how can this burden be distributed most equitably and with least danger to the efficiency of production?" He did not think we could "have our cake and eat it too."

Looking back on this talk many years later, Nourse said:

> This was a sweeping review of the economic situation since the Employment Act was passed. The Act was coming to its first real test. At this time we were getting past the first bloom of post-war boom and the question was coming up as to what we would do if there were a downturn. So this was the first opportunity for old schoolmaster Nourse to make this sort of review....[14]

The Council After Two Years

In June, Nourse could look back on nearly two years of experience as Chairman of the Council with a high degree of personal satisfaction. The Council was now a respected agency of government. It had built a fine performance record on the economic reports of the president and on its annual and other reports to the president. The president was recognizing the value of its advisory assistance on current economic problems. It had maintained a non-partisan professional position on economic questions, and it had kept free from political involvement. It had established excellent working relations with government departments and agencies, and it had developed valuable consultative relationships with groups representing industry, labor, agriculture, consumers, and state and municipal governments. It was working constructively with the staff of the Joint Committee on the Economic Report. Through its annual reports and the public addresses of Council members, it had greatly increased understanding of the Employment Act and the role of the Council in effectuating its objectives. The competence of its professional staff was widely recognized, and it was well organized to perform required duties. The Council members were working together on economic problems with a minimum of friction, although there was internal dispute on whether the Council or its members should testify before Congressional committees. However, this had not become a dominant issue, since the Joint Economic Committee was not putting pressure on the Council to appear at its hearings. Altogether, Nourse had good reason to believe that the Council's usefulness as a professional advisory agency for the president had been demonstrated, and he looked forward to greater attainments in the future. He could not then forsee how drastically operations of the Council were to be influenced by forces related to the coming presidential election.

This was a happy period in Nourse's personal life. He was enjoying the intellectual challenge of his position and the social advantages of official life in Washington. He and Mrs. Nourse frequently entertained at their home or at the Congressional Club, and they seldom missed a good stage offering at the local theatres.

Chapter XII

STICKING TO HIS GUNS
(1948-1949)

From the beginning Nourse believed that the Council of Economic Advisers should avoid any political orientation, and he had endeavored to establish it as a permanent nonpartisan professional agency in the federal government. When he accepted the appointment as Chairman of the Council in his letter to President Truman of July 29, 1946, it was with the understanding that the Council "is conceived as a scientific agency of the Federal Government" and that "there is no occasion for the Council to become involved in any way in the advocacy of particular measures or in the rival beliefs and struggles of the different economic and political interest groups." He sanguinely believed that the Council should be so respected for the objectivity of its economic advice that it should be able to continue with little change in different political party administrations.

As the 1948 presidential election campaign began to take form, it became plain that it would be difficult for the Council to escape political involvement, for it was apparent that "loyalty" to the president would be expected from the Council and its members. While sympathetic to the president's political needs, Nourse believed that the perpetuation and usefulness of the Council would be jeopardized should its members step over the line and openly advocate the president's economic policies. Keyserling and Clark saw no reason why they should not give the president their full support. They looked upon the Council as an adjunct of the party in power, and they were concerned with putting over its programs. They realized that they would probably be replaced because of their known political views should Dewey be elected, so they had everything to gain from Truman's election.[1]

Revision of the 1948 Midyear Economic Report

Plans for the midyear economic report were to be drastically affected by the political situation. President Truman was determined to use all of his resources for his election, and this caused him to look with favor on a recommendation of the Business Advisory Council of the Department of Commerce submitted on May 14. It was proposed that the annual economic report of the President be replaced by two reports. The first, by the Council of Economic Advisers to the president, "would be a purely factual report with no statements of policy. It would be a comprehensive summary of the principal factors in the current economic situation which would, over the years, be accepted as an unbiased report by all groups." The second report, the President's Economic Report to the Congress, "would be confined as far as possible, to such policy recommendations as he decided were necessary."

The idea of an independent Council report was not new. It dated back to the proposal for a national economic commission which was rejected by Congress when the Council of Economic Advisers was set up under the Employment Act of 1946. Many believed that there was need for an objective economic analysis by the Council to supplement the Economic Report of the President.[2]

The recommendation of the Business Advisory Council was made with regard to the President's Economic Report called for in January, and thus it did not apply to the coming midyear report. It was discussed orally at a meeting of the Economic Policy Committee of the BAC with the Council of Economic Advisers on June 9, but no commitments were made, and the subject was kept under advisement. It was Nourse's view that the recommendation raised a fundamental issue, for "if we made this sort of separation it would be practically impossible to keep from revealing differences between our conclusions and the President's policy decisions." However, Keyserling and Clark favored the change. According to Nourse: "Both my colleagues were eager to have the Council's report cover not merely factual but considerable interpretive material" (EPS, p. 217).

While this problem was deadlocked in the Council, the president advised Nourse, through Steelman, that he would very much appreciate it "if I were willing to have the Council's report differentiated from the economic report of the President in the mid-year document." He wanted at this time, said Nourse, "to show the world that his reports were straight economics and that the White House did not inject any politics into them" (EPS, p. 218). As Nourse could not oppose the president's wishes, he reluctantly agreed to the separation with the tacit understanding that the report of the Council would be limited to factual and technical matters, leaving interpretation and recommendations to the president's report.

It is possible that Truman's decision was made on the recommendation of Clark Clifford, who was then his principal adviser on political matters, and that Clifford was persuaded by Keyserling that the change would be beneficial. Keyserling, in his Truman Library Oral History Interview (p. 72), said that the Council's report was separated "at my suggestion from the President's report, his report becoming a short document of four or five pages hitting the highlights, supported by a very long Council document of a hundred or two hundred pages, which went to the Congress twice a year with the President's Economic Report."[3]

When this decision was made, it had been agreed already with the president that publication of the midyear report would be held up until after the Democratic nominating convention in mid-July so that it would not be considered a political document. Thus when the report was transmitted to Congress on July 30, President Truman had announced by this time in his acceptance speech that he was calling Congress back into special session on July 27 to enact anti-inflation legislation, and that in opening this session he had recommended a specific program to control inflation which was essentially the same anti-inflation program he had proposed to Congress in the November, 1947, special session. As Nourse later remarked: "Since all of this declaration of Presidential policy was now an accomplished fact, the Midyear Economic Report of the President had little *raison d'etre*." In fact, the president's economic report ran to only seven pages, and except for a summarization of the economic situation given in the Council's report, it did little more than emphasize his anti-inflation program. The report opened with a section, "A Time for Action," which declared that action to curb inflation should not be postponed, and it closed with his recommended program for inflation control as given in his message to Congress on July 27.

Printed with the president's midyear report was the Council's report to the president, "The Economic Situation at Midyear, 1948," under the signatures of the three Council members. It was a comprehensive document of 49 pages, with 65 additional pages of statistical and technical appendices. Nourse later maintained that its closing section, "The Issue Between Inflation and Stabilization," was not a brief for a direct control program, but a pro and con statement of the issue between inflation and stabilization. He admitted, however, that it was difficult to keep this section of the report objective in the face of the desire of his colleagues to make a case for the president's program.[4]

With this report, the Council stepped forward as a policy-influencing agency. From now on it would be difficult to hide the Council's views under the cloak of the President's Economic Report. It was obvious that in the future, the Council would find it hard not to testify before Congressional committees since it was independently expressing its views. This became clear soon after the midyear report was presented, when pressure was brought on the Council to testify in behalf of the president's anti-inflation program at the time of the special session of Congress called by the president when he made his acceptance speech. To understand this situation, we must briefly examine the special session and its aftermath.

The Special Session Brings Presidential Decision

President Truman's primary object in calling the special session of Congress on July 27 was to place the blame for inflation on a "do-nothing," Republican-dominated Congress. Should any achievement result, this could be claimed as a victory for the Administration.

The political strategy involved in calling the special session was outlined in an unsigned memorandum dated June 30, which gave the views of the Wardman Park caucus group of which Keyserling was a leading member.[5] It will be recalled that the special session of November, 1947, had been designed "politically" to set the stage for the 1948 presidential election with the strong backing of the Wardman Park group. It was believed that inaction on the president's anti-inflation proposals gave the president a strong campaign issue for 1948 and that the strategy which worked so well in 1947 could be advantageously repeated. The memorandum dealt with the question: "Should the President call Congress back?" The opening paragraph said: "This election can only be won by bold and daring steps, calculated to reverse the powerful trend now running against us. The boldest and most popular step the President could possibly take would be to call a special session of Congress early in August."

In support of this idea, the memorandum made five points of which the following were typical:

1. This would focus attention on the rotten record of the 80th Congress, which Dewey, Warren, and the press will try to make the country forget....

2. It would keep a steady glare of publicity on the Neanderthal men of the Republican party....

5. It would give President Truman a chance to follow through on the fighting start he made on his Western trip. It would show the President in action on Capitol Hill, fighting for the people, delivering messages to Congress at joint sessions in person, broadcasting his messages, leading

his party in a crusade for the millions of Americans ignored by the "rich man's Congress."

The memorandum saw no danger of the special session backfiring. It concluded:

> This Congress is so closely controlled by reactionaries and lobbyists that it cannot pass satisfactory bills to stop the disastrous inflation which is frightening the people. . . . On the issue of price control, which will be the hottest issue of this campaign, the Congress cannot possibly act. The present Congress cannot take any steps to curb prices or to prevent the people from watching the cost of living go higher and higher and higher. This Congress is run by men who cannot pass price-control legislation without losing their financial backers and incurring the wrath of the N.A.M., the U.S. Chamber of Commerce, and other such groups.

To present his legislative program for the special session to congressional committees, the president made Paul Porter, former administrator of the Office of Price Administration, his special assistant. Porter immediately called upon Nourse for help, and this forced the issue on whether the Council should testify in behalf of the president before Congressional committees, for as Nourse explained:

> Porter was not disposed to view my scruples on this matter tolerantly as had the Chairmen of various Congressional committees, members of the Cabinet, and the President himself. As he was mapping the strategy of his campaign for the President's 8-point "emergency" program, he came to my office to explain the part he wished to assign to the Chairman of the Council of Economic Advisers. When I said that this was not a part that, in the best interests of the Council and the President, I could play, he suggested that a subpoena from the appropriate committee might bring me into action. I replied that it would probably not be a course that a committee chairman would think it altogether wise to take, but that, if he did so, I felt sure Mr. Truman would challenge his right to summon one of the President's personal aides. Mr. Porter did not accept this answer very cheerfully. He seemed more impressed when I pointed out some difficulties that I might encounter in answering, to his complete satisfaction, certain enquiries as to strictly economic issues that congressmen might raise as to the proposed program [EPS, p. 221].

Porter then called for a presidential decision, and according to Nourse, "the issue brought sharp division in the Executive Office." He recorded what happened in his personal diary: "After numerous telephone conversations with Mr. Steelman, Mr. Clifford, Mr. Porter, and Mr Turner, and with lengthy conference on the Williamsburg between the President, the White House aides, and Mr. Porter, and after positions had been taken and reversed, as I recall it, four times within the week, the President's final decision was given me in his letter of August 3rd." In view of its importance to subsequent Council history, this letter is given in full (EPS, pp. 221-222):

Dear Dr. Nourse:

Mr. Paul Porter has raised with me the question of whether I would regard it as appropriate for members of the Council of Economic Advisers to testify before Congressional Committees concerning the anti-inflation program I have recommended to the Congress.

As you know, I have considered from time to time in the past the question of whether members of the Council should testify before Congressional Committees. I am aware of the difference between your views on this subject and the views of your colleagues in the Council. I respect these varying views, which I am sure all of you hold most conscientiously.

Under these circumstances, it seems that the wisest course in the present instance is to permit the members of the Council to be guided by their own convictions. Accordingly, I do not wish to induce any member of the Council to testify if he feels it inappropriate for him to do so; nor do I wish to restrain any member from testifying if he feels that to be an appropriate part of his duties.

I am informing Mr. Porter of this letter, with the expectation that he will make arrangements for testimony from the members of the Council if any testimony is to be presented by them.

Sincerely,

/s./ Harry S. Truman

President Truman's letter resolved a problem that had long been festering in the Council. It gave Keyserling and Clark White House approval to testify before Congressional committees, and it presaged that they could accept invitations to appear in behalf of the President's Economic Report in the hearings of the Joint Economic Committee. President Truman really ducked the issue by confining his decision to the "present instance," for it could be inferred that if he were to continue as president, members of the Council would be free to testify before Congressional committees if requested. At this time, Truman was in the midst of his uphill fight for reelection, and he was not averse to making use of the Council to support his candidacy.

The President's letter gave Keyserling the opening he desired. In Nourse's words: "Mr. Keyserling had already been diligently preparing material to present in support of the control program if he could get the 'go' signal from the White House. On August 4 he made his presentation before the Senate Banking and Currency Committee. . . . I had been invited to appear but had been excused by the Chairman of the Committee" (EPS, p. 222).

Keyserling and Clark were greatly pleased with the president's decision. It broke the deadlock so far maintained by Nourse that Council members should not testify before Congressional committees in behalf of the president. As Keyserling said in his Oral History Interview for the Truman Library (p. 53): "Porter said 'This is absurd. I need the help of the Council.' Then Truman decided 'We will let Nourse not go if he doesn't want to go, and we will let Keyserling go if he wants to go.' So I went." Nourse later said: "President Truman saw no reason why [the Council members] should not be regarded as combat troops to be thrown into the Congressional battle for his policies" (EPS, pp. 416-417).

As the campaign unfolded, Nourse, as a nonpartisan professional economist, scrupulously avoided any direct participation. On the other hand, Keyserling, who was closely allied to the Democratic Party, felt no scruples in doing what could be done "non-officially" to further the president's reelection. While he did not make speeches in behalf of the president, he considered himself a member of the president's team and provided statistical material and passages for his whistle-stop talks.

"Agriculture in a Stabilized Economy"

During the election campaign, Nourse continued his regular activities. At this time, the agricultural problem had come back into the national limelight following the inflationary effect of a poor crop in 1947. In view of this general situation, Nourse welcomed an invitation to address the annual meeting of the American Farm Economic Association in September on the subject, "Agriculture in a Stabilized Economy." This title was apt, for Dr. Theodore Shultz had just published a popular book, *Agriculture in an Unstable Economy*, which proposed a system of forward pricing for agriculture.

It was Nourse's view that "the industrial sector of the economy can suffer unstabilizing jolts from a badly managed or incorrectly directed agriculture quite as truly as agriculture can be rocked by industrial disturbances. Thus," he maintained, "there must be a simultaneous, coordinated adjustment of agriculture and industry." Nourse favored the return of agricultural adjustment to the market as fast as it was feasible. He thought that Shultz was saying: "The market can't do it so we've got to have a special trick here of forward pricing."

Nourse's main concern was to examine agriculture's responsibility in the economy, so he challenged his audience of agricultural economists with this question: "How can agriculture be so organized and farms so conduct their business affairs that agriculture as a basic industry shall make the maximum positive contribution to the stabilization of the economy as a whole?" He thought it unfortunate that measures had not been devised "to prevent a rather moderate agricultural shortage from having such profound inflationary consequences as those of the latter half of 1947 and 1948." When Nourse made this speech, it was generally hoped that the new Agricultural Act of 1948 might help agriculture better adjust to its problems in the years ahead. Although he did not refer to this new legislation, he recognized it by saying: "True economic stabilization requires the dampening of boom influences quite as much as it does the bolstering of a collapse. . . . We should be . . . determined to be tough-minded and fearless in dealing with the agricultural adjustment problems in 1949 and 1950." He saw "a grave testing time for agricultural adjustment principles in the years just ahead" and said: "Agricultural statesmanship must ease the farm industry from its wartime stilts."

"Economic Implications of Military Preparedness"

In view of the threatening international situation, James Forrestal, Secretary of the Department of Defense, had arranged for a National Military Joint Orientation Conference "for the benefit of prominent citizens from all groups" on November 10, one week after President Truman's reelection. The first speaker was George Kennan of the State Department, who stressed that "diplomacy needs to be backed up by impressive military power and even with diplomacy thus buttressed, we have to face the possibility of a need for military action at short notice." Following other speakers, including James Webb, Director of the Budget, Nourse was called upon to consider the probable effect of increasing costs for military preparedness on the civilian economy. In introducing his talk, "Economic Implications of Military Preparedness," Nourse admitted that, "until recently at least, the economist who strayed into a preparedness conference . . . was likely to find himself about as popular as the well-known skunk at the bishop's garden party."[6] However, he saw common ground on which military men and economists could work together—the fact that "in providing the means of modern war the whole structure of economic society is involved." He thought the problem could be characterized as a question of "harmonizing economic supply and military demand."

After examining how the conditions of post-war reconversion had given rise to a strong inflationary situation, he said: "If prospects for peace had improved, or even not grown worse, throughout 1947 and 1948, our ability to adjust our economy to the requirements of sustained peace-time prosperity would progressively have been put to the test. . . . If the practitioners of communism had not thrust us back into the danger of war, we would soon have been thrust forward into the difficulties of peace." He thought the problem of readjustment of the economy to peacetime conditions was now being postponed by an increased scale of military expenditures. Moreover, he saw serious repercussions if the cost of the defense program should be abruptly raised. It might unleash new forces of inflation that would be hard to resist and it might call for controls over raw materials, wages, and prices.

He believed that a substantial expansion in military expenditures would raise a fundamental question: "Would such a development simply defer the attainment of peacetime economic objectives, or would it make them more difficult of attainment over an indefinitely long future period?" He saw several dangers to be considered. The diversion of national resources to war goods would "bring a new threat to the educational institutions of the country. It would provide more specialized plants for war production of little use for peacetime needs. It would distort price and income relationships to the disadvantage of the 'weak or unfortunate' [and the] continuance of controls might prove habit forming and lessen the spirit of self reliance in our people."

Nourse made it clear that he was not offering any judgment on what the scale of military expenditures would be. He was simply attempting to look frankly "at the actual costs, present and future, of a military effort of stated magnitude." He completed his presentation by saying:

> If any moral is to be drawn from the objective analysis of this problem it would go to these points: (1) that those who are entrusted with our foreign relations must be wise as serpents and harmless as doves so that the need for military effort shall be held or reduced to the lowest possible point; (2) that those who are entrusted with the military effort display the prescience and the abnegation that will direct every dollar to the point of greatest effectiveness, and forego every outlay based on traditional practice, corps pride, or dispensable ceremony; (3) that the Government stand ready to introduce those measures of finance and control which will minimize the disturbing effects upon the economy; and (4) that the people at large face the necessities of the situation, make the sacrifices, and accept the disciplines which are entailed.

One of the speakers at this conference was Dr. E. T. Grether, who was on loan from the University of California to the National Security Resources Board where he was Director of Economic Development in charge of economic mobilization and planning. In his handwritten notes of this meeting, he recorded that "Nourse's statement made a profound impression, so much so that it was released."[7]

The Election Upset of 1948

In the fall of 1948 Nourse thought—like many others—that Thomas E. Dewey would be the next president of the United States, and he pondered how this would affect the future of the Council of Economic Advisers.

The prevailing attitude was well illustrated by a special election edition of the Kiplinger magazine *Changing Times* which was devoted to the subject, "What Will Dewey Do?" Much to the chagrin of Mr. Kiplinger, this publication hit the newsstands the day after the election. With regard to the president's economic advisers, it said: "The basic economics of the Dewey Administration will be orthodox. The advisers will be orthodox. This means middle-of-the-road as contrasted with either left or right. The Council of Economic Advisers, which advises the President on how to watch for booms and busts and how to avoid them, in due course will be remanned."

Never a strong partisan, Nourse hoped that Dewey if elected would make effective use of the Council. He thought it important that the Council be continued on an effective basis, and he believed that he might be in a position to help as a member, if not as chairman, during the transitional period when the Council was being reconstituted. He looked upon a change of administration as a real test of the Employment Act, and he was committed to the success of the Council as a permanent nonpartisan agency of government. He later explained how he saw the situation at that time:

> It was pretty well known that I was not in full accord with the other members of the Council and that they were, perhaps, better in tune with the Administration than I was. . . . I was pretty well disenchanted with the possibilities of getting anywhere unless there were a change in the Administration. And, like everybody else, I read the signs as meaning that there would be a change of Administration. I felt that if Dewey came in he would not care to have Clark and Keyserling as his economic advisers. I had no way of knowing whether he would want me or not. My position was that if he had an interpretation of the Council's role, which was more in line with what I had written to Truman in accepting the post and if he wanted me to go on, I would be glad to do so, not merely as a matter of serving him, but in a professional sense of seeing whether a more objective and scholarly or professional use of the Council could be developed within the Executive Office of the President.
>
> I knew some people that had worked with Dewey in Albany and I took occasion to speak with one or two of them to get their views on how Dewey would utilize the Council, and I was encouraged by their replies. My own estimate was this: Dewey was trained as a lawyer. He would appreciate the value of staff work, just as any lawyer in a big office needs to have professional assistance in working out his own policies and positions and opinions. . . .
>
> When the election returns came in, I remember very definitely my feeling that this was the end of my career in the Council. I would not find it rewarding to continue in the sort of Council which would develop under a still more cocky President, after he'd upset the dope and secured his re-election single handed.[8]

Although Truman's victory caused Nourse to come "rather rapidly to the conclusion that the difficulties and burdens of further service would be quite disproportionate to any possibility of accomplishing helpful results" (EPS, p. 272), he could not in good conscience leave the Council. In fact, he believed that he was needed more than before as a counterbalance on the Council. While he was in this ambivalent mood, he decided to draft a frank letter to the president to see if he could work out a better understanding with him on the future operations of the Council. This drafted letter—which Nourse printed in full in his book, *Economics in the Public Service* (pp. 272-274)—throws much light on how Nourse was thinking at that time. After some gracious preliminary remarks, he said:

> I have labored hard in the past two and a half years to lay a solid foundation for the Council as a permanent feature of the Executive Office, to establish effective relations inside and outside of Government, and to get systematic studies under way on problems that emerge from the declaration of policy of the Employment Act of 1946. Upon this foundation it should be increasingly possible to bring the product of the best thinking professional economists and of experienced business and labor leaders to your desk. All this preparation, however, will be relatively useless unless the Council has opportunity to be heard before final policies are determined and decisions for action made. Certain issues will have to be faced and appropriate adjustments made with reasonable promptness.
>
> Your decision as to the role you wish the Council to play in future and the way in which it can most helpfully serve you will be interrelated with the question of its chairmanship. I have indicated clearly in the past that I am suited to my present position only if it is intended to make the Council a strictly professional agency and to give it a really effective position as a channel for "economics in the public service." If it is in any way to be assigned a political role or to be allowed to stray over into political activities or lay itself open to political influences, you would want an entirely different kind of Chairman, and I would want to be relieved of the position at once because I feel that it would be impossible to accomplish results proportionate to the labor and strain involved.

Nourse did not send this letter. On November 15, before it was put into final form, he received a telephone call from John Steelman in behalf of the president at Key West requesting that he "personally" set up an intra-cabinet committee on anti-inflation policy. As Nourse later explained: "Since this looked like a promising development, with which I should cooperate to the fullest extent, I withheld the letter I had drafted" (EPS, p. 272).

Truman's request was just the tonic Nourse needed, for the splitting of the midyear report had been a victory for Keyserling and Clark, and they had won their contention that the members of the Council should be free to testify in Congressional hearings. At this time, Nourse needed assurance from the president that his leadership of the Council was valued. Thus Truman thinking from his own needs gave Nourse just what he wanted—an expression of appreciation. This unsent letter and Truman's recognition of Nourse's capacity explain a lot about both men. Truman was a political realist and Nourse was not inflexible. The battle for supremacy in the Council was not over. Nourse still hoped that his conception of what the role of the Council should and could be would eventually prevail.

Nourse later said that his unsent letter was in no way an offer to resign. "That letter was simply raising again the question of my suitability to the sort of Council that the President wanted and it would have been quite out of range of possibility for me to get out in November or December, just as the President was coming back to take the leadership with the new Congress. I simply raised the long time question."[9]

As this unsent letter could have been considered something of an ultimatum, it was perhaps fortunate that it did not go forward. Nourse needed a reaffirmation of the president's position, but he should have known from over two years of experience that the president saw the Council primarily from the standpoint of its political usefulness, and that with victory behind him, he would be less dependent upon bipartisan support.

Nourse Stands Pat on Refusal to Testify

The sweeping Democratic electoral victory, giving majorities in both houses of Congress, made it obvious to Nourse that the Joint Committee on the Economic Report would be reorganized under the chairmanship of Senator O'Mahoney. He therefore decided to visit O'Mahoney "on the Hill" to see how the Council could best cooperate with the Joint Committee. He found O'Mahoney jubilant over the election results, and he immediately made it clear that he expected Nourse to support the Administration's program. Many years later, Nourse recalled in the following words the nature of the interview:

> I have a very amusing picture of us, with O'Mahoney wagging his finger at me and expounding his position rather than trying to learn what mine was and how compatible they were. But I remember that the line he took was, "Now we've got the President re-elected and we're going to go ahead on a real program." He implied "we expect you to go along with us" and certainly he said: "We'll want you to come up and discuss this with the Committee." To which I said: "Well Senator O'Mahoney, you know perfectly well what my position has been on that for some time back and I don't think that I can change that position. The President is perfectly willing to have me interpret the Council in that way." So that ended the relationship. From there on he dealt with Mr. Keyserling and Mr. Clark, both of whom

were not only willing, but eager to assume the role of ambassadorship to the Joint Committee on behalf of the President's policies.[10]

The Cabinet Committee for an Anti-Inflation Program

While President Truman was recuperating at Key West after his election triumph, he had become, in Nourse's words, "considerably concerned about inflationary dangers and how they should be dealt with in his forthcoming economic report." He therefore decided to meet this problem by providing "a more definite procedure for integrating the advisory service of Cabinet officers and executive heads with that of the Council in developing the content and text of his Economic Report." This led him to request Nourse to set up a cabinet committee for an anti-inflation program to work with the Council in developing the Economic Report. Nourse was to use the Council in such way as he saw fit, "but the purpose was to secure continuous discussion of policy matters with the Cabinet members or other agency heads particularly concerned, so that they would be in touch with developments and . . . we would promote as much agreement as possible on all features of the program" (EPS, pp. 228-229).

This development gave Nourse much satisfaction, and he observed in his diary at the time: "I interpret it as meaning an important recognition of the work of the Council and as affording an opportunity to have our materials and views fully considered throughout the executive branch before policy decisions are arrived at." The response from the cabinet members was encouraging. Secretary Snyder (Treasury) and Secretary Sawyer (Commerce) called him to express their gratification at this development "together with proper pride that they had helped bring it about" (EPS, p. 229).

The announcement of the plans for the new committee was well received by the press and radio stations. J. A. Livingston, in his syndicated business outlook column (*Philadelphia Inquirer*, November 28, 1948), explained that the committee was designed "to avoid a fiasco akin to that of November 1947 when the President's anti-inflation proposals were laid low by the President's own team [who] failed dismally to make out a good case for hastily improvised legislation." He maintained that "naming the Chairman of the Council of Economic Advisers to this job is evidence of political imagination and savvy—even brilliance. If it sets a precedent, if future Presidents and future Cabinets are to be regularly briefed on the economic outlook, then their handling of massive affairs—such as the budget, taxes, public works and recommendations for legislation—will be more sophisticated." Livingston did not think that Nourse's appointment to the chair of this committee meant a repeat program such as that of the year before, for at the moment, "crucial economic indicators point to an inflation lull." Nourse himself looked upon the committee more as a stabilization committee than as an anti-inflation committee, and he was inclined to focus attention on economic stabilization rather than exclusively on the current inflationary threat (EPS, p. 229).

Upon the president's return to Washington, he and Nourse agreed on how the committee would work. Nourse at once invited five cabinet members (Treasury, Commerce, Labor, Agriculture, and Interior) and the Chairman of the Board of Governors of the Federal Reserve System to "constitute the nuclear committee," with the understanding that as particular problems arose other agency heads would be invited to sit in on the committee's deliberations. Meetings were held twice a week in the conference room of the west wing of the White House. "In the last few meetings all members of the Council were present, and the draft of its 'materials for the President in the preparation of his economic report' was in the hands of the members of the Cabinet Committee."

Nourse kept the president well informed on the progress of the work of the committee, and on December 31, the president sat down with the Council and the full committee to consider the materials prepared for him. As Nourse called attention to "salient points in the draft" where there was not complete agreement within the Council or among the members of the Cabinet Committee, the president said, after reading the controversial passages: "No. That's the way I want it to stand." After a final conference between the Council and members of the White House staff on minor editorial matters, "the Economic Report of the President went to the Government printing office" (EPS, p. 230).

Nourse was greatly pleased with the work of the Cabinet Committee, which he considered a step forward in the area of Cabinet-Council relations. He later said: "I regarded the arrangement as the high-water mark in the development of the Council into a position of intellectual helpfulness within the executive branch."

Nourse Submits Resignation

While Nourse was organizing the Cabinet Committee and getting it into operation, he became aware that persons unfriendly to him were telling the president that he had been trading with the enemy during the election campaign. Nourse could not let this charge go unanswered, so he wrote to the president on December 15 to deny the allegations, while offering his resignation should the president desire it. He said in his letter:

> I have reason to believe that you have been told that for some weeks or

months prior to November 2, I devoted a major part of my time and effort "in saving my skin" in the event that there was a change in administration. This is absolutely untrue. . . . I have been deeply concerned that the Council of Economic Advisers should become established on a high professional plane, with its members not subject to the vicissitudes of politics but retained or replaced solely on the grounds of their qualifications as objective economists [EPS, p. 274].

Nourse then went on to point out that before the election he had made it known that in the event of a change of administration he hoped that "replacements would be made solely . . . to serve the President as contemplated in the Employment Act, and that there would not be a merely political housecleaning." He continued: "I said that if there were a new President, and he wished me to remain for a time in order to give a new chairman or members the benefit of our initial experience I should be glad to remain and serve to the best of my ability for a reasonable time. In view of my age and the hard work and tensions involved in the job it was and still is my hope that I can be relieved at a not too distant date." Nourse closed his letter by saying:

In view of this and other considerations, I think it appropriate at this time to hand you my formal resignation. Of course, I am not backing away from my duties or responsibilities in connection with your forthcoming Economic Report or the coordination of anti-inflation policy among the several agency heads of the Executive Branch. However, I hope you will regard this resignation as being on your desk any morning after these immediate responsibilities have been fulfilled to the best of my ability and that you will pick it up and inform me of your acceptance on the first day when you feel that the service of this agency to you would be bettered by such a change in personnel.

Regardless of what he may have thought, the president did not acknowledge this letter. He was aware of Nourse's deep concern for the welfare of the Council, which would have made his behavior during the campaign natural to him. Moreover, he considered Nourse too valuable a man to lose just at this time. So Nourse continued at his post with the satisfaction that he had explained himself while tendering his resignation to be effective whenever the president might wish to accept it.

Although Nourse's letter was ostensibly written to meet the charge that he had worked with Dewey representatives to protect his position, it also reflected his deep concern with current developments in the Council, for after the election victory of Truman, he found "the boys raring to go." He had come to the conclusion that the attitude and behavior of Keyserling and Clark made impossible his interpretation of how the Council should function; and he saw little alternative to resignation. While the unsent letter had asked for the president's affirmation of his non-political stance, the second letter simply offered his resignation whenever Truman chose to accept it. Nourse later explained the situation in the Council at that time:

> The tendency of the election of Truman was to make Keyserling and Clark both feel that I was a brake on the wheel of progress and that they were the ones who really had the mandate for a Council service and the right posture, and that they were now free to go ahead with support of more active measures and new legislation of a rather definite sort. They were working privately, rather than having it brought to the table of the Council and having our Council policy and attitude thought through with reference to whether this was the time now for direct controls on the market prices and for directive stimulative activities on the production side, both of which would mean proposing new legislation.[11]

To understand Nourse's predicament, it is necessary to realize that Keyserling and Clark, with the assistance of Bertram Gross and others on the Council's staff, were then drafting unofficially in the offices of the Council a bill designed to implement in various ways the Employment Act of 1946. How this bill, to become known as the Spence Bill, came to be developed with the Council becoming, in Nourse's words, "an inadvertent participant," was well set forth by Nourse in *Economics in the Public Service*.

The Genesis of the Spence Bill

Nourse explained the emergence of the Spence Bill in the following way:

> It had been the philosophy of the Murray "full employment" bill of 1945 that when the Federal Government detected, through the projection of investment trends, a scale of private spending for business expansion and technological improvement inadequate to keep total spending up to the full employment level, it should itself embark on a spending-investment program sufficient to close this gap.
>
> This would call primarily for a shelf of public works but, since a stabilized economy calls for the maintenance of private enterprise in the major productive areas, it was recognized that, if the government undertook to bring spending investment up to a full employment level, it would have to look to mining, manufacturing and power industries, not merely the building of highways, reclamation works, and slum clearance projects.
>
> Any specific espousal of such a range of government activities in the private investment area had been talked down in Congressional debate and hearings on the "full employment" bill and had been kept from specific inclusion in the Employment Act of 1946. The Act did, however, pledge the government "to utilize all its plans, functions and resources for the purpose of creating and maintaining ... useful employment opportunities ... for those able, willing, and seeking to work."
>
> Those who had sponsored the more aggressive type of statute hoped to see this general declaration of policy followed by one or more supplementary

statutes as occasion might arise for government support to declining industrial activity. Such a need, according to thinkers of this school, might emerge in either of two ways.

[1] The advent of recession might call for prompt activity on the part of the government in the construction of large public works or stimulation of the construction of private works in volume sufficient to offset any sag in private capital formation.

[2] *On the other hand, as the inflation movement persisted and accelerated through 1947 and 1948, the argument was advanced that these price rises were due to, or aggravated by, the inability or unwillingness of private business, but particularly industrialists, to expand productive facilities fast enough. Thus the flow of goods was not proportionate to the flow of money, and market scarcity led to price inflation.* [Emphasis added.]

Numerous attempts had been made to have this view expounded in the Economic Report of the President, or, after the dual form of domucent was adopted, in the Council's economic review. The President himself did not at this time manifest any desire to espouse the policy of having government supersede private enterprise in this manner, and he declined to lend his support to various senators and representatives who wished to introduce legislation of this character. They were of course free to proceed without active Administration sponsorship, and this led in late 1948 and 1949 to the drafting of the so-called Spence bill.

Its proponents, both in Congress and in the executive agencies, sought a rendezvous in the headquarters of the Council of Economic Advisers. They had spiritual support from some staff members and from at least one member of the Council, and it was rather hard as a matter of principle to take the position that our good offices should not be available to the drafters of a law, helping them to bring its terms into conformity with the general policies of the President and the purposes of the statute under which our agency has been created. . . .

At all events, H.R. 2756, introduced by Representative Spence of Kentucky on February 15, 1949, did have what amounted to a legislative drafting bureau in the Executive Office but was presented as a private rather than as an Administrative measure. It was to be cited as "The Economic Stability Act of 1949" and was described as "a bill to implement the established national policy of promoting maximum production, employment, and purchasing power and for other purposes."[12]

To fully understand this situation, it should be realized that the dream of the original Full Employment bill had never died out. It had provided a formula for massive government spending to forestall the scourge of another great depression, which was believed to be an inevitable aftermath of World War II. While its supporters had accepted the Employment Act of 1946 as all that was politically feasible in the early post-war period, they did not give up easily. As the inflationary boom persisted, they began to consider how the Employment Act could be bolstered along the lines of the original full employment bill. Among those who held this view, perhaps subliminally, were Keyserling and Gross, both of whom had been active proponents of the full employment bill. With Truman's electoral victory, Keyserling and Gross believed that the time had come to amend the act so as to ensure full capacity operation of industry.

Nourse thought that the bill, if enacted, would weaken if not destroy the function of the Council of Economic Advisers. To Keyserling, the end justified the means, and if the Council of Economic Advisers were to be made impotent by the legislation being drafted, this was less important than the attainment of the bill's immediate objectives. Nourse, on the other hand, felt that the preservation of the Council as a nonpartisan advisory agency for the presidency was of the utmost importance.

The Nature of the Spence Bill

The provisions of the Spence Bill, as disclosed after the bill's introduction in the House of Representatives on February 15, fully justified Nourse's concern about the participation of the Council in its drafting. It was designed "to implement the established national policy of promoting maximum employment, production, and purchasing power" as provided for by the Employment Act of 1946. The bill declared that certain adverse conditions resulting from World War II "still exist and threaten to persist unless affirmatively remedied." These adverse conditions were held to have "impeded maximum production," "reduced the purchasing power of the dollar," and "jeopardized the condition of useful employment opportunities." The declared purpose of the bill was to utilize the powers and resources of the federal government to assist in overcoming these adverse conditions.

The bill was a very comprehensive measure. It provided for continuous standby price and wage controls and a system of voluntary priority and allocation devices which were to become mandatory upon a finding of necessity by the president. However, the heart of the bill was Title II, "Promotion of Production and Supply," which authorized outright construction by the government of additional industrial capacity. Section 205 (b) read as follows:

> Whenever the President determines that it is necessary in order to help achieve the quantity goals established under section 201 (b) for designated essential materials or facilities, he may, by or under contract with private enterprise, construct new plant facilities, or expand or rehabilitate existing plant facilities, including Government-built war plants, for the expansion of capacity and production. . . .

The administration of the act was to be vested in the president, who could delegate any and all responsibilities to government agencies as he deemed appropriate. He was to have authority to appoint an assistant to aid him "in the coordination of activities of departments, agencies, and officials of the Government under this Act." The compensation of this assistant was not to exceed $20,000 per annum which was more than the Council members received, and such assistant could appoint up to three assistants not subject to Civil Service Laws and the pay classification act. Nourse observed that "it might be inferred that such a functionary would greatly circumscribe if he did not actually supersede the Council of Economic Advisers." Nourse also considered it "notable" that the president was to be required to make a quarterly report to Congress of the operations under the act, and such reports were to be referred to the Joint Committee on the Economic Report, "which shall study such reports and from time to time transmit to the Senate and the House of Representatives the results of its studies" (EPS, p. 246).

The title of the act dealing with price and wage controls and with priorities and allocations was to terminate on June 30, 1951, but Title II had no termination date except that any corporation created under it "shall not have succession beyond June 30, 1954, except for purposes of liquidation unless its life is extended beyond such date pursuant to act of Congress."

The 1949 Economic Report of the President

The positive tone of the President's Economic Report of January 7, 1949, reflected Truman's firm political position after the November election. He could now speak with confidence on his plans for the next four years. The report also accepted the aggressive views of Keyserling on the need for economic growth as a cure for many of the nation's economic problems. It continued in the "dual authorship" form inaugurated in the midyear report of 1948. The new arrangement had been well received by the public, and Nourse accepted it without protest.

The key note of the report was declared in its opening statement: "Now is the time to formulate and execute a practical program of immediate and long range measures pointed toward stability and growth." The president saw price inflation being "halted or reversed," and he believed that this "should be looked upon as a desirable development to be welcomed rather than feared." He thought it marked "the beginning of a process by which a more stable condition can be reached after a long period of rising prices." However, he did not think that adjustments had proceeded far enough to justify a "cessation of concern about inflation."

In his legislative recommendations, the president proposed an increase in government revenues from taxation of $4 billion to provide a budget surplus to combat inflation, and he urged strengthening of rent, credit, price, and related wage controls. He also called for immediate action to deal with shortages of supply, a recommendation which gave encouragement to those who were drafting the Spence bill. On this he said:

> There are shortages of supply in certain critical areas which are so serious as to impede maximum production in an expanding economy and to limit programs related to national security.
>
> I recommend immediate legislation to deal with this problem of capacity and supply. It should impose upon the Government the specific responsibility and provide the funds to make careful surveys of future supply needs and productive capacity. It should further require that these specific studies be correlated with the general requirements of an economy operating at maximum employment, production, and purchasing power. To the extent that facts reveal the need, it should provide additional authority to deal more effectively with inadequacy of capacity and supply.

To provide for "balanced economic growth," the president recommended "pressing forward with programs of high priority needed to conserve or increase the strength of the nation." He said: "We cannot accept the dangerous idea that inflation's end will automatically bring about a period of stable prosperity. The country's need for productive Government expenditures must not be translated into false economy." In this section of the report the president said: "The Federal Government has an important role in the development of our material resources" so as "to relieve shortages in many of our most essential minerals and metals, our energy resources, especially electric power and oil, and some chemicals and fertilizer." Measures were also recommended for stabilizing agriculture, improving international economic relations, increasing housing, promoting urban redevelopment, and furthering education, health, and old age, disability, and unemployment insurance.

All in all, the report proposed a comprehensive and progressive program designed to meet the nation's discernible economic needs. Nourse considered it both constructive and reasonable.

The Council's Economic Review (submitted with the President's Report) provided tempered support for his recommendations. Nourse was satisfied that it "kept pretty well to the factual level" and "did not get over the line into policy recommendations of its own or arguments in support of policies enunciated in the Economic Report of the President." The outstanding feature of the Review was a comprehensive analysis of "Basic Objectives for Balanced Economic Growth," which gave particular attention to governmental programs essential to economic growth in the years ahead, taking into consideration the fact that "stabilization policy for the immediate future is still concerned mainly with restraining inflationary forces, breaking bottlenecks, and selectively adjusting the markets and prices of some commodities. The Council maintained that:

> Our analysis shows that over the ensuing years consumer income and expenditure should be increased both absolutely and relatively. The fundamental issue is: Will this result automatically through the interplay of prices and costs in the market place? Or will depression appear when the gap between potential output and effective demand of consumers and business becomes unmanageable as has happened in the past? Or can affirmative policies, as envisaged in the Employment Act, close or bridge this gap before it becomes a chasm?

Although preparation of the President's Economic Report and the Council's accompanying Annual Economic Review had occasioned a certain amount of strain among the Council members, Nourse felt that he could live with the reports as completed.

Dissention in the Council Increases

Although the President's Economic Report was a balanced document, its recommendations for government action to increase the production of scarce materials, should this be found necessary, gave encouragement to those who were drafting the Spence bill. In fact, Nourse was to say a year later that out of this report "there promptly came the Spence Bill." He went on to explain that this bill "was widely hailed by those who believed in it as a new action program by government to carry the Employment Act into effect. Those who feared this bill branded it as the opening wedge to nationalization of industry, and eventual state socialism." He then said:

> Certain members of the Council and its staff lent support to the Spence bill. They not only helped draft it, but gave assurance that it was in line with the Council's findings of fact and its private recommendations to the President. Such a course was not justified by any Council understanding, but this could not be made clear in view of the peculiar circumstances . . . for members of the Council unofficially and surreptitiously, to give such a measure a cloak of Council approval created an impossible situation to the chairman of the Council. [13]

Nourse was strongly opposed to this bill being designed with the help of his fellow Council members for expanding industrial production by government action, for he considered it economically unnecessary, and he feared that it "would do as much as anything would to prejudice a cooperative spirit between business and government."[14] He felt so keenly on this subject that he allowed his temper to boil over in a Council meeting early in January. He recorded this incident in his personal diary as follows: "When discussion got rather acrimonious in a Council meeting several days ago I told Mr. Keyserling and Mr. Clark that I had presented my resignation and that therefore they might entertain some hope that they would be relieved of my incubus on the Council in the not too distant future." He also said in this diary note: "I will not undertake to go through another annual or midyear report struggle with the present set-up. After two and a half years of experience, I regard it as impossible both internally and externally. We cannot organize and operate our staff satisfactorily to produce a product which will stand the test of any reasonable professional standards. Nor can we maintain proper external relationships" (EPS, p. 275).

There was no agreement in the Administration at this time that legislation to expand production of steel or other products would be desirable. On January 14, the Council examined the advisability of such action in a memorandum for the president, "Legislation to Effectuate Stabilization Policies." It concluded: "We do not yet have sufficient information to advocate the enactment of these proposals at this time."[15] While President Truman concurred, work on drafting the Spence bill was continued unofficially by Keyserling and Clark and others in the offices of the Council, with the support of important Democratic Congressional leaders. It was at this time (January 15, 1949) that Nourse gave a talk to the Harmonie Club in New York City which inadvertently disclosed the cleavage in the Council on this matter. In view of the controversy it aroused, it is essential that we see what was involved.

The Harmonie Club Incident

There is no full record of Nourse's Harmonie Club talk which dealt with "issues confronting business in 1949," for only the first two pages were prepared in rough draft. These two pages, however, show how Nourse was thinking at that time. "In my judgment," he said, "the master issue which American business faces in 1949 will be this: Can we maintain through this year and project into the next year a level of production and employment only a little below that of 1948?" Assuming that there would be no war or crop failure, he said: "I believe that we *could* produce that result. Whether in fact we do it, I am not so sure." Nourse termed the high employment of the past year "not really full employment" but a "state of overemployment, which was both a cause and effect of inflation." It was his premise "that we wish in 1949 to arrest the further march of inflation and to let out a little wind so that we may be safer and a bit more comfortable."

In the question period following the talk, Nourse disassociated himself "from proposals to have the government construct or operate industrial facilities," then a hot issue in connection with steel capacity. As reported by Nourse, "the New York *Herald-Tribune*, the *Philadelphia Inquirer*, and some other papers played up this episode as revealing 'sharp disagreement within the official White House family.' The *Inquirer* added: 'Leon H. Keyserling, vice chairman of the Economic Council, said today that his position in favor of the Presidential request had not changed. Keyserling is reputedly the author of the proposal. He declined to comment on Nourse's views'" (EPS, pp. 275-276).

This publicity was distressful to Nourse, for he had thought that his views were off the record. Of most embarrassment to him was an observation that he had made that recent administration statements went further than some would have liked and not as far as others would have favored. He had said that those in the first group were regarded as "old fogies" by those in the second, while those in the second group were regarded as "eager beavers" by those in the first. This was taken to imply that Nourse had Keyserling in mind as an "eager beaver."

Keyserling did not let this matter go without expressing his deep concern over the public exposure of a lack of complete unanimity in the Council. In a memorandum to Nourse on January 19, he said: "I do not think that we, as Economic Advisers to the President and in confidential relationship to him, should criticise at a public meeting . . . proposals which the President has already made . . . [or] use a public meeting [to express] favor or disfavor of important proposals which the President currently has before him for decision." Keyserling maintained that his actions had always been consistent with "the foregoing principles," and that in the many talks that he had made there had never appeared any story that attributed to him either a disagreement with his colleagues or a disagreement with the president. Rather piously he closed his memorandum with this sentence: "I feel very sincerely that this is the only kind of procedure that can prove workable for an institution such as the Council, and I want to urge it upon you for careful consideration" (EPS, pp. 276-277).

Nourse responded on January 22 with a three-page memorandum addressed to Keyserling and Clark, with copies to Clark Clifford and Charles Murphy of the White House staff. Nourse agreed that the propositions stated by Keyserling were altogether reasonable and sound, and restated principles "which I think all have sought to follow in the past and that I am sure we all intend to follow in the future." He then set forth the actual circumstances relating to the Harmonie Club speech and explained how his views were distorted by certain newsmen. He denied that he had involved Keyserling's name in any way. He finished his memorandum with this paragraph:

> The episode is of course most regrettable from the standpoint of the Council and not only distressing, but humiliating to me. If either of you wishes to discuss it further by memorandum or in Council meeting, I shall be happy to do so. All of us have been around Washington long enough to know that sooner or later everyone makes a mistake or gets a "raw deal". On several occasions in the past, I have been deeply concerned at positions taken by other Council members in radio speeches or public forum debates which seemed to me to put the Council on record on issues on which we had not taken a position or done the Council and staff work which would justify us in taking a position. I have not, however, been too seriously concerned about some individual departures of this sort, and up to the present we have fortunately escaped headline treatment on revealed divergencies. I hope that we shall be quite free of it in the future [EPS, pp. 267-268].

Although this incident blew over, it brought into the public arena a conflict in basic thinking between Nourse and Keyserling which was to grow in intensity during the ensuing months.

From then on, Nourse felt increasingly on his guard within the Council. He was aware that Keyserling, Gross, and other members of the staff were "participating in the work of drafting what became the Spence bill in the House, and a new farm bill in the Senate. But," as he later said, "they kept it off in a corner, not thinking of it as a Council matter, nor a matter of Council knowledge even, so there was a sort of subterranean strain developing there, a matter of policy, and in the way several people behaved."[16]

Nourse Continues to Speak Out

In the weeks following his Harmonie Club speech, Nourse expressed his economic philosophy in two public addresses. The first dealt with farm policy, while the second set forth his views on the aspirations of the Employment Act.

On January 25, Nourse addressed the Farm and Home Conference at the University of Kentucky on the subject, "Where Does the Kentucky Farmer Stand on Agricultural Policy?" Realizing that agricultural policy was then a delicate political subject, he provided copies of his proposed talk to both the president and Secretary of Agriculture Brannan, who gave it their approval. He expressed his theme as follows: "This is the year for agriculture to abandon any thought of freezing the scarcity levels of war and post-war years into their relations with the rest of the economy."

Nourse stated that agricultural policy was "one of the momentous factors in attaining the kind of stabilized prosperity contemplated under the Employment Act of 1946." He hoped that farmers would "consolidate the gains of the last twenty years by still further perfecting a system of agricultural price supports on a moderate level which provides support against disaster rather than perpetuating fortuitous high levels of wartime scarcity." He considered the Agricultural Act of 1948 an important step forward in recognizing the difficulties associated with over-rigid supports.

Nourse did not think it necessary or desirable to freeze farm prices at a high level or into a rigid formula. "What is sought," he said, "is to stabilize farm income within a reasonable range . . . but at the same time leave the price indicator enough freedom of movement so that it can continue to give the farmer-producer the continuous market guidance he needs in directing his productive efforts into the lines where the consuming public is relatively undersupplied and away from those lines where it is oversupplied." He believed that any attempt by farmers to overreach themselves might jeopardize the institutions built up "to safeguard farmers against dangers of collapse when production becomes abnormally large or demand abnormally low."

Speaking to the Bond Club of New York on February 8, 1949, on the subject, "Economics in the Public Service," Nourse declared that economics in the public service called for the best American thought and action to advance "the wealth of the nation." He thought that success in this endeavor largely depended upon whether each of the special interest groups—industry, labor, and agriculture—would "submit to the self-discipline necessary to hammer out an answer by the methods of science rather than trying to force a differential advantage for itself through the methods of group warfare."

He opened his address by saying:

> The Employment Act of 1946 constitutes a novel development within the American frame of democratic government. It very frankly introduces a machinery for dealing rationally—indeed, so far as possible, scientifically—with the broad issues of national economic policy. It thus raises planfulness to a higher level within that scheme of government. It should not, however, for a moment be thought of as proposing a "planned economy". It does not introduce any control or carry us one inch toward authoritarianism.

Nourse's main concern was to explain how the Council of Economic Advisers assisted the president in formulating economic policy, under the terms of the Employment Act. In his opinion, its function was to enable the Administration to use the analytical methods of social science to record major business trends, to detect spots of weakness, to devise means for meeting specific dangers, and to synthesize these factors "into an internally consistent legislative and administrative program." Nourse called the Economic Report of the President "a major state paper in which the President sets forth his economic statesmanship year by year."

Inflation or Deflation?

It became evident to Nourse in January that inflation was fast giving way to deflation. Keyserling and Clark could not agree. This difference of opinion was registered in the Council's regular monthly memorandum to the President on February 4. The majority opinion expressed by Keyserling and Clark held that there had been no change in economic signs since the President's Economic Report had been published in January. It concluded: "This is not the performance of a softening economy. The situation is strong, and there will now come into it the demands of labor for wage increases." Nourse's views were set off in a separate paragraph which read:

> Mr. Nourse believes that there are other facts than those cited above, additional developments not yet reducible to a statistical basis, and questions of business attitudes which lead him to an interpretation materially different from that contained in the remaining paragraphs of this memorandum. In a word, he does not believe there are clear indications that inflationary pressures are increasing or unabated, although developments are conceivable which might renew the process of inflation.

Nourse said later that this memorandum "had special significance in that it completely abandoned the attempt to have the Council speak with a unanimous voice in their appraisals and recommendations rather than revealing frankly to the President such real differences of view that might exist" (EPS, pp. 234-235).

Soon after this report was made, Nourse responded to some questions of reporters by saying that he viewed the current softening of prices as a sign of "healthy disinflation."

In their testimony before the Joint Economic Committee later in February (to be discussed later), Keyserling and Clark continued to stress the inflationary problem in the face of visible indications of falling prices. Nourse later said: "At a time when businessmen and the public were fearful about current price weakness in both agricultural and business lines, this emphasis on inflation dangers in the first forensic appearance of Council representatives evoked a great deal of comment on the value of the Council's work" (EPS, p. 236).

The March memorandum to the president was submitted by Keyserling and Clark, since Nourse was not in Washington. It pointed out that "the pulse of the economy is still strong." It maintained that the fundamental conditions "for very high-level employment and production in 1949 are all present. The only condition in sight which could materially alter the optimistic outlook would be if business on a large scale seriously reduced its investment plans. . . . If there should unexpectedly be a substantial downturn in business, there are elements in your proposed program designed to combat it just as there are elements in your program to combat the remaining inflational forces which are still present. In the economic situation as complex as the present one, the Government should have both types of weapons available so that they can be used promptly in the right combination" (EPS, pp. 236-237). The Council's quarterly report to the President on April 1 indicated that Nourse's views were now accepted by his fellow Council members (EPS, pp. 237-238).

Nourse Declines to Testify

With the reorganization of the Joint Committee on the Economic Report, it became evident that the Council would be called upon to testify in support of the president's economic recommendations. On January 29, Senator O'Mahoney, the new chairman of the committee, issued a press release which stated that among the first witnesses at the forthcoming hearings of the committee would be the three-man Council of Economic Advisers, headed by Edwin G. Nourse, and that they would amplify President Truman's program designed to curb high prices including "in the last resort authority to construct plants for production of such scarce materials as steel" (EPS, p. 268). On February 4, O'Mahoney sent Nourse a telegram inviting the Council to appear at the hearings on February 8. In sending the invitation only four days before the committee was to convene, it was understood that Nourse would decline to testify. In fact, as noted previously, he had made his intention clear to Senator O'Mahoney soon after the 1948 election. On the other hand, it was known that Keyserling and Clark were preparing testimony for the hearings and would respond affirmatively. As Keyserling has explained:

> It was established long in advance that I would appear before the JEC in early 1949, and I prepared testimony over a considerable period of time, as must be evident from its content including the charts. Dr. Nourse knew fully that the President [had decided that Council members could testify if they so desired,] knew that Dr. Clark and I would be appearing, and knew that I was working on the testimony with the help of staff. In a small organization, indeed, it would have been impossible for him not to know. The people on the Hill as well as elsewhere knew Dr. Nourse's position all along, and I presume that in not inviting Dr. Nourse to testify until a few days before the hearings was merely in the nature of a perfunctory courtesy, knowing that his answer would be "No."[17]

Nourse reported this situation as follows: "As February 8, the date for the hearings, drew near, and I had heard nothing direct from the Committee, I was naturally curious. On February 4 . . . a lengthy telegram from Chairman O'Mahoney was received at my office, inviting the Council to appear at the Joint Committee's hearings on the Economic Report of the President." This telegram said:

> . . . Secretary of Agriculture Brannan as opening witness will outline and discuss in broad terms the President's legislative recommendations as contained in his Economic Report, followed by members of the Council of Economic Advisers, who are requested to develop and amplify those major analyses and findings in the Annual Economic Review of current economic problems and prospective trends and developments which accompanied the President's report and to which consideration should be directed by the committee in accordance with the terms and purposes and objectives of the Employment Act. . . . I am wiring you because time is pressing and the law requires the Committee to file its report on March 1 [EPS, p. 269].

Nourse later said of this request: "The message was worded with notable precision. Anyone of normal political sophistication would realize in advance that the question of whether our analysis justified the President's recommendations would arise at every stage of the discussion."[18]

On his return to Washington on February 9, Nourse wrote immediately to Chairman O'Mahoney. He said: "Your telegram of February 4 inviting the members of the Council to appear at the hearings of the Joint Committee yesterday has only now reached me. . . . I understand that Mr. Keyserling and Mr. Clark freely and gladly accepted your invitation to appear before the Committee. If I had been here I would have had in good conscience to ask that I be excused."

Nourse stated his position in the following paragraph:

> I think that you are aware that I have always taken the position that the Council occupies a unique role of intimate and essentially confidential professional staff service to the President. It is my belief that this agency cannot over the years discharge this function effectively and without embarrassment either to the Chief Executive or to Council members if it is drawn out of the Executive Office into the political atmosphere of the Hill to discuss specific issues of policy on which the President has made his own recommendations. However perfect our agreement on these recommendations in the past or in the present instance, it is clearly foreseeable that the Council or individual members of the Council sooner or later will be in quite frank disagreement with some policy recommended by the President. We would then be confronted by a difficult and dangerous dilemma. Either we would have to "go down the party line", supporting this position by the best plausible arguments we could devise, regardless of our honest professional beliefs; or else we would have to debate and in the end criticize positions taken by the President.
>
> I would be much disturbed, here in the latter years of my professional career, to be put in the position which would be created by the first line

of action. As chairman of this agency, I am desirous of demonstrating the unique staff service that it is capable of rendering to the Chief Executive. Therefore, I would strongly regret being put in a situation where my testimony could be used to embarrass or weaken the position of the President.[19]

To ensure that his position was well understood, Nourse sent copies of his letter to all members of the Joint Committee. In reply, Senator Flanders said: ". . . after sitting in at various sessions of the Joint Committee, I concluded that the position you have taken is the only one it is proper for you to take." It will be recalled that in the fall of 1947, Senator Flanders had believed it desirable for the Council to testify at the Joint Committee hearings.

Nourse did not feel called upon to discuss this matter with President Truman, "since the Council's actions were in conformity with the latest instructions received from him." However, he still harbored the hope that his judgment would eventually be accepted. When he was invited several weeks later to have the Council testify on pending labor standards legislation, he wrote to President Truman expressing the hope "that we have a clear-cut statement from you that it is your wish that in future no member of the Council shall appear before a Congressional committee to discuss specific legislative proposals dealing with issues of economic policy. . . ." He went on to say: "I have a strong feeling that the participation [of Keyserling and Clark] in Congressional hearings a few weeks back was seriously harmful to the position and future usefulness of the Council. . . ."

President Truman responded on April 8 as follows:

> Replying to yours of April 6th, it has been my policy to allow the Council of Economic Advisers to follow their own viewpoint with regard to appearance before Committees. If you do not desire to appear it is perfectly all right with me. If the other gentlemen feel that they should appear, I would not interfere with that procedure. Other members of the President's staff, however, do not appear before Congressional Committees.

Nourse said of this letter: "Something new had been added in the closing sentence" (EPS, p. 270).

While this expression of the president settled the matter, it left Nourse in an untenable position. He could continue as chairman and refuse to testify, but his authority as chairman would be badly impaired if the other Council members were to represent the Council and thus the president in appearances before Congressional committees. Nourse later said that "the first real showdown between the political and economic interpretations of the Council's role" came with the hearings of the Joint Economic Committee in February, 1949. He charged that the other members of the Council "were not content to wait for the Council to win prestige and usefulness based solely on professional competence, mature judgment, practical realism and a stubborn refusal to let economic judgment be warped by political considerations. They wanted to advance philosophies or causes for which they had a personal enthusiasm. The most direct and dramatic means of gaining such personal influence was, of course, to go before a Congressional committee in active support of the President's program."[20]

The Hearings on the Economic Report

Chairman Joseph C. O'Mahoney opened the Joint Committee on the President's Economic Report on February 8[21] by saying: "We are probably facing this year the first real test of the Employment Act of 1946." He then called on Charles F. Brannan, Secretary of Agriculture, to present the general views of the Administration in detail. In his closing remarks, Secretary Brannan said: "The Administration, the Congress, and the people all realize that for the long pull, production is the answer to inflation and a prime requisite for continuing prosperity. We also know that while serious bottlenecks exist, and while production of essential items is lagging, the lack of balance is dangerous and protective substitutes for abundant production are needed." He also stated that "the Administration wants to use the least possible authority in achieving economic stability and growth but delay in achieving stability is extremely costly and we believe that we cannot afford to delay. . . . The Administration is firmly committed to action."

As the first Administration witness, Keyserling said: "I come here at the invitation of the Chairman . . . to discuss the Annual Economic Review of the Council . . . and the President's Economic Report of January 7." He indicated that in the course of his statement he would "take full account of the important and significant economic developments which have taken place . . . since the reports were submitted . . . and it will also enable me to address some remarks to points which have been raised in the Congress and elsewhere about these reports" (p. 8). He pointed out that:

> I am profoundly conscious of the fact that the role of the economist appearing before you is merely to analyse the economic situation and perhaps to suggest the relation of that situation to policy. It is not my function, but rather yours, to decide policies, because the tools for that purpose are not within the possession of the economist, and even if they were, the people have not entrusted the economist as such with that responsibility. So, if at any stage I transgress by stepping across the dividing line, it will not be by design, and I ask your tolerance in advance [p. 9].

Keyserling saw the economic situation as good. "I would like to say at this point that I hope that sensational magnification of some of the slight changes in the economic situation within the last month or so, some increase of unemployment in some places, will not be allowed to produce a fear psychology. I repeat that the economic outlook for 1949 is still bright, and I think that it can be kept bright by confidence combined with affirmative action" (p. 9). He did not think that one could be complacent. He saw danger that inflationary forces were rising and "there are some elements of increasing danger in the current economic situation.... Therefore, I submit that there is even greater need now than there was six months ago, or a year ago, for an effective and comprehensive stabilization and growth program..." (p. 11).

He went on to say: "May I suggest that the people who are now saying that we no longer need worry about inflation and should concentrate all our attention upon worrying about deflation are somewhat like the doctor who sends for the undertaker instead of realizing that there is still excellent chance to restore the patient to good health" (p. 11). In his analysis of the current situation, he said: "I would like to touch upon the question of capacity, and to point out why it seems to me that we are not in certain vital areas developing enough capacity for a growing and expanding maximum production economy."

Later in the hearings, the chairman said: "I suggest that you make clear to the Committee whether you are here as a proponent of continued inflation or as a proponent of some restraint upon inflation." Keyserling responded: "I am very definitely here pleading for restraint upon inflation. I think we need a rounded and balanced stabilization program." He saw in the industrial price situation prices "going too high and going too fast" (p. 77).

Keyserling gave considerable attention to "the question of whether sufficient capacities exist in certain basic industries to supply the needs of a stable and growing economy operating at maximum general levels of production and employment." He said: "I am in agreement with the proposition that, in some instances, capacity expansion is required far in excess of that indicated by current or revealed business plans if maximum production throughout the economy is to be maintained." He went on to say: "When we set forth the objective of constant growth at a rate of 3 percent or better per year, then it becomes relatively clear that some basic industries do not now have, and are not planning for, capacities adequate to the load of effective demand that will confront them if the objectives of the Employment Act are to be realized" (pp. 107-117).

In summarizing, Keyserling said: "Another depression within the next ten years ... could cost us about $800 billion in lost national income. Economic policy needs to concentrate upon this $800 billion question, and the answer we provide will shape our own future and largely determine our place in world affairs" (pp. 121-122). In referring to the Economic Report to the President on January 7, he said: "Nothing that has happened in the month since then ... has, in my judgment as an economist, altered the essential validity and urgency of this program in its entirety" (p. 125). He also said: "The main import of my statement ... has been to disclose the complete relevance and soundness of this guide laid down by the President. ... The Economic Report of the President ... was almost an exact appraisal of the difficulties which have begun to augment since then" (p. 129).

In his testimony, Clark stressed the necessity of controls for inflation and went even further than Keyserling in advocating government action to bring about increased capacity of steel and other basic products. He saw the expansion of productive capacity as of immediate importance and said: "The one way to stop inflation ... is to increase production." In response to a question from Chairman O'Mahoney on whether the government should actively operate plants to produce commodities, Clark said: "There is no reason to be greatly startled by suggesting that under some conditions the Government might produce commodities" (p. 440).

After Keyserling, Clark, and other government representatives had testified, the hearings were opened to other witnesses. Before they presented their views, Senator Taft called attention to the Spence bill (HR 2146) which was then being introduced in the House of Representatives. He thought that the committee "to a large extent" should consider this bill. Chairman O'Mahoney concurred: *"I think Senator Taft has correctly stated the issue. . . . I assume that it may be regarded as a summation of the President's Economic Report, so that it is, in fact, the question before this Committee"* (p. 488). (Emphasis added.)

One of the witnesses favorable to the Spence bill was Dewey Anderson, Executive Director of the Public Affairs Institute. He said: "I point out that the Spence Bill, which is the result of a long study on the part of various agencies of the Government, is an attempt to spell out in concrete fashion some of the recommendations that should be considered by this policy committee ..." (p. 507).

James Patton, President of the National Farmers Union, who had been a leading advocate of the original full employment bill in 1945, maintained that the election of 1948 gave the Administration a mandate for legislation of this type. He said: "It is my view that those who are unwilling to advocate the principles put forward by the President in his Economic Report, and the bill just introduced to put those principles into practice, have a very weak case indeed" (p. 650).

Those opposed to the ideas in the bill were vigorous in their criticisms. D. H. Kaplan, of the Brookings Institution, said that he was not afraid of the word "planning," but he thought the bill represented "the kind of intervention in the competitive market which, on balance, would be a disservice rather than an aid to the healthy readjustment and growth of our postwar economy" (p. 646).

Meyer Kestnbaum, president of Hart, Schaffner and Marx, was opposed to the bill as government intervention. He said: "The present situation is a highly dangerous one. . . . The thing to do now would be to allow the present trend of prices, which are beginning to soften, to develop without any great effort to introduce an inflationary movement" (p. 573).

Philip D. Reed, chairman of the board, General Electric Company, said: "It seems to me that nothing could be more drastically influential . . . than this bill. It is wrong in substance. It is very much more wrong, if that were possible, in terms of timeliness . . ." (p. 577, also p. 661).

Emerson Schmidt of the U.S. Chamber of Commerce said: "This bill is an essential negation. It would require an amendment to the Employment Act, because the Employment Act puts the responsibility on the Administration, that is, the Government, to promote a free-enterprise society, whereas this is the essential negation of a free enterprise society" (p. 598).

Bradford B. Smith, United States Steel Corporation, said: "The Employment Act of 1946 asserts that it is the policy of the government to foster and promote free competitive enterprise. Nothing would seem to me to be more clearly the antithesis of free competitive enterprise than Government ownership or operation of facilities, or close supervision of prices or production in nonfranchized industries" (p. 665).

Theodore O. Yntema, research director, Committee for Economic Development, provided a hard-hitting nine-point statement in opposition. He was concerned that the bill would delegate enormous power to the president. He said: "This is not merely an expansion of the power of the President: it is so great an expansion that it basically changes the character of the Presidency. It makes the President not an executive administering the law, but a czar administering the economy" (p. 669).

These prompt reactions from the business community indicated that it would be difficult—if not impossible—for Congress to enact the Spence Bill.

The Joint Committee divided sharply in reporting on the Economic Report of the President. The report of the seven Democratic majority members submitted on March 1 was largely a blanket endorsement of the policies recommended by the president. On the other hand, the report of the six Republican minority members submitted by Senator Taft on April 28 was highly critical of the President's Economic Report. It opened with the statement:

> We reject the basic philosophy of the President's Economic Report which, in effect, recommends that we set up in this country a planned and controlled economy and increase taxation for that purpose. The President's report ignores the broad powers already existing in the hands of the President . . . and carries on a crusade for more executive power, which we consider unjustified and dangerous. . . .

It was the minority's opinion that "the President's Economic Report threatens to become political propaganda rather than a scientific analysis" (EPS, p. 258).

Collapse of the Spence Bill

The storm of protest aroused by the Spence bill made clear to President Truman that it would be unwise to give this measure his support. Moreover, the economic situation was rapidly changing, and it could be argued that there was no longer need for heroic action such as this bill represented. Under these circumstances, Truman informed Keyserling through Clifford that he did not want him to advocate the bill in a scheduled speech. Keyserling realized that he could not oppose the president and cancelled his appearance. Without his advocacy, support for the bill soon petered out.[22]

Nourse was pleased to have the Spence Bill fall by the wayside, for as an economist he could not give it his support. Because of the circumstances beyond his control under which the bill was drafted in the Council's offices, he maintained a discreet silence on the proposed legislation and avoided becoming involved in the controversy which it aroused.

"The Gentle Art of Disinflation"

As it became increasingly clear in February and March that the long inflationary period following the war was giving way to deflation, the business community showed concern that depression might result. Nourse did not consider the economic situation unfavorable on the basis of the facts. He welcomed the transition from a seller's market to a buyer's market, for he considered this the "normal state of a productive and competitive economy." He thought it raised a fundamental question: "Are we going to show the ability of free business enterprise to meet the challenge of real competition, or can American businessmen make the grade only when we have the external stimulation of government orders and a deficit economy and its brief aftermath?"

He dealt with this question in a talk to the Executive Club of Chicago on March 18. He said: "I have called this speech 'The Gentle Art of Disinflation' to express my belief that we may, through the process of intelligent diagnosis of business conditions and economic needs, formulate and execute policies and programs to prolong our economic health. We may take off some fat, but we shall not die and need not really suffer." He went on to say: "I think you will agree with me that getting over the fever of inflation is a healthy process and that I am right in counselling my fellow citizens not to get jittery about one of the inevitable phenomena of convalescence." He saw a distinct difference between "corrective and orderly disinflation" and a "deflationary bust."

Nourse considered 1949 "our first real post-war testing year—the year of disinflation." To him, disinflation meant deceleration, not catastrophe. He thought "the real danger was that the current sense of uncertainty might be converted into a feeling of panic that could result in progressive reductions of business spending and consumer spending." He saw no reason for this to occur, for he believed that "with the volume of unsatisfied wants among consumers and the propensity to spend shown by steadily employed Americans, 1949 should show a sustained volume of consumer spending and hence employment only very moderately below last year."

In discussing this talk with him many years later, I said: "You were apparently quite concerned on the direction things were taking." Nourse replied: "Oh, yes. There's no question about that. By the spring of 1949 there was a shiver of apprehension moving through the business community."[23]

"Private Enterprise and Public Enterprise"

Three days later (March 21, 1949), in addressing the Economic Club of Detroit on the subject, "Private Enterprise and Public Enterprise," Nourse said: "While obviously we are passing out of the seller's market, we are passing into a healthy and husky buyer's market." He continued:

"Vigorous and skillful competitive pricing should keep that market alive for a long time ahead. For myself I do not believe that American business men want to rely on the artificial market in which war makes Uncle Sam the one big buyer and in which he has seemingly unlimited buying power derived from deficit spending. . . . I believe that American business enterprise expects to get back to conditions in which we show the world that free business under free government can keep resources used as steadily and fully as can authoritarianism and with much higher efficiency and fuller personal satisfaction."

He saw in the Employment Act "a declaration of residual public responsibility" based on a foundation of private enterprise. He thought it raised "planfulness" to a higher level in national economic policy, while it did not introduce any control or "carry us one inch toward authoritarianism." He asked this question: "Are the developments now going on under our noses soon to push us to socialism?" He answered with a resounding "No," saying that while we have socialized our economic institutions to a considerable degree, "we have not taken the one fateful step . . . of nationalization of industries." He said: "I am quite aware that there are people in Washington as well as Detroit who yearn and labor to that end . . . but in my opinion they are very much in the minority."

While he admitted that there were certain areas where public enterprise could render a desirable public service supplementary to private enterprise, he thought "the presumption for any economic activity was in favor of private enterprise," since "complex industrial and commercial operations cannot be conducted successfully by remote control." He saw public enterprise performing a facilitating role in providing a source of financing or in undertakings which required public control—such as the Bonneville Dam or Grand Coulee projects, but he did not think this implied socialism.

As Nourse and I looked back on this talk many years later, he denied that he had the Spence bill specifically in mind when he prepared this talk. He said that following Truman's election, businessmen were increasingly charging the government with "socialism," and he thought it desirable to scotch this socialism talk as a "bit of my professional role."[24]

Farm Policy Re-examined

Nourse brought his views on agricultural policy up-to-date in an address to the Farm and Home Week Conference at Cornell University on March 23, 1949. He noted that many people were becoming alarmed that growing industrial surpluses "might start cut-backs of employment, cracking prices, and the kind of depression that the country has frequently experienced in the past." It was his view that a business setback could be avoided or lessened "if only we keep cool heads, business courage, and a willingness to proceed on the necessary give-and-take of true collective bargaining."

Much of Nourse's argument followed the line of his Kentucky speech of two months earlier. He again indicated that the Agricultural Act of 1948 represented "an important step forward in recognizing that difficulties associated with over-rigid supports," but he thought that the "precise formulas for adjustments in support levels, including standards of discretionary action, need careful review and further testing against the criteria both of adequate farm income and of adaptability to meet specific commodity situations."

At this time, the House and Senate Agricultural Committees were working on a new farm bill, and on April 9, Secretary Brannan unveiled an ingenious plan for meeting the agricultural problem through "the use of compensatory payments to farmers to bring returns to them up to stated levels while permitting the products to move at free-market levels. This offered direct subsidies to farmers and low prices to consumers."[25] Nourse was not informed of this plan before it was submitted to Congress, and he found it subject to many weaknesses. However, as President Truman favored the plan as good politics, Nourse was estopped from expressing himself publicly on its economic soundness, although Keyserling did not hesitate to give the Brannan plan his early endorsement (EPS, p. 292). When the plan failed to gain Congressional approval, advocates of high support prices were successful in passing the Agricultural Act of 1949, which largely closed the door on the more moderate provisions of the Agricultural Act of 1948.

The Split in the Council

The refusal of Nourse to testify before the Joint Economic Committee and the willing participation of Keyserling and Clark made it obvious to alert observers that all was not well in the Council of Economic Advisers.

The internal disagreement among the Council members was brought into the open on March 29 by J. A. Livingston in his syndicated "Business Outlook" column which was headed, "Truman's Economists Split: Nourse Threatens to Resign." While the column gave no evidence that Nourse threatened to resign, it contained the sentence: "The resignation of Edwin G. Nourse, Chairman of the Council, is in President Truman's office." The opening sentence declared: "The Council of Economic Advisers, which was established by the Employment Act of 1946 to help the President develop a unified and workable economic program for the Nation, is itself now embroiled in an irreconcilable conflict."

Livingston went on to explain that Keyserling and Clark believed that the Council "must play a political role," while Nourse viewed the Council as a non-political, professional body. He held that Nourse "highlighted the rift" when he refused to testify before the Joint Economic Committee while Keyserling and Clark had gladly done so. He quoted the letter which Nourse sent to Senator O'Mahoney, Chairman of the Joint Committee, explaining why he could not "in good conscience" appear before the committee. He said that Keyserling and Clark believed the Council should: "1. Undertake economic studies; 2. translate these studies into recommendations to the President; and 3. see that the recommendations are put into effect—that is explained and defended before Congress." He pointed out that Nourse could not agree that there was need for strong controls on inflation in view of the recent downturn in prices; whereas Keyserling and Clark, in supporting the President's program before the Joint Committee, "had to emphasize the inflationary forces," for "otherwise they could not 'logically' ask for price controls."

Livingston concluded his column by saying: "As a result of the conflict the Council has lost caste in Washington. . . . How the President resolves the conflict will determine—in large part—the future vitality and usefulness not only of the Council but also of the entire Employment Act of 1946." This was not an easy problem for the president to resolve, for he valued the services of all three Council members and he was not greatly disturbed by their disagreement.[26] So he let the matter ride with the hope that it would work itself out. But the problem would not go away. In May, Drew Pearson, in his "Predictions of Things to Come," saw Nourse leaving the Council within two months.

The Economics of National Defense

At the request of Louis Johnson, Secretary of Defense, Nourse addressed the Second Joint Civilian Orientation Conference at the Pentagon in April on "The Economic Implications of Military Preparedness." As in the case of the first conference, he submitted his paper in advance to President Truman, who responded with the comment: "I think this is a good document" (EPS, p. 405). The continuing interest in national defense and the related problem of foreign aid led to a third Joint Orientation Conference on June 13, and again Nourse was invited to analyze the economic implications of a preparedness program. In each of these addresses, Nourse emphasized his belief that "sound policy and prudent action with reference to military preparedness must be carefully oriented to the actual capacities and limitations of the national economy." In his June 13 address, he said: "Preparedness for possibly prolonged international tension should not borrow resources from the future but build up the economic potential and strengthen the social fabric. Each long-run program must combine military preparedness with economic and financial preparedness, and last but not least, conditions of life that give the citizenry a deep conviction that theirs is a political, social, and economic system that is worth defending." He did not favor increasing the military budget simply to prop up a sagging economy, even though this might seem desirable. He would not agree "that the present level of military expenditures is really good for the economy and that 'more would be better.'"

Nourse did not think it proper to suggest "what program of military preparedness can or should be undertaken," for he believed that this was a problem to be answered by the Services, the president assisted by the Bureau of the Budget, and the Congress. His object was to present only a background of economic analysis against which technical and political facts would have to be measured.

Increasing Tension

Nourse had no illusions on the problems that would arise in coming to agreement with his colleagues on the 1949 midyear economic report. He recorded how he felt as work was begun on the report: "I had, just as a matter of self-respect, stated flatly at one of the first Council meetings in which plans for the mid-year report were discussed that I positively would not sign a review at midyear which included policy recommendations or whose analytical findings did not seem to me to be objective, consistent with and securely based on our factual data" (EPS, p. 278).

As work proceeded on the report, it became apparent to Nourse that "Mr. Keyserling was much disturbed by so much prominence being given to conflicts within the Council and was determined to have a report and so far as possible an entire Council program on which we were in explicit public agreement. Later he came to the opinion that Keyserling's conciliatory attitude was largely assumed "for the purpose of claiming that the ambitious proposals for extension of government power (inherent in the Spence and Murray bills) derived from Council analysis and had Council support" (EPS, p. 278). It should be noted that the Murray bill, known as the Economic Expansion Act of 1949, was then being drafted with the assistance of Keyserling and Gross.

Despite Keyserling's efforts to achieve harmony, Nourse found himself in sharp disagreement with Keyserling's thinking before the report was completed. "After one turbulent session," he said in a note to Clark, "it appears that we have come to the ultimate parting of the ways." Nourse thought his "intransigence" was "apparently good strategy for dealing with the impasse," for following his outburst it was possible to eliminate from the report the "untenable positions or objectionable kind of exposition" that had given Nourse so much concern (EPS, pp. 278-279).

Despite Nourse's efforts to keep the midyear report safe, he was surprised to find after the report was issued on June 13 that the "highly generalized and apparently innocuous language" of at least two passages was "being quoted in support of specific action which we refrained from accepting in the draft." Of most concern to Nourse was the interpretation given to a paragraph which called on the Congress to

> provide for a broad study of potential business investment, expansion and market opportunities under conditions of maximum use of our productive resources in a growing economy—conditions which the Employment Act of 1946 contemplates and which can be achieved if we have the confidence and determination to achieve them. This study should be designed especially to discover inadequacies in capacity in basic industries which may serve as limiting factors to expansion when the upward movement of business is resumed.

Referring to this matter in his diary, Nourse said:

> Of course I find no difficulty in subscribing to the desirability of having this issue probed deeply and competently. That would be no more than quickening and correlating the studies now being made by various agencies of Government and by outside agencies, the Council participating actively in raising questions, guiding study programs, and making application of findings. But now I find that this is conceived to imply the setting up of some new *ad hoc* body using perhaps as much as $6 million for what seems to be a precommitted study—this possibly attached to the Council. But beyond this, the passage cited and others of the Report are being represented as intended to support the Murray bill (S. 281). . . . The introduction of that bill was held up till after the midyear report was in. Then it was given a final redrafting and was offered as an implementation of the Employment Act of 1946 and of the President's Economic Report [EPS, p. 279].

Senator Murray's statement in introducing his bill, The Economic Expansion Act of 1949, on July 15—only two days after the Midyear Economic Report was issued—made clear to Nourse that Keyserling had done all that he could do to have the midyear report give this bill its full support. Senator Murray said:

> This bill is designed by the sponsors to carry out the recommendations in President Truman's economic program. While the bill is not being introduced at the request of the Administration, and while its sponsors take full responsibility for it, we feel that a careful study of the bill will reveal

the point-by-point similarity in form and substance to the analysis and recommendations contained in the President's Midyear Report [pp. 246-247].

To understand the concern that this bill gave Nourse, it is essential that we briefly examine some of its provisions.

The Economic Expansion Act of 1949

When it became clear that public enthusiasm could not be built up for the Spence bill, Keyserling and Gross had turned their attention to modification of a bill which had been introduced in January by Senators Sparkman and Murray as "The Full Employment Act of 1950." After many revisions in the spring of 1949, this bill emerged as "The Economic Expansion Act of 1949" on July 15, 1949, under the sponsorship of Senator Murray and a number of cosponsors. This bill expressed Keyserling's well-known views on the necessity of continuous economic expansion as a matter of public policy, as was evident in its title.

In introducing this bill, Senator Murray maintained that it did not include the controversial features of the Spence bill. He said: "It makes no provisions for controls or construction of plants by government." He went on to say: "It follows the logic of the President's Economic Report, in relying primarily upon the stimulation and encouragement of voluntary investment by private business and voluntary price and wage adjustments. The supplementary Government programs which it proposes, such as advance planning of resource development and public works and the improvement of social security, are in accord with the best business thinking of how to prepare ourselves against the possibility of a further economic downturn. . . . There are . . . no inconsistencies between the bill and the President's program, and the bill is as close to the President's program as it could be . . ." (EPS, p. 247).

It is significant that Senator Murray with a group of his colleagues from the Senate and House had met with the president in June to get him to take over the bill as an Administration measure and that Truman had declined to give it his blessing. Even before this, he had restrained Keyserling from addressing a meeting of the Americans for Democratic Action as an exponent of the bill. In reporting this incident, Nourse said that President Truman sent word to Keyserling on the morning of the meeting that such an appearance "would be regarded as an unfriendly act," and the appearance was cancelled (EPS, p. 246).

While Nourse was less critical of the Murray bill than of the Spence bill, he thought it of doubtful value. One feature of the bill gave him special concern—the way it would utilize the Council of Economic Advisers. Section 602 provided for an "Economic Cooperation Committee" set up by the Council. It was to consist of "not more than fifteen representatives of business, labor, agriculture, the professions and consumers." The committee was to advise or consult regularly with the Council with respect to its assistance to the president. It was to help achieve and maximize the objectives of the Employment Act and help disseminate information to improve understanding and cooperation in achieving the objectives of the Employment Act. This was a modification of Keyserling's plan for an American Economic Committee proposed in his 1944 Pabst Prize essay. Moreover, the Council was to cover the costs of staff services required by the Economic Cooperation Committee, per diem allowances for committee members, and publications of the committee. Provision was made in the bill for such costs and for the costs of the Council's studies required under various sections of the bill. These expenditures, not to exceed $500,000, were not to be included within the maximum limitation contained in the Employment Act of 1946. It was obvious to Nourse that the tail would wag the dog. Several other sections of the bill gave the Council a prominent role in developing and guiding national economic policies. For example, Section 202 provided:

> The Council of Economic Advisers may arrange from time to time for the holding of national, regional, or industrial conferences, including conferences at which representatives of industry, labor, agriculture, consumers, the professions, and government shall seek to formulate general principles and methods to encourage the development of such voluntary price, wage, and profit objectives and policies as will further the objectives of this Act.

Nourse Asks to Be Relieved

The first seven months of 1949 had been a frustrating period for Nourse, for he found himself in almost continuous disagreement with his colleagues in interpreting economic trends, in formulating economic policies, and in conducting Council operations. As the year progressed, he had felt that his colleagues were increasingly influenced by political considerations, and he found himself constantly on the defensive. He could not agree with their hesitation in recognizing that inflationary forces were subsiding, and he thought their testimony to the Joint Economic Committee on the President's Economic Report definitely proved that such appearances were non-productive and harmful. He differed from them on the advisability of granting the president extraordinary powers to undertake production of steel and other basic materials, and he found work with them on the midyear economic report "wearing to a high degree." In July he had come into open conflict with them on desirable budget policy, and he saw no way in which he could adjust his thinking to his colleagues' views. By early August he saw little possibility that the basic disagreement within the Council could be resolved, and he feared the situation would worsen, for Keyserling and Clark were strengthening their relations with the president and important leaders in the Democratic Party. He did not like to contemplate struggling with them on the next annual report to the president and on the Economic Report of the Council with the issues that would ensue. As he phrased it, he did not see how he "could go through another annual or midyear report struggle with the present set-up" (EPS, p. 276).

Under these circumstances, he decided to press his resignation offered in December, for it did not seem that President Truman would otherwise accept it. Apparently, Truman was not disturbed by the public knowledge of dissention in the Council, and he had shown no preference for the views either of Nourse or of Keyserling and Clark. He recognized that Nourse had a strong following with important members of his cabinet and with certain important agency heads and with the business and agricultural community, while he realized that Keyserling and Clark were entrenched with key members of his White House staff and with the progressive wing of his party, both in and out of Congress. On August 9, Nourse wrote to the President as follows (EPS, pp. 280-281):

Dear Mr. President:

On December 15 last I tendered to you my resignation, to be effective as soon as tasks to which I was then committed could be completed. I asked you to "regard this resignation as being on your desk any morning after these immediate responsibilities have been fulfilled. . . . In view of my age and the hard work and tensions involved in the job, it . . . is my hope that I can be relieved at a not too distant date."

I have not pressed for the acceptance of my resignation during the busy and troubled conditions of this spring, as I felt that I should serve through the completion of the Midyear Economic Report if you desired me to do so. That report has now been presented and appears to have been, on the whole, very well received both by the Congress and the public. I passed my 66th birthday on May 20 and during the past year have become convinced that I no longer have the physical resources to carry the responsibilities of the post. As today is the third anniversary of the swearing-in of the Council, it seems an appropriate moment to urge as much speed as possible in the selection of my successor. Considerations of efficiency suggest that he should be installed at least a couple of months before the time when the next annual Economic Report of the President is due.

I believe deeply in the soundness and value of the Employment Act and in the great possibilities of usefulness for the Council. I trust that these will be fully realized under the new Chairman.

Sincerely yours,

From this letter it is evident that Nourse hoped that his resignation would bring in a new chairman who might be able to improve conditions within the Council. As he said in his diary on the day he submitted this letter: "The issue must be faced now—either make possible a truly professional and non-political Council or let it be known for the political agency it so clearly is" (EPS, p. 280). He was no doubt wise to push his resignation at this time, for he could do little more to gain acceptance of his views, and diminishing returns were setting in.

The president did not directly respond to the letter, but two days later John Steelman gave him the president's views at a luncheon conference. According to Nourse, Steelman said: "Of course this had to come sooner or later. The only question is about timing in naming the new man. The President says we must have this all fixed up and [be] ready to send his name to the Senate the very minute your resignation is announced" (EPS, p. 281).

How Big Should the Defense Budget Be?

A problem of great national importance in the summer of 1949 was to determine the size of the defense budget for the fiscal year 1951. This was a subject of considerable interest to Nourse as shown by his three speeches on the economic implications of military preparedness.

With the intensification of the cold war in 1947, Congress had set up in the Executive Office of the President the National Security Council, comprised of the president and certain major officers of government. While the Director of the Budget was not an official member of the Security Council, he was drawn into active consideration of military policies in formulating his budget recommendations, and he in turn called upon the Council of Economic Advisers for economic advice. Perhaps because of this relationship Nourse was invited to participate in the staff meetings of the National Security Council during the spring and summer of 1949.

On July 1, the president called a meeting in the Cabinet Room of department secretaries and agency heads primarily concerned with the problem of national defense, and Nourse was invited as Chairman of the Council of Economic Advisers. The purpose of the meeting was to apprise the group that he intended to limit the defense budget for fiscal 1951 to $13 billion in a total budget of $41.8 billion. The preliminary defense budget estimates had been $30 billion, and the Department of Defense was then insisting on $24 billion.

The president opened the meeting by passing a letter to Nourse, which he then read to the group. It called for the help of the Council of

Economic Advisers "in firming up the program of this Government to be reflected in the 1951 Budget."

This letter read as follows (EPS, pp. 250-251):

My dear Mr. Chairman:

. . . .

The budget policy on which my ceiling determinations for 1951 are based is that of (a) holding governmental expenditures as closely as possible to present levels, and, in particular, (b) preventing the prospective large rise in the military area by adjustments in present plans. Even under this stringent policy the outlook is for sizeable deficits, at least in the next two years, under present tax rates.

I recognize that proper budget policies cannot be determined without recognition of the requirements for maintaining a healthy and secure economy. Therefore, I feel that it is necessary to re-evaluate the character and size of our major governmental programs before making final decisions with respect to the 1951 budget.

The same financial problems which prompt the memorandum to the National Security Council thus bear a direct relation to the responsibilities of the Council of Economic Advisers to advise me concerning the effect of our fiscal policies upon the maintenance of high employment and a sound domestic economy. I am requesting you to furnish me by September 1 your advice on the following matters:

1. The probable effect upon our economy of the governmental programs contemplated under the tentative ceiling determinations. . . .
2. The relative effect upon our economy of a substantial deficit which may continue for a period of years, as contrasted with (a) a lower level of governmental activity during the years immediately ahead, or (b) higher tax rates.
3. The economic consequences of the proposed resource diversion to military and foreign aid programs. In this connection I should specifically like to obtain your advice with respect to the relative economic impact of moderate changes upward or downward in the level of military and foreign aid programs from that proposed in the ceiling determination programs.

/s./ Harry S. Truman

Nourse thought that this request was "a rather striking gesture on the part of the President toward integrating economic analysis from the Council into the setting of a ceiling on defense appropriations at the time when budget totals and subtotals were being decided upon" (EPS, p. 249).

The Council immediately began work on the requested report, but it soon became "glaringly evident" to Nourse that the Council members would not be able to agree on the type of report required. Rather than wait until this report could be completed, Nourse had decided to press for acceptance of his resignation.

Conflicts on Council Administration

At this time, Nourse was finding it increasingly difficult to accept the views of Keyserling and Clark on work plans for the Council. In his diary for September 2 (EPS, pp. 284-285), he reported on a session of the Council in which they "expressed great dissatisfaction with the work of practically everyone on the staff. . . . Keyserling said that the Council itself could in two months time do the Economic Report without any help from the staff. . . . Clark indicated that he had been in complete disagreement with me at the time of the last Economic Report when I had said that I hoped they would leave major responsibility for the staff draft of the Economic Report to the Periodic Reports Committee. Clark held that the writing of the annual and midyear reports is our main job. Two years and a half of experience have given him no evidence that we are capable of getting answers to the problems that I have regarded as basic staff work. If we are to learn how to write the proper kind of annual and midyear reports we should practice having a full-dress report each month." Nourse observed: "This seems to me utterly stupid and wasteful as a theory of Council and staff work."

It was Nourse's view that

> Mr. Keyserling would have the Council itself draft much of the Economic Report and not begin with a staff draft as has been my procedure. He would have each Council member call on the staff for data or assistance on his particular aspect but would expect them to validate the Council member's view rather than make an independent appraisal. As to reconcilement of Council members' positions, he has always argued that the majority view should prevail and that the minority member should concur rather than dissent or dissociate himself from a majority view. I have said I cannot operate on this basis. I think differences should be made explicit . . . rather than devising slippery ambiguities which obfuscate the issues and can later be interpreted by any member according to his own liking.

He went on to say:

> Keyserling and Clark were quite impatient with my idea that, since we have to do a great deal of re-thinking of economic theory and business practices, the staff work is heavily weighted with refinement of issues and statement of *pros* and *cons* rather than setting forth dogmatic answers. Keyserling said that he knew it was quite possible to get prompt and definite answers to the problems. When he was in the Housing Administration he had in two and a half months prepared a report that was a perfect example of the succinct laying out of a major economic problem with its proper solution. . . .

Nourse thought that "some good is emerging from these discussions because we are shaping plans for lessening emphasis on some of the fields set up in our original organization chart, expanding at other points, and planning to re-define staff assignments along the lines on which experience shows we need more light. Personally," he added, "I should like to keep a fair slice of our funds uncommitted to regular staff salaries and be able to finance conference sessions of the best men on particular topics which had been formulated for study by the Council and staff. *But with the present personnel of the Council, we could not agree on how the questions were to be formulated and then conduct the conference in such a way as to be really fruitful."* (Emphasis added.)

In concluding his diary note, Nourse said: "In the present Council discussion I always speak as though I were continuing as Chairman even though I am fully decided to step out not later than early November. I have never heard a word from the President nor anything from Steelman since my luncheon conversation with him on August 11. [It is difficult to believe that Keyserling did not know what was going on in view of his intimate contacts with Clark Clifford and others on the White House staff.]

It is apparent from the foregoing that Keyserling and Clark did not concur with Nourse's concept of Council administration. This was a matter of considerable disappointment to Nourse, and he was later to say: "The concept of a 'coordinate' Council of three persons of diverse training, experience, and interpretation of the Employment Act made effective administration impossible" (EPS, p. 240). Here it should be said that Nourse's views on how the Council should function were not impracticable and that members of the staff generally agreed with his methods of administration. One who had a high regard for Nourse's administrative skill was Fred Waugh, who was highly respected throughout the Council. He later gave me his views on Nourse as Chairman of the Council, as follows:

> Dr. Nourse had very positive ideas about the staff of the Council. He wanted a professional, non-political staff. He wanted it to be on a Civil Service basis. He wanted a permanent, full-time staff of career economists, chosen solely for their ability. . . . Nourse knew how to use his staff. He gave it plenty of work to do. He wanted the staff to get accurate facts, to help analyse and interpret the facts, to suggest programs, and to help the Council draft reports. . . . When Nourse disagreed with the findings of his staff, he told them why in a friendly way that elicited further efforts.
>
> As Council Chairman, Nourse was always dignified, scientific, and objective. He was not content with abstract theory and statistical fact-finding. He insisted that the facts and the theory be used to find practical, workable ways of furthering the public welfare. He was impatient with partisan politics. . . .
>
> As a writer, Nourse was always careful and precise. He had a marvellous choice of words and phrases. He dictated beautiful prose to his secretary, Margaret Quill. He usually worked it over many times before it was pub-

lished. Of course, this was especially true of the Economic Reports, which were gone over dozens of times with a fine tooth comb.

I have had the good fortune to study under such renowned scholars and teachers as Alexander Cance, Wesley Mitchell, Allyn Young, John Black, Ragnar Frisch, Erich Schneider, Jan Tinbergen, and Francois Divisia. Some of these men had more technical ability than Nourse in such fields as mathematics and statistics. But none had more depth and breadth of understanding and none had equal ability to find workable solutions to important practical economic problems.

I have been lucky to work under a number of able administrators, including Alexis Clark, I. G. Davis, Nils Olsen, Howard Tolley, and Oris Wells. Doubtless these men knew their specialties more intimately than did Dr. Nourse. Some had much larger staffs. But none had so difficult a job of organizing and administering a new program as did Dr. Nourse. And none knew better than Dr. Nourse how to inspire a staff to do its best work and to like it.[27]

Council Disagrees on Budget Ceilings

The Council found it impossible to agree on the report called for by the president on budget ceilings. After protracted discussion during July and well into August, two reports were submitted—one by Keyserling and Clark and the other by Nourse. In presenting these reports to the president on August 26, Nourse said that he felt the majority memorandum "gave an unusually complacent view of moderate deficits, soon to be followed by comfortable surplus." He indicated that he could "not derive any such easy confidence from a reading of the discernible facts and forseeable trends." Keyserling then made a brief statement which, according to Nourse, "was practically limited to the assertion that there was really no significant difference between our two interpretations but that they thought the economy could stand the burden of such budget as he in his wisdom found necessary after examining all the conditions." Nourse went on to observe: "This seems to me to reflect the general tone toward the whole role of the Council. It seems to me completely to negate any proper function of objective professional advice for a Council of Economic Advisers. . . ."[28]

At the time, the president showed no partiality for either view and said that he would carefully consider both reports. However, when Nourse read the president's Pittsburgh Labor Day speech on September 5, he felt that the views of Keyserling and Clark had prevailed, for "deficit spending" was depicted as only a "scare word" to "turn the American people against the programs which the people want and need." Nourse was especially concerned with the following paragraph in the president's speech:

The selfish interests say we can't afford these programs during a boom because that would be inflationary. They say we can't afford them during a recession because that would be deflationary. They say we can't afford them during a war because we are too busy with defense, and we can't afford them in time of peace because that would discourage business. So according to the selfish interests we never can afford them. But the truth is—we can't afford *not* to put these programs into effect. We can afford them, we ought to have them, and we will have them.

To Nourse, the president's statement seemed a "casting to the winds of any economic analysis of the intricate process by which several segments of a total economy can be helped into workable balance and sustained high production. I seemed to discern a highly political and dangerously inflationary economic program."[29]

Keyserling had no doubt helped draft President Truman's speech, for it was a direct reflection of his views. One student of the period said that at this time, "Truman adopted Keyserling's figures and rhetoric."[30]

Nourse Finally Gets Action on His Resignation

Since he had heard nothing direct from President Truman on his letter of August 9, Nourse wrote a more urgent follow-up letter on September 9. In this he stated that he would "be leaving the Council no later than November 1." On September 12, Steelman telephoned Nourse to say: "The Boss has your letter. He doesn't like to cross this particular bridge just now. But, of course, he can't ask the man who is in to go on and on. It's quite a problem. Of course your successor will have to be someone of considerable prominence" (EPS, p. 286). Later in the month, Nourse reviewed with Steelman a list of possible appointees.

While he was awaiting President Truman's acceptance of his resignation, he continued with his regular duties without mentioning his intention to soon leave the Council. On October 17, his decision to resign became known through a commentator's column. It happened that on the following day, Nourse was scheduled to address a trade association group at the Mayflower Hotel on a program that had as its theme "The March of Progress," and this speech brought action from the president. The next day he accepted Nourse's resignation, saying tersely: "I have been increasingly aware of your desire to retire. . . . I must assent to your request to be relieved of your duties as of November 1." Nourse has described this speech and its aftermath as follows:

> Speaking from the economic side, I reviewed the enormous potentialities for progress within our grasp and then expressed concern lest policies and practices being followed in private and in public areas might seriously impede that progress. My speech had been written some days in advance,

and I was completely surprised when the belated story of my resignation broke the day before the meeting. The fact that the news was out did not infuse any added feeling into what I said on this occasion. Nor did it occur to me that I should withhold or modify my prepared paper. The press, however, seized upon my speech as either "a parting shot" to relieve my mind after I was out, or as an indiscreet utterance which caused prompt acceptance of a resignation which otherwise I might have been urged to withdraw. The facts as here cited make it clear that neither interpretation was correct.[31]

"The March of Progress—Economically"

In view of the stir that this speech caused, it is important to know the setting and something of its content. It was one of a series of talks on the march of progress in various areas given at the Golden Anniversary Convention of the National Retail Farm Equipment Association which followed an address on fifty years of progress of the Association. Other talks dealt with the march of progress in agriculture, in farm mechanization, and in government.

Nourse opened his talk on "The March of Progress—Economically" by saying that "the economic progress of this country has been fabulous since its founding, or during the last century, or in the fifty years spanned by the life of your organization." He thought the record of the war and post-war years had been outstanding, and he referred to the Employment Act "under which I have the honor to serve" as a "March-of-Progress Act."

While not making any prediction himself on future economic growth, he examined the optimistic projections of two persons "whom I may call colleagues." The first was by Dr. Harold Moulton, his former chief at the Brookings Institution, who, in his recent book, *Controlling Factors in Economic Development,* envisaged a doubling of population and an eightfold increase in general standards of living during the next century. The second projection was by his fellow Council member, Vice-Chairman Leon Keyserling, who in an address, "Prospects for Economic Growth," at a Democratic Party Conference in San Francisco a month previously, foresaw the annual output of goods and services being lifted from $262 billion in 1948 to about $350 billion by 1958, and a minimum income of $4,000 for almost every family in the latter year. Nourse thought these predictions proclaimed "an almost self-evident truth that, with our traditions, our training, and our resources, the march of economic progress from here on *should* be even greater—much greater—than the quite creditable record of the past."

But, he warned, "Those dreams of progress will go a-glimmering unless they are intelligently brought to pass. . . . In all seriousness I must say that as I look about me I am filled with real concern. I cannot indulge in easy optimism." He continued:

> As an economist, I do not see standards of life being raised adequately out of enlarged production when a great labor organization sees the current situation as the occasion for a reduction in the hours of work . . . or when the czar of coal orders a 3-day week (21 hours) with full pay for a redundant labor force. . . .
>
> I am filled with apprehension too when I look to management and see it choosing the costs of banked fires and the demoralization of the delicate adjustments of supply lines and distribution patterns rather than capitalistically venturesome re-examination of their practices of accounting and their theories of price making.
>
> I am uneasy when I see farmers demanding stimulative prices whilst Government accumulates gigantic surplus holdings, pays subsidies out of federal deficits, and imposes production allotments and marketing quotas.
>
> *I am not happy either when I see Government slipping back into deficits as a way of life in a period when production and employment are high,* instead of putting its fiscal house in order and husbanding reserves to support the economy if less prosperous times overtake us. [Emphasis added.]

He summed up by saying:

> If we are to maintain the march of economic progress, we must, individually and in groups, in private business and in politics, display industry, prudence, and self-discipline, and recognize that we can't get more out of the economic system than we put in, that collective bargaining in good faith and on solid facts is the road to a workable distribution of total product, and that monetary and fiscal tricks have no power of magic but are a slippery road to misery.

On its face, this was a sound and balanced statement, but it is doubtful that it was read objectively by President Truman. His attention was probably called to what may have been considered skeptical comments on Keyserling's growth projections, which he was increasingly endorsing, and to the inference that the government was slipping back into deficits as a way of life—a comment which he probably took personally in view of his recent depiction of "deficit spending" as only a scare word.

Final Days in the Council

Nourse's departure from the Council was marked by many expressions of goodwill from the staff and others in and out of government who recognized how hard he had worked to bring meaning to the Employment Act of 1946. None pleased him more than a personal handwritten note from Gerhard Colm, which is here quoted in full:

October 20, 1948

Dear Dr. Nourse,

I read today that the President has accepted your resignation and that ends the hope that you will be persuaded to stay on. I know that you wanted to resign but for us it is a sad decision. In these three years I have sometimes wished you had taken a different position on one or the other issue but such difference in views never interfered with my affection and respect for you.

I certainly have to thank you profoundly for your fairness, generosity, and confidence which I always felt in your relationship with me. For me you have been a demonstration of a truly democratic spirit for whom an argument has the same merit and weight irrespective whether it comes from a P 1 [the lowest professional government grade], or a recognized authority in the field. I hope that you will be willing to continue personal and professional contact beyond your term of office.

Because I want to continue this relationship, if I am permitted, in the same spirit of confidence and candor, I plan to write for you some comments on the final policy comments which you included in your speech of October 18th.

With my best and most sincere wishes,

I am always yours,

(signed) Gerhard Colm

Colm followed up on October 21 with a three-page letter in which he frankly questioned Nourse's views on the "government slipping back into deficits as a way of life." He said: "I do not think you can scold the Government for what it has not yet done and what it might only contemplate in the future. I admit there is a real case for a warning and perhaps that was all you intended to do, in which case I would have no criticism." Regrettably, Colm's full letter, which showed his high respect for Nourse as an economist, cannot be examined here.

The coolness of the president's letter accepting Nourse's resignation was offset by "a delightful little farewell reception" given by the Council staff at Paul Homan's home. Nourse later recalled this occasion with much satisfaction:

> They did something very nice by way of memento. They had become aware that I dabbled around in sculpture so they bought a very handsome illustrated book of sculpture and had it inscribed over at the State Department by someone who inscribed treaties with a beautiful little farewell statement on the flyleaf followed by the signatures of everyone from Keyserling and Clark down to the office messenger. I was really moved. I remember that after the presentation of this book I had to struggle for quite a little bit of time to get myself under control so that I could really make my response and say good-bye and express my affection and appreciation of what they had done over these years. We had a wonderful faculty group there, oh, excuse me, staff group. I think that saying "faculty group" was a reasonable slip of the tongue.[32]

It was appropriate that Nourse's last public expression was at a forum of the New School for Social Research on October 21, where the subject under discussion was "Can Business and Government Get Together to Maintain Prosperity?" Nourse was soberly optimistic and closed his talk with this paragraph:

> It may be argued that individual and group rivalry are the very essence of the competition that drives our economic system vigorously forward. This is undoubtedly true, but competition is most helpful and least harmful only after the competitive urge has been schooled by understanding of the nature of the economic process and disciplined to rules of sportsmanship. It must not be resigned to the mutual destructiveness of gangsterism if we hope to get together to maintain our common prosperity.

In closing this record, I have a feeling that it was unfortunate that Truman in a hasty moment accepted Nourse's resignation without expressing appreciation for his conscientious and effective services. If he had not valued his services so much he would not have deferred action so long on Nourse's proffered resignation. Nourse was not "fired." He was simply allowed to leave the Council. In fact, Dr. John Steelman, who was very close to President Truman throughout his term of office, assures me that Truman held Nourse in high regard, although he was sometimes exasperated by his preciseness of expression. He writes: "President Truman expressed to me on several occasions, both while and after Dr. Nourse served as Chairman, his high respect for the Chairman personally and as an economist. He appreciated the fact that Dr. Nourse saw his role and that of his associates on the Council as economic advisers to the President, and that only."[33]

With Nourse's resignation, Leon H. Keyserling, as Vice-Chairman, automatically became Acting Chairman of the Council of Economic Advisers and on May 10, 1950, he was appointed Chairman with Clark being appointed Vice-Chairman.[34]

Retrospective Note

Looking back on Nourse's career as first Chairman of the Council of Economic Advisers, it would be easy to conclude that he expected too much of human nature and that he should have been more flexible in dealing with his fellow Council members, the president, and political leaders. Had he functioned differently he might have survived longer in his political environment, but it is doubted that he would have contributed so much to the establishment of the Council on a permanent basis.

When Nourse accepted the appointment as Chairman of the first Council, he did so with his eyes wide open. He saw this agency as an instrument for bringing sound professional advice on economic problems to the president and the government, and he fought for this objective throughout his time in office. As Joseph A. Pechman has said: "Edwin Nourse was a strict constructionist in his interpretation of the Employment Act; he believed the council should give economic advice to the President, but argued strongly against participation by the council in the legislative process or in partisan debate."[35]

The predicament of Nourse was defined by the conditions that confronted him. He had to give leadership to a novel organization which was charged with bringing sound economic advice to the president. As stated by Don K. Price in his book *Government and Science,* "The story of Dr. Nourse . . . is the story of a professional economist who tried to protect his dual status as a professional economist and a confidential adviser to the President by refusing to be drawn into public testimony before Congressional committees."[36]

When Nourse left the Council, Keyserling and Clark had won acceptance of the view that Council members should be expected to testify on the president's economic program before the Joint Economic Committee and other committees of Congress. This was the practice when Keyserling was Chairman of the Council, and when Arthur Burns became Chairman in the Eisenhower administration, he recognized that he could not refuse to testify if demanded by Congress. He felt that Nourse had taken a "rigid position," and he endeavored to cooperate with Congress to the extent this might be deemed desirable.

With the benefit of hindsight, it is reasonable to assume that Nourse was too obdurate in holding to the position that the Council should not testify before the Joint Economic Committee or other Congressional committees and that if he had been as flexible as was Arthur Burns, this problem might have been resolved. But it should be noted that Burns and later chairmen of the Council came to this position with greater administrative authority than was enjoyed by Nourse. They were not plagued by a divided Council which limited the freedom of action of the chairman.

Nourse was in an untenable political situation. He was endeavoring to establish the Council as a nonpartisan professional economic advisory agency in an administration which was struggling for its political survival. Moreover, he was flanked by two associate Council members, with equal authority in administrative decisions, who were closely attuned to the political objectives of the party in power. After he did all that he could to withstand the internal and external pressures that militated against the philosophy he represented, there was little he could do but resign.[37]

Part Three

NEW FRONTIERS
(1950-1974)

Chapter XIII

ECONOMIST AT LARGE
(1950-1959)

Nourse had no definite plans when he left the Council on November 1, 1949. He was past retirement age and could not return to the Brookings Institution. He thought that he might find a suitable teaching opportunity at some academic institution and devote more time to the developing program of the Joint Council on Economic Education. He also had in mind writing a book based on his Council experience, but this could wait. His immediate concern was to reestablish his life as a private citizen. Moreover, he wanted to make clear his reasons for leaving the Council and do what he could to further the basic principles of the Employment Act of 1946. In general, he had faith that his future would grow out of his past. He was in fine mental and physical condition, and he was glad to be relieved of official duties. He was again a free agent —free to think of himself as an economist for the people.

As there was much interest in his views on economic affairs, he welcomed opportunities to express himself. The day after he retired, November 2, 1949, he gave an already scheduled address to the Ohio Chamber of Commerce in Columbus. He spoke as "an economist at large" on the subject, "Economic Therapy Under the Employment Act." It was much in the vein of his Council talks. He emphasized the importance of the Employment Act of 1946 and how it could be best utilized.

Requests for other talks soon followed and in the next 14 months he gave over 70 addresses to business, professional, and academic groups. These talks gave Nourse an outlet for his energies and an opportunity to express his ideas without restraint. Some years later, in reviewing with him this period of his life, I remarked: "You showed remarkable stamina for a man of sixty-six, after your three years as Chairman of the Council. One would have expected you to relax and take a few months off for recharging your batteries." He replied: "I was recharging my batteries while on the Council. Now I was ready to turn on the juice."[1]

Nourse soon realized that he would need to revamp his affairs to handle this new situation. He met this problem by setting up a temporary office on H Street, and with the assistance of his long-time secretary, Miss Margaret Quill, he was soon functioning as an independent lecturer on current economic problems. As this program expanded, he moved to more suitable offices at 1835 K Street, where he maintained his headquarters for the next few years. Several lecture bureaus wanted to sign him up, but he turned them down, for he desired to respond "to spontaneous requests" from those who desired his views on subjects of specific interest to them. He did not wish to be tied down in any way, for his first concern was to put himself *en rapport* with his audience. He referred to this period of his life as "a transition from being an economic adviser in the executive branch of the government to economic adviser to the public at large."

Up to this time, Nourse was inclined to charge but nominal fees for his lectures. Sensing this situation, one of his business friends advised him that business groups were accustomed to paying at least $500 as an honorarium for guest speakers. While Nourse was not averse to getting the going rate, he did not wish to cut off invitations from academic and civil groups who could not pay this much. So he varied his charges in accordance with the group's ability to pay. To non-business groups he said: "The fee should be dictated by your custom and the state of your exchequer." On some occasions where he had a particular interest, he spoke without charge. To his surprise, the lecture work proved to be quite remunerative. In one exceptional week he took in over $3,000.

Why Nourse Left the Council

Before we examine the nature of these public addresses, let us see how Nourse explained his retirement from the Council of Economic Advisers. At the time of his resignation, Paul Homan said to him: "Now you must make clear why you left the Council." Nourse agreed that this must be done, but he wanted to do it in his own way after the dust had settled. He had no wish to embarrass President Truman or display a pique that he did not feel. He therefore turned down an invitation to appear on the "Meet the Press" program, for he feared that he might be forced into a misstatement of his position. He was more interested in generous offers for his "story" from the *Saturday Evening Post, Reader's Digest* and *Collier's* magazine, and after careful consideration he decided that *Collier's* offered him the best opportunity to clearly express himself. However, when the proofs came, he was disturbed by the title given the article: "Why Dr. Nourse Broke with the President." Nourse felt that this "would never do, for it put it out of all perspective." Instead he suggested as a title: "Why I Had to Step Aside," which was used. As he later said: "I didn't have any ill temper. I had sadness that the institution hadn't developed up to the full measure of what I thought it should be." When the article came out in February, 1950, Nourse was greatly pleased with the way it was presented, with a fine color photograph of himself and an introductory note in which the editor said:

> In 18 years of Democratic rule in Washington, no one man's break with the White House has had deeper meaning than the resignation of Dr. Edwin G. Nourse as Chairman of the President's Council of Economic Advisers. . . . Dr. Nourse is no mere disgruntled politician or disaffected phony. . . . He quit his Council post as an act of intellectual protest against the things he saw done and the attitudes he met behind the top-level Washington scene. This is Dr. Nourse's own story of why he quit. He tells it with characteristic dignity, restraint and lack of sensationalism. But in it he raises one of the most important questions of our time: How far do we want to let political and personal bias go in swaying the official decisions which daily affect our economic lives?

In explaining the conditions that led to his retirement, Nourse said:

> I did *not* resign because of any doubts or disillusionment about the Employment Act of 1946 itself. . . . Nor did I resign because I felt that the Council of Economic Advisers itself was either inadequate or ill-designed to promote the purposes of the Employment Act. . . . My troubles stemmed entirely from the interpretation placed on qualifications for Council membership and from the way Council members interpreted the general instructions laid down in the Act. In the end, I felt that I had to step aside because I had become convinced that the Council of Economic Advisers could not, under present circumstances, be operated as the professional and non-political agency I had supposed was called for by the Employment Act of 1946.

In the body of his article, Nourse detailed the accumulating events that led to his decision to resign. While he endeavored to present his views in a dispassionate manner, he could not avoid stating how deeply he felt on the issues involved. He concluded his article by saying:

> I left the Council deeply disappointed over a purpose not fully accomplished, but stubbornly hopeful for the future. It will take time for future Presidents to learn how to use a non-political advisory staff agency effectively. It will take time for successive Council members to learn how to bring the most competent and realistic analysis of economic problems simply and effectively to the President's aid. . . . A position on the Council of Economic Advisers should come to be regarded as the highest recognition to which any economist can aspire after he has risen to mature stature in the profession. . . . Most of all, Council members must be above and beyond the temptation to make economic rationalization serve any predetermined conclusion or policy.

Telling his story gave Nourse peace of mind. He hoped that it would have a constructive effect on the future interpretation of the Employment Act and on the functioning of the Council of Economic Advisers.

The annual meeting of the American Economic Association in December, 1949, also gave Nourse an opportunity to throw light on his recent resignation. At this meeting a symposium on the Employment Act appraised in some depth the work of the Council of Economic Advisers. One speaker maintained that if a Council member could not go along with the economic views of the president, he should resign. Nourse held that members of the Council should strive for economic objectivity and not be swayed by political considerations. He thought that members should avoid placing themselves in a position subservient to the president. He said: "I, myself, am one of those old-fashioned girls who have no liking for being a kept economist, even of the White House." He was pleased that this "flippant remark" was well received.

Helping Build the Joint Council on Economic Education

Another activity that engaged Nourse's attention in 1950 was work with the Joint Council on Economic Education. Freed from his duties with the Council of Economic Advisers, he could now give his active attention to this organization of which he was named one of its two vice-chairmen in January, 1950. In this position he attended all meetings of its Board of Directors and Executive Committee, and he became, in the words of G. Derwood Baker (the Council's first President and Director), a "circuit rider" for the summer workshops held by the Joint Council in all parts of the country. As recalled by Baker:

> We paid him a modest per diem and travel expenses as he went from workshop to workshop; and he became an expert on workshop techniques and processes. He was as convinced as I that the unfettered play of intellectual forces was, for most workshop participants, a new and revolutionary experience. He would usually spend a day at each workshop giving a talk and participating in discussions. In his talks he emphasized the importance of economic education in the light of the public policy declarations of the Employment Act of 1946. . . . You can imagine how this movement appealed to a scholar and citizen of Dr. Nourse's caliber. It provided him with renewed contact with professional leaders across the country—and above all the teachers of youth.[2]

The summer workshop program expanded rapidly in the 1950s. While only 3 workshops were held in 1949, 6 were held in 1950, and by 1954 the number had increased to 31. One of Nourse's main concerns in these early days of the Joint Council was to attract the interest of professional economists, and within a few years the American Economic Association joined in the Joint Council's program. Nourse also shared with Baker a conviction that inadequate attention was being given in the high schools to the need for conservation of our natural resources—a subject that had attracted his attention while with the Council of Economic Advisers. Together they sought a grant from Resources for the Future[3] in order to carry on a pilot project in resource conservation. According to Baker, "Our proposal, and Dr. Nourse's prestige, were persuasive," with the result that a grant of $150,000 was made for 1953 and later renewed. Baker gave Nourse great credit for his assistance to the Joint Council in its formative years. He said: "I can assure you that his philosophy on the relationship between government and business enterprise influenced all our planning, and his counsel and prestige contributed mightily to our creditability. His tolerance, his scholarship, his humanity, and his gentle humor influenced the behavior of all who were privileged to know him."

A Campaign of Economic Enlightenment

Although Nourse found time for other interests following his resignation from the Council of Economic Advisers, most of his attention was demanded by his public lectures, and it is essential that we examine this activity in some detail. One thing that impressed me in reviewing Nourse's post-Council talks was their great variety of subject matter for a wide diversity of occasions. Many of the talks dealt with current economic problems of particular interest to business groups, while others dealt with broad economic and social issues for academic and professional audiences. Each talk was keyed to a particular group. Expressing himself in precise and effective language, he never talked down to his audience.

After reviewing these talks, I remarked to Nourse that he seemed to be carrying on an extension program of economic enlightenment. He liked this expression and observed that, while he was with the Brookings Institution, it had always been his position "that the worthwhile attitude of the economist would be featured by his willingness and the effort he would make to communicate with the large number of non-professional people who were dealing with economic problems." Although he spoke on many subjects, most of the talks emphasized the significance of the Employment Act of 1946. As he explained: "I was addressing different audiences and beaming my remarks to the phase of the economic situation and economic policy that seemed pertinent. But it was as expositor of the Employment Act as a new activist force in our national economic life—they were all related to that."[4]

Excerpts from several of these talks show how Nourse was thinking at this time. One that expressed his general philosophy was an address to the Institute of Economic Affairs at Pomona College, Claremont, California, on December 3, 1949. Speaking on the topic "The Welfare State—Where is the Point of No Return?" he answered that it was at that point where the government went so far as to operate business, to manage business. He drew a distinction between "social activism and socialization, in the sense of nationalization of basic industries." He said in his concluding comments: "It is not my judgment that the more active role that the people have assigned to their government carries the implication or inevitable consequence that the state will go into schemes of nationalization of industry or encroach dangerously on the operational area of business."

On January 24, 1950, he discussed the economic consequences of current government policies in addressing the Economic Club of New York City. He did not think that the President's 1950 Economic Report and the Report of the Council of Economic Advisers were "tough-minded in grasping operating realities." He said: "I think the first order of business for this country in 1950 is to turn from the easy acceptance of deficits as a way of life to the making of a specific and hard-headed plan of getting back to black ink and a long-run program of sound debt." In taking a conservative stance on the dangers in the current economic situation, he declared: "What I have said is no stupid negation of faith in the great potentialities of our country, expressed so exuberantly in the Administration documents. It is not selling the United States short. It is not subscribing to the doctrine of 'the mature economy' or long-run stagnation. It does not brand me as a renegade from the Employment Act or the national policy of maximum production and employment."

In February he gave a carefully prepared address for the Creve Couer Club in Peoria, Illinois, on the subject, "The General Welfare and the Pursuit of Liberty." He maintained that he was neither a proponent or opponent of the welfare state, but he said: "Welfare is our business." He concluded: "A good working balance between the individual and the group must be found. We can advance the welfare of the people and at the same time preserve the blessings of liberty."

Of more than ordinary importance was his Penrose Memorial Lecture, "Economic Analysis and Political Synthesis," for the American Philosophical Society in April. Nourse considered it his interpretation of the role of the Council of Economic Advisers "after having served as its first Chairman and having tried to establish a philosophy and organization for it." As Nourse later said: "This was where I really took my stand." He went on to explain:

> I interpreted the role of the Council as a professional body, serving the President with economic analysis, the best they could collate from other government agencies, from business, academic and all economic circles out-

side the government. It was their role to present him with an economic analysis of problems on which he would have to enunciate for the Congress, for the country and for the world an economic policy for the United States. I definitely differentiated this role of economic analysis by the Council from the President's role with his Cabinet and the whole Executive Branch in formulating policy on the basis of a political synthesis. Being guided by the professional economic analysis, he would then have to adapt policy to the political realities or exigencies as he and his political staff, in the Cabinet and in the independent agencies, might think constituted the best economic statesmanship or the best politics. But that was their problem and I took my position firmly on the separation of those two.[5]

Another of his self-revealing talks, "The Social Responsibility of Management from the Point of View of an Economist," was presented at New York University on May 10. Here he said: "I am proud to admit, if not to boast, that the economist is in fact an engineer. That is, a wealth engineer." Looking back on this talk many years later, Nourse said: "This comes to a very hard question as to whether we have economic science or, merely, economic technology. My position is that most of economics is technology, rather than science, and that we need to get those who are practitioners of the economic process to understand this relationship and see their own activities within this context."[6]

A few weeks later he followed up on the same theme in a commencement day address at his first Alma Mater, The Illinois Institute of Technology (formerly Lewis Institute). Speaking on the subject, "Technology and Public Service," he said: "There is a technology of living as well as a technology of nature's processes and we must master basic principles of social organization and operation if our American way of freedom is really to succeed."

Up to the coming of the Korean War in late June, Nourse was critical of large budgets for national defense financed by deficit spending. In addressing the annual meeting of the Chamber of Commerce of the United States on "The Battle of the Budget Bulge" on May 2, he said:

> I think that slipping into deficits as a way of life is threatening the industrial security of our country, on which we have to rely if the cold war goes on, and still more if a hot war develops. Continued deficits will threaten the value of, or public confidence in, the nation's basic monetary unit. And it is only upon confidence in that unit that the sustained activity and stable prosperity of all kinds of business can be built. . . .

He finished his talk by saying: "I think that if I were sitting in the Kremlin I would be quite complacent as I viewed the progress of the Battle of the Budget Bulge. Sitting in Washington, I am deeply concerned."

Following the North Korean attack, Nourse quickly adjusted his thinking to the new military situation, and he fully approved the imposition of war taxes as a much needed anti-inflation measure. However, he remained concerned that greatly increased budgets for military preparedness could weaken the economic strength of the nation. After the Korean War front was apparently stabilized, he gave his views on this matter in several speeches. On October 23, for example, in addressing the Iowa Bankers' Association, he recognized that "in the wake of the Korean episode, there has been almost a tidal wave of demand that our definition of military necessities be completely revised." However, he was apprehensive that military and diplomatic issues not be given a distorted emphasis at the expense of the basic strength of the economy. The following day, in addressing the Wisconsin State Chamber of Commerce on "Some Mid-Century Problems," he saw the short-run issue as preparedness, but he thought the main problem for a 10-year preparedness program was to assure that the nation would not be crippled by lack of productive capacity due to debilitating economic policies. Two days later, as a keynote speaker on "National Security" for a meeting in Boston of the Associated Industries of Massachusetts, he said: "We should face without flinching the lessons learned from Korea but not weaken the development of a sensible and workable program of national security for the years ahead." He feared that there was serious danger of stepping up our military program to a point where it would be self-defeating.

Nourse's last talk in 1950, "The Mature Mind—Not the Mature Economy," well expressed his basic conviction that better economic education was essential for the nation's economic guidance. In his address for the Association of Secondary School Principals at Syracuse, New York, on December 11, he examined the "mature economy thesis" as developed in the late 1930s which maintained that the dynamic forces of the economy had lost their potency and that this new situation demanded aggressive government planning and action. Nourse found this a pessimistic philosophy not grounded upon a sound interpretation of the economic facts.[7] What was needed, he maintained, was effective working of our present economic system. He felt that this called for well-informed citizens to direct and operate our free enterprise economy. He said: "It would be a sad commentary if, in this day when popular education has brought us such command of the technologies of material objects and natural forces, we should fail in our grasp of the technologies, that is, the applied social science, of the human mind and spirit associated in business ventures and in free political life."

The Nineteen-Fifties Come First

Many of the ideas given in these public addresses were incorporated in a little book published early in 1951 under the title *The Nineteen-Fifties Come First*. This book was prepared at the suggestion of President Edwards of Henry Holt and Company, who wanted the gist of Nourse's economic thinking for a small low-priced book that could be promoted with the business and general public. Nourse liked the idea and devoted much of the summer to it, when there was a lull in the lecture business. The coming of the Korean War made it desirable to postpone publication until its outcome seemed clear; the book also expressed his views on the economic questions arising from this incident.

This book enabled Nourse to round out his views "into a more connected treatment of basic and current economic problems." In his introductory chapter he explained how the book came to be written: "Much of the book is drawn from public addresses I have made during the past year to a variety of audiences from coast to coast. . . . It grew out of the spontaneous interest manifested by community groups, business associations, academic and professional bodies, and farm organizations." He found people confused "at the rapid march of new developments growing out of a gigantic war, the rush of technological progress, the challenge of Soviet Imperialism, the dilemmas that arise in trying to preserve and develop our system of free enterprise in a day when large units of economic organization have been thrust upon us." He thought that "perhaps they hoped that, having just been released from the Executive Office—focal center of national policy analysis—I might have some insights that would be helpful in their own thinking."

He stressed that he was writing definitely as a non-partisan, for he held that "economics knows no party line." He offered the book "in the spirit of science," saying: "While the social scientist cannot be as dogmatic as the natural scientist about what will happen, he can have illuminating and helpful insights as to what may happen. . . . He can make practical suggestions, as to how to promote the desirable, avert the harmful, or adapt to the inevitable. He can solve his problems only as he can persuade the minds of men."

He emphasized that the spirit of the book ("or the spirit that will animate the remaining years of my life") may be reduced to the single phrase "the spirit of '46. . . . That means devotion to the great purpose of raising and stabilizing the level of our economic life enunciated in the Employment Act of 1946. . . . My devotion to the Employment Act means that I concur with the general means proposed in the Act for promoting its purposes." He thought that "the essential feature of this important new statute is that it enunciates a national policy of mobilizing all our organizational resources, public and private, within our system of free enterprise, for a sustained high level of production with the correspondingly high level of national living." He did not see the economy as a great automatic machine in that "economic life is a vital but ever-changing relationship among men and women." He maintained that "we must fuse the dynamic spirit of competition and the no less dynamic spirit of cooperation," since both "are inborn in the hearts of men."

In his first chapter, which he arrestingly called "Big Brother or Self Discipline," he warned that the totalitarian conditions foreseen by George Orwell in his challenging book *1984* were not impossible to envisage. He thought that the central challenge of Orwell's book was not to permit "the extinguishment of the individual," which would be a reversal of our American tradition. He was concerned that such a process of extinguishment might be "subtly going forward among us today." But he did not think that Orwell's prediction need be consummated, for "the 1950's come first." These years, he asserted, "are still ours. During them we shall, time and again, be casting the dice of crucial, even fateful decisions. . . . Our children will have to live with their consequences in 1984." It was his hope that historians of the future would say that the 1950's were years when "free and smart Americans looked carefully on their way of life and found that in its basic features it was good; when they resisted dangerous proposals; . . . when they reinforced the strong points in the business and political structures they already had [and] devised new means to enlarge productivity and distribute its fruits more equitably."

Three major developments which he named "Political Agrarianism, Political Laborism, and Political Businessism" gave Nourse much concern, and he dealt with each in a separate chapter. He thought there was too much of a tendency toward turning to the state for achievement of aims by agriculture, labor, and business. He found that all groups seek security, even if it impaired the security of others. He saw the danger that "welfare" programs, if not carefully designed, would bring on government insolvency. It was his view that "security must be created—not conferred." He concluded that "there is no real security but collective security. What is done through accident, health, old age, or unemployment insurance is largely in sharing risks. These are palliatives or rescue operations to offset the individual's insecurity in an unstable world." He thought that while important, "the basic remedy or preventive medicine for the body politic will come only through systematic, and so far as possible, scientific action to stabilize the economy on a plane of high production." This would call "for intelligent cooperation by all the would-be beneficiaries."

Of great concern to Nourse was the threat of inflation, which he feared might become endemic. He was not opposed to economic expansion, but he believed it should come from improvement of national economic efficiency rather than be induced by governmental fiscal measures. He did not think that a little inflation was a good thing, for the tendency of inflation, once started, was to continue and to quicken its pace.

He was also greatly concerned that militarism not be rooted in our national life as a result of the Korean War. He thought the nation should be careful not to unbalance its economic machinery which, in the long run, would provide the best military protection. In a chapter on "Militarism as a Way of Life," he foresaw a growing influence of military budgets should the nation become more imbedded in a cold war philosophy. He felt that the nation had nothing to fear "more than fear itself." He thought that confidence in the nation's future was the best antidote for fear, rather than the size of the military budget. He said: "National security is an integrated whole, in which economic soundness is just as important as military force. . . . National security rests on the dollar, the government bond, and the price index just as much as it does on the tank, the atom bomb, and the radar net." If fear itself was our greatest danger, he thought that those makers of our military, industrial, and financial policies whose programs bring about a contagion of fear would have much to answer for.

Nourse concluded his book with a chapter entitled "Was 1950 Our Lost Weekend?" Here he observed that if the worsening of the American way of life should come about, it would be in large part because of "failure to deal intelligently and courageously with the conditions and the problems of today." He saw 1950 as a year when many achievements were registered and many opportunities were missed. He thought that the future would demand mature minds or people who would not struggle for maximum acquisition by fair means or foul, but who would seek "to make their best contribution to maximize total production, and then cooperate in patterns of distribution designed to keep the productive process going with both vigor and efficiency." He ended the book by saying: "I have spoken out frankly in the belief that it is better to face stern realities . . . than to deny or try to hide them. . . . For myself, I would rather risk criticism for being a partisan of hard-won solvency than live pleasantly as a collaborationist of inflation."

This hard-hitting little book distilled much of Nourse's thinking during the post-war inflation period. It shows how his thinking had become broadened by his experience with the Council of Economic Advisers, for he now saw government economic policy from the inside as made by men and institutions. It was a tolerant book—the work of an elder economic statesman who wanted to interpret what he had learned to the generation who would largely shape the future. He dedicated the book to "my wife—Ray Tyler Nourse."

The book was well received as the testament of a man concerned with our economic and political future, and it attracted much attention in business and professional circles. Several reviews lauded the book's frank, nonpartisan spirit. O. B. Jesness, for example, in the *Journal of Farm Economics* (August, 1951), said: "This is not a 'grudge' book. Those who know Dr. Nourse know it would not be. . . . The book is intended for the intelligent, serious reader. It does not present a series of dogmatic conclusions for acceptance or rejection. Instead, it recommends fundamentals which citizens . . . can recognize in arriving at judgments. The author has drawn on his excellent command of language to present a most readable and clear treatment. This book deserves all the interest it is receiving, and more." William N. Louks, in a full-scale review for the *Political Science Quarterly* (1951), called it a "timely book—profound in that it searches the basic economics of a free enterprise system for the elements of economic progress, and yet lucid to the 'man in the street.' . . . [If] a good book is a disturbing book, this is one of the best, for it leaves no ground for complacency with respect to our 1951 status. . . . It goes without saying that the author's opinions will be most unpalatable to those he declares guilty of impeding the public interest and threatening the very foundation of economic progress under a free-enterprise economic organization. . . . In the vernacular, he 'lays it on the line' without fear or favor utterly regardless of toe-treading." One review of particular interest was by his former close associate Leon Keyserling, his successor as Chairman of the Council of Economic Advisers.

Keyserling, in reviewing the book for the *Annals of the American Academy* (1951), said: "The author is pragmatic, not dogmatic; and he is stating and illustrating a philosophy rather than making a tabulation." He thought that the philosophy would "disappoint those uninformed persons who may have regarded Dr. Nourse as a 'reactionary' or even 'conservative' economist or political scientist." He then explained:

> He is modern and forward looking. He asserts that our economic fate is determined not by impersonal forces but largely by wise or foolish human action; that reasonable economic stability is not only attainable but also preferable to the recurrent depressions which were supposed to "purge" the economy of its weaknesses; that we cannot go back to a simpler or "free market" economy by fragmentizing big private economic organizations or big government; and that competition and cooperation are both useful and dynamic concepts.

Keyserling ended his review with the hope that in his next book Dr. Nourse "will return to the more complete detachment and objectivity which helped make some of his earlier works—such as his studies on productive and consumption capacity, and of the price system—among the finest contributions to the literature of American economic thought."

Nourse cut down on his speaking engagements in 1951 so he could work on a book based on his experience as first Chairman of the Council of Economic Advisers. His most ambitious project during the year was to prepare the Harvey Weil Lectures presented at the University of North Carolina in October. They dealt with the conditions that brought economists into the public service, and so they related to the book he was projecting. He also continued to devote much time to the work of the Joint Council on Economic Education.

During the following year, he served on a committee comprised of well-known agricultural economists assembled by the Farm Foundation under the chairmanship of Dr. O. B. Jesness of the University of Minnesota, to prepare a report on national farm policy. One of the problems that arose was harmonizing the views of the various committee members into a consistent statement, and Nourse assumed the task of being "master scrivener" for the report, "Turning the Searchlight on Farm Policy," which became known as "The Searchlight Report." This report presented a conservative and studious examination of the farm problem, and it questioned the desirability of heavy subsidies to agriculture. Nourse also found time to spend an academic quarter as a visiting professor at the University of Minnesota, giving courses on fiscal and administrative problems under the Employment Act. In the summer he delivered an address to the American Institute of Cooperation entitled, "Change Is Necessary to Meet Tomorrow's Problems." He raised this question: "Does the cooperative philosophy contribute some definite guidance toward the solution of agriculture's part of the problem of America's economic future?" He later explained: "I was reiterating my belief in the distinctive character and serviceability of cooperative organization as a self-help enterprise of farmers themselves, which was one of the best bulwarks against undue intrusion of government into the agricultural sector of the economy."[8]

Economics in the Public Service

On December 30, 1952, Nourse completed *Economics in the Public Service*, a book which he had been working on since his retirement from the Council. As a professionally trained economist going into a formative position with a new economic institution, he had thought it incumbent on him to keep a record of that experience so that he could interpret it afterwards to scholars who would want to look back on this development from the vantage point of later years. He conceived of this book as something that he could work on after he left the Council, but he did not wish to have it embarrass Mr. Truman while he was still in office. This gave him a goal to complete the book in 1952 so that it would be available to help guide the new administration when it took office in 1953.

Work on the book was facilitated by a fellowship from the Carnegie Memorial Foundation which was to last for two years, but it was extended to a third year. Thus he was under no pressure, and he worked on the book as time and opportunity permitted. In fact, many of the things that he did in 1950, 1951, and 1952 were helpful to this larger enterprise, for they helped give him perspective. He designed it to cover experience under the first six years of the Employment Act rather than confine it to the first three years while he was Chairman of the Council of Economic Advisers. His work with the Joint Council on Economic Education, his public lectures, his teaching at the University of Minnesota, and other activities were all germane to this task, for when Nourse had a major project in mind, such as this book, everything he did came to focus on it. For example, his Harvey Weil lectures on the evolution of economic work in government helped provide the foundation for the book.

While he called his book *Economics in the Public Service*, its subtitle, *Administrative Aspects of the Employment Act*, was more explicit, for it was essentially an investigation in political science. He made this clear in his foreword: "In the present volume I am frankly slipping out of my primary role as economist and assuming that related role of political scientist to which the economist must frequently turn if he is to do an adequate job of economic analysis and prescription."

He also explained the scope of his book: "In the present volume, I shall offer my personal interpretation of the national policy enunciated in the Employment Act, set this policy in its historic perspective, and discuss the steps that have thus far been taken to bring the Council of Economic Advisers to a position of usefulness consonant with the terms of the Act and worthy of the purposes which it was designed to express. In somewhat less detail and from a necessarily less intimate experience I shall discuss the parallel work of the Joint Congressional Committee on the Economic Report of the President."

Later in the book he gave his objective in these words: "This book was conceived primarily as a simple story of people in action—a narrative and descriptive account of one particular effort of free government to make itself better government, of free enterprise to make itself more fruitful."

The book was presented in three parts. In Part I, "Economic Science and Practical Policy," he explained how the Employment Act came into being. In this part he said: "The central proposition around which this book is written is that the Employment Act of 1946 constitutes an attempt to bring the tools of economic science, in this modern day, to bear more effectively on the formulation of practically successful policies for the conduct of the nation's business." Then in Part II, "We Start to Administer the Employment Act," he examined the problems that arose in putting the act into effect. It provided a "personalized" account of the installation of the Council of Economic Advisers and its administrative problems in getting under way and established. It gave a within-the-ring view of the vexing problems encountered—economic, political, and administrative. In Part III, "First Tries and Second Reflections," Nourse looked back over the first six years of the Employment Act to determine whether it offered lessons for the better utilization of the act in the future. He ended this part with a final chapter, "Evolution or Episode," which asked this question: "Does a study of the case history here recorded lead to the conclusion that the philosophy expressed and the machinery set up in the Employment Act mark a logical evolution from the institutions and traditions of our past, soundly adapted to the changing conditions of our present and outlook for the future?" Nourse's answer was positive. "I believe that the Act's declaration of policy is no mere episode in our history, but marks an irreversible—though as yet indeterminate—step in the evolution of our politico-economic life."

While Nourse endeavored to present his views as objectively as possible, he realized that he was not free of bias. He recognized this by saying: "Being who I am and what I am, I cannot look at the twelve Economic Reports of the President and the six years record of the Council of Economic Advisers and the Joint Economic Committee of Congress as acts in a spiritual vacuum." He presented the facts as he saw them in the light of his background and experience.

Economics in the Public Service gave Nourse an opportunity to explain and evaluate the problems that were involved in getting the Employment Act meshed into the operations of the government. No other person had held such a key position in the inception of the work of the Council of Economic Advisers or had a greater interest in having the Employment Act serve the nation's needs. It gave him much satisfaction to dedicate the volume to his sisters, Mary Augusta Nourse, "historian of the Far East," and Alice Louise Nourse, "novelist, Alice Tisdale Hobart," for since childhood they had shared each other's joys in intellectual achievement. The book also enabled him to do something that he considered of great importance. It provided a case study that could be used in reestablishing the work of the Council of Economic Advisers on a more effective basis.

Nourse recognized that the book did not deal extensively with the problem of full employment which had given birth to the Employment Act of 1946. He thought it more important to devote his attention to problems involved in the administration of the act. In a footnote to his foreword, he said: "I hope to embody in a subsequent volume under the title 'The Road to Full Employment—Without Serfdom' my analysis of the central economic problem with which the Council of Economic Advisers and the Joint Congressional Committee on the Economic Report of the President have to wrestle."

The Rebirth of the Council of Economic Advisers

As Nourse neared completion of his book, it was obvious that its publication would come at a propitious time. During much of 1952, the Council of Economic Advisers was under political attack, and its budget for the 1953 fiscal year was reduced by 25 percent. Moreover, Congress had stipulated that the budget cut would all be taken in the fourth quarter so that, in effect, the Council would be dismantled the following March unless the new administration provided funds for its maintenance. Thus, when President Eisenhower took office in January, the Council was in "limbo" and its future was "uncertain at best."[9]

This uncertainty was increased in February, 1953, when the new House Appropriations Committee rejected a supplemental request of the new Administration for $75,000 to enable the Council to function during the fourth quarter of the fiscal year. Instead, $25,000 was allowed the president for one economic adviser and a small personal staff. President Eisenhower then appealed to Styles Bridges, Chairman of the Senate Appropriations Committee, for sufficient funds to see the Council through the fourth quarter, stating in his letter to Bridges that it was his intention "to reinvigorate that body." The Senate Committee agreed to increase the appropriation to $60,000, but after conference between the two appropriations committees, the amount was fixed at $50,000, and no provision was made for more than one adviser and staff.

In early March, while the conference committee was deliberating on this matter, President Eisenhower nominated Dr. Arthur F. Burns for membership in the Council, with the understanding that he would become chairman when the Council was reconstituted. The *New York Times*, in reporting this action on March 7, observed that "with the Fair Deal slate wiped clean the President will begin to form an agency reflecting the economic thinking of his administration." This forecast was immediately borne out by events. "Within a week of Burns' nomination the appointments of the remaining Keyserling staff members were terminated and the Truman Council passed out of the picture. When Burns started to work on March 19 he was in the anomalous position of being a presidential adviser and also of having been confirmed in a body that did not exist."[10]

Burns had outstanding qualifications for this assignment, and his appointment met with widespread approval. As director of research for the National Bureau of Economic Research, he had the respect of the economic profession and of the business community. He was recognized as conservative in his economic views but broadly liberal in his social outlook. He had supported Eisenhower in the election and was generally sympathetic to the economic philosophy of the new administration. In selecting him for the post, Eisenhower relied on the advice of Gabriel Hauge, his administrative assistant for economic affairs and his economic adviser during the recent election campaign. It was Hauge who persuaded Burns to take leave from his work with the National Bureau and undertake the task of rebuilding the Council. Later Hauge was to say: "Bringing Arthur down was one of my most significant accomplishments."[11] Moreover, his sponsorship ensured that Burns would have a free hand and good working relations within the new administration.

Burns did not accept his new responsibility lightly. He was later to say:

I did not jump for the job, but took my time to accept. I was, after all, deeply involved in the work of the National Bureau. On the other hand, I was drawn to the post by the idea that there was an opportunity to serve and that the President thought he needed me. There was also a chance to rebuild the Council, which had fallen into pretty bad disrepute—witness the unprecedented action of Congress in giving it only a nine months' appropriation for fiscal 1953.[12]

With a small staff comprised of former Council staff members, Burns set to work on the task of reestablishing the Council, and it was not long before plans for the new Council began to take shape. On May 23, the *New York Times* reported that President Eisenhower would shortly ask Congress "to revive the moribund Council of Economic Advisers and make it the watchdog over the freer economy to which he is dedicated." The article went on to say: "Now that a decent interval has passed since the burial of the Fair Deal's council, the Republican Administration has made plans to recreate it in its own image." The article made clear that Eisenhower was determined "above all to eliminate the political coloration that got the old Council in trouble with Congress." This objective was to be achieved through giving the Chairman of the Council greater authority and prestige. He would be the "embodiment of the Council," and the other two members would not have status co-equal with him in relationships with the president. Thus the Council would speak with "one voice."

To establish this idea on a permanent basis, President Eisenhower on June 1 made it the subject of Reorganization Plan No. 9 (drafted by Burns), which would become effective in two months unless disapproved by Congress. Its primary feature was the designation of the chairman as the Council's operating head. No longer would the chairman be merely "first among equals," a situation that had "racked the Council during Nourse's Chairmanship."[13] As Burns later explained: ". . . under the [Employment Act] the three Council members not only had identical responsibilities, which is as it should be, but also had identical administrative powers, which can lead to confusion. This difficulty was eliminated by the reorganization plan which delegated to the Chairman of the Council the responsibility for administering its affairs and for reporting to the President on its work."[14]

While submitting Reorganization Plan No. 9, President Eisenhower—also with the advice of Burns—set up a new government instrumentality, The Advisory Board on Economic Growth and Stability, under the Chairmanship of the Council of Economic Advisers. This board was to be comprised of representatives from the major departments and agencies with a primary concern in economic matters. According to Burns, it "was designed to overcome another difficulty in the Council's operations—namely the want of regular governmental machinery whereby the economic thinking and planning of the Council could be brought continuously to bear on the work of the executive departments and agencies or whereby their economic plans could be continuously brought to bear on the work of the Council."[15]

With provision for the Council made by Congress in the 1954 budget, Burns was renominated and reconfirmed as a member of the Council in late July and designated its chairman on August 8, 1953, after Reorganization Plan No. 9 had become effective. At that time the professional staff still consisted of only three persons. Within the next few months, the other two members of the Council were appointed by President Eisenhower (with Burns's concurrence) and a professional staff recruited. Thus reconstituted, the Council was back in business.

The appointment of Burns gave Nourse much satisfaction, for he had great confidence in his judgment and economic competence. In endeavoring to launch the Council on a professional basis in 1946, he had enjoyed

Burns' cooperation and he had greatly appreciated a letter from him on February 23, 1950, following his own resignation from the Council. Burns had said: "It may be some years before the Council can become a body of economic statesmen, aloof from the turmoil of politics. If and when that happens, you will deserve the paramount credit. In my judgment you have added enormously to the prestige and dignity of our profession...." Nourse had kept Burns apprised of the book he was preparing on his Council experience, and Burns had agreed to review it when published. As the page proofs became available early in 1953, they were furnished to Burns, and they helped him decide whether he should accept, and under what conditions, appointment to the Council. It is here significant that Burns's recommendations for strengthening the Council recognized the two great handicaps that Nourse labored under as first Chairman of the Council—lack of clear-cut authority and lack of inter-governmental machinery to work with.

When Burns came to Washington, Nourse made himself available to help him in every possible way, and Burns was to say after Nourse's death: "As the first Chairman of the Council of Economic Advisers, he set a standard of integrity and scholarship that has never been surpassed and that still nourishes that institution.... [W]hatever success I achieved at the Council of Economic Advisers derived in very large part from the counsel he so generously gave me when I first came to Washington."[16]

How the Book Was Received

While the Council of Economic Advisers was going through this metamorphosis Nourse's book came out, and reviews were soon available in the leading newspapers. John Kenneth Galbraith, in his review for the *New York Herald Tribune* (April 19, 1953), considered the book an appraisal of a highly significant experiment in government. While he held that Nourse was primarily concerned with the reasons why the Council and therewith the Employment Act had failed in realizing their promise, he thought that the problems that had beset the Council were largely inherent in the over-promises of the act itself. Holding that "the maintenance of a high and increasing level of output and employment" had become "the major preoccupation of government in our time," Galbraith said: "There was never any hope of solving these problems with the new machinery; all that could have been asked was a small improvement in Executive and Congressional capacity for dealing with these issues. Such improvements we may have since had."

Galbraith questioned whether the "cold objectivity" prescribed by

Nourse for dealing with problems of economic policy was possible, in that economic and political issues were "inextricably tangled—even in the evaluations and attitudes of the economist himself." He doubted "the practicability of a politically detached and disembodied source of economic advice" and thought that if the economic adviser was to be "influential," he would have "to be committed to the whole program of his Chief, and that includes not only what is economically wise but what is politically feasible." This was the opposite of Nourse's view that the economic adviser should concern himself with what was "economically wise," leaving to the president and his staff the problem of what was "politically feasible." Nourse did not think that the economic adviser should strive to be "influential" in a political sense.

A more sympathetic view was that of Elliot Janeway in the *New York Times* (April 19, 1953), who said that "Edwin Nourse is naive enough to believe in the possibility of non-political, technical dedication to the public service, and he is as eloquent in expressing his faith as he was courageous in fighting for it." He considered Nourse's historical treatment of the early days of the Council "a tract for the times."

In a review for the *Washington Post* (April 19, 1953), Ernest A. Tupper said: "This is not a book about economics. It is a drama. It is a popular behind-the-scenes account of a piece of legislation—the Employment Act of 1946. Dr. Nourse, Mr. Leon H. Keyserling and former President Truman are the leading actors." After pointing out some of the problems that had impaired the usefulness of the Council of Economic Advisers, Tupper expressed the hope that President Eisenhower's promise to reinvigorate the Council and augment its influence would be fulfilled. He said: "There is a mass of evidence in Dr. Nourse's book to suggest the tragedy in not doing so." He held that the book provides "a wealth of information which should be invaluable in helping to raise the standards and to improve the effectiveness of economics applied in the interest of public service."

The first reviews naturally emphasized the newsworthy features of the book. A more balanced analysis was that of John Maurice Clark in the *American Economic Review* (December, 1953). He considered the volume an account of "a noble, controversial, and surprisingly difficult experiment in the organizing of government for integrated economic functioning," and he held that it represented "an enlightening contribution to American political-economic history." Clark recognized the difficulties under which Nourse had labored in endeavoring to provide through the Council "scientific" economic advisory service for the president. He questioned, however, whether members of the Council could be expected to provide advice on a confidential basis as called for by Nourse. He thought this demanded "great self-abnegation," almost "martyrdom, anonymous." Clark thought that the antithesis of anonymous advisorship would be "the concept of a political ministry without portfolio, charged with developing coordinated policy, which should be economically sound and should fulfill the mandate of the Act, and always subject to the President's approval." Clark thought that the practical problem of how the Council should function—as set forth by Nourse—threatened the success of the experiment, and he observed that much would depend upon the fresh start which the new administration had undertaken. He did not believe that the Employment Act could be "simply reversed."

It was not surprising that Leon H. Keyserling could not let the book go unanswered, for he felt that it misrepresented his own contribution to the Council. In his review for the November, 1953, issue of the *Annals of the American Academy of Political and Social Science,* he charged the author with self-serving bias and gave no recognition to the book's considerable merit. He said: "The core of the book is a defense of a position which plunged him as Chairman into numerous inconsistencies." Later in the review he said: "By late 1949 Dr. Nourse felt frustrated and resigned. His book, written before full recovery of perspective is designed to demonstrate that, on most problems which arose within the Council, the Chairman displayed not only the practical touch but also moral elevation, while his colleagues were not only unwise but suspect because they sought to help gain acceptance of policies which they deemed to be in the national interest. Such a book on its face is not a careful study in economics or political science, despite copious excerpts from a 'personal diary' to reinforce undocumented allegations." Although Keyserling maintained that Nourse's "political cause célèbre" had lost any standing, it is significant that Nourse's insistence that the work of the Council should be nonpolitical and nonpartisan continues to reverberate to the present day.

My own views on the book were expressed in a review for the *Journal of Farm Economics* (May, 1954). I asked this question: "Why does a man write a book like this? I think the answer is obvious—to help keep an adequate record of how things happened, how they looked at the time and from the inside, so that worthwhile lessons are not lost." I also said: "It is the biography of the birth and uncertain initial years of an institution, written by the family doctor who never lost hope for the patient, or his belief in its future.... We see the situation as objectively as the author can present it. To the extent that the author has a bias, it is expressed with candor and conviction. . . . The author has tackled a big problem—and the calipers for measuring his success in coping with it must also be big."

With the completion of his book, Nourse had less need for a business office so he found congenial quarters at 1785 Massachusetts Avenue, not far from the Cosmos Club where he enjoyed luncheon contacts. He gave up the services of Miss Quill, who was qualified for a high secretarial post in government, but she continued to do special jobs for him until her death some 10 years later. In view of his continuing active work with the Joint Council on Economic Education, his office became the Washington headquarters for the Council and it assumed the burden of rent.

"The Persistent Problems of the American Economy"

Nourse's main job during 1953 was to analyze for the Joint Council "The Persistent Problems of the American Economy" as a basis for assisting high school teachers in training youth for citizenship. His findings, published as an article in the November, 1953, issue of *Social Education*, the Journal of the National Council for the Social Studies of the National Education Association, were widely distributed as a pamphlet of the Joint Council on Economic Education. In this undertaking, Nourse was concerned with providing "a frame of reference" for the study of economics in high schools rather than a syllabus for use in instruction. He dealt with the subject from an institutional standpoint and stressed the fact that economic problems were centered in market conditions.

He examined economic problems under the following five headings: (1) Our National Resources, Their Conservation, Use, and Development; (2) Our Labor Force, Its Development and Utilization; (3) The Need for Capital and Means for Supplying It; (4) Forms of Business Organization and Management; and (5) Government and Economic Life. He thought the merit of this grouping lay in the fact that it "poses any so-called problem as a complex of many problematical elements." He recognized that the outline was not complete in that it did not cover specifically the interrelations of American economic problems with those of other countries, but he held that the same principles of analysis would apply also to the larger world economy.

In the middle 1950s, Nourse also took a great interest in the American technical assistance programs designed to help cooperating countries improve their economic efficiency. In connection with these programs, "productivity teams" comprised of well-qualified persons were given the opportunity to visit and study progressive American business concerns.

Nourse often met with these teams in orientation sessions held in Washington, D.C., and then after they had visited selected business firms, he met with them again in a round-up seminar to analyze what they had learned so that they would get the most benefit from their experience. On the whole, he thought the program "well worth while," and he looked upon his own efforts as a form of "unpaid public service." On one occasion he invited me to meet with a group from Africa which was interested in our American experience with farmer cooperatives.

He also became involved about this time with a continuing education program carried on by the Bell Telephone Company. It brought together for a three-week period a group of selected young and middle-aged executives in the Bell System for advanced management training. Nourse, as one of the "professors," gave his views on the changing economic situation and the current problems of the economy. Commenting on these meetings some years later, he said: "Those were very worthwhile meetings from my point of view. They gave me an intimate association with this group of first-rate executives. I had an opportunity to pick their brains just as much as they were picking mine." He continued to participate in this program for several years.

During this period, Nourse served as consultant on the business outlook for a number of business concerns. One of these jobs was for the Gulf Oil Company. He also met with the Fiduciary Council of New York at its quarterly meetings—giving them a rundown on the economic situation as a guide in their investment analysis for their clients, private and institutional.

This was a happy stage in his life. He had completed his book based upon his Council experience, and he was pleased with the way the Council was now functioning. His views were sought by Congressional committees, and he was not doing anything that he did not want to do. As he said to me in a luncheon conversation at that time: "I can select my own clients." His home life and social activities continued to give him much pleasure.

Could the Boom Be Continued?

Nourse followed with much interest the efforts of the Eisenhower Administration to stabilize economic conditions in 1953. He did not express himself on the economic situation until September, when he gave a talk to the Memphis Clearing House Association on "Recession Threats and Depression Safeguards." He then urged caution: "I think most people will agree that after 12 years of war and post-war boom, we have an economic bear by the tail." He thought that the Administration was taking proper steps in a fiscal way, but he also held that much would depend upon the good sense of business and labor leaders. He said: "If the Employment Act of '46 is interpreted by labor, by businessmen, and by government as meaning that we must always have lovely weather and a perpetual picnic, that no one will ever have to accept personal or group sacrifices for the common good, or that a provident government will take care of the market breakdown that results from our own failures to negotiate workable terms of trade, then it had better never have been passed." This was strong language for Nourse, but it exactly expressed what he believed.

Three months later, on December 10, Nourse addressed a private meeting of businessmen in Boston on "Productive Capacity and Business Performance." Admitting that productive capacities were adequate, he said: "I am not worried about the car—but how good is the driver?" He was amused that some people considered him a "prophet of disaster" because of his Memphis speech. For example, Benjamin Fairless, head of U.S. Steel, in an address entitled "What Kind of America?" had chided those who expressed concern about the economic outlook. This had been printed alongside Nourse's Memphis speech in the *Commercial and Financial Chronicle*. Fairless had prescribed "Detroit talk" as a sovereign remedy for economic ills. He said: "Whenever Detroit talks, it speaks the economic language of a growing dynamic America. . . . All in the world we really need is more 'Detroit talk,' and a full realization that nothing has got made or done by selling America short."

Nourse could not resist observing that he got a chuckle out of this emphasis by a "hard-bitten business executive" on the importance of talk "as a significant factor in the economic process," in view of the "derisive howls about the jawbone attack that arose when certain *Economic Reports of the President* made reference to psychological elements in economic behavior." Nourse went on to say that there were three current attitudes toward the economic situation which could be characterized as Detroit, Washington, and Boston talk. "Detroit talk" expressed the "jaunty optimism" of certain automobile manufacturers who saw "no possibility of depression unless we talk ourselves into it." In contrast, he thought that "Washington talk" reflected too much emphasis "on salvation of the economy by programs of government." He believed that there should be more "Boston talk," which would recognize the "intellectual process in helping the economy meet its problems." He believed that "the adjustment of our national business to a sustained level of high production needs to be approached as an economic problem or one of scientific management of the business process." He thought that the term "Boston talk" reflected the thinking of such Boston-based institutions as the Massachusetts Institute of Technology and the Harvard Graduate School of Business.

Nourse believed that the crucial issue for 1954 and the years ahead was "what policies big business, management, and organized labor leadership will follow in this testing time when the economy is poised between inflation and deflation." He thought that "if the irresistible force of union wage and security demands meet the immovable body of managerial resistance, what could be small but realistic adjustments to the normal completion of a boom can snowball into an unmanageable recession." He concluded this talk with this sentence: "The productive capacity of our economy has been unquestionably demonstrated in the years we have just passed through; the quality of private business performance—management, labor, and agriculture—is yet to be demonstrated in the years ahead."

In commenting on this talk some years later, Nourse held that it was consistent with other talks he was making at that time. He said: "It was the same stance which I had maintained in my advice to the government while with the CEA—that we shouldn't rely on magic drugs. We should not expect Washington to 'do it all with mirrors.' I thought that industry and agriculture and banking should strike a good balance among themselves with a minimum of corrective measures from government."[17]

In January, 1954, Nourse followed up with an address to the American Retail Hardware Association on this question: "How Shall We Reason About 1954?" It was his view that 1953 had been a year of adjustment under the new Eisenhower Administration and that the economy was in a fundamentally strong position. "Our major concern in 1954," he said, "should be to keep recessionary tendencies, already emerged, from snowballing into unmanageable recession," and this would call for "working out a practical non-boom way of life." He raised the question: "Can we take it? We have had 12 years of 'pie in the sky.' We have come to love inflation. . . . Voices are already raised for big doses of inflation to deal with the first faint signs of deflation."

As an economist, he believed that the new Administration was consistently overbidding its hand in its repeated assurances that a real recession would not happen because *the government will not let it happen.* While he admitted that this assurance kept the business public from "stampeding to the storm cellar," he felt that it encouraged everyone "to run to Washington" with demands for special aid for troubles that they should themselves "reduce in size by wise action." Here he made a challenging observation: "I do not believe in the inevitability of cycles in which busts must be as deep as booms are high. On the contrary, I believe that we are arriving at a stage of general economic literacy in which periods of readjustment could be proportionate only to the excesses or distortion of the boom period and would not check the march of economic growth and progress."

Nourse naturally took a great interest in the first Economic Report prepared by the Council of Economic Advisers under the chairmanship of Arthur Burns, and he was glad to participate in an evaluation of the report before the Joint Economic Committee on February 18, 1954. He was impressed by the high professional quality and workmanship displayed by the report, and he could not resist prefacing his comments with an expression of satisfaction "in behalf of the economics profession" on the way the Council of Economic Advisers was now functioning. He subjected the views in the report to careful examination and found himself in general agreement. However, he inferred from his analysis "that sound economic strategy for economic stabilization and recovery in 1954 would give maintenance of consumer buying priority over stimulus to plant expansion and modernization or the enlargement of profit incentives to operation." He was also less sanguine that "our present troubles will be over within a few months." Taken by and large, his attitude on the report was one of cautious approval.

Bigness and Countervailing Power

During the year, Nourse welcomed an opportunity to participate in the preparation of a comprehensive symposium review of two books that were attracting national attention: John Kenneth Galbraith's *American Capitalism: The Concept of Countervailing Power* (1952) and David E. Lilienthal's *Big Business: A New Era* (1953). This composite review, published in the May-June issue of the *Northwestern University Law Review*, brought together the thinking on these books of Nourse and several other well-known students of the American business enterprise system, including Edward N. Levi, Dean of the University of Chicago Law School; Arthur J. Goldberg, General Counsel of the C.I.O.; Senator Joseph C. O'Mahoney; and Wendell Berge, former Assistant Attorney General in charge of antitrust laws. We are here concerned with only Nourse's views as expressed in his lead-off essay. Nourse opened his statement by saying: "In these two books we find two doughty knights of the pen entering the lists of economic controversy. The scope of their argument and the weapons and tactics they use are marked by differences no less striking than is the fact that nonetheless they are joined in a common cause—the justification of bigness." He characterized the two books as follows: "Galbraith's book may be properly regarded as an economic brief for the defense in the case of *The Public Interest v. Power Groups* whereas Lilienthal's book might be filed as an economic brief for the plaintiff in the case of *Big Business v. Current Interpretation of Antitrust*." While Nourse did not consider himself an opponent of business bigness, he could not fully agree with either author. He saw a place for the regulation of big business by antitrust law, and he could not accept Galbraith's faith in the self-corrective action of power groups. He saw a "fundamental divergence in the views of the two authors. Whereas liberal Lilienthal would turn business loose to achieve the full fruition of its powers and reserve to the Federal Government only the power to police abusive practices, New Dealer Galbraith would put the Federal Government in the position of ultimate power and responsibility to make the economy work, redressing the weakness of group position or the faults of group bargains and production and marketing adjustments." Although he agreed that big business should not be considered in itself a crime by antitrust laws, he considered Lilienthal's views on the merits of big business rather extreme. He thought Galbraith's views on countervailing power even more exuberant. He said: "For him, alarms about concentration of economic power are unjustified. The disease engenders its own antibodies, and Nature cures all things. Some malaise, some lost time, some incidental expense of course, but neither death nor permanent injury to the body economic." Nourse could not refrain from pointing out that in Galbraith's model, "the Government plays the ultimate and crucial role."

Automation and Other Problems

The rapid spread of automation in the early 1950s caused the Joint Committee on the Economic Report in 1955 to set up a subcommittee on automation to examine its effects on the economy. As a student of industrial organization, Nourse was greatly interested in this new stage of technological development which promised to have a revolutionary impact on the economy, and he welcomed the opportunity to present his views at the hearings of this subcommittee on October 28, 1955. In his statement he made it clear that he did not look upon automation as nothing really new—"just more mechanization." He said: "It has its roots in mechanization, to be sure, but something new was added when electronic devices made possible the widespread application of the feedback principle." He believed the issue raised by automation could be expressed as follows: "Will it alter present economic relations in such ways as to disturb ... favorable economic conditions, or will our business system be able to translate these technological improvements fully and promptly into still greater prosperity and higher standards of living?"

For the long run, he was optimistic that our competitive economy could absorb automation into our economic institutions and practices. However, he maintained that "the smooth and beneficent assimilation of sharp and rapid technical change has to be effected through intelligent and even generous policies painstakingly arrived at by administrative agencies, private and public." He did not think that legislation was required to deal with the problems created by "so-called" automation, for he held that "to curb or redirect the process of scientific discovery and engineering application and the adaptations of business men and consumers to these changes would be utterly repugnant to the system of free enterprise and individual choice that have made our country great." He did believe, however, that public policy on economic problems related to automation "should be framed in the light of the fullest possible understanding of the integrated character of the price-income structure and behavior of our economy, with an eye single to promoting 'maximum production, employment, and purchasing power' for the whole people, not to serve the immediate interest of any special group."

He concluded his statement by saying:

> The declaration of the policy of the Employment Act set "free *competitive* enterprise" as a premise of its policy, and the historic argument for giving technological innovation free rein is that competition both maximizes its gains in production and distributes its benefits in purchasing power. One of the dangers of automation stems from some tendency toward rigidity, and this applies equally to concentrations of economic power in the hands of management, of labor, or of finance. The legislative recommendations of this committee in my judgment should be unremitting in their emphasis on maintaining real competition between centers of administrative control even when the operative units introduced by modern technology are necessarily large. But an optimum result depends on the mores of business above and beyond the structures set up in law. Each segment of an automated continuous process has a built-in responsibility to every other part through its mechanical interconnections. . . . Unless the responsible executives seek to integrate their operations to the prosperity of the whole economy . . . our economic process will disintegrate into wasteful struggles for individual or group short-run advantage. . . ."

Three years later, the Philosophy Library published a book, *Automation and Society*. It raised such questions as: "How will automation affect our lives?" "Will its results be beneficial or harmful?" "How can it be controlled?" Nourse contributed a chapter under the title, "What's New About Automation?" He made clear that "automation" was something more than an extension of old-fashioned mechanization, for as the "child of the vacuum tube and the transistor," it brought new developments to our industrial life with great economic, and hence social, implications. He thought that by introducing the principle of information feedback and continuous process, it promised to have an enormous impact on production and distribution methods. He was concerned that much of its potential benefit might be lost "through failure to make our economic structure and practice equally scientific." He believed it highly important that social scientists study this new development so that it could be assimilated into our social structure.

Another matter that greatly interested Nourse in 1955 was the exportability of our thinking on economic planning as expressed in the Employment Act of 1946. *Economics in the Public Service* had attracted attention in foreign countries, and several were interested in having something of their own like the Council of Economic Advisers. This led to correspondence between Nourse and various persons in England, Japan, Germany, and India. At this time a representative of the Australian government urged him to write an article on the experience of the Council of Economic Advisers for publication in Australia. Nourse was glad to comply, and his views were presented in the Australian *Economic Record* of November, 1955. In his article he indicated that under the chairmanship of Arthur Burns, the Council had come to a position of important "but unobtrusive" usefulness throughout the executive establishment. He concluded by saying: "Much has been learned from experience in both the executive office and in the Congress during the first nine years of operation of the Employment Act of 1946. Perhaps the greatest lesson learned has been the realization that such an intellectual approach to economic affairs is a permanent need of a democratic system."

During this stage of his life, Nourse examined any question that aroused his interest. Charles Morgan's play, *The Burning Glass*, which he saw at the National Theatre, greatly impressed him, for it posed a difficult moral question: Should scientific work be discontinued if it threatens to destroy civilization? In Morgan's play, a young scientist developed a device which he refused to turn over to government for fear that it might lead to wholesale destruction. Nourse played with the idea and made it the subject for a talk to the Washington Literary Society, but he could not "leave the issue alone," so he developed his views in article form for the *Virginia Quarterly Review* (Summer, 1955) under the title, "Nature's Power and the Conscience of Man." He considered this theme "central to social science in its inter-weaving with natural science." He saw this as the problem raised by the proliferation of atomic power, and he was intrigued by the question, "Can atomic energy be controlled by social science procedures?" He came to two conclusions: (1) that we cannot stop the advance of science with its "terrifically potential powers," but (2) that we may be able to restrict the control of these powers to nations that are not "trigger happy." In this article, which was widely reprinted throughout the world, he posed a problem which is still far from solution—perhaps the ultimate problem before the world today.

The Tenth Anniversary of the Employment Act

The tenth birthday of the Employment Act on February 20, 1956, was fittingly observed by the publication of a comprehensive symposium report issued by the National Planning Association.[18] It gave the views of participants in the passage of the Employment Act and of several who had been actively concerned with its administration. In addition to the statements made at the anniversary meeting, it included 17 related essays by professional economists, many of whom had served on the staff of the Council of Economic Advisers or of the Joint Committee on the Economic Report. It was the consensus that the Employment Act had been wise legislation. Ex-President Truman, in a letter sent for inclusion in the symposium report, said: "There is almost no other piece of domestic legislation enacted while I was President to which I would attach equal significance." In a like letter, President Eisenhower said: "This has been a momentous decade in the economic history of our country. Over these years the objectives of the Employment Act have offered sound guidance in furthering economic growth and stability." Of particular interest were statements made by the first two Council Chairmen, Edwin G. Nourse and Leon H. Keyserling, and a letter from the present Chairman, Arthur F. Burns, who was unable to attend the meeting.

In his paper, "Taking Root—Ten Years of the Employment Act," Nourse said that there had been and still were two divergent philosophies as to the scope and purpose of the act. He maintained that the first school of thought looked to the Employment Act "to launch the Federal Government on a comprehensive and continuous program for engineering optimum performance by the whole economy," and it "expected the Council of Economic Advisers and the Joint Economic Committee to draw blueprints for that program and keep them continuously revised." On the other hand, the second school of thought included those "who understood the Act as merely stating a broad objective or ideal goal toward which efforts should be directed and as introducing additions to our executive and legislative institutions which would aid the economy—both its private and its public sectors—in moving more competently toward that goal."

As an adherent of the second group, Nourse said: "I am disposed to argue that the first 10 years under the Employment Act accomplished about all that could reasonably be demanded." He believed that the first decade under the act had firmly planted "the concept of Federal responsibility for an integrated, consistent, and positive policy in support of economic growth and stability." He was well pleased with the way the Council was functioning as a non-political agency under the Eisenhower Administration, and he thought well of the work being done by the Joint Committee on the Economic Report. He held that it would take more time under successive administrations to establish the concept of professional economic advisership, but he believed that the "policy and procedures implanted by the Employment Act have taken vigorous root."

Keyserling, in his statement, "The Council of Economic Advisers— Tasks in the Next Decade," was less complacent on how the CEA should function. He envisaged the role of the Council being more positive and aggressive than did Nourse. He held that under the Employment Act, "the CEA exists primarily to help the President formulate, articulate, and obtain maintenance of the *policies* contained in his Economic Reports." He discussed a number of ways in which the Council could better "service" the president in the decade ahead, and he thought that if the Council were not to lapse into "innocuous desuetude," it would need to move vigorously along the following lines: (1) It should "reinstate its earlier practice of projecting in economic terms levels of employment, production, and purchasing power. . . ." (2) It should "set forth and evaluate the Federal Budget as an integral part of the National Economic Budget. . . ." (3) Its "projections should state quantitatively our basic national priorities and appraise their relative economic cost and necessity." (4) It should "make these projections on a long term basis. . . ." (5) It should "realize that it is not primarily an economic research agency, nor a statistical refinement agency, nor an interpreter of past trends, nor a pure forecasting agency. . . . It is primarily an agency to help determine needs and evolve policies and programs."

Keyserling held that the Chairman of the CEA should be the trustee of the president in advocating and defending his policies before Congress and the Joint Committee on the Economic Report, and he inferred that the views of Nourse represented a "cloistered concept" of the CEA.[19]

Arthur Burns, in his letter for the symposium, indicated that the Employment Act had become law in an atmosphere of economic uncertainty and had not won enthusiastic acceptance quickly. He thought that "much of the skepticism or fear that accompanied the passage of the Employment Act" had vanished. "Today," he said, "there is broad agreement that our economy is stronger than a decade ago, that the scope of free enterprise is larger, and that the Employment Act has provided serviceable procedures for promoting economic growth and reducing economic fluctuations."

The views of Alvin H. Hansen on progress made under the Employment Act during its first 10 years were of particular interest in the light of his acknowledged generative influence on the origination of the act. In his essay for the symposium report, he said: "The Employment Act of 1946 has truly set in motion a great educational force. . . . It is my distinct feeling that we have moved a long way from the generally prevailing economic illiteracy of a generation ago to at least a modicum of economic literacy." Hansen accorded Nourse much credit in the "initial launching of a wholly new venture in an atmosphere of widespread suspicion." He considered the appointment of a highly competent staff during the formative years "crucial." He thought the Employment Act was at long last "a firmly entrenched institution."

He noted that the "earlier view of the Council as potentially an independent entity, shifted under Keyserling's chairmanship, to the view that the Council should perform as an integral part of the political machinery and should indeed play a leading role as the chief economic advocate for the Administration in power." Hansen then said: "It is, I think, a fact that there is a widespread opinion throughout the country that this placed the Council in an unnecessarily controversial position." He thought that the Council under the chairmanship of Arthur Burns had "receded measurably into the background. It restricted itself more nearly, though not quite exclusively, to the role of assisting and advising the President."

Hansen aligned himself on the side of Nourse in his conception of the proper role of the Council on political matters. He said: "In my view, the Council should, strictly as technicians and not as political advocates, interpret the President's program before the public (preferably on rare occasions) and before Congressional Committees as requested." He did not think that Council members should be employed as policy spokesmen "else they tend to lose that objectiveness which is so essential to a staff agency." He said: "The Council members are economists, and they should not attempt to be something more than economists." He summed up his views as follows:

> The Employment Act of 1946 states specifically that it shall be the duty and function of the Council to assist and advise the President. It should not attempt the role of an independent entity operation on its own, ambitiously instructing the American people and the Congress with respect to its conception of "economic truth." It should not be a political arm of the party in

power. Its function is clearly to assume the more humble role of adviser to the President and of technical interpreter of the President's program.

Thus, Hansen generally concurred with Nourse on how the Council of Economic Advisers should function.

"Intellectualism on the Economic Front"

During the academic year 1956-1957, Nourse greatly enjoyed participating in a program set up by the national office of Phi Beta Kappa to revivify the intellectual spirit of its local chapters. Under this program, Nourse, as a visiting scholar, spent about a week at each of the following colleges or universities: The University of Kansas, University of North Dakota, Washington University (St. Louis), University of Arkansas, University of the South (Tennessee), Cornell College (Iowa), Dickinson College (Pennsylvania), and Sarah Lawrence College (New York). Local chapters made the arrangements for his contacts, and in several instances he gave a public address on "Intellectualism on the Economic Front," which was open to the faculty and all interested students.

These visits permitted Nourse to examine the intellectual life of a representative group of colleges and universities and enabled him to articulate his thinking on the kind of economic information needed for informed citizenship. There was no direct connection between this activity for Phi Beta Kappa chapters and his work with the Joint Council on Economic Education, although both programs were in keeping with his strong belief that the importance and quality of economic education could not be overstressed in a democratic society. He found this experience very congenial, for it brought him back into close contact with college students. He was pleased by the publication of his address on "Intellectualism on the Economic Front" in the *American Scholar*—the journal of Phi Beta Kappa—in its summer issue for 1958, as this enabled him to reach a much broader audience. This article is worth detailed scrutiny as an expression of Nourse's educational philosophy, but only a few of its points can be examined here.

He said in his opening statement: "We have become accustomed to thinking of general attitudes in the economic sphere as strongly marked by anti-intellectualism. The 'practical' businessman has scorned the 'theorist,' repudiated the 'planner' and openly opposed the very idea of comprehensive social welfare. Labor union officials and members likewise have been skeptical of 'long haired' leaders with policies based on analysis of the relation of efficient production and equitable distribution." Nourse felt that "these overt manifestations" were somewhat "paradoxical," for "covertly," both labor and management were moved by beliefs as to "what makes an economy tick." He thought that this fact held promise that eventually gradual change would bring a greater appreciation of intellectualism in our economic life. He considered the Employment Act of 1946 an important milestone in this development, for it was passed with "overwhelming support after searching public and congressional consideration." He saw it as "a real step to the nation's economic sophistication."

To make clear his thinking, he examined the epithet "egghead," which was being invidiously applied to those who believed that intellectual approaches would help strengthen the economic system. He thought that a distinction should be drawn between "hard-boiled" and "soft-boiled" eggheads. While the first group was rigorous in searching for cause and effect relationships, the "soft-boiled" eggheads were inclined to dilute intellectualism with emotionalism. Nourse had little sympathy for the latter group, members of which were "sometimes referred to as 'bleeding hearts.'"

Nourse summed up his thinking by saying:

> True liberalism is properly synonymous with intellectualism or the most objective application of social science to social betterment. . . . Intellectualism in the economic area is the clean cut of corrective surgery, the administering of distasteful medicine, and a disciplined regimen of life in contrast to the misguided affection of the indulgent parent. Liberalism, in my book, means deep concern for humankind as such, for universal opportunity and incentive for full realization of productive capacities and equitable sharing of the fruits of common endeavor. To move surely toward these goals the liberal must have his feet firmly on the solid grounds of economic efficiency, not lose his head in the pink clouds of emotionalism. By the same token, the true conservative is one who cherishes these age-old dreams of bettering the life of many and who would preserve and refine both the values and tools already found useful in that upward struggle. Intellectualism is the God-given faculty for objectively viewing and rationally weighing together the desired ends and the available means so that they may be combined in the most efficacious blend.

Clarifying the Full Employment Concept

The meaning of "full employment" intrigued Nourse from the inception of the Employment Act of 1946. After 10 years of experience with the act, he thought it time to examine which goals of employment were coming to "expression or acceptance" in our national economic life. He presented his findings in the *Review of Economics and Statistics* (May, 1956) under the title, "Defining Our Employment Goal Under the 1946 Act."

In introducing this article, he analyzed the full employment goal as it emerged in the original full employment bill (S 380) and how it was tamed in the legislative process leading up to the passage of the Employment Act. He recognized that the act "clothed but did not resolve two divergent views—minimalist and maximalist—of the goal to be sought through subsequent action, executive or legislative." He said: "The focus of disagreement then evident has persisted, simmering along at the low temperature of polite debate during years of prosperity but boiling up to sharp intellectual and political controversy as soon as we have moderate declines such as those of 1949 and 1954." He held that the divergence of views grew out of two basic concepts of the nature of our enterprise economy. "One may be called the filling-station philosophy; it is concerned primarily with a fuel supply poured in from outside. The other may be called the service-shop approach; it is concerned primarily with optimum adjustment of the working parts internal to the engine."

He went on to explain: "the filling-station approach is external to the policy and action of individuals, or firms and organized groups, and even of government except in its fiscal role. It is concerned with aggregate magnitudes on both the supply and demand side of the labor market—total labor force and total job offerings. It conceives our economy as an integrated mechanism where if output falls below theoretical capacity, the sovereign remedy is to 'turn on the juice' in the form of total monetary demand."

In contrast to the filling-station philosophy, Nourse favored the "service-shop approach which did not place all of the policy eggs in one statistical basket." Under this approach, he said, "the policy maker proceeds to make comprehensive diagnostic studies of the economy to discover any possible source of low performance. . . ." While he admitted that the two philosophies were not mutually exclusive, he thought that "the difference in emphasis [was] so great as to amount to a difference in kind when it [came] to sharp issues of employment policy, or more broadly, economic stabilization policies." Nourse maintained that the Employment Act represented a distinct shift from the "gap," or filling-station, approach to the "functional adjustment," or service-shop, approach to national economic policy. However, he noted that "acceptance of this eclecticism as the dominant note in administrative and congressional interpretation" during the nine years of experience under the act also reflected the "persistence and frequent recrudescence of the simpler total-demand philosophy of economic stabilization."

Nourse felt that the conditions from 1946 to 1956 had not really tested the Employment Act. He said:

With the concept of the labor force still unclarified, the reliability and pertinence of statistical measures under challenge, and the nature, timing and proper dosage of remedies in controversy, we have muddled through the post-war decade with an amazing degree of success. We must, however, bear in mind that the period, though hectic, was prevailingly buoyant. Whether the degree and kinds of economic sophistication we have displayed during these years will suffice if we are called upon to cope with a grimmer set of circumstances in the years ahead remains to be seen.

In closing his article, Nourse said that his main purpose had been "to broaden somewhat the empirical foundation on which to theorize about the nature and attainability of the employment goal we still see only under a glass darkly." He was then at work on a follow-up paper which he hoped would make more explicit what might be done. This was presented at the December annual meeting of the American Economic Association, which featured a symposium on "The Employment Act in the Economic Thinking of Our Times," with Nourse as moderator. His lead-off paper, "Ideal and Working Concepts of Full Employment," was on a subject of compelling interest to him. In his opening paragraph he set the stage for an analysis of the practical problems related to the concept of full employment:

> A decade of experience under the Employment Act of 1946 has served to uncover many complexities that inhere in the mere concept of full employment—quite aside from the yet greater complications that beset the attempt actually to reach such goals as we may set up. We need a concept that will be dynamic and at the same time realistic in that it views fullness of employment in perspective to the state of the arts—organizational as well as technological. It must recognize but not accept as fixed, the institutions and mores of our system of free enterprise and representative government. So oriented, it will envision goals high enough to gratify our socio-political aspirations but also be consonant with the limitations of means existing at any given time for their attainment. Thus my title links ideal with working concepts of full employment.

With this setting he explored the sociological, political, and psychological implications of the term "full employment." He thought that under the Employment Act, "it devolves on the economist . . . to furnish interpretations of the full employment goal that will sublimate political pressures, temper reformist dreams, and combine industrial and commercial workability with the scientists' ideal of systematic progress." He did not think the criteria given by the act provided "a consistent and tenable formula for the full employment ideal or adequate working rules for national employment policy." He said: "Our profession has further work to do toward conceptual clarification." However, he thought it was "an encouraging aspect of the economic thinking of our times . . . that the oversimplified goal of full or maximum employment is to so great an extent giving way to maximum production and the new formulation 'economic growth.'"

Nourse was apprehensive that the goal of full employment, no matter how measured, would encourage inflation. He said: "I am quite aware that many will not go as far as I do in refusing to accept price inflation or even price level stability as the only solution theoretically possible to the problems of full employment and economic growth. . . . It behooves these proponents of high pressure economics . . . to abstain from such ambitious definitions of full employment or of business expansion as will engender a degree of inflation that will call for the imposing of controls on prices, wages, or investments." He believed that "a better alternative than complacent inflation backstopped by standby controls is the self-discipline of groups under increasingly sophisticated leadership seeking to advance their group interest through promotion of a self-sustaining price-income structure competitively shaped to maximizing employment because it maximizes consumption." He went on to say: "Toward such a goal the Employment Act, with its socially oriented intellectual apparatus, will, I believe, mark an important milestone."

"The Changing Pattern of Our Economy"

As a social scientist, Nourse was greatly impressed by the changes in economic institutions that had come in his lifetime. He dwelt upon the significance of these changes in an address on "The Changing Pattern of Our Economy" given to the New Jersey Bankers Association at Atlantic City on May 22, 1957. In opening his subject, he said:

> With my own eyes I have watched the transition of America from a simple horse- and steam-powered technology to the age of jet planes, synthetic chemistry, antibiotic medicine, radio physics, and nuclear fission. Accompanying this physical progress, I have seen hardly less startling economic and social changes. I propose to take a quick look at this changing pattern of our free enterprise economy in what I regard as its most challenging aspect.

He desired to make clear that these changes had brought forth a "new economics" which was conceived "as human engineering based on scientific method."[20] He said:

> The new economics is concerned with those large units of business organization that are needed to operate our modern technology efficiently. It is concerned with those elite groups who are needed to guide the affairs of the large aggregations of Big Business (including Big Banking) and of Big Labor. The new economics is greatly concerned about the business policies of these administrators of the private economy and of how their policies are arrived at and how they are implemented.

He saw the new economics building a national economic machine based on the principle of private competitive enterprise that could achieve vigorous national growth and stability, with government playing a complementary and facilitating role. He was encouraged by the evidence of growing economic sophistication in business, labor, farm, and other organizations, and he looked forward to the day when business decisions would be based upon applied intellectualism. This address reflected Nourse's long-held faith that intellectualism offered "an approach to widespread and sustained prosperity," a belief in the ultimate professionalization of economic organizations for the best interests of society.

Nourse also examined the great change that had come in our economic life since the Great Depression in an article for the *1958 Yearbook of the National Council for the Social Studies*, entitled "New Viewpoints in the Economic Area." Contrasting the gloomy attitude on economic matters in the 1930s, he said: "Now we are talking confidently of a new world of perpetual boom." He found the great change in public thinking largely due to four general factors: the new outlook on physical productivity, a new emphasis on income security, changed attitudes toward spending and saving, and more pragmatic concepts of tax policy and the role of government.

He attributed the new outlook on physical productivity to the productive powers unleashed by World War II. "The resultant marriage of fecund science with fostering business enterprise has brought a change in the general outlook of economics from that of scarcity to that of abundance." While he thought that the new outlook on productivity was "dazzling," he was concerned with the question "Will it last?" He believed this would depend upon continued availability of resources, population growth, and other intangible factors. "To make the new type of abundance permanent and progressive," he said, "we must have wise public and sound private practices."

The new emphasis on economic security was evident in business pension plans and in state and federal measures. He thought it significant that the Employment Act of 1946 placed responsibility on the Federal government for providing "maximum employment, production, and purchasing power."

Nourse was impressed also by the change in individual and family attitudes toward spending and saving. The emphasis had ceased to be on thrift and was turned to free spending through various credit devices. Nourse thought that "today's economic thinking shows confidence in the attainability of a high-level balance between production and consumption, a smooth rhythm of earning, spending, saving, investing, that spells economic progress. There is less fear," he said, "of blind impersonal forces that bring periods of general disaster. There is new emphasis on confidence in scientific analysis, short- and long-range planning, and responsible administration. This new trend is manifest in both the private and public sectors of the economy."

Nourse saw developing a more pragmatic attitude toward taxes and the role of government in economic matters. He thought that the modern objective in economics was "to strike a balance between two equally vital concerns, (a) that taxation shall not be abused to destroy what we the people want, and (b) an equal concern that taxation and the government spending that goes with it shall be used under suitable conditions to create a larger measure of general well-being." It was his view that when "productivity rises to the level of present-day America, consumption must be widely shared. General well-being must be allowed to rise if the production system is not to stagnate." He went on to say: "Modern economic thinking sees the two processes (a) of distributing national productivity through incomes and prices in the market and (b) of redistributing this social product through government taxing and spending as complementary parts of a flexibly efficient and progressive economic system."

In his concluding paragraphs, Nourse pointed out that one keynote characterized today's economic thinking. "It is the recurring emphasis on 'management' and social responsibility." He did not think that "this progress in economic viewpoints" assured the millenium, in that human judgment "is fallible and human character is often weak or selfish. But," he averred, "as never before, we seem in our economic institutions and practices to be combining scientific method with social purpose."

Fellow of the American Farm Economic Association

At its annual meeting in 1957, the American Farm Economic Association embarked on a program of recognizing outstanding agricultural economists by designating them as "Fellows." Nourse was pleased to be included among the inaugural group of 10 which included his friends John Donald Black, Thomas Nixon Carver, Joseph Stancliffe Davis, Garnet Wolsey Forster, Asher Hobson, Theodore W. Schultz, Henry Charles Taylor, Frederick V. Waugh, and Milburn Lincoln Wilson. The citation of Nourse's accomplishments included this paragraph:

> As one of the senior statesmen among agricultural economists, Dr. Nourse has for many years inspired others in agricultural economics. He has incessantly pioneered the arduous pathway that agricultural economics has traveled during the past four decades in its attempt to attain professional maturity. During those years, he helped to establish the young and growing discipline on the firm foundation of complete and objective analysis, in-

tellectual integrity, and dedication to the preservation and strengthening of a progressive agricultural economy in a dynamic and expanding America.[21]

The Problem of Inflation

Inflation was attracting widespread attention in 1957. This was manifest in the formation of an informal organization which took the name "The National Citizens Committee to Curb Inflation." Nourse welcomed an opportunity to address a conference of this group held at the Mayflower Hotel in Washington, D.C., on June 24, 1957. Speaking on the subject, "Sowing the Seeds of Inflation," he explained how the inflationary situation had its roots in World War II and in the ensuing post-war years. He did not feel that the full responsibility for the continuous growth of inflation could be placed on government fiscal and monetary policies, although they had been of contributory importance. Rather, he said, "It is much nearer to the truth to say that the real source of inflation in post-war United States has lain in the market place—in the institutions and practices of labor union bargaining and corporation price administration." He then said: "We live in an age of big business, big labor, and big government and we had better learn to make its three big wheels mesh together as a producing machine of maximum efficiency, instead of becoming an 'engine of inflation.'" Nourse did not believe it possible for inflation to be curbed simply or swiftly by action of the federal government. He thought that this could be achieved only by self-restraint within the business community, and he wondered: "Have we all the intestinal fortitude to curb inflation and let the system work?"

The rapid rise in prices from 1955 to 1957 was of great concern to Congress, and this was manifested by the Senate Judiciary Committee in setting up a Subcommittee on Antitrust and Monopoly under the aggressive chairmanship of Senator Estes Kefauver. This subcommittee held hearings on the subject of "Administered Prices" in July and August, 1957. In opening the hearings, Senator Kefauver said that the subcommittee was "trying to come to grips with what is probably the nation's current No. 1 problem—the problem of inflation." He added: "We are concerned particularly with the extent to which administered prices in concentrated industries may contribute to this problem."

To get the hearings under way, five leading "experts on administered prices" were called upon to provide a general understanding of the problem. Nourse, as the lead witness, related the matter under consideration to the objectives of the Employment Act of 1946. It was his view that under the act, Congress had incurred "an obligation to reexamine from time to time the economic institutions or structures that it has authorized and the regulatory agencies that it has set up." He thought that reexamination of antitrust laws was thus called for. It was his opinion that the issue of monopoly and antitrust legislation could be stated thus: "Does present federal legislation . . . provide the best harness in which the power of individual and group enterprises can be applied to maximize total production? Does it facilitate the concentration of sufficient economic power at the proper places to get greatest progress, and does it deter the amassing of economic power in amounts or in places that result in sacrificing the good of the total economy to the lust for gain or control on the part of certain individuals or organizations?" He thought that "any combination that, in fact, restrains trade nullifies by so much the declared purpose of the Congress 'to promote maximum employment, production, and purchasing power.' It is in the context of such an issue that my comments are set."

The following thoughts expressed by Nourse in his presentation are worth quotation:

> It is my considered opinion that the economic institutions and business practices described by administered pricing grow naturally and properly out of the conditions of modern industrialism and that they may be so used as to promote both economic growth and business stability vigorously and consistently. But, as matters are currently developing, I am deeply apprehensive lest the actual administration of the prices of goods, of commercial services, and of labor are impeding or threaten to impede seriously the full and continuous use of the nation's productive resources toward satisfying the needs and wants of consumers.
>
> . . . .
>
> I do not subscribe to the view that, under the divergent but roughly or partially countervailing impact of administered prices and administered wages, we have effected a rolling adjustment to a state of continuous dynamic equilibrium and stabilized prosperity. I feel rather that we are just coming to the real testing time with reference to the quality of administration on both sides. . . . We are now confronted with the pressing problem of seeing to it that big business does not become managerial domination, that big labor does not become union dictation, and that big government does not become authoritarianism.
>
> . . . .
>
> There is inherent incompatibility between government accepting responsibility for maintaining full employment and stable prosperity and large units of business administration accepting no responsibility for making their administrative policies and practices conduce to maximum productivity of the economy.
>
> . . . .
>
> I have stated just one positive principle in my testimony: that I place reliance on the maintenance of a truly competitive situation, and I would like to see a clear reaffirmation by the Congress that no party—farm, labor, or business—shall be exempt from that antitrust principle or, as I prefer to call it, the competitive principle.

In view of the shifting economic situation as the year ended, Nourse's views on the 1958 Economic Report are of much interest ("A Tract for the Times," *Challenge* magazine, April, 1958). He prefaced his examination of the report by saying that it "must be read in the context of our current hysteria about space travel, persistent fears of inflation, and a widespread distaste for government planning." In looking back over previous Economic Reports, he found that the problem of inflation had been pervasive in both the Truman and Eisenhower Administrations. Turning to the 1958 report, he found that inflation was still a dominating consideration. He thought that the following sentences in the report stated the problem confronting national economic policy with clarity and frankness. "During much of the year (1957) the task of restraining inflationary pressures was paramount, and the policies were directed to this end. In the closing months of the year, and currently, the task has been to facilitate readjustments in the economy essential to the resumption of sustainable economic growth, but to do so without reviving inflationary pressures."

He thought that the following statement in the report skillfully blended optimism with realism and was an appropriate statement for the president to utter at that time. "As we look ahead in 1958, there are grounds for expecting that the decline in business activity need not be prolonged and that economic growth can be resumed without extended interruption. The policies of Government will be directed toward helping to assure this result."

While Nourse thought that the report glossed over the problem of adjustment of prices and incomes to a level of full use of our plant and labor force, he was pleased that this problem was not ignored as evidenced by the following "chaste words with pregnant meaning":

> There is no easy solution to the problem of maintaining high employment, vigorous economic growth and reasonably stable prices. But it is clear that the combination of policies and practices followed in the recent past by the various participants in our economic life has given results that in respects are unfavorable. There are critical questions here for the leadership of business and labor, as well as for Government. Business concerns must re-examine their policies and practices. Price increases that are unwarranted by costs or that attempt to recapture investment outlays too quickly not only lower the purchasing power of the dollar but may be self-defeating by causing a restriction of markets, lower output, under-utilization of capacity, and a narrowing of the return of capital investment. The leadership of labor must recognize that wage increases that go beyond prospective productivity gains are inconsistent with a stable price level.

Nourse felt that this statement properly laid responsibility squarely on the shoulders of business and labor for positive contributions to growth and stability. Moreover, he found the Economic Report entirely consistent with the conservative budget submitted to the Congress. He did not think the budget or the Economic Report would "satisfy those who are convinced that the Government should call out 'horse, foot, and artillery' to rescue the economy from the brink of an economic crash," but he believed that they represented "good statesmanship for a democratic government learning to use the intellectual aids of a Council of Economic Advisers and a Budget Bureau."

As the concern with inflation gave way to fear of depression, a National Conference on Keeping America Strong, held at the Statler Hotel in Washington, D.C., on June 28, 1958, gave Nourse an opportunity to speak on the subject, "Reaping the Harvest of Inflation." This was a sequel to his talk, "Sowing the Seeds of Inflation," of the preceding year. He said: "It behooves us now to examine the manner of harvest these seeds of inflation are producing." He thought that the current situation was showing how inflation "overstrains a boom and aggravates the ensuing recession. We are learning that the great fiscal and monetary powers of government . . . are not cures in times of recession, but merely palliatives—and dangerous ones at that." He pointed out that but a year before, the general public was complacent about the problem of inflation. "The country was zipping along on a pleasant highway of apparently invulnerable prosperity: why worry? This insouciance was fortified by assurances from the highest quarters that if some downturn should appear, the government had at its disposal the means of checking or reversing it and that the government possessed the skill and determination to use these weapons decisively and at the proper time." Now there was a demand that the government "do something," and Nourse was fearful that this situation would bring on policies designed "to get us off the unemployment horn of the economic dilemma" that would "impale us solidly on the inflation horn of this same dilemma." He ended his talk by saying: "I was astonished during the recent hearings of the Joint Economic Committee to note the number of witnesses who, after recognizing the threat to sustained full employment which stems from inflation, proposed the setting up of one sort or another of wage, price, or investment stabilization commission or authority. Is it possible that the harvest of inflation will be economic authoritarianism?"

Consultant on Dairy Marketing Problems

Nourse continued to keep in close touch with developments in agricultural economics and cooperative marketing while he was working on broader economic problems, but he did not return actively to these fields until 1957, when he was engaged by the Maryland and Virginia Milk Producers Association to serve as chairman of a technical committee to determine whether it would be advisable for the association to again place itself under a Federal Milk Marketing Order. This committee was set up at the suggestion of Herbert Forest, who was in charge of the Milk Market Order Program of the USDA. He recommended that Nourse be invited to serve as chairman of this committee, in view of his recognized competence as an agricultural economist.[22] Work on this committee called for economic and price analysis, which soon brought him back into active participation in economic and cooperative problems relating to the milk industry. This committee, under his chairmanship, recommended conditions for the proposed order that were found satisfactory by the association and the government, and no basic change has since been found necessary in the order established.

Growing out of his work on a new federal milk order for the Washington, D.C., market, Nourse prepared a paper for the annual conference of federal milk market administrators, November 12-13, 1958, in which he explained how the federal milk order system enabled the government to help maintain a supply and demand balance in the fluid milk markets. Later, in discussing this paper with me, he said: "I was there expounding an economic theory of coordinating prices in such a way as to adjust the national market supply to the national demand. I was simply applying, recapitulating the theoretical position that I had enunciated way back in 1919 in my article for the *Quarterly Journal of Economics* which I called "Normal Price as a Market Concept." He admitted that there had been great institutional changes since his 1919 article, but he believed that its underlying principle was still sound.[23]

In the mid-1950s the Maryland and Virginia Association had acquired the business of another cooperative that gave it a virtual monopoly in its operating territory. This caused the Anti-Trust Division of the Department of Justice to bring suit against the association on charges that it had unduly reduced competition. In developing its defense to this charge, the association employed Nourse in 1959 as a consultant to study the economic factors involved. In accepting this assignment, Nourse made it clear that he could not offer views on the legal issues in the case. He believed that the attorney for the association erred in placing too much reliance on the Capper-Volstead Act for protection, and he heartily approved the Supreme Court's decision (U.S. v. Maryland and Virginia Milk Producers Association) of May 2, 1960, which placed cooperatives in the same relation to the antitrust laws as other business corporations.

Suggestions on the Farm Problem

In a paper on "The Impact of Monetary and Fiscal Policy on Agricultural Business," presented at an agricultural industry conference at Cornell University in September, 1957, Nourse noted that agriculture was recognized as one of the major coordinate factors in the concept of planning for national economic growth and stability. He said: "It is not a special interest and should not be a pressure group, but a full partner in the effort to mobilize our business to perfect a free enterprise system. The basic philosophy of the Employment Act is *against* political action for private groups and *for* economics in the public service." Nourse did not think that monetary and fiscal policy—although important—reached the heart of the problems of agricultural business, which were related more to *market policy*. He therefore urged agricultural business "to exert its great influence toward curbing the monopolistic, restrictionary, and inflationary structures and practices of industry, commerce and finance [and] not join in the 'donkey race' of centrally controlled supply." He thought that agriculture could benefit from, and render benefit to, the economy by continuing and strengthening its distinctive business agency— the cooperative—as a means of getting the efficiencies of large size and skilled direction both in the sale of its products and in the procurement of farm supplies but he warned: "Its objective (should be) distributive and bargaining skill, not monopolistic power." He urged agricultural leadership to throw its weight behind a competitive enterprise interpretation of the Employment Act so as to help make the "anti-trust or pro-competitive" principle apply equally to industry, labor, and agriculture.

Several months later, in an interview with Carroll Kilpatrick for the *Washington Post* (1958), Nourse proposed that we should "move with all deliberate speed against the resistance and political involvement of those who support the high rigid price support program." He said that "the need is to get more farmers to stay on the farm." He recognized that farm policies could not be reversed overnight without economic chaos, and that was why he advocated "all deliberate speed." He thought it might take 10 years or more to get out of the present situation, but he believed a start should be made to reduce price supports in an orderly way so as to give farmers more freedom of choice in their farm management. He considered the soil bank program "a brave try."

Looking back on this interview several years later, Nourse thought that it epitomized his thinking on the farm problem at that time. "My whole thinking," he said, "was that good economic statesmanship would be assimilating the agricultural industry into the general industrial development of the country rather than setting it up as an area for special interventionist treatment."[24]

Prices in Relation to Economic Stability and Growth

Nourse was highly pleased when the Joint Economic Committee set up hearings in May, 1958, to deal with the "relationship of prices to economic stability and growth" and invited him to present his views at its first meeting. In his opening statement, he said: "I believe this committee is marking a new milestone in the interpretation and application of the Employment Act by conducting this series of hearings. . . . Such an inquiry is of the utmost timeliness just now as the policy set forth in the Employment Act is facing its first severe test."

He thought that the purpose of the hearings as stated by Chairman Wright Patman held great promise for the outcome of the investigation—that it was to be "an exploration of general economic processes which involve prices, price relationships, costs, and price policies . . . public and private [that] can contribute to . . . maximum employment, production, and purchasing power." This expression impressed him as being "in refreshing contrast to some of the oversimplified and over-mechanistic concepts of the employment problem that are still current."

Nourse felt that the stabilization of prices was implicit in the objectives of the Employment Act, although this was unstated. He did not see the desirability of amending the act to provide a specific price stabilization objective—a proposal then under Congressional consideration. He said: "I argue against such amendment on the ground that it would add more words of vague meaning and controversial interpretation without giving further practical guidance to policy-makers."[25]

"To understand the part that prices play in the interpretation and application of the Employment Act," Nourse said, "it is necessary to note a broad analytical difference among those who try to interpret usefully the objectives of the Employment Act." He described the two divergent groups as follows: "One group vigorously proclaims itself the exponent of 'high pressure economics' and ever-full (or over-full) employment (more jobs than applicants), with 'pressure' to keep it so exerted through positive governmental policy and action, fiscal and monetary." In the second group he included "the sober but by no means complacent economists like myself who call themselves exponents of safe-pressure stabilization with vigorous growth. We place primary emphasis on such fullness of employment as can stand on its own bottom and thus reflect internal stability in the market . . . and believe there is such a thing as inflationary over-employment, a condition in which production is at a destabilizing maximum of inventory surplus, excess plant building, and wage-price 'leapfrogging.'"

Nourse went on to explain that "to take this latter position is not to espouse the heresy of 'general over-production' but to stress the fact that misallocation of resources derives from faulty price, wage, and profit adjustments. As such it is to be attacked through specific market institutions, practices, and policies, not through the blanket devices of interest rates and tax level and only in emergencies through the processes of federal spending."

He maintained that "the 'high-pressure group' stresses growth, though they are not unmindful that market instability might retard growth, while the safe-pressure economists stress the functional balance of prices and incomes as the surest means to sustained growth in jobs, in production, and in real consumer purchasing power. Advance would be at as fast a rate as can be sustained within a competently administered market and fiscal process."

Nourse thought that this divergence in interpretation of the policy and responsibility of the federal government for economic well-being "very evidently hinged on price issues." Moreover, he thought that "a mandate for the price-income adjustment line of attack on the employment problem was clearly evident in the Employment Act's declaration of policy" and in the way the act had been interpreted in the 13 Economic Reports of the President so far submitted. He buttressed his position by citing past economic reports and then turned to the 1958 Economic Report recently submitted, which acknowledged as an "unfavorable feature in recent economic developments [that] four-fifths of the increase in gross national product in 1957 was accounted for by rising prices." He quoted approvingly the following paragraph of this report:

> There are critical questions here for business and labor, as well as Government. Business management must recognize that price increases that are unwarranted by costs or that attempt to recapture investment outlays too quickly, not only lower the buying power of the dollar, but also may be self-defeating by causing a restriction of markets, lower output, and a narrowing of the return on capital investment. The leadership of labor must recognize that wage increases that go beyond over-all productivity gains are inconsistent with stable prices, and that the resumption of economic growth can be slowed by wage increases that involve either high prices or a further narrowing of the margin between prices and costs. Government, for its part, must use its powers to keep our economy stable and to encourage sound economic growth with reasonable prices.

Nourse's examination of the language of the Employment Act in the perspective of its legislative history and in a review of its administration in the context of contemporary thinking led him to five general conclusions which are worth emphasis by full quotation:

1. Both the framers of the Act and those who have sought to forward its broad purposes of sustained high-level use of the nation's productive resources have been quite aware that they must deal with a complex interrelated process of prices and incomes.

2. There has been general recognition that there are three avenues of constructive approach to the maximum production problem: fiscal policy, monetary policy, and market (or private price-income) policy. Because of preoccupation with the current economic fad of aggregate demand as the antecedent rather than the concomitant of maximum production, there has been undue faith placed in monetary and fiscal policy as the means of attaining the ends of national growth and stability.

3. There is progressive disenchantment with monetary policy as a major means of achieving the objective of the Employment Act both because of inherent limitations and of political back-seat driving. Fiscal policy is still recognized as a powerful agency of growth and stability but one subject to similar political hazards in application. It is a basic limitation in both these types of control that they are aimed at aggregates, or the statistical artifact of a price level rather than specific functional price and income relationships. They may aggravate rather than correct the specific local situations where increased costs, disbursed incomes, and prices realizations attain or fail to attain so good a balance as to clear the market at full capacity operation. To the extent that such balance is not attained (or approximated) the compensatory or offsetting task thrown on public action (fiscal and monetary) is increased—with resultant failure or desperate resort to authoritarian controls.

4. In lieu of such a drift toward government control . . . we have the alternative deeply rooted in our traditions—"free competitive enterprise." This has two aspects. One is the "economic statesmanship" of corporation price-making executives, and a like concern for the welfare of the economy on the part of wage negotiating officials of large and strategically placed labor unions. Appeals to this important source of business efficiency and economic stability are consistently emphasized through the Economic Reports of the President from 1947 to 1958. I believe that such appeals are not fatuous. With growing economic sophistication and clearer sense of their responsibility on the part of executives of large industrial, commercial, and labor aggregations, we may hope to move closer toward the self-sustaining balance which both President Truman and President Eisenhower have repeatedly stated should be the contribution of private business. . . .

5. The greatest service this committee and the Congress can render at this juncture is to clarify the meaning of free competitive enterprise in this day of corporations and labor union giants. With the degree of concentration of economic power that has grown up at these centers and the institutional structures they now have it is quite possible for the free competitive enterprise of their leaders to work against rather than for the stabilization of the economy in a strong growth trend. We need to re-establish conditions of price competition instead of power competition. A full employment economy needs flexibility of its price and income structure to displace the built-in rigidities and ever widening institutions of "escalation", whether of farm

price supports, union contracts, cost-plus procurement, variable annuity insurance, government pay scales, and even proposed fixed income bonds.

To conclude his presentation, Nourse quoted the Economic Report of 1949, the last report submitted while he was Chairman of the Council of Economic Advisers. "The policy proclaimed in the Employment Act requires us to devise and adopt positive measures to stop this inflation and secure relative stabilization." He did not think that this responsibility had been diligently accepted in the intervening years but that instead "the easier but dangerous course" had been followed—which he characterized as acceptance of "inflation as a way of life."

Observations on the Economic Situation in 1958

As the business recession of 1957-1958 lifted, optimism replaced gloom, but Nourse saw no evidence that the new prosperity would be permanent. In an address on "The Economic Outlook" at a management conference held at Michigan State University on October 18, 1958, he asserted that the great wave of optimism sweeping the country was a fine tonic for vigorous business planning, but with his tongue in his cheek, he said: "We should of course move on confidently to the bright day when there will be two infrared roasted chickens in every electric refrigerator and two oversized and overstyled automobiles sticking out of both ends of every garage." He believed that the prudent businessman would wish to view the present situation with more perspective.

Looking back over the general post-war boom that began in 1946, he found it a result of six general factors: (a) re-equipping and re-stocking, (b) technological revolution, (c) early marriages and more babies, (d) an expansion of the middle class, (e) easy money and big government budgets, and (f) price inflation. He concluded: "What we have been witnessing is a dynamic enterprise society in a state of boiling activity, in a setting of revolutionary technological progress and great institutional changes." While he did not think that the force of these factors was spent, he asked in all seriousness: "Do you think we should keep things at 'the jumping boil' all of the time and expect the government to turn the heat on every time the economy simmers down to a period of consolidating its gains and laying the groundwork for the next surge forward? This, I think, is the fundamental issue confronting our business world today."

Nourse was fearful that a boom in 1959 would be inflationary—not soundly based on sustainable prosperity. He saw inflation as the greatest threat to the goal of sustained high level use of productive resources—human and material—the stated objective of the Employment Act of 1946.

He ended his address with this statement:

As I interpret our present economic situation and outlook, I would suggest that we are in a perfectly normal and not dangerously severe stage of shaking down to the mutual adjustments of new technology, new consumer patterns, new fiscal practices, and new strategies of private business management. If we accomplish these adjustments within a free enterprise economy with economic sophistication and mutual tolerance over a space of two or three years, I believe we shall be giving a good account of the American way of economic life. To insist that we must have forced-draft prosperity all the time—or chronic boom—is to invite destructive depression rather than to benefit from mild but not aborted corrective recession.

Several years later, when I brought this quotation to his attention, Nourse said to me: "My face doesn't get red as I hear that quotation. That's the intellectual-professional bed that I have made and I am content to lie in it."

Economic Justice

In August, 1958, Nourse presented a paper on "Economic Justice as a Social Goal" in a workshop, sponsored by the Joint Council on Economic Education in cooperation with the National Council of Social Studies and the National Science Teachers Association, held at Sarah Lawrence College. The object of the workshop was to determine how high school teachers of science and social studies could reinforce each other.

Nourse maintained that "justice" had an important place in economic thinking. He said: "We are getting away from the natural science concept of economics with its proscription of value judgments. We are moving over to the social science concern about motives and incentives as basic factors even in productive efficiency. . . . Social science emphasizes value concepts or ideals as defining ends toward which we shall use the methods of science to devise effective means. In this quest, issues of economic justice become matters of lively concern."

In his analysis he found the problem of justice closely related to labor and market problems. He raised the questions: "Are we allowing sources of palpable injustice to multiply or become entrenched? Are we reaching out to grasp larger or better grounded concepts of the kind of economic justice that would alleviate tensions or stimulate fuller realization of our productive powers in the future?" Nourse's strong ethical sense went back to his early interest in the subject of ethics while he was a student of sociology at the University of Chicago. To him, justice was a corollary of freedom.

Return to Academic Life—Pennsylvania State University

Nourse never missed an opportunity to work with an academic institution. It will be recalled that he taught a quarter at the University of Minnesota in 1952. From February 1 through May in 1959, he enjoyed a similar spell of teaching at Pennsylvania State University. He gave two courses. One was a class on price-making for advanced undergraduate and graduate students; the other was a seminar on fiscal policy for graduate students. Both were related to his past and current interests. He maintained residence at the university, but every two or three weeks he would return home over weekends. This gave him an opportunity to develop close contacts with the professors in the economics and business departments and those in other fields. He found this sojourn on a college campus very pleasant, and it was here that he composed his triptych "I Must Believe," giving his philosophy of life that he had been mulling over since he first became interested in thinking through his conception of religion while working with the Phi Beta Kappa program at Cornell College. On that occasion, at a seminar devoted to science and religion, he had observed that as the years ahead of him were shortening, he was more concerned to think about the place of religion in the social sciences. As he recalled: "This episode at Cornell College rather stirred up my thinking in this area which was stimulated by chapel services of a purely undenominational character at Penn State, and it moved me to set down my own thoughts in poetical form which spontaneously took the form of this triptych: 'I must believe that God is Life; I must believe that God is Mind; I must believe that God is Love.'" Nourse had his triptych attractively printed on what he called a "king-sized Christmas card" for distribution to his intimate friends, and it gave him lasting satisfaction. It is given as an appendix to this volume.

The Economics of Public Spending

In an article in *Challenge* magazine for March, 1959, Nourse examined what he called "The Dilemma of Government Spending." He was concerned with getting the subject of government spending into constructive perspective. To clear the record, he denied the allegation that he was always opposed to public spending, although he admitted that he had opposed fiscal programs which he interpreted as "*inflationary* public spending." He recognized that there was a "positive case for public spending as one integral phase of the total phenomenon of spending in all departments of the economy," and he maintained that "modern sophistication" had arrived at the point of realizing that the basic rule of economic progress is that "free spending is the life of trade." While admitting that the aphorism "we can't spend ourselves into prosperity" had a germ of truth in it, he thought it would be much more constructive to say "we can't hoard ourselves into prosperity."

He pointed out that business establishments and consumers had learned the desirability of free spending to achieve constructive ends, then said: "To call me an enemy of public spending—even big public spending—is a mistake. I have never been an enemy of public spending to arrest recession before it became depression or prudent spending for the enlargement of productivity. But," he continued, "I have always opposed politically pressured spending during the upper reaches of a boom, implemented by deficit financing, and engendering inflation. National policy is not a matter of categorical good and bad or absolutely black and white. It is a matter rather of expedient choices among alternatives, proportions, and priorities."

Nourse believed that the problem of government spending should be set in the perspective of a total interrelated economy—"not viewed as some new and malignant growth in our business life." He thought it desirable to examine the "fundamentally different attitude toward government spending than toward family spending and business spending." Starting from the oft-repeated proposition, "that government is best that governs least," he said: "It has seemed to many to follow as a corollary that that government is best that spends least." But he observed that "both the proposition and the corollary have been subject to considerable re-examination in recent years." He then observed: "It takes more economic sophistication for the public to see the functional relationship of public spending to national prosperity."

Nourse disagreed with the view that spending by the government represented the amount "the government draws out of the economy," for "obviously, every dollar that the government budget takes out of the company treasury and the family bank-roll is promptly put back into the national income stream in payment for personal services or the procurement of goods." He thought that the informed citizen could "legitimately quarrel" with government spending when it contributed to the process of "monetary inflation, wastes of over-staffing, subsidies to special interests, or encroachment on areas of economic activity which private business organizations could exploit, or when it resulted in poor allocation of the nation's resources."

He did not believe that public spending would necessarily result in inflation getting out of hand, provided that "the people are sufficiently business-like to tax themselves to pay the spending bills." He thought the books should balance over the years "by being overbalanced in boom times and underbalanced in recession years." He affirmed: "It is not an unbalanced budget in a given year that spells danger but *a budget out of control.*"

Admitting that public spending was abnormally high because of conditions "primarily forced upon us by the Kremlin," he said: "We need to be on our guard lest this threat be the excuse of padding the military budget with billions whose real function is to serve the vested interest of military (and ancillary) personnel and suppliers." However, he did not think that government spending would greatly decrease "even if peace broke out," for there were many needs that could be provided for "most economically and most beneficially on a community basis." He made clear that this did not mean that he espoused socialism. Rather, this would be necessary to strengthen our "free enterprise system toward growth and stability."

He ended his article by saying:

> Since a genuinely free enterprise system implies not only freedom of individuals to use the large corporation and the large union as their organizing agency, but also freedom of voters to use the local school district, the municipality, the state, and the Federal government to activate and direct our local and national productive resources, we shall in all probability in future see money flowing even more freely than now through public treasuries on its way back to the open market. Such, in my view, is the logic of a full employment high-productivity economy.

The Law and Economics

In 1959 Nourse wrote a full article review of Eugene V. Rostow's book *Planning for Freedom: The Public Law of American Capitalism* for the *Vanderbilt Law Review*. He admitted that he was prejudiced in favor of the book since Rostow, a legal authority, viewed the Employment Act of 1946 as "one of the most important statutes of this generation." Moreover, as an institutional economist, Nourse was deeply interested in the close relationship of law and economics. He considered the book "a sound and deeply perceptive treatment of issues that are crucial for the future success of our American way of economic life," and he particularly liked Rostow's characterization of the social sciences as "the professions of social action," since this got away from "the mechanistic and natural science" concept of economics which was then prevalent.

Although in general agreement with the author's approach, he thought that too much emphasis was given to the concept of legal control of the economy. Nourse believed that more attention should have been given to the creative, or leadership, role of business. He liked Rostow's general concept of planning as institutional guidance or self-discipline, but he felt that Rostow attributed more importance to law than to economics. It was his own view that the law simply provided a framework for economic institutions. He said: "In my reading of economic history, experiment and test of business practice have generally preceded evaluation and formulation in law." Nourse also thought that Rostow placed too much reliance on the use of fiscal and monetary tools for the control of the economic order, whereas he would have given more stress to the importance of market policy. Altogether, he welcomed the book as "an enlightening volume for professional lawyers, professional politicians, professional business executives or labor leaders, and for professional economists, too."

Keyserling-Nourse Rapprochement

The longstanding controversy between Nourse and Keyserling on how the Council of Economic Advisers should function was aired by the publication of a case study, *The President's Economic Advisers*, by Miss Corinne Silverman in 1959.[26] This study endeavored to present the background situation and the divergent positions held by the first members of the Council of Economic Advisers. Nourse, Keyserling, and Clark gave Miss Silverman their views in taped interviews, and they reviewed her report before publication.

Miss Silverman did not draw conclusions on the merits of the views expressed by the original Council members. She simply focused attention on the principle issue that divided them—whether members of the Council should testify before Congressional committees in support of the president's policies. To round out her study, she examined the way in which Arthur F. Burns dealt with this issue when he became Chairman of the Council in 1953.

The conflicting views of Nourse, Keyserling, and Clark were presented in their own words. Nourse believed that the Council was designed to provide the president with economic advice which he could use as he saw fit. He did not think that the Council members should consider themselves advocates of presidential policies. Keyserling, and to a large extent Clark, held that the Council members were representatives of the president and should support his policies in testimony before Congressional committees. They considered Council members to be trustees of the president.[27]

The disagreement of Nourse with Keyserling and Clark was not resolved when Burns took over as Chairman of the Council in 1953. He inclined toward Nourse's view that the Council was primarily a professional nonpartisan body, but he recognized that the will of Congress could not be ignored. While he did not refuse to testify when called upon by Congress, he endeavored to gain acceptance for the view that his testimony, other than on technical matters, should be given only in executive session. Nourse thought that Burns had wisely handled this difficult problem.

Burns was in sympathy with Nourse's efforts to make the Council purely a professional advisory body. This was expressed in the following statement of Burns, quoted by Miss Silverman:

> If there had only been the type of Council that Keyserling envisaged, I never would have accepted the appointment. I would have taken it for granted that the Council Chairman must, as a practical matter, support the President's views at public hearings, and I would not place myself in that position. But because there had been a Nourse I could conceive of there being a practical alternative and could try to find it. So Nourse did more than make my job easier by taking the position he did; because there was a Nourse my job was possible [p. 17].

Although Miss Silverman's study did not settle the fundamental problem on how the Council of Economic Advisers should function, it did make more clear the issues involved in the dispute between Nourse and Keyserling. It was evident that the two men represented two different philosophies of government, as distinct as had been those of Thomas Jefferson and Alexander Hamilton.

It is of interest that while the Silverman report was in process of preparation, Nourse wrote Keyserling thanking him for information he had supplied to Miss Silverman. This letter gives an insight into the personalities of both men.

September 6, 1958

My dear Keyserling,

. . . .

I find myself in hearty accord with the major proposition stated near the close of your covering letter: "There are usually two sides to most questions. . . . Future historians of this important measure will be benefitted by having [our views] side by side. . . ."

I congratulate you on having at length found the time necessary for completing such a document. Your contact with the development of the Employment Act was more intimate than mine in the year or so before we joined the Council, and it continued for some time after I left. Also, since your approach was different, this complementary interpretation of the issues will enable serious students to see the whole matter "better in the round."

I am in full agreement too that Miss Silverman's preliminary draft needs careful checking for errors of fact and interpretation. . . . I join you in the suggestion that in the process personalities should be reduced to the minimum necessary to elucidation of the substantive issues. Obviously they cannot be entirely eliminated since this is a case study of a personal episode.

While I winced at your repeated use of such expressions as "categorically false", "ex parte", "building up a record . . .", "personal and subjective allegation", "deliberate prevarication", "manifestly incorrect statement", "subjective and self-serving imputation", "personal attack and disparagement", "misstatement of fact", "personalized disparagement . . . based on personal pique", "comments unsupported by record", I shall make no comment on the specific points to which they refer. Even with the best of intentions, no one can do anything more than tell the truth *as he sees it.*

With best wishes,

Sincerely yours,

(E.G.N.)

This letter elicited an equable response from Keyserling and closed the record as far as Nourse was concerned.[28] Both men had had their say. The issue was not resolved, and the views held by Nourse and Keyserling continue to have their adherents. However, it is true that with the passage of time, the Chairman of the Council of Economic Advisers has become more of an advocate of presidential policies in Congressional hearings and in other ways than Nourse thought advisable.[29]

The Rosenberger Medal

Of all the honors that came to Nourse, none touched him more than the award of the Rosenberger Medal by the University of Chicago—his alma mater—on June 12, 1959. He was presented the award as "administrator, author, critic, research worker, scholar, teacher, and molder of private and public institutions." The presentation continued:

> In his long and important career he conscientiously and successfully worked to relate economics and other social sciences to the understanding and solution of many of the important problems of our nation and the world. His pioneering work at the Brookings Institution in developing an empirical and analytical description of the American economy; his roles as a student and critic of governmental farm programs during the 1930's; and his foresight and administrative ability in recasting and molding the Social Science Research Council and the American Economics Association were fittingly recognized when he was appointed the first chairman of the Council of Economic Advisers to the President of the United States, where he established a pattern of objectivity and independence which is now generally accepted as the appropriate role for that post.

"Some Questions Emerging Under the Employment Act"

For some time, Nourse had desired a forum where he could present to economists his explorations on how the Employment Act of 1946 could more effectively meet its responsibilities. Arthur Burns, the incoming President of the American Economic Association—who was in charge of the program for the December, 1959, annual meeting of the association—agreed that this would be a good subject for consideration, and he asked Nourse to lead a panel discussion on the subject, "Some Questions Emerging Under the Employment Act."

Nourse began his paper by saying: "The predominant force leading to the prompt and sweeping passage of the Employment Act was the fear of massive post-war unemployment," but he recognized a "latent apprehension" of "no less harmful inflation." He felt that 13 years of experience had shown that measures taken to get full employment resulted in "dangerous inflation" and that attempts to prevent inflation produced "intolerable unemployment." He said: "The continued rise in industrial price and service rates during the 1957-1958 recession while unemployment persisted or even mounted was highly disillusioning to many who had felt so confident that the use of fiscal and monetary powers by the Federal government could be relied upon to accomplish the national purpose of maximum production and real consumer purchasing power." Nourse attributed the unfavorable situation to "institutional inflation," which he defined as "an inflationary trend built into the market process through the institutions of the large corporation, the big union, and big government sensitive to the political pressures of special interest groups."

In his analysis, Nourse directed his attention primarily to "the price- and wage-making process as the source of cost-push inflation." He thought "both fiscal policy and monetary policy" were to a very important extent "captives of market policy or, stated more precisely, captive to market behavior, with its decisive administrative component." He then said: "To recognize this fact of our economic life today is to realize the sterility of the aggregate demand formula in the unique causative, explanatory, and correctional senses in which it has been so freely used in recent years." He maintained that "the tough questions ultimately raised by the Employment Act" were "not primarily or dominantly those of public action to compensate for failure of the private economy to effect sustained high production." Rather, he held that "they are basically questions of how to forestall such failure by improving the institutions of the market—for goods, for services, and for funds—and how to raise the mores of individual and administrative responsibility to a level compatible with the character of modern industry and trade." He was not opposed to "concentrations of private economic power as are needed for efficiency in . . . our fast advancing technology," but he saw the need for discipline in group behaviors of corporations and labor unions.

He saw the "basic questions emerging under the Employment Act" as being "how competition shall be defined in a day of Big Business and

Big Labor and implemented toward the attainment of national growth and stability." Believing that the "workability of a system of free competitive private enterprise under modern conditions pivots on the institution of collective bargaining," he was concerned that "reliance on collective bargaining between monopoloid equals on the management and the union side" would be "fatuous," since this produced "a price-raising spiral." This line of reasoning led Nourse to observe:

> In terms of purposes of the Employment Act it seems to me that something radical . . . needs to be done to check the erosion of that competitive flexibility that is needed for an enterprise economy to deal with real operative situations. We are inescapably confronted by two broad questions which have been too long evaded: (a) How great a centralization of decision-making as to the administration of capital resources shall we entrust to the corporations of the future and of labor resources to the unions of the future? and (b) What devices of public control or voluntary restraint can we introduce into the arthritic body economic, to restore to it the flexibility of price-income adjustment needed by an economy dynamic enough to measure up to the goals our own traditions set or that the pace of growth being set by communist countries requires of us?

He thought that this general problem called for more searching examination by economists. He rejected "the deceptively simple device of cutting the Gordian knot of our full employment vs. inflation dilemma by the use of direct government price and wage controls," for he did not feel that government could act "as the voice of God." He did, however, believe that the federal government could make a constructive contribution to a positive program through "a vigorous implementation of the policy explicitly stated in the Employment Act, namely 'to foster and promote free competitive enterprise.'" How to do this was to Nourse "the most pressing question that has emerged under the Employment Act," and he listed three ingredients for a solution:

> 1. Integration of our sprawling and confused statutes . . . under a basic policy law that declares a comprehensive principle of free competition.
>
> 2. Pressure for vigorous and consistent enforcement of this declared principle.
>
> 3. Realistic studies by the economic profession of the fundamental theory of large scale competition and the use of this enlarged understanding for the guidance of the courts and administrative agencies; and for systematic campaigns of general education in the operative requirements of a free competitive system.

It is not possible here to set forth fully Nourse's arguments as presented in his paper. He thought it obvious "that the program of systematic overhauling of our market legislation and administration needed to bring about a structure of corporate and labor institutions strongly conducive to the kind of competitive behavior among large operating units that is needed for stabilizing high production is a long range task—in fact, an indefinitely continuing one for a free society in a dynamic world. . . ." He asked this question: "Can we discover any hard core of theory as to the basic nature of our problem which might furnish theoretical keys to its solution?"

He then ventured to suggest two hypotheses "on a brazenly (but empirically) philosophical basis, rather than one respectably econometric or esoterically mathematical."

His first hypothesis was that the power of large corporations and big unions was becoming too centralized and called for a certain degree of decentralization. He was persuaded that a "basic reason why an irresistible force of union cravings meets an immovable body of managerial prerogative was that the scope of decision-making on wages and work rules has become too wide and its situs too far removed from the core issues that need to be resolved." He did not propose "a sweeping proposal for corporation-busting or union-busting" but simply a discriminating realignment of functions.

His second hypothesis was that a serious impediment in the path of fundamentally workable adjustments was the refusal of management to admit that the price of products should be considered as an integral part of the wage problem. "If management were to admit functional inseparability of these issues, it should expect labor similarly to treat wages in their relation to volume of employment, productivity, and actual rather than formulated living costs."

He summed up his views by saying: "In a word, our society is now laboring under a serious cultural lag, and will continue to do so until we can bring ourselves to substitute scientific method for "muscle" in the conduct of big-unit industrialism."

Nourse realized that his views which called for the improvement of marketing institutions (including labor organizations) would be disparaged by many economists as "hortatory." He answered by saying: "Only at our peril do we sneer at 'creeping admonitionism' and declare that 'statesmanship is for the statesmen' and thus that private statesmanship is 'for the birds'—even in the day of multi-billion dollar corporations and multi-million member unions and the still more powerful solidarities of both."

Nourse could not resist pointing out that "admonition" was a well-established fact in our national life. He said: "Business organizations carry on an elaborate campaign of admonition to their workers, their shareholders, and the public against the economic fallacies of labor, or government, and of 'liberals' generally. The unions conduct a parallel crusade to educate the public as to the errors of capitalist practices and theory . . . and of course, the political campaign, the legislative process, and the executive branch of government reek with admonition." Nourse looked upon admonition as "the distinctive economic weapon of a free society in its battle against authoritarian imperialism. If we allow it to rust or use it but feebly, we have not validated the inherent potentialities of a self-disciplined enterprise system and of economics in the public service."

Nourse's paper was a very important enunciation of his thinking on the efficacy of the Employment Act. It made clear his view that the objectives of the act could not be attained by government alone without a change in the character and performance of economic institutions. It emphasized his opinion—that there was need for a wider application of the intellectual process to our national economic affairs.

Chapter XIV

ECONOMICS PRACTITIONER AND PHILOSOPHER
(1960-1972)

In May, 1960, Nourse reached the age of 77. He could look back with satisfaction on his career, but he still had work to do. The 1960s were to be his harvesting years—one of the most productive periods of his life.

With the presentation of his paper on "Some Questions Emerging Under the Employment Act" at the annual meeting of the American Economic Association in December, 1959, Nourse felt that he could now devote more attention to other matters. He had decided not to press forward on the book he had projected as a sequel to *Economics in the Public Interest* until he could explore new developments in the administration of the Employment Act that might come under a new Democratic president.

Of continuing interest to him was his work as Vice-Chairman of the Joint Council on Economic Education, which had prospered in the past decade. It gave him much pleasure to expound on the significance of the Joint Council at a meeting of the Literary Society of Washington in March. He took this occasion to explain how the Joint Council was encouraging and improving economic education in secondary schools by holding three-week summer workshops for teachers. He called this a "first-aid program" and said that about 50 workshops were being held each year throughout the nation. The typical workshop was composed of about 50 teachers recruited through recommendations of high school authorities, and a full staff of 3 in the Council was giving direction to subject matter while a number of "curriculum specialists" were giving attention to practical problems. He was proud that the Joint Council had set up early in its life a "commission on the place of economics in teacher-training courses" and that, as a result, about 40 teacher-training colleges were pooling efforts to shape up a basic course in economics for teachers. He made the point that while standards and qualifications were set up for physicians, lawyers, electricians, plumbers, etc., no specific requirements were stipulated for giving instruction in economics. Nourse believed that there should be at least one comprehensive course in high schools on the "philosophy of our economic system."

At about this time, I was completing a historical case study of a large integrated regional cooperative organization that I had been working on for several years. Knowing of Nourse's considerable interest in what I was attempting, I suggested that he might like to contribute an interpretive foreword. This idea appealed to him, and to prepare himself fully, he read the galley proofs as they became available. The resulting foreword greatly pleased me, for it caught the significance of what I was trying to do and gave the book a fine send-off. In one of his sentences he said: "One point that particularly impressed me as I followed these annals was the value of cooperative organization as a yard-stick on the performance of commercial agencies and as a pace setter in adopting or adapting new technological or business discoveries to local requirements and particular farming situations."[1]

During this year, Nourse was doing whatever interested him. This included pondering on economic, social, and political developments; giving occasional speeches and advice as an economic consultant; and preparing articles and book reviews. As he said: "I am keeping myself delightfully busy but free of formal duties or punishing deadlines." In the summer, he and Mrs. Nourse happily celebrated their golden wedding anniversary. As the political campaign moved toward a climax with the election of John F. Kennedy as president, he began to develop ideas for an article on the economic outlook for the 1960s.

In the fall of 1960, the Brookings Institution moved from Lafayette Square to 1775 Massachusetts Avenue, just east of Dupont Circle. Its new facilities provided adequate space for guest scholars, and Nourse was granted a private office. This greatly facilitated his work, for it gave him ready access to the Brookings library and lunchroom and an opportunity to keep in touch with fellow economists and other social scientists. Moreover, his new office was within walking distance of the Cosmos Club, of which he was then a member of the Board of Management.

Nourse realized that great changes would come with the end of the Eisenhower Presidency, and he had followed closely the contest between Nixon and Kennedy. Living in Washington, D.C., he was denied at that time a presidential vote, but he was impressed by the thrust of Kennedy's promise to get the country moving again. His ponderings on the economic problems confronting the nation were set down in an essay that he completed just after the election. This was published as an article in the Winter (1961) number of the *Virginia Quarterly Review* under the title, "1960: The Hinge Between Two Decades."

"1960: The Hinge Between Two Decades"

In introducing his article, he said that the word "hinge" in the title was intended to suggest that "while the future is always an outgrowth of the past, the new decade will also have its own distinctive character." Furthermore, he said: "It attests my belief that as we move from one Administration—and indeed one Party—to another we have the opportunity for constructive economic maneuver . . ." He saw 1960 as a "momentous year" in our economic history.

In view of the serious problems confronting the economy, he thought that the decade ahead might well be characterized as "the Sobering Sixties." It was his view that "if we are to maintain the desired tempo of national economic life—or achieve 'full employment,' to repeat the rallying cry of 1945-46—we need to do a lot of homework on the basic rationale of a free economy in a day of burgeoning technology, 'exploding' populations, and exigent consumer demands at home and abroad."

Later in the article he said: "We need, in the Sixties, to demonstrate such mastery of the art of prosperity-with-preparedness as will prepare us to capture in some happier future decades the dream of full and enduring peacetime prosperity." He saw major problems arising in four phases of our economic life: "population, welfare, science, and the apparatus of free enterprise." Under the first heading he discussed the changing employment problem and the need for "upgrading our labor force." He thought the welfare issue would grow in importance, and said: "I doubt that the sixties can cope with the blessings of redundant productivity without finding ways of dividing this new abundance liberally with our underprivileged classes." He believed the solution would be "compounded of higher wages, lower prices, and enlarged public services." Science was an unpredictable area, but he thought it probable that the sixties might bring "new and perhaps more astounding break-throughs. We shall need to check and recheck our scientific goals in their social perspective during the Sobering Sixties."

Of particular interest to him was how the goals of a free enterprise economy could be achieved. He saw two questions needing immediate attention: (1) "How shall the boon of free private enterprise be assured both to capitalist management and organized labor?" and (2) "How shall the private market and the policies and programs of government be made complementary and harmonious?" On the first question, he saw the 1960s as a "showdown decade for the system of Big Business and Big Labor," since "the country cannot endure an economic cold war. . . ." With regard to the second question, he thought that an outstanding issue would be: "How shall private enterprise and public enterprise share the burden and opportunity of underwriting sustained national prosperity?"

He finished his article with this pertinent comment: "If the Sobering Sixties are in fact to mark our progress toward a wary partnership of labor and management and a pragmatic complementarity of private enterprise and public enterprise, the hinge period on which we swing toward that better day needs to be well oiled with both economic intelligence and group tolerance." It was clear that he did not see things in a simplistic frame. He saw developments as evolutionary, with one event causing another.

"Mr. Kennedy as Economic Statesman"

Nourse was very favorably impressed with the way President Kennedy took over his economic responsibilities. This was evident in an address entitled "Mr. Kennedy as Economic Statesman" that he presented to the District of Columbia Bankers Association at the Homestead, Virginia, on June 8, 1961. This address was given national circulation in the *Commercial and Financial Chronicle* (August 24, 1961).

He began by saying: "The concept of the President of the United States as an economic statesman—not merely a political and diplomatic statesman—is a creature of the twentieth century. It began with Theodore Roosevelt, gained clarity under Woodrow Wilson, and has become a criterion avowed by or applied to every President from Herbert Hoover forward." After elaborating on this idea, he turned his attention to the way President Kennedy had taken immediate steps to demonstrate his great interest in the economic problems of the nation by submitting a revised economic report and budget upon taking office. It was his view that "on the record so far, President Kennedy's economic statesmanship has appeared knowledgeable, discriminating, vigorous and at the same time, prudent."

With this background, Nourse examined certain questions that might furnish "guidelines for economic statesmanship" in the years ahead. He considered of prime importance this question: "Will Mr. Kennedy be the economic statesman who leads the way to integration of Big Business and Big Labor into a pattern of peaceful co-existence reasonably geared to full use of national resources privately owned and managed?" The president's action in promptly setting up an Advisory Committee on

Labor-Management comprised of top business and labor executives on a continuing basis under the rotating chairmanship of the Secretaries of Commerce and Labor struck him as a most promising step forward. He was hopeful that the president's thinking would not be distorted by the "recent widespread preoccupation with fiscal and monetary policies and programs."

The Federal Milk Order Study Committee Report

In March, 1961, Nourse was brought back into the mainstream of agricultural economics by a request from Secretary of Agriculture Orville L. Freeman that he serve as chairman of a committee of 18 highly qualified marketing economists who were directed to make an evaluation of the federal milk order system administered by the Department of Agriculture and present recommendations pertinent to its future.[2] Work on this project required much of Nourse's attention during the next 12 months before the report could be submitted to the Secretary on March 16, 1962.

At this time there were two opposing schools of thought on how the milk order program should be conducted. One group, in tune with the then current concept of supply management, favored giving the federal government greater control over the milk marketing process. The other group believed that the system should be kept decentralized and free of government direction to the extent possible. The members of the committee represented both philosophies in varying degree.

As chairman, Nourse immediately sought to get agreement on certain broad principles which he submitted in draft form. With slight revision, this draft served as the committee's basic statement of policy and became Part I, or the introductory part, of the report. It traced the development of the milk marketing order system and found that it was performing a constructive and useful role in serving the interests of both producers and consumers. However, in the body of the report, the committee sharply differed on the desirability of giving the Secretary of Agriculture a greater degree of control over the total milk supply.[3]

As a result of the disagreement within the committee, the conclusions of the report largely sidestepped the basic issue which was set forth in an "addendum" signed by Nourse and nine other members of the committee.

> That issue [said the "addendum"] was characterized as a choice between (a) continuing the low-pressure, educational, analytical, and pragmatic policies and practices of the marketing order system as it has been evolving vs. (b) a change of pace and indeed of direction which, its proponents

allege, would cope more decisively and speedily with the persistent problem of large and growing surpluses of milk and its products, i.e. official "supply management" or, ultimately, government control.

The dissenting group frankly expressed its opposition to any approach toward supply management and said in the concluding paragraph of the "addendum":

> We are unable to accept the trend toward extension of government control proposed by the recorded majority in this report. We admit that under the more self-reliant philosophy expressed in the present order system, with its multi-managerial organization, results are slow of realization and beset by ever-recurring new problems, as technology, consumer behavior, and the normal clash of individual or group interests have to be dealt with. The same may be said of the free enterprise system as a whole and of the democratic pattern of government within which the entire economy has its setting. But we believe its results justify its continuance.

In effect, this dissenting "addendum" had more influence than the somewhat ambiguous conclusions of the formal report. According to a statement in the *Washington Post* (May 2, 1962), "There was little in the report to [Secretary] Freeman's liking. Not only did 10 of the 18 committee members turn down his proposals to control milk production; the group also rejected suggestions supported by Freeman that milk move freely throughout the Nation." Following publication of the report, no direct change was made in the federal milk marketing order system.

Serving as chairman of this committee was a taxing experience for Nourse, although he greatly enjoyed the intellectual challenge that was involved. It is probable that without his courage, competence, patience, and conciliatory efforts no report could have been agreed on. George N. Pederson—then General Manager of the Twin City Milk Producers Association—who was a member of the committee, has given us this picture of how Nourse functioned as chairman:

> It was a unique experience, indeed, to be closely associated with a man who had such a broad understanding of the economics of agriculture, and was so keenly alert and interested in others' viewpoints on the subject. The manner in which he chaired this committee's activities was a creditable display of leadership, understanding, and ability. His mind seemed to have the capacity of an electronic brain to store, and then repeat almost word for word, entire discussions carried on by the individuals of this group, some of whom had national and international reputations as agricultural economists. I shall never forget the many occasions when he sat in his usual position at the head of the conference table, perfectly still and quiet. From all appearances, he might very well have been sneaking an afternoon siesta, for he seemed to be dozing. But then, all of a sudden, when discussion seemed to be waning—or on the other hand, it might have become argumentative in nature—he would, without the benefit of a note of any kind, summarize everything that had been said in the most articulate and beautiful language I have ever heard.[4]

"The Degradation of the Agrarian Dogma"

It afforded Nourse "distinct personal pleasure" to give the Benjamin H. Hibbard Memorial Lecture at the University of Wisconsin on March 20, 1962. He chose for his subject "The Degradation of the Agrarian Dogma," a topic suggested by the book of Henry Adams, *The Degradation of the Democratic Dogma.* He was concerned with examining whether there was life in the "agrarian dogma," which had been a pervasive philosophy in American agriculture down to World War I. "All that I shall essay," he said, "is to set forth some retrospective ponderings of an aging scholar who has observed and, in some small way, participated in the economic evolution of the agrarian segment of American life over the past half-century."

He opened his subject with an interpretation of the agrarian dogma. He thought the concept could be identified by four distinguishable but subtly intermeshed elements: "(1) economic individualism, or free enterprise; (2) neighborliness, or community cooperation; (3) respect for learning, or native intellectualism; and (4) social conservatism." He found these elements synthesized in a general social attitude of rural people, reflected by their spokesmen in a "generally quiescent but at times aggressive class consciousness" which had been aptly called "agricultural fundamentalism" by Joseph S. Davis. This agricultural fundamentalism, in Nourse's opinion, had reached its "apogee" in the nonpartisan Farm Bloc in the early 1920s and in subsequent farm relief legislation.

Nourse then examined the great changes in agriculture that had come with government programs and concluded that they did not represent degradation so much as transformation of the agrarian dogma. He did not find that "free enterprise was abandoned" by the acceptance of corporate big business in agriculture. Nor had there been any downgrading of the mutual self-help idea in the large cooperative organizations through which farmers render for themselves marketing, purchasing, and other business services. Moreover, it was apparent that interest in scientific agriculture had expanded rather than decreased and that rural conservatism had become less rigid or doctrinaire than in pre-World War I days. As to the "overriding charge that the farmer had bartered his birthright of independence for government largesse at the price of government control," Nourse considered the broad trend toward more active participation by government in national economic affairs to be "irreversible"—but not necessarily harmful. On balance, Nourse saw arising an economic sophistication and social broadening of the agrarian dogma which could mean "an ennobling" of it.

The Evolution of U.S. Agriculture

In celebrating its 100th birthday on May 15, 1962, the United States Department of Agriculture sponsored a World Food Forum. One of the panels featured an address by Henry A. Wallace on "The Evolution of U.S. Agriculture as Related to Changes in Economic and Institutional Patterns." As moderator of this panel, Nourse provided an introductory statement in which he said:

> Now as I look back over the past century of evolution of American agriculture I am struck by two features. First, what we call agriculture today is not at all the same thing as the farming business of the late 19th century and early 20th. Many erstwhile activities of the family farm have gone to town or been superseded by industrially produced products. At the same time, the source of capital and business leadership for the supply of food and fiber is increasingly to be traced to urban centers, rather than merely rural vision, daring, or opportunism. But a second process of economic transfusion has been no less significant. By building up large cooperative enterprises and developing the overhead service functions of general farm organizations and of government, farmers have, in turn, penetrated into realms of industrial processing, commercial distribution, supply of farm-used materials, and several branches of finance, all formerly pre-empted by urban agencies.

He noted that "since the post–World War I collapse of agriculture, the American farmer has been in violent transition from a past of triumphant individualism into the troubled adolescence of an unfolding life of highly organized groupism." He did not believe that agriculture could remain a "sort of third estate" within the economy. "It must accept and participate actively in the shaping of an integrated national economy in its international setting and responsibilities." He saw the "ineluctable forces of technology and business genius making the farmer—in the best sense of the term—an organization man . . . whose level of economic sophistication, democratic discipline, and referendum power will be the ultimate determinant of the course of our future agricultural evolution. This means that our agricultural group is committed to living dangerously." He spelled this out as follows:

> They need to see that, in seeking to be an active force, not a passive pawn, in the world of general business, the farmer shall not overreach himself and lose either his pocket book or his soul. Similarly, he must guard against seizing short-run profit or security by yielding to advances of non-farm corporate enterprise, only to find himself, in time, short of his own freedom of enterprise. Finally, he must be alert to see that the role of government shall continue to be limited to legislation and administrative service that assures equality of opportunity and flexibility of choice and adaptation, and does not slip into hampering rigidities and government control.

He ended his introductory statement by saying: "The future evolution of American agriculture should be shaped toward optimum use of our national resources, natural and human, not toward the attainment of maximum market or political power. I believe that in the century on which we are now embarked, the public interest will more and more outrank class interest as the touchstone of both private and government policy."

The Future of Milk Marketing Orders

In June, 1962, shortly after the Federal Milk Marketing Order Program Committee submitted its report to Secretary Freeman, the American Dairy Science Association sponsored a symposium of leading marketing economists to appraise the federal milk marketing orders.[5] Dr. Harry C. Trelogan, Administrator of the USDA's Statistical Reporting Service, as moderator made clear that the objective of the symposium was to present "an objective treatment of the subject" in accordance with the principles of social science.

Nourse's job on the symposium was to examine "What Lies Ahead for Federal Milk Marketing Orders: Objectives and Means." He introduced his analysis by saying:

> What lies ahead for us will not develop as a result of unescapable economic determinism. It will be built by our own hands, our own wills, our own value judgements. It will be the product of our traditional system of free but not anarchistic business enterprise, working within a responsive but also at times restrictive democratic system of national government. The future of the fluid milk industry is within our keeping.

After weighing many unsettled issues, Nourse concluded his paper by setting forth two "guidelines" that might help in engineering the road ahead for the marketing order system. He thought of most importance was the guideline provided by the Employment Act of 1946. He pointed out that "this epoch-marking statute declares a 'continuing policy and responsibility of the Federal government' to integrate its 'plans, functions, and resources' in an active role in the economy. Secondly, it provides that these services of a democratic government to its citizens shall be carried out 'in a manner calculated to foster and promote free competitive enterprise and the general welfare.' That," said Nourse, "seems to me both a clear and (if I may use the word) noble guideline for the Order system today and in the future." For a second guideline he accepted the criterion of "the public interest" as repeatedly set forth by President Kennedy.

Nourse saw the milk marketing order system as "a prime opportunity for demonstrating the economic superiority of voluntary group action coordinated through the good offices of a cabinet officer, equipped with a professional staff." He maintained that

> we should recognize and be proud of the fact that the Milk Order System has already pioneered a kind of institutional development in price sophistication which has as yet been barely begun in the industrial and labor areas. I hope we shall continue to perfect what we have so well begun and perhaps contribute some lessons to industrial management and collective bargaining out of past experience—and, still more, for our future program.

He summed up his presentation by saying:

> You may say what I have outlined as my hope, rather than my prophecy, of what may lie ahead for the Milk Marketing Order System is idealistic. I plead guilty, but, in defense, I remind you that idealism is the essence of the scientific way of life, seeking to discover and attain the highest goals by identifying and measuring the forces of nature—and working with these innate forces. Whether you grant that economics is a science or not, whatever lasting achievements it makes will be by the use of scientific methods of identifying and measuring the forces of the market and putting itself in line with those forces.

"The Promise of American Capitalism"

For some time, a pair of questions had been giving Nourse much concern. What is American capitalism? How does it differ significantly from Communism? He took seriously Khrushchev's boast "We will bury you" as meaning "American capitalism." Nourse thought that the meaning of capitalism deserved careful thought and could not be taken for granted. He brought his ideas together in an article for the *Virginia Quarterly Review* (Summer, 1962) under the title "The Promise of American Capitalism."

Nourse held that the word "capitalism" could be looked at from three points of view. In one sense "it signifies property—saved from past labor to make future labor more productive." This conception of capitalism was not distinctive to so-called capitalistic countries, for in this basic sense, Soviet Russia was built on capitalism controlled by the state. In a second sense he found that "capitalism is the price-profit-wage (and dividend) system by which we operate a market economy." It was the use of the term "capitalism" in a third sense that seemed most important to him—the designation of capitalism to express "the mystique through which our physical plan and commercial processes reflect our economic, and hence social philosophy." He said: "It embodies the composite of theories and beliefs of our business, labor, and agricultural community as to how the modern capitalistic system *ought* to be run, or *needs* to be run."

Nourse believed that the meaning of capitalism in this third sense could be better understood by tracing its evolution through four stages. First there was Owner Capitalism, or Proprietary Capitalism, in which the owner-capitalist was "the whole works." Then, with the development of the modern corporation, came the age of Managerial Capitalism, in which management was the controlling factor. Eventually, when labor became well organized, it demanded a voice in the control of Managerial Capitalism—with the result that capitalism became Laboristic. Nourse saw a fourth stage now emerging—"an all-embracing and coordinated structure of modern capitalism" that he thought could well be named People's Capitalism, for it would represent capitalism "*of* the people, *by* the people, *for* the people."

It was his view that People's Capitalism complemented "the traditional and well-proven institutions of the free market with an increased amount of activation and financial implementation of national resources through governmental policy-making, fiscal and monetary administration, and institutional regulation." He held that this maturing public philosophy was well established in our national life, and said: "Its future hopes of still richer fulfillment and its peril of arrest or retrogression now ride with the guidon of John Fitzgerald Kennedy."

Nourse finished his article by saying: "In the words and actions of the President may be seen touches of prophetic insight as to what American capitalism may become." He went on to say:

> But the mind and heart of the people must be lifted up if he is to march at the head of a victorious army of free capitalistic enterprise. The minds of the people must be sharpened to comprehend the novel issues raised by new technology and accompanying concentrations of economic power . . . to preserve the dynamism of the individual and still achieve the full efficiency of large organization. The hearts of the people must be fortified to renounce the ways of economic war among special-interest groups and to seek honestly such rewards as match their several contributions to the joint economic enterprise, these contributions to be evaluated by the tools of scientific method.

This article reflected Nourse's fundamental idealism and his belief in evolutionary progress. He saw capitalism as a concept which could become of greater value as a force in itself if its meaning were more thoroughly explained, understood, and recognized.

"Lessons for Farm Economists from Recent Anti-Trust Decisions"

A subject of much concern to agricultural economists in the early 1960s was the relationship of antitrust laws to cooperative associations.

This general problem was given a thorough airing in a group of papers presented at the annual meeting of the American Farm Economic Association held at the University of Connecticut on August 19, 1962. One of the principal speakers was Nourse, who spoke on the subject, "Lessons for Farm Economists from Recent Anti-Trust Decisions: Desirable Public Policy." This topic gave him an opportunity to relate recent antitrust developments to the needs of agriculture. He dealt with his subject in historical perspective, going back to the legislative and judicial actions of the past 50 years which had invested farming with a high degree of public interest.

After reviewing cooperative experience in the light of developments under the Agricultural Marketing Act and the Agricultural Adjustment Act, Nourse said:

> The cooperative marketing movement has had two basic purposes over the years. One is to secure maximum efficiency in the physical handling of its members' products, educating growers as to market requirements and demand limitations as a guide to their individual farm management, and serving them with expert and aggressive leadership. That this business efficiency phase of farmer cooperation is in the public interest is, I think, not open to question. But the issues as to the second phase of agricultural cooperation—namely, market power—are less clear and controversial.
>
> How far did the Congress intend or will the Supreme Court—in the light of its recent decisions—permit farmer cooperatives to amass market power and use it by what devices toward price enhancement? Here there is a definite conflict of interest between the special group and the general interest of the economy in optimum allocation of national resources.

It was in this setting that he analyzed the significance of three 1960 Supreme Court decisions which definitely made clear that cooperative marketing associations were generally subject to the same basic antitrust laws as other business corporations. Although the Capper-Volstead Act of 1922 had encouraged the development of strong cooperative marketing associations, he did not think it gave them unlimited freedom to engage in non-competitive practices. "Personally," he said, "I do not discern in recent Supreme Court decisions any threat to the future health and vigorous growth of economic organizations among farmers, including such integration, both horizontal and vertical, as is called for by the progress of technology and of business organizations in other segments of the economy."

I attended this meeting and remember vividly the personal conditions under which Nourse gave his talk. Shortly before noon I noticed him standing at the back of the auditorium where the morning session was being held. He was in a startling condition, with a gash over his left eye which he was covering with a handkerchief. He explained that he had slipped on something going downstairs to the men's room in the basement. (Later, a man who had seen him fall headlong down the full flight of stairs told me that he was surprised that the fall had not killed him. Nourse was a big man, and his fall was impressive.) As Nourse had no room on the campus since he had come to the meeting only to give his talk, we went to my room in a nearby dormitory. He laid down on the bunk with compresses over his bruised forehead, while I got him toast and milk for lunch. He would not hear of seeing a doctor, for he was determined to give his talk. By 2 o'clock, when the program started, he was ready and bandaged, but in a weak condition. It was a long session and Nourse's talk came near the end. When he rose to speak, he asked permission to read his paper sitting down and then subsided into a chair. Although he was in fair voice, I was aware that he was under severe strain. He was relieved that his talk went so well, and after the meeting he took the bus back to the airport and was off again for Washington. Two days later he was to present an important statement to the Joint Economic Committee. He was a natural Spartan.

The Limitations of Macroeconomics

In appearing before the Joint Economic Committee on the State of the Economy and Policy for Full Employment on August 21, 1962, Nourse said: "I deplore the exaggerated emphasis that professional economists have in recent years been giving to the 'macroeconomic' part of the total economic progress—important as it undeniably is *per se*." While he concurred that the fiscal and monetary policy area was of great importance, he said:

> But in the last analysis, the problems emerging with reference to both these functions . . . are kept manageable or are rendered insuperable by the way in which the private sector of the economy is functioning. Even fiscal and monetary policy cannot be adequately analyzed and formulated in isolation from the processes of the private business world—collective wage bargaining, administrative price setting, capital formation and investment.

He thought it important that "our basically private enterprise system operates so well . . . that its shortcomings will not have to be 'compensated' by frequent and massive fiscal and monetary manipulation." Nourse saw in evidence

> a cult of economic magicians, who claim that fiscal and monetary action alone can, in any time of business sluggishness, so stimulate the private economy that a desired rate of acceleration will be induced. They regard this response as bankably certain. Tax abatement or enlarged government spending, they argue, can be undertaken in magnitudes great enough to insure effectiveness, with confidence that prompt growth in the volume

of national production, multiplication of jobs, fattening of profits, and easing of credit will preclude a budget deficit and indeed create a Treasury surplus as well as a rise in level of general consumption.

Nourse then said: "This consummation, so devoutly to be wished ... seems to me to rest on over-simplified assumptions about the fundamental nature of free enterprise, business motivation, consumer behavior, and collective wage bargaining."

In his testimony, Nourse applauded President Kennedy for establishing a continuing Advisory Committee on Labor-Management relations by Executive Order on February 16, 1961, "as a sort of summit conference between the Departments of Commerce and of Labor and the prime ministers from organized labor and big business," and for convening in May, 1962, a White House Conference to determine the proper relationship between government and business and labor. He was of the opinion that "a succession of such conferences ... might really help effect a break-through from what threatens to become a stalemate in our economy."

Should the Employment Act be Amended?

At this time, Nourse was greatly interested in the views expressed by Arthur F. Burns in an article entitled "Reflections on the Employment Act." While he had high respect for Burns as an economist, he could not accept his position that the Employment Act should be amended "so as to broaden its explicit objectives." In a three-page letter to Burns (October 20, 1962), he made clear how he differed with him on this general point. His views are quoted in some detail, for they give a good idea of how his mind worked on a problem of this sort.

> You may say that efficiency, price stability, and national economic growth are such basic and enduring principles [that they] should be explicit in the economic constitution. But these are all terms of indeterminate and controversial meaning among economists and others. I am still unconvinced that any brief statement of these goals more explicit than those now in the Act in general terms could be agreed to and effectuated. I would be glad to see the language you would propose to those ends—without jeopardizing the flexibility with which national policy needs to be directed to changing situations. You claim that full employment has ceased to have the primacy it had in 1946 (a debatable proposition), but I believe a case could similarly be made for the proposition that the problem of growth ... may not always have the exigency it now has for our national policy. I suspect we have more to lose than to gain by trying to broaden and sharpen the terms of our economic constitution of 1946 ...

He went on to say:

> It seems to me that your indictment runs not so much to the terms of the

law as to the inadequate performance of the Executive Branch and the Congress during the last fifteen years. . . . You yearn for "speedy if not automatic procedures . . . needed to strengthen our defenses against recession" . . . but your economic theology seems to me one-sided in its reliance on fiscal and monetary measures and its neglect of market processes in a broad sense—primarily the institutions of corporation price making and union wage "bargaining." . . .

He continued by saying:

I need not bore you with even the barest statement of my concern for equal emphasis on the functioning of the private sector. . . . Nor will I lengthen this too long letter with comment on your resurrection of the "supreme court of economics" proposal which, I believe, wisely was rejected in 1946. For the Council of Economic Advisers to be assigned that role or for a still more supreme court of economic omniscience to be set up would fly in the face of all my beliefs about a "free enterprise" (private and public) society.

The Income Tax Cut Question

Nourse and I had a good talk on December 17, 1962, after his return from speaking engagements in California and Utah. He had found bankers and businessmen strongly behind the president's espousal of early and substantial tax reduction. He said that in his western talks he had taken the position unequivocally that this was an instance of pressing the panic button when there wasn't any panic and that a big tax reduction was not the economic prescription that was best for the patient, our economy. He thought that the pressure for a tax cut came more from Walter Heller, the Chairman of the Council of Economic Advisers, than from President Kennedy. In fact, he thought that the president had been a balance to his economic advisers rather than the opposite. He said: "Mr. Heller came in yelling for quick and drastic tax reduction in the first year of the Administration. Mr. Kennedy has moved slowly, and, in fact, the papers report now that the Administration has practically agreed to let the thing go over another year. It seems to me that he has been wiser than his economic tutors."

Later in our talk I asked him whether he felt that Heller was keeping his objectivity and scholarly qualities under the pressures of his post. He replied that this was rather a hard question to answer, in that Heller entertained a considerably different philosophy of what would constitute economic statesmanship. He thought that Heller had "put most of his eggs in the fiscal and monetary basket," while he thought it desirable to give more attention to the different issues involved in the growth and stabilization of the economy—especially questions of industrial management and of labor policy and organization.

Nourse could not accept Heller's interpretation of the role of the Council and, particularly, his role as chairman. He said: "There he is finding quite congenial, a positive, aggressive policy which the president seems to accept and approve and expects from him. That means he has cast himself in more of a role of policy-maker, more of a role as attorney for policies than I think is the soundest interpretation of the Council as an institution in the Executive Office of the President." He went on to say that he and Burns had essentially the same views on the role of the chief adviser, while Heller's interpretation, with the approval of the president —almost at his behest—was a more combative and improper role. "I have sometimes said that my interpretation is that the Council should be coach whereas the president's interpretation, which Heller accepts, is that the Chairman of the Council should be a player on the field, not a coach on the sidelines."

On January 15, 1963, we discussed the president's State of the Union address of the day before, in which he proposed a very substantial reduction of the Federal Income Tax over a period of three years. Nourse gladly gave his comments. "My position has been right along that I did not concur in the widely prevalent idea that taxes at the rate they are being levied are what is holding the economy back. I think the pattern of our economy has changed so that from here on we will be not only a big business, big labor, big government economy but we will be a high tax economy. I have even predicted that probably taxes in the long run —that is in the decades ahead—will tend to be higher, not only absolutely but even relatively to the GNP. Now, that means I am not in sympathy with the president's position." He continued: "On the other hand, I am not sure that the multifarious effects will be serious. It is so much yearned for and so much approved that it will have a psychologically stimulative or nourishing effect at the present time. . . ."

Later in our interview, he said: "I don't give the same importance to the use of fiscal measures to stimulate the economy that many people do. I feel that what is retarding the economy more is the 'obdurate' position of both labor and management leaders which causes them to fail to get together and do those things which will make for peaceful adjustment of the several parts of our economy."

"Government Discipline of Private Economic Power"

Nourse had long held that the efficient functioning of the American private enterprise system was essential to the attainment of sustained business prosperity. Since the 1930s he had been concerned with the problem of administered prices in a competitive economy, and he had taken great interest in the investigation of this subject by Senator Estes Kefauver's subcommittee on Antitrust and Monopoly for the Senate Judiciary Committee. It will be recalled that he was the first witness called by this subcommittee in 1957.

In 1962 the subcommittee had asked Nourse and a number of other economic and legal authorities for their written views on appropriate public policy relating to administered prices. Nourse presented his considered thinking under the title, "Government Discipline of Private Economic Power," which was published in 1963 with the other papers supplied to the subcommittee under the title, *Administered Prices: A Compendium on Public Policy*.[6]

In introducing his subject, Nourse thought it appropriate to clarify the actual meaning of the term "administered prices" as it related to the issues of concentrated economic power and antitrust policy and action. He said: "Administered prices are a natural outgrowth of modern industrial and commercial enterprise. The term is simply descriptive of the way much of our business is (and has to be) done under the complexities of modern technology." He held that it was the "distinctive feature of the administered price phenomenon that the large-unit executive can significantly influence the volume of market supply, and also the character of available product and attendant services. Clad with these powers, he is in position to adopt and implement a price (and congruent production and marketing) policy. He can set up goals and targets of specific price and overall profit and then adjust company operations toward the attainment of those objectives." While he did not hold that the makers of administered prices were emancipated from the basic laws of supply and demand, he thought that "unless checked" they might "acquire an inordinate measure of control over supply factors." He recognized that modern technology engendered big business and big labor, and that "their modus operandi" was through administered prices, including collective bargained wage rates. He believed that if the powers of big business and big labor were not to become absolute and thus "corrupt absolutely," central government would need to impose discipline over their actions.

Nourse felt that the question in need of analysis was: "What could or should the Congress do . . . about this dilemma of private power in a free society?" It seemed to him that six possible approaches might be considered, namely: "trust busting; removal of anti-competitive practices by government itself; price fixing; waiting periods; selective prosecution; and admonition." His views on each of these approaches are briefly presented.

(1) With reference to "trust busting," he held that it was "wholly illusory to suppose that a workable or helpful bill of particulars could be written into our antitrust law." He said: "Administered prices and collectively bargained wages are prime movers in our economic system and must be dealt with as such. Both must be treated in conformity with the same economic principle, i.e. competition as the master organizing force in a free economy, though with appropriately different methods."

(2) He believed that government itself was partly responsible for the building up of concentrations of economic power through subsidies of various kinds, and that it would be necessary "to make a fearless attack on Government favoritism or special economic privilege complementarily to a continuing campaign to vitalize competition in the private market."

(3) He did not think that general price fixing by government agencies could serve as a substitute for privately administered prices. He said: "I, for one, reject the idea of a necessary forward creep of governmental price fixing. . . ."

(4) Neither did he think that any system of requiring industrial concerns to provide advance notices on price changes could be practically employed.

(5) While Nourse did not favor generally restrictive programs as being either "enforceable or desirable," he thought that a more positive selective appoach might be employed that would retain "the élan of big business efficiency while still protecting the public from continuing or mounting abuse of concentrated power." What he had in mind was something quite different from a general program of "trust busting." He thought it would be salutary if antitrust action were directed against certain carefully selected industrial or labor organizations to determine whether they were operating in the public interest. He maintained that "vigorously directed and adequately financed prosecution of antitrust cases . . . must be a mainstay of our program to sustain competition and arrest or reverse monopolistic growths of market power," but he favored restricting such action to cases of major import.

Nourse believed that "antitrust prosecution should be only incidentally punitive in character," and he held that it should be "primarily a means for a civilized business community to explore and rectify the frontier between good and bad business structures and conduct. . . ." He therefore proposed that attention be addressed toward growing problems arising from "conglomeration" or from corporate expansions that acquire a "significant and progressive centripetal pull on the resources of the economy." He explained the problem as follows:

The big name company becomes the Mecca for aspiring executives, technicians, and even scientists. What it can offer in salary, promotion, bonuses, and sheer prestige enables it to skim an inordinate share of the cream of talent from the personnel market. Likewise, its greater accumulation of capital enables it to seize enterprise opportunities whose size and hazard shut out lesser firms and, when it needs to supplement its own capital formation, it is a preferred applicant at the major sources of credit. Recent experience indicates also that it stands at the head of the line when attractive opportunities of profit are presented by fat government contracts for goods and services. [Thus] the super corporation becomes a pool of funds and talent self fed from the springs of its own superior ability to capture profits and elude or absorb losses.

Nourse was aware that it would be difficult, if not impossible, to develop any adequate apparatus of scientific measurement to evaluate the consequences of very large concentrations of economic power, but he thought that recognition of the public interest provided a valid criterion that might well be employed in examining this problem. To him, "the true goal of antitrust as a disciplinary force in the economy was not to assure perpetually correct conduct throughout the business community." Rather, he thought the first duty of the Antitrust Division should be "to detect spots where normal enterprise transcends wholesome growth and becomes a malignant tumor on the body of our economy."

In order to "get down to cases" from the plane of abstract generalization, Nourse nominated General Motors Corporation and the International Teamsters' Union for explorative treatment. He said:

The General Motors Corporation seems to me a clear—in fact, the clearest—example of the centripetal pull of an overblown industrial complex that we have. . . . A no less strong presumptive case is presented by the International Teamsters' Union. . . . Exploration of these two outstanding concentrations of economic power, with the best resources of legal talent and economic analysis, and the Supreme Court's findings as to the public interest in an economy of maximum growth and stability would go far toward defining what the American way of life is to be.

(6) While Nourse believed that discriminating application of antitrust procedures offered the best strategy for dealing with concentrations of economic power, he did not feel that this alone was enough. He thought that such "positive controls" should be "complemented" by peaceful persuasion toward socially beneficial conduct. As a strong believer in the benevolent force of enlightened public opinion, Nourse held it incumbent on wise and responsible members of the community not merely to promote good economic conduct on the part of their "less enlightened or more willful fellow executives and fellow citizens." Nourse viewed admonition as a positive educational force for bringing about constructive developments in a democratic society.

Nourse ended his paper by examining a suggestion that responsibility for maintaining competition might be placed on the Council of Economic Advisers or some other government agency—such as a proposed Consumers Department. He did not believe that this responsibility could be centered in the Council of Economic Advisers, in that the Council was designed to serve in an advisory capacity within the Executive Office of the President rather than as a "national economic policeman" for all agencies of government. However, he thought that the Council in its advisory role could be immensely helpful to the Attorney General and his Antitrust Division in formulating policies, in selecting cases for judicial test, and in formulating issues for trial.

Neither did Nourse look with favor on proposals for placing responsibility for maintaining competition on other specific agencies of government. He thought the heart of the issue was not one "of administrative structure but of intellectual conviction." He believed that only when all of the departments and agencies of government were "imbued with and loyal to" the principles of competition as the basic organizing and adjusting force in a free enterprise economy would the problem of maintaining competition be adequately dealt with.

Public Policy on Administered Prices

Following up on the views expressed in the compendium on administered prices, the subcommittee held hearings to examine these views in greater detail in May, 1963.[7] In the opening session, Senator Kefauver, as chairman, said that the subcommittee's investigations so far completed had found that price competition—the assumed "protector of the public interest"—was "conspicuous by its absence." He called on Nourse first as the "dean of the delegation" to present the essence of his views and congratulated him on arriving at his 80th birthday. In response, Nourse focused attention on three major issues: "(1) the selective and exemplary character of an effective antitrust program, (2) the exploratory and educational possibilities of antitrust prosecution, and (3) the complementary role of admonition." To promptly make his position clear, Nourse said:

> I do not share the view of those who assert that "the antitrust approach has failed and we must now turn to other means of disciplining private power. . . ." I believe that a policy of vigorously followed, wisely directed, and adequately financed prosecution of abuses of concentrated private power must be a mainstay of our effort to "foster and maintain free competitive enterprise" as stipulated in the Employment Act of 1946. . . . As against the shotgun or blunderbuss attacks of wholesale trust busting, I support a carefully aimed rifle attack at strategically or tactically important targets. . . . By defining the line beyond which a private business

collective in a challenged situation is, or would in reasonable prospect be, trenching on the efficiency and equity of the economy, each prosecution— win or lose—would have the maximum educational value for private promoters and managers and make the maximum contribution to an architecture of private business that will achieve for large unit competition under sophisticated direction all that, or more than, atomistic competition was supposed to do through the automaticity of some "invisible hand".

Nourse also emphasized that

vigorous but discriminating application of the antitrust laws needs to be complemented by peaceful persuasion toward conduct beneficial to the economy. This should proceed both through public discussion and group self-discipline and through official admonition. . . . Such admonition has educational value in interpreting economic goals and policies to the business community and in persuading individuals and organizations that their policies and practices should contribute to the achieving of these national purposes or at least not heedlessly frustrate them.

In the discussion which followed Nourse's presentation, one of the recognized experts on price competition present at the hearing—Gardiner C. Means, the man who had coined the term "administered prices"—said: "I want to see vigorous prosecution under the antitrust laws, and I would strongly recommend the kind that Dr. Nourse has suggested."

Although Nourse's proposal for directing antitrust actions toward carefully selected market-dominating firms has received much favorable attention in recent years, it has not been fully tested in a significant way. It is of interest that John M. Blair, a leading authority on economic concentration, said in 1972: "If the competitive approach is to have any degree of success, the FTC and the Antitrust Division *must mobilize their resources to have the greatest strategic effect* on what is happening in the more concentrated industries and on what is being done by the largest corporations with substantial monopoly power." (Emphasis added.)[8]

Cooperative Business Integration

Nourse examined the future of the dairy industry for an Agricultural Industries Forum held at the University of Illinois on January 29, 1963.[9] He concluded that the major factor in the future of the dairy industry and of other areas of agriculture as well would be the industry's business and economic integration. He saw the cooperative movement "fast coming of age as Big Business in a world of big-unit organization; industrial, commercial, and financial," with local assembling and shipping associations being an important wheel in the cooperative machinery. He maintained that "the power line of effective cooperation must run clear through to a central organization of size and character commensurate with the nature of the economic problem to be coped with." It seemed to him that "the rising confidence of self-help dairy organization" gave "a perfect setting for a vigorous integration movement in the dairy industry," vertically and horizontally. He admitted that he was presenting "an idealistic picture" of what dairy cooperatives could accomplish to improve the conditions of their industry, but he stoutly maintained that "idealism is the stuff of progress and economic stability." He pointed out that what put men in orbit and enables Telstar to speak in one flash around the globe is the fruition of the idealistic thinking of scientists. "Are we then to say that scientific methods and scientific devotion to ideals is less needed in or applicable to the field of economic organization and operation? If we are not ready to lead in scientific marketing, we are bound to lag in the economic position of our chosen industry."

The Death of Mrs. Nourse

With the death of his wife in March, 1963, Nourse lost his lifetime partner. She had been ailing for many months from hardening of the arteries, but he had stoically carried on with his work. For the memorial service for Mrs. Nourse—held appropriately at the Young Women's Christain Association building in Washington, D.C., where she had devotedly served the association in many capacities over the years—Nourse prepared a tender and appreciative tribute for impersonal presentation by one of her friends. The following sentence conveys some of the beauty of its prose:

> Lovely outwardly and equally lovely in spirit and graciousness, she moved among us beloved by all.

Harold G. Moulton, who was a close friend of the Nourses during most of their married life, was greatly touched by Nourse's tribute. He remarked to me after the service: "This is the best thing Edwin ever did."

Nourse realized that life must go on, and he continued his activities without interruption. His elder sister, Mary, made her home with him and they understood each other.

Protecting His Records

The illness and death of his wife made Nourse realize that he could not live forever, and he began assembling his papers for the use of scholars who might later have an interest in them. During 1963 and 1964, he gathered his papers and correspondence for the years when he was Chairman of the Council of Economic Advisers, 1946-1949, for the Truman Library at Independence, Missouri. He also prepared two statements to accompany his papers for the use of scholars who might be interested in appraising the initial years of the Council of Economic Advisers: (1) "The Professional Background of the First Chairman of the Council of Economic Advisers," and (2) "Public Utterances of the Chairman of the C.E.A., 1946-1949."[10]

He also assembled his papers and available correspondence for his full professional career for deposit in the historical archives of Cornell University. Knowing of my interest in preparing a biography of him, he furnished me with copies of many of the documents that were deposited in the Truman Library and Cornell University archives. He took a considerable interest in providing me with background information on his life for my biographical needs, and from time to time, from 1962 to 1965, we would have interviews using a voice recorder.

"The Not So Dismal Science of Economics"

Nourse continued his crusade for better economic education in an article published in the March, 1963, *NEA Journal* which he called "The Not So Dismal Science of Economics." He believed that the term "dismal science" was no longer apt as a characterization for economics, in that economic problems were being increasingly examined "in the hopeful context of social and behavioral science."

In view of the stress then being given to fiscal policy, his views on this subject were of particular interest. He defined fiscal policy as "the rationale of government spending and ways of financing it mainly though the tax machinery." He made clear that modern conditions called for increased spending to serve needs that only government could meet. He thought that "the intrinsic problem of fiscal policy is to see that funds are put back into the money stream at a place where they have a more vitalizing or socially meritorious effect than they would have had at the place from which they were diverted."

It was Nourse's contention that economic problems could be looked at basically in only three ways: (1) "on the basis of personal hunch, girded with 'the valor of ignorance'; (2) through the eyes of group or special interest, with a leaning toward power solutions and short-run opportunism; (3) with concern for the public interest and loyalty to the intellectual process of diagnosis by analytical procedures and of willingness to participate in indicated methods of long-range and widespread correction." To Nourse, "each citizen of a democratic economy must make this choice."

The Steel Price Situation

In a conversation on April 12, 1963, Nourse and I discussed whether the president was acting wisely on the steel situation. Nourse said: "I was not one of those who resented the president's intervention last year," although he thought it had been handled clumsily from a business relations point of view. He felt that the steel companies had made a "stupid move" in the first place and that since then Kennedy had followed "a pretty wise course," in that he had not jumped in and thrown his weight around in this situation.

> He has taken the attitude which seems to me impeccable that when, as, and if price increases are really called for and really feasible from the standpoint of market demand, that the government would stand aside and let the business process work itself out. He has, on the positive side, maintained just the amount of sustained pressure that was desirable. In essence, the White House was watching and if the advances made were stupid, or let us say outside of guidelines such as the Economic Report has set up, then the industry should be warned that he wouldn't hesitate to be the defender of the public interest. I think this is a pretty good example of the basically private enterprise market system with watchfulness exerted by government.

On Milk Marketing Policy

On October 2, 1963, Nourse undertook the job of summarizing a Milk Marketing Policy Forum for the Southeastern States, sponsored by the North Carolina Extension Service at Asheville, N.C. He observed: "The word 'policy' indicates an intellectual approach to business and economic problems. This approach aspires to develop both better structures and better practices for the intelligent administration of the affairs of its members as a coordinated group." He pointed out that

> the political system laid down by the Founding Fathers had freedom as its bedrock—freedom of speech, of religion, and of business association. That included, indeed headlined, freedom of economic enterprise. In our pioneer stage this meant individual free enterprise. In the nineteenth century this doctrine gave larger place to freedom of group enterprise—as exemplified by the business corporation and its counterpart, the cooperative association, and by the labor union. The political doctrine of freedom in business spawned Big Business and Big Labor and posed the continuing problem of reconciling the efficiencies of size and the rights of the individual and the claims of both with the claims of that amorphous but ultimate entity, "the public". Thus the traditional political tenet of free private business enterprise came to be increasingly parallelled by assertions of and recognition for public enterprise. In other words, if the free enterprise of individuals or of groups having special interests fails to achieve reasonably full use of our productive resources or reasonably equitable distribution of the fruits thereof, we the people assert our right to exercise our freedom of public enterprise to activate and regulate some part of the economic system.

He went on to say:

> The Milk Marketing Order System is an extremely interesting economic expression of this political democracy. . . . The milk marketing section of the Marketing Agreements Act of 1937 is an idealistic statute. It responds to the consumer's demand or need for an adequate and dependable supply of pure and wholesome milk and to the producer's demand for full and equitable access to all technologically and economically available markets. It is an expression of our belief in competitive free enterprise, our aversion to monopoly, and our respect for government as servant of the whole people.

This interpretation, he said, was supported by the Federal Milk Order Committee in its report to Secretary Freeman, and he thought it was pertinent to the development of milk marketing policy for the Southeastern States.

What Lies Ahead for Cooperative Marketing?

I was privileged to participate with Nourse in a panel discussion on what lies ahead for cooperative marketing at the annual meeting of the Milk Marketing Administrators held in Colorado Springs at the Broadmoor Hotel on September 17, 1963. This program was designed to give the administrators of the milk orders a broad view of developments in the entire field of cooperative marketing.

As first speaker on the panel, Nourse spoke on the "totality" of the cooperative movement and its general line of evolution. He said that the federal milk marketing orders could well claim to be the most sophisticated development of the "orderly marketing concept"—the goal of the Founding Fathers. He thought that the "common denominator" in the "vigorous cooperative movement of today" was "not coercive power but constructive *business* efficiency." He emphasized "business efficiency" rather than "distributive efficiency," because he saw the cooperative movement as something much broader than merely marketing activities. He maintained that "the improved organization of the complete economic process from farmer to consumer which a mature cooperative organization effects does put the farmer in a strong position, income-wise. That is the whole purpose and *end* in view. But the *means* to that end is not muscle, to borrow the labor union phrase, but brains, i.e. the know-how of economic adjustment industry-wide."

Nourse was of the opinion that dairy cooperatives were proceeding along sound and wholesome lines in emphasizing marketing administration and skill rather than seeking "immunity from antitrust as a power device." He believed that the Supreme Court's decision which struck down the claims of the Maryland and Virginia Milk Producers for immunity from the antitrust principle was a healthy development which "undergirded" constructive cooperative thinking. Nourse presented his views in an informal, direct way and was responsive to questions engendered by his talk. There was much interest in his views.

What Would Economic Literacy be Like?

Since 1948, Nourse had been active in the program of the Joint Council on Economic Education, for he believed that economic literacy was a requirement for effective democratic government. His work with the Council had caused him to examine the question of what economic literacy would be like, and in an article for *Challenge* magazine, March, 1964, he set forth his views on this subject.[11]

It was his view that economic literacy demanded a reasonable competence of the largest possible proportion of the population in administering their individual, family, and company business affairs, and similar competence as voters to choose among rival candidates to administer the public business and to vote yes or no on state and local bond issue proposals or other referendum questions.

Nourse held that *certain qualities* identified the economically literate person and safeguarded against gullibility in economic matters. First was "the ability—the habit, if you please—of searching for cause-and-effect relations." Second was "the capacity—again, the habit—of weighing alternatives thoughtfully before making choices in action or belief." Third was "objectivity, or the ability to think scientifically." This was "possibly the quality most difficult to inculcate or acquire because the individual is so personally involved."

His experience had led him to believe that the most promising area of education for economic literacy was in the high schools, since the colleges took little interest in training students in economic citizenship. He held it to be an "educational scandal that a majority of that smug class holding a baccalaureate degree or better does not know anything coherent about the institutions and processes of the economy they live in." He continued: "With shame for my own profession, I have to confess that an important reason is that basic economics has been made a dismal science or an esoteric craft by most college teachers instead of a throbbing reality and a responsible avocation for all good citizens." He was, however, encouraged by the "great awakening" of interest and concern about economic education at the secondary school level and in the programs of adult education.

He concluded his article by saying: "We have economic illiteracy on the run and are pressing the attack. A reasonable objective now is economic sophistication."

Key Witness in Important Cooperative Tax Cases

Nourse's last major contribution to cooperative theory and development came in the spring of 1964, when he served as an expert witness on two important income tax cases of plywood workers' cooperatives in Oregon and Washington. The question before the courts in both instances was whether a workers' cooperative was eligible for income tax exemption on amounts distributed as patronage dividends to worker-members as owners and participants in the enterprise.

To understand these cases, it is necessary to know how these plywood workers' cooperatives were organized and how they carried on their operations.[12] Each of these associations consisted of a few hundred plywood workers who held prescribed amounts of capital stock to qualify for membership. The members subscribed to other requirements of membership and elected the directors, who provided management. The associations purchased the raw materials required for manufacturing operations, and the worker-members prepared the finished plywood products for sale. All labor, except for some specialist labor, was performed by the members, and all of the proceeds from sales after deductions of business costs were returned to members in the form of patronage dividends calculated upon the hours of labor performed by each member. Interim payments of the patronage dividends were paid in the form of nominal wages, and at the end of the operating year the balances belonging to the members were paid or credited to them.

In 1964 there were some two dozen plywood-worker cooperatives functioning in Oregon, Washington, and California, which together manufactured about 15 percent of the plywood produced in the United States. These associations were treated as other business corporations by the Internal Revenue Service and were compelled to pay federal income taxes on margins after deduction of business costs.[13]

In 1962 the Linnton Plywood Association of Portland, Oregon, and Puget Sound Plywood, Inc., of Tacoma, Washington, decided to take legal action to establish their rights to tax treatment as true cooperative associations. Their decision to challenge the status quo followed a ruling of the Internal Revenue Service in 1961 that the net proceeds of the plywood worker companies were not excludable from gross income for tax purposes. Both of these associations were organized under the cooperative laws of their respective states. The Linnton case was tried before the Oregon District Court in Portland, while the Puget Sound case was tried before the Tax Court of the United States in Seattle. Although both cases were decided favorably for the associations, the Puget Sound decision, which followed that on the Linnton case, was more comprehensive and was of controlling importance.

To bulwark their legal positions, the attorneys of both associations sought the assistance of Nourse as expert witness in view of his recognized standing as an authority on the cooperative form of business enterprise. He was intrigued by the problems involved and gladly agreed to serve both associations.

The primary issue in the two cases was whether the plywood workers associations were organized and operated as true cooperatives. It was the contention of the Internal Revenue Service that these organizations were little different from other business corporations and should not be accorded special tax treatment as cooperative associations. Of vital significance was the question of whether margins after payment of operating costs belonged to the worker members in proportion to their labor contributions.

In his testimony on both cases, Nourse traced the history of worker cooperatives in the United States and displayed a comprehensive knowledge of the theory and practice of cooperative business organization and operation. He centered attention on the fact that the worker cooperative members were the participants as well as the owners of the enterprise and maintained that all the proprietary benefits should ultimately accrue to them. He clarified the meaning of the term "patronage dividend" as used by the plywood workers associations in the following way:

> The culminating feature of cooperative practice is its vesting of all rights to pecuniary benefits of the joint undertaking in the members who are active participants in the joint enterprise. This "equitable sharing" in the benefits is widely referred to as a "patronage dividend"; but the phrase is inept and likely to lead to misunderstanding of the distinctive character of the cooperative association. The word "patronage" came into general usage naturally because of the fact that the Rochdale Pioneers operated a store, but "participation" is a much more accurate term to describe the basis of "equitable sharing" in an operation of producing and marketing associates. ... Cooperation is a distinctly first-person arrangement of business affairs. "Participation distribution" would be a much more accurate designation. Cooperative distributions are not dividends on capital but terminal settlements of the individual member's participation in a mutual enterpise or pooled operation.

In view of the importance of the issue, the attorneys for the Internal Revenue Service repeatedly tried to get Nourse to admit that the cooperative overages or margins of the plywood workers associations were no different in an economic sense from profits in a non-cooperative enterprise. According to Kelsey B. Gardner, a retired and highly respected United States Department of Agriculture cooperative expert, who was present at the hearings: "Dr. Nourse came out the victor in this interchange which was vitally essential to the position of the plywood workers. ... His self-possessed, masterful way of taking care of this important point undoubtedly contributed to the Tax Court's unanimous approval of the cooperative side of the case."[14]

In the Puget Sound Case (Puget Sound Plywood, Inc., v. Commissioner of Internal Revenue), Nourse presented his testimony before Judge Allin H. Pierce of the United States Tax Court in Washington, D.C., on March 15, 1964. The case had been opened in Seattle, but Judge Pierce adjourned it to Washington, D.C., so that he could personally hear Nourse's testimony. The transcript of the hearing, which ran to 77 pages, makes clear that Judge Pierce found Nourse's views of great importance, and in his opinion on the case, rendered on June 5, 1965, he fully approved of Nourse's general argument. This is evident from a footnote reference in his opinion in which he said: "In the instant case, the history and characteristics of cooperative associations were developed extensively in the testimony of Dr. Edwin G. Nourse. ... He is one of the outstanding authorities on the subject of cooperative associations in the United States and foreign countries." In the text of his opinion he also referred favorably to Nourse's view that "the more accurate designation of amounts allocated by cooperative associations would be 'participating distributions' rather than 'patronage refunds.'"

Judge Pierce's opinion concluded with the following statement:

> We have herein before found as an ultimate fact, and we here hold, that the right to the fruits and increases of the cooperative efforts of petitioner's worker members (i.e. margins) was vested in and retained by such workers, and *not* in and by the cooperative association as a separate entity. And we further hold that the amounts of such margins, which for the taxable years here involved were equitably allocated to the worker members as patronage dividends pursuant to a pre-existing legal obligation, are excludable from the petitioner-association's gross income for Federal income tax purposes.

The Puget Sound Plywood decision was immediately hailed as "a landmark case for cooperatives" by the National Council of Farmer Cooperatives in a legal Tax Memorandum issued on June 23, 1965. The memorandum stated that "the language of the opinion and the Court's thorough and detailed analysis is important to anyone with an interest in cooperative tax matters." It attributed much significance to Nourse's testimony in achieving this favorable outcome.[15]

Nourse's testimony in both the Linnton and the Puget Sound plywood cases displayed his broad knowledge of cooperative theory and practice and his ability to cogently present and defend his views, and the decisions in both cases reflected the impact of his thinking. His work and the outcome of these tax cases gave him much satisfaction, for he considered the cooperative form of business enterprise an essential part of the American free enterprise system. He thought that cooperative enterprise could be employed effectively in many ways in the economy, and he was appreciative of the opportunity to help expand its use in the field of production.

"Witch's Brood"

On May 23, 1964, Nourse presented an autobiographical essay to the Literary Society of Washington. He called his paper "Witch's Brood," for he was interested in showing how he and his sisters, Mary and Alice, reflected in their lives some of the qualities of their ancestors. He opened his paper by saying:

> I am a son of a witch. I submit this not as a character reading but as a documented fact of history. To be specific, I am the son, eight generations removed, of Rebecca Towne, born in Yarmouth, England, in February 1621, married to Francis Nurse in August 1644 and hanged on July 19, 1692, by the God-fearing people of Salem, Massachusetts, for the sin and crime of witchcraft.

It was his conviction that his devotion to principle was a heritage from Rebecca Nurse, who had refused to belie herself in the face of death. He was delighted with the response of many friends to whom he sent copies of his essay. He enjoyed particularly a letter from a Presbyterian minister who saluted him as "Dear Son of a Witch."

"Life and Taxes"

Nourse watched the growing acceptance of the "new economics" philosophy, as ably expounded by Walter Heller, Chairman of the Council of Economic Advisers, with a considerable amount of skepticism.[16] He voiced his apprehension in a reflective essay for the *Virginia Quarterly Review* (Autumn, 1964) under the title, "Life and Taxes." In using this title he dissociated himself from the "macabre cliché 'death and taxes,'" which he transmuted to "Life and Taxes," to give recognition to the fact that fiscal policy was "one of the great life forces in our economic world."[17]

This article provides an excellent expression of Nourse's economic thinking in contrast to that of Heller and the dominant school of economists who were then following his lead. He voiced his views in a tolerant good-humored way, for he was not so much opposed to the economic reasoning implied in the tax cut emphasis of the "new economics" as in determining whether the projected program would work in the long-run interests of the nation.

He introduced his analysis by examining the evolution of modern economic thinking in the United States with its increasing emphasis on fiscal policy and public spending. He thought that the present Administration was making for itself "a rigorous theology" with "tax manipulation as the chosen instrument." He considered the tax program adopted in February, 1964, "as good a clinical case . . . in full employment theory and fiscal science as could be devised." He then explained: "We are challenged to analyze tax processes as an integrated part of an evolving high-production economics, not an esoteric specialty of a splinter group." Later in the article he pointed out: ". . . the tax issue has been chosen by the Administration as its major theater of operations in the economic struggle." He asked this question: "Has the Administration, with its $11-billion-plus tax reduction, fashioned a sound plank well fitted into a platform of economic statesmanship for the New Frontier?" His answer was a "regretful 'No.'" He then said: "The present program does not seem to be consistent with the basic propositions of the 'compensatory' economic model of the New Economics. Nor is it faithful to the socio-economic standards programmed at the inauguration of the Kennedy regime in 1961."

The rationale of compensatory fiscal policy, according to Nourse, called for fiscal balance over the full period of the business cycle. There would be

> treasury surplus in boom years, and deficits in unprosperous years. The boom-time surpluses would act as a safeguard against inflation and would build up reserves . . . to finance protective and stimulative programs when recession appears or depression threatens. But now we have adopted a program to lower taxes substantially, go on enlarging government spending, and add a quite sizable new deficit to the national debt—all at a time when government statistics and business reports have been recording new highs in GNP, in profits, in employment, and in private spending.

Nourse went on to say: "These economic indicators were, seemingly, regarded as irrelevant or at least far subordinate to two more recently emphasized criteria of fiscal policy, namely *growth rates,* and the *gap* between two statistical artifacts—aggregate performance of the economy and a theoretical but categorical overall potential. . . . Thus, we were confronted with a crisis by definition and a crash program to meet it."

According to its advocates, said Nourse, "massive tax reduction" would provide "continuing stimulus to consumption spending by families and investment spending by business firms." This would bring increased employment and "produce revenues so ample that deficits would 'melt away' permitting further tax reductions." Nourse did not think it was as simple as that. He believed that it would be difficult to reverse direction and raise taxes or cut public spending should this be needed. "In short," he said, "I am not sanguine as to the ability of a fiscal 'shot in the arm' to bring robust health and continuing growth . . . to the economy while . . . other causes of economic sickness or low vitality persist and are not given searching diagnosis and vigorous treatment." He had in mind such factors as the growing "rigidities in the private economy, because of great self-serving concentrations of private economic power" and the challenge of "conglomerate mergers of multi-billion dollar corporations which exert a centripetal pull on the nation's resources of capital and talent."

He feared that too much emphasis was being given to a "speculative" solution of our economic problems, and that if it were not successful, there was no alternative that could "snatch victory from defeat." He continued:

> They could not repeat the dose with another like tax cut or a comparable slug of public spending without such massive deficits as would undermine confidence at home and abroad and thus be self-defeating. Even more glaringly, they could not reverse their move and raise taxes or cut public spending. They would have squandered a major resource which the government should have in reserve against the day of real emergency. It is a serious shortcoming of the macro-economic approach to tax policy that . . . it cannot be redirected flexibly if at all to new "intelligence" or changed circumstances.

Nourse could not help but be cautious. His reading of economic history and his long experience in economic analysis made him suspicious of easy answers, even if they had strong professional support from a major part of the economics profession and met with widespread popular appeal.

The White House Conference with Past CEA Chairmen

The presidential election campaign of Senator Barry M. Goldwater soon made it clear that his economic views—which called for the dismantling of government economic machinery upon the advice of Milton Friedman—were not generally attractive to economists (*New York Times*, July 31, 1964). President Lyndon B. Johnson took advantage of this situation by convening a meeting in the White House with the four past chairmen of the Council of Economic Advisers along with Walter Heller, the present Council Chairman. His object, he said, was "to get advice from all sources."

According to the report on this meeting (*New York Times*, August 20, 1964), a wide measure of agreement was registered on the good state of the economy. Heller summarized the meeting by saying that its dominant note was one of broad consensus. However, Arthur Burns denied that the meeting was "a lovefest" with an "embracive consensus of thinking."

The separate views of those who participated in the conference were made clear in an article in the *U.S. News & World Report* on September 14, 1964. Nourse thought it a good time "to stop, look, and listen." He was not worried about inflation, but he thought that "modest credit tightening" by the Federal Reserve might be in order. In response to the question: "Will the economy grow enough to yield annual tax cuts?" he said: "I am somewhat skeptical of being able to do all things at once—bring the good society, an end to poverty, and give everybody a tax cut for Christmas." Arthur Burns held that the economy might be on the threshold of an inflationary rise in prices and thought that the tax cut might overstimulate the economy. Raymond Saulnier likewise saw the danger of inflation and the possible need of tighter credit. On the other hand, Leon Keyserling was not concerned about possible inflation. In fact, he favored monetary expansion and lower interest rates. While Walter Heller did not anticipate any immediate danger from inflation, he believed that the government had various tools that could be used if needed to head off trouble. In reply to the question: "Are annual tax cuts something Americans can expect?" he said: "Our Federal tax system is so powerful that each year it generates about 6 billion dollars more revenue on the average than it did the year before. The 6 billion is the Federal Government's share of the 'normal' growth of more than 30 billion dollars a year in gross national product. That money could be used either to retire debt, cut taxes, increase federal spending, or broaden the flow of federal funds to states."

On Fiscal Policy

An editorial in the *Washington Post*, October 15, 1964, stated that Arthur F. Burns had joined the growing group of economists who were convinced that annual tax reductions were required to maintain a high rate of economic growth. It quoted a recent statement by Burns in which he recommended that the federal government "embark prudently on a systematic program of annual tax reductions" and proposed that Congress plan for five annual tax cuts of 4 percent beginning in 1966. The editorial said that there was "a growing bipartisan consensus in favor of regular tax reduction" and closed with this sentence: "The maintenance of a high rate of economic growth may well hinge on the willingness of the next Congress to place . . . annual tax cuts high on its agenda."

Nourse could not let this proposal go without comment. In a letter to the editor published in the *Post* on October 24 under the heading "Off with Fiscal Fetters," he said: "What a wonderful message of hope you bring. . . . Your citation of Professor Arthur Burns limits the rainbow to 4 per cent for five years . . . but at 4 per cent a year, it would be only 25 years before we would be entirely free of our fiscal fetters." This hypothetical prospect led Nourse to say: "There was a Midwestern farmer, so the story goes, who so begrudged the cost of the grain his cows consumed that he began a program of mixing 4 per cent of sawdust in their ration each month. This made his cost sheets look better and better, but the supply of milk dwindled and the farmer's herd began dying off. The fool cows just didn't understand modern fiscal policy."

"Untaxing as a Way of Economic Life"

In the April, 1965, issue of *Challenge,* Nourse carried further his analysis of the tax reduction program of the New Economics then being vigorously pushed by the Johnson Administration. He gave the article the challenging title, "Untaxing as a Way of Economic Life." In his opening statement he set the stage for his presentation.

> The theory and practice of political economy in the United States are in the midst of a veritable revolution. Federal Government spending and taxing have arisen from a mere routine of public housekeeping to a major role as determinants of national prosperity and individual well-being, co-ordinate with the process of the private market or, as some of the *avant-garde* would say, superior to it.

In his analysis, Nourse pointed out that the Employment Act of 1946 made fiscal policy a "preoccupation of the Executive and the Congress, with intellectual commerce travelling a two-way street between the government and the business public and the electorate." He noted also that since 1918, direct taxation of incomes, individual and corporate, had become "the dominant means of financing an expanding program of Federal spending." He believed that future historians would "rate 1964 as a pivotal year in the evolution of our American way of economic and political life," for in February of that year, "the people's representatives . . . launched a daring fiscal experiment in massive tax cutting as a means to perpetuate a long-running business boom," which was in effect ratified by the presidential election in November.

It seemed to Nourse that the theoreticians of the Johnson Administration had "carried to the extreme the New Economics which had been developing over the past two or three decades" and had abandoned such "old-fashioned rules of fiscal responsibility" as a budget balanced over the span of a business cycle in favor of what might be called "an open-end formula of public enterprise and risk-taking." He described how the theory was supposed to work as follows:

> According to the untaxing theory of maximum employment and accelerated growth of the economy, larger "disposable" income left in the hands of consumers will so stimulate the market for both goods and services that merchants will enlarge orders and manufacturers so expand orders that jobs multiply. Similarly, larger retained profits in the treasuries of business concerns will enable them to expand and improve plant, embark on new ventures and create additional jobs. As the national product mounts, the lowered taxes on a larger income base soon wipe out the initial increase in the deficit. After a few years of this growth, the economy would be spinning off an annual surplus of some 5 to 7 billion dollars—a year-to-year dividend whose wise disposition would be the continuing problem of national fiscal policy and over-all economic statesmanship. . . .

Nourse believed that the tax-reduction program "presented an unprecedented opportunity and serious responsibility . . . to see whether we can learn something definitive from this daring experiment in actual use of a thus far untested economic statecraft." He was not content to accept without qualification the view of Arthur F. Burns that with a "normal rate of economic growth" declining rates of taxation would provide "sufficient revenues to meet any modest increase in Federal spending that may be needed." For himself, he had "considerable misgivings" about the possibility that a "normal rate of growth . . . could be maintained" with only "moderate increases in the Federal spending program." He saw many national problems emerging that could only be met by national leadership and federal financing—"air and water pollution, slum degradation, 'crime on the streets,' psychotic breakdown, educational lag, and transportation muddle." He thought that science-technology would need to be nourished with central government support, and he did not believe that businessmen, the professions, and citizens would "be content to have this source of our progress subsist on what is left after a continuous process of year-by-year tax reductions."

He foresaw that there would need to be a great expansion in government expenditures to meet the growing demand for services that could only be provided by government, and he was apprehensive that such needed expenditures could be adequately provided through the mechanism of a tax-reduction program. It was his general conclusion that

> there is a strong popular appeal in the current emphasis on continuing tax

reductions. The appeal is all the stronger for right-thinking citizens when such a program is linked with assurances that the very act of untaxing will generate revenues that remove the need for vacated taxes in the future. But lightening the fiscal responsibility on those relatively most able to meet it rather than providently lightening the burden of poverty and frustration of the twenty percent of our people who are ill-housed or fed, ill-educated, or ill-trained or placed, seems to me not the most promising way to realize our national potentialities for becoming a truly great society. Holding out to the public an expectation of continuing tax reductions—while yet a solvent base for such cuts is only a dream in a theorist's eye—is not responsible economic statesmanship.

It should be realized that the throttle had not yet been opened on the Vietnam war when this article was written.[18]

How Independent Should the Federal Reserve System Be?

In a talk on June 19, 1965, Nourse discussed with me the controversial address given by William McChesny Martin, Jr., Chairman of the Federal Reserve Board, on the subject: "Does Monetary History Repeat Itself?" His address, given at Columbia University, had attracted much attention and it had disturbed the economists in the Johnson Administration.[19]

Martin found "disquieting similarities between our present prosperity and the fabulous 20's," and he warned against a disaster such as that which occurred in the years from 1929 to 1933. His views brought forth a bitter response from Congressman Wright Patman, who almost accused Martin of being un-American because he did not go all out for economic growth. Nourse thought that Martin was right in urging caution, and on June 5, when the subject was hot, he had written him as follows:

> Dear Mr. Martin: I hope you are not too busy to let me hand you an orchid. Noting your remarks to the Society of American Business Writers—only the latest of many wise utterances of yours—I say: Thank God that the Fed is still an independent agency. And double thanks that it has a chairman so uniquely sophisticated, so articulate, and so tempered withal. Mr. Patman asserts that the system's "unbridled freedom just isn't compatible with representative, democratic government". On the contrary, I see it as exemplifying and defending our traditional two-party philosophy against financial autocracy.

After showing me a copy of the letter, Nourse said: "Now that paragraph expresses my position with precision. What Patman is talking about is financial autocracy. He would have the politically-oriented Congress of the United States dominate our credit system. On the other hand, we have set up an independent agency as a uniquely comprehensive and adequate facility for diagnostic study of how the private economy is functioning and for prescribing the monetary policies which are intelligently geared to the stabilization of the viable apparatus of commercial credit."

Nourse believed that "the Council of Economic Advisers was oversold on the activist doctrine that the government through fiscal and monetary policy can keep the economy running at full employment and maximum sustained growth of the gross national product." He said: "They don't want to have anyone else have his hand on the driving wheel. They are so confident in their ability to fabricate policies that will accomplish these results that they don't want to have the issues debated."

Nourse maintained that "the Federal Reserve people have not pursued, or felt that they had a right to pursue, policies that were dictated only by the desires or needs of the business community. They have had to defer to the needs of the federal government in its financing and debt management. To be specific, it might be their judgment that for the good of the economy a restrictive policy of interest rates should be followed but realize that if that were done it would tighten up the money market in such a way that refinancing of certain issues of the public debt would be difficult if not impossible. In conference with the Treasury, they have followed the middle-of-the-road course which seems to reconcile private interest with the public interest. I think that is as it should be."

Nourse saw a relationship between the Martin controversy and the tax-cutting issue. He said:

> In a different way Martin is doing just what I was doing in my recent article, "Untaxing as a Way of Economic Life." He is questioning the confidence of those who go ahead with stimulative measures regardless. . . . Martin is doing what I advocated should be done on fiscal policy. With his board and staff he is studying the results of monetary actions as they go ahead. The import of my article was not to say that tax cutting is wrong philosophy but to say that it is a philosophy which can be, and in my judgment is, in danger of being carried to excess. A blind reliance on the stimulative effect of tax reduction is sure to result in such an inflation as would make the yield of taxes at the lower rate inadequate for the carrying on of the full program. While I accepted the activist philosophy, I was simply expressing some caveats as to whether the tax cuts could be carried out indefinitely.

The Death of Harold Moulton

In December, 1965, Nourse lost his former chief, Dr. Harold Glen Moulton. They had been close friends for more than 50 years, and Moulton's death deeply affected him. More than any other he had lived Moulton's life and career with him and helped him establish the Brookings Institution as a going concern.

At the memorial service held at the Brookings Institution on December 18, Nourse was naturally the principal speaker. In beautiful prose he sketched the high points of Moulton's life and endeavored to preserve the memory of his unique personality and permanent significance. He termed the Brookings Institution "a lasting memorial to Harold Moulton" and said: "It was he who brought the inchoate dream of an enlightened businessman, Robert Brookings, down from cloud nine and objectified it practically in the busy workshop that was then 26 Jackson Place." In his word portrait he stressed the humanness and greatness of the man and spoke of the "warm glow of friendliness and the keen sparkle of intellectual power that we, his co-workers, loved and admired." It was a tribute that would have given Moulton great satisfaction.

With Moulton's passing, Nourse became the grand old man of the Brookings Institution, for he had been Moulton's partner in the formative years of its development. He was now the bridge between its pioneer days and its fruition as a great modern institution for economic and social research. It was appropriate that the office assigned to Moulton adjoining the library was now turned over to him, and he was to enjoy its use during the remaining years of his life.

The Twentieth Anniversary of the Employment Act

Nourse took great interest in the symposium to commemorate the twentieth anniversary of the signing of the Employment Act of 1946 held on February 23, 1966, in the Washington Hilton Hotel by the Joint Economic Committee. He was not included among the speakers, but after the presentations were made he was asked to open the discussion from the audience. I was present at the meeting and recall how he stepped to the podium with a mischievous air and said: "I feel like the little boy who thought he was creeping under a circus tent and found himself at a revival meeting." He had a paper in his hand but he only used it for the last sentence which he wished to state precisely.

In his comments he observed that the program "spread a rich intellectual feast but hardly a balanced diet" in that most of the speakers were former members of the Council of Economic Advisers. In view of the fact that the Congress had stipulated in the Employment Act that the government, in pursuing the goals of national growth and stability, "should rely on the assistance and cooperation of industry, agriculture, and labor," he was surprised to find no witness present from "these sectors of the private economy." This situation caused him to raise this question: "Did the passage of the Employment Act mark a subconscious or intentional departure from or revision of the traditional principle of 'checks and balances' and toward monolithic central government?" His point was well received, and several later speakers supported it. Among them was Leon Keyserling, who recalled how the first Council under Nourse had endeavored to enlist the active cooperation of all segments of the economy.

As a follow up to the one-day symposium, interested persons were invited to express their views for publication in an addendum to the hearings.[20] This enabled Nourse to explain more fully what he had in mind in the question he had asked. "This invocation of the principles of checks and balances was not intended to be applied to the familiar political doctrine of 'separation of powers'—legislative, executive, and judicial." Rather, he said that his intent was "to expand or transpose this well-proven theorem to the economic realm. There we find a comparable differentiation, organizational and operational, between three major economic functions: fiscal, monetary, and market, which make up the total economic process."

Nourse's main concern was that the fiscal function might be given dominating attention while inadequate consideration was given to the role that private institutions could play in effectuating the purposes of the Employment Act. He set forth his thinking as follows:

> The fiscal function is *sui generis* an exclusive prerogative and responsibility of government. During the last 20 years, national policy-making for growth and stability has been preoccupied with a newly propounded theory of fiscal activism and the problems of its applications to political practice. This intensive attention was, at the time, natural and even desirable in terms both of operational experimentation and of popular education. The next 20 years should see further refinements in the technology of fiscal stimulation and stabilization. But these years should also see improved voluntary coordination of the philosophy and the administration of the monetary function and the market function along with our now accepted fiscal activism, not an attempt to dominate them. *We need unity of purpose rather than unitary control.* [Emphasis added.]

As for "monetary management," Nourse thought that it would require perhaps more "searching and imaginative experimentation" than "fiscal technology." He believed that the Federal Reserve System "turned away from the European tradition of a central bank, tied servilely to the national exchequer and established a voluntary federation of thousands of locally autonomous member banks, organized into a national credit pool —a system that honors the principle of private enterprise in the banking business but raises it to the high level of national efficiency and safety compatible with modern industrial capitalism." He maintained that the Fed was "by no means a law unto itself. It is a responsible partner of fiscal administration and market administration in the effectuation of the purposes of the Employment Act. While it acts as a check on both these other members of our economic troika . . . it is itself checked by the impact of fiscal operations on the one hand and the impact of administered prices and of collectively bargained wages on the other."

Nourse believed that the action of the Fed in applying the monetary brakes in December, 1965, had been "salutary" and might soon be needed again "since fiscal devices [are] patently defective in their reverse gear." Later in this article he said: "Success in the grand purpose of the Employment Act . . . will not be advanced by rigid welding of the monetary function to the fiscal function but through flexible articulation between fiscal and monetary. . . ."

Turning to a consideration of the market function, he repeated his original question as follows: "Did the passage of the Employment Act express an intention to curtail the independence of private business and bring it in some significant new way within the ambit of national economic management? Or has the experience and experimentation of these 20 years indicated that such change is necessary for accomplishment of the purposes of the Act?"

Nourse could not agree with those who favored increasing central governmental control over the economic process. He concluded his article with these words:

> I venture to predict that history will adjudge the years 1946-66 a period in which complementary governmental action, fiscal and monetary, was broadly accepted—even measurably understood—as an indispensable and permanent part of the structure of our technologically ordained capitalism. But, to consolidate this gain, the next 20 years must produce a no less revolutionary development of private business structures of equal economic sophistication and a new sense of national solidarity superior to class interests. . . . We need to move forward to a uniquely productive and progressive system of collective bargaining between private and public free enterprise.

Updating Our Persistent Economic Problems

Nourse brought up-to-date his 1953 views on the "Persistent Problems of the American Economy" in an article for *Social Education* (April, 1966) under the title, "Current Aspects of our Persistent Economic Problems." He found three fundamental economic problems challenging scholars and all thoughtful citizens: (1) the population dilemma, (2) the challenge of "Laboristic Capitalism," and (3) the changing relationships between government and business.

Of particular interest was his discussion of the third problem under the heading, "The People's Business and the People's Government." He held that the Employment Act of 1946 had greatly expanded the role of the federal government in our economic life and that this had brought

Edwin G. Nourse, an economist at large—ready for anything. © Karsh, Ottawa.

Nourse with a group of economics teachers at a Joint Council on Economic Education workshop in Pittsburgh, July, 1953.

Nourse conferring with friend A. D. H. Kaplan at a Joint Council on Economic Education workshop in Nashville, July, 1953. (*Nashville Tennessean* photo.)

Meeting of the Agricultural Policy Committee, September, 1954. Seated: Nourse, Margaret G. Reid, John D. Black, Jesse W. Tapp, Louise L. Wright, Murray R. Benedict, Calvin B. Hoover. Standing: Obed A. Wyum, Orville Poland, Oscar C. Stine, Donald R. Murphy, Harry B. Caldwell, Andrew Stewart, Theodore W. Schultz, Quentin Reynolds.

Nourse with Eugene Meyer and Frank Pierce at American Assembly, Arden House, October, 1954.

Conference at Harvard Graduate School of Business, mid-1950s. Dean Donald David is second from left and Meyer Kestnbaum is at right. (Photo by Hansen-Cambridge.)

Nourse receiving the Rosenberger Medal, University of Chicago, 1959.

Mr. and Mrs. Nourse on their golden wedding anniversary, 1960.

Nourse with son Tyler and grandson Chip, early 1960s.

Past Chairmen of the Council of Economic Advisers, White House, August 19, 1964. From left: Arthur F. Burns, Leon H. Keyserling, Walter W. Heller (Chairman at time of photo), Nourse, Raymond J. Saulnier, Gardner Ackley (successor to Heller).

Two of Nourse's cooperative friends. Left: Raymond W. Miller, President of the American Institute of Cooperation from 1945 to 1948. Right: J. Kenneth Stern, AIC President from 1950 to 1969.

Nourse at his last public address, May 29, 1965.

Nourse giving oral history interview at his home, 1966.

Nourse with author, 1969.

Nourse in 1971.

Nourse with son Tyler, 1973.

a "new intellectualism" in dealing with economic problems. He found that what economists had expounded as a "price-organized society" had become a "price-and-tax organized society." He was of the opinion that the freer use of "the people's government to energize and stabilize the people's economic life unleashes new productive powers—and exposes the people to new social or political dangers." It was his fear that the power "to accelerate" the economy would, if not wisely disciplined, lead to an inflationary breakdown.

He ended his article with this statement: "Whatever problems continue to persist in our economy will need the thoughtful and enlightened considerations of citizens who have had economic courses in high school and college. Economic education of students provides the tools of analysis and reasoning which they must have in order to be counted upon to help solve the problems that will persist in their adult lives."

"Early Flowering of the Employment Act"

The somewhat complacent consensus of economists at the twentieth anniversary celebration of the Employment Act that the act was at last functioning effectively caused Nourse to feel that a more sober analysis was called for. He set forth his views in an article entitled "Early Flowering of the Employment Act" for the Spring (1967) number of the *Virginia Quarterly Review*.

This perceptive and temperately expressed essay appraised attainments under the Employment Act. Nourse used the term "early flowering," for he thought that 20 years was "obviously only a short span in the life of an institution conceived as a permanent part of our governmental machinery." He thought the current situation called for "a serious look forward" more than a "complacent glance backwards."

It was his opinion that the Employment Act had taken "firm root in government understanding and public confidence" during the Eisenhower years and that the Kennedy-Heller partnership had "stimulated vigorous growth both in the performance of the economy and in popular understanding of its rationale." While he characterized progress under the Eisenhower Administration as "competent but conservative," he thought that explorations under the New Frontier could be called "bold—even a bit doctrinaire" in that "they prescribed a massive dose of tax cutting under a generalized theory of 'fiscal drag'" and stressed "tax abatement as a source of maximized national productivity—with 'feedbacks' into an indefinitely continuing succession of tax cuts." While this gave "a welcome prospect for business, consumers and surely politicians," Nourse thought that the New Men should not count their chickens when first hatched. He suggested that they "keep evaluations tentative until the first brood grows to maturity and begets offspring that, in turn, have been tested under varying conditions."

The problem of inflation brought on by the tax cut was already giving concern, "but," he said, "the inflation of prices is not the only . . . threat confronting a high-pressure economy. There is also a danger of inflation of central government authority and debasement of the decision-making role of administrative centers in the private business sector."

Nourse thought that the New Economics was placing overemphasis on fiscal policy. He said:

> The fiscal function of taxing and public spending is by its very nature an exclusive prerogative and responsibility of government. But the monetary function and the market function both have no less disinctive roles of service and no less valid jurisdictional claims. They are bound to confront us with sharp and recurrent dilemmas of private vs public responsibility and capability for national growth and dollar stability under the Employment Act. During these first twenty years of the Act policymakers have been preoccupied with a newly propounded theory of fiscal activism and with the problem of its application to political practices. This preoccupation was, in the circumstances, only natural and indeed necessary in terms both of practical experimentation and of popular and professional education. But future years will demand improved understanding of the monetary function and the market function in voluntary coordination with the fiscal function, not subservient to it.

In another passage he said:

> The Employment Act had not a word to say about the choice of strategic weapons in the campaign for maximum employment or about who should have a finger on the trigger for their use. . . . Success in the grand purpose of the Employment Act . . . will not be advanced by rigid welding of the monetary function to the fiscal function but through flexible articulation between fiscal and monetary functions. . . .

Nourse was particularly concerned that the market process be given more recognition. He said: "The market process of prices, wages, and services rates; of capital formation, investment, and dividend payments; of consumer choices and selling pressures does not lend itself to the 'aggregate' treatment central to the New Economics as do fiscal budgets and monetary maneuvers." He finished his article with these sentences:

> If we are to pass from the early flowering of a five-year boom on to the steady harvest of fully used national resources, successive Presidents and their economic advisers, successive Congresses and their economic committees, successive generations of business and labor leaders must activate and also restrain each other in a common purpose and shared responsibility for democratic wealth-generating enterprise and a free choice market. That, I think, was the intent and also an operative requirement of the Employment Act and should be a first order in the coming years.

It was generally agreed in early 1967 that the "sizzle" of the six-year boom was over. In an interview article for the *U.S. News & World Report* for April, 1967, four past chairmen of the Council of Economic Advisers gave their views on the immediate and longtime future—Nourse, Keyserling, Saulnier, and Heller. It was Nourse's opinion that "we have created an extraordinarily long boom. It would not surprise me to see the economy enter a more sedate phase." He did not expect a sizable slump in business, because our "growing sophistication of leadership helps insure against old-fashioned cycles." However, he found that "we are overbought—with heavy credit outstanding. We are housed up, auto-ed up, applianced up. We could live on the fat for a year and not seriously miss it." Looking ahead, Nourse expressed concern about continuous and deep deficits in the federal budget. He said: "We are about to find out whether we can 'handle our liquor' or will become alcoholics."

"The Employment Act and the New Economics"

In the Autumn (1969) number of the *Virginia Quarterly Review*, Nourse appraised the significance of the New Economics in the light of the Employment Act of 1946. His article, "The Employment Act and the New Economics," was his last published statement on the nation's economic problems.[21]

It was his view that the "on-going process of interpretation and application" revealed the potentialities of the Employment Act in shaping its operations to "ever-changing" circumstances. He divided the 22 years of experience under the act into three periods, "the shake-down cruise of the Truman regime, the re-examination period under President Eisenhower, and the period of dashing economic and political innovation under the Kennedy-Johnson succession, with Walter Heller as its presiding genius." Nourse focused his attention on this third period, which brought into play the so-called New Economics.[22]

He thought that the essence of the New Economics could be put in the form of six major propositions, which are here stated in brief. (1) "For full use of national resources . . . government must be equivalent to the productive capabilities of the economy." (2) "These capabilities are now so technologically great and growing, at full employment of national resources, there would be a surplus of goods and services above the buying power of the private sector at existing rates of taxation and government spending." Therefore "these tax rates will act as a 'fiscal drag' on the economy and must be lowered (or government spending expanded) if it is to attain that full productive potential." (3) It is technically possible to "prescribe the dosage and the timing of tax (and public spending) adjustments so as to alleviate 'fiscal drag' and facilitate a full employment balance of maximum production and purchasing power." (4) "Removal of fiscal drag . . . will so unleash productive potential that lower tax rates applied to an expanded national income will soon change deficit into surplus and call for another cut in tax rates—or facilitate the funding of larger social programs." (5) "This fiscal policy must be kept flexible." (6) "Monetary policy is the natural partner of fiscal policy. The cost and availability of money—i.e., credit—must be varied locally and changed more swiftly than fiscal policy and action."

The primary manifestation of the New Economics philosophy was "the creative tax cut" of 1964. In Nourse's words, this represented "a more daring and more professionally designed experiment with a total economy than we had ever experienced before."

While admitting that the New Economics had largely achieved its declared ends, Nourse could not agree that "even seven years of well-sustained prosperity" established "a verified set of principles for future generations." He believed that the "somewhat equivocal state of affairs at the close of the third period of the Employment experimentation" raised two important questions: "(1) Is the pleasant conclusion that we now have put the cycle of boom and depression permanently behind us demonstrable, valid, or perhaps premature? (2) Do we now have the tools, the skills, and the popular acceptance that make the continuous successful 'management of prosperity' . . . an assimilated part of our 'mixed system' of American Democracy?"

To Nourse, the lessons of the 1960s from New Economics experience were "less clear and reassuring" than they were to Paul Samuelson, who, as "the Pope of American Economics," had jauntily remarked in one of his magazine columns: "Now that the data for the 1960's are virtually in, I can say 'I have seen the past, and it works.'" As Nourse looked into the future at the end of 1969, he thought three broad generalizations could be made on the unfolding trend of economic statesmanship, namely: (1) "There is widespread consensus . . . that central government . . . has a permanently large role to play complementary to the basic enterprise sector of the economy. . . ." He thought that this proposition of the New Economics could be regarded as "well synthesized into our traditional two-party system." (2) "There is no similar consensus as to the major strategy and style of tactics to be followed. The Heller *et al.* massive fiscal stimulation produced an inflationary overdose not promptly correctable under our free-wheeling political structure and practice. The present Administration is presented with the task of disinflating the price structure and the structure of expectations . . . on which the longest-ever boom of the 1960's was built. . . ." (3) "The time is ripe for a next step in applying the basic methods of scientific analysis and generalization to the empirical observation of the three periods of experience in Employment Act political economy. . . ." Nourse thought that this could "mark a new high level in the intellectualizing or scientizing of the politico-economic process in the United States" that could round out the scope of the New Economics, improve its balance, and correct some of its shortcomings.

Nourse believed that the New Economics had given inadequate consideration to the market system "which, after all, administers nearly four-fifths of the total flow of the national wealth." He thought that the institutions and practices in that area might disclose "the Achilles heel of the New Economics theory of high-speed growth without inflation." He could not overlook the domination of commercial life by Big Business, Big Labor, and Big Finance, and it seemed to him that "wider dimensions of political economy—including the regulatory as well as the fiscal monetary policies of Big Government"—were needed to cope with this situation. To him, "these big collectives" were "inimical to the theory and technology of the New Economics," since both the giant power machines of Big Business and Big Labor had "devised and installed ratchet mechanisms by which the force of large scale competition of prices and wages is constantly upward and only in extraordinary cases downward." Nourse concluded that "a high-pressure economic policy thus creates the dilemma of market power versus market control." He did not believe that "the New Economists served their generation well" with their prime emphasis on the dismal dogma of "fiscal drag" and the pleasant promise of "fiscal dividends" each year. He believed that "leaders and people will have to be re-educated to the duties of citizenship, the enormous social needs of the impending years, the difficulties of curbing the arms race, the space race, and the power of the industrial-military complex." These problems, he asserted, "would not resolve themselves" but would have "to be faced —now—courageously—and as objectively as possible."

"What Can You Do for Your Country?"

While Nourse worked on his social science book (as described in the next chapter), he watched with interest the efforts of the Nixon Administration to stabilize the economic situation. Following the presidential nominating conventions in the summer of 1972, he was tempted to write a popular article on the economic outlook under the title, "What Can You

Do for Your Country?" He gave it the more expressive subtitle "Political Economics for 1976." He thought that either Nixon or McGovern would "face the dilemma of full employment vs. inflation." It is unfortunate that his manuscript was not published, for it provided a searching examination of the economic conditions then confronting the nation.[23]

Looking back, he thought it regrettable that President Kennedy had turned from a constructive approach to champion the "bold and unconventional economic strategy of tax cuts as espoused by the 'new economics.'" He noted that President Johnson had adopted Kennedy's program "to advance the New Frontier to the fair horizon of the Great Society" and pushed this program with zeal even as the Vietnam drain increased and federal deficits rose from $8.8 billion in 1967 to $25.2 billion in 1968, so that "by the time he abdicated his position as President the new economics as a science-and-technology of normalized growth and stability was in serious trouble. Instead of normalized prosperity without inflation, there was persistent unemployment . . . together with a pace of inflation that frustrated domestic policies and programs and was undermining our position in international trade and the foreign exchange system."

As a result, said Nourse, President Nixon in 1969 found himself "in a box—boarded in by rising prices, escalating wages, soaring Federal deficits, and unprecedented foreign exchange and trade difficulties." As quarter after quarter followed, "he had swallowed his campaign pride and economic prejudices and used his executive powers to find some escape from his predicament . . . but the dimensions of the problem were grotesquely out of proportion to the corrective power of these devices for the source of the difficulty was deep-seated in the economic institutions and behaviors, both governmental and private, which had developed over several past decades."

As Nourse looked ahead—just before the election of 1972—to the bicentennial year 1976, he saw the need "for fresh economic thinking and self-abnegating action at the centers of leadership in government and, in the private sector, by capitalist managers, labor generals and resentful consumers." This would require that "the people's government and the people themselves accept sustainable relationships between civilian and military expenditure programs, and the level and structure of individual and corporation taxes."

He believed that the next president (whether it be Nixon or McGovern) and the next Congress would be "challenged sharply to provide leadership toward opening frank and fruitful communications among business and labor leaders, government officials and social scientists on pressing issues in the private sector." Nourse did not think that full employment could be attained by further lightening of taxes or without adding new taxes. He realized that it would call for belt tightening, "but," he said, "the gains in human welfare for the disadvantaged classes would rise faster than the sacrifices entailed for the well-to-do and rich. That is the basic principle of welfare economics."

Chapter XV

SEARCHING TO THE END
(1965-1974)

During the final years of his life, Nourse's dominant interest was to complete a book on the meaning and significance of social science. It was begun as an essay, but as he became more and more involved in his subject it took form as a book, and the manuscript for the book became, in his words, his "unfinished symphony."

The project reflected his lifetime interest in the concept of social science. It will be recalled that as a graduate student at the University of Chicago he had liked to think of himself as a social scientist working in the field of economics and that later he was an active worker and leader in the Social Science Research Council.

The Beginnings of the Book

As Nourse later explained, the genesis of the book went back to 1949, when Vanniver Bush gave him a copy of his challenging treatise, *Modern Arms and Free Men*, which "depicted an all-embracing threat to our human estate as a 'harsh materialism' supposedly based on the findings of science." Bush had thought it essential to "expose the depth and breadth of this danger and to combat acceptance of it as a necessary outcome of the work of modern science." He had said: "The whole affair is a ghastly fallacy. Science has been misread. Science does not exclude faith. And faith alone can meet the threat that hangs over us." Bush's conclusion did not satisfy Nourse. "To me as an institutional economist," he said, "it seemed that scientist Bush turned transcendentalist made less of a case than might or could be made. The fact and the nature of the threat were solidly grounded in his exegesis of modern physics, chemistry, and biology; but the concept of 'bulwark' was less clearly drawn or impressively supported."

It was Nourse's view that Bush had limited his coverage of science to the physical and biological sciences and had ignored the potential contributions of the social sciences. He believed that the limitations of the "natural sciences" called for a greater recognition of the values of social science, which was a blind spot in their thinking.

While Nourse had been skeptical of Bush's views, they were dormant in his mind until Bush reiterated them in the May, 1965, issue of *Fortune* magazine under the title, "Science Pauses." At this time, Nourse was recuperating from a hip injury and he had plenty of time to get his own ideas in order. He then decided to "draft a commentary and extension of the area of discussion using the title 'Science Pauses—but Not Too Soon.'" It was his idea that "science should not pause until it had bestowed its benevolent services on the field of human nature as well as on the field of physical and biological nature." As he explained:

> Where Bush had only doffed his scholar's cap rather casually to the great company of men of good will who would follow natural science where it leads but reach beyond in aspiration, I undertook to show that some (not all) of the aspirations of this great company had been and were being brought to slowly enlarging fulfillment by the use of methods analagous to, but not identical with, the techniques of the physical and biological sciences. For this work the rubric Social Science has come into common use but also has fallen under continuing attack. Whereas Bush dismissed all questions of the meanings and goals of human life, free will, and reasoned choices, as forever "beyond the ken" of science, I spoke up for a "great company of men of good will"; realists and scholars but not victims of the materialistic fallacy, who are carrying the methods and attitudes characteristic of science over into the systematic study of Man-in-Society, where human life discovers and/or generates much of its meaning, its challenges, and its spiritual fruition.

When Nourse found that *Fortune* was not interested in "subjecting its readers to further dialogue on this plane of discussion," he decided to dig more deeply into the problem with the purpose of presenting his views in a little book somewhat comparable to James B. Conant's *On Understanding Science* (1947). In fact, he projected the book under the title, "On Understanding Social Science," which he admitted was stolen from Conant "in broad daylight." He liked Conant's view that "we need a widespread understanding of science in this country, for only then can science be assimilated into our secular ethical pattern. When that has been achieved we shall be one step nearer the goal which we now desire so earnestly, a unified coherent culture suitable for our American democracy in this new age of machines and experts." While Bush strictly limited his conception of science to the physical and biological sciences, Conant noted that "an increasing number of intelligent citizens believe that the social sciences rather than the physical and biological sciences hold the keys to the future." This was in accord with Nourse's belief that "widespread understanding of the architecture of our major social structures and the functioning of the major social processes need to be assimilated into our culture pattern at least as much as the understanding of 'natural science.'"

In starting work on the book in the fall of 1966, he didn't give himself a deadline for its completion. He wanted to reflect and study how light could be thrown on the field of social science and assess its importance. He didn't want it to absorb his time so that he could not work on his other interests. He still had much writing to do in economics, and he wanted to be free for other things that might come up. He looked on the book as a standby job that could be worked on as opportunity permitted.

It was at this time that Nourse agreed to be interviewed for the Cornell University Oral History project. Dr. Gould P. Colman, then in charge of this program, invited me to be the interviewer, since it was known that I was planning a biography of Nourse. In making arrangements for the interviews, Colman came to Washington in September and met with us at the Cosmos Club. He explained that he was interested in finding out for historians how Nourse's professional career had unfolded. I had already assembled a file of Nourse's writings and copies of his books that would help me guide the interviews. In this connection, Colman asked Nourse if he had kept any record of his early years in the form of a diary, notes, clippings, letters or correspondence. Nourse responded: "Not a scrap. I was brought up on the eleventh commandment: 'Don't take yourself too damned seriously.'" Fortunately, he had a retentive memory and could recall vividly the events of his life from childhood.

We started our interviews in October and continued semimonthly for about a year. As we completed tapes we sent them to Colman, and he would return the typed transcripts for us to correct and return to him. It was delightful to work with Nourse, for he got great enjoyment in recalling the events of his life. We would usually start an interview with a little warm-up off-the-record talk and plan the discussion for the day. Then we would turn on the recorder and begin our interview. Sometimes when Nourse wanted to explain something that he didn't think should be on the tape, he would interrupt the interview before we went on. When we finished a session, we would have a little talk on what we would cover next time, and in our next interview we would pick up things he wanted to get on the tape. We held the interviews in his upstairs study at his home where he kept his books and papers.

In my interviews with Nourse, he would often tell me of the book he was planning on social science, and in December he handed me a copy of a draft foreword he had written with the heading: "How this book came to be."[1] As a matter of fact, he was putting the flag up for a book that had yet to be. At this time he had in mind a book of perhaps seven chapters in two parts that would run to about 200 pages. The first four chapters would deal with the meaning of social science in relationship to the entire field of science. The last three chapters would examine recent developments in the three main social science fields—sociology, economics, and political science.

As Nourse completed several of his chapters in 1967, he passed them on for me to review. He was quite enthusiastic on the progress being made and was confident that he was going to have a worthwhile book. When he came to his 85th birthday in May, 1968, President Kermit Gordon of the Brookings Institution arranged a birthday luncheon in his honor, and Nourse, in response to the friendly comments of those present, told of the book he was writing, which he called his "unfinished symphony," for he didn't know whether he would ever finish it. In the next year he largely completed what he had originally set out to do, but he didn't publish what he then had written, for as he later said:

> As my writing progressed and the dramatic developments of the late '60s unfolded around me, I was loath to leave my commentary at the level of social science theory. What was its relevance to the turbulent current scene? It seemed to me that the activist movement, in its justified dissatisfaction with things as they have evolved, was in the way of throwing out the baby with the bath-water and fleeing to anarchy and anti-intellectualism instead of a better ordered way of human living.

How he coped with this problem will be discussed after we examine the way he was carrying on his affairs during this closing period of his life.

Nourse in His Ninth Decade

At this stage of his life, Nourse was growing old gracefully. He was getting much pleasure from daily activities, and he felt that he had much to live for. His faith in human progress was unabated, and he found his work exhilarating. He was young in mind, spirit, and interests, and he said to me on one occasion: "I protest, I am not a sour-bellied old man."

After 1969 he lived alone at his home on Jocelyn Street in Chevy Chase, Washington, for his elder sister Mary, who had been with him since his wife's death, had to move into a nursing home where she died in 1971. Mrs. Elizabeth Gerald, who had served as housekeeper for the Nourses since 1958, continued to keep house for him. She would come three days a week, get his groceries and supplies, and prepare a hot lunch for him. He was quite dependent on her, and she even took over care of the lawn. He was not lonely, for radio and television kept him up-to-date on public affairs and provided entertainment. He no longer attended the meetings of the Washington Literary Society, but he maintained his interest in the theatre. Up to the end of his life, he subscribed for four tickets in the middle of the second row for productions of the Theatre Guild at the National Theatre. When the Guild began to use the Kennedy Center Theatre, he would arrange theatre parties which consisted of an early dinner at the Cosmos Club before the performance. His son Tyler usually accompanied him and drove him and his guests to the theatre. On a number of occasions my wife and I were guests, and these were very pleasant occasions, for Nourse was a consummate host.

He did much of his work at home in an upstairs bedroom that he had made into a study, while he also spent several mornings a week in the office provided him by the Brookings Institution. As he could no longer drive his car because of his failing eyesight, he got down to his office and back home by the Connecticut Avenue bus. Frequently his son Tyler drove him to Brookings on his way to work and then stopped off for an evening chat on his way home. Nourse greatly enjoyed his downtown office, which enabled him to keep in touch with the world. It was located adjacent to the Brookings library, and he was often to be found looking for a book in the stacks. He did his own typing and when he got something in fairly good shape, he would have it typed by a Brookings Secretary. It was a convenient arrangement, for he could get his lunches at the Brookings cafeteria, where he could eat with staff members and friends. Occasionally he would go over to the Cosmos Club a few blocks away for a luncheon engagement.

One of his pleasures was attending the monthly luncheon meetings of a group of former Brookings associates which some of us called "The Brookings Old-Timers Group." It had begun meeting in 1963, while Dr. Moulton was still alive, and it usually brought together some 20 of us who had been connected in some way with the Brookings Institution down through the years. It was designed to enable old friends with a common interest in Brookings to get together to recount their experiences and exchange views. It was a very informal organization with no elected officers, and it was kept together by Esther and Evelyn Breck, who rounded up participants by telephone. Sometimes members of the Brookings staff would be invited to give talks on work they were doing, but in general, the meetings were simply social affairs. Nourse looked forward to these gatherings and rarely missed one.

An attachment that gave Nourse much pleasure during this period was with Professor Monroe (Mike) Newman of Pennsylvania State University and his wife Ruth. He had formed a friendship with the Newmans while he was a visiting Professor at Penn State in 1959, and this ripened into a rich relationship in 1965 when Mike spent a year in Washington as a member of the staff of the President's Appalachian Regional Commission. Soon afterwards, he became Research Director of the Commission and came to Washington monthly up to the end of Nourse's life. He usually brought Ruth with him, and they always had good get-togethers with Nourse, who was much interested in Mike's work, which continued his long concern with national resources use. It gave him great pleasure to sponsor Mike for membership in the Cosmos Club, which strengthened their bond of friendship.

During these years, my wife and I also kept in close touch with Nourse, for we had many common interests. Frequently we would have him over to our home for a meal and a good talk. He was meticulous in repaying hospitality, and often he would entertain us at the Piccadilly or Normandy restaurants near his home on Connecticut Avenue. Several times we drove him out to the Meadowlark Inn in Poolesville, which provided good food and pleasant surroundings. His appetite never flagged, and he always insisted on paying the bill. Once we drove him to Reston so that he could see how the new town was developing. It was always fun to be with him, for he enjoyed life.

It should be noted that Nourse valued and responded to women. He understood them, for he had been raised largely by his two sisters, and he was sensitive to feminine values. His own married life had been a continuing romance. He liked my wife, Carol, and she had a warm affection and admiration for him, which dated back to 1929 when the Nourses were among the few guests at our wedding. Whenever he came in contact with me, he would say: "How's Carol?" and he would be really interested in my reply. Carol greatly enjoyed entertaining him, and she would think of things that he might like to eat. She would say to me, "He has a sweet tooth." Sometimes we would have some simple meal that she knew he would fancy, such as lamb stew. He remembered her birthdays, and in 1971 he invited us over to his home so that she could select her birthday present. He gave her the choice of two beautiful antique oriental items—one a mosaic vase and the other a pewter jug. When Carol found it difficult to decide, he said: "Take both. I can see you like them."

Women greatly appreciated Nourse's warm interest in their lives. When Evelyn Breck retired as editor of Brookings Institution publications, he wrote to her as follows:

Dear Lady Editor:

I am quite sure that if all the editors in the world were laid end to end they would reach one definite conclusion: authors of economic manuscripts are a rather sloppy and somewhat peevish lot. But I am no less sure that if all of us who have passed under your editorial pencil could be added up, we would agree that you have been both a patient and perceptive *redacteur,* sharp at catching either a verbal or a logical slip but helpful thereafter in finding ways to make the inexplicable crystal clear.

After having been published in many places, I hereby proclaim: you are my favorite editor. And I take particular satisfaction that it was on a book of mine, x years ago, that you began the editorial career that has been so fruitful.

With cordial welcome into the ranks of us who are retired but continue to be active.

Sincerely,

(Edwin G. Nourse)[2]

As Nourse's life extended, he was saddened by the loss of many of his lifetime companions and friends. One of the first to go was John Maurice Clark in 1963, and a few years later he was deeply affected by the deaths of Harold Moulton and Gerhard Colm. He realized that he had reached an age when such losses were to be expected, but it was not easy for him to give up those with whom he had shared so many joys. He was deeply touched in 1965 when his longtime secretary and assistant, Margaret Quill, died, for she had been both his friend and partner. It gave him much pleasure to provide financial assistance for her niece's education, for he knew that Margaret would have appreciated this consideration. He found the loss of his sister, Alice Tisdale Hobart, who died in California in 1967, particularly hard to bear, for they had been confidants from childhood. When his old friend, Henry C. Taylor, died in 1969, I drove him to the Quaker Memorial Service. After many had spoken of Taylor's rich life and fine qualities, Nourse rose and said: "There is one thing that no one has brought out about our good friend. Henry Taylor was a fighter. He fought for his principles." Later Taylor's niece said that he had caught the real spirit of the man.

As his life slowed down, Nourse took a great interest in the affairs and good fortune of his friends. For example, it gave him much satisfaction in 1971 when Arthur Burns was appointed Chairman of the Board of Governors of the Federal Reserve System, and he greatly appreciated Burns's thoughtfulness in inviting him to his swearing in at the White House. Nourse was impressed by the ceremony and pleased that President Nixon recognized him.

It should also be noted that Nourse and Keyserling maintained an amicable relationship during this period. It gratified Nourse when Keyserling, at a White House Conference of all past chairmen of the Council of Economic Advisers in 1964, said in effect: "I agree with the analysis given by my former boss, Dr. Nourse." Several times Keyserling entertained Nourse at his home, and they carried on a friendly correspondence. In 1966, Nourse remarked to me: "I have always had a very pleasant contact with Keyserling on those infrequent occasions when we happen to be thrown together." He thought the record of their correspondence would make clear that there was no great rift between them.[3]

In the years from 1966 to 1969, Nourse took a real interest in the book I was writing on the rise of American cooperative enterprise. I had begun this volume with his encouragement many years before at the Brookings Institution, but its completion had been deferred until I could retire from government service. When the book came out, I dedicated it to him as "Dean of Scholars in American Cooperative Enterprise," and he was delighted with this tribute. From 1969 to 1973, I was busy writing the second volume of my history of cooperative enterprise in the United States, and he continued his deep interest in what I was doing. As the date of publication neared, he generously arranged to purchase 100 copies for distribution with his compliments to economists—an encouragement that meant much to me.

Although Nourse gave up active work with the Joint Council on Economic Education in 1964, he attended Washington Council meetings up to the time of his death. He never lost interest in this program.

Giving with a Purpose

As Nourse came to the closing years of his life, he was not a rich man, but from a good income over many years from professional service wisely invested, he had accumulated substantial savings which gave him the ability to do things that he considered important. His career had been devoted to education, and it was natural that he would use his savings to expand educational opportunities for disadvantaged youth.

One of his first ventures into giving, except for a few "pet charities,"[4] was to help finance the Legal Defense and Educational Fund of the National Association for the Advancement of Colored People. This fund was established in 1939 and received its "tax-deductible" status in 1940. Following the Supreme Court's decision in 1954 against desegregation of public schools, Nourse had become a member of the "Committee of 100" to help the Legal Defense Fund further the educational rights of black people, and as a member of this committee he provided a thousand dollars or more annually for this program as long as he lived.⁵ Moreover, he encouraged his friends by letter or conversation to support the Legal Defense Fund.

Nourse's interest in the work of the Legal Defense Fund encouraged him to examine the educational programs of black colleges, and he was attracted by the effective work being done by the Hampton Institute under the leadership of its president, Dr. Jerome Holland, whom he knew as an alumni Trustee of Cornell University. When Hampton embarked in 1966 on a Centennial Campaign to greatly expand its program and facilities by 1968, he was so impressed by a brochure prepared for this campaign that he decided to attend a luncheon meeting of the United Negro College Fund at the Mayflower Hotel on March 28, where he could look up Holland and find out more about Hampton's program in the area of business and economics. Holland was deeply appreciative of Nourse's interest, and this led to another interview and correspondence which gave Nourse assurance on the soundness of Hampton's plans. On May 30, 1967, he sent Holland a letter enclosing shares of common stock with a value of $52,000 as a contribution to Hampton's Centennial Campaign. He also said: "This gift does not necessarily close the book for us. If some matters work out as I hope they will, I may be in a position to add a little something more in 1968."

Holland was so pleased by this expression of Nourse's interest that on June 2, 1967, he wrote him as follows:

> Since this stock is worth $52,000, I would like to use these funds to start the Edwin G. Nourse Professorship in Economics. In view of the fact that you stated in your letter that a future gift may be forthcoming prompts me to start this endowed professorship. It will probably take me a year to find a good person, and with some luck, I may be able to make some additions to this amount. . . . Again, many, many thanks, and with your cooperation, I believe that we may start the professorship within a year or two.

Nourse replied on June 13, 1967:

> The plan you projected for making my gifts to Hampton the nest-egg for the endowment of an Edwin G. Nourse Professorship in Economics is very pleasing to me and I hope you will be able to initiate it with a young Ph.D. of great promise—perhaps from Cornell since you have exchange relations there *and* since you and I are both Cornellians. I shall hope that developments in the economy and the stock market during the rest of this year or early next will make it possible for me to approximately double the present gift.

Holland was happy to have Nourse's approval of the professorship. On June 22, he said in a letter to Nourse:

> It is my hope that we may secure the necessary funds and encourage a

young teacher-scholar to accept this endowed chair by September 1968. If I do not secure the $400,000 endowment by that time, I believe that I can subsidize the professorship out of some special college funds. However, keep your fingers crossed as I may not make it.

In January, 1968, Nourse sent Holland additional shares of stock which brought his contribution up to $100,000, and later in the year he made further contributions. Moreover, he was so interested in what Holland was trying to do that he wrote to several friends with the thought that they might wish to help fund the professorship. He typed the letters himself and they indicated how much the proposed professorship meant to him. In writing to Mrs. Katharine Graham, President of the Washington Post Company, he said: "Recent events have impressed it on my mind that nothing is so important in solving or at least ameliorating our racial problem as improving educational facilities for young Negroes who show capability and ambition." To William McChesny Martin, Chairman of the Federal Reserve Board, he said: "I feel that creating opportunities for bright young Negro youths to get the training that will enable them to become small proprietors or get in line for executive jobs in larger companies is about as fundamental a thing as we can do at the present juncture." Nourse was pleased with the response to these letters, which brought in several thousand dollars for the professorship.

By the end of the year, it appeared that the chair would soon be formally established. On December 1, 1968, Holland wrote Nourse as follows: "Many thanks for contacting your friends on behalf of this program. The College plans to move forward in seeking a person for this position for the 1969-1970 college year. It will have a real meaning to our academic efforts at Hampton Institute. Your willingness to pledge $44,000 in order to bring your grant up to $200,000 is deeply appreciated."

Unfortunately, it was not possible for Holland to start the professorship as early as he had planned. In 1969 he was busy completing his book *Black Opportunity*, and the following year he became Ambassador to Finland. Nourse accepted the delay with good grace, for he was confident that in time the chair would be established. He was highly pleased with Holland's book, and he gave me a copy as a birthday present. It gave him much satisfaction to attend a dinner given in Holland's honor before Holland left for his new post.

Nourse had always been grateful for the encouragement given him at Lewis Institute, which became the Illinois Institute of Technology, and at one time he had contributed funds to help expand its program. Therefore, when he was in Chicago with his sister Mary in 1966, it gave him a special satisfaction to provide a fund of several thousand dollars to enable the

Institute's English Department to offer an annual cash prize for the best composition submitted during the year. He was gratified by how well this program worked out.

When Antioch College opened a branch at the new town of Columbia, Maryland, Nourse was greatly interested, for he liked the Antioch idea of combining periods of education with periods of practical training experience. He was particularly attracted by the plans of its associated school of law located in Washington, D.C., for he had long been concerned with the relationship of law to economics and government, and he found in Dean Edgar Cahn of the Law School a man highly congenial to his thinking as an institutional economist.[6] In the years 1972 and 1973 he made contributions to the Antioch Law School amounting to over $125,000.

As a loyal alumnus of the University of Chicago, Nourse took a continuing interest in its program of research and education for human betterment. In July, 1971, he transferred to the university common stock with a market value of approximately $100,000, as he wanted to give something to the university which had meant so much to him and his sisters throughout his life. He was very proud of his doctor's degree from the University of Chicago, and his attachment had been strengthened when it awarded him the Rosenberger Medal in 1959. As in the case of his other benefactions, he got his satisfaction internally, for he said little of the gift to his associates.

In this same month, July, 1971, Nourse decided to give support to the effective work being done by Meharry Medical College of Nashville, Tennessee, in training blacks for the medical profession. He therefore wrote to Dr. Lloyd C. Elam, President of the College, as follows:

> As a social scientist, I am convinced that "Black Capitalism" is a snare and a delusion but that capable and ambitious young men and women will have a greatly improved place in American Capitalism in the future. On the other hand, I believe black professionalism has a great prospect of reward and service. It seems to me that you are going at the medical phase of this matter in the right way. Therefore I take pleasure in sending you herewith shares of common stock with a market value of approximately $46,000. With best wishes for the continued success of Meharry.

This gift gave him so much satisfaction that he transferred additional shares of stock with a value of approximately $57,000 to Meharry in December, 1972, and supplemented this in December, 1973, with additional shares valued at $4,000.

Thus Nourse made gifts for purposes that he believed in, to an amount totalling more than a half million dollars. He liked to put his money where his heart was.

Changing His Focus

As indicated above, Nourse had largely completed work on the book he had planned to write on social science theory by 1970, and he was concerned with making it relevant to the turbulent questions of the day. He was asking himself: "What have I learned as a social scientist that can be used to help solve the critical social and economic problems confronting the nation?" This gave him a new perspective and a practical focus for his writing. He was then beginning to think of his book as a distillation of his experience to help guide unsettled youth.

When we finished the oral history interviews in 1967, we decided to follow up later with other interviews to complete the record, and this led to an interview on January 23, 1971, in which Nourse brought me up-to-date on the status of his book. He then said that he had been working on the book on and off for more than five years because he had been troubled by the inadequate public understanding of social science. He said: "I wanted to strike a blow for recognition of the importance of social science vis-à-vis so-called natural science, for this thing had been nagging at me for years. I wanted to see what I knew and thought and understood after 60 years of working in various parts of this field." He said that he had projected the book, under the title "On Understanding Social Science," in two parts: "One a broad picture of what scientific method and attitude are, illustrated by the physical and biological sciences, and then developed in terms of the several social sciences." While he had largely completed what he had set out to do, he had come to feel that there was a need for a third part which he tentatively called "Sophisticating Our Democratic Society." He held that democracy was the essence of our system and that "now we have some new problems and new methods that are sophisticating it under the challenge of the so-called new confrontation." He thought that one way of getting the third part into a manageable frame of reference would be to divide it into two chapters, "Adult Protests and Proposals" and "The Agony and Ecstasy of Unfolding Youth." He was then working on these chapters.

In this interview, Nourse emphasized some of the ideas he was developing in his book. He saw all branches of science joined in "a seamless web" in which one form of science merges into another. He said: "We all work in our branches of experience and understanding, measurement where possible, analysis and hypothesis, to see what understandings we can get in a given field. There is a great deal of free trade between the several provinces of science." He made much of the point that social science deals with active, participating subject matter in which the subject matter itself talks back and interprets itself to the social scientist. He used the term "negotiative science" to indicate how the social scientist and his data influence each other. He did not see any universal generalizations applicable to the social sciences comparable to the laws of gravity and thermodynamics, except possibly "that human beings are polarized between two great qualities, the quality of competition leading to aggression and the quality of cooperation, leading to altruism and human brotherhood." It was his "more hopeful hypothesis" that "we are polarized between that competitive, aggressive instinct, and the other one of working together, of cooperation in a variety of forms which have not only preserved the human species so far but have brought enormous elements of progress, of civilization." He believed that it was the mission of social science to show the way in which the institutions of our society could be perfected, or at least improved, to better conditions and relationships.

This glimpse of Nourse's thinking at this time shows that his book was gradually taking form but that much remained to be done on it. It was apparent that he was changing his focus to emphasize what social science could do to help solve current critical problems, and this would involve gathering of new material, much reworking of manuscript already written, and the writing of several additional chapters. While the new direction for his book excited him, he did not find it easy to express just what he wanted to say. One problem that gave him much concern was to find a more suitable title for the book, for as he came to see it as a testament for the guidance of young people, the title he had planned to use, "On Understanding Social Science," no longer seemed appropriate. For a time in 1972, he planned to call his book "This Old Grey Head," an idea he got from Whittier's poem "Barbara Fritchie" (Shoot if you must this old grey head / But spare your country's flag she said). Counseled by friends that this title would repel the young, he finally settled on the other half of Dame Fritchie's admonition, "Shoot If You Must," with the subtitle "A Veteran Social Scientist Looks at the NOW Generation." He thought that this name for the book would recognize the legitimacy of social protest.[7]

Nourse Surmounts a Crisis

Nourse's greatest handicap in completing his book was deteriorating sight. When he saw an eye specialist in 1971, he was informed that the chances for a successful operation on his cataracts were about 50-50. As he could not contemplate blindness, which would foreclose completion of his book, he decided to struggle on without the operation. In 1972, as he found it increasingly difficult to read anything without a reading glass, he employed a young woman to come to his home several times a week to read materials to him, but she was not trained as a secretary and could not help on manuscript work.

Then in the late summer, his problems became almost insuperable when he had a fall and injured his pelvis. This made it almost impossible for him to use his upstairs bedroom and study. To overcome this obstacle, his son Tyler installed a downstairs toilet, and Nourse began using his sun room as a bedroom and his dining room as a place where he could work. It was at this time that he gave up use of his Brookings office.

It was now apparent to him that if he were to complete the book at home he would need to have clerical assistance. So he put a want ad in the newspaper to find a helper. Fortunately the ad attracted the attention of Mrs. Peggy Gagan, who had just come to this country from England with her husband, who was then editor of Reuters Economic Division in Washington. As she later explained:

> I first met Dr. Nourse in October, 1972, when I answered an advertisement of his for someone to help him with his work on a book; to be his eyes as he was nearly blind. After my husband had made enquiries among his staff to find out "Who is this wonderful old man that Peggy has just had an interview with?" and checking him up in the current Who's Who, I took the job. Armed with these facts I was of course quite nervous when I reported for work on the following Monday. Mostly I think I was worried that my English accent would grate on his ears during the long spells of reading which he required; but no, he said he was delighted with my clear enunciation because his hearing was getting so much worse.

The arrangement worked out happily for Nourse, as it gave him just what he needed—competent professional help and the companionship of a pleasant woman. This is indicated by the following statement of Mrs. Gagan:

> I remember we used to thoroughly enjoy our sessions of dictation or reading—when I would stress a different syllable from the American pronunciation or use the long "o" in such words as "progress" or "process" neither of us ever came up with a really satisfactory reason for the difference. He was a wonderful dictationist and used to come up with some new (to me) word in a sentence and then ask "How does that sound?" Sometimes I would reply: "Why not use the simple basic English word?" He would laugh and say: "But I am not writing simple basic English—I am writing for the with-it young American." My reply was generally: "O.K., you know best, you're much younger than I am," which always brought a delighted grin to his face. After one session with a lot of teasing and laughter he turned to me and said: "Peggy, it's such *fun* working with you"—a remark I shall treasure for the rest of my life.[8]

Indian Summer

1973 was the Indian summer of Nourse's life. Several things were to give him much satisfaction during the year, such as the celebration of his 90th birthday and the second marriage of his son. With the assistance of Peggy Gagan he was making excellent progress on his book, and except for near blindness, he was feeling quite well. Fortunately I was able to spend quite a little time with him during this year. I will draw on some of my contacts to give an impression of how he responded to his 90th year.

On February 13, I called him on the phone to see how things were coming along. He was quite excited by a visit he had just had with Dean Edgar Cahn of the Antioch College of Law located in Washington, D.C. Cahn was greatly interested in his ideas of institutional economics and fascinated by the way he had developed his studies of cooperative enterprise in relationship to the law. He reported that he had given Cahn copies of his books—in some cases the last copies—for the Law School library. He was anxious to arrange a meeting for Carol and me with Dean Cahn and his wife Jean, who was co-dean, for he thought we would be congenial. A few weeks later, Nourse invited us to have dinner with him and the Cahns at the Cosmos Club. He arranged it so that we could use his tickets to take the Cahns on to a play at the Kennedy Center while he returned home by taxi.

Early in March, I went over to see Nourse at his home on a Saturday morning to help him make up a list of those to whom he wished to have copies of my soon-to-be-published book sent with his compliments. He then suggested that we go upstairs to look over his files for materials that I could have for my biography of him. His eyesight was so poor that I had to identify items, but this didn't handicap us, for he knew what he had in his files. I gathered about a carton of manuscripts, reprints, and correspondence that have since been invaluable to me. As we chatted, I indicated that it was two years since we had our last tape interview for the Oral History project and that I would like to bring the record up to date. He said that he was finishing the first part of his book and might have a little time later in the spring, but this did not prove feasible.

Soon afterwards, Carol and I drove Nourse over to the home of Bernard and Peggy Gagan in Arlington for dinner. Peggy was looking out for us, and she welcomed Nourse with the tender affection of a lovely woman for a gallant elderly man. She was delighted that he had brought her a bottle of Drambuie as a "delayed" birthday gift. She had prepared a fine baked ham dinner on which we all did well, and after dessert we had a lively conversation around the table on economic and political affairs. Bernard, who followed economic matters closely for Reuters, was well informed on the American economic and political situation, and he knew many persons prominent in official Washington. It was pleasing to see Nourse actively participating in economic conversation and getting so much joy from expressing his views.

On May 5, his son Tyler, whose first marriage had ended in divorce, was married to Stephanie Gorski, an attractive young divorcee with a baby daughter Sarah, nearly one year old. Nourse realized that Tyler needed a mate and a settled home life, and he liked Stephanie, who was a professional psychologist. Carol and I attended the wedding held at the Unitarian Church in Kensington, and it was pleasant to see Nourse dolled up for the occasion. It was apparent that he greatly enjoyed the ceremony and the reception which followed at Tyler's home in Rockville, where Tyler's son Chip (Edwin Wallis) and daughter Gayle (Rebecca Gayle), in their early twenties, helped entertain the guests. Bernard and Peggy Gagan brought Nourse in their car to the wedding and the reception.

We celebrated Nourse's 90th birthday in advance at the May 10 meeting of "The Brookings Old-Timers Group." The meeting was held in the Round Table room, and a beautiful birthday cake was brought in with lighted candles while an elegant brown necktie was presented on behalf of the group. We all sang "Happy Birthday," and Nourse was so touched that he felt that he had to say something. He was reminded of an old German farmer from his Iowa days who was asked to say something under similar circumstances. He had said: "The ghost is villin—but the meat is veak." Although Nourse was in good voice, it was apparent that his body was frail. He didn't speak long, but he recognized Barbara Moulton as a longtime family friend and recalled how he had come to the Brookings Institution (then the Institute of Economics) in 1922 at his own invitation to assist her father, Harold G. Moulton, in starting its program of work. Dr. Robert D. Calkins, former President of the Brookings Institution, then paid a fine tribute to the contributions Nourse had made to the Institution, and the group gave personal testimony on what Nourse meant to them. Among those who spoke were Harold Rowe, Lynn Edminister, Mollie Ray Carroll, and Mildred Maroney. It was a heartwarming occasion, and I was greatly pleased when Nourse later told me that I had been a good chairman.

Nourse's birthday was more formally celebrated the following week with a luncheon arranged by Kermit Gordon, President of the Brookings Institution. I took Nourse down to Brookings in advance by taxi so that he could get a couple of pages of his book typed and give Moe Frankel three chapters for review. The luncheon was a very cordial affair, with some 25 old friends present. While lunch was being served, Herbert Stein, then Chairman of the Council of Economic Advisers, read an appreciative letter to Nourse from President Nixon. After a birthday cake was brought in and "Happy Birthday" was sung, Gordon made a felicitous talk in which he recognized Nourse's contributions to the Brookings Institution and called attention to the great changes that had come in population, growth of GNP, and other economic indicators since 1883, the year of Nourse's birth. He pointed out that Nourse's life reached almost halfway back to the adoption of the Constitution in 1789. At the close of the luncheon, Gordon said: "On his 85th birthday Dr. Nourse promised to be present for his 90th birthday and here he is. We will look forward to your 95th birthday." Nourse quietly responded: "Don't overplay your hand." The occasion elated him.

The celebration of Nourse's birthday culminated with a family dinner at the home of Tyler and Stephanie Nourse on May 20. This was a pleasant affair, for Nourse shared honors with Sarah Elizabeth, Stephanie's daughter, who was having her first birthday. Tyler's children, Chip and Gayle, were there, and Stephanie served a delicious rib roast with Yorkshire pudding. After Nourse blew out the candles on his birthday cake, Tyler asked me to propose a toast. I felt greatly honored to toast him as "a great American and a great scholar," and all responded with warm affection. After dinner, birthday presents were opened for Nourse and Sarah. I was sorry that Carol couldn't be with us because of a bad cold, for her present of a little book on cats was a big hit with Sarah. We gave Nourse a copy of Earl Warren's new book, *A Republic if You Can Keep It*, which Peggy Gagan could read to him. Chip said that he venerated Warren, and this got us into a discussion of the Watergate situation. Nourse hoped that it would not be found necessary to impeach President Nixon, and Chip remarked: "Isn't it wonderful to be alive during the greatest crisis of the greatest nation in the world today?" I was pleased to be included in this intimate family party and see the fondness of Nourse's family for him. He philosophized a little during the evening and said that he still found a lot to live for. Although his eyesight was almost gone, he exuded a sort of spiritual happiness to those around him. We all agreed on his verdict: "A damned fine party!"

During the next few months I was able to spend more time with Nourse. I realized that he was pushing hard to complete his book and I wanted to be of all possible help. As he could not read by himself, he welcomed my reading to him articles in the newspapers and magazines on current economic and political developments. It was at this time that *Challenge—The Magazine of Economic Affairs* was being reinaugurated by Myron E. Sharpe, and it provided many articles that were of great interest to both of us. Nourse was an absorbed listener, and he gave rapt attention to whatever article was under consideration. Occasionally he would interrupt to comment on some point, and at the end of the article he would indicate how it struck him.

The first *Challenge* article that I read to him was in the form of an interview with Herbert Stein (then Chairman of the Council of Economic Advisers) on "The Principles Behind the Policies." In our next session I read to him an article by Leon Keyserling on "What's Wrong with Economics." He was favorably impressed with its spirit and content, but he thought it covered too much ground for one article. We followed up by reading an interview with Walter W. Heller, "Let's Tailor the Policies to Fit the Problems." This was vivaciously written, and while Nourse admired its jaunty style, he thought Heller was often carried away by flights of fancy. He believed that Heller had moved toward his way of thinking and was "less positive than a few years back."

Several of our sessions were devoted to the reading of *Galbraith and the Lower Economics*, a recently published book by Sharpe. We began by reading the book flaps, the preface, and the first two chapters, for, as Nourse said, "this is the way to read a book." He found the book challenging, but he wondered if it fully expressed Galbraith's thinking. While Nourse's preoccupation was in finishing his book, he enjoyed the diversion of having such economic material read to him. He was then reworking his final chapters and such material was pertinent to his needs.

While we were having these reading sessions, Carol and I would enjoy having Nourse over to our home for meals where we would have discussions on general topics of interest. With our encouragement he would reminisce on significant events in his career. He always brought along a few pages of his manuscript for me to read to him, for this gave him ideas on how he could better express himself. He was glad to get our reactions and gave them serious consideration. One of the subjects that was then concerning him was how to state his ideas on secular religion so as not to upset deeply religious people.

When my book was published in June, I took a copy over to Nourse which I inscribed "To My Permanent Chief." He hefted it and was pleased with its appearance. As his eyes wouldn't permit him to read the book by himself, I read the introduction and cover material to him and several passages where I had quoted from his writings. He was greatly pleased with my expression of appreciation for his help in my acknowledgements. I told him how my neighbor, Mrs. Madge Becker, had remarked, when I showed her the book, "What a heavy book." He gently said: "I wouldn't call it a heavy book. I would, however, call it a weighty book."

For some time, Nourse had wanted to entertain us at the Meadowlark Inn in Poolesville when the weather was bright. It looked the right kind of a day on September 28, so we took advantage of it. We had a lively conversation on our way, during the meal, and on our way home. He loved to get out into the open country, even though he could see little of it, and he liked to have us describe what we saw. He could just make out the white fences, and this gave him a thrill. We spoke of something relating to age and I said: "I really don't feel my age," and Nourse responded: "Neither do I." As a man of 90, he was remarkably quick on the uptake. He enjoyed having the opportunity to reflect on things past, and on that day he told us of his first teaching job in Utah and of the background of Mrs. Nourse. I mentioned a good review of my book by Alfred Stedman and of the honor I had received in being named "Cooperative Communicator" of the year. I said that it made me feel a bit smug, and he remarked: "I think it's all right for you to purr a little over it." When we took him home, he wanted us to come in and listen to a few pages that he had dictated into a recorder. He played them back and then wanted our criticisms. I offered a comment or two, and then he wanted Carol's reaction. She hesitated and then asked if the word "hopefully" as used was not a bit overworked. Nourse was absolutely delighted that she had caught this.

When I visited Nourse on November 3, he looked a little tired, but he soon livened up as we began talking. I had a number of things to talk over with him, so he let me have the first round. I read to him a letter from Alfred Stedman which gave him much pleasure, for Stedman spoke highly of his contributions to agricultural economic policy in the 1930s. Then I read an item in the *Washington Post* in which Ken Galbraith wanted to know what the president's economists were doing, and a review of Galbraith's latest book in the *Wall Street Journal* by Herbert Stein, Chairman of the Council of Economic Advisers. Nourse said that it increased his respect for Stein as an economist. We then settled down to read passages of Galbraith's new book, *Economics and the Public Purpose*. Nourse thought this a good title, for it was something like the title of his own book, *Economics in the Public Service*. He thought that many of Galbraith's views parallelled his own, and I said: "I think that you preceded him in much of your thinking." He wasn't so sure of this, but he said: "I am as much of an iconoclast as Galbraith, but with a different approach."

Nourse then told me of how his own book was coming along. He was getting Part I typed up so that he could send it to a publisher for consideration. He had prepared a one page introduction for this part of the book at my suggestion. I liked this so much that I shook his hand and said: "Don't change it. It's just right." When I got home I recorded how he impressed me on this visit:

> As we got into our conversation on his book, I enjoyed watching Nourse as he talked. He has a benign, expressive face which lights up as he talks. His hair is now grey but still thick and his sideburns frame his face in a very attractive manner. As he talks his hands lie in his lap and they help him express his thoughts. He makes very interesting gestures that really help him convey his meaning. He doesn't wear glasses any more, for his eyesight is gone, but one isn't conscious of this when he talks. His gift of enthusiasm remains high and the joy of work is still apparent. He appreciates very much the approbation of the young, and he remarked on the helpful comments of his granddaughter on one of his chapters. We talked about the present cult of young people, "doing one's thing," which I termed a cult of selfishness. Nourse didn't blame the young for having it, for as he said: "It's the fault of our civilization."

A week later, on November 10, I drove over to get Nourse to have supper with us. As we were walking from his house to the car with Nourse holding on to my arm for support, he slipped and slid on to his back. He was not hurt, for his big coat cushioned his fall, but his large frame made it a real job to get him back on to his feet. The fall worried me, but he made nothing of it. However, he must have been shaken up, for he was ready to go home about 9 o'clock, when generally he stayed until 10 o'clock. (This disturbed Carol, so I called him on the phone the next day and was relieved that he was in good spirits.) Our evening together was very pleasant. We had drinks in front of a fire, and Carol had prepared a fine meal of Swiss steak with apple pudding for dessert. Nourse was in a reminiscent mood, so after supper he told us of his life as a boy in Illinois. I read to him the introduction to Walter Lippman's book, *The Good Society*, which I had borrowed for him from the Bethesda library so that he could review it again. This led him to a discussion of the books by Macaulay and Bagehot which had inspired him when he was a student at Cornell University. As usual, he had brought along a few pages of a chapter for me to read to him, and this gave him ideas for changing a few words. He would have me attach a card with a paper clip so that he could later make a correction with the help of Peggy Gagan. He seemed to be well pleased with the way his book was shaping up, and we had no idea that this would be his last visit to our home.

I wasn't able to visit Nourse again until December 9. We sat on the big couch in his living room and had a fine conversation. The Watergate situation was dominating the news, and Nourse quoted Lord Acton:

"Power corrupts and absolute power corrupts absolutely." He had just heard Joe Fisher's talk on TV which indicated that he was going to run for Joel Broyhill's seat in Congress. The announcement didn't surprise him, for he was aware of Fisher's political interests and ability. He said that he had told Fisher on some recent occasion that he had a flair for national politics that shouldn't be denied. He was greatly interested in a paper I was preparing on the Capper-Volstead Act for a Symposium on Cooperatives and the Law to be held at the University of Wisconsin in April. I read to him a statement by Thomas E. Kauper, Assistant Attorney General, Antitrust Division, which indicated that the Capper-Volstead Act was under serious attack and a statement in response by Kenneth D. Naden, Executive Vice-President of the National Council of Farmer Cooperatives. As a careful student of the Capper-Volstead Act from the time of its passage in 1922, Nourse recognized my subject as of basic importance to cooperatives. He thought that the large dairy cooperatives might have gone too far in interpreting the act for their own advantage and were apt to get their fingers burned.

At this time, Nourse was quite pleased with the way his book was coming along. He gave me two chapters for reading at home so that I could give him my suggestions when we next got together. In our conversation I mentioned a brief prepared by my friend Harold McCoy, formerly Secretary of the Interstate Commerce Commission, on the regulatory agencies, and he said: "Could I have a copy? I'm greatly interested." It pleased me to see how he maintained his enthusiasm for a subject like this. He appeared to be in good physical condition, although his hearing was giving him trouble and he was planning to visit an ear clinic to see if a hearing aid would help. I had to speak loudly during our conversation, even though I sat near him.

As the year came to a close, Nourse could see his book nearly ready for publication. He now had a title for the book that satisfied him, and he was completing a foreword to explain what he hoped his book would accomplish. He titled it "How This Book Came to Be," but it differed greatly from the foreword he had tentatively written under this title when he began writing the book. *Then* he was primarily concerned with gaining recognition for social science in the total field of science. *Now* he placed his emphasis on how social science could help youth meet the difficult problems of modern life. This foreword was a victory for Nourse, for it was evidence that he envisaged the book largely finished at last. In closing this foreword he said:

> The present book is obviously not a scientific treatment or a formal study of social science as a distinctive discipline. It may best be viewed as a

"position paper", setting forth one personal interpretation of our twentieth century social evolution and its present crises.

Whatever your reading style or habit of thinking, *understanding*—the basic theme of this book—is a highly personal experience, intellectual and spiritual. It is not, however, an exercise in loneliness. Each newcomer to the human pilgrimage is met by the challenges and enlightenments of those who travel by his side, and of those who went before and left their record.

And so, as you continue your private quest for some satisfying understanding of the social life of which you are an inescapable part, I proffer my services as a sort of *habitant* guide and companion for a short span of that pious journey.

The End of the Trail

During and following the 1972 presidential election campaign, there was a feeling among economists that the Council of Economic Advisers had become too closely allied with the political objectives of the Nixon Administration. On the initiative of Eileen Shanahan, Washington Bureau correspondent for the *New York Times*, a panel discussion was arranged for the annual meeting of the Allied Social Science Associations in New York on December 29, 1973, to consider "How Political Must the Council of Economics Advisers Be?" It was sponsored by the American Economic Association and the Society of Government Economists. The speakers on the panel were limited to past chairmen or members of the Council. They included Herbert Stein, the current Chairman of the Council, past chairmen Walter Heller and Arthur Okun, and several former Council members.

As Nourse was greatly interested in the subject under consideration, his good friend Mike Newman attended the panel discussion and gave Nourse a full account of it in a letter dated January 1, 1974. He reported that the meeting attracted a large and "fascinated" audience and said: "Virtually every one of the speakers used your precepts of proper Council member behavior as a model to which they compared post-Nourse behavior. None of the former council chairmen was mentioned with the frequency or respect with which your term of office was treated. Throughout the give-and-take there was a unifying theme of respectful regard for the advisory path you had charted."

Although Newman was no doubt biased in Nourse's favor, the edited discussion published in *Challenge* (March-April, 1974) indicated to a high degree the extent to which the standards set by Nourse as first chairman were still pertinent. When I later read the discussion to him in early March, he commented: "It was no doubt toned down in the editorial process."

Nourse's health deteriorated rapidly in the new year. His hearing gave him increasing trouble, and with his son's help, he got a hearing aid which provided some benefit. He wasn't able to get outdoor exercise, and his energies were low. I went over to see him on Sunday mornings and read to him items that I thought might be of interest. I kept him informed on progress being made on my paper relating to the Capper-Volstead Act, and this pleased him. Frequently he lay on a couch in his dining room which now served as his office, and he didn't get up. His main concern was finishing his book, which he felt was nearly ready for publication.

In January, Hampton Institute was preparing a brochure to develop support for the Edwin G. Nourse Professorship in Economics and Business, and Nourse asked Mr. Nathaniel B. Smith, who was representing the Institute's Office of Development, to work with me on its content. Later I told Nourse of my suggestions to Smith, and he was quite content.[9]

In February, Nourse was able to have the first seven chapters of the book sent to McGraw-Hill for review, but he found it impossible to revise the remaining five chapters before he died because he had to labor paragraph by paragraph with the aid of Peggy Gagan. He was working under almost insuperable difficulties, but he refused to give up.

In early March, Nourse had another fall, and he had to have a blood transfusion at the hospital. I saw him there soon afterwards and was concerned that he wasn't making a stronger recovery. Peggy Gagan, who was continuing to help him on his manuscript, reported over the phone to me: "I think the dear old chap is on the way out."

I had my last good visit with him on a Sunday morning in late March. He was then in bed and mentally responsive, but it was evident that his vitality was ebbing. I read to him several pages that he was revising, and when I left he characteristically asked me to take home some chocolates for Carol that were in a box on his book shelf.

The following Saturday afternoon, Carol and I went over to see him. His faithful housekeeper, Mrs. Elizabeth Gerald, was concerned with his condition. As she talked with Carol, I went into his bedroom. He had failed greatly since my last visit, and he was delirious. However, he recognized me and said: "Joe, here's a card, get a paper clip," for he wanted me to mark some passage in his manuscript for later consideration. I took the card and he attempted to express himself, but I realized that his words were confused and that he had lost control of his mental processes. I watched him for several minutes, for he was unconscious of me, and then I left with the feeling that his life was slipping away. When I got home, I reported my visit to his doctor, and that evening he was taken to Suburban Hospital in Bethesda where he died the following night (April 7). One of the last persons to see him was Peggy Gagan, who visited him at the hospital shortly before his death. She tells the story this way:

> I worked with him for five half-days a week right to the end of his life and well do I remember that last week. He was (much against his own wish) in bed and obviously getting weaker, yet he had this burning desire to finish his book so that "some of the up-and-coming young fellers may be able to learn something from this 'Veteran Social Scientist'". I left him as usual at lunchtime on Friday and then was told on Saturday that he had been taken into hospital. Sunday evening I went in to see him because I had to go to New York the following day. I found him much weaker and had a terrible feeling that he would not last much longer. Dr. Nourse died soon after I left him on Sunday evening" [Letter from Peggy Gagan to author, May 26, 1977].

Sadly, he had not been able to complete his "Unfinished Symphony," which is abstracted in Appendix B.

A Proper Leave-taking

In a conversation after the death of his wife, Nourse had told me that he hoped any memorial service for him would be held at the Brookings Institution. He had taken a great interest in helping arrange the memorial service for Harold G. Moulton, so I had some idea of what he would like for himself. Soon after Nourse's death I passed word to Kermit Gordon that he had expressed a wish that the Brookings Institution would honor him with an appropriate service, for he considered Brookings his intellectual home. Gordon received the suggestion graciously and immediately made arrangements for a service in the Brookings Auditorium on the afternoon of April 17.

It was a proper final salute to Nourse, for the ceremony was simple, without music or lavish display of flowers. Back of the speakers' table was a portrait of Nourse furnished by his son Tyler. In his introductory remarks Gordon well expressed the spirit of the gathering:

> We meet today to honor the memory of our friend Edwin Griswold Nourse. Some of us who are gathered here knew Edwin Nourse mainly as a scholar whose distinguished work at Brookings over two decades won him the presidency of the American Economic Association. Others knew him mainly as a public servant who served the nation with wisdom and integrity as the first chairman of the Council of Economic Advisers. Still others among us knew Edwin Nourse as a man of conscience who sought through quiet benefactions to raise the downtrodden. But all of us knew him as a rare human being who combined distinction of intellect and strength of character with civility, humor, and personal warmth.
>
> A memorial service is often a time for grief and sadness, but except as

mortality itself is a vein of sadness in the human condition, there is little to be sad about as we reflect on the richness and abundance of this life that spanned ninety-one years. To live for ninety-one years is a privilege vouchsafed to few of us. To Edwin Nourse it was a boon that enabled him to prolong the search for truth and sustain his service to man.

Gordon then called on four friends to speak about the Edwin Nourse they knew from separate vantage points. As one who had come to work with Nourse in the early days of the Institute of Economics before it was merged into the Brookings Institution, I reviewed his career up to the time of his retirement from the Brookings Institution in 1946. Then Joseph Fisher, President of Resources for the Future, told of his relations with Nourse on the Council of Economic Advisers and of his continuing association with him. Stanley Ruttenberg described his work with Nourse on labor problems and as a colleague in the Joint Council on Economic Education. The final speaker was Professor Monroe Newman of Pennsylvania State University, who knew him as an educator and intimate friend during the last 15 years of his life.[10]

All of the talks were brief, and the service lasted but one hour. Then there was a reception in the lounge which enabled friends to speak of the man they loved and admired. Coffee, tea, and punch, with cakes and sandwiches, were served. It was a pleasant gathering which Nourse would have liked. It was a proper leave-taking for one of the great pioneers of the Brookings Institution.

Chapter XVI

THE MAN AND HIS WORK

In the foregoing chapters I have shown how Nourse's career unfolded. I have also tried to convey something of the spirit of the man through quotations of his own thought and through explanation of the conditions which confronted him. His life was one of remarkable consistency, for he built on what he learned. As a young man he had a searching curiosity which attracted him to the social sciences—history, political science, sociology, and economics. Although he built his reputation in the field of agricultural economics, he was never restricted to this field, for he looked upon himself as an economist with a special interest in agriculture. One thing led to another. Agricultural economics opened studies in agricultural cooperation, and work with cooperatives led to an examination of their legal environment and institutional arrangements.

As the problems of agriculture became increasingly political, he studied the governmental machinery relating to farming. And so it went. Increasingly he became concerned with the solution of national economic problems, while he maintained his close interest in the economic and social problems of agriculture. His interest in the total field of social science never flagged, and probably no one contributed more to the advancement of research in all social sciences from 1926 to 1945 than he, through his leadership in the Social Science Research Council. When he was invited to serve as the first Chairman of the Council of Economic Advisers, it was in recognition of his outstanding record as an economist and social scientist who was knowledgeable on the problems of government. As Nourse widened his experience, he moved to new areas of thought. His professional career was cumulative to the very end of his life.

While his versatility and high productivity are reflected in my record of his life, I do not feel that my account adequately brings out his distinctive personal qualities. I am therefore adding this final chapter to help explain the nature of the man. I have divided it into three parts: (1) a consideration of his working methods, (2) expressions of contemporaries to indicate how they saw him, and (3) a summing up of his major contributions.

Working Methods

I was always impressed with the way Nourse worked. He never allowed himself to be distracted by unessential activities. One of my early memories of him at the Institute of Economics was the way he came out of his office in the morning to look over the mail before his secretary could sort it and bring it in to him. He would quickly pick out the junk material and drop it into a wastebasket and then gleefully return to his desk with his "bag" of important letters and documents. He kept his attention on what really interested him. I was also impressed with the way he prepared a manuscript. After getting his ideas in order, he would dictate first drafts to his secretary and then revise them until they satisfied him. In this way he captured the flow of his thought and got the stimulation of his secretary's response. To him, secretaries were partners.

In an interview with Nourse in the early 1960s, I said that I would like to dig into his research procedures and techniques—his working rules as a scholar. He replied that my expression "working rules" was "apposite." He said that his first tendency was to say: "No, I don't have any. But as a matter of fact I do have principles—let's call it that and not inflexible rules. My way of working is to have something of a vision or outlook on a field that is significant or needs treatment. Then my procedure characteristically would be to jot down a title under which it might appear and then to start to outline the organization for it, the scope of the treatment, and its major divisions and perhaps write something that could be a sort of precis for it. We had a phrase at the Institute of Economics that 'a study will grow under your hand.' That was Harold Moulton's expression and I think an admirable one. You just have a vision—that was in our procedure. If a staff member was going to do a study he had to prepare a memorandum indicating what he proposed to do, why it was important, and the scope within which it would be manageable. It would set forth the depth and plan of development, the materials to be used, contacts to be made, whatever. It might need to be redrafted before approval as a project. Then it would have sailing orders, and it would continue to grow under the author's hand. We had a review committee to ensure good work but in every case, the author had the final word. It was his book and he took responsibility."

He did not think that one could gather all of the materials necessary for writing a book and then sit down and write it. He was impressed with the great number of graduate students who went through all of the course work for a doctor's degree who never got the degree because they couldn't complete an acceptable dissertation. They would say: "I've gathered all my materials but I haven't got them organized and expounded yet." Nourse said:

> There is no such thing. You cannot in my judgment gather all your materials for a study and then start to organize and interpret them. This cames back to the formula "growing under your hand." You have a general view and you begin to select pertinent materials and to discard and to amplify and to analyze and you keep writing as you keep gathering material. I think that is the thing which graduate students should be apprised of and trained in so that their writing of a thesis would not result in so many situations where they say: "I've got everything done but the thesis."

Nourse thought that "one great flaw in much social science research came from treating problems in cross sections without a longitudinal or historical perspective." He said:

> I always want to see how a situation has developed. Because I am an institutional economist primarily I want to see how an institution, how patterns of human behavior, how the functioning of the economic process is working at the present with a long past behind it and a future ahead which we try to probe. I think the shortcoming of a good deal of work comes from lack of a broad social science content. I might add that the reliance on mechanistic methods and the vogue of the digital computer at the present time have dangers. While the computer has unquestionable value, it needs to be used with care.

This led to a discussion of how Nourse became an institutional economist. I wondered if he had been attracted by the work of John R. Commons and others labelled as institutional economists. I observed that I didn't think he came to this approach through that direct conduit. Nourse replied: "That is quite true. I had great respect for Commons, Wesley Clair Mitchell, and others who were known as institutional economists, but my approach was an innate characteristic of my budding scholarship. I developed along parallel lines rather than as an intellectual son."

I enquired whether exploratory reading helped him determine whether something was worth being done. He replied that his analytical efforts largely grew out of his past work. He gave the following example of how one job led to another.

> *Industrial Price Policy and Economic Progress* was in a sense the amplification of things which I thought were inadequately dealt with in *Income and Economic Progress*. While *Industrial Price Policy* did not fully meet the needs of what I wanted to do, it was a good springboard for my more

detailed book, *Price Making in a Democracy*. That emphasized the necessity of economic statesmanship by private officials, and when it was done I projected a follow-up book to be called *Business Executives as Professional Men*. I saw the need of trying to develop professional standards for corporate executives and labor union officials as they were the administrators of large blocks of resources at strategic points of the private economy.

I said: "I take it that you like to work in areas where you can see some purpose, some timeliness to your efforts." He replied:

> Yes, I think that again is an expression of my temperament. I have been concerned with things which have meaning to me. At the Brookings Institution we were not interested in writing books that would eventually say the final word after the problem was dead or at least moribund—or to write books that would go on the shelves for only a handful of people to read. Our whole philosophy was to take a pressing current problem, bring good scientific economic analysis to bear on it within a reasonable time period, and do the best book that we could do within those limitations.

I asked him: "How much perfection do you strive for?" and his answer was: "As much as the time allows." He said that at the Council of Economic Advisers,

> We had to hit problems on the wing. . . . If I have time I am a perfectionist and yet I know when I have got something to the stage of diminishing returns or at least I think I do. I come to a point where I say: well, that's the best that I can do. This problem is going to go on. It's going to change. My thinking is going to go on and I'm going to get new insights, but I regard this as a piece of workmanship which I can turn loose at this stage.

We went on to discuss the use of hypothesis as a research technique. I said that I thought there was something to be said for the use of hypothesis in the sense of starting out with something to be tested. I enquired: "Is this something of an unconscious state of a good researcher, or should he build a formal hypothesis?" Nourse answered: "I think this varies according to the temperament of a man. One could go through an exercise in quite formal logic, starting with an hypothesis, and developing it by very careful technical stages from there on. I'm not as precise as that. I do have my preconceptions, my assumptions, my tentative conclusions which amount to hypotheses, and I work along from them but it's a rather informal procedure rather than a precise one."

I referred to something I had learned from working with him. I said: "Instead of taking hard things first you encouraged me to take the easy steps first. You suggested that if I did know something about my subject to get that down and then extend my knowledge from the part I knew to the unknown. Have you followed that in your own writings?" Nourse replied: "Yes, I think that would be true. On any empirical study your experience would give you something of an outlook and general approach—you might say an hypothesis as to what the nature of the functioning of an institution would be; its effects, strengths, checking yourself as to whether you have the facts and whether you have reasoned correctly about them."

He looked on intellectual work as a collaborative process. He said that when he was writing something, he would think of someone who was a master in that field and he would say to himself "I wonder what J. M. Clark or Gerhard Colm or some other person would think of this, and I would check my writing against what they had written or I would get their ideas on what I had written. When possible, I would confer with them." This led us to the problems of group research. Nourse thought there was a danger in team research that workers would lose their individuality and initiative. He was concerned with the growth of diploma mills and Ph.D. factories and thought that it was a shortcoming of the profession that more emphasis was not given to the encouragement of independent original research work.

Nourse believed that there was a need for social science to provide a harness for the natural sciences. He said that the dominant effort in economics for the last hundred years was "to ape the natural sciences and try to get the same degree of precision, and the same methods of demonstration, proof, and prediction that was then regarded as possible for the physical and biological sciences." Remarking that "now, even the natural sciences are taking probability in place of absolute proof," he saw a division between economists who wanted to be natural science economists and those who wanted to be social science economists. He said: "The latter want to make economics basically scientific while recognizing that it doesn't have the mechanistic qualities that natural science has."

In response to my question, "What do you stand for as an economist?" he said:

> I stand for the institutional position as I interpret it in economics. I am interested in the institutions which we have set up as a framework of our economy which we have built up out of ideologies and psychological reactions. This is all tinged with a heavy pragmatic tone that doesn't have anything like the precision or rigidity of mechanical processes or the predictability of mathematical manipulations. I consider that the social scientist uses the scientific approach to phenomena which cannot be simplified or quantified as in the natural science fields. Instead of an exposure toward mathematics it has an exposure toward philosophy, a most imprecise side of human learning.

Nourse realized that institutional economics was not the dominant school of economics. He said: "It has been definitely subordinated to the

Cambrian fiscal, monetary, cycle theory." He thought that business cycles did not have behaviors, that only people—groups—have behaviors. He agreed with Ed Mason of Harvard that institutional economics was a component part of current economics, and said: "While it has not been absorbed, it has not lain sterile." He hoped that in the period ahead it would come more into its own.

He traced his own evolution as an institutional economist to his interest in history, which made him concerned with seeing economic institutions in their historical or evolutionary setting. He was further encouraged along this line by his work in sociology and political science. He thought that these subjects provided a good foundation for being an economist and said: "Many of our mechanistic and mathematical economists suffer from the lack of it."

He was impressed with the close relationship of law to economics, and he had found it necessary to concern himself with legal institutions in his studies of cooperative organizations. Looking backwards, he thought that a better title for his book, *The Legal Status of Agricultural Cooperation*, would have been "The Legal and Economic Foundations of Agricultural Cooperation." He greatly admired the legal thinking of Holmes, Brandeis, Cardoza, and Stone, and he was particularly impressed with the contribution of Earl Warren. He said: "I believe Earl Warren is going to go down in history as a great Chief Justice not because he is, in the traditional sense, a great jurist, but because he has brought a somewhat different emphasis into the contribution of the Supreme Court. He has freed the Court from some of the travails of its old legalism under due process and has made interpretation of the public interest a factor in decisions which shape the course of judicial precedent." He realized that many people of traditional legal training and legalistic outlook objected to this view. "You know," he said, "the tremendous protest that under his leadership sociological considerations rather than legal principles governed the segregation decision of '54." Nourse liked an expression in the *New York Times* that the Court had undergone a change from being "custodian of the nation's property" to becoming "trustee of the national conscience." He said: "I think that is the essence of Warren's place on the Court, and I think that will be his important place in history."

In speaking of his favorite economists, he referred to Alfred Marshall and John Stuart Mill as being "congenial to me." He also had great respect for A. C. Pigou and his *Economics of Welfare*. He said that in a sense, John A. Hobson was the "intellectual daddy of what we did at Brookings on the Price and Income books." Turning to American economists, he placed John Maurice Clark "right up to the head of my list" because of his social science approach. He also had a very high regard for Wesley Clair Mitchell because of his social science point of view. He admired the institutional economics writings of John R. Commons and said: "I would have been very happy if I could have incorporated him in my graduate training period." He thought his long association in the Social Science Research Council with top-flight men in the various social sciences had been an invaluable influence on his professional development.

Nourse felt that the approbation of his colleagues had been a driving force in his career. One friend had said that what keeps people going is affection. Nourse thought that he would use the word "recognition" rather than affection. However, he said that it was quite heartwarming when his own alma mater—the University of Chicago—conferred on him the Rosenberger Medal.

I was often struck by his use of words or phrases to give precision to his meaning. Once when he had used the phrase "by the vicissitudes of politics," I enquired how he had acquired his vocabulary. I asked him whether this was something he had worked on conscientiously. He responded by saying:

> I do take pains with my writing. I ponder whether a given word really conveys the idea I'm trying to express. I use a dictionary quite freely and when I go to the dictionary, I don't just grab out one definition. I look at the synonyms and antonyms and I look at the etymological derivation of the word. I may say that I take a good deal of care in honing down the verbal tools that I use in my craft. The mathematicians make a great deal out of the precision of mathematical symbols and the equations into which they put those symbols. In general, they take a rather contemptuous or condescending (that's a better word) attitude toward "literary" economists. My philosophy is just the opposite—that we have two means of communication, one by verbal symbols and one by mathematical symbols. And I am concerned to see that my expository or argumentative equations (if you please) use verbal symbols precisely and put them in relationships which move us toward a solution of the problem we're dealing with.

How Others Saw Him

From the foregoing chapters it is apparent that Nourse was a well-liked and highly respected man throughout his professional life. This was attested by those who worked with him as he advanced from one position to another. The admiration of his colleagues was reflected in his election to the presidency of the American Farm Economic Association and the American Economic Association and the chairmanship of the Social Science Research Council. He was held in high esteem by those whom he came in contact with—business, farm, and labor leaders, members and officials of cooperative organizations, lawyers, scientists, government officials, colleagues and students, and others whom he met in all walks of life. To convey some idea of how his contemporaries saw him, I am here drawing on the recollections of several associates who knew him well in various capacities.

One who formed a close attachment to Nourse in the early days of the Brookings Institution was Lewis L. Lorwin, who was then writing his classic book *The American Federation of Labor*. Nourse took a great interest in this book, for he thought its concept of collective bargaining might be adapted to the cooperative marketing practices of American farmers. From 1932 to 1934, Lorwin conducted a round table seminar on social and economic planning which brought together government experts, trade association executives, and others interested in this subject. Lorwin later recalled that "Nourse was the only member of the Brookings hierarchy who came to these meetings and he was the speaker at one of them." As a fellow member of the Brookings Council, Nourse impressed him by "his manner, his light touch, his earthy humor, and his good common sense." Based upon his association with Nourse at the Brookings Institution and his contacts afterwards, Lorwin said: "My image of Edwin G. Nourse is that of a kindly, generous man, with a keen sense of justice, wise in his judgments, humorous in the expression of his thoughts arrived at on the basis of careful and competent scholarship, a man close to earth —a realist—and yet moved by large human ideals and values" (Letter to author, December 10, 1963).

John K. Anderson, as manager of publications for the Brookings Institution, maintained almost daily contact with Nourse from 1929 to 1946. Following Nourse's death, he recalled the pleasure of this relationship.

> During all the years of our association I was constantly surprised by the breadth of his knowledge and the balanced perceptiveness of his decisions. He always took the broad view, but never overlooked the small points which, if not considered, might lead to knotty problems later on. In discussion meetings his was often the calm comment that led to an orderly and acceptable decision. During the formative years of the Brookings Institution "E. G." maintained a steady pace, always producing pioneer articles or books in his special field. He was the strong right arm for our President, Harold G. Moulton. A real scholar, a gentleman, and a great economist— that is the way I shall always remember my valued friend—Dr. Nourse [Letter to author, June 28, 1974].

In Chapter XII, I quoted Fred Waugh's high assessment of Nourse as an administrator. Few people had a better opportunity to evaluate Nourse, and few were so well equipped to do so. For many years he had worked closely with him on various marketing problems, and he was the first person invited by Nourse to serve on the top staff of the Council of Economic Advisers. In writing to me on June 29, 1964, he summed up Nourse's economic philosophy as follows:

> Above all Nourse has faith in economic education. He sees that no group, whether farmers, wage earners, or businessmen, can prosper for long by actions that hurt others. He knows that enlightened self-interest calls for prosperity and employment throughout the economy without inflation. Being a strong advocate of democracy, he is most anxious that all citizens have some understanding of economics so that they will support an effective program to avoid depressions, to encourage economic growth, and to maintain a satisfactory distribution of purchasing power. He is an advocate of government economy and . . . yet, he never insisted on an annual balanced budget at all costs. He is a strong supporter of private enterprise. Yet, he favors a strong government, with a flexible economic program that can be quickly adjusted to changing needs.

Another of Nourse's close associates on the Council of Economic Advisers was Gerhard Colm. The aspect of Nourse that most impressed him was his fairness and open-mindedness. He expressed this as follows:

> When Dr. Nourse invited me to join his staff he knew that I was perhaps a bit more of a "Keynesian" than he was. However, he said that he would not expect me to join his staff unless I was assured that I could have some impact on the work of the Council. All through the years of our cooperation there was an occasional difference in emphasis, he being a bit more conservative than I am. Nevertheless, he always lived up to what he told me at the beginning. He gave me ample opportunity to express my views. We had lots of discussions but I would not remember any instance in which a difference on emphasis developed into an unpleasant argument. In short, what I try to say is that I learned to respect Dr. Nourse not only as a scholar but also as a gentleman through and through [Letter to author, May 14, 1964].

Joseph L. Fisher, who became President of Resources for the Future, Inc., and later United States Congressman from Virginia, was recruited by Nourse to work on natural and human resources development problems for the Council of Economic Advisers in 1947. He recalled how Nourse was always eager to have him participate in interagency study groups. "I realized that I was dealing with a broad-gauged economist interested in human and social problems, technology, and the scientific aspects of natural resources. I think a more traditional and narrower economist would not have opened up the work of the Council of Economic Advisers and the Presidential Economic Reports to broad study of the human aspects of natural resources" (Letter to author, July 2, 1973). Fisher continued his friendship with Nourse up to the time of Nourse's death, and at the memorial service for Nourse he said: "Kind, generous, broad in outlook, professional, thoughtful, a pioneer into his seventies and eighties, Dr. Nourse was one of the considerable economists of this century. Those of us who worked with him were always his colleagues, including the younger ones, perhaps especially the younger ones, which added to our sense of worth and to the affection in which we held the man."

Of particular interest is the assessment of Leon Keyserling, who worked closely with Nourse in establishing the Council of Economic Advisers. At the time of Nourse's death he wrote to Nourse's son as follows:

> Despite some sensational exaggeration in the press during the 1940's when your father and I were together on the Council of Economic Advisers, our relationship was always pleasant. Moreover, our only important disagreement was with respect to the political science issue of whether the Council should testify before Congress, and even about this we never quarreled. Far more important, we were in agreement on most economic issues, and I gained the highest regard for your father's knowledge and wisdom as an economist.
>
> Your father was certainly not really a "conservative" economist as that term is generally used, and here again the reporting in the press has been at fault. He certainly did not disbelieve in the vigorous use of fiscal and monetary policies by the Government. But he differed from many of the Keynesians, and I agreed with him as he well knew, in that he did not hold the naive notion that fiscal and monetary policy could work unless the adjustments of prices and wages and profits in the private economy were reasonably in balance. All subsequent experience has vindicated his position, and has proved that he had a much broader view than most economists when he was active. I should add only that your father was certainly favorable to the need for social programs to help the unfortunate and unprotected. And he was always a delightful person to work with, respecting the views of others even while he had conferences in his own [Letter to J. Tyler Nourse, April 11, 1974].

Nourse had a very high regard for Paul Hoffman's leadership of the Committee on Economic Development and for his later work in international stabilization. In turn, Hoffman was very favorably impressed with Nourse's work as an economist. He later said:

> I have the greatest admiration for the contributions Dr. Nourse has made to our economic need. It was his pioneering work in the field of economic planning that gave entirely new respectability to this activity. When he took over as Chairman of President Truman's Economic Policy Board, the very word "planning" was looked upon with the deepest suspicion. By the competence of his endeavors, he proved that penetrating analysis of the state of the economy and sound planning fortified rather than vitiated our free enterprise system [Letter to author, May 22, 1963].

Karl Brandt, a Director of the Food Research Institute and a member of the Council of Economic Advisers in the 1950s, was proud of his relationship with Nourse. Writing me on December 20, 1963, he said:

> I have known Dr. Nourse for probably thirty years as a scholar whose contributions to knowledge were always far above the current of agricultural economists, whose thoughts had always the independence of

scholarly statesmanship. . . . When President Truman appointed him as the Chairman of the newly-formed Council of Economic Advisers, it simply was the natural selection of one of the wisest economists who had a thorough grasp of the whole range of issues in economic policy including the complex problems of agriculture. . . . It has been one of the really great privileges of my professional life to have had the encouraging support and confidence of this great scholar.

John W. Snyder, as Secretary of the Treasury, was a firm supporter of Nourse's work as Chairman of the Council of Economic Advisers. He expressed his high respect for Nourse as follows:

I considered Dr. Nourse's work on the Council of Economic Advisers as exemplary. Working with him on the economic programs of the day was both productive and refreshing. I believe that his efforts to establish the Council of Economic Advisers on a sound basis were continuously dedicated and inspirational in a very trying period. I would like to state that in my opinion Dr. Nourse exercised the soundest of positions on the economic questions facing the Council of Economic Advisers. I felt that he continually emphasized the importance of free competitive enterprise. He and I concurred completely on the necessity of maintaining a strong, sound economic position for our country, emphasizing that we could not do all the splendid things that the nation would like to do for its citizens and for its foreign allies if it permitted continual deficit financing in its fiscal affairs [Letter to author, June 7, 1975].

One who knew Nourse intimately for more than a third of a century was Raymond W. Miller, a past President of the American Institute of Cooperation and a nationally-known public relations counselor. To Miller, the outstanding quality of Nourse was integrity. He said to me in 1975: "Nourse was so ingrained with this concept of integrity that it dominated his thinking and made of him one of the most honored and respected men of his time. When he wrote a paper or a book or made an address or taught a class, he said what Ed Nourse thought and no one else. A man expressing the ideas he evolved from his God-given talents, was the Ed Nourse I knew and admired."

The impact that Nourse made on his associates in the field of cooperative enterprise was well expressed by J. Kenneth Stern, who was President of the American Institute of Cooperation from 1950 to 1969. Writing to me in 1974, he said: "My memories of Dr. Nourse are almost tempered with reverence for the man and his ideas. What he said was as true as if it came from the Bible. So many economists today get mixed up and confused by politics and changing times. Dr. Nourse was as solid as the Rock of Gibraltar."

Willard F. Mueller, Professor of Economics at the University of Wisconsin, came to know Nourse quite well when he was Chief Economist of the Federal Trade Commission in the 1960s. In a letter to me of January 2, 1974, he said:

Dr. Nourse has the unique quality of having made enduring contributions to many areas of economics; the field of cooperatives and agricultural economics, the field of industrial organization; and in his latter years to public policy formulation of macro economics. As one of the first members of the CEA he set an example in trying to keep "politics" out of the CEA. Yes, Dr. Nourse is one of those rare economists who has left an enduring imprint on many phases of our profession.

William H. Nicholls, Professor of Economics at Vanderbilt University and a staff member of the Council of Economic Advisers during the Eisenhower Administration, provides this terse assessment of Nourse's qualities:

My own impressions of Nourse were (a) his kindliness and loyalty in encouraging the work of younger men in fields of common interest; (b) his amazing breadth of knowledge and interests, making him not only an economist but a social scientist in the broadest sense of this word; (c) his intellectual and physical vigor even in the last twenty years of his life; (d) his gentlemanly mien, appearance, and behavior, which made him so attractive to non-professionals, especially those participating in his economic education programs; (e) his high qualities of "economic statesmanship" which (perhaps sometimes naively) he wished to attribute to business and labor leaders as well; (f) his basic mule-like stubbornness and persistence, which was very admirable in such broad matters of principle as his relations with President Truman during his Council chairmanship but which, for persons like myself with even small differences of approach or outlook from his own, at times became exhausting and even annoying despite the greatest of graciousness on his part [Letter to author, May 28, 1963].

Joseph J. Spengler, Professor of Economics at Duke University and a President of the American Economic Association, thought that Nourse set a standard for the economics profession. In writing me on June 18, 1973, he said:

My impression of Nourse was of a quiet, self-contained, judicious man who did not rattle easily and who carried conviction. I was always impressed with his work in support of flexible pricing—work far more important now that Big Trade Unions, Oligopolies, and Conglomerates have taken over control of the American economy and pursued policies calling in turn for bailing out by an inflation-minded Congress. I can think of no greater national need than flexible pricing and the removal of all institutional barriers to such pricing. . . . Careful inquiry, essential empiricism coupled with an adequate amount of theory, a sense of the country's institutional set-up, and a recognition that in the absence of flexible pricing the American economy could not function effectively—these seem to be the values and elements that permeate Nourse's work.

When Nourse wrote he wrote not only for the professional economist, but also for the intelligent layman even as Alfred Marshall did. He was not interested in shrouding his necessarily imperfect knowledge in the tongues of a technocratic Babel or in highly circumscribed models which abstracted out essential matter. Along with his effort to be clear was Nourse's companion effort to make it fairly easy for policy makers to picture options, selections which would make for material improvement. In essence Nourse was a statesman as well as an economist. . . . We as a profession might do well to emulate his insightful yet always humble approach.

James Washington Bell, longtime Secretary of the American Economic Association, had a close working relationship with Nourse for many years. In a letter of August 2, 1963, he said:

> Ed is a competent scholar; everything he does reflects ability and experience. He is cooperative and industrious, diligent and painstaking; he is friendly and likeable, trustworthy and inspires confidence; he is effective and resourceful and produces expected results. He is willing to compromise but not with insincerity nor self-aggrandisement—to wit: his clash of personalities with his associates on the CEA. Ed has qualities which any scholar or scientist must admire. I can only express a profound wish, namely, that all economists and political scientists in academic, business and political life were as honest, sincere, objective, non-selfseeking and able as Edwin G. Nourse. If we had more men like Ed in our Universities and in business and government posts then this would indeed be a superb economy, a happy society and a better world.

Bell softened his accolade by saying: "Ed did have a sense of dry humor, and enjoyed a joke even when he was the butt of it, but his reserved dignity and self-effacing manner was a bit disarming when it came to horse-play."

Among Nourse's ardent disciples was M. L. "Moe" Frankel, President of the Joint Council on Economic Education, who worked intimately with him from 1952 up to the time of Nourse's death. Writing me on June 6, 1973, he said: "I became a student whenever I was in his presence. But this was only a small part of the warmth, the incitement, the judiciousness, the integrity and high values that were part and parcel of Ed." He enumerated Nourse's contributions to economic education and the work of the Joint Council as follows:

> (1) He enthusiastically lent his support, his leadership and his counsel to the formation of the Joint Council. (2) The original guidelines "objectivity, nonpartisan and nonpolitical activity, academic freedom and responsibility" are attributable to Ed. (3) The concept of "Joint" in our name and its reflection in the make-up of the Council was another good idea he brought to our philosophy. (4) His work as Vice Chairman helped weld together a diverse group into a unified body. (5) He never missed a meeting, and set an example in his unflagging interest in the work of the Joint Council. (6) He helped guide the Council through many difficult decisions. He helped establish its publications policy. (7) He was a tireless worker. His prolific writings on economic education were invaluable. (8) He recognized the need for integrating economics in all courses in schools. (9) He enlisted the support of the American Economic Association which led to partnership of the AEA and the Joint Council.

Monroe Newman, Professor of Economics at Pennsylvania State University, enjoyed a rich and intimate friendship with Nourse during the last 15 years of Nourse's life. In speaking at Nourse's memorial service, he expressed his understanding of Nourse as a man in the following words:

Edwin Nourse was an educator who saw in education one of the paramount institutions of human evolution. He was convinced that education could further human progress by informing today about the options for tomorrow built on the experience of yesterday. . . . His self concept did not require the grandstand play of public pronouncement. Rather his philosophy of social science, social service, and social evolution required the careful demarcation of the boundaries between analysis and advocacy, between commitment to an institution and a process and a goal, and commitment to an individual or a group or an office. To live his philosophy required courage, and he was a courageous man. He could look life in the eye and, as a realistic analyst, he could see its majesty and its mis-step, its vitality and its venality, and still be an optimist who . . . could repeatedly assert *I Must Believe*. His courage enabled him to look death in the eye and face its prospect alone and blind, if need be.

Edwin Nourse was the imposing patriarch of warm and human fatherly sentiments; a man of wit, robust humor, and zest for living. He was confidently modest and never was convinced in his innermost self that he could be awesome, physically or intellectually or morally. . . .

Edwin Nourse was forever inquisitive, forever wanting to know the changing values of his fellows and particularly of the young. We went with him to the National Collection of Fine Arts when it opened a few years ago and inwardly wondered how he was reacting to the modern non-objective art we found on display. To our pleasured amazement he appreciated it, and helped us appreciate it, and revealed to us for the first time his responsibility for the creation of some of the art work in his home. He wanted to see the latest plays and movies. He did not approve of all he saw and actively speculated on their significance. . . . His was a young, incisive, expanding mind and intellect at 90.

His last major project was, characteristically, a book intended for the young. . . . Edwin Nourse was a painter with words, and he was the ultimate humanist who lived his humanism. One of his great joys over the years was to work on this book, and one of our greatest joys was to see how his mind evolved and perfected his ideas.

During the last two years of his life, Nourse was increasingly dependent for services and companionship on his secretary, Mrs. Peggy Gagan, and his part-time housekeeper, Mrs. Elizabeth Gerald. Mrs. Gagan remembers Nourse as a "truly remarkable man. He had an incredible memory with almost total recall of events that had occurred many years previously. He was totally 'with it' in his outlook, keeping up to date with modern thought and ideology. This was evident in the way young people loved to talk with him just as he did with them. To him they were persons with views and ideas to be respected" (Letter of May 26, 1977). Mrs. Gerald recalls how Nourse would talk to her of his "unceasing efforts to help black people improve their image through higher education" and of people they knew in common. She said: "Although he was wholly preoccupied with the writing of his book, he still liked to hear a little 'local gossip' about what was happening in the neighborhood. He was a dear man, not at all a cantankerous old man. . . . I remember my time with

Dr. Nourse with great pleasure and happiness" (Letter of April 6, 1977).

These various impressions provide some insight into the man as he lived and worked. He was a gentleman and scholar of the old school who always tried to do what he thought was right. I think all will agree that he was no ordinary person.

Contributions and Accomplishments

I once asked Nourse what he would like to be remembered for. In response, he said that he hoped that he would be thought of as something of a pioneer in helping adapt our economic and social system to the rapidly changing needs of the twentieth century. From my own examination of his career, I believe his contributions and accomplishments can be grouped under 12 interrelated headings.

1. *Agricultural Economics*: He established his reputation in this field. It is significant that he produced the first well-rounded textbook in agricultural economics and that his incisive writings and addresses and his inspiring personal leadership broadened the scope and significance of this subject. His effective work in building a well-rounded department of agricultural economics at Iowa State University led to his presidency of the American Farm Economic Association and national leadership among agricultural economists. His eminence as an agricultural economist was recognized in 1957, when the American Farm Economic Association named him as one of the first Fellows of the Association.

2. *Economics*: Although Nourse built his professional reputation as an agricultural economist, he was broadly trained as a general economist, and he always considered himself an economist with a special interest in agriculture. His competence as a general economist was recognized when he was made Director of the Institute of Economics of the newly formed Brookings Institution in 1928. The output of the Institute of Economics in economic literature, including several books written by Nourse, was so outstanding that he was elected President of the American Economic Association in 1942. By then he had become nationally known for his studies of industrial organization and low-price policy which recognized the social responsibility of business leadership. No economist has done more to champion and give meaning to the concept of free competitive enterprise. As the first Chairman of the Council of Economic Advisers from 1946 to 1949, he did much to help harmonize government and business economic policies.

3. *Cooperative Organization and Operation*: Nourse's studies of agricultural economic problems led him into the field of agricultural coopera-

tion. He was one of the first to understand that the industry of farming could only be developed on an effective basis through integrated cooperative associations which brought farmers together in strong business organizations. His pace-setting studies of cooperative enterprises in the 1920s and 1930s gained for him national standing as an outstanding theorist and exponent of cooperative organization and operation and exerted great influence on the character of cooperative advancement. He was one of the founders of the American Institute of Cooperation in 1925, and he provided unique leadership to this organization for many years. In 1968 the American Institute of Cooperation recognized his creative activities in helping build strong cooperative organizations through the establishment of an annual Nourse award of $1,000 "for distinguished and scholarly research and the best doctoral dissertation by a Ph.D. candidate on a subject relative to U.S. agricultural cooperatives." In 1975 the Cooperative League of the U.S.A. recorded his name in its Cooperative Hall of Fame.

4. *Marketing Theory and Practice*: Nourse was one of the first economists to recognize marketing as a separate field for economic enquiry. His doctoral thesis at the University of Chicago in 1915 was an empirical study of the Chicago Produce Market, and it provided a foundation for later studies of the marketing process. While his major contributions in marketing were related to cooperative organizations, he maintained a broad interest in the entire marketing field. His book *Marketing Agreements under the AAA* has helped guide the marketing agreement program of the U.S. Department of Agriculture to the present day. Nourse believed that marketing was a neglected area in economic thinking, and he emphasized its importance while Chairman of the Council of Economic Advisers.

5. *Research Administration*: Nourse was not only a scholar in the field of economics. He was also an effective administrator of economic research programs. He demonstrated his capacity to devise, supervise, and coordinate programs of economic and social research while at Iowa State University, and he expanded this capacity at the Brookings Institution and at the Council of Economic Advisers. He imparted his enthusiasm to others and enlisted the cooperation of those working with him. His own high standards influenced those with whom he came in contact, and he was able to delegate responsibility and select the right persons for specific tasks. He developed team spirit among his colleagues, for he gave them opportunities to express themselves and he saw that they received recognition for their contributions. As an administrator, he understood the involved human factors, and he was critical of bureaucratic procedures and complex administrative machinery.

6. *Educator in Economics*: Nourse was a natural teacher. He believed in the importance of education in the field of economics. He thought the purpose of research in economics was to find the answers to problems and that the end product of research should be its application in education. He considered it essential to train the public and particularly young people in what he called "economic literacy." He looked upon his writings as materials for educational use. All of his work was designed to improve the knowledge of others. When he resigned from the Council of Economic Advisers, his first thought was to carry on a program of economic enlightenment, and he found in the Joint Council on Economic Education an instrument to carry on this mission. As he neared the end of his life, his main concern was to finish a book that would give guidance to coming generations.

7. *Social Science*: Nourse looked upon himself as a social scientist, and he sought to apply social science thinking to the field of economics. His interest in social science was kindled when he was a student at Cornell University and a graduate student at the University of Chicago. From 1926 to 1945 he actively participated in the work of the Social Science Research Council, of which he was chairman from 1942 to 1945. It is significant that his last professional effort was to be devoted to a book designed to improve understanding of social science and gain recognition for its potential importance. Few have done more to further the cause of social science and apply it to the improvement of our national life.

8. *Economic Historian*: Trained as a historian in college, Nourse looked at economic and social problems in the light of their historical roots. He grounded his thought on the experience of the past, and his books and articles show his mastery in this field. Nourse was a proponent of his concurrent history conception that data for future historians should be gathered while an event or development was taking place. His studies of contemporary institutional developments have proven of great value because they were made with an understanding of the historical past with an eye on the historical future. It was Nourse's belief that an investigation of an economic institution "must be grounded on patient and fearless study of its past as well as its present manifestations and disinterested discussion of the issues on their merits."

9. *Organizational Builder*: Nourse realized that organizations must be created and supported if desirable objectives were to be carried forward. He took a great interest in helping set up and maintaining organizations to achieve attainable ends, and he endeavored to build them solidly. Among the organizations that benefited from his continuing interest and care were the American Economic Association, the American Farm Economic

Association, the American Institute of Cooperation, the National Council of Farmer Cooperatives, the Social Science Research Council, and the Joint Council on Economic Education. When he became Chairman of the Council of Economic Advisers, he saw it as an opportunity to build an efficient economic advisory service for the benefit of the nation, and after his term as chairman, he did all in his power to further the objectives of this agency as set forth by the Employment Act of 1946.

10. *Political Science*: As a social scientist, Nourse realized that there was a close relationship between economics and political science. It was apparent to him after World War I that the economic problems of the nation—agricultural and industrial—could not be divorced from government policy, and many of his studies examined the governmental machinery that influenced economic conditions—the Federal Farm Board, the Farm Credit Administration, and the Agricultural Adjustment Act. He felt that economists working in the public interest had to understand the political environment that confronted them. He considered the establishment of the Council of Economic Advisers a vital experiment in political science as well as in applied economics, and as its first chairman he took pains to relate the meaning of the Employment Act to political theory and practice. It is significant that he gave his book *Economics in the Public Service* the subtitle "Administrative Aspects of the Employment Act."

11. *Economic Theory*: It should be noted that Nourse was not greatly interested in economic theory as an abstract subject. He was more concerned with the application of economic analysis to specific problems. However, one should not overlook his contributions to economic theory. His 1919 article in the *Quarterly Journal of Economics*, "Normal Price as a Market Concept," helped set the stage for the advancement of marketing studies. He was a close student of price policy, and he developed a pragmatic theory of pricing. He applied the idea of collective bargaining to the whole economic process. He helped refine the theory of business organization, with emphasis on the social responsibility of business leadership. He did much to help clarify the concept of free competitive enterprise. As Murray Benedict, one of his longtime friends, has observed: "He was an all-around able economist who brought sound principles of economics to bear on many important national problems."

12. *Economic Literature*: A record of Nourse's contributions and accomplishments would not be complete without referring to the importance of his writings. Nourse wrote to be explicit and understandable. His distinctive and readable prose did much to raise the literary level of the economics profession, and it brought sound thinking to many who

otherwise would not have been interested in economic problems. His 12 books and many articles provide a treasure-trove of information which can be drawn on for the guidance of future generations.

* * * * * *

It is impossible to assess the ultimate importance of any man in his own lifetime. In the perspective of history—if the world escapes the holocaust of nuclear war—is it not reasonable to think that Nourse's name will stand out as one of the great creative economic, social, and perhaps moral leaders of the United States during the twentieth century?

Appendices

Appendix A

I MUST BELIEVE

A Triptych by Edwin G. Nourse

I

I must believe that God is Life
Since cells appeared where had been
Only cooling crust or barren sea,
After the swirl of flaming gas;
Since plants of simplest form and dullest mien
In time took on the glory of effulgent bloom,
With fruits that nourished, stems and leaves that sheltered
Higher forms of living things;

Since plants found motion (of a sort) that helped them live;
Burrowing to the hidden damp that, sucking up,
They married to the fecund sun with midwife air
To work the miracle of growth;
Creeping, vine-length by vine-length, to possess a larger living space.
Or—trusting, patient, to generations new—
Migrating as air-borne seed or stream-borne slip
To pioneer the barren land, ameliorate its half-born soil;
Indomitably fruitful, to multiply and populate.

I must believe that God is Life
Since creatures lately risen from the slime—
All sludgy yet—impatient proved;
And bridged in time the span from rooted life to muscled locomotion,
Not passive adaptation;
Since sentient, moving, choosing beasts—
With many a straggler species left behind
To vanish or accept a role vicarious to higher forms of life—
At length achieved a prototype of God on earth
An animal that could reason, that could aspire,
That can create—and can destroy.

II

I must believe that God is Mind
Since instinct life soared up to power of thought.
Above mud-wasp and nesting bird.
Above the woodsman beaver and the chambering ant,
Arose man-the-builder, with gift from God
To be himself, in ever-larging crafts, creator.
Not long content to pile up Nature's stones in rude abode and temple,
From some mysterious inner dream, he shaped those piles
To lines imposing and to chiselled beauty.

Nor did he find him long content merely to tan and braid,
To plainly spin and simply weave the fibres that he found at hand.
From somewhere came the urge to pigment bright
And pattern with imagined beauty,
Till clothing more than meets the call of comfort's need;
Both shrines a mystic modesty and stirs a subtle provocation,
Whilst beautied hangings and symbolic vestments
Speak out the wakened soul of man.

I must believe that God is Mind
Since, above mere animal grunt and warning cry of beasts,
Beyond mating call of bird and wailing bleat of young,
The human species was vouchsafed the miracle of ordered speech;
Devised written symbols for constituent sounds
And gave to thought the needed tool
To traffic in ideas and so to grow as conscious being;
Find meaning in the past experience of the race
And their depictions of imagined realms of soul.

I MUST BELIEVE

I must believe that God is Mind
Since from aeons' plod of slowly growing craft
To work his will on objects seen and handled
There burst a forward rush of power to master by more subtle technics
Vast forces that man could neither hear nor see, to touch was death.
Inside the smallest grasp of microscope,
Outside the farthest reach of Palomar's lens,
With revelation from radio wave and cosmic ray,
Through thought he harnessed power to break his chains to earth
And reached a hand-breadth toward
The million-galaxied realm of space and endless time
(both abstract concepts of his finite mind)
To limn a vision of God's other-worlds more valid
Than the opulent dreams of John on Patmos Isle.

Thus man grows large enough to see how finite small he is
Within the infinitely great;
Yet feels the kinship sure between his growing mind and God.
And so, himself a fleeting spark of that great Mind,
He gains the grace to feel a sense of awe
Of what is—and must remain—beyond his ken,
And stubbornly insists that life shall have a meaning;
To find it is his Holy Grail.
With inner urge to seek it out,
He walks his laboring days on earth
In proud humility as son of God.

III

I must believe that God is Love
Since love it is that raises humankind farthest above the beast.

After the primal biologic urge that gave the rude mechanics
Of life's renewal, there flowered and towered
The slow-perfecting sacrament of man-and-woman mating.
Beyond the fecund instinct of hatching bird
And vixen fetching home her kill to feed her young
There bloomed, in slowly-moving time,
The spiritual bonds of mother-love
That trains the young in body, mind, and spirit.
Beyond promiscuous mating or the season's call to breed,
Man learned the arts of gentle wooing and mutual choice,
Routing the marriage broker and the yoke of royal houses
For purposes of state or fortune spliced to fortune.
And from the loving tie of man and woman, child and parent,
Grew up the family circle of gentle discipline and free God-worship;
Parental sacrifice to give each rising generation
A better life than had the last,
And grateful urge through all of life to pay—in help to others—
A debt to parents gone and all who toiled to build our heritage.

I must believe that God is Love
Since man's humanity to man
Stops not at bonds of blood and cousins close
But reaches out beyond the line of color, speech, and creed;
Beyond the prideful line of tribal power,
To learn the loving loyalty of patriot to motherland
And nations federated to the betterment of man—
The earthly manifest of God's domain.

'Tis love alone that keeps the egocentric urge to live and master
From being a prison of the individual soul
And death-warrant of all humankind.
For man, unleashed upon his world through power of mind,
Would be no more than prattling, dressed-up, ravaging beast
Had he not been dowered with the fire divine of love,
That blooms in sacrifice, in service, and in seeking out
That "something outside ourselves that makes for righteousness."

Appendix B

THE "UNFINISHED SYMPHONY"

As Nourse worked on the social science book he prophetically called it his "unfinished symphony." Struggle as he would, he could not finish it before his death. This is greatly regretted, for the chapters that were completed promised a book with rich insights into the applicability of social science to the major problems of our times.

Since it is doubtful that Nourse's thinking on social science as expressed in the manuscript will ever be available in book form, it seems desirable to provide here a brief abstract of its contents as it neared completion. He then envisaged a book with two main parts. Part I, in seven chapters, would explain the meaning and significance of social science. Part II, in five chapters, would show the evolution of social science thinking in economics, politics, and sociology, and deal with two serious current problems—ethnic alienation and the generation gap.

As explained in Chapter XV, Nourse increasingly saw his book as a primer for young people, and he wanted to attract their attention. He therefore was planning to name the book "Shoot If You Must!" and use as a subtitle "A Veteran Social Scientist's Response to the Now Generation."

In his first chapter, "Science a Seamless Web," Nourse endeavored to convey the meaning of the word "science." His opening sentences declared: "Science weaves a seamless web of Man's hard-won understanding of his world and himself. It is a stout and richly-patterned fabric having three distinguishable breadths—physical science, biological science and social science—but no selvage edges." He maintained that science is better described than rigorously defined and that "the historical description of Pan Science can be seen as a triangulation of scientific atitude, scientific methods, and scientific scope or findings. . . ." He thought the scientific *attitude* "of insatiable curiosity, diligence in the amassing of evidence, open-mindedness to new hypotheses, and caution in the drawing of conclusions apply universally to all who aspire to the dignity and service of science." He did not find such universality in scientific *method*, since "techniques of exploration, instruments of discovery, and logic of interpretation must be adapted to the particular subject matter, physical, biological, or social." While "elaborate and precise instruments of discovery and measurement are essential in the physical field, subtle means for gaining intellectual and spiritual insight are no less essential in the field of societal life." He considered the *scope* of Pan Science to be as wide as human curiosity.

Nourse then explained what was involved in the physical and biological sciences and showed how they were intimately interrelated to the social sciences, which he termed "the sciences of human togetherness." He indicated that the social sciences "study the structures of legal compact and community convention that people set up in their pursuit of happiness and efficiency. These social institutions and behaviors constitute the man-made culture that synthesises the community's economic, political, educational, juridical, religious, artistic, and recreational activities." He said: "My own understanding of this domain of thought and action and my personal interpretation of the nature of the social scientist's vocation reflect my seventy years as student, teacher, practitioner, critic, rebel, and designer."

He then presented "an overall look at the three conventional subdivisions of social science—economics, politics, and sociology. Economics," he said, has "traditionally been defined as the science of wealth; its sources, its expansion or erosion, its measurement, distribution, and protection of property rights, individual and community." He pointed out how the classical economists of the eighteenth and nineteenth centuries sought to emulate physical science by formulating mechanistic laws which, if understood and obeyed, would trend toward an automatic equilibrium of supply and demand in the prices of a free market. It was believed that "private enterprisers, doing what came naturally to promote their own interest, would best promote the total interest or wealth of the nation." He thought that twentieth century economics may better be described as "a social science of general welfare—material and psychic." He continued: "Instead of leaving the economic process to natural forces, it aspires, through skilled and prudent management, to bring the planet's resources of materials and energy to full fruition, to develop the varied capabilities of the whole population, and to evoke their active participation and cooperation. Instead of *laissez faire*, this is to be accomplished through painstaking engineering of community enterprise and national purpose. . . . Central government plays a greatly enlarged role through exercise of its innate fiscal, monetary, and regulatory powers." Thus he said: "Economics bridges into politics."

Nourse accepted the description of political science as "the science of power, individual, group or societary," in that "it examines acquisition or allotment and exercise of power, functional interrelationships, and need or means of containment." He said that "political scientists aspire to learn the principles of human competition and cooperation, of personal ambition, group tolerance, and human brotherhood that make civilization possible." He held that the scope of political science reached from the single acts of individuals to the largest conceivable pattern of world government.

Nourse saw the third and youngest branch of social science—sociology— "as the culminating and integrating science of intellectual and moral *values* that suffuses each ethnic or national way of life. It is thus a synthesizing discipline, complementing the elder sciences of wealth and power with its own investigations of other functional relationships such as education, jurisprudence, religion, recreation, and the fine arts. It aspires to promote understanding of these and other facets of group structures and behavior by which the total way of life may, more and more, move toward the Good Life for humankind. . . ." To Nourse it was the science of the total culture.

He also briefly described what he termed "two bridge sciences"—anthropology and psychology—in that they were related to both the natural and the social sciences. He said that *anthropology*, the science of Man, has "one solid abutment in the area of biological science, where ethnologists examine the physical and mental characteristics of the various races," and "another solid abutment in the area of social science, where cultural anthropologists examine the different races', tribes', nationalities' distinctive cultures, ancient and contemporary." He pointed out that the anthropologists "perceived that subsistence activities, trade, government, religion, and native crafts are all intermeshed parts of a people's way of life" and introduced or popularized the expression "culture—tribal, racial, or national." He classified *psychology* as a bridge science since it "has one end firmly anchored in biology's understandings of the physiological, chemical, and psychic properties of the human brain and nervous system and the other end implanted in the group behaviors of business, politics, and every department of societal life."

Nourse considered these bridge sciences of great importance.

> In its psychiatric phase, social psychology explores the sources of conjugal failures, racial and religious antagonism, crime waves, and generation gaps. The psychological mediation between management and labor, between bureaucracy and the individual, and between "the criminal element" and the agencies of rehabilitation is obvious. It, and also anthropology, should serve to bridge the chasm of misunderstanding or hatred between races or regional subcultures. They should also serve as bridges of reconcilement between the special interests of economic, political, or even religious factions and the policies and strategies of national solidarity. They help to explain the pathological nationalist behavior persisting or now mounting in India, Pakistan, Israel and its Arab neighbors, Ireland, Korea, and Vietnam.

He thought that history and statistics should be described as "science helpers," for they served all scientists. He saw them as technologies rather than as social sciences proper. He finished his chapter with this paragraph:

> As the scope of physical science runs from atomic structure to the infinities of limitless time and space; as biologic science runs from the inexplicable spark that lit the flame of life to the awesome capability of selective geneticists to guide the course of organic evolution; so the scope of social science spans the range of human life from the individual act to the ultimate balancing of world power between international capitalism, international laborism and sovereign nationalism.

In his second chapter, "Science and Technology: Of Nature and of Society,"

Nourse examined the interrelatedness of science and technology. He did not accept the commonly held view that "technology is applied science," since generally technology preceded the application of a science. He pointed out that

> a great body of sound operative method was developed by rank amateurs long before scientists were available to explain why these arts had been successful, and how they might be made more dependable and be given added potency and refinement. . . . It was not until the eighteenth and nineteenth centuries that science got the lead in its own hands. In several areas, practical technology came to the end of its rope, unable to solve some new problems by the methods of mere trial and error. . . . Fortunately at this juncture, the reserves of theoretical science came to the rescue.

This led to a "reciprocative or complementary relationship" between technology and science. As he summed it up, "science, both natural and social, is technology-feeding and technology-fed." Or, to express this differently, "technology in its varied fields of action is science-fed but also science-feeding."

Nourse found the social sciences uniquely endowed with a fourth dimension of intellectual choice or moral value. He said: "They share the scientific code and manual of objective attitude, meticulous measurement, vigorous analysis of data, disciplined but courageous hypotheses, guarded generalization, and repetitive testing." But because of the difference of their subject matter, "they require special methods of investigation and interpretation and their own ways of formulating their findings. Unlike natural scientists," Nourse said, "social scientists undertake to deal objectively with the subjective phenomena of life. They analyze consumers' preference and producers' enterprise and acquisitive urge; politicians' and voters' wants. . . ." He then examined some of the techniques and methods peculiar to social science, such as the community survey, model building, and the opinion poll. He concluded his chapter by saying:

> It may seem that the methodology of social science is primitive and feeble as compared with the elaborate, precise, and powerful instrumentation and rigorous analytical and synthesizing techniques of the natural sciences. But the labors of discovery directed by social scientists toward understanding the complex and everchanging societal process are met half way by the processes of self-revelation constantly operating in the fields of economic, political, and other social action. Social science, because it deals not with the inarticulate orders of nature but with Man's mental-spiritual character, pursues methods of discovery distinctively its own and seeks to arrive at principles helpful to the individual in joint action with his fellows.

Nourse called his third chapter "The Distinctive Character of Social Science." He opened it by saying: "The phenomena and problems on which social science seeks enlightenment are those of the individual in group action. . . . It might even be said that social science is the scientific treatment of social variety and change—hallmarks of the human species." To him, society was "an artifact of creative humankind. Whereas, the subject matter of the natural sciences is the discovery and delivery of the rich stores of knowledge from Nature's quarry and mine, the social sciences are concerned with Man the architect as he builds and continually rebuilds the domicile, the workshop, and the temple of his early living."

He did not find any "real intellectual discontinuity between the life sciences and the social sciences [since] the latter simply move on from the analytical study of the human animal at the instinctive level to comparably systematic and analytical study of the organizations and practices that *he develops* for the amelioration and enrichment of the common lot." He recognized that "the social structures we erect in this process are unstable as compared with the enduring architecture of the physical universe. They are evanescent, as we abandon what we find was inept or what has become unworkable, as we shape our own evolution to enlarging knowledge and our expanding vision." Therefore, said Nourse, "the principles we derive [in the social sciences] have less universality than those of physical and even biological science," and the methods of investigation of social scientists "are distinctively their own."

He pointed out that in both the physical and biological sciences "the materials which are being explored and exploited are themselves passive, inarticulate or, in the nature of the case, disfranchised. They are clay in the hands of the potter. They cannot talk back to the scientific investigator, veto his program of manipulation, elude his instructions or commands, or challenge his findings." On the other hand, he said: "The subject matter of social science is human *life* . . . the sociologist, economist, or politicist, must grapple with the indomitable—indeed ever growing—complexities of associated human behavior."

He then said:

> Since the subject matter of social science is human, it follows that the methodologies of the social science must be humane. The sociologist may not dismember families or set up new domestic patterns in a community to suit his purposes of enquiry, however vital. The politicist cannot recast political structures and existing civil rights in various ways in order to test his theories of casual relationships or of social improvements. Nor can the economist redistribute a community's wealth or coerce business conduct in order to learn how the machine ticks or could be made to operate productively. He can only give professional advice.

He added: "Social science is committed to the quest for objective knowledge about subjective individuals and group behavior. It seeks to learn how self-conscious human beings erect and operate the organized apparatus of civilized economic, political, and cultural existence, why they behave as they do, and how individuals are conditioned by their social environment. To see these matters in the round, social science methodology relies heavily on statistical evidence, on psychological analysis, and also on organized dialogue between social theorists and articulate practitioners of associated human life."

Nourse held that social science moves forward—even as does natural science—on the pragmatic principle, "Does the given theory work in practice?" The answer could be found only through the process of negotiating and arriving at a consensus.

This line of thinking led to his conception of social science as "negotiative science." He said: "The core problem of societary life . . . becomes one of offsetting frustrations against achievement, and the task of social science begins with the finding of ways of identifying or defining categories of human interest to be served and of measuring, weighing, or rating any given one against others. It focuses on methodologies of evaluation and group choice, phenomena unknown to the physical sciences, and present only in rudimentary, instinctive form in the higher subhuman animal species."

Nourse saw "group choice as a—perhaps *the*—central factor in the social process." He thought that the vivid term "trade-offs" reflected the fact that no value "stands on its own bottom as an absolute or independently measured magnitude." Nourse saw trade-offs as pervasive in the determination of group choices, for each member of society must eventually face the necessity of giving up in some measure the thing he least requires to gain in some measure the thing he most desires. He said: "Practice of trade-offs constitutes the bootcamp in which to acquire the social discipline we know as consensus."

To him, the term "trade-offs" described equally well:

> (1) the elegant analytical process of which economic, political, and other social scientists invoke or derive theoretical principles in the computation of ideal programs in a universe of simplified assumptions and rational conduct; and (2) the cruder but more vital two-way discovery and mutual education in the continuing stream of business competition, political struggle, and the accommodations demanded by family life and all other interpersonal relations.

Nourse held that social science provides a rational approach to such questions as "How much and what kinds of freedom can most advantageously be traded off for what kind and degree of civil order and national growth and prestige? How much of private enterprise, creative and acquisitive, can wisely and safely be traded off for what desiderata of national economic efficiency, social security or human justice?"

He finished the chapter by saying: "A distinctive merit of the negotiative technology of the social sciences is that it recognizes the qualities and honors the aspirations of the individual at the same time, or in balance with, its recognition of the primacy of society."

His fourth chapter, "Individualism, Identity, Membership, Morals," which he subtitled "Self and Society," followed up on his interpretation of social science. He set the stage with the following introductory paragraph:

> To understand the edifice we call society, we need to gain progressively better understanding of the bricks and mortar of which it is constructed; the persons who make up its membership and the cohesions which hold them together. *But hold it!* That metaphor, though suggestive, is both imprecise and misleading. It implies that the units of the material are uniform in size, shape, and composition; and that there is a static character

in the total structure. Society is more like an elaborate mechanical apparatus whose working parts are different in shape and function but closely related in operation. *But again hold it!* Society is not just a machine. It is an association of human beings, different in character and function, but consciously adjusted to each other in a working process. Democratic societies are solicitous about the individual; individuals today have become increasingly solicitous about the individual; individuals today have become increasingly solicitous about themselves and aggressive as to their rights and the satisfaction of their wants.

In this chapter he examined the meaning and value of such concepts as "personal identity," "belonging," "constructive dissent," and "personal morals." He thought that personal morals "traced the spiritual profile of individualism," that the individual's moral sense grows with his education and accumulating experience, and that his moral code is not static but changing from infancy to full maturity.

He concluded this chapter by saying:

> Again and again the individual comes to the cross roads where he must decide whether he will conform to a law that he regards as morally wrong, obey under protest and a moral commitment to work for change, engage in civil disobedience and take the consequences, or resort to methods of surreptitious evasion. It is in the name of conscience that sensitive and highminded young folks alienate themselves from the prevailing industrial order, which they charge with being grossly materialistic, unjust, and repressive of individual rights, human dignity, or their personal "identity." The frequent and massive flouting of the law and custom among our youth and certain ethnic minorities in recent years should prompt fresh scrutiny of our understandings and beliefs about personal morals and their relation to social ethics.

In his Chapter V, "Social-ism: Tribal, National, International," he endeavored to make clear that his use of the word "social-ism" was not misunderstood. He explained that this hyphenated word was intended to bring out the distinction between social solidarity and the class concept of Marxism. He said it "pairs social-ism and individual-ism."

He introduced this chapter with two paragraphs:

> As individualism is a quite diverse pattern of personal choices and action for self-direction, so social-ism is a systematic but slowly changing pattern of community or national custom, policy, and action, conventionalized and/or legalized. This is a system of group direction: by the People in democracies, by the Party in communist countries and empires.
>
> Social direction had its beginning far back in the dawning of civilization. It was indeed the source and substance of their dawning. . . . Social organization moved on from mere instinct, unreasoned fumbling, and familial cohesion, to common purpose, reasoned planning, and programs of group action. The first manifestation of this development was the primitive tribe.

Nourse then examined tribalism as "the basic social institution" under the heading "From Biologic Fact to Social Artifact." He followed this with a section, "Tribalism Before Nationalism and After," which showed how nationalism grew out of tribalism while tribalism continued in various ways. From there he moved on to internationalism as a logical next step in social development. One manifestation of internationalism was the formation of multi-national corporations.

The final section of the chapter dealt with "Internationalism's Challenge to Human Nature." In this he said: "The United Nations may be viewed as the current prototype prospectus, or ideal draft, of an ultimate multi-national self-evolving apparatus of technical and sociological planning and school of harmonized human behavior." By 1945 "it seemed plausible that men of many nations could federate and function in a parliament of man." But he went on to add: "In the last analysis, however sociologically sound the purposes of the U.N. as an institution of inner-directed social evolution, and however well-designed and adaptable its structure, its success must ultimately depend on the moral leadership of outstanding individuals and the willingness of the masses to follow that leadership on an ascending and sometimes rocky road. The U.N. model of internationalism is and always will be in the spiritual predicament of personal morals and social ethics."

Nourse called his next chapter "Personal Morals and Social Ethics," and he subtitled it "From Individual Conscience to Social Science." Holding that personal morals and social ethics are the very essence of the theory and practice of democracy, he said: "Since the social process is polarized at the extremes of personal identity and social cohesion, it follows that democratic government will be similarly polarized between individual conscience and prevailing law and convention, or between personal morals and the social ethic." He looked upon "the social ethic [as] the culminating manifestation of the social process, derived from experience and animated by discussion, spiritual evaluation, and negotiated choice."

He saw social direction gradually evolving through discussion, negotiation, and mutual accommodation. He said: "The social ethic is a long accumulation of experience of successive generations in situations both routine and innovative." Out of the interplay of individuals and social groups he saw developing a recognition of social science as a means of improving man's estate.

However, Nourse found the world scene one of "massive contradiction," for "along with the wide expansion of international cooperation . . . there are still bitter clashes due to disparities of national conditions, with sharpening conflict between authoritarian communism and the democratic way of life." Moreover, in the domestic sector, with an enormous advance in the ideology and practice of welfare democracy, there is a continuation "of bitter in-fighting between special interests and between institutionally advantaged and disadvantaged classes." He thought the basic sociological issue for the next stage of social evolution would be: "Can a democratically self-perfecting human society surmount the materialism, selfishness, ignorance, and lethargy of voters, officials, and business managers?"

Nourse had great faith in the possibilities of social science as a means of

THE "UNFINISHED SYMPHONY"

solving the problems confronting the nation and the world. He expressed this faith in closing the chapter:

> Social science does not furnish individuals and organized groups with a set of mechano-mathematical laws and explicit rules of conduct which they have only to apply in any given instance. It does equip them with tools of measurement and analysis to quantify and qualify their reasoning, and elucidates criteria of evaluation and choice of action. Thus social science is comparable to the engineer's handbook and the philosophers' dialogues, a reference work to be consulted from day to day by all who seek seriously to give their lives full meaning and to make their best contribution to the salvation of the race.

He then said: "With this luminous horizon and advancing frontier of laborious revelation, social science becomes secular religion."

His Chapter VII, "Social Science as a Secular Religion," explained just what he had in mind. He recognized that by nature, man was a religious being as attested by history and archeology, and by modern anthropology and psychology. He said: "The most primitive folk sensed the presence of mysterious and mighty powers outside and above themselves. . . . As civilization advanced, religions of fear and punishment were modulated to one-god religions of omnipotent power, omniscient wisdom, and universal beneficence. Their theologies posited love between humanity and deity and among all members of the human family. This entailed service of person to person and of banded groups committed to the betterment of the race. . . ."

In time, philosophers arose who turned to "reason rather than yearning and instinct for the nurture of belief and the fortification of faith in the spiritual future of mankind's tenancy of earth. For them, such matters as direct revelation, divine intervention in human affairs, or the hope of a new life after physical death were subjects for continuing analysis and debate rather than personal longings and dogmatic assurances."

The development of natural science "only three or four centuries ago opened a new lane of intellectual travel . . . primarily concerned with things earthy or secular. It turned away from the personalized gods of love and hate and mere whim and an anthropomorphic God of episodic intervention in earthly processes and human affairs. Through inspired hypotheses, honest testing, and open-ended dicta, it seeks a progressively richer and truer cosmology of Nature's order and discernible means for avoiding or mitigating human catastrophies and for utilizing natural forces and materials for human purposes."

Then, "barely a century ago," the social sciences took shape as "an integrating movement toward a global science of self-evolving society." It extended "man's understanding of his own nature and capabilities for the orderly improvement of human life. . . . Economics rose from science of wealth to science of welfare; politics from science of power to science of human rights; education from rote learning to personality development; jurisprudence from precedent to social relevency. Beneficiated by psychology and anthropology, the social sciences began to coalesce into a comprehensive science (and technology) of self-evolving human life."

Nourse went on to say: "Social science is the student and the illuminator of the ubiquitous negotiative process by which individuals, interest groups, and nations find the common ground on which they can work together to achieve the largest, practicable fulfilment of their disparate desires. . . . The goals envisaged by social technologies, whether in public or private affairs, and their undergirding social science—common aspirations and personal commitment—are basically the same as those that have animated religions of many forms in all ages: salvation for the individual within the brotherhood of the group, achieved through the communion of its individual members. Social science would integrate—but differentiate—the total culture and the congeries of cultures that constitute human society."

"Social scientists," said Nourse, "no less than transcendental religionists stand in awe before the infinities that run 'from everlasting to everlasting' seeking to put man 'in tune with infinities.' As social science advances, mankind gains systematic and communicable knowledge about the mind and conscience of the individual and about the mysterious forces of common purpose and cohesive action of new generations conceiving ever higher goals of human life and the ultimate reality on earth of a full and honest brotherhood of man —our human or, if you prefer, divine estate."

"This," he explained, "is secular religion." He held that it "does not subvert or denegrate the aspirations or commitments of sacred religions, past, contemporary, or future." Rather, he said "does it reinforce and refine their aspirations for a good social life and furnish generally applicable instrumentation for their sincere practice and continuing growth."

Nourse himself was a deeply religious person. His own profession of faith was expressed in his triptych "I Must Believe," from which a few lines are here quoted:

> I must believe that God is Life
> Since cells appeared where had been
> Only cooling crust or barren sea,
>
> I must believe that God is Mind
> Since instinct life soared up to power of thought.
>
> I must believe that God is Love
> Since love it is that raises humankind. . . .

At the time of his death, Nourse was quite satisfied with the chapters which were to comprise Part One of his book, and he was then endeavoring to perfect the five chapters he was planning to have in Part Two. He set forth what he had in mind for these chapters as follows:

> As readers move on from Part One to Part Two, they are likely to feel a distinct change of pace. Instead of Part One's broad generalizations about group behavior, man-made institutions, and social evolution, these chapters come down to concrete situations of our own time and our own country. . . .

> These five chapters should serve to illustrate the application of social science principles to the guidance of social technology and, reciprocally, show the contribution that the continuing flow of social group experimentation and negotiation makes to the enrichment of social science.

He had most of the manuscript prepared for these five final chapters, and if his health had not failed him, he would have been able to finish them in a few more months. Here it is possible only to briefly explain from his drafts what he planned to include in these unfinished chapters.

Chapter VIII, "Economics from Acquisitive Wealth to Social Welfare," was to examine the great changes in American economic institutions since the turn of the century. It was to explain how the doctrine of laissez faire gave way to social direction as manifested by trustbusting and emphasis on conservation and labor reform in the early 1900s. He was impressed by the great strides forward which came with the Federal Reserve Act of 1913, the strengthening of antitrust legislation, and the constitutional provision for federal income taxes. "What was new in all this," said Nourse, "was obsolescence of laissez faire and the beginnings of a role of societary responsibility undergirded with scientific capability—a conceptual and operational scheme of ends, means, and human guidance."

Nourse went on to explain how World War I brought stronger governmental institutions and greater power to business corporations and how the New Deal, following the Great Depression, inaugurated a democratic welfare economy which was tested by World War II. This in turn led to the Employment Act of 1946 to provide for post-war prosperity, which Nourse termed "A Declaration of Economic Interdependence." He followed this with a review of experience under the Employment Act, which caused him to say: "Progressively from Theodore Roosevelt to Richard Nixon, the Federal Government has abandoned laissez faire and become an active, perhaps ultimately, dominant partner in our national economic life. . . ." He completed this chapter with the following paragraph:

> The fast pace of economic evolution in the twentieth century has shaped three major economic technologies, capitalistic, laboristic, and governmental, into structures and practices that have outrun our understanding and our economic science. . . . In this tri-partite evolution, the simple economic science of an automatically self-adjusting competitive mechanism has become egregiously inadequate, but no basic principle or principles of national or multinational competition has yet emerged. . . . The accommodations worked out by management-labor bargaining has permitted lush quantitative growth but at the price of unmanageable inflation, less than full employment, deterioration in the quality of national life. Economics is thrown back on the necessity of scientizing a tri-power economics that will provide workable competition among giant private organizations and cooperation between them and an activist People's government.

In Chapter IX, Nourse turned his attention to the place of political science in modern society. He first drafted this chapter under the title "Political Science and American Democracy" with the subtitle "Political Planning for National Welfare." In later revisions he changed the title to "American Democracy and the New Politics" and "Political Evolution Toward a Democracy of Welfare" before he finally settled on the title "The Political Technology and Science of Large Collectives" with the subtitle "Harmonizing the Exercise of Power."

From the various drafts of this chapter, it is apparent that Nourse was endeavoring to trace the evolution of our political system in the United States. He dealt with the objectives of government and the changes made to adjust democratic institutions to meet needs as economic and social problems increased. From a relatively simple government it became a complex system of strong governmental agencies; suffrage was expanded and election laws were changed. Executive direction and local control grew in importance, while planning and regulation assumed greater significance as strong national government became a feature of modern life. The separation of powers was maintained but adapted to new conditions. Nourse viewed these developments as beneficial—particularly, the greater use of political science in guiding governmental operations. He saw the Employment Act of 1946 as a great step forward in governmental administration.

In his draft material for this chapter he said:

> Political science undertakes to discover the basic principles of equilibrium—dynamic equilibrium—in the body politic, just as economic science seeks to discover the basic principles of dynamic equilibrium—growth in productivity *cum* financial stability—in the economy. This sort of dynamic equilibrium in the political process has been designated in the caption of this chapter as "harmonizing the exercise of power."

Nourse called his Chapter X "Sociology: The Total Culture as a Synthesis." He defined sociology as "the science and technology of total culture, the types of human action—economic, political, educational, juridical, and esthetic —that compose it, the nature and degree of their integration, the ways of cultural transmission and assimilation." He held that "sociology is concerned with both the physical environment and human capabilities, yearnings, and institutional structures that jointly determine a people's characteristic way of life." He said: "Sociology moves on from empirical descriptions of a society's institutions and behaviors, to analysis of the rationale of individual and group relationships and their changes, particularly the perennial challenge between individual and society."

He held that "a culture is an acquired way of group life." He said: "In simplest terms, a people's culture is the aggregate of its structures and practices of sex and family relations, its techniques of subsistence and shelter, of governance, religion, music, art, and recreation. . . . This total way of life is embodied in traditions, tabus, conventions; in property laws, civil rights and criminal penalties; in military establishments, ecclesiastical systems, and business organizations; in scientific findings and artistic expressions. A total culture is not the mere co-existence or aggregation of the disparate actions of a given population mass; it is a functional synthesis . . . with continual feedback from today's performance of tomorrow's plans." He also said: "A total culture is no monolithic mass but a pillared structure gradually architected by a whole people . . . A democratic culture reasonably well integrated by the active participation of its members, though it imposes discipline, is not a social straight-jacket. . . ."

Nourse pointed out that "it is the chosen vocation of sociologists to gain understanding of the basic forces underlying and shaping action patterns of our society and the manner in which and the degree to which they can be integrated in a national or regional way of life, orderly but not rigid, scientific in character but sensitive to spiritual and aesthetic considerations."

He recognized that historically, cultures have been formed or transmitted by parents, priests, and professors or teachers. In time, he said, education came to have a predominant importance, and with education came research, or "the production of knowledge." He then said: "This growing responsibility, in both theory and practice, of the people's government for the people's education and the research that gives it depth and direction is an outstanding feature of our cultural evolution and hence is a central concern of sociologists and, more broadly, of the whole field of social science."

He thought it very important that a new method of acculturation had emerged in the form of the "mass media," which provides through press, radio, and television rapidly processed information. Nourse said: "In an authoritarian country, mass media are an agency of indoctrination and control. In our democratic way of life, they serve as a first, empirical step in the social-scientific procedure of data marshalling, evaluation, choice, and synthesized action. In their kaleidoscope picture, the scholar or thoughtful layman can discern those cohesive elements of *consensus* that make a society workable and those outlets of dissent that keep it progressive and reasonably comfortable."

Nourse considered consensus and dissent essential in a democratic society. "A total culture is given dynamic stability by the differences among its people quite as much as by their similarities and agreements." He thought that checks were necessary to provide social balance, or to express this differently, that social balance derived from a harmonization of dissents.

In his last two chapters Nourse dealt with the "extraordinary social turbulence" since World War II which reached a peak in the 1960s. He called these chapters "Ethnic Fractures in Our National Solidarity" and "The Agony and the Ecstacy of Youth's Unfolding." In introducing them, he expressed the view that future historians might appraise the second half of the twentieth century as a period of basic redesigning of our economic, political, and social system. He believed that the current drive to make our national thinking and action more relevant to emerging circumstances or neglected problems was bringing out wider, livelier, and better-informed debate than was possible in any earlier period.

Nourse saw social science as being "on the threshold of vast new discoveries about the techniques, individual and social, by which new powers and beauties of the human estate may be attained or its vulnerabilities safeguarded." He went on to say: "Science is accumulative and irreversible—though always subject to challenge and refinement. The race cannot repudiate or obliterate its intellectual past and start in a new direction. . . . Each generation passes civilization's torch, dimmed or brightened, to the next."

With the great expansion of governmental agencies brought about by economic and social changes, Nourse saw "a great deal of intelligent negotiation between central and local authority . . . to the end that national purposes may be adapted to widely varying local conditions and local choice of priorities." He was optimistic that "the major goal of community participation could be reached without running the risks of ethnic separation or susceptibility to revolutionary violence." He said: "Personally, I am impressed with the vigor, tolerance, and reliance upon social-scientized negotiation with which political-economic protests are being considered and the accompanying proposals are being winnowed."

The problem of harmonizing the ethnic interests of our population, dealt with in Chapter XI, had long been of much concern to Nourse, and he believed it merited special attention. He recognized that while immigrants from European stocks could be largely assimilated into our common democratic culture, there was a substantial minority of the population comprised of American Indians, Mexican Americans, Orientals, and Afro-Americans who could not be merged in the melting pot process. While he felt that substantial progress was being made in harmonizing the interests of these ethnic groups, he realized that much remained to be done to give them a sense of belonging and participation. After carefully analyzing this general problem, Nourse concluded:

> No racial or regional stock can shed its distinctive physical, mental, and spiritual identity just by moving to a new environment. Change can come rapidly through intermarriage, but there are many tabus and aversions to check that amalgamation. The popularization of scientific knowledge and attitude in our society facilitates the development of a total culture of common purpose with an enriching society of ethnic identities, all giving scope to a wide range of individual differences in lively but peaceful co-existence. . . . We know better than to try to fuse all ethnic groups into one dull mass. . . . For our social building we choose not the drab uniformity of sandstone but the rich patterns of nature's noblest building material—marble. In the marbleized culture that is continuously being worked out in our democratic society, the black subculture is sure to supply a strong and ever-present note. This with a sprinkling of Oriental, Chicano, and Indian communities, will round out our democratic pattern of social democracy E Pluribus Unum.

Nourse was sympathetic to the rebellion of youth which challenged the values of our industrialized society in the 1960s. This was evident from his final chapter, "The Agony and Ecstacy of Youth's Unfolding," which he subtitled "Dreams, Drugs, and Discipline." He thought that "the hidden dreams and expressed demands of each new generation reflect the unfolding of the individual's physical and mental powers and spiritual perceptions. He believed that the "encounter between the retiring and advancing generations calls for mutual respect and mutual curiosity; appreciation of each for the credibility of the others' views and values. There is neither place nor occasion for mutual disparagement or for the alienation of either party from the common enterprise of human fulfillment and social betterment." He believed that young people could be either "apprentice builders" or "juvenile destroyers," and he held that "social science provides them with help in finding their place in the endless procession of the generations instead of floundering in a generation gap." He concluded the chapter with this paragraph:

> The young dissidents and demonstrators of the sixties perhaps did better than they knew in getting acceptance of the proposition that juveniles have a basic human right to be heard, and that society, in its own interest, must consider and respond to their protests and proposals. But the right to be heard entails a duty to bear true witness to their peer group's honest anguish and the reality of their dreams.

Nourse planned to bring his book to a close with an afterword which he had prepared before his final illness. In it he said:

And so, patient—or impatient—reader, I press the "Stop" button on my tape recorder. No summary chapter seems called for; just a brief Afterword to rhyme with the Foreword to my social scientist's response to the NOW GENERATION. There, I combined endorsement of the NOW generation's intention of betterment with a word of counsel: to your ardor for reform, add understanding of the tools of modern social science needed for stout and beautiful re-building, and the skill to be acquired for their use. Here, I simply add three wistful comments on the current scene and outlook. First is full agreement with activists' unwillingness to accept the human condition as they find it. Second is profound disappointment that coalescence of many elements of social protest in the 1960s has so far subsided or been fragmented. New and greater crises press upon us, and new possibilities of daring but science-based innovation open before us. Third is my accumulated faith in humanity's innate commitment to its own betterment; and that social science is fashioning better and better tools for the achievement of that religious commitment. I must believe that God is universal Life, the creative human Mind, and all-brotherly Love—expressed in mutual helpfulness.

Appendix C

SELECTED BIBLIOGRAPHY OF NOURSE WRITINGS

(Chronologically listed)

Books

Agricultural Economics. Chicago: University of Chicago Press, 1916.
The Chicago Produce Market. Boston and New York: Houghton Mifflin Company, 1918.
American Agriculture and the European Market. New York: McGraw-Hill, 1924.
The Legal Status of Agricultural Cooperation. New York: Macmillan, 1927.
The Cooperative Marketing of Livestock (with Joseph G. Knapp). Washington: Brookings Institution, 1931.
America's Capacity to Produce (with associates). Washington: Brookings Institution, 1934.
Marketing Agreements Under the AAA. Washington: Brookings Institution, 1935.
Three Years of the Agricultural Adjustment Administration (with Joseph S. Davis and John D. Black). Washington: Brookings Institution, 1937.
Industrial Price Policies and Economic Progress (with Horace B. Drury). Washington: Brookings Institution, 1938.
Price Making in a Democracy. Washington: Brookings Institution, 1944.
The Nineteen Fifties Come First. New York: Henry Holt and Company, 1951.
Economics in the Public Service. New York: Harcourt, Brace and Company, 1953.

Parts of Books

"Agriculture," Chapter VIII in *Recent Economic Changes in the United States*

(Report of the Committee on Recent Economic Changes, Herbert Hoover, Chairman, Textbook Edition). New York: McGraw-Hill, 1929.

"Agriculture," Chapter XXIII in *Government and Economic Life*, Volume II. Washington: Brookings Institution, 1940.

"What's New in Automation," a chapter in *Automation and Society*. New York: Philosophical Library, 1958.

"New Viewpoints in the Economic Area," in *New Viewpoints in the Social Sciences*, (Twenty-eighth Yearbook of the National Council for the Social Studies, Roy A. Price, editor), 1958.

Bulletins

"A Preliminary Survey of Land Tenure in Arkansas," unnumbered bulletin, University of Arkansas. Fayetteville: November, 1919.

"Cooperative Livestock Shipping in Iowa in 1920" (with C. W. Hammans), Iowa Agricultural Experiment Station Bulletin 200. Ames: July, 1921.

"Fifty Years of Farmers' Elevators in Iowa," Iowa Agricultural Experiment Station Bulletin No. 211. Ames: March, 1923.

Articles and Addresses

"The War and the Back to the Land Movement." *North American Review*, February, 1915.

"What is Agricultural Economics?" *Journal of Political Economy*, April, 1916.

"The Cheapest Source of Increased Food Supplies." *Scientific Monthly*, February, 1918.

"The Revolution in Farming." *Yale Review*, October, 1918.

"The Place of Agriculture in Modern Industrial Society." *Journal of Political Economy*, Part I, June, 1919; Part II, July, 1919.

"Normal Price as a Market Concept." *Quarterly Journal of Economics*, August, 1919.

"Will Agricultural Prices Fall?" *Journal of Political Economy*, March, 1920.

"Corporate and Cooperative Farming." *Youth's Companion*, April 13, 1920.

"Harmonizing the Interests of Farm Producers and Town Consumers." *Journal of Political Economy*, October, 1920.

"The Outlook for Cooperative Marketing." *Journal of Farm Economics*, April, 1922.

"The Economic Philosophy of Cooperation." *American Economic Review*, December, 1922.

"The Proper Sphere of Governmental Regulation in Connection with the Marketing of Farm Products." An address to annual meeting of the American

Economic Association, December, 1922; *American Economic Review*, March, 1923.

"Some Fundamentals of Cooperative Marketing." An address to Fifth annual meeting of the National Association of State Marketing Officials; *Proceedings*, Chicago, December, 1923.

"Some Economic Factors in an American Agricultural Policy." Presidential address to annual meeting of the American Farm Economic Association, December 29, 1924; *Journal of Farm Economics*, January, 1925.

"Organization and Purposes of the American Institute of Cooperation." An address to the American Institute of Cooperation; *American Cooperation*, Volume I, 1925.*

"Recent Trend of Cooperation Among Cooperatives." An address to Seventh annual meeting of the National Association of State Marketing Officials. *Proceedings*, Chicago, November-December, 1925.

"History and Structure of Cooperative Livestock Marketing." *American Cooperation*, Volume I, 1926.

"Potential Development of Functions and Service by State Federations of Farmers' Elevators." *American Cooperation*, Volume II, 1926.

"The Outlook for Agriculture." Address to annual meeting of the American Farm Economic Association, December, 1926; *Journal of Farm Economics*, January, 1927.

"The Evolving Idea of Cooperation in the United States." *American Cooperation*, Volume I, 1928.

"The Trend of Our Agricultural Exports." *Journal of Political Economy*, June, 1928.

"Some Economic and Social Accompaniments of the Mechanization of Agriculture." Address to annual meeting of the American Economic Association, December, 1929; *Proceedings of the American Economic Association*, March, 1930.

"What Can the Farm Board Do Toward Production Control?" *American Cooperation*, Volume I, 1930.

"An Evaluation of the Livestock Marketing Work of the Federal Farm Board." *American Cooperation*, Volume II, 1931.

"Cooperative Structure and Farm Board Policy." *American Cooperation*, 1932.

"The Cooperative Marketing Movement Under the New Deal." *American Cooperation*, 1933.

"The Farm, the Cooperatives, and the Government." *American Cooperation*, 1934.

---

*Addresses to the annual sessions of the American Institute of Cooperation are published (in Washington, D.C.) in annual proceedings under the title *American Cooperation*.

"Is the AAA Doomed?" *Farm Journal*, August, 1935.

"What Cooperatives Should Know About America's Capacity to Produce and Consume." *American Cooperation*, 1935.

"Certain Post-War Trends in Agricultural Cooperation." *American Cooperation*, 1937.

"Fundamental Significance of the Agricultural Adjustment Concept." *Journal of Farm Economics*, May, 1938.

"Monopolistic Practices and the Price Structure." Address to annual meeting of American Academy of Political Science, November 9, 1938; *Proceedings of the Academy of Political Science*, January, 1939.

"The Meaning of 'Price Policy.'" *Quarterly Journal of Economics*, February, 1941.

"The Nature and Future of Private Enterprise." Address to Congress of American Industry, National Association of Manufacturers; published as a pamphlet by N.A.M., December, 1941.

"Democracy as a Principle of Business." *Yale Review*, March, 1942.

"Collective Bargaining and the Common Interest." Presidential address to American Economic Association, December, 1942; *American Economic Review*, March, 1943.

"The Place of Cooperatives in Our National Economy." *American Cooperation*, 1942-1945. (No sessions of the American Institute of Cooperation were held during the war years, 1942-1945. This volume consisted of contributed articles.)

"Serfdom, Utopia, or Democratic Opportunity." *Public Administration Review*, Spring, 1946.

"From Dogma to Science in Cooperative Thinking." *American Cooperation*, 1946.

"Economics in the Public Service." Address to annual meeting of the American Economic Association, January, 1946; *American Economic Review*, May, 1947.

"Public Administration and Economic Stabilization." Address to annual meeting of the American Society for Public Administration; *Public Administration Review*, 1947.

"The Position of Agriculture Under the Employment Act of 1946." *American Cooperation*, 1947.

"The Problem—Market Absorption." *Printers' Ink*, October, 1947.

"The Employment Act and the Act of Employment." *Dun's Review*, November, 1947.

"The Role of the Council of Economic Advisers." *American Political Science Review*, November, 1947.

"Why I Had to Step Aside." *Collier's*, February 18, 1950.

"Economic Analysis and Political Synthesis." Penrose Memorial Lecture, April 20, 1950; *Proceedings of American Philosophy Society*, August, 1950.

"Changes Necessary to Meet Tomorrow's Problems." *American Cooperation*, 1952.

"The Persistent Problems of the American Economy." *Social Education*, November, 1953.

"Nature's Power and the Conscience of Man." *Virginia Quarterly Review*, Summer, 1955.

"Defining Our Employment Goal Under the 1946 Act." *Review of Economic Statistics*, May, 1956.

"Ideal and Working Concepts of Full Employment." Address to annual meeting of the American Economic Association; *American Economic Review*, May, 1957.

"Administered Prices and All That." Address to annual meeting of the Western Economic Association, Salt Lake City; *Proceedings*, August, 1957.

"Prices and Policy Makers." *Challenge*, December, 1957.

"Intellectualism on the Economic Front." Address to chapters of Phi Beta Kappa in 1957; *American Scholar*, Summer, 1958.

"The Dilemma of Government Spending." *Challenge*, March, 1959.

"Some Questions Emerging Under the Employment Act." Address to annual meeting of the American Economic Association, December, 1959; *American Economic Review*, May, 1960.

"The Hinge Between Two Decades." *Virginia Quarterly Review*, Winter, 1961.

"The Promise of American Capitalism." *Virginia Quarterly Review*, Summer, 1962.

"The Not So Dismal Science of Economics." N.E.A. (National Education Association) *Journal*, March, 1963.

"Government Discipline of Private Economic Power." A statement included in *Administered Prices: A Compendium on Public Policy*, pp. 245-261. 88th Congress, 1st Session. Senate Subcommittee on Antitrust and Monopoly, Senate Committee on the Judiciary, March, 1963.

"What Would Economic Literacy Be Like?" *Challenge*, March, 1964.

"Life and Taxes." *Virginia Quarterly Review*, Autumn, 1964.

"Untaxing as a Way of Economic Life." *Challenge*, April, 1965.

"Current Aspects of Our Persistent Economic Problems." *Social Education*, April, 1966.

"Early Flowering of the Employment Act." *Virginia Quarterly Review*, Spring, 1967.

"The Employment Act and the 'New Economics.'" *Virginia Quarterly Review*, Autumn, 1969.

Notes

Notes

NOTES

Chapter I

1. The character of Rebecca Nurse has been dramatized by Arthur Miller in *The Crucible* (1952). For more complete historical information on Francis and Rebecca Nurse, see Marion L. Starkey, *The Devil in Massachusetts* (New York: Alfred A. Knopf, Inc., 1949), and Charles Sutherland Tapley, *Rebecca Nurse* (Boston: Marshall Jones Co., 1930).
2. Apparently Henry Nourse took little responsibility for "Rafe," who grew up with his relatives in the West. Edwin Nourse came to know his half brother after his parents moved to Illinois, but Rafe was then more like an uncle than a brother, for he was over 20 years Edwin's senior.
3. For a tender and appreciative portrait, see the book by her daughter, Alice Tisdale Hobart, *Gusty's Child* (New York: Longmans, Green and Co., 1959).
4. Ibid., p. 6.
5. Ibid., pp. 18-19.
6. To get the flavor of Edwin's relationship to his sisters while he was growing up, see Alice's book, *Gusty's Child*, op. cit., pp. 14-40.
7. His sister Alice later explained that Edwin "had consented because he was fearful lest he be left out of the family circle; and yet, child as he was, he even then challenged any dogma and when he appeared before the deacons to be questioned, it had cost him dearly to express what he really did not believe." See Hobart, op. cit., pp. 20-21.
8. As quoted by Fred C. Kelly, *George Ade—Warmhearted Satirist* (New York: The Bobbs-Merrill Company, 1947), p. 101. This book gives a very good account of all aspects of Chicago's life in the 1890s. As Kelly said: "Chicago was some laboratory."
9. Robert Morss Lovett, *All Our Years* (New York: The Viking Press, 1948), p. 55.
10. Hobart, op. cit., p. 13.

Chapter II

1. The City White referred to the white buildings of the Chicago World's Fair of 1893. At the same time the City Gray was arising nearby in the form of the gray buildings of the University of Chicago. How the alma mater came to be written by Lewis in 1898 is told by Thomas Wakefield Goodspeed in *A History of the University of Chicago* (Chicago: University of Chicago Press, 1916), pp. 452-453; see also p. 438.
2. Cornell Oral History Interview with Edwin G. Nourse by Joseph G. Knapp, 1966-1971 (Cornell University Library, Ithaca, N.Y.), pp. 63-64.
3. Cornell Oral History Interview, pp. 38-39.

4. See Alice Tisdale Hobart, *Gusty's Child* (New York: Longmans, Green and Co., 1959), pp. 40-41.
5. For a full description of Cornell during the years when Nourse was a student, see the illuminating book by Morris Bishop, *A History of Cornell* (Ithaca, N.Y.: Cornell University Press, 1962).
6. For an account of the Cornell typhoid epidemic of 1903 and its effect on Cornell, see Bishop, op. cit., pp. 421-422.
7. For more complete information on Carnegie's benefaction, see Bishop, op. cit., p. 422.
8. See the delightful presentation of this tradition by Carl Becker, *The Cornell Tradition: Freedom and Responsibility*, an address that he gave on the university's 75th anniversary (Ithaca, N.Y.: Cornell University, 1940).
9. See Bishop, op. cit., pp. 324-325.
10. For further information on the development of agricultural education at Cornell, see Bishop, op cit., pp. 364-383; Gould F. Colman, *Education and Agriculture: A History of the New York College of Agriculture* (Ithaca, N.Y.: Cornell University, 1963); and Henry C. and Anne Dewees Taylor, *The Story of Agricultural Economics* (Ames, Iowa: Iowa State College Press, 1952), pp. 356-358.
11. According to Morris Bishop, they were "a group of powerful scholars . . . unforgettable to those who sat twice weekly in their classes." He vividly described them as follows: "There was Charles H. Hull, '86, omniscient, whimsical, with his five-minute sentences that always came out, and with a rare gift for the telling phrase. . . . There was Ralph Catteral, a master in the blending of high thought and low comedy; and Henry Augustus 'Gussie' Sill, so warm and kindly, who carried on a perpetual war with Catteral; and of course there was George Lincoln Burr." Bishop also quoted Professor Burr's view on his aspirations in teaching history, which is here of interest as a reflection of the spirit of the history faculty at that time: "I want my boys and girls to be broadened and deepened, mellowed and sweetened, by living the life of other men and other days, by living the larger life of cities and of people, by living themselves through all their past into the present." These men, with the exception of Burr, whose field Nourse had already studied at Lewis Institute, were Nourse's teachers of history, and he took full advantage of the intellectual feast they provided. See Bishop, op. cit., p. 395.
12. For a vignette of this fabulous character—Professor Edward B. Titchener—see Bishop, op cit., pp. 621-623. See also p. 326.
13. Hoxie was later to gain national recognition for his pathfinding studies in the labor field. For a beautiful tribute to the man and the importance of his work, see Walton Hale Hamilton's essay, "Robert Franklin Hoxie," in the *Dictionary of American Biography*, s.v. "Hoxie, Robert Franklin."

Chapter III

1. One of my neighbors in Washington, D.C., Mrs. Edna Snow (nee Bohn), was a teen-age girl in Ogden when Nourse taught in the high school. In the 1960s she recalled Nourse well as a "beau to my older sister's crowd—a racy crowd that didn't smoke, didn't drink, and they made fudge." To her, Nourse was "tall and stately, and terribly good looking, and learned." But from her vantage point then as a "pestering younger sister," he was "something of a stuffed shirt without a bit of sense of humor."
2. Soon afterwards, Nourse purchased Horace Plunkett's newly published book,

The Country Life Problem in the United States, to obtain more information on the subject.
3. Cornell Oral History Interview, pp. 105-106.
4. The information for this section has been drawn largely from Nourse's recollections as given in his Cornell Oral History Interview, pp. 109-125.
5. No one who did not know the old South Water Street market before it was moved to the suburbs to make way for Wacker Drive in the mid-1920s can appreciate the squalid, untidy mess that was the old South Water Street market. As a graduate student at the University of Chicago in 1923-1924, I got well acquainted with the market in connection with terminal market studies.
6. Letter from Dr. Mollie Ray Carroll to author, April 6, 1973, with a brief memorandum on "Institutional Economics at the University of Chicago, 1914-15."

Chapter IV

1. Cornell Oral History Interview, pp. 128-129.
2. Since the Harvard Business School financed the trip, Nourse was of the opinion that he was being looked over as a possible addition to its faculty. Although no offer was made, it is interesting to speculate on how Nourse's career might have unfolded had he been lured to Harvard at that time.
3. See the chapter, "Agricultural Economics Finding Itself," in Henry C. and Anne Dewees Taylor's *The Story of Agricultural Economics* (Ames, Iowa: Iowa State College Press, 1952), pp. 80-98. The establishment of the American Farm Economics Association in 1919 brought about a harmonization of the conflicting views of those who favored the farm management and of those who favored a more general approach.
4. See essay by E. T. Grether on "Edwin Griswold Nourse" in *The Journal of Marketing,* April, 1958, p. 417.
5. Letter from Joe C. Barrett to author, December 4, 1964.
6. Letter from Joe C. Barrett to author, December 22, 1964.
7. Letter from Brooks Hays to author, July 8, 1965.
8. Letter from Charles S. Stewart to author, November 10, 1964.

Chapter V

1. Letter from Frank Robotka to author, April 28, 1964.
2. Russell C. Engberg, then on the staff of the state Extension Service, saw the possibilities of making Nourse's article into an interview article for *Successful Farming,* and in this form it gained widespread attention in Iowa and nearby states. (Letter from Russell C. Engberg to author, August 30, 1964.)
3. For full information see Joseph G. Knapp, *The Advance of American Cooperative Enterprise: 1920-1945* (Danville, Ill.: The Interstate Printers & Publishers, Inc., 1973), pp. 13-15.
4. The study group also included William G. Eckhardt, an official of the Illinois Agricultural Association and a member of the Committee of 17; J. G. Brown, President of the Indiana Farm Bureau Federation; Harry G. Beale, Treasurer of the Ohio Farm Bureau Federation; E. L. Rhodes, Kansas State Extension Service Specialist; and Herman Steen, Economics Editor of the *Prairie Farmer* of Chicago.
5. See "Report of Mid-West Committee on Essential Features of Pacific Coast

Producers Cooperative Associations and Discussion," *Proceedings of the Farmers Marketing Committee of Seventeen*, November 4-6, 1920, Chicago, pp. 1-26. Multilithed.
6. For a résumé of Robotka's cooperative contributions in profile see Richard Phillips, "Frank Robotka: The Gadfly of Cooperation" in Joseph G. Knapp and associates, *Great American Cooperators* (Washington, D.C.: American Institute of Cooperation, 1967), pp. 429-433.
7. Cornell Oral History Interview, pp. 168-169.
8. Edwin G. Nourse and C. W. Hammans, Iowa Agricultural Experiment Station Bulletin No. 200.
9. See Edwin G. Nourse and Joseph G. Knapp, *The Cooperative Marketing of Livestock* (Washington, D.C.: The Brookings Institution, 1931).
10. Letter from Frank Robotka to author, April 18, 1964.
11. Edwin G. Nourse, Iowa Agricultural Experiment Station Bulletin No. 211.
12. See the *Journal of Farm Economics*, April, 1922, pp. 80-88.
13. See Knapp, op. cit., pp. 7-16, for discussion of Sapiro's influence and views.
14. For a brief summary of this article with an expression of its importance, see Orion Ulrey's profile, "Edwin G. Nourse—Pioneer in Cooperative Theory and Education," in Joseph G. Knapp and associates, *Great American Cooperators* (Washington, D.C.: American Institute of Cooperation, 1967), pp. 368-370. For a condensation of this article, see Martin A. Abrahamsen and Claud L. Scroggs, *Agricultural Cooperation* (Minneapolis: University of Minnesota Press, 1957), pp. 161-183. In introducing this article, the authors say: "Perhaps the most outstanding article dealing with cooperative principles is that developed by Edwin G. Nourse some thirty-five years ago under the title 'The Economic Philosophy of Cooperation'. This article long has been recognized as a bench mark in this field."
15. Cornell Oral History Interview, pp. 176-178.
16. Letter from A. H. Hausrath to author, December 6, 1966.
17. Letter from O. B. Jesness to author, June 25, 1973.
18. Letter from Frank Robotka to author, April 28, 1964.
19. Ibid.
20. Ibid.
21. "Development of the Field of Economics at Iowa State," an informal paper prepared for internal use of the Department of Economics at Iowa State University, September 4, 1973. Multilithed.
22. Letter from Murray R. Benedict to author, June 25, 1973.
23. Papers and Proceedings of the Thirty-fifth Annual Meeting of the American Economic Association, March 1923, pp. 198-208.
24. Cornell Oral History Interview, p. 184.

Chapter VI

1. For more complete information on Brookings, see Hermann Hagedorn, *Brookings, A Biography* (New York: Macmillan, 1936), especially Chapters XV and XVI.
2. Ibid., p. 267.
3. Proceedings of the Fifth Annual Meeting of the National Association of State Marketing Officials, Chicago, 1923, pp. 14-24.

4. Letter from Fred Waugh to author, June 29, 1964.
5. Author's interview with Roscoe Saville, June 10, 1974.
6. At that time, Moulton favored the use of italicized topic sentences to lead the reader through ensuing discussions. In this way, the argument marched along cumulatively to the final conclusions. This form of exposition was suitable for certain types of books, but it was too mechanical for Nourse's temperament, and he made little use of it in his subsequent writings.
7. Charles B. Saunders, Jr., *The Brookings Institution: A Fifty-Year History* (Washington, D.C.: Brookings Institution, 1966), p. 34.
8. *Journal of Farm Economics,* January 1925, pp. 1-21.
9. For more complete information on the early history of the American Institute of Cooperation, see Joseph G. Knapp, *The Advance of American Cooperative Enterprise: 1920-1945* (Danville, Ill.: The Interstate Printers & Publishers, Inc., 1973), pp. 79-87.
10. See Cornell Oral History Interview, pp. 205-212.
11. Proceedings of the Seventh Annual Meeting of the National Association of State Marketing Officials, Chicago, 1925, pp. 7-13.
12. See Orion Ulrey's essay, "Edwin Griswold Nourse—Pioneer in Cooperative Theory and Education," in Joseph G. Knapp and associates, *Great American Cooperators* (Washington, D.C.: American Institute of Cooperation, 1967), pp. 366-378.
13. Engberg, who had known Nourse while on the farm management staff at Ames, had completed all requirements for a doctor's degree at Columbia University in the summer of 1925. He was planning to return to Columbia the next year to complete his dissertation on "The Effect of Business Cycles on Agriculture" under Professor Wesley Clair Mitchell, when he wrote to Nourse seeking a job. Nourse was interested in his thesis subject and immediately suggested that he join the Institute, where he could work on this topic. Mitchell strongly urged that Engberg take advantage of this opportunity. Engberg has always been grateful to Nourse for his help at this stage of his career which, in his words, "represented a tremendous break for me." (Letter from Russell C. Engberg to author, June 21, 1974.)
14. Letter from Lynn R. Edminster to author, September 16, 1974.
15. It is of interest that Brookings set forth his own ideas on what should be done on the agricultural problem in a little book, *Economic Democracy* (New York: Macmillan, 1929). In a chapter on "Agricultural Corporations," he said: "While the much-discussed development of agricultural cooperative associations will no doubt render an important service, any system of production and distribution which leaves the individual small farmer the owner of his farm, with personal freedom of operation, can never develop anything like the efficiency of the modern corporation. Through the corporation the farmer can receive a good bond for the value of his farm, and in addition, by working under the direction of a centralized authority, may enjoy not only a liberal wage for his services, but every opportunity for personal development and advancement."
16. Author's interview with Edwin G. Nourse, January 15, 1963.
17. Letter from Murray R. Benedict to author, June 25, 1973. Benedict held that the inception of the fellowship program displayed "the sureness and wisdom of the Nourse Touch," for it was a program much needed at the time. It is of interest that under this program, well over a hundred persons were assisted. Many were to become national leaders in the agricultural economics profession.
18. The formation of the Brookings Institution is well explained by Saunders, op. cit., pp. 35-40.

Chapter VII

1. See *Recent Economic Changes in the United States* (New York: McGraw-Hill Book Co., 1929), Chapter VII, "Agriculture," pp. 547-602. This volume of over 900 pages gives the report of the Committee on Recent Economic Changes, which was initially chaired by Herbert Hoover. Most of the book is devoted to reports of investigations made by a special staff which worked under the direction of Wesley Clair Mitchell and Edwin F. Gay for the National Bureau of Economic Research. Nourse's chapter on "Agriculture" represented one of the special studies made for the National Bureau. This book provides a good record of the substantial progress made by most elements of the nation's economic system during the years from 1922 to 1929.
2. *Recent Economic Changes*, pp. 909-910.
3. For more complete information on the provisions of the Agricultural Marketing Act of 1929 and the role assigned the Federal Farm Board in effectuating its purposes, see Joseph G. Knapp, *The Advance of American Cooperative Enterprise: 1920-1945* (Danville, Ill.: The Interstate Printers & Publishers, Inc., 1973), Chapter VIII, "The Federal Farm Board Experiment," pp. 120-122. See also Murray B. Benedict, *Farm Policies of the United States, 1790-1950* (New York: The Twentieth Century Fund, 1953), pp. 239-240.
4. Cornell Oral History Interview, pp. 258-261.
5. See *American Cooperation, 1930* (Washington: American Institute of Cooperation, 1930), pp. 24-31.
6. This address was one of many sponsored by the National Council on Radio in Education. Its committee on economics, which worked in cooperation with the Brookings Institution, included Moulton and Nourse among its members.
7. At this same meeting, Nourse gave Sapiro credit for being a great evangelist of cooperation. "In terms of his addresses he made a great contribution to the movement. In terms of his ability to evangelize, to get people to hit the sawdust trail, he has never had a peer in this country. There can be no question that he opened the minds of people to the cooperative movement. And he did another thing . . . he brought the cooperative movement into the field of finance in this country and got bankers to see cooperation in a way they never had seen it before." *American Cooperation, 1932*, pp. 69-70.
8. For a discussion of the conditions that led to the formation of the Farm Credit Administration, see Knapp, op. cit., p. 240. For information on how the Farm Credit Administration developed, see Chapter XIV, "Building the Cooperative Farm Credit System, 1933-1940," in Knapp, op. cit., pp. 246-287.
9. See Cornell Oral History Interview, pp. 272-273.
10. Apparently the idea of having these men as codirectors appealed to Nourse early in the consideration of the project. Davis was of the impression that he and Black were brought in to help persuade the Laura Spellman Rockefeller Foundation that it should support the project, but Nourse's recollections indicate that arrangements for carrying on the study were made after funds for the study were assured.
11. For extended views see *American Cooperation, 1933*, pp. 42-55.
12. As expressed by Charles W. Holman, Secretary of the American Institute of Cooperation. *American Cooperation, 1934*, p. 7.
13. Ibid., p. 44.
14. Ibid., p. 152. See also statements by H. R. Tolley, Assistant Administrator of the Agricultural Adjustment Administration, pp. 46-62, and Mordecai Ezekiel, economic adviser to the Secretary of Agriculture, pp. 77-91.

NOTES

4. Letter from Fred Waugh to author, June 29, 1964.
5. Author's interview with Roscoe Saville, June 10, 1974.
6. At that time, Moulton favored the use of italicized topic sentences to lead the reader through ensuing discussions. In this way, the argument marched along cumulatively to the final conclusions. This form of exposition was suitable for certain types of books, but it was too mechanical for Nourse's temperament, and he made little use of it in his subsequent writings.
7. Charles B. Saunders, Jr., *The Brookings Institution: A Fifty-Year History* (Washington, D.C.: Brookings Institution, 1966), p. 34.
8. *Journal of Farm Economics,* January 1925, pp. 1-21.
9. For more complete information on the early history of the American Institute of Cooperation, see Joseph G. Knapp, *The Advance of American Cooperative Enterprise: 1920-1945* (Danville, Ill.: The Interstate Printers & Publishers, Inc., 1973), pp. 79-87.
10. See Cornell Oral History Interview, pp. 205-212.
11. Proceedings of the Seventh Annual Meeting of the National Association of State Marketing Officials, Chicago, 1925, pp. 7-13.
12. See Orion Ulrey's essay, "Edwin Griswold Nourse—Pioneer in Cooperative Theory and Education," in Joseph G. Knapp and associates, *Great American Cooperators* (Washington, D.C.: American Institute of Cooperation, 1967), pp. 366-378.
13. Engberg, who had known Nourse while on the farm management staff at Ames, had completed all requirements for a doctor's degree at Columbia University in the summer of 1925. He was planning to return to Columbia the next year to complete his dissertation on "The Effect of Business Cycles on Agriculture" under Professor Wesley Clair Mitchell, when he wrote to Nourse seeking a job. Nourse was interested in his thesis subject and immediately suggested that he join the Institute, where he could work on this topic. Mitchell strongly urged that Engberg take advantage of this opportunity. Engberg has always been grateful to Nourse for his help at this stage of his career which, in his words, "represented a tremendous break for me." (Letter from Russell C. Engberg to author, June 21, 1974.)
14. Letter from Lynn R. Edminster to author, September 16, 1974.
15. It is of interest that Brookings set forth his own ideas on what should be done on the agricultural problem in a little book, *Economic Democracy* (New York: Macmillan, 1929). In a chapter on "Agricultural Corporations," he said: "While the much-discussed development of agricultural cooperative associations will no doubt render an important service, any system of production and distribution which leaves the individual small farmer the owner of his farm, with personal freedom of operation, can never develop anything like the efficiency of the modern corporation. Through the corporation the farmer can receive a good bond for the value of his farm, and in addition, by working under the direction of a centralized authority, may enjoy not only a liberal wage for his services, but every opportunity for personal development and advancement."
16. Author's interview with Edwin G. Nourse, January 15, 1963.
17. Letter from Murray R. Benedict to author, June 25, 1973. Benedict held that the inception of the fellowship program displayed "the sureness and wisdom of the Nourse Touch," for it was a program much needed at the time. It is of interest that under this program, well over a hundred persons were assisted. Many were to become national leaders in the agricultural economics profession.
18. The formation of the Brookings Institution is well explained by Saunders, op. cit., pp. 35-40.

Chapter VII

1. See *Recent Economic Changes in the United States* (New York: McGraw-Hill Book Co., 1929), Chapter VII, "Agriculture," pp. 547-602. This volume of over 900 pages gives the report of the Committee on Recent Economic Changes, which was initially chaired by Herbert Hoover. Most of the book is devoted to reports of investigations made by a special staff which worked under the direction of Wesley Clair Mitchell and Edwin F. Gay for the National Bureau of Economic Research. Nourse's chapter on "Agriculture" represented one of the special studies made for the National Bureau. This book provides a good record of the substantial progress made by most elements of the nation's economic system during the years from 1922 to 1929.
2. *Recent Economic Changes*, pp. 909-910.
3. For more complete information on the provisions of the Agricultural Marketing Act of 1929 and the role assigned the Federal Farm Board in effectuating its purposes, see Joseph G. Knapp, *The Advance of American Cooperative Enterprise: 1920-1945* (Danville, Ill.: The Interstate Printers & Publishers, Inc., 1973), Chapter VIII, "The Federal Farm Board Experiment," pp. 120-122. See also Murray B. Benedict, *Farm Policies of the United States, 1790-1950* (New York: The Twentieth Century Fund, 1953), pp. 239-240.
4. Cornell Oral History Interview, pp. 258-261.
5. See *American Cooperation, 1930* (Washington: American Institute of Cooperation, 1930), pp. 24-31.
6. This address was one of many sponsored by the National Council on Radio in Education. Its committee on economics, which worked in cooperation with the Brookings Institution, included Moulton and Nourse among its members.
7. At this same meeting, Nourse gave Sapiro credit for being a great evangelist of cooperation. "In terms of his addresses he made a great contribution to the movement. In terms of his ability to evangelize, to get people to hit the sawdust trail, he has never had a peer in this country. There can be no question that he opened the minds of people to the cooperative movement. And he did another thing . . . he brought the cooperative movement into the field of finance in this country and got bankers to see cooperation in a way they never had seen it before." *American Cooperation, 1932*, pp. 69-70.
8. For a discussion of the conditions that led to the formation of the Farm Credit Administration, see Knapp, op. cit., p. 240. For information on how the Farm Credit Administration developed, see Chapter XIV, "Building the Cooperative Farm Credit System, 1933-1940," in Knapp, op. cit., pp. 246-287.
9. See Cornell Oral History Interview, pp. 272-273.
10. Apparently the idea of having these men as codirectors appealed to Nourse early in the consideration of the project. Davis was of the impression that he and Black were brought in to help persuade the Laura Spellman Rockefeller Foundation that it should support the project, but Nourse's recollections indicate that arrangements for carrying on the study were made after funds for the study were assured.
11. For extended views see *American Cooperation, 1933*, pp. 42-55.
12. As expressed by Charles W. Holman, Secretary of the American Institute of Cooperation. *American Cooperation, 1934*, p. 7.
13. Ibid., p. 44.
14. Ibid., p. 152. See also statements by H. R. Tolley, Assistant Administrator of the Agricultural Adjustment Administration, pp. 46-62, and Mordecai Ezekiel, economic adviser to the Secretary of Agriculture, pp. 77-91.

15. Ibid., p. 70.
16. For further information on the progress of the Agricultural Adjustment Administration in the 1930s, see Chapter XIII, "The Triple A and Cooperative Marketing" in Knapp, op. cit., pp. 227-245.
17. Nourse was to continue his interest in the marketing agreements procedure up to the end of his life. He felt that it was a unique American contribution in the field of governmental-cooperative relations not fully recognized for its valuable contribution to better agricultural marketing. See Chaper XIV.
18. Cornell Oral History Interview, pp. 296-297.

Chapter VIII

1. Although his deep involvement in the economic problems of agriculture had largely precluded him from working actively in the general economics field, his article, "Normal Price As a Market Concept," published by the *Quarterly Journal of Economics* in 1919, was definitely a contribution to general marketing theory.
2. Author's interview with Isadore Lubin, February 15, 1965.
3. Letter from Joseph J. Spengler to author, June 18, 1973.
4. With the abolition of the Graduate School, Leverett S. Lyon directed its transformation into a Training Division. The Institution's commitments to the students in residence were fulfilled, and the last class of Ph.D.'s was graduated in 1930. From 1928 on, predoctoral and postdoctoral fellows were appointed annually. They participated in seminars, worked with the staffs of the research divisions, and took their degrees at their home institutions. Charles B. Saunders, Jr., *The Brookings Institution: A Fifty-Year History* (Washington, D.C.: Brookings Institution, 1966), p. 46.
5. Ibid., pp. 43 and 44.
6. Ibid., p. 47.
7. For more complete information, see Harold G. Moulton's "President's Report on the Institution's Financial History, 1916-1952." This document gives a record of source of funds for the years covered.
8. For information on the symbiotic relationship of the Falk Foundation to the Brookings Institution, see Agnes Lynch Starett, *The Maurice and Laura Falk Foundation: A Private Fortune—A Public Trust* (Pittsburgh: Historical Society of Western Pennsylvania, 1966), pp. 26-29. For detailed information on grants to Brookings Institution, see Appendix E, *The Cumulative Record of Grants*, pp. 254-256.
9. Moulton felt a great responsibility to the Falk Foundation in completing this project as fast as possible. He was action-minded, and he believed that work on the "capacity to consume" volume called for his active intervention. In view of the heavy pressure of the big AAA study, Nourse was quite willing to relinquish direction of this volume.
10. See Cornell Oral History Interview, p. 296. Dr. George Terborgh, who was at this meeting, recalls Keynes as being somewhat condescending and arrogant on this occasion. (Author's interview with George Terborgh, November 10, 1974).
11. Letter from Colin Clark to author, May 17, 1963.
12. Cornell Oral History Interview, pp. 764-767. In his touching memorial service tribute to Moulton in 1965, Nourse referred to "Moulton's gallant capitulation" on one occasion. This was the incident he had in mind.
13. Saunders, op. cit., p. 59.

14. Cornell Oral History Interview, p. 237.
15. Saunders, op. cit., p. 59. For more complete information on Brookings Institution developments during the 1930s, see pp. 43-62.
16. Nourse enjoyed very much his active work with this committee which brought him into close association with such distinguished social science leaders as Charles Merriam (political science), Wesley Clair Mitchell (economics), Arthur M. Schlesinger (history), and Robert Redfield (sociology). See Cornell Oral History Interview, p. 223.
17. This was issued as Bulletin 45 (1940) under the title, *Critiques of Research in the Social Sciences: II.*
18. Mrs. Eleanor C. Isbell, Research Associate of the Social Science Research Council, informs me that she was given this report as part of her "education" when she joined the Council. She states that the minutes of that meeting provide a good picture of Nourse in action as a member of the Council. (Letter from Eleanor C. Isbell to author, September 21, 1973.)

Chapter IX

1. For more complete information on the war activities of the Brookings Institution, see Charles B. Saunders, Jr., *The Brookings Institution: A Fifty-Year History* (Washington, D.C.: The Brookings Institution, 1966), pp. 62-69.
2. Bell was impressed with the gracious and capable way in which Nourse accepted and handled his heavy responsibilities, in that "most presidents find their duties so exacting that they seek relief from their regular occupations and some get leaves-of-absence." (Letter from George Washington Bell to author, July 1, 1963.)
3. Published in *American Economic Review,* March, 1943.
4. Many years later, Nourse admitted that he "overstated" his position at that time. "The receptivity that I had had to the innovation involved in Farm Board and stabilization corporations and my tempered attitude of objective evaluation of Triple A and other measures, my attitude toward the New Deal in general—was not quite in line with my avowed minimalist declaration. . . . I was looking backward at my past position rather than around at what was taking place and of my own participation in the process." See Cornell Oral History Interview, pp. 301-303.
5. See Robert Nathan, *Mobilizing for Abundance* (New York: McGraw-Hill Book Company, Inc., 1944). This book presented a lucid analysis of the economic problems confronting the nation and offered helpful solutions for them. George Soule reviewed *Mobilizing for Abundance* and *Price Making in a Democracy* in the May 15, 1944, issue of *New Republic* under the title, "Business and Its Doctors." He found little basic disagreement in the two books and said: "Business has now what may prove to be a last chance to listen to its doctors."
6. See also his discussion of papers on "The Structure of Post-War American Business" in the *American Economic Review* (March, 1944). Here he said: "The roles of individual business and of government are co-ordinate. Each can help the other" (p. 131).
7. A typed copy in Nourse's files gives no information on time or place of presentation, but it was apparently given as an address to business leaders.
8. See Cornell Oral History Interview, pp. 297-299.
9. Gordon found this a very happy arrangement. He wrote me (June 11, 1973) that "Nourse provided all the help I could possibly need. . . . All through the

study he was available as a sympathetic counselor, but left me entirely to my own devices in carrying on the study. When the book came to publication Nourse insisted at the highest possible policy levels . . . that it should be published in precisely the way that I had completed it: and he carried the day." Gordon considered Nourse "a pioneer in the field now loosely referred to as industrial organization. His work in this area paved the way for much later work by a younger generation of economists."

10. Among those who carefully read and offered suggestions on the early draft chapters were Harold B. Rowe and Kurt Broun of the Brookings staff; Dean Robert D. Calkins, School of Business, Columbia University; Dean E. T. Grether, School of Business Administration, University of California; Professor R. A. Gordon, Department of Economics, University of California; Professor William S. Hopkins, Economics Department, Stanford University; and Professor Sumner H. Slicter, Department of Economics, Harvard University.

11. The conditions that led to the establishment of the National Science Foundation are set forth by Don K. Price in *Government and Science* (New York: New York University Press, 1954). See Chapter II, and pp. 47-64.

12. I was working on this book when Nourse became Chairman of the Council of Economic Advisers. While he was with the Council, I continued to submit chapters to him, which he conscientiously reviewed. Because of my other obligations and the lack of interest in cooperative studies in the Brookings Institution after Nourse's departure, I did not get out the book we had planned. However, I used much of my manuscript in *The Rise of American Cooperative Enterprise* (1969), which I dedicated "To Edwin G. Nourse—Dean of Scholars in American Cooperative Enterprise."

13. Published by the Chicago University Press in 1944.

14. Compare the views of J. M. Keynes on this book as expressed in a letter to Hayek on June 18, 1944. Keynes found himself "morally and philosophically" in agreement with the book, but he could not accept Hayek's attack on all planning. He said: "Moderate planning will be safe if those carrying it out are rightly oriented in their own minds and hearts to the moral issue." See R. F. Harrod, *The Life of John Maynard Keynes*, (London: Macmillan & Co., 1951) pp. 436-437.

15. See Lewis L. Lorwin, *Time for Planning* (New York: Harper & Bros., 1945), pp. 14-15. Lorwin's interest in planning went back to the early days of the New Deal. As a member of the staff of Brookings Institution, he then promoted a well-known seminar on the subject in the Institution's Round Table Room. Lorwin recalls that Nourse was the only member of the Institution's staff having a vital interest in these meetings. (Letter from Lewis L. Lorwin to author, December 10, 1963.)

16. These hearings (on S 1730 and S 1823) led directly to the Employment Act of 1946, signed into law by President Truman on February 20, 1946, and brought Nourse's qualifications for chairmanship of the Council of Economic Advisers to the attention of Senator Murray, who was a cosponsor of this legislation. For the detailed story of how this act came to be passed, see the illuminating book by Stephen K. Bailey, *Congress Makes a Law* (New York: Columbia University Press, 1950).

17. Nourse reproduced this letter in his memoir, "The Professional Background of the First Chairman of the Council of Economic Advisers" (August, 1963); prepared for inclusion with his papers for the Harry S Truman Memorial Library. He was later informed by Bertam Gross (his administrative assistant in the CEA) that he (Gross), as staff assistant for Senator Murray, had drafted the letter for Senator Murray's signature. Without doubt, however, it also

represented the views of Senator Murray. See Cornell Oral History Interview, pp. 326-327.
18. For detailed information on the evolution of the "Full Employment Bill," see Bailey, op. cit., and Robert Lekachman, *The Age of Keynes* (New York: Random House, 1966), pp. 165-175. See also Nourse, *Economics in the Public Service* (New York: Harcourt, Brace & Co., 1953), pp. 49-75, and especially pp. 69-74.
19. A copy of this unpublished article is filed with the Nourse papers in the Truman Memorial Library.
20. For a full discussion of the intense interest which developed in economics during World War II, see Paul T. Homan, "Economics in the War Period," *American Economic Review* (December, 1946), pp. 855-871.
21. Cornell Oral History Interview, pp. 323-324. For Nourse's extended views on how his professional career had fitted him for this new development, see his memoir, "The Professional Background."

Chapter X

1. Much of the material for chapters 10 through 12 has been drawn from Nourse's book *Economics in the Public Service*, which has the subtitle *Administrative Aspects of the Employment Act* (New York: Harcourt, Brace, and Company, 1953). This book recorded Nourse's experience while Chairman of the Council of Economic Advisers. As an advocate of the concurrent history method of studying economic institutions, he set down in a personal diary his interpretation of events as they took place so that he or others could later draw on this material. Many excerpts from this diary—which is filed with the Truman Memorial Library—were incorporated in this book. References to it are recorded parenthetically with the initials "EPS."
2. Cornell Oral History Interview, p. 337.
3. The Full Employment Bill of 1945 is available as an appendix to Stephen K. Bailey's book *Congress Makes a Law: The Story Behind the Employment Act of 1946* (New York: Columbia University Press, 1950). In this section, I have drawn heavily on Bailey's book, which provides authoritative information on the gestation of the Employment Act.
4. Robert Lekachman, *The Age of Keynes* (New York: Random House, 1966), p. 173. He also said: "As soon became evident, forecasting in the 1945 state of the art failed to project the movement of the economy with enough precision to define appropriate compensatory action. . . . It is even conceivable that Congress did an unwitting service to the reputation of economists by its refusal to retain this key section of the bill [relating to the National Production and Employment Budget]."
5. See Bailey, op. cit., pp. 170-171 and 226-227.
6. *Memoirs of Harry S Truman.* Volume I, *Year of Decisions* (New York: Doubleday and Co., Inc., 1955), p. 493.
7. For Keyserling's own account of his background, see his Oral History Interview by Jerry H. Hess, May, 171 (Harry S Truman Library, Independence Mo., 1975), pp. 1-4. See also Corinne Silverman, *The President's Economic Advisers*, Inter-University Case Study #48 (University, Ala.: University of Alabama Press, 1959).
8. Silverman, op. cit., p. 4.
9. The winner of the First Prize of $25,000 was Herbert Stein, later to be a

Chairman of the Council of Economic Advisers. The judges for the contest were Wesley C. Mitchell, Director of the Bureau of Economic Research; A. F. Whitney, President of the Railway Trainmen; Clarence Dykstra, President of the University of Wisconsin; and Beardsley Ruml, well-known economist-businessman.

10. For Keyserling's account of his participation in the development of the Employment Act, see his Oral History Interview for the Truman Library, p. 25-32. See also his article, "The Council of Economic Advisers since 1946: Its Contributions and Failures," in the March, 1978, *Atlantic Economic Journal*, pp. 17-19, in which he said that the original Full Employment Bill "was very far from my idea of desirable legislation, which I envisaged as a plenary statute to set goals for full employment, production, and purchasing power, and to unite all of the significant economic policies of the federal government in an integrated attempt to reach these goals. This indeed had been the basic theme of my 1944 Pabst essay. . . . The bill as finally enacted was very close to my work on the subject. It differed mainly in its apportionment of responsibility between the President and the Congress along established and conventional lines; my Pabst essay, based upon long experience as a worker in both the legislative and executive branches, advocated a larger participation by the Congress in the process of defining the goals and formulating the policies geared toward full employment. My essay also contemplated larger participation in the process by representatives of the general public. After more than three decades of experience with the Employment Act of 1946, the Humphrey-Hawkins Full Employment and Balanced Growth proposal moves largely in the direction of this wider participation."
11. Quoted by Edward S. Flash, Jr., *Economic Advice and Presidential Leadership: The Council of Economic Advisers* (New York: Columbia University Press, 1965), p. 23.
12. For additional information, see Silverman, op. cit. p. 3; Nourse, op. cit., pp. 111-112; and Flash, op. cit., p. 21.
13. Flash, op cit., pp. 23-24.
14. *In Memoriam: Edwin Griswold Nourse, May 20, 1883–April 7, 1974* (Washington, D.C.: The Brookings Institution, 1975), pp. 13-14.
15. Cornell Oral History Interview, p. 352.
16. Ibid., p. 351.
17. Ibid.
18. Ibid., pp. 347-348.
19. Ibid., p. 304.
20. Keyserling, in recalling this episode, said: "Steelman and his boys completely rewrote the report and sent it back to us. This I regarded as entirely improper quite aside from the fact that they did a job inferior to ours. I thought it was a basic issue. Nourse was inclined not to fight on it, but we did make a fight on it, though a pleasant one. We revised it again and brought it back to what we had in mind." (Truman Library Oral History Interview, p. 41.)
21. Cornell Oral History Interview, p. 388.
22. *The Truman Presidency* (New York: The Macmillan Company, 1966), p. 161.
23. Ibid., pp. 162-165.
24. See Truman Library Oral History Interview, pp. 55-103.
25. It is obvious from his Truman Library interview that Keyserling enjoyed being part of the Administration's team. He had the full support of the liberal bloc in the Democratic Party, for they considered him the strong man on the

Council, the defender of the faith, and an economist they could depend upon. See Alonzo L. Hamby, *Beyond the New Deal: Harry S. Truman and American Liberalism* (New York: Columbia University Press, 1973), pp. 81, 148, 182, 197, 303.

26. Cornell Oral History Interview, p. 368. Keyserling, in reviewing the manuscript for this book (December 1, 1978), commented as follows: "They were not referred to me *qua* CEA member nor for Council attention at that stage, and I knew they would come to the Council later for review and comment."

Chapter XI

1. There had been no problem of relationship with the Joint Committee on the Economic Report during 1946. The committee had been set up before the Council began operations under the chairmanship of Senator Joseph C. O'Mahoney, but Congress had adjourned soon afterwards. With the congressional defeat of the Democratic Party, it was apparent that the committee would be reconstituted under a Republican chairman. Senator Robert A. Taft became chairman in January, 1947.
2. It should be noted that the problem was not pressing at this time. The Joint Committee on the Economic Report was not really organized to report on February 1 as required under the Employment Act of 1946. No hearings were held, and only a nominal two-page report was made on January 30. The president informed Nourse that this report was "wholly innocuous." Edwin G. Nourse, *Economics in the Public Service* (New York: Harcourt, Brace, and Company, 1953), p. 187.
3. Cornell Oral History Interview, p. 355.
4. For more detailed information, see Appendix B, "The Council's Plan of Staff Work," *Economics in the Public Service*, pp. 469-472; see also pp. 155-158.
5. See *Public Administration Review*, Autumn, 1947, pp. 85-92.
6. Nourse included this address as an appendix to his book, *Economics in the Public Service*, pp. 475-488. (It was misdated in the book as being given on May 14, 1948.)
7. Letter from G. Derwood Baker to author, January 22, 1975.
8. For more complete information on the efforts of the Truman Administration to arrest inflation, see Craufurd D. Goodwin and R. Stanley Herren, "The Truman Administration: Problems and Policies Unfold," in *Exhortation and Controls: The Search for a Wage-Price Policy, 1945-1971*, Craufurd D. Goodwin, Editor (Washington, D.C.: The Brookings Institution, 1975), pp. 44-48.
9. Quoted by Goodwin and Herren, op. cit., p. 46. Chester Bowles expressed the same idea as follows in a letter to the president on November 5: "If we can load the blame for all that has happened and all that is likely to happen squarely on their shoulders, I believe we will be richer by five or six million votes in 1948."
10. Keyserling provided a suggested draft for this message on November 11. Goodwin and Herren, op. cit., pp. 46-47.
11. Goodwin and Herren, op. cit., p. 48.
12. For more complete expression of Keyserling's views on this matter, see his Oral History Interview for the Truman Library, p. 54 and p. 122.
13. Nourse highly applauded this sentence which he attributed to Gross. He said: "The thing that I was particularly tickled about in that article was that he said 'Congress, in its wisdom, set up its own advisory apparatus in the Joint

Economic Committee and furnished the President an advisory staff arm in the Council.' I particularly liked his expression 'it did not attempt to bestride the two functions' and that was exactly the position that I took although, subsequently, he departed from it." (Cornell Oral History Interview, p. 408).
14. Cornell Oral History Interview, pp. 409-410.

Chapter XII

1. It is of interest that Keyserling thought that Nourse's unwillingness to testify in support of the president at Congressional hearings was due to his desire to maintain his position on the Council should there be a change in party administration. In his Oral History Interview for the Truman Library (p. 54), he said that "Nourse made a public issue of it by telling people around the country that we just wanted to support the President politically, which put us in an almost impossible position. And it later developed that what he was really concerned about was that in 1946 the Republicans had taken the Congress and he thought that Dewey was going to be President [in 1948], and he was in private consultation trying to assure that he would stay on in the next administration and therefore he did not want to be identified politically with the President he was serving."
2. For more complete discussion, see Edwin G. Nourse, *Economics in the Public Service* (New York: Harcourt, Brace, and Company, 1953), pp. 70-75; pp. 216-220; and pp. 398-399.
3. In an interview with the author on April 5, 1975, Keyserling pointed out that the split report corrected a situation of concern to Truman. He said that having all in the president's economic report was artificial in that it made the president mouth economic principles that were alien to him.
4. Edwin G. Nourse, "Why I Had to Step Aside," *Collier's*, February 18, 1950, p. 54.
5. In his Oral History Interview for the Truman Library (p. 101), Keyserling said: "I do not recall this specific memo, and my guess would be that it was prepared at the White House—perhaps by Clifford. However, the memo in substance is so close to the 'political' phrases of the agreement reached by the Ewing group that I am confident that it may be fairly said that the memo derived from the deliberations of that group." A copy of this memo was attached as an appendix to Keyserling's interview. The original is filed with Clifford's papers at the Truman Library.
6. Nourse later explained that he had deemed it advisable to get White House approval on this talk. "I felt that this pushed me out into a position where I could not escape being regarded as a spokesman for the Administration. I therefore submitted this manuscript to the White House and received clearance before it was delivered" (EPS, p. 405). This address was reproduced as Appendix E in *Economics in the Public Service*, pp. 485-495.
7. Letter from E. T. Grether to author, October 14, 1977. For a full analysis of the economics of preparedness at this time, see his paper, "Preparedness for War and General Economic Policy," in the Proceedings of the American Economic Association, May, 1940. In his concluding sentences he said: "Never in peacetime have we faced this problem of controlled balance in the economy involving broad decisions as to the size of the civilian expenditures in relation to those of the military establishment. . . . It will require consummate wisdom and skill in national economic and foreign policy and in administration to maintain reasonable balance under these conditions."

8. Cornell Oral History Interview, pp. 416-418.
9. Ibid., pp. 418-419.
10. Ibid., pp. 425-426.
11. Ibid., pp. 420-421.
12. *Economics in the Public Service*, pp. 242-243. For more complete discussion, see the section on "The Spence and Murray Bills," pp. 240-248. Edward S. Flash, Jr., in his book on the Council of Economic Advisers, *Economic Advisers and Presidential Leadership* (New York: Columbia University Press, 1965), p. 124, states that "in 1949 Keyserling, Bertram Gross, and other staff members were active proponents of the Spence and Murray Bills as resurrections of the original Full Employment Act. Like Truman, Nourse would have nothing to do with either of the measures, neither of which were considered by Congress."
13. Nourse, "Why I Had to Step Aside," p. 54.
14. See Craufurd D. Goodwin and R. Stanley Herren, "The Truman Years," in *Exhortation and Controls: The Search for a Wage-Price Policy, 1945-1971*, Craufurd D. Goodwin, Editor (Washington, D.C.: The Brookings Institution, 1975), p. 63.
15. Ibid.
16. Cornell Oral History Interview, p. 424.
17. Letter from Leon H. Keyserling to author, September 11, 1975.
18. Nourse, "Why I Had to Step Aside," p. 55.
19. For full text of this letter, see Appendix C in *Economics in the Public Service*.
20. Nourse, "Why I Had to Step Aside," p. 54.
21. *Hearings Before the Joint Committee on the Economic Report*, Congress of the United States, Eighty-first Congress, February 8-18, 1949. (Washington, D.C.: U.S. Government Printing Office.)
22. In his Oral History Interview for the Truman Library (p. 187), Keyserling reported that he was scheduled to talk to a group of businessmen in New York, when Clifford called him and said: "The 'Boss' thinks it would be best if you didn't go and make that talk." Keyserling commented: "And, of course, I made an excuse and called it off. I wasn't prepared to fight the President on the Spence bill, and I was really a little bit out of line." Keyserling has also supplied me with the following information with regard to his support of the Spence bill. "The sum and substance of the matter is that I did not feel at the time that the President's official program to deal with the economy during the recession of 1949 was entirely adequate or dealt sufficiently with some outstanding long-range problems. I never expressed publicly any disagreement with the President's program. . . . There came a time when the Spence bill was under consideration, when I learned that the President did not want it pushed, and from that time forward I ceased to interest myself in it. Before that I did encourage those who were developing interest in the Spence bill. I never regarded it inappropriate, on the part of those in high Government positions, to maintain an informal and off-the-record interest in proposals which went further than the President was prepared to espouse, so long as they were not inconsistent with his program and supportive of his objectives." (Letter from Leon H. Keyserling to author, August 28, 1975.)
23. Cornell Oral History Interview, p. 438.
24. Ibid., p. 431.
25. See Murray R. Benedict, *Farm Policies of the United States, 1790-1950* (New York: The Twentieth Century Fund, 1953), pp. 479 and 484-485.
26. In his memoirs, Truman said of the Council members: "These were eminently

qualified men. They differed in point of view, and in the years ahead were to disagree strongly. I knew this when I appointed them. I believe I was well advised in their selection by the very fact that they were not of one mind." *Memoirs of Harry S. Truman.* Volume I, *Year of Decisions* (New York: Doubleday and Co., Inc., 1955), p. 495.

27. Letter from Frederick V. Waugh to author, June 29, 1964.
28. For more complete information, see Nourse's personal diary note, *Economics in the Public Service*, p. 283. See also Nourse, "Why I Had to Step Aside," p. 56.
29. See Nourse's article, "Why I Had to Step Aside," p. 56.
30. See Alonzo L. Hamby, *Beyond the New Deal: Harry S. Truman and American Liberalism* (New York: Columbia University Press, 1973), p. 302. He also said: "Truman's approach was cautious, but by abandoning the balanced budget, by stressing economic growth, Truman indicated that he had adopted the liberal expansionism of his most articulate economic adviser" (p. 333).
31. See Nourse, "Why I had to Step Aside," p. 56.
32. Cornell Oral History Interview, pp. 442-443.
33. Letters from John Steelman to author, May 3, 1975, and June 3, 1975. Steelman also respected Nourse's efforts to keep the Council "out of politics" and "start it on the right pathway." He thought Nourse's position that Council members should not testify before Congressional committees "for or against" administration policies "was right." He said: "In my 20 years of Government service I did not meet a greater man than Dr. Nourse."
34. In his Oral History Interview for the Truman Library (p. 107), Keyserling said that the president "offered me the job right away, and in fact the President said spontaneously when he got Nourse's letter of resignation, because Clifford told me this, 'Now we can appoint Leon.' Now, these other forces came in, and they did succeed in delaying it, but there was never any offer to anyone else." For a comprehensive analysis of Keyserling's term as Chairman of the Council from November 1, 1949 to March 31, 1953, see Edward S. Flash, Jr., *Economic Advice and Presidential Leadership: The Council of Economic Advisers* (New York: Columbia University Press, 1965), Chapters II and III, pp. 18-99.
35. Joseph A. Pechman, "Making Economic Policy: The Role of the Economist," General Series Reprint 311 (Washington, D.C.: The Brookings Institution, 1976).
36. Don K. Price, *Government and Science: Their Dynamic Relation in American Democracy* (New York: New York University Press, 1954), pp. 180-181.
37. For a discussion of the insuperable problems of Nourse as first Chairman of the Council of Economic Advisers, see Paul T. Homan, "The Place of the President's Council of Economic Advisers," *Proceedings of the Western Economic Association*, September, 1953. Homan served as one of the top staff members of the Council during Nourse's term as chairman. In an interview with the author on April 27, 1966, he gave Nourse credit for establishing the Council as a professional organization.

Chapter XIII

1. Cornell Oral History Interview, pp. 451-452.
2. Letter from G. Derwood Baker to author, January 22, 1975.
3. Resources for the Future, Inc., Washington, D.C., was established in 1952 as a nonprofit corporation to advance the development, conservation, and use of natural resources through programs of research and education. It has been supported largely by grants from the Ford Foundation.

4. Cornell Oral History Interview, p. 458.
5. Ibid., p. 408.
6. Ibid., p. 470.
7. For a good critique of the mature economy thesis, see George Terborgh, *The Bogy of Economic Maturity* (Chicago: Machinery and Allied Products Institute, 1945).
8. Cornell Oral History Interview, p. 483.
9. Edward S. Flash, Jr., *Economic Advice and Presidential Leadership: The Council of Economic Advisers* (New York: Columbia University Press, 1965), pp. 103-104. Keyserling is of the opinion that this paragraph in the text "misconstrues the matter of funds for the Council" (letter from Leon H. Keyserling to author, January 3, 1979). He calls my attention to his explanation of what happened in a letter to the editor of the *Journal of Commerce*, December 31, 1968, in which he said: "I was successful in having the Council cut restored in full, and without difficulty. . . . The method chosen to help was unusual and sprung from the fertile brain of Senator O'Mahoney. He suggested that . . . the Council be permitted to spend the fiscal 1953 reduced appropriation in nine months rather than twelve. This was agreed to without any significant opposition anywhere. It had precisely the effect of permitting us to spend at the originally asked for rate and not to have to reduce our activities in any way, as the amount alloted was authorized to be spent from July 1, 1952 to March 31, 1953." Thus, in effect, the responsibility of maintaining the Council was passed to the incoming Administration. For full exposition of Keyserling's views, see his *Journal of Commerce* letter quoted above.
10. Flash, op. cit., p. 105. Keyserling, in his letter to the author of January 3, 1979, objects to the words "Keyserling staff" as being "categorically incorrect" in that "very few staff were added after Dr. Nourse left the Council. Initially, I conceded to Nourse the privilege of selecting the original staff members, and took part only in the selection of Colm and Gross, who turned out to be two of our best staff members. Nor were all those on the staff when I left terminated. At least, David Lusher and Frances James were retained. . . ."
11. Ibid., p. 102.
12. Ibid., p. 103.
13. Ibid., p. 105.
14. Arthur F. Burns, *Prosperity Without Inflation* (New York: Fordham University Press, 1957), p. 86.
15. Ibid. Keyserling, in his letter to the author of January 3, 1979, maintains that this paragraph gives "a complete misunderstanding of what had been happening all along under Nourse and Keyserling. We developed such relationships quite as fully as at any later time, and my files are filled with evidence of this. . . ."
16. *In Memoriam: Edwin Griswold Nourse, May 20, 1883-April 7, 1974* (Washington, D.C.: The Brookings Institution, 1975), p. 21.
17. Cornell Oral History Interview, p. 515.
18. *The Employment Act—Past and Future*, Edited by Gerhard Colm, February, 1956.
19. Although he did not refer to Nourse in his text, it was clear from a footnote that he had him in mind.
20. The term "new economics" as used by Nourse should not be confused with the "new economics" of the 1960s, which will be discussed in the following chapter. Leon Keyserling referred to the "so-called 'new economics'" of the 1930s in an article, "Everybody's Problem: Prices, Wages, Profits," *Harper's Magazine*, March, 1948, p. 2.

21. For complete citation, and citations of the others honored, with portraits, see "Proceedings of the Annual Meeting of the American Farm Economic Association, August 28-31," in the *Journal of Farm Economics*, pp. iii-xiii, December, 1957.
22. Letter from Herbert L. Forest to author, December 10, 1966.
23. Cornell Oral History Interview, pp. 609-610.
24. Ibid., pp. 602-604.
25. Burns, on the other hand, favored such an amendment on the ground that it would strengthen efforts to deal with inflation. See Arthur F. Burns, *Prosperity Without Inflation* (New York: Fordham University Press, 1957), pp. 71-73.
26. This case study in public administration and policy formation was made under the Inter-University Case Program and was published as Case #48 for the ICP by the University of Alabama Press, University, Alabama, 1959.
27. Keyserling thinks that this sentence might be "misinterpreted." In his letter to the author of January 3, 1979, he states: "I regarded myself as a trustee of the economic policies I have always believed in, and valued my relationship with the President as a more effective means of achieving these policies than any other relationship. I determined Truman's economic thinking far more than he determined mine, and I determined his policies far more than he determined my actions."
28. In his letter to the author of January 3, 1979, Keyserling explains "that the strong language that I used [as quoted by Nourse] was not an initial criticism of or attack upon Nourse, but rather my response to some of the things he said about me in *Economics in the Public Service* and some of the things that Miss Silverman picked up from that book in the review. I never initiated a published criticism or attack directed against Nourse."
29. It is significant that the different viewpoints of Nourse and Keyserling flared up in a symposium held at the annual meeting of the American Economic Association in December, 1973. This symposium was held because there was a widespread sentiment among economists that the Council had become "too political." Several participants held that political predisposition of Council chairmen endangered the validity of economic advice. For a report on this meeting, see *Challenge* magazine, March-April, 1974.

Chapter XIV

1. See Joseph G. Knapp, *Seeds that Grew: A History of the Cooperative Grange League Federation Exchange* (Hinsdale, N.Y.: Anderson House, 1960), Foreword, pp. vii-ix.
2. Nourse was recommended for this post by Herbert Forest, Director of the USDA's Dairy Division, who was in charge of the federal milk order program.
3. See *Report to the Secretary of Agriculture by the Federal Milk Order Study Committee* (USDA, Washington, D.C., December, 1962).
4. Letter from George N. Pederson to author, June 12, 1968.
5. See "Symposium Appraisal of Federal Milk Marketing Orders," *Journal of Dairy Science*, November, 1962, pp. 1397-1410.
6. See *Administered Prices: A Compendium on Public Policy*, Subcommittee on Antitrust and Monopoly of the Committee on the Judiciary, U.S. Senate, 88th Congress, 1st Session, Pursuant to Senate Resolution 56 (1963).
7. See *Public Policy on Administered Prices*, Hearings before the Subcommittee on Antitrust and Monopoly of the Committee on the Judiciary, U.S. Senate, 88th

Congress, 1st Session, Pursuant to Senate Resolution 56 (Part 29), May 21, 22, and 23, 1963.
8. See John M. Blair, *Economic Concentration: Structure, Behavior and Public Policy* (New York: Harcourt Brace Jovanovich, Inc., 1972), pp. 614-620. Blair was chief economist to the Senate Antitrust and Monopoly subcommittee under Senator Kefauver.
9. Nourse was unable to present his paper in person because of the illness of his wife.
10. These documents provide invaluable information on Nourse's behavior as first Chairman of the C.E.A. In the first, he endeavored to show how his professional career had fitted him for this post. In the second, he explained how in his 50 public utterances in the form of speeches, articles, or interviews he endeavored to set a precedent that would "not plague his successors." As chairman he did not think it "proper to take a public position as protagonist of any particular politico-economic policy or program of the Administration," while he thought it "both proper and desirable to reaffirm in various concrete situations" his devotion "to the purposes of the Employment Act" and to urge "the assistance and cooperation of industry, agriculture, labor, and State and local governments to effectuating these purposes."
11. Nourse participated for the last time in a workshop seminar of the Joint Council held at the University of Nebraska in May, 1964. However, he was to continue his active interest in its affairs to the very end of his life.
12. For comprehensive information, see Katrina V. Berman, *Worker Owned Plywood Cooperatives: An Economic Analysis* (Pullman, Washington: Washington State University Press, 1967).
13. For full discussion of the tax problems of these associations, see Chapter 11, "The Income Tax Question," in Berman, op. cit., pp. 165-179.
14. Letter from Kelsey B. Gardner to author, January 18, 1967. Gardner also served as an expert witness for the associations in these cases. It was he who recommended that Nourse be brought in as an expert witness because of his vast knowledge and understanding of the cooperative form of business enterprise.
15. Karl D. Loos, who was counsel for the Puget Sound Plywood Association, informed me in a letter of April 25, 1973, that "there can be no doubt that the Judge attached great importance to the testimony of Dr. Nourse. In my opinion, Dr. Nourse was the most important single witness of the entire case. . . . I believe the testimony of Dr. Nourse was also of great importance in persuading the government not to appeal the Tax Court decision." Robert M. Kerr, who was counsel for the Linnton Plywood Association, likewise informed me in a letter of May 29, 1973, that Judge Solomon in the Linnton Plywood case accepted and placed strong reliance upon Dr. Nourse's explanations of the basic characteristics and methods of operation of workers' cooperatives. He states: "I am sure that Dr. Nourse's participation in this case and in the similar litigation involving Puget Sound Plywood, Inc., in the United States Tax Court was a major factor in the determination of the Federal income tax status of workers' production cooperatives which are not only organized to operate, but also actually operate, on a true cooperative basis."
16. The term "new economics" became popular in the early 1960s to represent the activist economic policies of the Kennedy Administration. See Joseph A. Pechman, "Making Economic Policy: The Role of the Economist," Brookings Institution, General Series Reprint 311, 1976, pp. 54-56.
17. In reviewing this talk in his syndicated column, J. A. Livingston in the *Washington Post*, December 14, 1964, said: "Even eternal Benjamin Franklin needs

updating. In an essay which sparkles with youthfully crisp phraseology, Nourse reconstructs Franklin's famous and overworked apothegm to: 'In this world nothing is certain but life and taxes.' "

18. As Robert A. Gordon has pointed out in his valuable history of American economic experience, *Economic Instability and Growth: The American Record* (New York: Harper and Row, 1974), p. 155, "The happy combination of rapidly expanding output, falling unemployment, and relative price stability ended in the latter part of 1965. In July President Johnson announced the beginning of expanded American involvement in Vietnam. Government expenditures began to rise rapidly while the expansionary effects of the fiscal stimuli applied in 1964-65 were still being felt; business expectations improved still further, and the rise in business investment accelerated. Thus, just as full employment was being reached, a new and powerful expansionary stimulus was injected into the economy. . . . The American economy entered a period of demand-pull inflation that persisted . . . until restrictive policies in 1969 helped bring on a new recession. . . ."

19. A condensed version of this address was carried in the *U.S. News and World Report,* June 14, 1965, under the title, "A Speech that Jolted the Stock Market."

20. *Invited Comments on Directions for the Future* (Twentieth Anniversary of the Employment Act of 1946: An Economic Symposium), Supplement to Hearings before the Joint Economic Committee of the 89th Congress, 2nd Session, 1966.

21. In information printed in the *Review's* "Green Room" section on its authors, Nourse said: "I am fully occupied—on a no-pressure basis—in writing a book which I refer to fondly as my 'Unfinished Symphony', because I have considerable doubt that I shall ever finish it and find a publisher. More formally, this opus is titled 'On Understanding Social Science'. . . . The present essay is excerpted with some modification from a chapter on 'Economic Science and Economic Statesmanship' ". A full account of Nourse's work on his "Unfinished Symphony" will be given in the following chapter.

22. For a classic statement of the philosophy of the New Economics by its leading exponent, see Chapter II, "The Promise of Modern Economic Policy," in Walter W. Heller's *New Dimensions of Political Economy* (Cambridge, Mass.: Harvard University Press, 1966), pp. 58-116. Nourse greatly admired Heller's writing ability and thought that Heller had broadened his views under the conditions of 1967 and 1968.

23. This manuscript may have been submitted to the *Virginia Quarterly Review* or some other publication, but there was no evidence of this in his records. Nourse frequently prepared an article to clarify his thinking on some subject and then made no effort to get it published.

Chapter XV

1. Information on the beginnings of the book has been drawn largely from this document and interviews with Nourse.
2. *Letters to the Editor,* a volume of letters in tribute to Evelyn Breck, Brookings Institution, December, 1964.
3. Cornell Oral History Interview, pp. 443-444.
4. When I interviewed him in 1967, he mentioned that he had long been "a steady supporter" of the Seeing Eye Dogs movement for the blind, the Star Commonwealth for Boys in Albion, Michigan, and the Berkshire Boys' Farm in Massachusetts. These benefactions give some idea of the man. See Cornell Oral History Interview, p. 562.

5. James R. Robinson, Secretary of the "Committee of 100," states in a letter to the author (December 19, 1976) that "Dr. Edwin G. Nourse was a major contributor to the Legal Defense Fund. His annual gifts ran as high as $3,300.00, usually in stock, and his last gift came in 1973."
6. Joel Seligman in his book *The High Citadel* (Boston: Houghton Mifflin Company, 1978), refers to the Antioch Law School as "the nation's first law school-public interest law firm," as a "highly personalized expression of the educational theories of its founding co-deans, Edgar and Jean Cahn." (For more complete information, see pp. 363-369.)
7. In the revised foreword that Nourse prepared for the book in December, 1973, he made his meaning clear by paraphrasing it to read: "Attack, as you should, what you find base or stupid in our present way of life. But do not ignore or put down the honest efforts of those who went before you constructing a broad Highway of Science for you to travel and extend; and fashioning a set of scientific tools for you to use, to expand, and to refine."
8. Letter from Peggy Gagan to author of May 26, 1977.
9. The brochure was issued later in the year, and a substantial amount was obtained to help fund the professorship which was established in 1977. (Letter from Laron C. Clark, Jr., Director of Development, Hampton Institute, to author, May 18, 1977.)
10. In 1975 the Brookings Institution brought together these talks and other tributes with a portrait of Nourse by Karsh in a beautifully published brochure entitled *EGN*.

Index

INDEX

Administered Prices: A Compendium on Public Policy, 409 ff.
Administered prices and public policy, 181, 372-374, 412-413
Administrative methods, 322-324
"Admonition," 391-392
Advisory functions, 250
Agricultural Act (1948), 244
Agricultural Adjustment Act (1933), 129-130
Agricultural adjustment concept, 135
"Agricultural and Industrial Balance in the United States, The" (Nourse), 45
Agricultural cooperation, 59-60, 70 ff., 90-92, 97-102 (*See also* Cooperative enterprise)
Agricultural courses, 24-25, 56-57, 63
Agricultural credit problems, 107, 128-129, 196
Agricultural Economics (Nourse), 50-52, 63
Agricultural integration, 67 ff.
Agricultural Marketing (Weld), 63
Agricultural Marketing Act (1929), 118, 120, 121
Agricultural planning, 134-135
"Agricultural Surpluses as a Concern of Cooperatives" (Nourse), 126-127
"Agriculture" (Nourse), 145-147
Agriculture in an Unstable Economy (Schultz), 283-284
Altgeld, Peter, 14
American Agriculture and the European Market (Nourse), 93-94, 107
American Capitalism—The Concept of Countervailing Power (Galbraith), 358-359
American Economic Association, 179-180, 336
American Economic Review, 44
American Farm Bureau Federation, 64, 70

American Farm Economic Association, 92 ff., 371-372; presidential address, 97-98
American Institute of Cooperation, 97-99, 103, 112, 131-133, 142, 196-198
American Marketing Association, 256
American Retail Federation, 255
Anderson, Dewey, 308
Anderson, John K., 472
Annual Reports of Council of Economic Advisers, 228-231 (1946), 266-267 (1947)
Anti-inflation Committee, 289-290
Antioch College of Law, 450, 454
Anti-trust decisions, 403-404
Aquinas, Thomas, 42
Arkansas, Governor's Adviser, 49
Arthur, I. W., 82
Automation, 359-361

Bailey, Stephen Kemp, 210, 225
Baird, Frieda, 128-129
Baker, G. Derwood, 258-259, 337
Ball, E. W., 93
Barrett, Joe C., 56, 57
Baukage, H. R., 163-164
Beaman, Harriet Augusta, 2, 4-7 (*See also* Nourse, Mrs. Edwin Henry)
Becker, Carl, 178
Becker, Madge, 456
Behavior of Prices, The (Mills), 171
Bell, James Washington, 179, 477
Benedict, Murray R., 82, 113, 482, 517 (note 17)
Benner, Claude, 89, 128-129
Big Business: A New Era (Lilienthal), 358-359
Black, John D., 93, 100, 113, 128-130, 371
Bliss, Director, 62
"Bottom up" cooperative procedure, 90-91

535

Bradfute, Oscar, 94
Brand, Charles J., 108
Brandt, Karl, 474-475
Brannan, Charles, 300, 304, 306, 313
Brannan Plan, 313
Breck, Esther, 444
Breck, Evelyn, 444, 446
Breeder's Gazette, 109-110
Brindley, John H., 62-63
Brookings Graduate School, 95-96, 149, 514 (note 4)
Brookings Institution, 115, 142, 150, 159, 175, 374, 430, 463
"Brookings Old-Timers Group," 444, 455
Brookings, Robert S., 85, 86, 87, 110-111, 517 (note 15)
Brough, Hillman, 48-49
Bryan, William Jennings, 13
Budget Bureau, 251
Budget policy, 256-257
Budget problems, 248-250, 268-269
Burns, Arthur F., 156, 330, 348-351, 358, 363-364, 386-388, 406, 425-427, 446
Bush, Vanniver, 440-441
"Business Executives as Professional Men" (Nourse), 193-194, 202, 205, 207
Business Leadership in the Large Corporation (Gordon), 192-193
Butz, Earl, 196

Cahn, Edgar, 450, 454, 532 (note 6)
California Fruit Growers Exchange, 67, 72, 73
Calkins, Robert D., 455
Canadian Journal of Banking, 65
Canning, John B., 42
Capitalism, meaning of, 402-403
Capper-Volstead Act (1922), 74, 79, 376, 404, 460, 462
Carnegie, Andrew, 22-23
Carnegie Corporation, 86-87
Carnegie Institution, 150
Carroll, Mollie Ray, 45, 455
Catteral, Ralph, 25, 27
Challenge—The Magazine of Economic Affairs, 456 ff.
"Changing Patterns of Our Economy, The" (Nourse), 369-370
Changing Times (Kiplinger magazine), 286
"Cheapest Source of Increased Food Production, The" (Nourse), 58
Chicago in the 1890s, 5, 6, 11
Chicago Produce Market, The (Nourse), 52-55
Chicago World's Fair (Columbian Exposition), 11-12
Civil War atmosphere, 10
Clark, Colin, 156
Clark, John D., 205, 220-221, 229, 232-233, 242, 248, 265, 269, 273, 278, 282, 287, 292, 298-299, 302-303, 305, 308, 313-314, 322-323, 329, 386
Clark, John Maurice, 352-353, 446
Clayton Amendment, 73
Clearinghouse Movement, 114-115
Clifford, Clark, 234, 237-241, 251, 263-265, 270, 279, 281, 299, 310, 323
Coker, Francis W., 183-184
"Collective Bargaining and the Common Interest" (Nourse), 179-180
Colman, Gould P., 443
Colm, Gerhard, 223, 226, 233, 248, 252, 327-328, 446, 473
Committee for Economic Development, 192
"Committee of 17," 70-71
"Committee of 100," 447-448
"Commodity type cooperatives," 137-138
Commons, John R., 457, 471
"Compensated Dollar," Nourse's views on, 44
"Compulsory Cooperation," 138
Conant, James B., 441-442
"Concurrent history" concept, 129, 168-169, 345-346
"Conglomerate mergers," 424
Congressional testimony disagreement, 243-244, 264-265, 269, 273, 281-283, 303-306
Congress Makes a Law (Bailey), 211
Consulting jobs, 355 ff., 375 ff.
Controllers Institute of America, 253
"Cooperation American Style," 70
Cooperation in Agriculture (Powell), 63
Cooperative business integration, 413-414
"Cooperative Commonwealth" concept, 79
Cooperative enterprise, 29, 37, 52, 56, 59-60, 63-64, 67, 69-80, 88-92,

94-105, 107-115, 117-129, 131-134, 137-138, 143-144, 181, 196-198, 260-261, 345, 375-376, 394, 397-404, 413-414, 416-419, 422, 447, 452, 455, 461, 463, 470, 475, 479-480, 514-515 (note 2), 516 (note 14), 519 (note 17), 530 (note 15)
"Cooperative Livestock Shipping in Iowa" (Nourse and Hammans), 75-76
Cooperative marketing—an evaluation, 417-418
Cooperative Marketing of Livestock, The (Nourse and Knapp), 122-123
Cooperative production, 419-422
Cooperative success, fundamentals of, 78
Cooperative tax cases, 419-422
Cooper, Thomas F., 112
Copeland, Melvin T., 50, 53
Cornell, Ezra, 21
Cornell Law Quarterly, 109
Cornell University oral history interviews, 442
Cornell University student life, 21 ff.
"Corporate and Cooperative Farming" (Nourse), 68
Corporate farming, 67-68, 140-141
Council of Economic Advisers: administrative procedures of, 323-324, 427-428; annual reports of, 228-233, 266-267; functions of, 212-214; rebirth of, 349 ff.; staff committees in, 247 ff.
Coverdale, John, 64
Cunningham, E. H., 71
Curtis, C. F., 62-63, 68

Dairy marketing problems, 375-376
Davis, Chester, 133
Davis, Joseph S., 106-107, 129-130, 156, 371, 399
Day, Edmund E., 129, 170-172
Defense budget (1949), 321, 322
"Defining Our Employment Goals" (Nourse), 366-369
Deflation, 302, 303, 311
"Degradation of the Agrarian Dogma, The" (Nourse), 399
"Democracy as a Principle of Business" (Nourse), 178-179
Dewey, Davis R., 44
Dewey, Thomas E., 201, 277, 285-286, 291

Diener, Matt, 9, 16
"Dilemma of Government Spending, The" (Nourse), 383-385
"Does a Pig Have More Sense than a Sophomore?" (Nourse), 81
Dollinger, Miss, 15
Downers Grove, 6 ff., 39
Drury, Horace, 160-163, 165
Dyson, Lowell K., 143

"Early Flowering of the Employment Act" (Nourse), 433-435
Eastman, George, 150
"Economic Analysis and Political Synthesis" (Nourse), 338-339
Economic development, Nourse's views on, 501
"Economic Expansion Act of 1949," 316-318
Economic growth, 428
"Economic Implications of Military Preparedness" (Nourse), 284-285
Economic Indicators, 271
"Economic Justice as a Social Goal" (Nourse), 382
"Economic Literacy," 418-419
"Economic Philosophy of Cooperation, The" (Nourse), 78-79, 516 (note 14)
Economic reconversion, 260-263
Economic Reports of the President, 235-236, 267-268, 295-296
Economics in the Public Service (Nourse), 245-246, 345-348, 351-354
Economic situation in 1958, 381-382
"Economic Stabilization in a Troubled World" (Nourse), 274-275
"Economist and His Job, The" (Nourse), 174-175
Edminster, Lynn, 103, 455
Eisenhower, Dwight, 348-350, 352
Elam, Lloyd C., 450
Ely, Richard, 72
"Employment Act and the Economic Future, The" (Nourse), 226-228
"Employment Act and the New Economics, The" (Nourse), 435-437
Employment Act of 1946, 205 ff., 212-216; amendment to, 407; tenth anniversary of, 362-365; twentieth anniversary of, 430-433
Engberg, Russell C., 102, 515 (note 2), 517 (note 13)

Erdman, Henry E., 139
"Ethical Values of the Economic Process, The" (Nourse), 37-38
European recovery plans, 271, 272
European trips, 94, 143
"Evolving Idea of Cooperation in the United States" (Nourse), 113-114
Extension Service experience, 57-59
Ezekiel, Mordecai, 101, 128

Falk Foundation, 151 ff.
Farm Credit Administration, 128-129, 167, 196
"Farmer's Mysterious Malady, The" (Nourse), 111
Farm Foundation, 345
Farm Journal, 133
Farm policy, 301, 312-313
Fay, C. R., 143
Fayetteville, Arkansas, 48 ff.
Federal Farm Board, 118-125, 145
Federal Milk Order Study, 397-398
Federal Reserve policy, 428-429, 431-432
Fellow of American Farm Economic Association, 371
Fetter, Frank, 25
Field, James A., 32, 50
Fifty Years of Farmers Elevators in Iowa (Nourse), 76
"Fiscal drag," 437
Fiscal policy, 405, 415, 424-425, 434
Fisher, Irving, 44
Fisher, Joseph L., 461, 464, 473
Flanders, Ralph, 265, 305
Flash, Edward S., Jr., 221
Foreign aid study, 251-252
Forest, Herbert, 376, 529 (note 2)
Forrestal, James, 284
Fortune magazine, 441
Frankel, M. L. "Moe," 455, 477
Free enterprise, 163
Freeman, Orville L., 397, 401, 417
Freeman, Ralph E., 164
"From Dogma to Science in Cooperative Thinking" (Nourse), 197-198
"Full Employment Act of 1945," 201, 208
Full employment, clarification of, 366-369
Futrall, John C., 47-48, 57

Gagan, Peggy, 453-454, 457, 463, 478

Galbraith, John Kenneth, 351-352, 358-359, 457-458
General Motors Corporation, 411
"Gentle Art of Disinflation, The" (Nourse), 311
Gerald, Elizabeth, 443, 462, 478
Germany's Capacity to Pay (Moulton), 89
Golden wedding anniversary, 394
Goldenweiser, E. A., 25-26, 245
Goldwater, Barry, 424
Gordon, Aaron Robert, 192-193, 520-521 (note 9)
Gordon, Kermit, 443, 455-456, 463, 465
"Government Discipline of Private Economic Power" (Nourse), 409-410
Government spending, 323-324, 339, 383-385
Graham, Katherine, 449
Grant, Ulysses S., 13
Great Depression, 119
Grether, E. T., 54, 185-186, 285, 525 (note 7)
Gross, Bertram, 219, 225, 292, 300, 315
Guard, Samuel, 109-113

Hadley, Arthur T., 30
Hall, Arnold B., 31
Hamilton, Walton Hale, 42, 96
Hampton Institute gifts, 448-449
Hampton Institute professorship, 462, 532 (note 9)
Hansen, Alvin H., 201, 208, 364-365
Hardy, Charles O., 158, 175, 244
Harmonie Club incident, 298-300
"Harmonizing the Interests of Farm Producers and Town Consumers" (Nourse), 66-67
Harper's Magazine, 201
Harriman, Averell, 268
Hart, Schaffner and Marx Prize Essay, 43, 50
Harvey Weil Lectures, 345, 346
Hauge, Gabriel, 349
Hausrath, A. H., 80
Hayek, Frederich A., 198
Haymarket Square riots, 14
Hays, Brooks, 57
"Healthy Disinflation," 302
Heller, Walter W., 407, 408, 422, 424-425, 456

INDEX

Hibbard Memorial Lecture, 399
Hill, James B., 26
History teachers, Cornell, 25
Hobart, Alice Tisdale, 160-161, 347, 446-447 (*See also* Nourse, Alice Louise)
Hobson, John A., 470
Hoffman, Paul, 192, 258, 474
Holland, Jerome, 448-449
Holman, Charles W., 94, 97, 98
Homan, Paul, 223, 248, 328, 334, 527 (note 37)
Horton, Donald C., 85-86
Howard, James, 65
Hoxie, Robert Franklin, 26, 30, 31
Hulbert, Lyman S., 118
Hull House, 32

"Ideal and Working Concepts of Full Employment" (Nourse), 368-369
If Christ Came to Chicago (Stead), 12
Illinois Institute of Technology, 18-19, 339, 449
"Impact of Monetary and Fiscal Policy on Agricultural Business" (Nourse), 377
"I Must Believe" (Nourse), 383
Income and Economic Progress (Moulton), 157-159
Income tax cut, 407
Industrial Price Policy and Economic Progress (Nourse and Drury), 160-165
Inflation and related problems, 372-375
Inflation control, 263-267
Institute of Economics, 84-87, 102-103, 148-149, 159-160
Institutional economics, 123, 469-470
"Intellectualism on the Economic Front" (Nourse), 365-366
International Correspondence School, 30
International Institute of Agriculture, 94, 143
International Teamsters Union, 411
Iowa Farm Bureau Federation, 64, 71, 75
Iowa Non-stock Cooperative Law (1921), 73
Iowa State College, 62-83
"Is the AAA Doomed?" (Nourse), 133

Janeway, Elliot, 352

Jenks, Jeremiah Whipple, 26
Jesness, O. B., 80, 100, 101, 142-143, 344-346
Johnson, Louis, 305
Johnson, Lyndon B., 438
Joint Council on Economic Education, 258-259, 333, 336-337, 354, 365, 382, 393, 447, 477
Joint Economic Committee, 242-244, 273-274, 288

Kahn, R. F., 165
Kaplan, A. D. H., 259, 309
Kefauver, Estes, 372, 413
Kennan, George, 284
"Kennedy as Economic Statesman" (Nourse), 396-397
Kennedy, John F., 394, 396-397, 401, 403, 404, 407, 416
Kestnbaum, Meyer, 309
Keynes, John Maynard, 143, 153, 191-192, 200, 208, 521 (note 14)
Keyserling, Leon, 205, 216-221, 225, 229, 232-233, 237-242, 247-248, 263, 265, 269-270, 273, 278-279, 283-285, 286-287, 292, 298-300, 302-303, 305-308, 310, 313-320, 322-326, 329, 344-345, 352-353, 386-388, 523 (notes 10 and 20), 525 (note 1), 526 (note 22), 527 (note 34), 528 (notes 9 and 10), 529 (notes 27 and 28)
Kilgore, B. W., 94
Kilpatrick, Carroll, 277-278
Kiplinger, W. M., 286
Knapp, Carol, 445, 457-459, 462
Knapp, Joseph G., 101 ff., 112, 119, 122, 196, 353-354, 394, 404-405, 447
Korean War, 339, 340, 343

Labor-management relations, 406, 438
Land tenure study, 57-58, 60-61
Lane, Laura, 102, 104
Large-scale cooperatives, 91-92, 137-138
Larmer, Forest, 89
Laughlin, J. Laurence, 32, 42, 44-47
Laura Spellman Rockefeller Foundation, 129, 150
Law and economics, 385-386
Lebergott, Stanley, 201
Lecturing campaign, 337-340
Legal Defense and Educational Fund, 447-448

*Legal Status of Agricultural
  Cooperation* (Nourse), 107-111
Lekachman, Robert, 210
Lewis, Dean, 40-41
Lewis, Edwin Herbert, 19-20
Lewis Institute, 18-20, 339
"Liberalism," 366
"Life and Taxes" (Nourse), 422-423
Lilienthal, David E., 358-359
Linnton Plywood Association, 419 ff.
Lippman, Walter, 159, 459
Literary Society of Washington, 393, 422, 445
Livingston, Joseph A., 289-290, 313-314, 530-531 (note 17)
Loos, Karl D., 530 (note 15)
Lorwin, Lewis L., 199, 472
Louks, William N., 344
Low-price policy, 158, 161-162, 165, 168, 181-183, 190-191
Lubin, Isadore, 148-149
Lyon, Leverett S., 158

Macaulay, Thomas Babington, 459
McCoy, Harold, 460
McCracken, Harlan L., 156
McGovern, George, 438
Macklin, Theodore, 100
Macroeconomics, 405
Management Review, 185
"March of Progress, Economically, The" (Nourse), 326 ff.
"Market Absorption," 261
Marketing Agreements Under the AAA (Nourse), 137
Marketing contracts, 72 ff.
Marshall, Alfred, 420
Marshall, Leon C., 45, 47, 50
Martin, William McChesney, 428, 449
Maryland and Virginia Milk Producers Association, 375-376
"Mass Media," 503
May, Mark A., 169
Mead, Elwood Sherwood, 23-35
Mead, Margaret, 35
"Meaning of Price Policy, The" (Nourse), 177-178
Mechanical Engineering, 164
Mechanized Agriculture, 119-120
Meharry Medical College gifts, 450
Meyer, Eugene, 192
Midyear economic reports, 259-260, 278 ff., 315-316
Military Joint Orientation Conferences, 284, 285, 314-315
Military preparedness, 284, 314-315, 339-340
Milk Marketing Administrators, 417
Milk marketing orders, 397-398, 401-402, 417
Milk Marketing Policy, 416-417
Miller, Raymond W., 196-197, 475
Millis, Harry, 119
Mill, John Stuart, 470
Mills, Frederick, 171
Mitchell, James C., 73, 107
Mitchell, Wesley Clair, 117, 164, 467, 471
"Monetary management," 431
"Monopolistic Practices and the Price Structure" (Nourse), 165-166
Moody, Dwight L., 4
Morgan, Charles, 361
Mormon cooperative activity, 29
Moroney, Mildred, 455
Moulton, Harold G., 68, 84, 87-90, 95, 103, 110-111, 115, 148-149, 151, 153, 157-158, 168, 326, 429-430, 446, 467
Mueller, Willard F., 475-476
Murphy, Charles S., 237, 270, 340
Murray, James E., 200-221, 315 ff.
Murray, Phil, 224
Myers, W. I., 108

Naden, Kenneth D., 460
Nathan, Robert, 189
National Association of Manufacturers, 176, 227
National Cooperative Council, 126
National Council of Farmer Cooperative Marketing Associations, 100
National Council of Farmer Cooperatives, 421
National Livestock Producers Association, 75
National Security Council, 320
"Nature and Future of Private Enterprise, The" (Nourse), 176-177
"Nature's Power and the Conscience of Man" (Nourse), 361-362
"Neo-Sapiroism," 127
New Deal and cooperative marketing, 131 ff.
"New Economics," 435-437
Newman, Monroe, 445, 477, 478
"New Viewpoints in the Economic

INDEX

Area" (Nourse), 370-371
Nicholls, William H., 186-187, 476
1984 (Orwell), 342
Nineteen-Fifties Come First, The (Nourse), 340-345
"1960: The Hinge Between Two Decades" (Nourse), 395-396
Nixon, Richard, 438, 446, 456
"Normal Price as a Market Concept" (Nourse), 55-56, 376
"Not so Dismal Science of Economics, The" (Nourse), 415
Nourse, Alice Louise (sister), 5 ff., 31 (*See also* Hobart, Alice Tisdale)
Nourse Award, American Institute of Cooperation, 480
Nourse, Edwin Griswold (general information only): ancestry and birth, 3-5; childhood and high school, 4-15; college training, 18-27, 31-36, 41-46; farming experience, 39-40; final days and death, 461-464; marriage, 35; professional positions, 29-30, 33-38, 40-41, 47 ff., 61 ff., 84 ff., 115 ff., 148 ff., 175 ff., 205 ff., 345, 382-383; working methods, 466-471
Nourse, Edwin Henry (father), 3 ff., 22
Nourse, Mrs. Edwin Henry (stepmother), 8, 22
Nourse, Edwin Wallis "Chip" (grandson), 455, 456
Nourse, Mrs. Harriet Beaman (mother), 4-7
Nourse, John Tyler (son), 84, 444, 453, 455-456
Nourse, Mary Augusta (sister), 5 ff., 347, 443
Nourse, "Rafe" (half brother), 4, 513 (note 1)
Nourse, Mrs. Ray Tyler (wife), 160, 414 (*See also* Tyler, Ray)
Nourse, Rebecca Gayle (granddaughter), 422, 455-456
Nourse, Mrs. Stephanie Gorski (daughter-in-law), 456
Nurse, Francis, 3
Nurse, Rebecca, 3

Ogden High School, 28 ff.
Okun, Arthur, 461
O'Leary, James J., 185
O'Mahoney, Joseph C., 163, 165, 208, 221, 288, 303-304, 306
On Understanding Science (Conant), 441-442
"On Understanding Social Science" (Nourse), 441
"Organized Labor and Economic Stabilization" (Nourse), 257
Outlook Conferences, 90
"Outlook for Agriculture" (Nourse), 104-107
"Outlook for Cooperative Marketing, The" (Nourse), 76-78

Pabst Essay Contest, 217, 318
"Participating distributions," 420-421
Pasvolsky, Leo, 191-192
Patman, Wright, 211, 378, 428
Patronage dividends, meaning of, 420
Pattee, Richard, 97, 98, 101
Patten, Simon N., 34
Patton, James, 308-309
Pearson, Drew, 314
Pechman, Joseph A., 330
Pederson, George N., 398
"People's Capitalism," 403
Perisho, Dean, 36, 38
Persistent economic problems, 354, 432-433
Phi Beta Kappa visiting scholar, 365-366
Phillips, Cabell, 237-238
Pierce, Allin H., 421
Pigou, A. C., 470
"Place of Agriculture in Modern Economic Society, The" (Nourse), 65-66
"Place of Cooperatives in Our National Economy, The" (Nourse), 197
Planning, 198-199
Planning for Freedom (Rostow), 385-386
Plywood workers' cooperatives, 419-422
Political Science, 272, 344, 501, 502
Pooling practices, 72
Porter, Paul, 281-282
"Position of Agriculture Under the Employment Act, The" (Nourse), 260-261
Post-war price policy, 190
"Post-War Trends in Farmer Cooperation" (Nourse), 143-144
Powell, G. Harold, 63
Prairie Farmer, 81

President's Economic Advisers, The
 (Silverman), 386-388
Price, Don K., 330
Price fixing, 83, 410
Price, H. Bruce, 100
Price Making in a Democracy
 (Nourse), 180-192, 200
Price policy, 177-178
Price policy and government, 187 ff.
Pritchett, Henry, 86
Production control, 122, 125-126
Production Credit System for Agriculture, The (Butz), 196
"Productivity, Capacity and Business Performance" (Nourse), 356-357
Prohibition Party, 13
"Promise of American Capitalism, The" (Nourse), 402-403
"Proper Sphere of Government Regulation, The" (Nourse), 82-84
Psychology, 25, 26, 32
"Public Administration and Economic Stabilization" (Nourse), 252-254
Public enterprise, 311-312
Puget Sound Plywood, Inc., 419 ff.
Pullman strike, 14
Purnell Act of 1925, 112
Putnam, George L., 52

Quill, Margaret, 334, 354, 446

Racial problems, 449, 503-504
"Reaping the Harvest of Inflation" (Nourse), 375
Recent Economic Changes in the United States, 116-118, 518 (note 1)
"Recession Threats and Depression Safeguards" (Nourse), 355-356
Redfield, Robert, 169
Reed, Philip D., 309
Religion, 23, 500
Reorganization Plan No. 9, 350
Reuther, Walter, 224
"Revolution in Farming, The" (Nourse), 59-60
Rieve, Emil, 274
Road To Serfdom, The (Hayek), 198-199
Robinson, Walter, 94
Robotka, Frank, 65, 74, 81-82
Roosevelt, Franklin, 201
Roosevelt, Theodore, 26
Rosenberger Medal, 388

Rostow, Eugene V., 385-386
Ruml, Beardsley, 98, 522-523 (note 9)
"Rural Conservatism" (Nourse), 32-33
Ruttenberg, Stanley H., 224, 464

Salant, Walter, 252
Salem witch hysteria, 3
Samuelson, Paul, 436
Sankey, Ira D., 4
Sapiro, Aaron, 70-71, 77-78, 100, 107, 114, 127, 518 (note 7)
Saturday Evening Post, 34
Saulnier, Raymond, 425
Saunders, Charles B., Jr., 95
Saville, Roscoe, 93
Sawyer, Charles, 289
Schlesinger, Arthur M., 169
Schmidt, Emerson, 309
Schultz, Theodore, 283, 371
"Science Pauses" (Bush), 441
"Science Pauses—but Not Too Soon" (Nourse), 441
Sculping, interest in, 149, 478
"Search Light Report, The," 345
Searles, O. M., 15, 16, 28, 40
"Serfdom, Utopia, and Democratic Opportunity" (Nourse), 199-200
Shanahan, Eileen, 461
Sharpe, Myron E., 457
Sill, Harry, 23, 25, 27
Silverman, Corinne, 386-388
Small, Albion W., 32, 33, 42
Smith, Bradford B., 309
Smith, J. Russell, 35
Snyder, John W., 289, 475
Social activities, 17, 20, 84, 276
Socialism, 311-312
"Social Responsibility of Business, The" (Nourse), 338
Social science, 441 ff.
Social Science Research Council, 103, 112-113, 129, 151, 160, 168-173, 194-195
Sociology, 32-33, 502-503
"Some Fundamentals of Cooperative Marketing" (Nourse), 91, 92
"Some Questions Emerging Under the Employment Act" (Nourse), 389-392
Southern Pacific Railroad experience, 30
"Sowing the Seeds of Inflation" (Nourse), 372
Special sessions, 263 ff. (1947),

INDEX 543

280-282 (1948)
Spellman, William J., 92
Spence Bill, 292-295, 296, 298, 308, 309, 310
Spencer, Herbert, 30
Spending, 129
Spengler, Joseph J., 149, 476
Stedman, Alfred, 453
Steelman, John, 223, 234, 271, 281, 287, 320, 329
Steel price situation, 416
Stein, Herbert, 456-458, 461
Stern, J. Kenneth, 475
Stewart, Charles S., 57
Stine, Oscar C., 105
Stocking, George W., 183
"Suggestions for Economic Stability and Growth" (Nourse), 378-381
Supreme Court decisions, 133-134, 470

Taft-Hartley Act, 239, 251
Taft, Robert A., 243-244, 265, 268, 271, 306, 310
"Taking Root—Ten Years of the Employment Act" (Nourse), 362-363
Tax policy, 423, 425-429
Taylor, Henry C., 90, 92, 94, 98, 371, 446
Teachers' workshops, 336
Teaching experience, 29-30, 33 ff., 36-39, 40-41, 48 ff., 63 ff., 282-283, 345
Technical assistance work, 354-355
Tenneson, Ruby, 58-59
Testimony before Congressional committees, 242-248, 264-266
Thomas, Elmer, 208
Thompson, Sam H., 164-165
Three Years of the Agricultural Adjustment Administration (Nourse, Davis, and Black), 140-143
Titchener, Edward B., 25
Tobriner, Matthew, 109
Tolly, Howard, 133
Trelogan, Harry C., 401
Truman, Harry S., 205-207, 215-216, 226-229, 237-244, 250-252, 264, 268, 277-279, 282, 284, 287-289, 305-310, 313-314, 319-321, 324-325, 329, 352
Truman Library records, 414-415
"Trust busting," 410
Tucker, Ralph S., 164
Tugwell, Rexford G., 216

Tupper, Ernest A., 352
Turner, Robert, 281
Tyler, Ray, 29, 30, 35 (*See also* Nourse, Mrs. Ray Tyler)
Typhoid epidemic, 22-23

Ulrey, Orion, 101-102
"Unfinished Symphony," 443, 463, 491 ff.
University of Arkansas, 47 ff.
University of Chicago, 30-33, 41-46, 388
University of Minnesota, 345
University of North Carolina, 345
University of Pennsylvania, 382-383
University of South Dakota, 36-39
"Untaxing as a Way of Economic Life" (Nourse), 426-427

Vermillion, South Dakota, 36 ff.
Vietnam War, 438
Vincent, George Edgar, 32-33
Vocabulary, importance of, 471

Wagner, Robert, 208, 216, 220
Wallace, Donald, 164, 223
Wallace, Henry A., 54, 64, 129, 132, 133, 401
Wallace, Henry C., 64, 68
Wallace's Farmer, 64, 68
"War and the Back to the Land Movement, The" (Nourse), 43
Wardman Park group, 237, 241, 263, 280
Warren, Earl, 456, 470
Warren, George F., 25, 52, 92, 105, 106
Wartime Control of Prices (Hardy), 175
Washington Post, 267, 398
Waterman, Julian S., 48
Waugh, Frederick V., 92, 223, 248, 323, 472-473
Wealth and Income Study, 152 ff.
Webb, James E., 222, 251, 257, 284
Weld, L. D. H., 63
Wells, Orris V., 145
Wharton School of Finance, 33-35
"What Can You Do for Your Country?" (Nourse), 437-439
"What is Agricultural Economics?" (Nourse), 50-51

"What's New About Automation?" (Nourse), 335
White, Andrew D., 21
Why Co-ops (Knapp), 196
"Why I Had to Step Aside" (Nourse), 335
Wigglesworth, R. B., 249-250
Willcox, Walter F., 25
"Will Farm Prices Fall?" (Nourse), 67-69
Williams, Carl, 127-128
Willoughby, William F., 85
Wilson, Elizabeth, 89
Wilson, M. L., 128, 133, 371
Wirth, Louis, 169-170

"Witch's Brood" (Nourse), 422
Wolfe, A. B., 183
Worker cooperatives, 419-421
Working, Elmer J., 89
World Nutrition Conference, 143
Wright, Chester Whitney, 32, 42, 50

Yale Review, 59-60, 184
Yntema, Theodore, 309
Young, Brigham, 29, 30
Youth problems, 451, 505
Youth's Companion, 7, 12, 68, 111

Znaniechi, F., 171